SOCIAL COMMUNICATION IN
ADVERTISING

SOCIAL COMMUNICATION IN
ADVERTISING
CONSUMPTION IN THE MEDIATED MARKETPLACE

Third Edition

William Leiss
Stephen Kline
Sut Jhally
Jacqueline Botterill

Third Edition revised by Jacqueline Botterill

Routledge
Taylor & Francis Group
New York   London

Published in 2005 by
Routledge
Taylor & Francis Group
270 Madison Avenue
New York, NY 10016

Published in Great Britain by
Routledge
Taylor & Francis Group
2 Park Square
Milton Park, Abingdon
Oxon OX14 4RN

© 2005 by Taylor & Francis Group, LLC
Routledge is an imprint of Taylor & Francis Group

Printed in the United States of America on acid-free paper
10 9 8 7 6 5 4 3 2

International Standard Book Number-10: 0-415-96676-0 (Softcover)
International Standard Book Number-13: 978-0-415-96676-4 (Softcover)
Library of Congress Card Number 2005001364

Library of Congress Cataloging-in-Publication Data

Social communication in advertising : consumption in the mediated marketplace / edited by William
   Leiss ... [et al.].-- 3rd ed.
       p. cm.
       Previous edition entered under William Leiss as author.
   Includes bibliographical references and index.
   ISBN 0-415-96676-0 (pb : alk. paper)
   1. Advertising-Social aspects. I. Leiss, William, 1939-

HF5827.S63 2005
659.1'042--dc22   2005001364

Taylor & Francis Group
is the Academic Division of T&F Informa plc.

Visit the Taylor & Francis Web site at
http://www.taylorandfrancis.com

and the Routledge Web site at
http://www.routledge-ny.com

Contents

Preface to the Third Edition

The original three authors began the research for what became the first edition of this book—published in 1986—about twenty-five years ago. At that time the academic study of advertising was still largely confined to the fields of marketing, economics, and consumer behavior. To be sure, there was a semi-popular literature as well, which was usually highly critical of the contents of advertisements, but its coverage of the topic was haphazard, for the most part: One got the distinct impression that the authors of such works found the details of the material they were criticizing to be distasteful, to say the least, and thus intrinsically unworthy of serious analysis.

All this began to change in the early 1980s, as a cohort of scholars and writers began to take an entirely new look at this material. Historians, sociologists, business-school professors, social theorists, psychologists, and communications researchers entered the fray in increasing numbers, bringing a spate of entirely new perspectives and research methods to bear on this subject matter. The serious study of advertising was thoroughly transformed in the process. This new generation of commentators opened up the wide vistas of history and culture, on the one hand, and entered deep into the physiognomy of individual advertisements—the structure of their aesthetic design, persuasive techniques, and specific representations of persons and goods—on the other. Much of this literature is referenced in the chapters that follow. But if we were asked to single out one title from this era, one contribution that best pointed the way to a new appreciation of its subject, it would be the marvelous book written by the historian Roland Marchand, *Advertising the American Dream,* published in 1985: A work by an author whose insight, sophistication, and breadth of view set a high standard for everyone else who would venture into this territory.

Whether these authors were positive, negative, or indifferent to what they found in these products or what they thought about those who created them, they were all united on one simple point: There was more here than met the eye. Advertising practices were a fundamental part of a modern market economy, the first economy in history based on moving masses of goods to the entire population. Each individual example of advertising practice could appear to be an unremarkable or degraded expression of "low culture," an unworthy addition to humankind's cultural heritage. But taken as a whole, and taken seriously as a social and institutional force, the enterprise of advertising and its products had a deep structure and a larger significance.

Authors tried to grasp this larger significance, as we have said, starting from a wide variety of analytical frameworks, such as social theory or history. Our approach in this book is based on a communications perspective, as the title indicates. We maintain that, beginning at the turn of the twentieth century, and continuing through the turn of the twenty-first century, modern advertising has been responsible for nothing short of a revolutionary transformation in the techniques of persuasive communication. Designed initially for the selling of goods, in the era in which the mass consumer markets were being born, advertising practice developed over time an increasingly sophisticated understanding of how social communication works. Now, today, that understanding is used to market not just consumer goods, but also to construct dialogues in society involving complex ideas as well—political messages (and political figures) of all kinds, but also advocacy by environmental groups, large corporations, special interest groups trying to change social values and to influence lifestyle choices, and many others. Over a century of continuous development, and moving closely in step with regular innovations in communications technologies, advertisers taught all of us how rich, diverse, and simply fascinating are the ways in which a message can be conveyed.

For this has been, without a doubt, a process of educating our sensibilities. This point can be illustrated by comparing two ad formats, one from around 1900 and another a century later. In chapter 2 the reader will find a discussion of the communicative format of the old *Sears Catalogue,* which remained a venerable institution, especially in rural areas, throughout the entire first half of the twentieth century. An illustration, taken from the 1908 edition, accompanies this discussion, showing the complete reliance on a print-based form of expression, relieved only by stylized drawings; the target audience was expected to digest a truly immense quantity of words in order to get the message. Contrast this with the extraordinary British tobacco ad campaign of the early 1990s by the brand "Silk Cut," which relied entirely on pure visual imagery, with no words whatsoever, for its message strategy. The imagery, showing a bolt of purple silk (purple was the brand's signature color) being cut by huge scissors, or patched with a band-aid after having been cut, had no accompanying text in the body of the ad itself. Rather, the ad designer was relying on the government anti-tobacco health message, required by law to be printed along the bottom panel of the layout, to trigger the reader's set of mental associations and thus to "release" the promotional meaning for the product. An entire century of consumer experience with new communicative formats and strategies—researched, planned, and designed by ad agency personnel, and implemented in a series of discrete stages—was required in order for anyone to be able to understand what those Silk Cut ads were about.

Part I of this book shows how and why the advertising profession was able to carry out this mission of broad social significance. We show how agencies were positioned at the intersection of major institutional pathways which ran between the media (print, radio, television, etc.) and the public, between corporations selling goods and the public buying them, and, increasingly, between the advocates of social and political ideas and the public. To be sure, ad professionals and the agencies they worked for did not control the traffic moving along these pathways, but they have occupied a unique and strategic position there, one that enabled them to shape the way in which the new forms of persuasive communication would penetrate deeply into the crevices of social life.

Both the first (1986) and second (1990) editions of this book presented a unified conceptual synthesis, called "cultural frames for goods," which sought to draw together all of the separate strands mentioned in the preceding paragraph, as arrayed in a series of four discrete phases. Of course, in those editions our story ended in the 1980s. Much has happened since, which is why we have prepared this new edition, which extends both the analysis of advertising content, and the synthesis under the rubric of cultural frames, into the present. In this third edition the entirety of Part II is devoted to a detailed portrayal—including the sociological determinants, marketing strategy, and advertising content—of what we call the "fifth frame." Many new ad illustrations from the period 1990–present, drawn from both television and print media, are included in this new edition. There appears to be a paradox in what is happening now, at least in television broadcasting, which makes the contemporary era quite different from earlier ones: In the past, one might have said that ads portrayed reality while program content supplied the fantasy. Now, however, so-called "reality shows" increasingly dominate programming, while advertising content plays ever more subtly on our fantasies. But this phase too shall pass, at some point, as our seemingly endless fascination with the selling of goods provides advertisers with renewed encouragement to experiment on us with clever forms of messaging.

The new member of our author team, Jackie Botterill, did the lion's share of the work for the third edition. She substantially revised the material in Part I (chapters 1–7) that is drawn from the second edition, wrote all of the chapters (8–16) in Part II that are substantially new except for short sections brought forward from the earlier work, and updated the concluding chapter (17). In addition, she added new industry research as well as two entirely new advertising studies, one magazine and one television, and developed the central category for the fifth frame, *mise-en-scène*, which enables us to make sense out of what has been happening in advertising practice over the last decade or so.

Jackie Botterill would like to thank two doctoral students at the University of Calgary. Pam Buckle's considerable editorial and research talents greatly enhanced this book and Chad Saunder's research and technical skills, combined with his unwavering "can do" attitude, were indispensable for bringing this project to completion. William Leiss acknowledges the support of funding provided under the auspices of the NSERC/SSHRC research chair in risk communication and public policy (1999–2004), Haskayne School of Business, University of Calgary.

W.L.
Ottawa

PART I

Advertising and Media

CHAPTER 1

Introduction

This book examines the role of advertising and promotional communication in the expansionary phase of the market economy during the twentieth century. There are a number of obvious reasons for doing so. Advertising is after all a major sector in the global economy—part of the broader system of production, distribution, and consumption in the global marketplace. According to the Senior Vice-President and Director of Forecasting for Universal McCann, Robert Coen, global advertising in 2003 was a $471 billion business, more than half of which, $249.2 billion, were U.S. advertising expenditures (Coen 2003). Although the numbers fluctuate, agencies employ roughly 165,000 employees in the United States and 20,000 in London.

The willingness of corporations to speak to consumers directly in media subsidized the development of our information and entertainment infrastructures—from newspapers and billboards to the Internet. Promotional communication permeates and blends with our cultural environment, punctuating our television watching, saturating our magazines and newspapers, and popping up in our Internet surfing, movies, and video games. In short, advertising has become an accepted part of everyday life. The symbolic attributes of goods, as well as the characters, situations, imagery, and jokes of advertising discourse, are now fully integrated into our cultural repertoire. Children sing jingles while playing. Dinner party guests talk about their favorite (or most reviled) ads. Some spectacularly successful advertising campaigns have become legendary artistic statements: for example, the 1984 Macintosh Computer that "premiered" on the Super Bowl and, in London, Bartle, Bogle and Hegarty's (BBH) Levis' Laundrette advertisement. It is their prominent discussion of consumption that leads some commentators such as James Twitchell (1996) to compare advertising to a religion for its honest celebration of consumer goods as the key to contemporary American life-ways.

We agree with Twitchell that no other discursive practice in modern society exemplifies the tensions underlying the expansionary phase of market society. Since the 1950s, these tensions have provoked a growing debate about the role that advertising plays in the marketplace. Celebrated by the enthusiasts of marketing as the informational tool that empowered the consumer and critiqued by mass culture gurus for turning consumers into dupes, the advertising agency seemed to embody all that was both good and bad in the changing relationships between producers and consumers. Some styled it a mirror, reflecting back to us our deep-seated material visions of well-being.

Others felt it was a persuasive force articulating new consumption patterns which impacted on the ongoing social, economic, and cultural practices of the consumer society. Advertising thus became the lightening rod for critics who accused it of all manner of evil from accelerating environmental destruction to breeding a generation of super-sized children. We will explore all of these ideas throughout this book.

A century ago in North America and Western Europe, the forms of privileged discourse that touched the lives of ordinary persons were church sermons, political oratory, and the words and precepts of family elders. These discourses informed our relationships to goods, to each other, and to our social world. Such influences remain with us, but their prominence in the affairs of everyday life and their rhetorical force and moral authority have diminished considerably as the marketplace expanded and as the mass media grew in prominence.

Over the course of the preceding century, the marketplace itself has become a significant medium of social communication. The space left over in personal life has been filled largely by what we call the mass media's *discourses through and about objects*. We intend this seemingly awkward phrase to convey the following basic idea: Communications among persons, in which individuals send "signals" to others about their attitudes, expectations, their sense of identity, values, intentions and aesthetic expression, are strongly associated with, and expressed through, patterns of ownership, preference, display, and use of things. We also intend this phrase to convey something more specific—namely, that a significant portion of our daily public talk, thought, and action within the expanded market setting is about consumer goods and what they can do for us or should mean to us.

Our own analysis starts by acknowledging that within all human cultures the relationship between persons and nature is fundamental to our survival. We extract, make, and consume nature in the form of goods to meet our needs. But we also find that in transforming nature into goods, we are fabricating important channels of social communication. Goods-in-use mark honor, prestige, and rank; bind us in affection, love, and friendship; designate moments of celebration; denote safety and trust; and serve as a catalyst for fantasy and reflection. Clothing, tools, bowls, beads, and many other things invoke myth and tell stories through their display and use (both everyday and ceremonial), and as a part of the broader system of social transactions within the family, the community, and the market. Whether the ceremonial sharing of food in the community, the bartering over value at the fair, or the ritualized gift-giving at marriages, objects are enchanted with a profound range of meanings because they are embedded within the warp and weft of social relations we call "material cultures."

We believe that the modern consumer culture shares with earlier economic relations this fundamental characteristic: Material objects produced for consumption in the marketplace not only satisfy needs, but also serve as markers and communicators for interpersonal distinctions and self-expression. These symbolic markers are the mediating communicational elements that connect people and the consumer goods they use to satisfy their wants. In a market economy, too, goods are communicators—symbolic markers that embed consumption practices in daily social interactions and exchange.

What chiefly distinguishes our contemporary society from earlier ones is not only the sheer volume of goods and services available to consumers in a market economy, but also the sheer intensity of the promotional effort whereby marketers seek to link consumer needs to the characteristics of the products they sell. Economically speaking, the expansion of the marketplace has seen a profound growth in the production and distribution of material culture, that is, the totality of goods and associated services circulating in a modern industrial economy. On the symbolic level, we have seen a parallel expansion of the associated discourses about commodities and their modes of production and consumption.

As we survey the development of the contemporary market economy we are impressed not only with the enormous expansion of our material culture during the twentieth century, but also the changing meanings that surround the expanding world of goods and the ways these goods are used by consumers in everyday life. We argue, therefore, that advertising's role within the relations of production and consumption forged in the mediated marketplace should be seen as not only economic, but as cultural as well.

Our main point is a simple one: Advertising is not just a business expenditure undertaken in the hope of moving some merchandise off the store shelves, but is rather an integral part of modern culture. Its creations appropriate and transform a vast range of symbols and ideas; its unsurpassed communicative powers recycle cultural models and references back through the networks of social interactions. This venture is unified by the discourse through and about objects, which bonds together images of persons, products, and well-being.

This book sets out to historically *trace the changing discourses through and about things* within the expanding mediated marketplace. Our analysis of the market's expanding role in material culture does not assume a bifurcated world in which economy and culture are inherently opposed—quite the opposite. It insists that although the accounts of the market economy provided by business (mostly concerned with commodity exchanges for money) and of sociology (mostly concerned with the meanings of goods and their social use) often differ, both are necessary for the understanding of the role played by advertising in the changing discourses through and about goods. This is because in a mediated marketplace, goods are the point of contact between commodity relations and the broader channels of social communication. This is also why we think advertising's discourse through and about objects is a useful interpretive key for tracing aspects of our consumer culture.

The marketplace has become a preeminent institution in the consumer society because it is the point of access to material culture and the expanding discursive space in which the meanings of social consumption are transacted and negotiated. People in contemporary society also come together in "taste cultures," "lifestyle groupings," "demographic cohorts," or "ethnic communities," which represent distinctive consumption patterns. Such subsidiary social formations can be both temporary and quite informal in nature but are tracked by business through marketing research and are targeted by all sorts of promotional communications building a feedback loop between producers and consumers into the social communication of the marketplace. As the marketing practices became more adroit at assessing this social dimension of consumption, so too advertising became a "privileged" form of social communication—meaning that we accord what it says a place of special prominence in our lives.

We refer to the markets' social communication about consumption as privileged in two senses. First, in our market-industrial societies (North America, Western Europe, Japan, and a few others), economic affairs and marketplace transactions occupy a preponderant place in public life. For example, much of our political debate deals with managing the national and international market economy as a means of maintaining uninterrupted growth in our material culture. The talk about our economy's fortunes has come to overawe everything else and, indeed, forces most other concerns to be expressed in its terms and language. A hockey game becomes "an entertainment product on the ice," and delivering the goods to consumers becomes the "bottom line" for both corporate and state enterprises. Second, at the individual level the discourse through and about objects sidles up to us everywhere, beckoning, teasing, haranguing, instructing, cajoling, and informing our daily interactions with each other in most settings. Even if we go off on weekend wilderness quests, we do so in a team wearing branded jackets and armed with solar-powered stoves.

As national consumer products flooded shops, so did the social communication in and through goods. In the expanding consumer marketplace goods became "doubly articulated"—first, in terms of the meanings and uses imputed to them by consumers in their daily lives; second, by the promotional discourses of corporations that advertised them in the marketplace. The historical growth of the marketplace is experienced in and through the expanding social communication about consumption generally.

Advertising as Persuasion in the Marketplace

Vance Packard started his enormously popular *The Hidden Persuaders* by explaining that it was about the way many of us are being influenced and manipulated—far more than we realize—in the patterns of our everyday lives.

Large-scale efforts are being made, often with impressive success, to channel our unthinking habits, our purchasing decisions, and our thought processes by the use of insights gleaned from psychiatry and the social sciences. Typically, these efforts take place beneath our level of awareness (Packard 1959, 11).

Citing the use of motivational research (using focus groups of audiences to discover the basis of behavior, particularly consumer behavior) by growing numbers of advertisers, Packard attempted to show that consumers were becoming creatures of conditioned reflex rather than of rational thought. Most important, he alleged, this manipulation took place at a subconscious level. Packard's criticism was not leveled at all advertising but only that which is underhanded and covert; indeed, for most advertising Packard had nothing but praise, referring to many advertisements as "tasteful, honest works of artistry." His main theme, however, concerned the obnoxious character of what he regards as devious forms of advertising.

Packard's dark vision of the manipulative and hidden impacts of advertising was reinforced by Wilson Bryan Key's discussions (1972 and 1976) of the alleged technique of subliminal perception in advertising. Key was concerned not so much with the use of motivational research and non-rational techniques of persuasion, but with ascertaining whether techniques impossible to perceive at the conscious level of awareness are concealed within the construction of the advertising message itself and whether they can influence behaviour. For example, Key claimed to find the word "sex" baked into the surface of Ritz crackers and deeply symbolic sexual imagery used in the depiction of ice cubes in alcohol advertising.

This "secret technology," he asserted, "modifies behaviour invisibly, channels basic value systems and manages human motives in the interest of special power structures. . . . Subliminal stimuli assault the psyches of everyone in North America throughout each day of their lives" (Key 1976, 2). Neither Packard nor Key, it should be noted, was ever able to point to actual instances in which such alleged manipulative techniques induced consumers to do anything that they would not otherwise have freely chosen to do. But at least Packard could point to actual programs for motivational research; no other commentator, either within the advertising industry or outside it, has ever corroborated Key's assertions about advertising practices, nor is there any evidence that motivational effects result from subliminal stimuli. The popularity of these attacks appears to rest on the general impression they create that advertising is a powerful and omnipresent apparatus with better knowledge of consumers than they have of themselves, and that this knowledge is used to manipulate them into buying goods they do not need.

Business spokespersons often admit that in the past advertising was deceptive and was used to solve problems of under-consumption in an economy that had become newly capable of producing consumer goods in great profusion.

In his book *Marketing: Concepts and Strategy*, Martin Bell conceded that national advertising of the 1920s and 1930s did indeed seek to escalate consumer demand: "The high-powered, skilful manipulator of consumer opinion, using personal salesmanship and aggressive advertising, took charge in many American businesses. His was the specialized task of selling the goods that had been mass produced and mass distributed. He found that almost anything could be sold with enough expense and effort" (Bell 1966, 7).

But during the 1930s, social criticism of this aggressive approach also increased. In response, the marketing industry, recognizing the limits of aggressive persuasion, framed a new orientation based on two key strategies: (1) intensive market research and (2) the effective design of new products. This replaced the practice of merely churning out whatever goods manufacturers thought would be useful to people, and then looking for ways to flog them. The new strategy was given a name: the *marketing concept.* "The marketing concept starts with the firm's target customers and their needs and wants; it plans a co-ordinated set of products and programs to serve their needs and wants; and it derives profits through creating customer satisfaction" (Kotler and Turner 1981, 31). Marketers and advertisers became the apostles of a liberal conception of the marketplace, discovering (not creating) consumer needs, designing products to meet them, and using advertisements to communicate the availability and desirability of products.

Proponents of the marketing concept believe that contemporary marketing and advertising are the very lifeblood of our complex, market-oriented economy. Marketing techniques are used to make goods more meaningful and thus overcome some of the disadvantages of the specialization of labor, through which most persons become unfamiliar with the characteristics of mass-produced goods. The marketing system should be seen as a provisioning technology and cultural resource that confronts the enormous task of matching tens of millions of consuming units with tens of thousands of producing units. Its strategies are based on the premise that the consumer, as ultimate decision maker, is a rational problem solver who takes full advantage of this communication technology.

The marketing concept involves the integration of the "four Ps": *product* (shaping and designing products to meet consumer needs); *price* (pricing appropriately to generate sales); *promotion* (promoting sales through advertising, store displays, and selling strategy); and *place* (placing products in appropriate retail outlets). In this view advertising is a small part of a broader business project—the component of the "marketing concept" which links a corporation's survival to the way it helps people to match their needs with products, thus making a valuable contribution to the efficiency and freedom of our expanding market economy.

Implicit in the marketing concept is the assumption that the most efficient way for the market to function is to allow consumers to direct producers, rather than the reverse. Under classic liberal theory, the market behavior of consumers is based upon deliberate and calculated action. Rational consumers faced with many products will only purchase those they truly require to satisfy their wants; rational producers of goods (in the face of competition from other marketers) will only produce what consumers' want. Thus, the self-interested actions of buyers and sellers together within the free, competitive market will ensure the most efficient functioning of the system. Bell has outlined how the consumer behaves according to the rational approach. The satisfaction of a want involves four stages: (1) the recognition of a want, (2) the search for means to satisfy the want, (3) the evaluation of competing alternatives, and (4) a decision. Advertising plays its part in the search and evaluation stages (Bell 1966).

Advertising figured prominently in our public discussions of the market economy as it became a favored business practice—the leading pillar of modern marketing practice (price, product, distribution, and promotion). Public controversies intensified as corporations invested in advertising to influence consumer opinion and behaviour in their battles of survival—rather than lower prices or develop new goods. Merchants sometimes fanciful attempts at "sexing up" their wares seemed at odds with the pat marketing concept that imagined a rational consumer who chooses among goods based on the product information discussed in advertising. Social critics questioned whether it was possible to describe advertising's role in the modern marketplace with such simplistic models of consumers' decision processes.

The launch of commercial television in the 1950s especially provoked some within academic circles to see the growing spectre of commercial persuasion as symptomatic of a fundamental malaise in the market economy.

Once again, we note the importance of Vance Packard's book in this context. The *Hidden Persuaders*, published in the early 1950s, opened a window into the marketers' account of what they did by exposing the "depth psychology" techniques they employed. For many, this book evoked consumers' increasingly uneasy relationship with the onslaught of media advertising. There were two important challenges launched by Packard's critique: First, its account of marketing as a form of manipulation situated advertising within the theories of communication and culture, rather than within economics. Second, this exposé of previously hidden marketing practices called marketers' integrity into question. Depth psychology had given marketers a tool for subverting rationality, it could be argued. Granting advertisers unfettered access to media channels, therefore, allowed them to gain control over the psychic reins of the consumers' desires and satisfactions. Although Packard himself was resolutely a liberal, his arguments seemed to confirm the long-standing dogma of Marxist critics that advertising creates wants in people for things they do not need.

The understanding of advertising as primarily persuasive communication has been much debated since the 1960s by political economists concerned about the changing power relationships between producers and consumers in the market economy. We will return to some of these arguments later. Defending advertisers against such attacks, marketers ridiculed the idea of themselves as all-powerful psychic manipulators. Their basic contention is that the informed consumer and the responsible producer remain the cornerstones of the democratic market system. After all, those marketing goods do not strive to create wants but rather to discover what wants exist and to design and manufacture products to respond to those wants. Nor is the consumer a manipulated and controlled dupe, they retorted, but rather a free agent who searches the market for suitable means to satisfy his or her own needs and desires. Advertising actually plays a minor role in market transactions by informing consumers about the result of the manufactures attempts to keep up with the demand of consumers.

In a seminal article entitled "The Economics of Information" (1961), discussing the relation between advertising and its use by consumers, George Stigler justified advertising as an important source of consumer information. Provisioning oneself with goods takes time—one needs to "search" for products in an increasingly complex marketplace; advertisers provide a service for which consumers are willing to pay, since it reduces their search costs and improves their choices. These costs are associated with the time that would be spent talking to salespeople, reading pamphlets, and cruising the shops, which are now more easily accomplished by paying attention to advertising. Stigler admitted his remarks were perhaps more appropriate to classified and retail advertising, but suggested that the same logic applied to more spectacular brand advertising on television: "The assimilation of information is not an easy or pleasant task for most people and they may well be willing to pay more for information when supplied in an enjoyable form" (1961, 222). Advertising itself must become an attractive and accepted form of popular entertainment to earn its privileged place in the market economy. In this sense information designed to persuade consumers is a legitimate, even welcome aspect of market competition by most consumers.

The advertisers were rightly offended by this accusation of manipulation for what they felt was legitimate persuasion. Manipulation involves outright deception (lying or falsehood), whereas persuasion is supposed to harbor only allowable exaggeration and embellishment—what is known in the trade as "puffery" (Aaker and Myers 1975, 567–77). This distinction has been important to the advertising industry in redefining the boundaries of debate about its advertising. In essence, it says that while advertisers are not to lie, they are not necessarily bound to tell the whole truth and nothing but the truth: a vital distinction. Nor are they to be restrained in their attempts to communicate product information vividly and dramatically. Alvin Achenbaum, then senior vice-president at J. Walter Thompson, put it this way: "To the degree that an advertiser intends to deceive his prospects and succeeds, he is manipulating... But what constitutes deception is not always clear-cut. And to say that emotion, subjectivity, incompleteness are deceptive is not necessarily so" [*sic*] (Moskin 1973, 48).

Advertising after all is only one among many sources of market information in the free marketplace of ideas, and there is no good reason for singling it out for special attention. In Canada, a Royal Commission report on consumer problems stated bluntly, "the view that persuasion is bad... must be rejected out of hand. Persuasion is an inherent part of the democratic process." Rotzoll et al. (1976, 20–21) told us that "under the assumption that man is rational, it is quite appropriate to attempt to persuade. For it is assumed that rational man will be able to detect truth in the clashing views of self-interested individuals in the economic marketplace in the same manner that his discerning nature would enable truth to arise in the political arena."

Theodore Levitt (1970) agreed: Since the relationship between product use and symbolism is a fundamental part of all human interactions with objects, there cannot be anything wrong in principle with advertising's participation in this universal process, so long as its audiences are not subject to acts of outright deceit. Information and persuasion from uncounted sources swirl around all the individuals who live, work, and shop in this setting. Both informative and persuasive communications are vital and indeed necessary ingredients of decision-making processes in politics, in social relations, and in the marketplace. Advertisements include both communication formats but constitute only one ingredient in the mix, and not a particularly outstanding one at that. In short, there is nothing special about advertising. Supporting this standpoint, even a group of Toronto theologians upheld the position that persuasion is "legitimate and valid and entirely defensible" because the consumer is always more than a mere spectator in events (Oliver 1981). In order to legitimate this type of persuasion, the advertising industry has had to redefine what constitutes social influence in the marketplace as simply providing consumers with information.

Gradually the term manipulation faded from the debate. But as Michael Schudson (1984) pointed out in his book, *Advertising the Uneasy Persuasion*, the economists' account of advertising also comes loaded with ideological baggage, depending on what we mean by information, choice, and persuasion. At first glance, much of the national advertising we encounter today contains neither much information nor much explicit persuasion. Most people, we think, would agree that appeals to people's emotions and feelings are perfectly legitimate part of the social communication about goods. As Schudson also reminded us, in all cultures goods have been part of our most intimate moments and social rituals. If advertising is to be criticized at all, he continued, objections should be directed not at its lively symbolic representations, but rather at specific acts of omission or distortion it creates in the marketplace. We largely agree. So can we conclude that consumers acceptance of marketing persuasion is a rational process that empowers them?

In their detailed review of studies of consumer choices, Driver and Foxall claimed, "the depiction of consumers as rational, problem-solving beings is actually a highly limited description of buyer behavior" (1984, 87). Most people seem indifferent to much of the "information" about goods already circulating around them and express very limited interested in obtaining more: "For many purchases a decision process never occurs, not even on the first purchase" (Driver and Foxall 1984, 92). Rather, most purchasing decisions appear to be strongly influenced by interpersonal communications, especially word-of-mouth information.

Impulse and routine are most typical of consumer's "low-involvement" purchases; the consumer seems "essentially passive," selecting among products without spending much time or thought seeking information. The whole enterprise of shopping (except perhaps for consumer durables, fashion clothing, and personal care items) is a social occasion. Driver and Foxall (1984, 93) therefore conclude that advertising seems to have "no power beyond engendering passing interest and, perhaps, cursory comparative evaluation; it is certainly, of itself, incapable of building preference or conviction."

The key phrase in this passage is "of itself": The problem is that the defenders try and draw a line between the market economy and the market culture and advertising as business communication and advertising as social communication. We refuse to accept this arbitrary distinction, for clearly the market's social communication about goods is more complex than that. What strikes us as a crucial flaw in this way of thinking is the artificial line economists draw between the social and economic relations we establish with goods. Although they rightly rejected the manipulation model of social communication, the economists account also provides a very limited reading of the role that advertising plays in the consumer culture. Indeed, perhaps the least interesting question we can ask of a particular advertising campaign is whether it actually increased the sales of the product, for the answer is only of interest to those that staked their hopes on its particular product story.

As Andrew Wernick (1991) pointed out, navigating one's way within market society requires constant attention to the modes of consumer behavior as the arena wherein pleasure and the good life can be found. Hardly surprising, then, that we pay enormous attention not only to our own and to others' consumption styles as we consider what is fashionable or trendy—or as appropriate to our own social situation. Nor that we turn to the media or to celebrities for guidance in this complex task. To these discourses on consumption advertising provides some additional clues about how to live life and find well being in contemporary market society. Although advertisers inundate consumers with the symbolic meanings and lifestyle references, in the final analysis consumers determine which ones are most meaningful to them. The associative meanings which advertising projects onto goods are often recognized as fantastical and silly, as motivated purely by the interests of sellers. That 98 percent of goods introduced into the marketplace fail despite the intensity of promotional efforts launched on their behalf, testifies not only to the urgency with which marketers feel they must communicate with consumers through advertising, but also to the general ability of consumers to filter advertisers' persuasive appeals. That consumers exercise limited choice in the market or see through advertising persuasive strategies does not imply that advertising's social communication is benign or inconsequential.

Going Beyond the Rhetoric

For too long the debates about advertising have been much too narrowly concerned with advertising's role in promoting particular goods and services in "superficial" ways. Many individuals hold contradictory and sometimes diametrically opposed views on advertising, mirroring the divergence of opinion in society as a whole. Advertising has given rise to harsh criticism ever since it became prominent in the national media, on the grounds that it has a negative impact in general—for example, that it encourages people to over-value "material" things in life. Advertising has been accused of creating wants, the manipulation of psychological processes, and the promotion of unworthy ideals. On advertising's behalf we have reviewed the rational information model of consumer choice, the nature of persuasion, and the importance of symbolism in forming the individual's sense of satisfaction. On neither side do we get very far.

The critics turn out to be interested chiefly in attacking the materialist ethos in general and, except for brief rhetorical flourishes, pay little or no attention to the actual workings of advertising. Suggestions that subliminal messages hidden in ads affect us without our being aware of their influence are alarming, although this sort of claim usually turns out to be groundless. Serious criticisms of advertising have been around almost as long as their target has and doubtless will remain with us, ranging from idle, general unease to sharper, more specific forms of attack. The continued debate lends support to the common perception that advertising has some influence on serious issues in modern social lives.

One overall observation about advertising's critics will be ventured here. Objections directed at advertisements, the industry, and its alleged social impacts are often indirect attacks on the materialistic ethos of industrial society, or on capitalism in general as a social system; these are critiques of society masquerading as critiques of advertising. We have not presumed to evaluate their merits, but we do think that when advertising is used as a surrogate for these larger concerns its critics are aiming at the wrong target.

Thus, the debate about advertising is often vaguely cast. Both the usual criticisms and the usual defenses often end up at the same point, although they arrive there by quite different routes. In the defenses, as in the criticisms, we are hard-pressed to identify either advertising's uniqueness as a form of modern mass communication or its unique place and function among the many overlapping social forces in modern life. Most people working within the industry today no longer cling to the notion that advertising exerts a strong influence on consumer behavior, for their research has illustrated that "by and large, advertising does not act forcefully via intra-personal, mental processes to create attitudes which determine behavior" (Anonymous, 10 Top Purchaser Influencers, 2003, Halliday 2003). Most agencies argue that advertising works broadly to enhance the cumulative brand values associated with products. It is the cumulative and broad impact of advertising messages where their influence is to be felt. Even advertising researchers Driver and Foxall, for example, concede "the aggregate effect of advertising on a materialistic society may be very great" (Driver and Foxall 1984, 98–104).

Indeed, advertising's overwhelming presence today leaves little doubt that it is a factor to be reckoned with. In part, society tries to keep tabs on what the industry is doing by regulating it. Laws and industry codes of ethics are supposed to discourage unfair or misleading practices. All regulation is an attempt to work out a compromise among parties with conflicting viewpoints, but regulating advertising has not, by and large, ended the disagreements about its influence or appropriateness. Looked at in depth and as a whole, the ways in which messages are presented in advertising reach deeply into our most serious concerns: interpersonal and family relations, the sense of happiness and contentment, sex roles and stereotyping, the uses of affluence, the fading away of older cultural traditions, influences on younger generations, the role of business in society, persuasion and personal autonomy, and many others.

How do we react to this omnipresent discourse about the impact of advertising and marketing as a central discourse of? Typically, with matters that are major fixtures in everyday life, that are regarded as permanently troublesome but also indispensable—such as public education—we are ambivalent. So it is with advertising. Extensive public opinion surveys show that a high proportion of people enjoy ads as an art form, think that neither our economy nor the mass media could exist without advertising, and regard it as playing a generally positive role in society. In a major Canadian survey, respondents were asked whether the public school system or advertising had the greater influence on society—54 percent identified schools, 42 percent advertising. In the same study, an equally high proportion responded that good products do not have to be advertised at all; that ads cannot be believed, make products more expensive, do not influence consumer choice, and cause people to spend money on things they do not need. In another major Canadian survey, 60 percent of respondents agreed with the statement: "Most advertising is an insult to one's intelligence" (Canadian Radio-television and Telecommunications Commission 1978).

The Social Communication Approach to the Study of Advertising

Our emphasis in this book is on analyzing advertising's role as a primary form of social communication within the new institutional context of twentieth century. We acknowledge that it is impossible to study advertising as a privileged form of social communication without reference to both the changing practices of marketers, on the one hand, and the emerging institutions of commercialized media, on the other. For this reason our approach is both historical and contextual.

By virtue of the media's saturation of everyday life and of the expanding scope of marketing as a strategic activity, advertising must be recognized as a special (and uniquely problematic) business institution because it lies at the intersection of the economy and culture. Situated between producers and consumers in the expanding marketplace, and between media and audiences in the mass media system, advertising became a key site of negotiation between the economic and cultural spheres. As the model (Figure 1.1) visualizes, agency

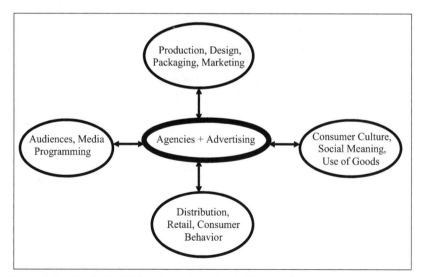

Figure 1.1 The Role of Advertising Agencies in Modern Society.

practice is linked to many aspects of modern commodity circulation, including the production, design, and marketing of goods, their communication to audiences through the media programming sphere, their distribution through retail outlets and the patterns of consumer behavior, and the incorporation of goods into broader cultural meaning and practices.

Rejecting the limited economic debates, some scholars have celebrated advertising for its positive contributions, not only to rising standards of living but also to the expanding range of lifestyle choices, social diversity, and aesthetics articulated in our material culture (Twitchell1996; Richards et al. 2000). Increasingly, advertising has been acknowledged as a form of artistic expression in its own right and as an inspiration to the arts in general; each year, prizes are awarded at an international competition held in Cannes (site of the famous film festival), and a collection of the year's best television commercials makes the rounds of movie theaters. Many youth and media professionals see advertising design as a "high art form of the postmodern era" and the leading edge of fashion and design (Nava and Nava 1992).

While we agree that advertising's place within our economy and culture can no longer be considered as separate issues, these new culturalist defenders downplay advertising's historical contribution to the expansion of the American material culture, preferring instead to see it only as an autonomous part of the postmodern popular culture system (Fowles 1996). But we seek to show that, far from being an autonomous agent, advertising is part and parcel of a highly industrialized, market-oriented society. We believe that advertising's impact on our social attitudes, values, aesthetics, and interactions can only be appreciated when it is analyzed in its institutional context as part of our mediated promotional culture.

In what follows we will attempt to situate the communicative power of advertising in the context of successive commercialized media channels, and the promotional relationships being forged between various sectors of cultural production in the media-driven (or "mediatized") marketplace. In so doing we hope to provide a broader and more complex characterization of the advertising industry: As an industry, advertising mediates between commodity production and cultural production; as a message form, it adopts, revises, and shapes other cultural message systems; most importantly, through research it appropriates the social structure and cultural dynamics of market society, and recycles them as strategies targeted toward segments of the population—making the marketplace into an oscillating feedback loop.

Thus, advertising is a channel through which social change is constantly mediated—both a discursive practice contributing to cultural and economic change and a representational practice wherein such changes can be witnessed and interpreted. This is not to say that advertising is the central determining factor in the expansion of the consumer society; rather, we present it here as an indispensable sector that helps us interpret the underlying historical developments that have been forged in the mediated marketplace over the last half century.

We argue, therefore, that advertising is best studied as a form of social communication about material culture, as an institution within which the market economy and culture are coordinated and negotiated, and as a cultural resource used by individuals for a variety of reasons, many of which may have little to do with the purchase of the product presented in an individual advertisement. To address advertising in this way requires us to take a broad view our subject, one which is built upon two pillars: history and culture.

The pillar of history is reflected in the consensus that we can grasp the implications of present-day practices best by seeing how they were composed and put into place during the preceding century. Older advertisements are a treasure house of fascinating and often amusing illustrations of how people and products used to look; exhuming and examining them is a pleasant chore. They are also a condensed and graphic representation of certain aspects of life in times past. Robert Atwan and his associates put together a selection of ads spanning the twentieth century in their book, *Edsels, Luckies and Frigidaires* (1979), and remarked quite accurately that "advertisements tell us in miniature a great deal about an entire civilization, its actual material life and interlocking collective fantasies."

Even a cursory glance at the past helps to persuade us that what exists now is by no means the inevitable outcome of prior events, that things could be other than they are. For example, if some of the businesspeople who controlled media industries in the 1920s had had their way, there would be no commercials on radio and television. Had this happened, we would have grown up knowing only non-commercial broadcasting, which would appear normal to us, and under such circumstances most of us would be offended at the very idea of having commercial messages on the electronic media. Our present-day situation, considered by itself, always appears at first glance to be a world that is whole: everything seems to be linked naturally to everything else. Thus, to understand the present we must first, so to speak, disassemble it. In this book, we will devote a good deal of space to inquiries into the historical evolution of various institutions: consumer goods marketing, the mass media of communication, popular culture, and the advertising agencies. Then we will put the pieces together again.

The advertising industry is a complex mechanism, made up of many parts, and its products reflect that complexity; by taking it apart and reassembling it we hope to show how it works. This type of historical analysis has fallen out of fashion with some historians, who have rejected the idea of reducing complex histories to epochs and great meta-narratives. In their place historians have offered in-depth analysis of particulars—minor practices and local events, for example, rather than large-scale, universal or global concepts. The alleged justification for this alternative approach is that these "mini-narratives" are always situational, provisional, contingent, and temporary, and make no claim to universality or ultimate truth. However, the flaw in this approach is a poor understanding of what most historians have actually done. In point of fact, most historical studies are miniatures—accounts of working-class life, of women's roles, of the creation of business empires, of resource industries such as the fur trade and the fishery, of forms of oppression such as slavery, and so on.

This traditional study of our past is indispensable for understanding both how the present came about and what the future possibly holds. Without it the world we observe in our surroundings appears natural to us, and it is easy to take it for granted. We can understand today's world, however, only if we step back from it and realize both how novel it is, compared to all past societies, and how it came into being.

The second pillar for the study of advertising is culture. Many controversies about the real or imagined effects of ads on specific aspects of attitudes and behavior are bound up with our cultural traditions. We have in mind, however, the more general issue of how advertising systematically responds and contributes to cultural changes.

The least important aspect of advertising's significance for modern society is its role in influencing specific consumer choices—whether wise or unwise—about purchasing products. The debates about advertising still focus too greatly on advertising's role in shaping individual consumer choices. Advertising's defenders maintain that a modern economy relies upon the provision of both straightforward factual information and persuasive messages to consumers; regulation and industry professionalism controls blatantly misleading or deceptive statements. Advertising's critics argue that consumers get very little useful information from advertisements and could make more sensible choices if they were not bombarded constantly with (often misleading and deceptive) messages about products. Both of these positions have limited understandings of advertising by narrowly apprehending the role of advertising in culture.

Then what is advertising about, if it is not about influencing consumer choices? To avoid misunderstanding, we wish to emphasize a key point here: All forms of advertising, from classified ads and grocery store flyers to nationwide TV campaigns, transmit some information about goods or services from those who own them to those who may wish to acquire them. Furthermore, it is reasonable to assume that such information has some influence on some of the decisions about acquiring goods and services that most people make every day.

Exactly what kind of influence is exerted on which people, and whether or not this influence is beneficial for society, are matters of longstanding controversy that will not be settled in the near future, or perhaps ever. Meanwhile, both modern society and advertising have been undergoing major changes that have affected every aspect of their interaction: the type of persons addressed by advertisements, the type of information presented in them, the media through which they are transmitted, and so forth. The entire social context and social significance of advertising has altered radically. If we continue to think about advertising as being mostly about the transmittal of specifics about item X from person (or company) A to person B, we will remain unaware of the most interesting and important developments affecting it.

The twentieth century witnessed a dramatic and sustained rise in the real income and purchasing power of the average person in Western consumer societies, where most people have access to a huge and constantly changing array of goods. At the same time, technological innovations in mass communications transformed the message formats for advertisements themselves. Billboards now include moving images, magazine promotion is no longer typeset but digitally rendered, the color and sharpness at which photographic images can be rendered has improved greatly, indeed so advanced are modern image techniques that older techniques such as black and white images, or cartoon-pixilated images, are employed within contemporary design to invoke nostalgia or retro sentiments. Improvements in image production might be understood as contributing to the very important shift within twentieth-century advertising away from heavily text-based messages to images. The shift to images was accompanied by a trend toward advertisers devoting less copy to talking about products, and more to claims about how those products could benefit people's lives. Understanding advertising's role requires attention to the context of the production of its messages, to the technology utilized, and to the changing habits of mind and techniques employed by its practitioners.

From Product Description to Social Communication

Over the course of the preceding century, advertisers constructed a vast, diverse, and continually changing library of messages that both schooled consumers in the use of objects and offered guidance about personal maintenance, appropriate values, and correct behavior for social acceptance. In short, advertising offered models of the good life and insight into how to achieve personal pleasure and social success. We argue that the vast library of commercial fables, fairy tales, and troupes represents something more than salesmanship. It can be understood as a cultural discourse in and through goods.

The linking of goods to social dialogue introduced a profound influence within the discourse in and through goods, but it arose out of the more focused interest in formats, which attracted audience attention. Similarly, advertising developed within the nexus of a great many contradictions, which often strengthened the unique quality of its messages instead of distracting from it. For example, several studies of the industry emphasize the interest in shaping messages which please the cultural elite, including other advertising practitioners. At the same time the practices of advertising are also influenced by the need to "speak to people on the street." In attempting to close the divide between aesthetic and pragmatic communicational concerns, advertisers popularized high and modern arts and were often more in tune and willing to react to changing public sentiments then many other institutions.

As twentieth-century consumer societies matured, advertisers demonstrated this key communications aspect of the consumption process more and more clearly, particularly through dramatic changes in marketing and advertising strategies. Herein lies the real importance of advertising in modern society: It is the privileged discourse for the circulation of messages and social cues about the interplay between persons and objects. The discourse through and about objects is privileged—that is, it occupies a special place in our lives—for three reasons. First, because the state of our economy is the predominant concern in public affairs. Second, because messages about goods surround us through our interactions with communications media. Third, because our interpretation of the social world is formulated against the backdrop of these messages. In comparison with the importance of this service, advertising's transmittal of details about product characteristics is a trivial sidelight.

To appreciate the discourses undertaken in and through goods requires careful attention to the context of the production exchange and use of goods and the role of mass media and advertising. In this chapter we address a few of the key moments of the emergence and evolution of consumer society. In broaching this complex subject we pay particular attention to the changing relations between persons and their relationships to consumption. In later chapters, we will assess the significance of changes in communications media and associated changes in advertising practice that were occurring and interacting at the same time.

Advertising helped industrialism to bring products associated with a refined lifestyle to the ordinary person. Keeping workers poor made less and less sense as the factory system's astonishing productive capacities became apparent—the only arena capable of absorbing the system's output was the one occupied by those who had been poor for so long. The modern economy, one based upon systems of production linked to consumption, emerged.

In seeking to analyze and understand this discourse and its historical evolution, it is necessary to weave together and synthesize elements from a number of different perspectives within the general domains of history and culture. Following the history of advertising, we find that agencies became uniquely positioned within the cycle of production and consumption. Agencies undertook a specialized function, but worked in conjunction with other important professionals—one of the most important being media professionals. The history of print, radio, and pay-per-view television testifies that media can be commercially viable without advertising subsidy. However, the advertising subsidy took root and helped to shape the growth of the modern communications industries.

The flow of money, reasonably straightforward at first, became exceedingly complex. In the late nineteenth century, producers began to allocate a proportion of their income to advertising. At first, the money went directly to the media; later it was channelled through advertising agencies, which took a proportion of the billing as their sales commission. Consumers pay this advertising subsidy to the media as part of the price of a product. The proportion varies across industries—manufacturers of cosmetics, personal-care products, and household goods allocate a high proportion of all expenses to advertising. For example, up to 50 percent of the cost of a perfume may be attributed to expenditures on advertising. Advertising now accounts for almost all revenue for the broadcast media (except in public networks such as the BBC or PBS, public radio, and pay-per-view satellite), 75 percent for the newspaper industry, and from 60 to 100 percent of income for magazines.

Advertising became the crucial bridge between the activities of selling products and communication as both spheres expanded rapidly. This is a simple but much overlooked aspect of its significance in modern society. The commission system was dissolved in the 1980s, and now advertisers often pay for media and advertising separately, but these new practices have not severed the advertising subsidy to the media. One of the major uses of this bridge, then, was to help allocate a proportion of the income accruing to industry from consumers to the development of media. Money, influence, and information crossed the bridge. The media, in turn, adjusted to these new sources of revenue by setting up departments and services (such as market and circulation research) to accommodate their growing relationship with agencies and advertisers, thereby diverting funds from editorial, programming, and internal development efforts. Agencies also bridge the work of marketers, product designers, consumer researchers, promotional specialist public relations experts, and direct marketing professionals.

Table 1.1 summarizes our main argument and findings about the development and the place of advertising as social communication in modern culture. It reflects our belief that only through an integration of insights from a number of different approaches is it possible to fully understand the role of advertising in the discourse through and about objects. Table 1.1 draws upon five main perspectives to aid us in this objective.

First, we focus on the broad economic changes that characterize the transition in societies from largely agricultural and artisanal (craft) modes of production to a predominantly industrial mode of production. This transition

Table 1.1 The Development of Media, Marketing, and Advertising

Media for Advertising	Newspapers/Magazines	Radio	Television	Television	Media mix
Marketing Strategy	Rational	Non-rational	Behaviorist	Segmentation	Anthropological
Advertising Strategy	Utility[a]	Product Symbols[b]	Personification[c]	Lifestyle[d]	Demassifying[e]
Period	1890 1910	1920 1940	1950 1960	1970 1980	1990 2000
Elements in Ads	Product qualities/price/use	Product qualities; Symbolic attributes	Product; Person prototype	Product; Activity: person-setting	Brand image; Media world niches
Metaphoric-Emotive Themes in Ads	Quality, useful, descriptive	Status, family, health; white magic; social authority	Glamor, romance; sensuality; black magic; self-transformation	Leisure, health; groups; friendship	Authenticity; spotlighting; reflexivity; diversity; transformation of objects
Cultural Frames for Goods	Idolatry: Products are abstracted from process of production, presented as pure use-values	Iconology: Products are embodiments of attributes, configured in social judgment	Narcissism: Products are personalized and satisfaction is judged in interpersonal terms	Totemism: Products are emblems of group-related consumption practices	Mise-en-Scène: Products are props for the self-construction of changing scenes and life-scripts

* Pre-1890: Posters and billboards.

[a] See Figure 1.2. [b] See Figure 1.3. [c] See Figure 1.4. [d] See Figure 1.5. [e] See Figure 1.6.

necessitated not simply the adaptation to new ways to produce goods, but also required the development of new mechanisms for the distribution and circulation of goods.

Second, we draw upon socio-cultural perspectives in seeking to understand how these economic changes influenced how people related to goods. We pay special attention to how the cultural forms that give meaning to the world of things undergo a drastic repositioning, such that in the consumer society marketplace institutions come to replace the family, community, and religious institutions that were important in agricultural societies and earlier forms of industrial society.

Third, we look to the specific manner in which these economic and socio-cultural changes were institutionally mediated by the emergence and development of two key symbiotically-related industries: the commercial mass media and the advertising agencies. In terms of the mass media, we focus on the way the successive integration of newspapers, magazines, radio, and television into the sphere of marketplace communications profoundly influences the nature of the discourse through and about objects. Different media offer different potentialities for advertising formats and strategies. This dimension is reflected in the "Media for Advertising" categories in Table 1.1. The commercial media are the delivery system for advertisements, which are actually planned and created by advertising agencies who act on behalf of their manufacturing clients. It is important to find out how the agencies and advertisers are thinking about consumers and ways to appeal to them. We identify five main phases in the development of marketing strategy throughout the twentieth century.

Fourth, we analyze advertisements from all periods of the twentieth century to see how the economic, socio-cultural, and institutional contexts influence their form and content. The advertising text reflects a *negotiation of meaning*. Advertising is privileged, as we have suggested, but the decoding of intended messages is not assured: The interpretive labor of audiences must be engaged for meaning to be released and transmitted. The encoding practices of advertisers are informed by an imagined or mobilized target audience. The construction of the audience occurs in the latent projections of advertising industry creative departments and formally through the research loop that feeds information about cultural trends and target market taste into design practices. A wide variety of changing strategies—which amount to intuitive guesses about the marketplace—are devised by advertisers, and those deemed useful are repeated and spread throughout the promotional system forming a historical record from which to derive insight into the changing social cultural dynamics of a particular historical moment. We identify five main stages in the development of advertising strategy. (See lines three to six in Table 1.1, as well as Figures 1.2–1.6.)

Fifth, drawing upon our previous analysis of advertising content, as well as three recent case studies, we can see how this framework impacts upon our general understanding of goods and the ways in which they are integrated into the process of satisfaction and communication in the consumer society. In particular, we focus on the predominant set of images, values, and forms of communication in any period that provide what we call a "cultural frame for goods." We find the product promoted and the unique characteristics of the target audience, particularly their gender, nuance the cultural frame, still we feel it is possible to identify five major cultural frames that have historically given some definition to the relationship between people and things (see below and Chapter 6, especially Table 6.1).

We have described our general approach to the understanding of advertising as a form of social communication. More specifically, as we proceed, chapter by chapter, to first take apart and then reassemble the mechanism of modern advertising and its linkups with other social institutions, we shall run through the following steps. In Part I we put our workbench in order by arranging and inspecting the principal arguments concerning the relationship between advertising and society. chapters 2 and 3 sketch the main differences between the earlier form of industrial society and the consumer culture that has replaced it over the course of the twentieth century. We now have a society unique in human history—one wherein most individuals depend on a continuously growing array of marketed goods for the satisfaction of their needs. This has been made possible by the succession of technological triumphs in industry, by the rationalization of the market economy by manufacturers and financiers, and by the long and bitter struggles of workers to win a decent standard of living and a semblance of social democracy.

Chapter 4 traces the emergence of the mass-communications-media modern society, from print (newspapers and magazines) to broadcasting (radio and television), and attempts to foster a proper appreciation of these media as autonomous institutional actors. By the end of the nineteenth century, the print media had established new forms of communication; created the public that they addressed; and, above all, set up the fertile interaction between media strategy and audience segment—all this before the sale of commercial advertising space began to generate significant revenues. So well-established was the framework for the transactions between media and their audiences by this time that, when the new electronic broadcasting media appeared on the scene, they slipped relatively easily into the mold established by the print media. Chapter 5 follows the formation of the modern full service advertising agency which developed in tandem with the mass media and the expansion of consumer culture. The first service performed by advertisers was the selling of space within the media, but over time, creative, research, and accounting departments were added to the focus on media.

The story of a muslin sack

THE real wonder-story of the tobacco that is smoked by *more millions of men* than all other good tobaccos *combined*—

GENUINE
"BULL" DURHAM
SMOKING TOBACCO

In quaint old Durham, North Carolina—that's where the story starts.

That's where those golden leaves first grew in the sunny fields of Greene's farm. That's where they first filled those simple muslin sacks with good, sweet, native tobacco—fifty-two years ago.

No thought then of fancy packages—or of "processes" for improving on Nature.

Just surprisingly good tobacco! *That* was what they had *discovered* —that was what interested those critical Southern smokers who gave a rousing welcome to "Bull" Durham as the greatest tobacco they had ever tasted.

And then the soldiers came. They came—and smoked—and were captured!

Scattering to their homes all over the nation, they carried the fame of this wonderful smoke.

Wasn't that Durham postmaster busy with letters from up and down the land asking how to get *more* of that "Bull" Durham!

And—for over half a century, just because it's so down-right *good*, it's been *earning* and *winning* and *hold-*ing new friends faster than any other tobacco ever grown.

Faster! Twenty-two million pounds — 362 million packages — were sold and smoked last year! Yet this was merely the normal growth over the year before.

That sack might have been displaced by a fancy box. But the increasing millions of smokers who have an affection for this plain, convenient muslin cover have shown that *they* want the value where it belongs—in the tobacco. You can't smoke the cover!

"Bull" Durham has stood the long test. Its purity—its natural, undoctored goodness as a smoke—have held and splendidly multiplied its friends—have won for it the leadership over all the tobaccos of the world.

Figure 1.2 Utility: A Discourse about Product Quality.
Source: Courtesy of The American Tobacco Company.

Figure 1.3 Product Symbols: A Discourse about Social Values and Tastes.

Figure 1.4 Personalization: A Discourse about Individual Feelings.
Source: Courtesy of Bristol-Myers Canada Inc.

Dubonnet s'il vous plaît

Figure 1.5 Lifestyles: A Discourse about Social Groups and their Activities.
Source: Courtesy of Schenley Industries.

Figure 1.6 "Demassifying": A discourse about creating self distinction and uniqueness in a massified world.
Source: Alfred Dunhill Fragrance

Can we devise a way to look at ads so that—out of their own form and content—they yield up this story? We take up this challenge in chapter 6, where we present our own research design for analyzing advertisements, as well as the results obtained in two extensive applications of it: One looks at modern television commercials; the other involves a large sample of magazine ads drawn from the period 1910–2000, providing detailed information about what was happening in ads over the entire course of the twentieth century. In the total system of advertising, the agencies turned out scene after scene and act after act of a never-ending drama of consumer satisfaction, using images of people, products, and forms of well-being as their players. Our research design enables us to follow each of the players and its lines separately, as well as to keep track of their interactions, revealing significant patterns in each period and changes in them over time.

Chapter 7, "Goods as Communicators and Satisfiers," seeks to put the pieces back together again. Anthropological studies tell us that, in human societies, material objects have always served to convey meanings and messages about rank, status, privilege, roles, caste, sex, class; about how such social subgroups were formed; and about what rules groups devised to dictate their conduct to each other. We look at the modern consumer society as an anthropological type and find that the age-old function of goods as communicators is now combined with the special capabilities of the new technologies of mass communication, the immense productive resources of modern industry, and the diverse array of lifestyle models for personal satisfaction, to generate the discourse through and about objects. Advertising makes all this possible, for it is the place at which industry, media, and lifestyles converge.

Chapter 7 concludes with a fuller explanation of the stages of development outlined in Table 1.1. The role of advertising as a form of communication contending that the success of both the advertising message formats, and the major shifts in their content—from description of the product to the linking of persons, products, and settings in symbolic representations—was not due primarily to their intrinsic merits as artistic creations. Rather, ads evolved alongside other, more general changes in society that loosened up and diversified the range of approved cultural models that guide the search for personal satisfaction. These models were later baptized "lifestyles."

Part 2 is devoted to a detailed study of advertising in the post-1980s period, beginning with an introduction to some of the key debates of consumer culture in chapter 8. Chapter 9 provides an exploration of some of the changes that accompanied the rise of a consumer culture, as an extended commercial media system brought advertising and promotion into ever more spheres of everyday life, including the stylization of goods and the rapid cycling of the fashion system. Our study reveals intensive discussion of the processes of "dematerialization" and "demassification," or what is taken to be a heightened attention within consumer culture to the symbolic aspects of goods and where sectors of the population develop lifestyles fashioned in opposition to mass society. Each of the major institutional components that set in motion the interplay between society and culture, media, and advertising is examined in turn.

Chapter 10 traces the evolution of the mass media after the 1980s as media reorient themselves in the light of new computer technologies and telecommunication innovations and the deregulation of the media spectrum. The interest of advertisers increasingly shifts from the national to global and more refined market segments—advertisers became particularly fixated upon those groups for whom aesthetics were highly important, young people and ethnic groups. Intensive study was undertaken to inform message designs to please these prized market segments. Network television, the traditional fulcrum of the advertising industry, was challenged by advertisers' embrace of new media options and below the line promotion, mixed and cross media strategies.

Chapters 11 and 12 look at the transformation of the full service agencies many of whom had their services unbundled and repackaged into either boutique advertising services or brought under the wing of massive global communication conglomerates. Agencies learned to operate on a triple front: They stood between industry and media, helping to create new forms for messages about products; between industry and consumers, helping to develop comprehensive marketing campaigns; and between media and consumers, helping to do the research on audiences that led to what we know as "market segmentation." While "agencies like to refer to themselves as experts in marketing communications" (Varcoe 1981, 67), the creation of advertisements is more a process of negotiation both within the agency and in its relations with media, clients, and audiences than it is a set of mechanical and technical routines.

Advertising campaigns today (as opposed to the individual finished ad) do not originate in one person's genius or drive but in a complex process of intra- and inter-organizational decision making and problem. Within the mediated marketplace advertising became just one component of a much larger promotional effort, and the integration between agencies and popular culture providers was fully integrated. Particular attention is paid to the role of the creative people, their acceptance within consumer culture, and how they learned to negotiate with savvy audiences no longer easily plied by the smoke and mirror routines of the advertising trade.

Our analysis of the post 1980 advertising industry and the consumer culture literature revealed advertiser's interest in addressing particular market segments. In chapters 13, 14, and 15 we present case studies that explore how advertisers along with other cultural intermediaries mobilized consumer segments by developing a template for understanding the habits and tastes of particular audience niches. Our attention is focused upon how market researchers and advertising agencies articulated these lifestyle groups and translate them into market segments. Chapter 13 details the construction—during the early 1980s—of the "yuppie" or young urban professionals, their unique consumption patterns, and enduring legacy within advertising circles. The yuppie became the object of ridicule for a so-called "Generation X," youth market that was detected in the late 1980s.

This grouping of disaffected young people later created its own distinctive style. We argue that in negotiating a relationship with Generation X, the industry developed new techniques that intensified the commodification of youth culture. We find advertisers involved in institutionalising practices to address complex lifecycle factors, generational conflict, and intensive cultural pirating into their marketing efforts. Generation X became of particular concern to advertisers because of their anti-commercialist attitudes. In addressing this market, advertisers brought a new intensity to youth marketing. Chapter 14 is a study of some of the dominant themes which advertising creatives used to engage the disaffected Gen-X audience within targeted television campaigns.

Chapter 15 explores the formation and modes of address used by advertisers in the 1990s to speak to the "culturati"—a highly educated and affluent audience who developed lifestyles and consumption habits to distinguish themselves from the mass. We examine how *Vanity Fair* magazine captured this cultural aspirant class and how the advertisements in this publication spoke to their particularly cultural anxieties.

What do these changing patterns mean? These two chapters open the discussion of Part 3, "The Theater of Consumption". Chapter 16 looks at a number of areas in which advertising has been especially controversial in recent years (for example, advertising to children, and tobacco/alcohol advertising), in the light of both industry and governmental attempts to regulate the contents of ads. These attempts have never been very satisfactory. Modern advertising draws upon so many diverse cultural resources, and is so dependent upon collaboration with its audience for constructing the meaning of its messages, that the rather clumsy tools of social regulation almost inevitably fail to achieve their objectives. We conclude that the only effective way of constraining advertising's impact, in those areas where social concerns about that impact are sufficiently grave, is to deny or restrict access by advertisers to specific audiences or media. In chapter 17, we seek to pull the threads together, returning to the question of the possibility of achieving satisfaction within the mediated marketplace.

CHAPTER 2

From Traditional to Industrial Society

Over three hundred years ago a set of practices and sensibilities emerged as the age of modernity. Within the sweeping set of changes—economic modernization—we have a specific focus on the changing relationship between persons and goods and, of course, the role of advertising in that process. Our discussion is organized around three broad social transitions: in this chapter, the transition from traditional to industrial society; in chapter 3, from industrial to consumer society; and in chapter 4, developments in the consumer society after the 1970s.

Traditional cultures—by which we mean all human societies in the period before the coming of industrialization—place great importance on the group, social obligation, and the stability of social rank. In such societies, which persist to this day in many parts of the world, individuals are completely dependant upon one another for survival, and, hence, are strongly motivated to adhere to group values and beliefs. In these societies, people generally learn to accept their fate, as few opportunities exist, short of marriage and war, to change their status. Traditional cultures weave new experiences into those of the past. Even here, a traditional form of fashion operates within the group—in the form of social norms for dress (including gender differences), ornamentation, and so forth—and is used to clearly demarcate social roles, thus cementing the group and the individual's place within it. The modest number of goods that are available in daily life are either produced locally by known craftsmen, self-made within families, or traded for in regional markets. Elites within these societies, of course, have access to a broader assortment of goods, but their consumption is also undertaken with the maintenance of cultural heritage, extended family relations, and local community norms in mind. Because inheritance is a key means of goods exchange in such societies, goods are made to last.

With the coming of modern societies, economic relations start to be mediated through a market that privileges long-term growth and an open-ended future. Individuals now work within new non-familial or craft settings. They are paid wages and conduct their exchanges through money, rather than by barter or trade, which permits a wider freedom with respect to their selection of goods. The population is more mobile as people moved to areas where better opportunities for employment exist. Social interactions are continuously in flux, and people come into contact with more strangers in daily life. Industrialization produces many more goods than craft networks, and over time these goods are made available not just to elites but to wider sections of the population.

A fashion system that emphasizes style, novelty, and continuous change became an important dynamic not just in clothing but in all types of goods. Fashion became institutionalized and specialized workers—including advertisers, product designers, and marketers—work within production cycles to stylize and popularize goods. The tastes of the new bourgeoisie or business class were prominent in early industrial society; however, over time the turnover of fashion accelerated and styles became pluralized, diminishing the power of any particular set of style leaders to dominate the fashion scene. Media and advertising offer a vast array of different styles, drawn from celebrity circles, fashion runways, experts, and the street, offering a prodigious symbolic outpouring that became readily available to consumers, who increasingly negotiated their sense of self, affiliation, satisfaction, and pleasure through commodities.

Pre-Industrial Society in the West

Within the agrarian feudal society that emerged between 1100 and 1600 AD, serfs produced goods on land overseen by the monarchy, church, and noblemen. Physical survival depended upon a group effort and people worked together within extended family and craft networks. Children were apprentices in the family craft enterprise, learning at the knee of their parents. Many children inherited their careers from their parents: If father was a blacksmith, the son was likely to be a blacksmith also. Children were also loaned out as indentured laborers. The work undertaken was largely agrarian, with some craft production and service functions for the wealthy. A serf's obligation to his lord was understood as a personal one: Resources and labor were given in exchange for protection, even though sometimes that protection was not delivered. That said, the common people did not blindly follow the dictates of religion and the nobility; indeed, the lack of bureaucratic processes to track people left most quite free from scrutiny of the powerful. Their behaviors were more regulated by family and close community members.

Traditional consumption was not particularly thrifty. The concept of thrift and prudence emerged out of a more affluent money culture. In traditional societies where resources continued to be scarce, consumption was more seasonally and communally orientated. In years of bountiful crops people ate heartily, and in lean years they starved. People were not particularly motivated to produce more goods for stockpiling, as there was little incentive to do so where there was little security from raids and plunder. When times were good, celebrations of gluttony were held in the winter season when stocks could not be replenished. These rituals were more important then the potential hardships such celebrations might later bring, as they served to bind people together and distribute resources

(Giddens 1995, Burke 1978). Holiday rituals were typically structured around pattered cultural practices such as song, dance, theater, and feasting, and took a great deal of time away from work.

Members of the elites often hosted these periodic carnivals, allowing the lord to provide a feast, or bread and circuses, which was an important political gesture. Traditional societies displayed their wealth in acts of consumption (pageantry, carnivals, potlatches, processions). Wealth was communally displayed and funneled into monuments, edifices, guildhalls, and cathedrals (Buchan 1997). Consumption was organized around the social group, rather than the individual or family.

Goods were produced locally and in limited number. Goods circulated slowly through inheritance and carried conversations, stories, and lore—the meanings of ancestry—with them. Tools of production were handed down from one generation to the next; for example, the term "heirloom" denotes passing down the loom used for weaving to one's children. On their journey from one generation to the next these goods accumulated a great deal of meaning. As Giddens (1991) has noted, rituals—the lifeblood of traditional cultures—were often enacted through the use of enchanted objects. Goblets were used in religious rituals, swords in honoring rank. These ritual objects were not subject to fashion, but rather were invested with uniqueness, as possessing eternal and timeless qualities: Sir Arthur did not tire of the search for the Holy Grail, Aladdin did not change his lamp every season, nor did the priest look for a new challis for every Mass. Indeed, the longer the object was in ritual circulation, the more its significance grew.

People, like goods, circulated slowly through traditional cultures and had relatively fixed meanings. Mobility was limited. More generally, one's place in the world was more inscribed at birth. War and marriage were two of the few channels for social mobility. The cosmology of the Great Chain of Being ordered the feudal world, placing God in the topmost position, followed by angels, monarchs and nobility, priests, craftspeople, peasants, and all the animal kingdom. Group values (modesty, obedience, religious faith) were prized over individual values (self-expression, self-esteem, creativity). People were encouraged to submerge their personal interests within that of the group. The cosmology of fate oriented people to see forces outside the self (nature, God's will) as playing a greater role in shaping one's life than did individual will. There was less psychological emphasis upon the potential for change, as the role of the past, ancestry and generations weighed heavily on the traditional mind. Self-transformation through work, enterprise, education, or stardom is a modern idea.

Sumptuary laws, which restricted the possession of luxury goods to certain classes of people, testify to the attempts made by early elites to use goods as explicit markers of social rank. The rationale offered in the literature of the day was that only the elite possessed the capacity to use such goods in an appropriate manner: "In the preindustrial period, social commentaries would argue that people could only handle a modest array of goods or they would become disorientated. This belief helped to keep people attached to their station in life and did not challenge the dominant social interests of the elite classes" (Douglas and Isherwood 1981).

Limiting the circulation of goods not only maintained privilege but also kept status competition in check. For the vast majority, consumption was regulated by availability and dictated by labor, rank, and ritual. Richard Sennett (1978) noted that fashion in the seventeenth and eighteenth centuries marked social rank. People's last names (Black, Baker) often indicated the type of work they performed—as did their clothing. Bakers, fishmongers, and shoemakers all wore unique uniforms that distinguished their profession. Wigs, ribbons, the color, texture, and amount of fabric used in a garment, all offered clues of social standing and gender. During celebrations people often donned different clothes to mark ritual space. Styles changed slowly, with the greatest change occurring in the upper classes. British elite emulated Paris fashion, for example, but it took many years for styles to migrate from one place to another. Clothing was not considered to be an expression of the individual's personality, and although individual variations in style did occur, they were not encouraged as they would be in the modern era.

Early Industrial Society

Industrial society emerged within an expanded money economy. As early as the thirteenth century, money began to be used in Europe as a medium of exchange for labor and land, and over a vast stretch of time wage labor began to replace traditional craft, family, and feudal production. This widespread money economy is seen as particularly important within the transition from traditional to industrial society (along with the Enlightenment, the Protestant reformation, secularization, and science). The sociologist Georg Simmel provides a richly descriptive passage that neatly summarizes the profound changes that were set in motion by the commodification of labor:

> The...level where the person is actually excluded from the product and the demands no longer extended to him, is reached with the replacement of payment in kind by money payment. For this reason, it has been regarded, to some extent, as a Magna Carta of personal freedom in the domain of civil law...The lord of the manor who can demand a quantity of beer or poultry or honey from a serf thereby determines the activity of the latter in a certain direction. But the moment he imposes merely a money levy the peasant is free, in so far as he can decide whether to keep bees or cattle or anything else. (Simmel 1990, 285–6)

Simmel recognizes how the new relations provided more freedom for individuals to act outside of the traditional social relationships of family, serf, and guild. Individuals earned their own money and acquired goods in the marketplace, becoming less dependent on the older networks of barter and social obligation. The lord and the peasant were unleashed from their traditional rustic diets, no longer confined to the food or goods produced locally. Money and the expansion of the marketplace enabled the purchase of goods outside of the local area, greatly widening the sphere of available goods (Buchan 1997). The practices and values of the modern marketplace began to support more independent and impersonal relations between people.

As agricultural production improved people migrated from the countryside to the city in search of work. Local and small-scale family and craft production was replaced by new working arrangements in which many people labored together. Craftworkers had been responsible for all aspects of production, whereas industrial production cycles broke work down into smaller tasks. The production cycle was made up of specialized functions. New lines of work emerged such as engineers, shopkeepers, accountants, and bankers, and other white collar workers. This division of labor, factory arrangements, and increased use of machines quickened the pace of production. Goods were produced more quickly, and improved transportation and communication facilitated the expansion of market exchange across time and space. People began to consume goods made by unknown others. Mobility was a key feature of the new marketplace relationships. Ideas and practices were exchanged along with goods. Linked intimately with craft labor, the old ways of life could not stamp their accumulated meanings on the anonymous products that were beginning to pour off the assembly lines. The unity and continuity of daily life in village settlements could not be sustained amid increasing urbanization, especially when workplace, domicile, and commerce were separated. Traditional society was fading away.

The new relations gave those who owned the factories power over a vast workforce. The traditional labor force had not been closely monitored, but the expansion of commerce brought more disciplining, tracking, recording and techniques of control and coordination over workers for maximum productivity and efficiency. Factory owners and shopkeepers seeking to teach the new discipline of market relations—regular hours and work days, punctuality, subordination to the machine, wage income as the sole means of subsistence—to a workforce steeped in peasant rhythms had encountered a recalcitrant and often hostile audience who had little reason to be grateful to its teachers. Employers lamented their employees' love of cheap but debilitating spirits and the "Blue Mondays" that shortened the working week; their frequent absences for long celebrations of traditional festive occasions, or just for going hunting, or attending to domestic business; and their stubborn resistance in general to the new work discipline that offended customary practices and the profound sense of personal dignity rooted in them.

These themes are nicely illustrated in a splendid essay by the historian Herbert Gutman, who also shows how European immigrants to North America constructed defenses against oppression out of their popular cultures: "Peasant parades and rituals, religious oaths and food riots, and much else in the culture and behavior of early twentieth-century immigrant American factory workers were...natural and effective forms of self-assertion and self-protection" (1977, 66). Both secular and religious elements in transplanted ethnic communities were called upon to sustain labor solidarity, especially in the bitter and all-too-frequent strikes. Group traditions supplied not only the means to struggle against degradation and injustice, but also to retain a foothold in a remembered world via an elemental coherence fashioned out of custom, venerated objects, ancient loyalties, and intergenerational memory.

But the highly restrictive codes of personal behavior shaped by the closed worlds of religious values, traditional cultural rituals, and distinct ethnic communities could not survive the more subtle blows of industrialism. The cultural relativism resulting from the quick amalgamation of so many different groups; the erosion of the economic function of the extended family; and the dawning of a new type of leisure time, highly individualized in nature and no longer bound to the traditional collective forms of popular entertainment or domestic routine, all eroded the viability of older community structures. Although many people continued to profess a belief in religion, the long and steady decline in church attendance began for all Western nations, with the exception of the United States.

Hierarchy, inequality, and power have shaped all societies, but were distinctly patterned in modern society. One of the most astute critics of the new relationships of industrial production was Karl Marx, who marveled at the immense power of the new systems of production, seeing in them as offering for the first time in history the means of unshackling society from scarcity and ameliorating the inequalities and hierarchies of the past. Yet he also argued that the promise of industrialization could not be actualized, because in the new relations of production divided people, producing not simply more goods, but social classes and systemic inequality and continual economic crisis as well. The new arrangement of production allowed property and labor to be controlled by a privileged few, whose interests in deriving an adequate return for their capital investment held inordinate sway within society.

The novels of Charles Dickens display some of the most vivid and enduring representations of the new relations of production. His famous *Christmas Carol* (1844) is a moral tale of the new industrial economy. Bob Cratchet works long hours into the Christmas holiday time in a dank, cold office. This lack of observance of winter rituals differed sharply from the practices of traditional cultures, in which holiday participation was communal and required, due its important in holding people together. Feudal society celebrated over one hundred annual holidays, which were reduced to eleven "bank holidays" in the industrial period.

Industrial society relies on the more abstract and impersonal relations of the market to bond people collectively, and thus ritual takes on new meaning and function. Dickens' tale draws a contrast between traditional social obligations, in which providing for winter feasting demanded community contribution, particularly from the wealthy, to modern relations, where Cratchet, like all workers, is responsible for using his individual wages to undertake a privatized feast for his family. Despite his long hours of work, however, Cratchet barely earns enough to maintain his family, let alone finance a celebration. The new relations of production permit the surplus value of his labor, which might have contributed to the festivities, to be redirected and hoarded by the owner of the business, Ebenezer Scrooge. The accumulation and growth of funds overshadows and disrupts traditional social bonds.

Critics of industrial society might focus on the plight of Bob Cratchet, but the early modern sociologist Max Weber was interested in what drove Ebenezer Scrooge to submit so forcefully to his work. What could explain Scrooge's ability to steel his emotions, choose coffee over alcohol, work so hard, and horde instead of squander his wealth? Weber argued that the expansion of capital could not in itself explain the dynamics of capital. People's willingness to participate within the new relations of production was not driven from without, but from within: The question of the motive forces in the expansion of modern capitalism is not in the first instance a question of the origin of the capital sums which were available for capitalists uses, but, above all, of the development of the spirit of capitalism. Where it appears and is able to work itself out, it produces its own capital and monetary supplies, as the means to its ends, but the reverse is not true. (Weber 1958)

Weber argued that religious ideas from traditional culture did not disappear, but rather were reworked in the new industrial setting. Within Protestant communities, work became associated with a calling of God. To undertake Gods' work on earth brought heavenly rewards—labor was given a divine reason to be. Weber located a work ethic which valued efficiency, productivity, thrift, discipline, and hard work within particular social groups, and suggested that this work ethic provided the motivation necessary to build industrial society.

Figure 2.1 provides a sketch of early industrial society. It suggests that within Western Europe and North America, at least until the turn of the nineteenth century, social classes were by and large formed directly through the operation

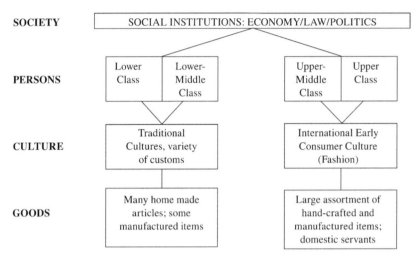

Figure 2.1 Industrial Society about 1900.

of economic and political institutions (the marketplace and the government). In other words, persons were formed into social classes as a direct result of how economic and political power was distributed; the lower class was defined by poverty and oppression, the upper class by wealth and political influence, and so forth. In everyday life—in types of housing, dress, recreation, for example—the social classes existed in quite distinct spheres, although, of course, the dividing lines between them were not always rigid, especially in North America, and some social mobility always existed.

Cities

Cities that grew with industrialization were stimulating and exciting, but for workers used to the slower pace of close-knit rural communities, city life brought new anxieties about how to interact with strangers. Several people from the outlying countryside who attended the 1893 Chicago Exposition fainted because they found its unfamiliar esthetics and novelty overpowering. Simmel noted that individuals dealt with their new urban environment by adopting an intellectual, blasé, and detached modern attitude, which would have been alien to their former boisterous and highly social traditional cultures. This new attitude was bred in the city: "There is no psychic phenomenon which is so unconditionally reserved to the city as the blasé outlook." (Simmel 1971, 14) Simmel described the modern attitude as a defense mechanism:

> Thus, the metropolitan type—which naturally takes on a thousand individual modifications—creates a protective organ for itself against the profound disruption with which the fluctuations and discontinuities of the external

milieu threaten it. Instead of reacting emotionally, the metropolitan type reacts primarily in a rational manner, thus creating a mental predominance through the intensification of consciousness, which in turn is caused by it. (Simmel 1971, 12)

At the height of the industrial revolution in Britain, the mid-nineteenth-century Victorians began to fashion a romantic vision of the family and children as sites of refuge away from the chaotic and alienating relations of the new industrial order. The private domestic space became an idealized site of pleasure and respite from the world of work. Walter Benjamin described the man about the city as a *flaneur*, and noted that he engaged with the wonders of the city less as an absorbed participant than a silent detached observer (Adornoand Adorno 1955). His enjoyment was a private exercise. Within traditional or small-scale societies individuals had communicated to one another in public. Indeed to avoid doing so would bring suspicion, concern, or moral condemnation. Quite the opposite occurred in the city: Individuals became largely silent in one another's presence. Individuals lived in closer contact with a mass of others, but interacted less, and speaking in public about anything more than the weather, could draw suspicion. Modern relationships have therefore tended to be characterized as more impersonal and instrumental than traditional relations.

Anthony Giddens has argued that the dissolving of traditional social relationships left the modern individual with much more responsibility over his or her self-identity. Indeed, according to Giddens modern subjects have no choice but to participate in the joy and conflict of self-construction.

> In the post-tradition order of modernity, and against the backdrop of new forms of mediated experience, self-identity becomes a reflexively organized endeavor. The reflexive project of the self, which consists in the sustaining of coherent, yet continuously revised, biographical narratives, takes place in the context of multiple choice as filtered through abstract systems. In modern social life, the notion of lifestyle takes on a particular significance. The more traditional loses its hold, and the more daily life is reconstituted in terms of the dialectical interplay of the local and the global, the more individuals are forced to negotiate lifestyle choices among a diversity of options. (Giddens 1991, 81)

Like Simmel, Giddens noted that the joys of modern independence came at a cost. Traditional social relations were often brutal, cloying and fatalist, but they offered citizens something modern society cannot: a sense of deep and enduring security. The freedom modernity affords the individual from social relationships has been purchased at the expense of existential torment and anxiety. Don Slater (1997) argues that modern society produced not only goods, but also a mass identity crisis. Beginning in the late eighteenth century a therapeutic ethos, or a great preoccupation with the care of self,

self-development and self-fulfillment, began to blossom. In art, popular con-versation and even the workplace a new discourse emerged allowing greater reflection on emotional processes, ideas of repression, and placing new atten-tion on the impact of one's childhood and its accompanying traumas and trib-ulations. This emphasis on the self can still be found in contemporary self-help books and is a dominant preoccupation within the media and advertising.

Industrial Style Cultures

Aesthetics, fashion, and style are uniquely woven together within modern society. Traditional cultures prized cohesion and group solidarity, therefore did not promote a wide spread fashion culture. Grant McCracken argues that, prior to the sixteenth century, consumption was focused on the group and its heritage; the status of the nobleman's family was of great importance. Goods did not belong to the individual; rather they were on a migration from the past generation to the future generation of the family. Goods were chosen for their durability and were prized for the amount of patina, wear, or aging they displayed. New goods were selected for the value they could bring to the fam-ily dowry and their durability. The act of acquiring goods, therefore, inspired a contemplation of the group and the existing ensemble of goods.

McCracken writes that in the sixteenth century these traditional bounds of consumption began to break down and the seeds of change were sown in the courts of Queen Elizabeth I. Queen Elizabeth took control of directly adminis-tering all the resources of her lands. Noblemen had to go directly to the Queen to undertake their activities and the desire to win her favor became intensive. She disciplined her subjects by encouraging them to participate in consump-tion rituals in London for her benefit:

> Elizabeth, for her own political reasons, had learned to use consumption as a means of creating a vast theatre devoted to the aggrandizement of her power as a monarch. She had also learned to use it as a device for the impoverish-ment of her potentially over-mighty subjects. Noblemen, on the other hand, found themselves spending reactively. Elizabeth demanded that they do so. The unaccustomed presence of social competitors prompted them to do so as well. The escalation of this spending meant that they were very soon the slaves of competitive consumption. (McCracken 1991, 16)

Status competition within the royal court led to a breakdown of the tradi-tional relations of consumption. Noblemen, consumed to please the Queen, competed in court to win her approval. The Queen situated herself as the ul-timate arbitrator of taste. Goods were not longer selected for their durability and heirloom quality, but for their ability to serve as display. Consumption was not undertaken with family or community in mind, rather more independent-ly. The long-term view of consumption shifted to the immediate concern of status competition. The patina, the signs of wear, and durability of the good became less important; fashion and novelty were valued in their stead. The plane of reference for goods shifted from local to pan-European. "Goods no longer needed to be able to assume the patina of long-term ownership to satisfy the symbolic needs of their owners. Noblemen increasingly looked away from the local in their consumption towards 'pan-European' standards" (McCracken 1990, 15–16). The transition to individual consumption, cosmopolitan tastes, and fashion became increasingly important through the modern period.

Fashion and status competition tended to be confined to the privileged sectors of society. The social elites in society are considered to have a particularly unique relationship to the entire structure of consumption patterns. Those within dominant positions are thought to entice the desire to emulate in those in subordinate positions. The elites became experimenters of modern consumption, developing unique pallets, because they enjoyed wider access to goods. The fruits of international trade and colonialism supported development of more cosmopolitan tastes, and an enjoyment of the exotic.

Richard Sennett noted that a variety of complex factors, lead to a change in the domain of style in the nineteenth century. Victorian culture began to inherit more mass produced goods, as production increasingly shifted from a focus on large-scale industry (ship building, processing of steel, experimentation with industrial chemicals), toward the production of mass consumer goods. The private homes of the Victorian industrialists became a reception area for the mass of new goods turned out by the new industrial focus on consumer products. The expansion of the private domain was interwoven with the emergence of new romantic attitudes about the self. Sennett noted that for the Victorian, fashion began to be not only a means of marking social rank, but also an expression of one's inner self. Identity began to be constructed through goods.

In the private sphere, a division of labor was forged between men and women. While men concerned themselves with the practices of industry, women oversaw many of the home and society issues. Elite wives dedicated themselves to the upkeep of the home and the management of staff, the cultivation of the children, social events, and some engaged in society work. The task of maintaining a house required a dedication to keeping up one's knowledge about the newest goods of the market place. The act of acquiring goods changed as shopping emerged a practice by which one did not simply go into the market to acquire goods, but to look and evaluate them. Thackeray noted in his novel, *Vanity Fair*, published in 1848: "The delightful round of visits and shopping which forms the amusement, or the profession as you may call it of the rich London lady" (chapter 12).

The practice of shopping was interwoven with the new forms of displaying goods. The city became a site of fashion and consumption with its early citadel, the department store. Rosalind Williams has spotted in French thought of the period the evocation of what she calls "dream worlds of the consumer." At this time, the large urban department stores were established. Traditional stores required people to ask for goods across a counter. The innovation of the department store was to lay goods out before the consumer for their private contemplation in surroundings that provided them with the maximum luxury in choosing, touching, and trying on goods. Shopping did not require a purchase; individuals could simply look at the goods or "window shop." The department stores engaged in the visualization of goods through such efforts as mannequins, store displays, and arrangement of goods in stylized layouts. A visit to the department store provided one a window to the world of fashion.

At the same time as the urban department store evolved, industry began to show a great interest in innovation and the ideas of progress. Progress and shopping were united in the great expositions that had started with the Crystal Palace in 1851, where the wonders of science, technology, and machinery were at the forefront. The transition from production to consumption was completed at the Paris Exposition of 1900: "At the 1900 exposition the sensual pleasures of consumption clearly triumphed over the abstract intellectual enjoyment of contemplating the progress of knowledge" (Williams 1982, 59–60).

In 1899 the American economist Thorstein Veblen noted a change in elite consumption patterns. Elites began to flaunt their wealth in conspicuous or ostentatious displays of consumption. Traditional cultures had stigmatized wealth, often linking it to sin and corruption, but the patterns of consumption described by Veblen announced the celebration of wealth and its display in goods. The late-nineteenth-century elites consumed not to impress the Queen but to impress and distinguish themselves from others below them. Because the vast majority of people worked exceedingly hard to survive, one of the richest sites to illustrate superiority was indulging in the antithesis of work: leisure. The man of leisure does not mark his affluence by simply consuming more: "The quasi-peaceable gentleman of leisure, then, no only consumes of the staff of life beyond the minimum required for subsistence and physical efficiency, but his consumption also undergoes a specialization as regards the quality of the goods consumed. He drinks freely of the best, in food, drink, narcotics, shelter, services, ornaments, apparel, weapons and accoutrements, amusements, amulets, and idols of divinities" (Holt 2000, 190).

The new consumption patterns required a redirection of energies. According to Veblen the role of the male shifted, from a display of aggression, strength and resourcefulness to the control and display of his ability to "discriminate with some nicety between the noble and the ignoble in consumable goods." The man of leisure was required to learn "how to live a life of ostensible leisure in a becoming way." (p.68) Veblen described the beginnings of the process whereby the tastes of the lower classes would be focused upon imitating the tastes of the classes above.

Yet, at this moment industry's cleverness was beginning to devise passable mass-produced imitations of objects that the poor had only dreamed of owning in the past, fueling their aspirations by creating cheap consumer goods in large quantities. Commentators started to fret about the leveling of tastes, that is, the collapse of the distinction, formerly so clear, between items of refined design possessed by the rich and the rough possessions of the poor. Mass production of goods did not efface status so much as to put status into flux and broaden the field for competition.

Interwar (1918–1936)

The interwar period lay down some of the key foundations of consumer society. Into the nineteenth century, industry was largely taken up with the project of developing and taming the systems of production. Few systematic efforts were made to intervene in the cycles of consumption. Demand appeared to obediently follow supply. It took industry time to shift from its "productionist" focus and to realize the importance of consumption within the new social arrangements. Until quite recently, our thinking about consumption was almost primitive. Reinforced by economists, a powerful cultural tradition lauded the moral benefits of hard work and obedience to authority and concentrated its attention on increasing production; the process of consuming the things so assiduously produced was regarded as a less worthy enterprise, which in any case would take care of itself.

Indeed, as the economic historian A. O. Hirschman has noted, attacks on "consumerism" are as old as the literature on economic development itself: The new productive possibilities, which began to be glimpsed in the eighteenth century, have always led to fears that the availability of new types of goods would corrupt society and individuals alike (Hirschman 1982, ch. 3). However, innovations during this period suggest that mass consumption was beginning to be acknowledged as something desirable.

Money was required for consumers to acquire the wide array of goods made available in the modern marketplace; and during the early twentieth century there emerged a change in attitude toward the social condition and low wages of the working class. A variety of competing theories have been advanced to explain these social reforms. One version sees the change stemming from within the working classes and their hard-won battles, organized by unions, to create workplace reform. Another view situates the impetus of change within liberal guilt. It became more difficult for the elite to ignore the vast inequalities of the lower class who had fought to preserve their privilege during the war. In Britain some of the most ardent supporters of working class reform hailed from privileged families. The stark disparities between classes, once considered the natural order of things, were subject to greater scrutiny. Another credits the state and the political will of governments, particularly left-wing governments, to instill social reforms. And still another locates these reforms within a structural adjustment and a slowly emerging understanding that increased consumption across a wider number of the population could fuel production, economic growth, as well as suppress political discontent.

But access to money alone was not enough to explain the expansion of consumption during this period. The older social mores and cultural restrictions associated with the popularizing of consumption had to be reworked, and they were within the "mass market." This idea was most clearly expressed in the United States, and can be seen in the work of the American writer Simon N. Patten (1852–1922). In his *The New Basis of Civilization* (1907), Patten argued that society should preach not renunciation of desire but expansion of consumption and should accept as its goal the attainment of a general state of abundance (in Horowitz 1980, 303–4). Patten's call for plenitude marks the origin of what has been called "the culture of consumption." The shelves of the stores and the cupboards of the nation were envisioned as the reception area for a vast abundance of goods. Not just the elite, but also all citizens were to be invited to enjoy the mass goods of industrial production.

The popularization of financial tools, once the privilege of elites and industry, for the personal consumer market contributed to the mass market. In Britain, consumer credit was pioneered by department stores that embraced the idea of mass consumption long before the banks. The expansion of consumer credit enabled people to acquire goods outside of the cycle of paycheck and savings. Large ticket items could be brought home without wait. The hording and saving privilege in the early industrial period was outdated by this new technology. Goods circulated more quickly.

Older cultural traditions continued to flourish particularly in large reception cities. In North America, immigrants had brought a variety of traditions with them from Europe and elsewhere. Consumer articles still included many things made partially or completely at home, and activities in popular culture (festivals, ceremonies, entertainments) still showed the strong influence of regional, ethnic, and linguistic differences. This is why we represent "culture" as standing between "persons" and "goods": For the most part, cultural traditions defined acceptable consumption patterns for each group, and in so doing these traditions shaped the sense of satisfaction individuals felt in their uses of things, however, the power of influence of these older cultural traditions were much less strong than they had once been.

The transition from older to newer forms of community was traced in a famous 1929 sociological study based on research done in Muncie, Indiana, in 1924, *Middletown*, by Helen and Robert Lynd. In seeking to depict the cultural changes that had occurred in the preceding thirty years, the Lynds chronicled what they saw as the systematic replacing of personal interactions with services for which cash payment was made. They also thought they detected a fundamental shift in attitudes toward work; what had once been a considerable source of intrinsic personal satisfaction was becoming chiefly a means of earning income–a change that more recent studies have confirmed as being deeply entrenched in popular attitudes (Coleman and Rainwater 1978). The Lynds saw what Richard Wightman Fox has also pointed out: Already in the 1920s, consumption had begun to serve as "compensatory fulfillment" for the older, largely interpersonal, forms of life-satisfaction that were disappearing (Fox and Lears 1983, 125).

Judging from the great popularity of the "anxiety format" in advertising during the period between the two world wars, the new social self was tormented by anxiety as it looked for a safe niche in largely uncharted domains of social approval. Jackson Lears quotes a classic example from a Brunswick toilet seat ad of 1930. Beneath a scene of well-dressed women drinking coffee the text runs as follows:

> "And...did you notice the bathroom?" At that moment the hostess re-entered the room. She had just barely overheard. But it was more than enough. She began talking about Junior, about bridge, anything—but like chain lightning her mind reviewed the bathroom. She saw it suddenly as a guest must see it, saw the one offending detail that positively clamored for criticism. (Fox and Lears 1983, 25)

The detail in question was a wooden toilet seat! The charming aspect of this tale is that two generations later the descendants of these allegedly anxiety-stricken women, responding to the beat of a different peer-group drummer, scoured junkyards and used furniture stores for the surviving population of old wooden toilet seats, carefully refinished them, and reinstalled them proudly in their bathrooms. At the time, the new interest in reclaiming the once downtrodden markers of modernity was not recognized by contemporary industry advertising. By the 1990s, however, they would come to understand the new interest in downward consumption that became favored by the new middle class.

Stylization

Modern market-industrial societies are noted for a progressive specialization of production, distribution, and promotion. In the interwar period, a new set of workers including product designers, marketers, advertisers, and consumer researchers became linked to the production process. These new workers devoted their attention to the preparation of goods for the consumer marketplace. The task of displaying the communicative function of goods was institutionalized. Our focus will be upon the role of advertisers, but their work cannot be separated from that of the product designers, marketers and consumer researcher. We shall refer to these workers as "cultural intermediaries," for they all worked to unite they cycle of production and consumption, economy and culture.

It is difficult to separate the work of the marketer from that of the advertisers. However, marketers tend to concern themselves with all aspects of selling techniques, distribution, pricing, promotion, design, and advertising, whereas advertisers concentrate on the communicative aspects of marketing. Marketers carved a role for themselves as consumer spokes people, heroes of consumer—some of the most reverent defenders of consumer sovereignty. In the shift to a more consumer-focused economy, those who professed to be the voice of the consumer enjoyed considerable power. Those who interpret the term "marketing" as coterminous with social exchanges see marketing activity as "essential to satisfying all the functional prerequisites of society"—generating meaning in the environment, role differentiation, communication, and social cohesion (Levy and Zaltman 1975, 2–4). If marketers are the strategists for the selling of goods, advertisers are concerned with the representation of commodities. It seeks to school consumers about the world of goods. From a marketers' perspective consumers are those who purchase, who will potentially purchase, or who are unwilling to purchase a given product. They see their job as removing any barriers and opposition to consumption; and communicating to consumers through advertising became one important means.

Andrew Wernick (1991) has provided a unique analysis to show how product designers, advertisers, and consumer researchers were united to become integral to the entire culture of consumption. For Wernick the expanded role of the product designers and advertisers marked a key link between economic and cultural spheres. He explained this link by exploring the practices of the Wedgwood firm, which mass-produced pottery in Britain in the eighteenth century. Although Josiah Wedgwood lived long before the age of quantitative consumer research, he had an intimate feel for cultural dynamics, and sought to incorporate this knowledge into his mass production designs. Of all the designs Wedgwood could have chosen for his mass-produced dinnerware, he elected to replicate Roman pottery. As ancient markers of a previously powerful civilization, the Roman pots emitted a sense of symbolic potency. The original pots were rare, displayed in museums, the arbiters of cultural state at the time, which made them very distinctive. When mass-produced, the pots fed the taste buds of aspirant classes who hungered for status markers.

But Wedgwood went beyond simply choosing a culturally potent object to reproduce; he aggressively promoted his designs. Wedgwood arranged to have his Roman pot replicas displayed in museums. The publicity of the pots was fused to their design, to form a commodity sign. Wedgwood's early interventions would become common practice for industry. Advertisers, marketers, and consumer researchers became professional producers of commodity signs. Although goods had always been traded in the marketplace, in the modern market setting goods were now *designed* for the express purpose of being widely available to many consumers. Goods were "aestheticized," both in their material design and representation for maximum cultural acceptance and minimum rejection. These practices indicated a fusion between cultural and economic processes: Culture itself became a commodity at the same moment that style became an important business strategy.

In the interwar period the types of practices undertaken by Wedgwood to promote his mass-produced pottery were institutionalized in the work of the product designer, advertiser, and consumer researcher. Industrial society "made" or "produced" goods, but in the consumer society goods would be "designed." This growing importance of the product designer within business cycles marked a new institutional emphasis on the "look" or stylization of goods. Many of the goods promoted to a wide American audience until the 1920s were, to put the point simply, quite ugly. American product design had enjoyed a reputation for innovation and good engineering, and little else.

When American products were exhibited in the Crystal Palace in Great Britain in the first world exhibition (1851), they were met with derision by the European press because of their ugliness, and with admiration by the same press for their efficiency and effectiveness. Neither the McCormack Reaper nor the Six Shot Repeater Pistol manufactured by Colt was much to look at, but both were genuine engineering advances. When it came to other products, American industrial product design was so much based on the copying of European models that the French and Swedes were afraid to exhibit their glassware and carpeting in the United States.

Product design was developing very differently in Europe. With few notable exceptions, such as the arts and crafts movement in Britain and the early years of modernist design, products associated with care, quality materials, and the attentions of a professional "designer" were usually conceived of and produced only for the upper classes. European designers tended to see themselves as either being in service of the rich or in service of "art." In other words, they either created things that were modeled on the past expressions of class privilege, or they sought to develop a philosophy of design and the built environment that was based on abstract notions of what was good for people.

Design in Europe, then, was either a very highly developed decorative art—as was the case with Art Deco—or else it was an aspect of an applied philosophy of the built environment, such as the modernism that was epitomized in the German architectural school known as Bauhaus. More than simply creating a style of building construction and industrial design, the Bauhaus developed a philosophy that combined a social vision with aesthetic and engineering principles. This applied philosophy enriched the entire design field, through its insights into the social and cultural implications of an increasingly technological and industrialized human environment.

Design in America was different. Early American experience had emphasized the necessity of efficient and reliable tools and weapons, be they the double-bit axe or the Kentucky Flintlock rifle. Product design was informed by the spirit of durability, mechanical ingenuity, and the no-nonsense approach of the engineer. While in America various periods and groups had produced beautiful objects and craft traditions (Quaker furniture is just one example), no tradition of product design as such existed except for those brought by settlers and immigrants. If the Americans did have a tradition, then, it was one of survival, entrepreneurship, ingenuity, and the ideology of equality.

The distinctions between American and European design is illustrated in the example of automobile design. Invented in Europe around the 1890s, the automobile became one of the most coveted of consumer objects. However, in Europe in remained the privilege of the elite. German and French car designers concentrated on producing luxury automobiles for the rich. Drawing upon the designs of those who build ornate horse drawn coaches, European automobile designers produced an elaborate chassis. European automobile designers also showed concern for the function and precision of automobile engineering. European manufactures such as Rolls-Royce, Mercedes Benz, and BMW came to epitomize luxury automobiles to American audiences.

American designers distinguished themselves by designing for a wider market than that of the social and economic elites. The production techniques of Henry Ford most clearly exemplify some of the foundations of U.S. design and mass production. Ford developed assembly-line arrangements which increased the speed of production, enabling larger numbers of goods to be produced at lower cost. Whereas in 1908 a typical automobile could cost $5,000, Ford's experimentation with "push" production enabled his simple Ford Model-T to be produced very quickly, and the economies of scale afforded by mass-production drove the cost down to $850. When Ford introduced the conveyor belt, cars were produced even more quickly and the price was driven down to $350, making the Model-T affordable for many who had a decent wage. When the Model-T production was stopped in 1928, 15 million cars had been produced and sold. While this figure represented a small section of the total population, it was enough to move car ownership well beyond the elite. The status value of the car changed, and new forms of distinction would have to be created.

The Ford Model-T was also a very durable product: Ford thought a person would only need to buy one and it would last a lifetime. It would be reliable, it would be easy to service and repair, and it would be made in just one color, black; it would be so cheap that everyone could have one. As American design historian Arthur Pulos (1986) put it, the product would be a "type form." In other words, the product, having reached its most developed form, would be reproduced thereafter just as it was; henceforth, there would be no need to tinker with its design. The idea of a type form is a producer's dream, because the production line could be set up, laborers trained, and the product endlessly turned out without the need for reengineering. But the conception of a type form did not prevail in America. Ford's emphasis on mass production and utility was challenged by General Motors, which began to compete for the mass market by emphasizing style and fashion. Ford assumed that the consumer's only interest was utility, not beauty and style. GM proved him wrong.

Roland Marchand (1998) provides a brilliant history of the emergence of stylizing in the source of consumer taste. Marchand's history shows that if Ford can be considered the key innovator of modern production processes, General Motors is most assuredly the hero of modern consumption. In 1926 a manager at General Motors named Weaver began to popularize a new approach to business. Weaver was a fan of the emerging consumer research studies. He saw within the studies a means to distinguish and advance GM over its primary competitor, Ford. The research provided the means to incorporate consumer insight into design decisions. He argued this was one of the best strategies to increase sales and to improve the esteem of the corporation in the eyes of consumers.

In 1933 Weaver's idea was approved by the board of the company, who charged him with the task of developing a comprehensive survey of GM customers. This project was to evolve into the formation of a GM Customer Research division within the company. Weaver stressed the importance of researching not simply large markets, or generic consumers, but actual (and potential) customers, an approach that seemed "to value individuals and to pay attention to their personal preferences." Weaver also pioneered the form of consumer research that concentrated on specific market segments, for example motoring enthusiasts, rather than the undifferentiated population. According to Jean Converse's authorative research on the history of survey research in the United States, by isolating an elite group for special questionnaires GM made a notable contribution to the advance of survey research, foreshadowing the "diffusion research" or "cool hunting" of the late twentieth century.

Weaver concentrated on calibrating the public's interest in style, that is, on their tastes. He argued that the decisions made by designers were most important because they took a broad view of progress and engineering, which evaded the layman who could not be expected to "project himself very far beyond that which he sees and experiences in his daily life." However, the layman did possess practical information, which could help the designer such as "social desires for style, appearance, comfort, appointments, which . . . do not lend themselves to laboratory research." Weaver began his study of GM customers by interviewing GM sales people about the "frequent change in design, actual and desirable rates of automobile obsolescence and customer preferences in styling" (Marchand 1998, 92).

His elaborate questionnaires asked consumers to rank the many car designs pictured. For example, one part of the questionnaire entitled the "face of the car" asked consumers to select the one they liked the best from six grill styles. A comment under the draft questionnaire notes: "In contrast to most mechanical products (or rather to a greater degree than is the case with many other mechanical products) motor car design must give consideration to style as well as utility." GM studied the timing of car purchases and learned about consumers' interests in new models and features. They constantly changed the style, color and features of the car, and brought out the idea of a production season in which new cars were introduced every few years. Weaver argued that producers should see the consumer as "the hub about which all our activities revolve and cementing all of our public relations with a more liberal measure of human understanding" (Marchand 1998, 92). The "Fordist" emphasis on an unchanging, parsimonious design was augmented by a new emphasis on style and fashion.

Consumer insight was institutionalized into the processes of production. Instead of appealing to consumers' interest in price, durability, and utility, General Motors emphasized style, luxury, and consumer choice. Consumers' interests were recorded and integrated into production. Instead of producing one car and trying to sell it to everyone, General Motors segmented its cars for different markets and linked them to different trademarks with bold names like Cadillac, Pontiac, and Buick. Cadillac competed for the American luxury car market against European designs, whereas the Buick served middle-class buyers.

GM was an ardent fan of advertising, whereas Ford was not. Consumer research revealed that consumers were flattered that the car company was interested in their opinions. Ad agencies played an indispensable role in GMs efforts, heralding the openness of the company and its interest in hearing from consumers. The twin dynamic of expert production engineers and designers with the practical logic of motorist could bridge the "gulf between the customer and those responsible for guiding the destiny of the institution" (Marchand 1985, 92). GM also embraced consumer credit to a much greater extent than did Ford. Henry Ford's sensibility remained rooted in the work ethic that prized thrift, hard work, and saving. Ford instilled saving schemes, which helped workers, save for a car, but he rejected the idea of consumer loans, leaving others like GM to profit within what was to become the lucrative field of car financing.

One of the best-known American designers of the 1920s was Raymond Loewy (discussed in Forty 1986; Hillier 1983; Pulos 1986). Immigrating to the United States from France following World War I, Loewy began his career in fashion advertising and illustration. By the 1930s he was redesigning products for industry. It was also in this era that he, along with Walter Dorwin Teague,

Henry Dreyfuss, and Norman Bel Geddes, founded and institutionalized the American product design profession. Indeed, probably no one contributed more to the public image of the designer than did this technological romantic, who was in love all his life with transportation and the image of speed, and whose designs were characterized by a slenderness and grace.

Loewy and other early designers all sought an idiom or style. That is to say, they worked within a systematic set of expressions. The idiom he is most often identified with, and which he helped to popularize in the 1930s, is "streamlining." Streamline design was characterized by its appearance of being aerodynamic. When applied to planes and cars it was functional; however, when applied to furniture, pencil sharpeners, and manure-spreaders, streamlining was an evocation of the fascination with a forward-looking progress. This idiom had a futuristic feel to it, as did much of the design that Loewy produced. In the Depression world of shortages, unemployment, and bank foreclosures, there was a great deal of appeal to objects that bespoke a utopian future.

Many of the designs that came out of Loewy's large firm lasted for decades. His office produced the Singer Sewing Machine logo, as well as those of International Harvester, Shell Oil, and Coca-Cola. Like the Lucky Strike cigarette package, which he redesigned before World War II, many of Loewy's designs are still in use. The Greyhound Scenicruiser, the red Coke dispenser of the 1940s and 1950s, the Gestetner Machine, the Studebaker, numerous train locomotives, the Avanti, Air Force One of the Kennedy era, even the interior of the Sky Lab: All of these and more flowed from his own fertile imagination or from those working under his supervision. Following his death in 1987, a commemorative edition of *ID*, a trade journal of the American product design profession, called him "one of the greatest form givers in America."

The essence of Loewy's approach is best captured in his credo, known as the MAYA dictum. MAYA, an acronym for "most advanced yet acceptable," was the article of faith on which Loewy's fortunes rode. Loewy reasoned that people wanted novelty, but not too much novelty. In short, anything too new frightened people and they would not buy such a product. Thus, if new technology permitted moving an automobile's external gas tank under the vehicle, a fake gas tank was left on top. The consumer who had expected to see the gas tank there still saw what he or she expected, even if it now contained a hideaway extra seat. The MAYA dictum was not invented by Loewy, but he gave it its most elegant articulation.

The MAYA principle was not the only motivating force in Loewy's design imagination. His overall intent was to simplify the lives of the people who, like himself, kept running into poorly made and unimaginatively conceived products. His Gestetner commission of 1929 is a good example of his approach. Prior to its redesign, the Gestetner Copier looked like an industrial printing machine. The guts of the machine were exposed, it was messy to operate, and because its moving parts were exposed, it was dangerous to use—not the sort of thing you would want high-school student or teachers operating. Upon receiving the commission, Loewy sheathed the machine in a metal covering, altered the handle a bit, and produced the device that two generations saw in nearly every school in North America. The machine was now safe and hardly messy at all, except when one had to change the stencils. In this simple redesign, Loewy demonstrated the use of design to eliminate the characteristics of products that inhibited their wider use.

Although he was born in and trained in Europe, Loewy's approach was distinctly non-European. For example, he never believed that design could produce an eternal masterpiece, and he would have had serious doubts about Pulos's assertion of type-form. As far as this "master form-giver" was concerned, every design was just a step in the evolution of the product. While Loewy might have called it an evolution toward technical perfection, it often meant simply cosmetic or surface design. This approach meshed well with the increasing "fashionableness" of material culture: If every product was but a step in its own endless evolution, what better justification could there be for annual style changes? Whatever we may think of this, it was an approach consistent with the attitudes of a man whose autobiography was entitled *Never Leave Well Enough Alone*. Loewy designed not in the service of elites or art, rather with populist dreams and pleasures in mind.

Design in America was reinvented in order to serve an entirely new social purpose. The modernist designers of Europe were talking about the social implications of technology and design: designing products from the inside to the outside, debating the nature of function, and applying a formal method to design. At the same time, their American counterparts were concerned with making products visually interesting and appealing in order to increase sales. It is not entirely true that all American design was on the surface only; ergonomic research was done, and there were scientific approaches to design. But it is the surface design of American goods that became known universally and associated with the consumer utopia that the United States was perceived to be.

The popularity of the Loewy's designs and of General Motors' stylized cars illustrates how the material culture of industrial society had begun to give way to a more fashion-driven consumer culture, in which idioms and their variations (as well as the idioms that were to displace them) would come to play a key role. Fashion is a process, and style or idiom is its currency. The discovery by professionals of the significance of the human propensity to create ensembles or stylistically or expressively coherent complements of goods contributed to an increased drive toward the fashion-orientation of our entire material culture. What is distinctive about the consumer society is the enormous assortment of goods available to the individual—and how the characteristics of those goods constantly change. A dramatic rise in real income, discretionary spending, and leisure time also meant that a far higher proportion of the marketing effort could be devoted to human wants not directly tied to the basic necessities of life.

Commodity Representations

Designers concentrated on the shaping of the object world, and as their role in production cycles expanded, so did an explosion in the numbers of commodity representations. One no longer had to go to the store or out on the street to see the latest offerings of the marketplace, because during the interwar years goods were shown through advertising within an expanded media system. The literature in the field is consistent. Advertisers taught industry how to produce stylized goods for consumer culture. First, advertising agencies in the 1920s and 1930s encouraged manufacturers to change their goods and to employ designers to achieve those changes. Second, a number of the innovators of American product design either began their careers in advertising, or else they moved into product design, from such things as theatre design, through the connections that were being made for them by the advertising industry.

Stuart Ewen (1988) has drawn attention to the discovery of design by the advertising profession. He points out that Earnest Elmo Calkins, partner in the agency Calkins and Holden, was one of the earliest proponents of coordinated image management in America. Advertisers were challenged to persuade producers to pay more pay more attention to the appearances of things, to enable advertising to do its proper work by surrounding its products with attractive images. As one of the great pioneers in this endeavor, Earnest Elmo Calkins, put the point in his 1927 article (as cited by Ewen 1990, 45) entitled "Beauty, the New Business Tool":

> The first step toward making the advertising attractive was to make the goods attractive. It was frequently necessary to introduce the article sold into the advertisement, or at least its package, and most products and packages were so ugly or so commonplace they spoiled the picture; and thus began that steady, unremitting pressure on the manufacturer to make his goods or packages worthy of being placed in an artistic setting. Bales and boxes and cans and wrappers and labels and trademarks were revised and redesigned.

Calkins and his associates, together with the manufacturers they won over to this new way of approaching the marketplace, worked their magic on fashion goods, cosmetics, automobiles (led by General Motors), the General Electric products, radios and phonographs, and so on. And they went on to promote change in the whole area of retail merchandising as well, particularly in department stores (Ewen 1988, 45ff). In the 1920s, this business visionary began pioneering creative services and arguing that businesses had to recognize the relationship between product appearance and consumer preference. Calkins and his partners advocated a systematic integration between aesthetics and industry, and they hired two men who would be among the founders of the American design profession, Walter Dorwin Teague and Egmont Arens. Teague, who began his career as a graphic designer of advertisements, went on to redesign products such as the Kodak Brownie and later the Bantam Special cameras. Arens, who began as an editor and writer, became a leading specialist in packaging and product design. It was Arens who coined the phrase "consumer engineering" to explain his philosophy, which was that industry had to match its products to the public's interests and demands.

Calkins was a major influence on the consciousness of American industry in his day. His argument that good mechanical function was not enough soon began to gain converts: If people were to be compelled to buy, then it would be through an appeal to their sense of the attractive or the expressive, not merely the useful. Attractiveness and expressiveness could be achieved through design, and consumer engineering could then help to stimulate the compulsion to buy. If American business were to thrive it would have to appeal to the feeling of pleasure in ownership and consumption that the ordinary citizen was presumed to have. It is not surprising that manufacturers themselves were product- or utility-focused. If left to their own devices, they would quite naturally privilege the purely useful qualities of their goods. As the Ford example suggests, early manufacturers conceived of the market as interested in utility and price. Advertisers helped producers learn that there was a much wider spectrum of consumer interests beyond utility.

The Sears Catalogue

One of the earliest sources of pictures and information about consumer goods was the print catalogue, which though the mail-order format also formed an important distribution channel for those goods and contributed to the assembling of a mass national audience. The department store provided a new site of consumption for those in urban centers, but interest in bringing rural populations to the national goods producers required extending their markets into rural areas. The vast stretches of American countryside made it difficult and expensive to build distribution outlets in every tiny hamlet. The evolution of the catalogue and mail ordering was an ingenious method that helped to integrate rural communities into national markets.

What at first might appear as nothing more than a mundane publication useful for the outhouse, upon closer inspection is actually one of the most outstanding social documents to appear regularly at the turn of the century: the Sears catalogue. Richard W. Sears began his career in 1887 as a railroad station agent, thus serving the most important transportation system of the time.

Some small manufacturers who were plagued with surplus goods hit upon the practice of shipping consignments to local merchants who had not ordered them. If the goods were refused, they offered them to the station agents at cut-rate prices, suggesting that they resell them to other agents on the line or to anyone else they encountered.

Sears soon discovered that this was a profitable sideline, in part because station agents were bonded and thus could be relied upon to honor their commitments. Sears went on to become one of the great media and advertising innovators of his time: By 1907, Sears, Roebuck and Company were printing six million copies a year of their catalogue, and their total readership was undoubtedly some multiple of that (Boorstin 1973, 118–29). Nor was the catalogue a slender volume; the 1908 edition was almost twelve hundred pages long and contained nearly three million words, the equivalent of about thirty average-size books today. Sears himself wrote much of the copy.

The arrival of the catalogue became a major social event, especially in rural areas. In the early days, people wrote letters about their lives when mailing orders to the company, and lonely farmers inquired of Sears whether they might acquire wives through its facilities. One of the authors of this book grew up in rural Pennsylvania in the 1950s and can remember the special excitement among children when, twice a year, the Sears catalogue arrived in the mail. In the early years, the catalogue contained not only advertisements for goods but also much puffery about the reliability of the firm, including testimonials from its bankers in Chicago, evidence that people had to be persuaded to put their hard-earned money in the mail and engage in transactions that were not face to face (similar techniques were undertaken during the 1990s to encourage Internet shopping). There were drawings of the firm's headquarters and of the factories where the goods were made: safes and stoves in New Jersey, cameras in Minnesota, shoes in New Hampshire, furniture in New York, guns in Connecticut, wire fence in Indiana, and saws in Michigan.

Page after page of densely printed, unadorned text at the front—up to four thousand words per page—explained the firm's criteria for ensuring high quality and low cost. And the company managers knew the social etiquette of small towns: A special section explained that the goods would always be shipped to the railroad terminal in unmarked packages, so that local merchants (who might well include the buyer's employer) would not discover the disloyalty of customers who were, of course, known to them personally.

This catalogue merchandising was enormously successful. Yet, curiously enough, the Sears catalogue was not itself a forward-looking enterprise. In fact, it can serve as a metaphor for the industrial age that was coming to a close, an age dominated by a system of manufacturing with a hitherto undreamed-of productive capacity that had been erected helter-skelter at the price of enormous human suffering. The industrial age had come into being without any notion among the captains of industry who were its leading figures that it could offer material abundance to the masses who toiled in its service.

The Sears catalogue itself stood at the transition point between the industrial and the consumer age, promising to bring "luxuries to thousands who formerly enjoyed only the necessities." It is not the content of its message, however, but its language and imagery—in other words, its communicative format—that looks backward in time. The missionary approach of the catalogue as a whole, with its implicit promise of general abundance, and the strategy for communicating it, are inconsistent and at war with each other. The task of the advertising industry beginning in the 1920s was to resolve and overcome this inconsistency.

In the first place, the catalogue's message content is saturated with what we might call "artisanal" or "craft" values; it refers to goods in ways that presuppose an intimate knowledge of functions and uses or an interest in acquiring such knowledge about unfamiliar items. It is addressing a population that, for the most part, produces and consumes the goods it needs rather than purchasing them. The catalogue did not present goods as if they were mass-produced in factories, but treated them like the things that people used to make for themselves, except for the fact that they were now available in much greater numbers and variety. The text remains innocent of the marketing outlook that one must forge innovative selling tools in order to dispose of a world of goods that have not been (and indeed could not be) made by the consumer personally.

A nice example is provided by the frequent illustrations of the factories where the goods are made: They look like icons, not actual places of production. There are exterior views only, in peaceful, landscaped settings with no workers or machinery visible; the text calls attention mostly to their size, even giving the exterior dimensions of some buildings. (Such illustrations, emphasizing the size, efficiency, and order of the mass-production factory setting, were common in this period.) In short, this is a symbolic representation of the industrial age, referring only in abstract terms to its immense productivity—and concealing the pervasive ugliness, social conflict, and environmental degradation that accompanied it. The implicit message is that nothing has really changed in the social world of values and behavior in the coming of industrialism.

Artisanal values pervade the catalogue's circumlocutory rhetoric and its meticulously detailed descriptions of the many objects on offer. The introductory section to the 1908 edition, emphasizing the high quality of the company's products, mentions the expertise of its buyer for harnesses, an expert harness maker trained in a small country firm who oversees the curing and tanning operations of the suppliers as closely "as if he were the owner." His mission is straightforward: "He is only called upon by us to know everything about a harness." The lead-in for this edition is a seven-page story about the newest cream separator, which is analyzed in loving detail (see Figures 2.1a–2.1d). The catalogue was directed primarily at a rural audience, so it is not surprising that its opening pages should focus on farm needs; but the amount of space devoted to one item and the exhaustive scrutiny of its characteristics reveal much about the underlying values being appealed to. Lest the reader think that other needs were neglected, we hasten to add that bicycles receive four full pages of densely packed text, followed by five pages devoted to bicycle parts. Coming upon almost twenty pages of text and illustrations for pianos and organs, the reader is admonished at the outset to "read every word in the pages that follow"!

A high proportion of goods made of multiple components are first shown intact and then broken down into their subordinate units, which are, of course, also for sale separately. Craftspeople are concerned with how a thing is put together, with "what makes it work," and with being able to repair rather than to discard it. Industrial goods are meant to be unambiguous in their utility and, in a sense, the fact that they are shown in their component parts is an assurance that they have nothing to hide, that there is nothing frivolous or unnecessary to them. The commitment to craft values also dictates linguistic style. Heavy matter-of-fact, overlong, and repetitive descriptions of product qualities predominate—interspersed far too infrequently with fanciful observations—and preachy exhortations appeal to the good sense of the potential buyer, who, as a careful, sagacious, and, above all, highly suspicious consumer ever alert for the slightest whiff of chicanery, clearly can judge the products' highest standards of craftsmanship.

One should not be misled by the frequency with which the buyer is addressed directly, as "you." The emphasis is always on the product and its marvelous attributes, constituting the "active" dimension in the message format; the text is devoid of personal references, and in those twelve hundred pages there are few drawings of people except for the clothing section where they look like mannequins. (Magazine advertisements at this time were already including many more illustrations of persons). The flat, self-assured tone that characterizes so much of advertising text in this era is deceptive, however, for some of its seemingly candid and innocuous statements are just hyperbolic nonsense. In the notorious patent-medicine field, most advertisements were simply fraudulent, but a few were downright sinister. Here is just a part of the pitch from *The Cosmopolitan* magazine of December 1899 for the "Turkish Bath Cabinet," which appears to be just a large wooden box that fits snugly around a person seated on a chair with a small alcohol stove that supplies enough heat to cause sweating:

> Our Cabinet is recommended by 27,000 best physicians, and it will cure Nervous Troubles and Debility, Sleeplessness, Obesity, Lagrippe, Neuralgia. Cures Rheumatism [we have offered for four years a standing reward of $50.00 for a case not relieved]. Cures Woman's Troubles, Headache, Gout,

Figure 2.2a

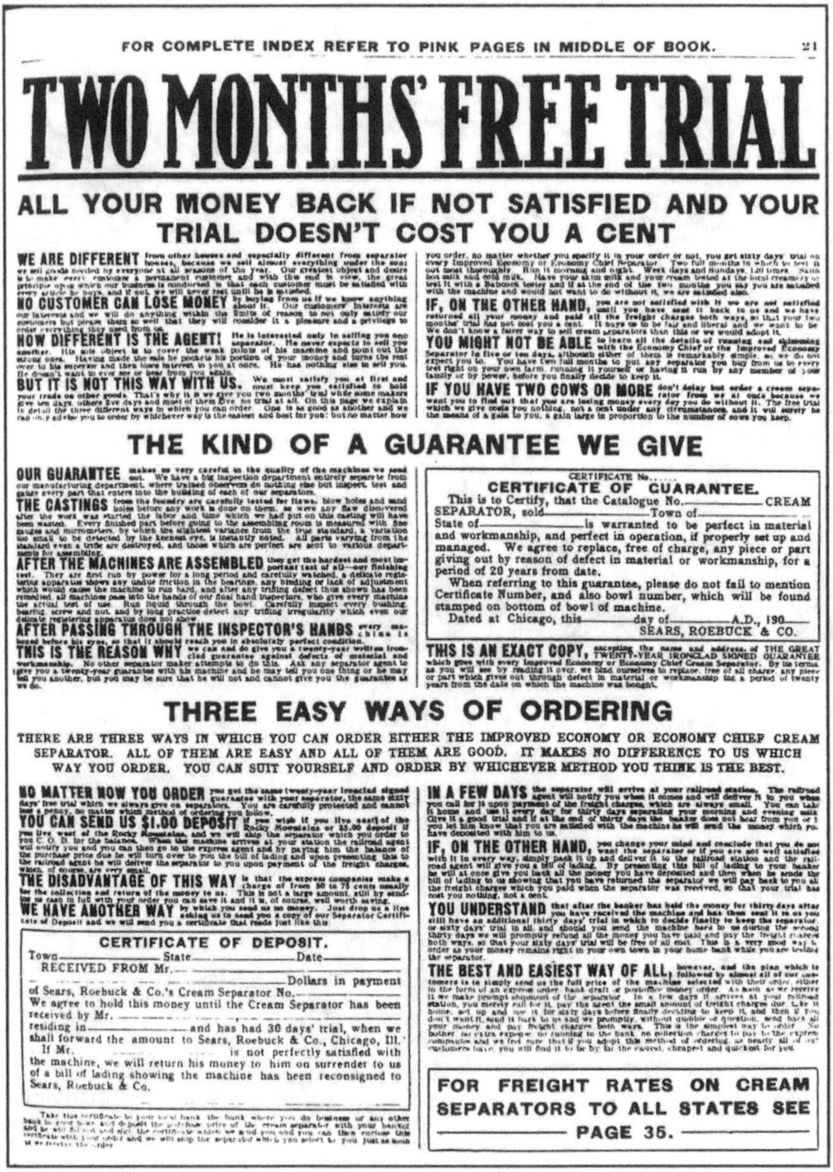
FOR COMPLETE INDEX REFER TO PINK PAGES IN MIDDLE OF BOOK. 21
TWO MONTHS' FREE TRIAL
ALL YOUR MONEY BACK IF NOT SATISFIED AND YOUR TRIAL DOESN'T COST YOU A CENT
WE ARE DIFFERENT
NO CUSTOMER CAN LOSE MONEY
HOW DIFFERENT IS THE AGENT!
BUT IT IS NOT THIS WAY WITH US.
IF, ON THE OTHER HAND,
YOU MIGHT NOT BE ABLE
IF YOU HAVE TWO COWS OR MORE
THE KIND OF A GUARANTEE WE GIVE
OUR GUARANTEE
THE CASTINGS
AFTER THE MACHINES ARE ASSEMBLED
AFTER PASSING THROUGH THE INSPECTOR'S HANDS
THIS IS THE REASON WHY
CERTIFICATE No......
CERTIFICATE OF GUARANTEE.
This is to Certify, that the Catalogue No.——CREAM SEPARATOR, sold——Town of——State of——is warranted to be perfect in material and workmanship, and perfect in operation, if properly set up and managed. We agree to replace, free of charge, any piece or part giving out by reason of defect in material or workmanship, for a period of 20 years from date.
When referring to this guarantee, please do not fail to mention Certificate Number, and also bowl number, which will be found stamped on bottom of bowl of machine.
Dated at Chicago, this——day of——A.D., 190——
SEARS, ROEBUCK & CO.
THIS IS AN EXACT COPY,
THREE EASY WAYS OF ORDERING
THERE ARE THREE WAYS IN WHICH YOU CAN ORDER EITHER THE IMPROVED ECONOMY OR ECONOMY CHIEF CREAM SEPARATOR. ALL OF THEM ARE EASY AND ALL OF THEM ARE GOOD. IT MAKES NO DIFFERENCE TO US WHICH WAY YOU ORDER. YOU CAN SUIT YOURSELF AND ORDER BY WHICHEVER METHOD YOU THINK IS THE BEST.
NO MATTER HOW YOU ORDER
YOU CAN SEND US $1.00 DEPOSIT
THE DISADVANTAGE OF THIS WAY
WE HAVE ANOTHER WAY
CERTIFICATE OF DEPOSIT.
Town——State——Date——
RECEIVED FROM Mr.——
——Dollars in payment of Sears, Roebuck & Co.'s Cream Separator No.——
We agree to hold this money until the Cream Separator has been received by Mr.——
residing in——and has had 30 days' trial, when we shall forward the amount to Sears, Roebuck & Co., Chicago, Ill.
If Mr.——is not perfectly satisfied with the machine, we will return his money to him on surrender to us of a bill of lading showing the machine has been reconsigned to Sears, Roebuck & Co.
IN A FEW DAYS
IF, ON THE OTHER HAND,
YOU UNDERSTAND
THE BEST AND EASIEST WAY OF ALL,
FOR FREIGHT RATES ON CREAM SEPARATORS TO ALL STATES SEE PAGE 35.

Figure 2.2b

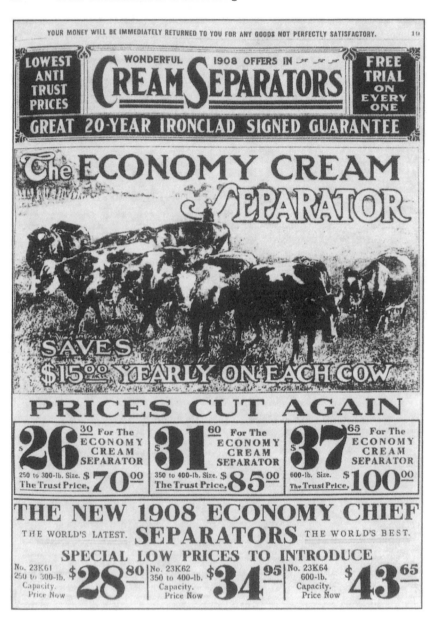

Figure 2.2c

Figure 2.2d

Piles, Dropsy, Diabetes, all Blood and Skin Diseases, Liver and Kidney Troubles. With the Cabinet, if desired, is a Head and Complexion Steaming Attachment, which makes clear skin, beautiful complexion, cures and prevents pimples, blotches, blackheads, skin eruptions and diseases.

The manufacturer claimed one million satisfied customers. Note especially the way in which the promised cure takes on everything from diabetes to pimples. This is not really a medical claim at all, but a random juxtaposition of words held together only by the ad's commitment to the matter-of-fact communicative format. It is a narrative form gone mad, a universe of discourse that resembles nothing so much as an uninspired version of Alice in Wonderland. Many other nostrums were touted for piles, headaches, debility, nervousness, "blood diseases," and so on (the lists are often remarkably similar). The 1902 Sears catalogue offered "Peruvian Wine of Coca," just one of a flood of cocaine-based elixirs (including the original formula for Coca-Cola and a failed imitator that carried the brand name "Dope Cola") that reached a wide market in the twenty years after 1885 (*Life Magazine* May 1984).

Whether the text was (at least in retrospect) utterly fraudulent or absolutely frank and honest, as in Sears' ads for bicycles or cream separators, its appearance and rhetorical style were identical. In the honest ads, there is a charming undertone of genuine pride in the technological accomplishments that were making such useful devices so widely available to those who deserved to have them; yet there is a slightly intimidating undertone as well, for, as far as the Sears catalogue is concerned, the dominant image is of the immense, startling ingenuity of industrial technology itself. The handwriting is on the wall, however: Although the words paid homage to artisanal values, the life and society sustained by artisanal labor was fast vanishing.

The success of the catalogue encouraged business to seek other representational formats for goods. The discourse in and through goods expanded. Consumers were offered a wide stream of commodity images and messages to consider. Their knowledge of the world of goods was enriched by a method which did not demand their physical presence. In some respects, the mail-order catalogue was a precursor of the modern mass media. Unlike newspapers or magazines of the period, it was sufficiently comprehensive to project a vision of an entire consumption universe of products to satisfy all wants—including wants conceived only in the act of perusing the catalogue itself. Together with the urban department stores, it promised an all-embracing, unified, and ordered mediation between persons and their social environment. The catalogue was also a very important instrument which both reflected the idea of a mass market and simultaneously contributed to its formation.

But it could not serve for long as such a model because its communicative format was too restrictive. Great ingenuity had brought mass-produced consumer goods to the marketplace, but the passage from industrial to consumer society called for bold and fresh initiatives. And advertisers took up the challenge. They would also unit marketing efforts, the media, designers and consumer research. While amount of wealth still arbitrated the goods one could own, the representations of goods offered in catalogues and the mass media were freely available to all.

CHAPTER 3

Advertising in the Transition from Industrial to Consumer Society

I think the most important element in success in ad writing is the product itself. And I can't say that often enough. Or emphasize it enough. Because I think that a great ad campaign will make a bad product fail faster. It will get more people to know it's bad. And it's the product itself that's all important and that's why we, as an agency, work so closely with the client on his product—looking for improvements, look for ways to make people want it, looking for additions to the product, looking for changes in the product. Because when you have that, you are giving the people something that they can't get elsewhere. And that is fundamentally what sells. (Bill Bernbach, founder of BBD advertising agency, cited in Twitchell 1996, 8)

The social transition we have been discussing occurred in North America and the more industrialized parts of Europe in the 1920s. Frederick Lewis Allen provides a finely detailed retrospective of it for the United States in his famous bestseller, *Only Yesterday* (1931). The opening chapter contrasts the beginning and end of the decade as reflected in the life of an ordinary citizen. Almost every detail would later be recognized as a landmark event in the constitution of a consumer society. New forms of popular entertainment, new vehicles of mass communication, and new consumer products of immense popularity were being stitched together to form a new popular culture, a rich and coherent network of symbolic representations and behavioral cues, to replace the older cultures then fading away.

Popular entertainment brought innovative musical styles, movies, and the "star system" that created famous personalities. The motion picture industry affected communications as well as entertainment; newspapers became easier to handle with the advent of the tabloid format; above all else the decade witnessed the arrival of radio broadcasting, which subtly penetrated and blended with the mundane routines of domestic activity. Radio was more than a technological novelty providing efficient channels for advertising and popular entertainment; in one powerful stroke it integrated nuclear family units (once tightly bound to local communities but now isolated and dispersed) into a larger association unique in human history: a national consumer culture.

Certain products that would soon dominate the consumer culture began to invade personal lives. Automobiles were beginning to be sold on styling and symbolic values; the number of privately owned cars more than tripled during the decade. Cigarettes more than doubled in sales, and smoking in public by women was becoming acceptable. Cosmetics, new personal-care products, and much freer clothing fashions for women were also having a social impact. (A changing image for alcoholic products did not appear at this time in the United States because of Prohibition, but it would do so later.)

Lodged at the intersection of all these currents was national consumer advertising, which had just arrived as a recognized profession, an accepted partner with industry, and an inescapable presence in daily life. This was advertising's golden age, not merely because advertisers had grasped its almost unlimited transformational capabilities, but because society as a whole almost completely agreed with its key premise, that the road to happiness was paved with more goods and services. Stephen Fox commented, "More than ever before or since, American culture and American advertising converged on a single point" (1984, 79). We would modify this judgment somewhat by pointing out that the next postwar decade (the 1950s) displayed much the same convergence of opinion.

The first stages of integration of advertising with the new technologies of communication, continuing innovations in industrial production, and new popular cultures oriented around consumer goods, were in place by the end of the 1920s. These integrating forces included the blending of commercial sponsorship, national personalities, and programming content in radio broadcasting; the general use of famous personalities (including movie stars) in advertising; and the heavy emphasis in national advertising on certain key goods (automobiles, tobacco, personal-care products, later alcohol). Most important were the systematic studies of population statistics, opinion polling of media audiences (George Gallup got his start in the 1920s), and psychological research on consumer motivations. All of these factors were explicitly intended to fuse, through marketing and media, the intentions of industry and the consumer into a single grand strategy for mutual benefit.

Advertisers

Advertising relies on the host of the media to distribute its messages. The contribution of the commercial media in the formation of the modern marketplace cannot be overemphasized. At the beginning of the twentieth century, advertisers began to forge their alliance with the media. The press welcomes the additional funds offered by advertising and by 1920 it accounted for about two-thirds of all newspaper and magazine income. It was not simply that commercial messages flowed through the media, but how media offered a new way of linking a mass of people across time and space as audiences. The popular cultural representations produced by the media and advertising became a key cultural resource, a shared resource in a fragmented landscape for individuals dislodged from traditional relationships.

Roland Marchand noted how early romance magazines and the tabloid press competed in offering personal advice on popular pleasures to help people navigate through the complexities of modern life. Advertisers learned many tricks about how to engage audiences from the media, as they continue to do so today. There exists a symbiotic relationship between the media and advertising, and advertisers learned how to engage audiences from the media, as media also learned from advertisers' promotional techniques. Daniel Boorstin's concept of "consumption communities" acknowledges how popular styles and expenditure patterns among consumers became a principal force for social cohesion in the twentieth century, replacing the ethnic bonds that people had brought with them to the industrial city. Advertising was understood to be the unifying force that brought these new communities into being: "Advertising could not be understood as simply another form of salesmanship. It arrived at something new—the creation of consumption communities" (Boorstin 1973, 145).

The assembly of audiences by the commercial media was a crucial linchpin in the formation of the consumer society. Advertising takes place through the communicative challenges offered by the commercial media. Advertisers are knowledgeable about consumers, but they specialize in audiences, translating consumer targets into an audience target. The size and type of audiences advertisers sought influenced the expansion and character of the mass media. Radio stations in the 1920s began to broadcast nationally in order to assemble wider audiences for advertisers. Two decades later television networks formed for the same purpose. The technologies and media owners who were able to deliver these national audiences were handsomely rewarded and in turn reproduced and expanded their networks, some globally.

Daniel Pope noted "industry's need for advertising" around the turn of the century to help businesses negotiation the industrial, urban society with its new forms of communication. The amount of advertising channeled through the media during this period expanded, but more important than the volume of advertising, which began to emerge in the 1920s, was the fact that "the lead in advertising had passed to manufacturers of nationally distributed, brand-named goods" (Pope 1983, 30). Heavily promoted brand names became key features of the twentieth-century marketplace. Many large-scale national U.S. brands began to expand globally during the 1920s and achieved worldwide recognition and markets. The media offered the means of bringing disparate mass of people together, albeit perhaps in superficial ways, and brands became a symbol of unusual constancy within a modern landscape of constant change.

To communicate successfully requires knowledge about one's audience. Consumer and audience research was developed to fulfill this function. Deciphering the modern consumer was a difficult task, but the rewards in doing so were great. More than any other institution, marketers and advertisers listen carefully (both strategically and selectively) to consumers and make serious efforts to adjust to shifting consumer and cultural sentiments, when it is commercially viable to do so. Just as GM allowed its product designers to set the tone for its new products, which was then refined by consumer input, so advertising agencies followed the practices of the creative department and their expert knowledge of communication design, while also encouraging consumer input through focus group evaluation of designs. Artists and copywriters become key players in the agency's creative department. They produced a range of commercial formats, often less out of strategic premeditation than through trial and error.

Marchand noted that males from elite educational institutions, who lived in urban centers and earned above-average wages, dominated the early agencies. These factors separated those known in the advertising business as "creatives" from the early public they spoke to—predominantly was female, less wealthy, and less literate. Agencies institutionalized the importance of speaking to "people on the street," as their livelihood depended upon their ability to establish dialogues with consumers. The creatives' unique social position, and the production tasks they were saddled with, led them to blend of elite and popular tastes, at once schooling the elites in the popular pleasures of the lower classes and also creating aspirations in the lower classes by associating commodities with high art.

Advertisers were forceful modernizers and their preferred aesthetic in the 1920s was modern art. Calkins (discussed in the preceding chapter) was among the first to advocate the use of modern art in advertising, suggesting that modern art techniques such as those developed by the European avant-garde movements of Surrealism, Cubism, Expressionism, and so on, were very well suited to developing powerfully expressive advertisements. What made these techniques so ideal in Calkins' mind was the fact that they possessed immense communicative power. In this, Calkins anticipated and promoted an approach to advertising that is still in place today. As the art historian John Walker pointed out in his *Art in the Age of Mass Media* (1983), the artistic avant-garde has become and remains the R & D (research and development) department for the commercial industry. Advertisers during the interwar period also devoted a great deal of time heralding and explaining the new and complex goods of the industrial market to consumers.

For example, the advertisement in Figure 3.1 explains for a female audience the addition of ethyl (tetraethyl lead compound) to gasoline by suggesting that adding lead to gasoline is like adding grated cheese to the family's macaroni supper dish. The ad strategy is simply to draw an analogy between a thoroughly familiar activity and social role (mother making dinner) and an unfamiliar activity (choosing the correct product for the car); it should be noted that the effect is achieved largely with visual imagery.

Figure 3.1 Advertising's strategy for the new consumer—associating something unfamiliar with something well known.

As Marchand has written, advertising was to become the "apostle of modernity" for its audience, going beyond its role as the seller of goods to develop broad "strategies for accommodating the public to modern complexities" of twentieth-century life (1985, 9). The larger social role that advertising came to play in modern society had its basis in a simple fact: The vast outpouring of new consumer products from assembly-line production would not sell themselves. In other words, prospective consumers had to be told not just what the new product could do, but why it was important that they should adopt the type of life made possible by that product. For example, the safety razor could not be sold on the basis of its technical attributes alone; the male populace had to be persuaded that good society in the modern age approved of the universal clean-shaven look. This strategy involved promoting the product in close association with an account of what we may call the social benefit that the consumer could be expected to derive from the activity associated with the product. The philosophy on which this marketing approach was based soon spread, in the 1920s, throughout the advertising industry. Marchand (1985, 24) observed:

> The result of this trend toward emphasis on consumer satisfactions was called "dramatic realism"—a style derived from the romantic novel and soon institutionalized in the radio soap opera. It intensified everyday problems and triumphs by tearing them out of humdrum routine, spotlighting them as crucial to immediate life decisions, or fantasizing them within enhanced, luxurious social settings.

Marchand showed how advertisers worked at creating successful formats for calming popular concerns about the decay of traditional values and the triumph of "new ways"—formats such as parables, tableaux, and visual clichés. For example, many ads dealt with women's roles, some providing reassurance that there was still an important place for the woman as the superintendent of the home (now filled with marvelous domestic appliances). Thus, a 1928 Canadian ad for "Magic Baking Powder" (Figure 3.2) began: "Some people say that modern mothers are not such good home-makers as were the mothers of olden days. But that's not true. Human nature doesn't change a great deal."

Early advertisers placed emphasis not on the characteristics of the products but with important ingredients in the lives of individuals, such as social roles. The text acknowledges that modern mothers in cities tend to do less home baking for their families than did their predecessors, but it goes on to assure readers that despite this mothers still care for their children. In the course of selling a fairly simple product, the ad tells a reassuring story about the maintenance of traditional family roles and interpersonal relations in the context of changing social conditions. Such easily repeatable formulas—used time and again so that consumers became intimately acquainted with them—served as a bridge between the older, familiar, and traditional world that was disappearing and the new mass-consumer age.

Figure 3.2 Advertising reassured people that traditional roles would not disappear in the modern era.
Source: Courtesy of Nabisco Brands Ltd. ("MAGIC" Baking Powder is a product of Nabisco Brands Ltd. and "MAGIC" is a registered trademark of Nabisco Brands Ltd.)

Such matters are by no means trivial. Today, in many traditional cultures around the world, the provision of food by the mother for the family's evening meal persists as an indispensable daily function, an essential part of an overall social role. Such functions often change, but they cannot be eliminated without providing substitute functions or rationalizations (for example, that the suburban mother requires more time for new activities, such as shepherding the children to social activities in the family automobile) that are likely to win social approval. In the consumer society, advertisements became an important means for transmitting cues, in specific forms consistent with product messages, about new styles of personal behavior.

The foundation stone for everything that was to emerge from this culture was a new type of personality and social self based on individuality. Gradually set loose from restrictive behavioral codes by the crumbling of older cultures that measured persons against fixed standards of achievement and moral worth, persons became oriented instead to the ever fuller consumer marketplace—a marketplace that had begun to address them as individuals. Jackson Lears argued that the popularity of psychological principles stemmed from a wide spread feeling of unreality felt among the population. In response a "therapeutic ethos" flourished. With the erosion of social group supports for personal identity sustained by older cultures, the generation and maintenance of selfhood became a lifetime task for individuals—an endless series of exercises in self-improvement, personal development, self-expression, mental and physical tone, "selling oneself," cultivating approval, "winning friends and influencing people," continuing down to the present outpouring of manuals for teaching self-assertion.

Lears saw the therapeutic ethos as a cultural response to the uncertainties introduced into the social environment by urbanization, industrial technology, and market relations. He also suggested that it prepared fertile ground for the rising prominence of national consumer product advertising, in that the "longings for reintegrated selfhood and intense experience" could be employed by advertisers "to arouse consumer demand by associating products with imaginary states of well-being." The erosion of older cultures created a void in personal life. For all practical purposes, there was a new slate on which to write, and advertisers seized the pen: "The decline of symbolic structures outside the self has been a central process in the development of a consumer culture, joining advertising strategies and the therapeutic ethos" (Fox and Lears 1983, 17–21).

Marchand suggested that early advertisers helped consumers adjust to the tribulations of modernity. Advertising humanized and personalized abstract corporations whose massive scale and power worried them. It told consumers that the new commercial arrangements enabled them to retain all the intimacy of the village as well as the excitement of modern society. Public relations techniques and advertising during the 1920s provided corporations with a soul to detract from the popular opinion, which deemed corporations greedy, inhuman, and uncaring. By promoting a vision of their social consciousness, businesses were able to fend off government interventions. Yet, while the captains of industry wanted to appear to be pillars of the community, there is very little evidence to suggest that they were interested in or took any responsibility to cure social ills.

Advertisers and marketers in the interwar period also began to stress to producers that what was important for the sale of goods was less a fixation on the product, and more attention to the consumer. Richard Pollay divided the communication function of advertising into two aspects: "informational" and "transformational." Through the informational function, consumers are told something about product characteristics; through the transformational function, advertisers try to alter the attitudes of consumers toward brands, expenditure patterns, lifestyles, techniques for achieving personal and social success, and so forth. After studying a sample of magazine ads covering the period from 1900 to 1979, Pollay (1984, 73) concluded, "There are clearly some large-scale historical trends in advertising copy, in particular the trend toward selling consumer benefits rather than product attributes and the trend toward creating favorable attitudes rather than communicating cognitive content."

Messages about necessities such as food could be incorporated within broader transformational message formats, which culminated in the present life-style image. Just as most individuals in the consumer society had been freed from concentrating on the bare necessities of existence, so marketers and advertisers could now, for the most part, safely ignore life's humdrum aspects and play freely, and apparently endlessly, with structures of imagery for the consumption process.

In summary, the interwar period saw the institutionalization of some key processes that helped to facilitate consumer society including increased wages and a more democratic consumption ethic, consumer credit, retailing and distribution techniques, and the institutionalization of marketers, advertisers, product designers, and research in production cycles. Neil Harris has pointed to a number of important changes during this period: more attractive product design and store merchandising, the power of the movies in conveying images of extravagant consumption, more striking photographic reproduction in magazines. Harris suggested that some prominent contemporary novelists, notably Sinclair Lewis, had noticed this and had begun to examine "the relationship between the objects of consumer desire and the creation of personality" (Harris 1981, 211–12). The "world of goods" was increasingly a key feature of personal and social experience for most people.

The expansion of the modern consumer society was stalled in the 1930s by an economic depression in the United States, and the outbreak of war in

Europe in 1936. War brings not only an outward contemplation of the enemy, but also an inward contemplation about the type of society that is being defended. The advertising industry found itself in an uncomfortable position. As we have seen advertisers were able to professionalize and expand their economic role by convincing businessmen that agencies alone held the key to understanding and communicating with consumers. However, their ability to sell this idea was made easier because firms could write off advertising as a legitimate expense of doing business, according to the income tax code.

During the war politicians reviewed these tax benefits, and advertising was threatened with a loss of its tax status, which would have been a severe blow to the advertising industry. Agencies banded together to find a means to prove they were worthy of preferential treatment. Their solution was to contribute to the war effort, by working through the Advertising Commission. Agencies contributed to the design of government war propaganda. This strategy did more than protect agencies' tax haven status; it helped to build a relationship between advertisers and the government, and to position agencies as national treasures. When war ended in 1945, the advertising industry was well positioned to contribute to the great economic boom that ensued. Advertising became significantly embedded within business practices, and organized to defend of its interests.

The Post-1950 Expansion

There was phenomenal economic growth in the United States, Britain, and many other developed countries in the two decades after the war. The economic recoveries of Germany and Japan were nothing short of miraculous. David Harvey (1989) maintains that the Bretton Woods Agreement, which fixed European currencies to the U. S. dollar, as well as agreements to support the reconstruction of Europe (the Marshall Plan), created a uncommon truce between "big business, big government and big unions" that facilitated a period of relative economic stability. Although the idea of the mass market was born in the interwar period, it received its fullest articulation during this period. Against the backdrop of fears of nuclear annihilation and paranoia of Communist insurgence, Americans began to spend their way to prosperity.

The steadily-increasing real wages of blue-collar workers made them more attractive to marketers. Progressive state initiatives including housing subsidies welfare and redistribute tax measures expanded further the number of people on the roll call of potential consumers. Businesses had refined their mass production techniques and were able to produce more goods, cheaper than ever. Cities have always been ethnic mixing pots, but during this period the city became a reception area to new waves of immigrants who came to America, Canada, and Britain as they opened their protective borders to obtain workers to fill positions in their booming industries.

Marketers worked ever harder to encourage business to address consumer needs. The popularity of television consolidated the mass nation audience, and the mass consumer brands (mostly American) of the 1920s were revitalized and expanded nationally and globally. A very profitable packaged goods sector appeared. Consumer credit and the department stores expanded, and the use of credit cards transformed personal debt from a mark of moral failing to a necessary aspect of everyday life. Many new technologies, perfected through the war—improved electrical systems, automobiles, communication services—were applied to the consumer markets. Everyone was destined to have a big car, a single-family home, cheap electricity, a television set, and new appliances.

In America 78 million children were born between 1948 and 1964, and the habits and attitudes of this so-called "baby-boom generation" would have a considerable impact on later consumption patterns. The cherished nuclear family, with married man and woman and exactly 2.3 children, came into being, if but for a brief moment in history. Demand for housing grew, as people began to think about the best place to plant their roots and raise their families. The widespread availability of automobiles fuelled the idea that people could escape the ethnic mixing, pollution, crime and moral deviance of the city for what was thought to be the wholesome paradise of the outlying suburbs. Governments were particularly benevolent to the returning soldiers and offered many new subsidies, and supported the new families with homeowner grants and support for children, helping make suburban family life a reality.

The series of new towns bearing the name "Levittown" can be seen as a prototype of the American suburb, and its formation and history has been thoughtfully documented by the art historian Peter Bacon Hales. The first in the series, built beginning in 1949, was situated on a vast and then-barren track of land on Long Island, near New York City. William Levitt, the construction magnate who lent his own name to his project, applied "Fordist" mass-production techniques to create affordable housing. Cost, efficiency, and speed of production were the first-order concerns. The suburb dwellers relied on the car, thus roads were laid out on a grid to facilitate uniformity and ease of mobility. A very appealing feature, which distinguished the suburb from the city, was that single-family houses were detached and surrounded with generous amounts of space for a front and back yard.

Levitt had perfected his housing design techniques in the Army, where he built barracks during the war. His later houses were very simple prefabricated designs that consisted of two bedrooms, a kitchen, bathroom, and living room. Employing factory-line production techniques, workers operated under a strict division of labor and each house was laid out identically for maximum efficiency and speed of production. For example, one person was responsible for painting just the windowsills of the houses. Levitt kept wages down by avoiding unionization. The result was a high turnover of workers, but because the tasks of building were so simple and the pool of laborers so large, Levitt simply replaced the workers who left with new ones.

The layout of the house sought to minimize costs and create efficiencies in building them. For example, although it would have been more convenient for the bathroom to be placed between the bedrooms, it was placed near the kitchen so that additional plumbing pipe was not required. Levitt had also learned from his army experience the importance of consistency of supply and secured a vertical integration with a few wholesalers and lumberyards, to ensure low costs and a steady supply of known parts. Mass production techniques, vertical integration, simple uniform designs and massive economies of scale enabled post-war families to purchase homes for less than $8,000. With the assistance of the U.S. Department of Veterans Affairs housing subsidies, it was possible for ex-GIs to acquire a home with little or no down payment and a reasonable monthly mortgage.

Although cost and rapid construction were the first-order concerns within the design of the suburb, it was also conceived with families in mind. For example, the kitchen included a very large window above the sink and work space to allow mothers to watch her children playing in the front yard and street, the center of the community. The window, of course, also permitted neighbors to look in to one another's homes, in a way that city brownstones had not. Later large glass windows were added in the back to permit parents to watch their children playing the back yard. Levitt also conceded to one very important expense in the home. In a gesture to technological progress, he designed many of his living rooms around built-in television and hi-fi systems. Families might have been physically removed from the action and cultural stimulation of the city, but television gave them an electronic window on the world.

The massive purchase of goods that equipped these new homes fuelled industry. The fashion system was not only extended to clothing and cars, but increasingly all products. Color became increasingly important—turquoise refrigerators filled kitchens and two-tone cars cruised the roads. Advertisers helped consumers learn the fashion trends, and understand what was "in" and what was not. The popular embrace of the suburb was considered a sign of the wondrous powers of the mass market to provide higher standards of living for the public. The market brought a new sense of democracy in which luxury items such as cars, washing machines, and television sets became the possession of the majority. Politicians celebrated the arrival of the classless society—did not all these white goods and television sets show that everyone was now middle class now?

Critics were quick to respond, contending that mass culture was not a promised land of democracy, but rather a homogenizing cage of alienation. They called Levittown homes "cookie-cutters," uniform boxes that obliterated individual distinction, rendering their inhabitants the equivalent of sheep kept in identical pens. Cultural critics saw Levittown as the end of individualism, and the erosion of cultural standards to the lowest common denominator. Those who chose to live in the suburb took on the character of their one-dimensional homes. Herbert Marcuse was a key spokesperson of this attack on mass culture:

> We are confronted with one of the most vexing aspects of advanced industrial civilization: the rational character of its irrationality. Its productivity and efficiency, its capacity to increase and spread comforts, to turn waste into need, and destruction into construction, the extent to which this civilization transforms the object world into an extension of man's mind and body makes the very notion of alienation questionable. The people recognize themselves in their commodities; they find their soul in their automobile, hi-fi set, split-level home, and kitchen equipment. The very mechanism, which ties the individual to his society has changed, and social control is anchored in the new needs that it has produced. (Marcuse 1964, 9)

Levitt made a token effort to distinguish the houses by varying the window lines and colors of the houses slightly; however, this did not fool the critics. Yet it was not the critics that had to be satisfied with the homes, but the people who lived in them. Levittown salespeople struck upon a wonderful idea for making the uniform houses attractive to customers. While walking prospective buyers through the barren new suburbs, they encouraged potential customers to see the homogenized ugliness of the house and yard as a blank canvas upon which they might script their own personalized creations.

Women, who remained largely outside of the workforce during this period (only 29 percent women between twenty-five and thirty-four were in the workforce in 1961), devoted their time to raising family, tending to the needs of their working husbands, and learning about consumer goods to engage in the project of decorative arts. "*Life* ran a contest, seeking the best-decorated Levittown house, and the winner was a rather startling red-themed Mandarin-Revival Sino-Asian extravaganza." As the affluence of the original owners grew through the 1950s, they added additions and engaged in the project of updating the look of their home. Home decoration became a serious sport in America (Hales 2004).

These diverse but interconnected changes affected the principal channels of public intercourse and also the smallest details of everyday life. For example, they are represented both in the character formation and values of individuals. David Riesman, writing against the backdrop of 1950s America, summarized these changes in his book, *The Lonely Crowd* (1950), by contrasting "inner-directed" and "other-directed" characters. The former's goals are set early in life and remain largely unaffected by later events; the latter are influenced continuously by what is happening around them, and their goals shift with circumstances. Inner-directed characters emphasize production, and other-directed characters, consumption. The other-directed character is open to ever-shifting environmental influences, especially peer-group pressures. Older extended family and ethnic community bonds were unraveling, urbanization and the personal anonymity it confers were proceeding apace; and individuals were being confronted more and more with the fact of incessant change in everyday life, as industrial technologies and design were applied to proliferating consumer products. Riesman contended that there had been a shift from inner- to other-directed thinking as the predominant character type in modern society.

The phrase "keeping up with the Joneses" entered the vernacular at that time. The Joneses were a fictionalized marker for the idea of keeping tabs on the goods of others. In the United States after the war, income became the single most important status indicator: "Income is of overwhelming importance in how Americans think about social standing" (Coleman and Rainwater 1978, 220). Income provides access to whatever visible and tangible tokens of success happen to be most prized at any given moment. A standard conversation starter was to ask a new acquaintance what they did for a living, a common practice which allowed strangers to read on another's social and economic standing which were now less clearly read in their clothing.

During the 1950s, companies followed the trend of General Motors by including marketing departments as part of their institutional structures to coordinate with advertising agencies and consumer researchers. Consumer research was increasingly done out of house because companies often could not resist attempting to sell their product to research subjects, which tainted the objective nature of the results. The inclusion of scientific consumer research, once celebrated in the 1920s, now elicited concerns from commentators, who began to observe that marketing and advertising was not serving our rational needs but instead influencing us without our being aware of it, affecting us behind our back, so to speak.

In 1959 Vance Packard wrote *The Status Seekers*, which condemned the "keeping up with the Joneses" mentality he saw pervading U.S. culture. In that same year John Kenneth Galbraith published a complex critique that sought to draw attention to the wider systemic changes cultural intermediaries were having on traditional economic practices. In *The Affluent Society* (1958) and later in *The New Industrial State* (1967), Galbraith celebrated the productive capacities of the market, seeing growth as good for two reasons: first, industrial production provides high levels of employment, and second, societies which attempt to produce goods to satisfy the needs of consumers are to be commended: "Consumer wants can have bizarre, frivolous, or even immoral origins, and an admirable case can be made for a society that seeks to satisfy them" (Galbraith 1958, 140).

However, what concerned Galbraith about the affluent society was that society was no longer addressing real consumer needs but the needs of industrial growth. Traditional economic theory assumed that consumers are the most important decision makers in the economy, controlling what and how much is produced as manufacturers of goods respond to consumers' purchasing patterns. This is known as the theory of consumer sovereignty. Galbraith thinks that to be accepted, this theory must convince us that consumer wants and needs are *independently determined*—in other words, that wants and needs originate with the consumer.

According to Galbraith, the institutionalization of marketing, advertising, and consumer research within the processes of production deprived the theory of consumer sovereignty of its explanatory power. The institutions of salesmanship and advertising cannot be "reconciled with the notion of independently determined desires, for their central function is to create desires—to bring into being wants that previously did not exist" (Galbraith 1958, 141). Galbraith thereupon reversed the theory of consumer sovereignty ("the accepted sequence") into what he labels "the revised sequence," in which producers clearly control demand. In this new sequence, the business firm is the key decision maker and the system operates in the firm's interests, not the consumer. Galbraith argued it was impossible to contend that growth was fulfilling consumer needs. The eradication of real human needs created great damage in such areas as resource use, the environment, and labor-management relations, and created greater inequalities. Discussion of inequality ceased to rouse the debates it had in the interwar period: Galbriath noted that wealth and income no longer carried the same prestige as they had in the first half of the twentieth century, as so many people were now affluent. He noted that the wealthy were no longer conspicuous consumers, but appeared to be under consuming. Galbraith therefore advocated social welfare and tax measures to redistribute wealth more equitably.

Stuart Ewen (1976, 36), too, saw the underlying dynamic of the system of needs as being based not on the interests of consumers but rather on "the real, historic needs of capitalist productive machinery." Ewen calls attention to a transition period in the 1920s, when advertising messages shifted from focusing on products to defining consumers as an integral part of the social meaning of goods. As the trade journal *Printer's Ink* noted in the 1930's: "Advertising helps to keep the masses dissatisfied with their mode of life, discontented with ugly things around them. Satisfied customers are not as profitable as discontented ones" (Ewen 1976, 39). If advertising's task were to create demand in consumers rather than simply to reflect their innate desires, it would have to stop talking merely about the product and incorporate direct references to the audience as well. Advertisers, therefore, effected a "self-conscious change in the psychic economy" (Ewen 1976, 39) by flooding the marketplace with suggestions that individuals should buy products in order to encounter something in the realm of social or psychological experience that previously had been unavailable to them. Material objects thus came to play an increasingly important role in social interaction and everyday life as symbols of prestige and status.

In an important and influential essay first published in 1962, Raymond Williams wrote that the social and symbolic significance conferred upon goods by advertising shows us that it is wrong to regard modern society as being too materialistic, as putting too much emphasis on the possession of goods. Rather, in his way of looking at this issue, we are not materialistic enough. If we were sensibly materialist, in that part of our living in which we use things, we should find most advertising to be of insane irrelevance. Beer would be enough for us, without the additional promise that in drinking it we show ourselves to be manly, young at heart, or neighborly. A washing machine would be a useful way to wash clothes, rather than serve as an indication that we are forward-looking or an object of envy to our neighbors. But if these associations sell beer and washing machines, as some of the evidence suggests, it is clear that we have a cultural pattern in which the objects are not enough but must be validated, if only in fantasy, by association with social and personal meanings which in a different cultural pattern might be more directly available (Williams [1962] 1980, 185).

Williams distinguishes between a rational use of goods, based on their utility alone (what they can do for us), and an irrational use of goods, based on what they symbolize (what they mean to us): a distinction between use and symbol. Thus, capitalist consumption is characterized by irrationality because of the symbolic system of meaning within which goods are located. But note that for Williams any symbolic system is irrational, for rationality is based only on utility, only on the objective performance features of the product. For goods to take on any other meaning is unhealthy. Fred Inglis also sees the consumption of objects based on such arbitrary characteristics as socially harmful:

> Attainment of the values is signaled by acquiring the appropriate objects, using them, throwing them away and acquiring replacements. Continuous and conspicuous consumption is the driving energy of this fiction.... The objects advertised are drenched in a certain light and smell. They give off the powerful fragrance of the very rich and instead of leaving the object in an intelligible domestic world, remove it to a fantastic one. (Inglis 1972, 17)

Once again, the contrast is between an intelligible domestic world and a fantastic one, between use and symbol. One of the cornerstones of the critical approach appears to be, then, that goods should have no meaning over and above their functions as conceived in strictly utilitarian terms, because any additional meaning is false.

Critics have not only attacked the content of advertising, but have also zeroed in on its mode of presentation, which favors persuasion rather than sober decision. In their study of the rhetoric of advertising, Gunnar Andren and his collaborators distinguish between non-rational influences, or persuasion, and rational influences, or argument. The latter operates in the public or consumer interest whereas the former does not. The rhetoric of advertising (the form of presentation) would have to conform to a particular set of criteria if the communication were to qualify as sensible guidance to the consumer. Andren (1978, 112) concluded, not surprisingly, that advertising does not contain sufficient information to be the basis of reflective choice among products, and that "advertising does not serve the consumer or the public interest."

At the heart of both critiques lies the claim that from the economic necessity to create demand, and from the existence of the technological means to achieve it, arose advertising's power to induce false needs in people.

The Creation of False Needs

There are two variations on this theme, the best known of which is found in the work of Herbert Marcuse. Here, false needs are defined as those that are superimposed upon the individual to aid repression and that

> perpetuate toil, aggressiveness, misery, and injustice: Most of the prevailing needs to relax, to have fun, to behave and consume in accordance with the advertisements, to love and hate what others love and hate, belong to this category of false needs. Such needs have a societal content and function which are determined by external powers over which the individual has no control.... No matter how much such needs may have become the individual's own, ... they continue to be what they were from the beginning—products of a society whose dominant interests demand repression. (Marcuse 1964, 5)

The only true needs, it would appear, are for nourishment, clothing, and housing. When pressed for a definition of who decides which needs are true and which are not, Marcuse retreats into the distant (socialist) future and answers that individuals themselves must define these, but only when they are truly free to give their own answer. This is impossible as long as they are "kept incapable of being autonomous, as long as they are indoctrinated and manipulated."

In a similar vein, the French "situationist" writer Guy Debord suggests that the whole enterprise of the consumer society is simply fraudulent: "When economic necessity is replaced by the necessity for boundless economic development, the satisfaction of primary needs is replaced by an uninterrupted fabrication of pseudo-needs, which are reduced to the single pseudo-need of maintaining the reign of the autonomous economy" (Debord 1970, 51).

Thus the claim is that without advertising people would not develop false needs, nor would they try to satisfy such needs in misdirected ways through purchasing non-essential commodities. According to Raymond Williams (1980 [1962]), much of human satisfaction takes place in nonmaterial domains, where objects are largely inconsequential, but the magic system of advertising distracts us by channeling all needs through the object-laden rituals in the consumer marketplace. Thus, it is alleged, the capitalist marketplace controls the basic pattern and content of social interactions: Leisure, play, and other personal activities increasingly are absorbed by a kind of generalized fashion consciousness that connects our activities with the inescapable presence of commercial objects.

Such manipulation is illustrated, for example, in the way that advertising encourages people to think of themselves as consumers rather than as producers. Advertising addressed both production and consumption domains: While creating demand to solve the problem of over-production, advertising would simultaneously persuade workers that the satisfactions not available in the workplace were available in consumption; though they could not control the conditions under which they labored, they could buy consumer goods and thus control, in some measure, their personal lives. In this vein Judith Williamson (1978, 13) wrote, "In our society, while the real distinctions between people are created by their role in the process of production as workers, it is the products of their work that are used in the false categories invoked by advertising, to obscure the real structure of society by replacing class with the distinction made by the consumption of particular goods."

In his 1970 book, *The Consumer Society,* the French writer Jean Baudrillard noted the great emphasis upon "things" that had accompanied the transition from industrial to consumer society:

> There is all around us today a kind of fantastic conspicuousness of consumption and abundance, constituted by the multiplication of objects, services and material goods, and this represents something of a fundamental mutation in the ecology of the human species. Strictly speaking, the humans of the age of affluence are surrounded not so much by other human beings, as they were in all previous ages, but by objects. Their daily dealings are now not so much with their fellow men, but rather—on a rising statistical curve—with the reception and manipulation of goods and messages. (Baudrillard [1970] 1998, 50)

Baudrillard therefore agreed with Galbraith that a major transition had taken place in Western cultures, and accepts the characterization that the older industrial society had been replaced by a consumer society. He too believed that the role of advertising within business cycles dissolved the ability to make a credible defense for the idea of consumer sovereignty. However, he rejected the notion that consumer society was an affluent society, and more radically, he argued there were no "real needs."

For Baudrillard affluence is created not through the acquisition of more wealth, but through a balance of status competition. Equality is not to be found in the number or type of goods people own, but in the quality of their social relationships: "Poverty exists neither in a small quantity of goods, nor simply in a relation between ends and means; but is, above all, a relation between human beings." Baudrillard emphasized the structural inequalities that accompanied the transition to a consumer society: "Every society produces differentiation, social discrimination, and that structural organization is based on the use and distribution of wealth (among other things). The fact that a society enters upon a phase of growth, as our industrial society has done, changes nothings in this process." No real progress had been achieved, he maintains, because the important point is not the growth in wealthy but its distribution—and wealth is ever more unevenly distributed in a mature consumer society.

Baudrillard finds true affluence in the nomadic hunting-and-gathering tribes of the Australian outback and the Kalahari Desert (as described by the anthropologist Marshall Sahlins), who live in a manner most would recognize as poverty. They have few things and their attachment to them is weak. Objects are easily thrown away to lighten travel loads. Everything produced is shared with the group and they expend only the amount of energy necessary to maintain their way of life. This does not mean they are frugal; indeed many of their practices are gluttonous and wasteful. Yet, because they are not burdened by the designs of production and economic calculation, they appear to enjoy life. Their apparently carefree existence is supported by their trust in the plentitude of nature and in how they share resources and control status competition among themselves.

Baudrillard rejected Galbraith's idea that human needs would find satisfaction if only they were unsullied by advertising. Status competition excites much more voracious needs than advertising. Affluence is the very symptom of inequality not its potential cure. Galbraith's promotion of social welfare programs is a misplaced strategy stemming from a misguided analysis. For Baudrillard, supporting the poor is not only a waste of money, and ineffective, it reinforces inequalities. That the lower echelons of society have been able to acquire television sets, video games, and cars is not a sign of affluence, for it only drives elites to seek new levels of consumption for distinction, which when "massified" by the marketers turns the engines of consumption, enabling profit to be made for private interests. The expanded sphere of consumption has an expanded domain of status competition as the key source of its growth.

The inequality of the sphere of production continually reproduces inequalities that fuel status wars which create a continual expansion of needs as people attempt to distinguish themselves from each other. The fears of over-production are no longer a concern within consumer culture. This is because the inequalities produced by the growth society assure continual status competition, hence continual interest in resources for distinction. Baudrillard announced that the "conspicuous consumption of the great capitalists...is over. Indeed, the rich feel almost duty-bound to under-consume." Both Galbraith and Baudrillard noted a key shift within consumption patterns; in the postwar period, the wealthiest segments undertook a less visible and ostentatious consumption. This development makes perfect sense to Baudrillard, who views it as a tactic of social distinction. Within a society where elite tastes are massified, the taste of the rich migrates from economic display to cultural display:

> Galbraith, for example, confuses the "under-consumption" of the rich with the abolition of criteria of prestige based on money. Now, admittedly, the rich man who drives a 2CV no longer bedazzles. What he does is subtler: he super-differentiates himself, super-distinguishes himself by his manner of consuming, by style. He maintains his privilege absolutely by moving from conspicuous to discreet (super-conspicuous) consumption by moving from quantitative ostentation to distinction, from money to culture. (Baudrillard [1970], 1998, 54)

Some elites expend a great deal of expense and exercise of cultural capital in order to live Spartan lifestyles. Consider those who live in urban centers such as New York, London, or Paris who purchase large properties, filling their massive loft rooms with nothing but a single bamboo mat, a plant, a stone water feature arranged according to the principles of *feng shui*. Minimalism and stark modernism are favorite styles of the new elite. Within a consumer society space is at a premium and the massive outpourings of the mass marketplace contribute to a great deal of clutter. How better for elites to distinguish themselves than to fill precious space with absolutely nothing—or at least, very little. More importantly, minimalist and modern tastes require the exercise of considerable cultural knowledge to be appreciated. This style speaks of a refined palate. What is implied is that income alone can no longer assure status; rather, cultural consumption and the use of signs to create distinction has become an important cultural dynamic.

The sin of advertising is not that it creates needs. Needs are far too complex to be enticed by a singular advertising message:

> We know how consumers resist particular precise injunctions, how they rove over the gamut of objects with which they might fulfill their needs, how advertising is not all-powerful and sometimes induces opposite reactions, and what substitutions there can be between one object and another to meet the same needs. (Baudrillard [1970] 1998, 53)

Advertising does not manipulate needs; rather it produces signs used in the new war of status competition and cultural consumption. Advertising is like the city, it creates a spectacle of competition and desire:

> Consumer society is propelled by a continual competition in social standing and the city is the site of the greatest spectacle of competition. The language of cities is competition itself. Motives, desires, encounters, stimuli, the endless judgments of others, continual eroticization, information, the appeals of advertising: All these things make up a kind of abstract destiny of collec-

tive participation, set against a real background of generalized competition. (Baudrillard 1998, 65)

The signs produced within advertising and the fashion system are arbitrary; their meanings are derived through their relationship to other signs. Advertisers produce a prodigious outpouring of signs of continually changing images. They contribute to, but do not control, the shifting and unstable code of interpersonal competition. This code makes possible the elaborate conversation that takes place in and through the objects and symbols of the marketplace.

The Sense of Satisfaction

We often think of consumption as a private affair: It is up to the individual to allocate his or her time and resources as a consumer in order to experience an adequate sense of satisfaction and well-being. Even the most casual observer can see, however, that marketing and advertising do not regard the consumer's search for satisfaction in this manner. Their full realization, which took hold in the 1920s, of how much the act of consumption goes beyond the private enjoyment of the individual marks a major turning point in modern society. The transformational function of advertising, as noted above, is to change consumers' attitudes toward products and brands. The new approach of the industry was far more broad and more radical: The consumer, not the product, was to be henceforth the key ingredient in the message system.

Two main features of this new approach stand out with increasing clarity in marketing and advertising from the 1920s onward. First, at the heart of the sales effort are images of persons and social groups, that is, visible expressions of human contentment in the associations between persons and products. The emphasis on social affiliation was increasingly augmented by an emphasis on self-satisfaction, individual gratification, and living life in the moment and with openness to change. Second, these images are embedded in background settings made up of both natural and cultural environments. Taken together, they mark the transition from a market-industrial society to a consumer society. Illustrations of both will be presented and discussed at different points in this book.

In the preceding section, we introduced some of the special characteristics of these two types of society. Here we shall identify the impact of the transition on the satisfaction of needs in the consumption process to show why marketing and advertising had to concentrate on these two key features (images of persons and settings for satisfaction).

Beginning in the last quarter of the nineteenth century, the market-industrial system pulled individuals away from traditional sources, such as handicraft objects, of need satisfaction and toward the marketplace, which was being filled with increasing quantities and varieties of mass-produced products. Starting in the 1920s, the coming of the consumer culture constructed an entirely new social framework for need satisfaction specifically tailored to a market-oriented society and based on the realization that individuals required help in learning bow to find satisfaction amid the great array of new products.

In fact, all human cultures devise socialization processes to teach men and women how to match their needs and wants with the satisfactions possible within socially approved ensembles of material objects and cultural practices. We will give a brief account of these processes, adapted from William Leiss's 1976 book, *The Limits to Satisfaction*.

Two general aspects of needs maybe labeled the "material" and the "symbolic." Humans are natural beings that are dependent upon the material world of nature for the maintenance of life, yet we rarely appropriate the fruits of this world as they are found in the environment. Rather, we transform them into specific types of goods—foods, clothing, ornamentation—according to the limitless ideas, images, and symbols fashioned by the human mind.

This point is easy to understand if we think about the traditional cultures that may be part of our family background or that we may have seen recreated at ethnic festivals or seen portrayed in film and television productions—Greek, Basque, Navaho, Japanese, Burmese, Kurdish, Ethiopian, the Indians of Peru. Each group has distinctive types of foods, clothing, housing, personal ornamentation, religious practices, and popular entertainments that provide socially approved forms of need satisfaction. These are the formats within which all members of the culture are expected to find an adequate sense of contentment and self-identity. A culture never imposes absolute uniformity; all cultures provide for variation and for greater or lesser degrees of individual expression within those basic formats. But all attempt to control deviance and maintain the viability of established customs, and to channel the individual's needs for physiological maintenance and psychological self-expression so as to ensure that some adequate match for them may be found in the existing ensemble of traditional objects and cultural practices.

A primary objective for traditional cultures is to maintain continuity and stability in these formats for need satisfaction. Indeed, their relative success in so doing is why we can still recognize an ethnic group by a particular style of embroidery on costumes, a characteristic food dish, or a special object crafted for festivals that has been part of its activities from time immemorial. Changes, including borrowings from other cultures, certainly occur over long periods of time, but every effort is made to preserve some continuity with the past, even if there remains only a fading memory of how things used to be done. This is the general pattern for every human culture that ever existed down to the point in our own century at which the market-industrial society was poised to undergo its metamorphosis into the consumer society.

Market exchanges have played a significant role in almost all human societies that are rooted in permanent settlements. This in itself does not mean that marketplace transactions determine the forms of need satisfaction or even have a major influence on them. The primary determinants are cultural traditions, which orient needs to specific, relatively stable sets of material things and to the accepted ways of carrying out everyday life with them.

However, as far back as the sixteenth century the system of price-directed market exchanges gathered strength in modern European societies. The field of satisfaction began to be concentrated increasingly in marketplace transactions (Mukerji 1983). More and more individuals received cash incomes and were required to purchase consumption goods, rather than producing most of what they required for themselves and obtaining the rest in local barter arrangements. But only when the market system was combined with industrialization and sustained technological innovation, bringing both mass production and rapid changes in the assortment of goods, did the revolutionary effects of the new system make themselves felt in everyday life.

As we have seen, the market-industrial society led to dissolution of the distinctive and relatively stable forms of need satisfaction created by traditional cultures. Industrialization uprooted great numbers of people from age-old rural settlements and relocated them in cities; only in the early stages could their traditional cultures sustain them amid the poverty of urban industrial life. As the tradition-bound forms of need satisfaction began to disintegrate, the marketplace itself began to assume the tasks of instructing individuals how to match their needs and wants with the available stock of goods and consumption styles.

Quite simply, individuals need guidance on what foods to choose and how to prepare them, on how to dress and wear ornamentation, on how to select and arrange their home furnishings, on how to entertain guests, and on innumerable other points of daily life. When traditional cultures have been weakened and the field of satisfaction filled with an ever-changing variety of unfamiliar, mass-produced goods, such guidance, or social cues, must be furnished in other ways. In the consumer society, marketing and advertising assumed the role once played by cultural traditions and became the privileged forum for the transmission of such social cues. This was not inevitable; beginning in the 1920s marketers simply seized the opportunity to put the transformation of consumer attitudes at the heart of the sales effort.

In a consumer society such as our own, where private business firms are the predominant institutions in the marketplace, the transmission of social cues for consumption styles is generated by these firms' wishes to deliver messages about products and services. It does not follow automatically, however, that such wishes are the most important element in the social impact of marketing and advertising. Having oriented the population toward marketplace transactions as the forum for need satisfaction, the market society then broke with the fundamental proposition of traditional cultures—that there is a virtue in fixed and stable forms of satisfaction—and instituted the radically different idea that enhanced satisfaction could be found in discovering new wants and experimenting with new products and consumption styles in order to gratify them.

Consumer culture did more than simply "massify" elite tastes; rather, it began to erode the very criteria by which status was once accorded in and through goods. The wealthier classes (being ever more closely attuned to international currents in fashions and tastes) had already become accustomed to drawing upon an ever-widening array of consumer articles, both handicraft and manufactured, shipped from every corner of the globe. The wealthy remained the relatively exclusive possessors of particular goods because only they could bear the expense, but because price not cultural policy was now the ultimate arbitrator for consumption, business interests could argue that their practices were inherently democratic and encouraged freedom. The massive outpourings of advertising and particularly an interest in brand competition led advertisers to present a great pluralization of stylized consumer goods enabling people to articulate their position less with a class affiliation than with a style affiliation.

The consumer culture is differentiated by voluntary and temporary affinities between persons who share a set of tastes and complementary values—a lifestyle. These affinity groups have been categorized as "market segments" by marketers and are also the object of audience research (by media firms) and market research (by goods producers), as coordinated by advertising agencies. In addition, the separate domains of persons and goods have collapsed and been absorbed into a more general, fluid setting where symbolic constructions play with an infinite variety of possible pathways to personal satisfaction. The functions of older cultural traditions in shaping consumption patterns and the sense of satisfaction for individuals have been taken over by media-based messages through which are circulated a great assortment of cues and images about the relationship between persons and goods. In other words, the realm of consumption practices, or the marketplace itself through messages about products and their possible meanings for an individual, gradually absorbed the functions of cultural traditions in providing guideposts for personal and social identity-telling one who one is or where one belongs or what one might become in life.

The consumer culture, we have argued, began to gather strength during the 1920s and was firmly rooted by the 1960s. Figure 3.3 represents the assimilation of cultural traditions into the common framework and the rise of a realm of popular culture that cut across income and wealth strata in the population.

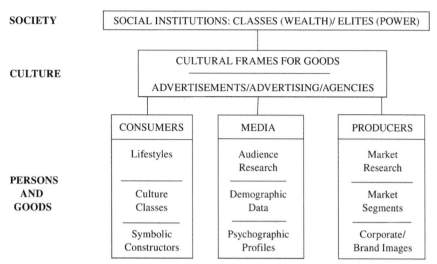

Figure 3.3   Modern Consumer Culture.

The discourse in and through goods expanded as goods became an increasingly important part of people's leisure time and the way they communicated with others.

Figure 3.3 suggests that social class and elite distinctions are in part hidden in the consumer culture by the flow of symbols across social groupings, as in the use of symbols signifying upper-class status in consumer goods ads directed at the ordinary person. The flow of symbols stands between social institutions, which embody the uneven distribution of wealth and power, and the democracy of consumption, in which equal access to the symbols of status and influence is guaranteed to everyone on the same terms. Diagram 3.1 also illustrates the central place of media institutions in the consumer culture and the place of advertising as the unifying force through which the flow of symbols and meanings is managed.

Finally, the phrase "Cultural Frames for Goods" is our designation for what holds together the message system about the relations between persons and objects in the consumer culture. A cultural frame is the predominant set of images, values, and forms of communication in a particular period that arises out of the interplay between marketing and advertising strategies, the mass media, and popular culture. We have identified five cultural frames over the course of the twentieth century; each is explained and illustrated in the final section of chapter 6 as we attempt to show how national consumer product advertising has become one of the great vehicles of social communication in contemporary society.

Conclusion

We have traced the evolution of a consumer society. A system of mass production provided a vast sea of goods. The rising wages of individuals and availability of consumer credit enabled a wider number of the public to engage in the expanded domain of consumer goods. A fashion system calibrated on seasons and turn over of product lines brought a new dynamism to the circulation of goods. Goods were increasingly stylized, and designs were informed by consumer research. Goods were not simply designed for utility but also for pleasure.

The institutionalization of a marketing, advertising, and media system provided individuals with increased exposure to representations of goods. People began to embrace the differences offered by the marketplace including and experimented with new colors and design. Up to the 1950s, there remained a strong community emphasis on consumption. Women remained the dominant shoppers looking after the household. Family consumption remained important, as did the keeping up of appearances for neighbors, and the tastes of economic elites and society people continued to hold sway. People looked to the department store, the fashion house, the designer, and advertising for guidance on consumption. But by the 1960s something began to shift within consumer society. Galbriath recognized that elites have given up their conspicuous consumption habits and were under-consuming. Baudrillard argued that display of economic wealth was becoming less important than cultural display. And most importantly, a generation of young people was coming of age and was examining the value of their parents mass consumer society with its suburban lifestyles.

CHAPTER 4

Advertising and the Development of Communications Media

Communication in pre-industrial societies was predominantly personal and oral in direct, face-to-face interactions in local markets, where barter and trade were the basis of economic activity; in places of worship, where ritual and sermons organized spiritual life; in courts and chambers, where officials held audiences; and in homes and communities, where the roots of cultural life were sunk deep in the soil of everyday social interactions. Communication—the transmission of ideas, feelings, attitudes, and experiences—was not mediated by technologies of communication.

However, as is the case today, communication flows were superintended by dominant institutions. Lines of authority and personal contact were well delineated, and ruling interests used whatever means lay at their disposal to transmit the versions of custom, belief, superstition, law, and power that suited them best. What distinguishes pre-industrial times from our own is that contact with social authority occurred through personal intermediaries. In modern society, direct and personal interaction is no longer the exclusive form of communication; it is now powerfully augmented and, to some extent, supplanted by interactions mediated by new technologies.

The Rise of Mediated Communication and Commercialized Media

During the last century, the process of exchanging ideas has become all but totally dependent upon mechanical and electronic infrastructures for symbolic reproduction and distribution. DeFleur (1970, 77) highlights this aspect in his "media diffusion curves" (Figure 4.1), reminding us of the speed with which successive waves of communication technology have been invented and assimilated into modern life (see also DeFleur and Ball-Rokeach 1989).

We follow DeFleur in concentrating on the mass media, rather than other point-to-point communication technologies, such as the telegraph, telephone, telex, and computer, whose effects have been felt mostly in the realm of business. The mass-consumer media are most closely related to the processes of cultural formation. We also follow Michael Real (1971), therefore, in preferring the designation "mass-mediated culture" to the more common "mass culture," for, whatever the nature of popular culture today, the instruments for transmitting it—the media—indisputably have a "mass" quality about them. What happens in and through them is dictated by audiences counted in the tens or

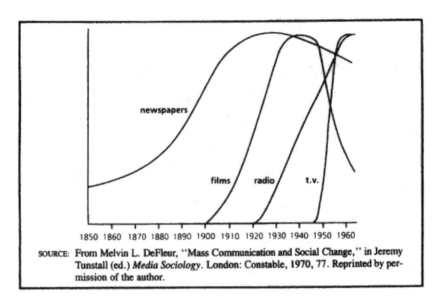

SOURCE: From Melvin L. DeFleur, "Mass Communication and Social Change," in Jeremy Tunstall (ed.) *Media Sociology*. London: Constable, 1970, 77. Reprinted by permission of the author.

Figure 4.1   The Diffusion Curves for Four Media with Ordinate Standardized.

hundreds of millions and by monetary transactions of similar dimensions. We have adapted this concept in our own phrase, "mediated communication."

There is a double mediation in the communication patterns of modern industrial society. First, during much of their daily lives, people are communicating through technologies rather than face to face. A technological means becomes the focus of the transmission and reception process, and the qualities of the technology and the forms in which it allows messages to be exchanged in these technological channels influence the patterns of communication. Innis (1951) and McLuhan (1964) have shown us that human experience and communication structures are influenced both by the perceptual and the social possibilities of a medium of interaction.

The second mediation is institutional. The panoply of communications organizations that create the technology, own or control the channels, and produce the messages also intervenes in the activities of human communication. These semi-autonomous organizations and the broader institutional framework in which they operate have become a major shaping force in the cultural life of modem society.

Taken together, both aspects have been active at the core of our cultural life. The spillover effects of this double mediation seep down into the farthest reaches of modern society, for the development of mass-mediated communication has been part of a historical process in which many of the other major institutions in our society—family life, religion, politics, business, education—have been realigned. Thus, communication technologies have a dual nature. They are channels through which information and interpersonal contact can flow and mix, binding together an otherwise dispersed and disparate population. They are also part and parcel of the institutional structure in a capital-intensive industrial economy, putting power and authority at the service of particular groups for particular purposes. This point should be kept firmly in mind throughout the remainder of our discussion.

Industrialism and the rise of mediated communication proceeded side by side. For example, the coming of mass media was facilitated by the effects industrialization eventually had on leisure time. As the length of the working day declined and the more puritanical aspects of the work ethic weakened, labor became less an end in itself and more a means of gaining access to life's necessities (and, later, luxuries). The time and energy no longer expended on work was available for other purposes, such as activities that contributed to the realization of personal goals.

The mass media seized upon this opportunity and began to reflect back their audiences' new interests and concerns as leisure-oriented consumers through popular films, radio programs, magazines, and newspapers. Their success (and later that of television) is proved by dramatic growth in audience sizes, which was the direct result of their quick adoption of communications forms and contents that focused on popular entertainments. The spheres of working life, business, and serious political and social issues were by and large relegated to well-segregated slots occupied by news and documentaries, except when they were refashioned to suit drama or comedy. Immense talent and resources were assigned to the task of making the style and substance of the mass media conform faithfully to the concept of "light entertainment." New cultural institutions arose to cater to the insatiable appetite of audiences for the media's products. Names like Beaverbrook, Hearst, Warner, and Disney became household words as the profile of communications as a social force became more distinct.

The prominence of mediated communication is very much bound up with the social functions it serves. Light entertainments make few demands upon their audiences, and so can be amusing accompaniments to rest periods when the working day is done or therapeutic aids to recuperation from stress. No less significant is their simple filling of free time; contact with the mass media absorbs about half the daily time released by the reduction in hours of work over the last century. Thus, it is fair to say that one has replaced the other as a form of activity.

The adoption of mediated communication into the rhythm of daily life also implied the development of new industries which supplied the technologies that enabled every household to enter into the flow of mediated communication. The realm of culture itself was industrialized. Moreover, each successive medium became a consumer product to be sought after—in the case of television, before it was even clear what it was actually going to offer. Up to 3 percent of consumer spending was funneled into communication and culture, and the modern living room took on the characteristics of a node on the communication networks. The industrial organizations playing a part in this cultural market—RCA, General Electric, Westinghouse, and so many others—found their fortunes rose with the importance of this new sector of the economy. The communication sector was becoming a distinctive and often autonomous actor in industrial society.

The rapid urbanization after 1900 was a factor in the development of mediated communication, as it was in the emergence of industrial production and distribution mechanisms. Commercial newspapers first flourished in centers where both business interests and readerships were concentrated. Radio and television were particularly appropriate for urban situations, for the transmission cost is the same regardless of the size of audience within the broadcast basin.

Ironically, spatial concentration of the population led to decreasing levels of interpersonal contact. The mass media very soon began to fill the gap with productions such as soap operas that recreated situations of everyday life. For urban populations, which are a concrete manifestation of the anonymity inherent in the concept of "audience," mediated communication gained a human face through their favorite stars.

But mediated communication is in itself a form of social organization, made up of the relations of media and audiences and the nature and influence of the messages that flow through these channels. Thus, the evolution of the print media, especially the newspaper through its contribution to informing and educating wider reaches of the public, into the so-called free press was considered one of the foundations of emerging political democracy. Advertising and the expansion of the commercial media were linked to the maintenance and growth of the market economy; it seems almost inconceivable that we could enjoy the benefits of industrial democracy without the activities of the commercial media

Thus, the historical development of the commercial media deserves close attention. In what ways and to what degree has advertising shaped the growth of the mediated communication that is so important to the conduct of every aspect of contemporary life? In the sections that follow we will outline the development of the modern media and the institutional framework in which they operate, showing how advertising-through the rise of mediated communication—has had a fundamental impact on society as a whole. We will focus our efforts by exploring three thematic areas.

The first is the establishment of commercial media themselves. Toward the end of the nineteenth century, advertising had become the key to the operation of the media, as the largest generator of its revenue. Commercialization, which was also based on increasing readerships and lower costs, not only became accepted as the best economic basis for newspapers, but also as the best guarantee of freedom from government interference. From then onward, the idea of the commercial press and the free press became synonymous and would continue to govern the evolution of the mass media institutions under successive waves of technological innovation. As a result, advertising considerations began to influence greatly the operations of media, particularly their orientation to content and programming and the organization of audiences in terms of social, spatial, and temporal qualities. The competition for audiences through programming became the *sine qua non* of all media. This is our second theme.

The process of development and change of audience patterns for different media became crucial to the communications system. The introduction of a new medium, which carved out its own relationship to an audience, implied changes in audiences for other media as well. Special-interest periodicals helped to create the mass audience base of the daily newspapers. Magazines, which cultivated the first mass nationwide audiences, increasingly lost them to broadcast media—first radio and then television.

Currently, newspapers address broad-based local readerships (far more stratified by social class in Britain than in North America), while most magazines seek national or regional readers defined quite precisely by interests, tastes, and social stratum. Radio, once a mighty national force, is now largely a local medium with audiences stratified by age; its continued high profile in daily life is a function of its concentration on music programming, which turns it into an accompanist to an almost unlimited range of other activities, irrespective of time or place. Television, in the hands of the networks, segregates its audiences rigidly in terms of time slots, but as a communications medium it is unsurpassed for its capacity to generate and hold the attention of audiences that are scaled in millions.

Our third theme is the very fact that the media are commercial, which makes them an important communicative genre in their own right, exploring the meanings of personal and social interactions as well as the meanings of goods in relation to those interactions. They confer a place of special importance to advertising's discourse about products. The average citizen now spends literally hours each day engaged in this discourse, not with friends, family, and neighbors, but through the mediated representations of posters, television, radio, and newspapers. Media have made commercial messages inescapable.

In expanding the discourse about goods, advertising accommodated itself to the communications environment. Advertising as communication evolved in response to the abilities of the audience to make sense of messages and in response to the ideas, styles, and forms that were being explored in other genres and other media. Within the proliferation of mediated communication a dialogue of forms occurred. Eventually the diffusion and intermingling of diverse currents of thought and action became synergistic, as ideas or styles arising in one medium or genre were transferred to others and adapted, refined, enhanced, or changed in form and emphasis.

For example, early prose styles for newspapers were modeled on letter writing, whereas later ones borrowed from novels and the periodical press. Radio absorbed performance modes directly from the theater, the cinema, and recorded music. Television undoubtedly has been the greatest synthesizer, turning to its purposes features drawn from all previous media forms. Visually oriented formats in art, photography, film, and television expanded and enhance in the population as a whole the understanding of the communicative skills that are founded upon symbolic, dramatic, imagistic, and metaphorical construction.

Positioned at the hub of the commercialized media, advertising has been in a position to assimilate all these influences and to bring them together in new ways. In some senses, it can be regarded as the quintessential communications form of the modern era. Its noteworthy features in this context are its condensing of ideas, its skilful combination of language and imagery, its breadth of thematic and social references, and its accessibility to and acceptance by wide audiences that may even cross linguistic and cultural barriers. Its efficiency as a communicative form has, in turn, affected other media productions, including serious film, television programming for children, and visual art. Most notable has been the expansion of advertising's social role; it has become one of the bases for governmental, political, and corporate efforts at persuasive influence through communication.

In the following sections we will place the emergence of advertising and the debates about its social role within the historical matrix that led to the rise of mediated communication and the emergence of our commercialized media institutions. In addition to the publications cited in this account we lean heavily on the work of A. Smith (1979), James Curran (1977), and E. Turner (1952).

The Origins and Development of Commercial Media

Newspapers

The development of the printing press marked the beginning of the industrialization of communication processes. The invention of typography resulted in "the first uniformly repeatable commodity, the first assembly-line, and the first mass-production" (McLuhan 1962, 124). With the invention of the printing press, modern society embarked on a long march that would usher communications into the marketplace as a product to be bought and sold rather than as an activity, and as an important part of the production and consumption process. The early products of the press were frequently read in a group setting; the eighteenth-century newspaper was a common property read by a large number of coffee-house devotees or by cooperative readership groups. As prices fell and content changed, the newspaper gradually began to define a more private and individual relationship with the reader. As specific readerships developed and were identified, the medium was segmented in order to cater to the range of interests within family units and social groups. All subsequent media developments have extended this trend toward communication as a privately owned and personally used household good. The Sony Walkman is probably the best and most extreme example of fragmentation of the audience.

The emergence of the daily newspaper brought about an equally significant shift in the *forms* of communication, introducing a radical change in the style and organization of the written word as well as in the distribution and availability of knowledge about the world. In becoming an essential channel for the social dialogue of modern democracies, the news has assured itself a special place in the institutions that govern mediated communication. (Moreover, as news increasingly emphasized the timeliness of information, the first repeatable commodity also became the first disposable commodity; few things are as uninteresting as yesterday's news.) The commercial press and the other businesses that sprang up around it are, therefore, prototypes for all the subsequent social transformations created by the industrialization of communication.

"The history of communications from the 1700s until our own century is largely the history of the Press" (Williams 1962, 22). It was by no means an untroubled history, for by the eighteenth century the press had ceased to be so carefully controlled as to be almost an organ of the state and had become a central feature of political factionalism. The repeal of the Licensing Act in 1695 had ended the broader phase of censorship control over the press in England, and the printing industries embarked on a period of growth linked to the expansion of newspapers. The Stamp Act of 1712 was moderately successful as a new form of control on the burgeoning press that continued in some form until the middle of the nineteenth century. It used market as opposed to political means to restrict circulations, imposing a duty of one pence per published page and an advertisement tax of one shilling per insertion (regardless of size) per issue. This effectively raised the price of publication and maintained the newspapers' dependence on sponsors and subscriptions from committed supporters. Advertising only defrayed a little of the cost of printing, so the coffee houses and other public forums for newspaper reading were crucial to maintaining the newspaper. These public places either provided newspapers free or rented them at very low cost. Circulations therefore rose more slowly than readerships as relatively few subscribers could regularly afford papers for their personal use. Political parties and factions within them based on coffee-house cliques became associated with particular newspapers.

Subsidies to the press through various means became an important instrument for disseminating partisan views.

Papers were voraciously read and debated at the coffee houses. Improved transportation and mail service encouraged wider circulation, giving a provincial as well as metropolitan slant. Since timeliness was crucial to political activity, demand for up-to-date news increased constantly. Average circulations were one to two thousand copies with some of the larger papers reaching about twelve thousand. In spite of increases in advertising and stamp duties, by 1753 total circulation in Britain had tripled from the 1711 level of 2,250,000; by 1776 it had reached 12,230,000, and by 1811 it had doubled again.

During the nineteenth century, the expansion of the press in both Britain and North America was connected to the development of new technologies for printing, as well as the rise of new readerships and new reasons to publish. A hand press might produce 150 copies per hour, and typemaking and typesetting were still cumbersome processes. The development of the Koening cylinder printing method and of steam presses brought the printing rate up to over a thousand sheets per hour. By 1827, the *London Times* was printing four thousand sheets on both sides daily.

Advertising volume increased dramatically with the growth in numbers of publications, in issue size, and in circulations and the appearance of a profusion of new products from manufacturers, especially after the repeal of the Stamp Act in Britain in 1856. In the United States, spending on advertising rose from $15 million in 1870, to $39 million in 1880, and to $71 million in 1890. By 1908, spending had reached over $140 million, with the lion's share going to the print media, particularly newspapers. Advertising revenue provided new capital and new profits for media businesses that were not used to large profit margins. The infusion of capital was invested in new print technologies that made daily circulations of over 100,000 (and up to one hundred printed pages per issue) possible for the first time.

From the advertisers' point of view, a problem with newspaper ads was the editorial restrictions imposed on style by the publishers. All ads at the time more or less resembled modern classifieds; the only variations permitted were in spelling, the use of repetition, and (on occasion) the use of bold type. Advertisements, which frequently were grouped together, dignifying the front page and set apart from the editorial content, were each only allowed to occupy a limited amount of space. In the late 1880s and early 1890s, Joseph Pulitzer and William Randolph Hearst introduced not only a new style of journalism but also a new look for advertising. These twin decisions marked the beginning of the modern commercial press.

When Pulitzer took over the New York *World* in 1883, he intended to make newspapers readable to new immigrants and to the lower-middle classes by using simple and accessible language. He adopted anti-establishment stances, advocating curbs on business, defending unions, and agitating opinion on a whole range of domestic issues. The format of the newspaper included exciting headlines and display presentations in advertisements. Within a year, his paper was selling 100,000 copies daily, and within ten years the total circulation of morning and evening editions was 374,000. These stylistic innovations opened up display advertising throughout the industry.

The creation of a press independent of political or party factions and of a specific circulation base of loyal subscriber-supporters, a press free to find its own niche purely in terms of its market success in winning and holding readers, was the final and most important step in the long process of commercializing the press. The commercial revolution in the daily newspaper was partly brought about by the development of advertising as a genre. The adoption of display ads and illustration techniques made possible by new print technology were part of the impetus for the expansion of advertising revenue.

Magazines

During the long maturation of the reading public in modern society, magazines carved out a special niche in mediated communication located somewhere between newspapers and books and borrowing ideas and writing styles from both (Peterson 1963). Magazines underwent several periods of development and transformation, during which they were influenced by—and, in turn, themselves influenced—other media.

Magazines were the first major competitors with newspapers for advertising, and they remain a significant part of the advertising marketplace today. Their own innovations in forms and styles reflected, in part, their search for a market niche, defined not only in terms of who their audience might be but also in terms of finding new ways to reach this audience. The Sunday periodical press in England was the first print medium to win substantial audiences for a popular press, achieving circulations of over 100,000, even under the disadvantages of The Stamp Act and advertising taxes (Williams 1961).

In Britain after the lifting of the advertising tax in 1856, a new range of magazines emerged to tap the potential reading audience as occurred in the United States, where no national newspapers existed to advertise the newly available branded goods in the 1880s. *Pickwick* and *Penny Magazine* in Britain and *Harper's* in the United States thrived on serial fiction and light matter lifted from digests of other literary sources. Stories taken from newspapers added breadth, and the absence of copyright laws made these literary efforts cheap to produce. In the United States, low postal rates for printed matter under the Postal Act of 1879 helped to ensure national distributions, meaning that reading publics could be organized around interests and attitudes. Religious and farm journals were very successful, and company-sponsored journals like the Canadian *Massey's Illustrated,* published from 1882 by the Massey-Harris farm machinery company, were often well respected. Many of these journals were not dependent upon advertising (they often, however, accepted it when offered), but rather on circulation and various forms of subsidy.

During this time, magazines thrived without the need for advertising revenue, and many of them, such as the better literary and religious journals, viewed it as a matter of pride not to sully their pages with ads. "Quality" literary magazines like *Harper's, Atlantic,* and *Scribner's* were wholly dependent on circulation, and indeed were only persuaded by the famous ad-man, J. Walter Thompson, to accept advertising after long refusing to do so. (*Reader's Digest* held out until 1957.) The leading women's magazines, *Godey's* and *Peterson's,* maintained low-profile advertising policies for much of the latter half of the century; the *New York Ledger* (400,000 circulation) did not accept advertisements.

In the 1880s, other journals were specifically created for advertising. E. G. Allen launched the *People's Literary Companion* as a pulp magazine to advertise a soap powder for which he owned the marketing rights. He scattered his ads throughout sixteen pages of stories, fashions, and household hints, charging subscribers fifty cents a year; he quickly achieved a circulation of 500,000. The *Companion was* the first "mailorder journal," so named for the types of advertising it attracted and upon which its economic security was founded.

The most famous magazine success story of the times was that of Cyrus Curtis. Curtis owned *Tribune and Farmer,* a somewhat successful weekly, from which he spun off *Ladies Home Journal The Journal* began with a circulation of 50,000, and as a result of a huge advertising campaign on its behalf this shot up to 400,000, confirming Curtis's faith in advertising as the foundation of the magazine industry. By 1895, circulation was 750,000. Building on this model, Curtis launched the *Saturday Evening Post,* which by 1910 had a circulation of over 2 million.

The popularity of magazines was stimulated by faster linotype typesetting and the invention of halftone technology. A pioneer was the weekly *Canadian Illustrated News,* which combined these techniques with the new paper made from wood pulp, which took ink differently from rag paper and made illustrations of a far superior quality. Advertising rates for this journal were the highest in Canada, but its combination of superior illustration and longer lead time than the daily newspaper proved attractive to readers and advertisers alike.

Munsey's *Journal,* a light topical magazine filled with illustrations as well as illustrated ads, was one of the first to exploit the dynamic relation between advertising and magazines. In 1893, its price was reduced to ten cents a copy and one dollar (formerly three) for a year's subscription. The result of this pricing strategy was a fantastic increase in circulation and a flood of ads. *McClure's* and *Cosmopolitan* followed suit, and the era of cheap general magazines had begun. By 1905, there were twenty magazines with circulations of over 100,000 in the United States with a combined audience of 5.5 million readers. Almost all included liberal amounts of advertising (some up to one hundred pages of it), using lots of display type and illustration. Much the same was happening in Britain, where *Tit-Bits, Pearson's Weekly,* and *Northcliffe's Answers* became the models for high-circulation, advertising-based periodicals.

The periodical press in the nineteenth century laid the groundwork for all subsequent developments in the commercialization of the mass media. The illustrated magazines, leading the way with innovations in photographic and color reproduction techniques, altered the print media and advertising industry alike, because they demonstrated the economic vitality of cheap, high-circulation journals that relied on advertising revenue. It was soon quite apparent that their popularity with advertisers rested on their acceptance of a whole new range of display possibilities for the ads within their covers. They brought fame and honors to their owners, who developed print empires based on exporting the capital resources, together with the marketing concepts pioneered by these journals, into the newspaper domain. And, finally, the illustrated magazines established many of the methods of promotion and distribution that would serve well in the later evolution of all commercial media institutions.

The Commercialized Print Media at the Turn of the Century

At the end of the nineteenth century, a number of forces, each of which had been gaining momentum on its own track for some time, were beginning to coalesce: the upsurge in industrial productivity, and the recognition that disposing of its output required adequate domestic markets; the change from a rural to a predominantly urban population, creating anonymity, mobility, and a widening distance from historical and cultural roots that prepared the ground for new patterns of everyday life, socialization, and consumption; the rapid growth of two print forms of mediated communication, newspapers and magazines, brought about, at least partially, by the ceaseless pace of technological innovation that offered the means of reaching a mass audience cheaply with a better quality product, including great improvements in graphics (halftone illustrations and rotogravure printing).

The fledgling advertising profession began to look beyond its original menial role of serving as brokers for media space, gaining recognition as an independent force along with manufacturers and the media. Later these three forces would be joined by consumers; later still, advertising began to regard itself as occupying the strategic point at which the others converged. At the turn of the century, the commercialization of newspapers that sought audience loyalty simply on the appeal of the paper's contents allowed advertising to assume a prominent role in the mass media.

As advertising became a major source of funds for the press, there was a reciprocal impact on the stance that newspapers and magazines assumed toward their audiences. Publishers began to regard their publications not so much as products to be sold to readers, but more as vehicles that organized audiences into clearly identifiable target groups that could be sold to advertisers; the audiences themselves became the products generated by the media industry. The selling of audiences to advertisers would later become an explicit and highly refined media marketing strategy. Our point here is that the framework for this approach existed by the end of the nineteenth century. As the mass media spectrum enlarged to include radio and television, of course, a regular reshuffling of the primary target audiences for each medium became part of the game. For example, major national daily newspapers were an important channel for national brand advertising until the 1950s, when it was attracted increasingly to television, and all but a few leading papers had to rely thereafter upon local and classified advertising.

Thus, competition from other media has repeatedly challenged the newspapers' pre-eminence as an advertising medium and forced them to make continual adjustments to the advertising market. For example, sectionalization, which became widespread during the 1960s, programs advertising into concentrated, topic-specific units; food preparation hints run with supermarket ads, market information with business ads, travel columns with package tour ads, and so forth. Sectionalization achieved for the newspapers the same results as segmentation did for magazines, namely the ability to address special audiences (theatergoers, sports fans, women interested in fashion) that advertisers wish to target. As a by-product, multiple readership improved because detachable sections could be read simultaneously by different members of the family.

Many of the innovations in newspaper design, such as the liveliness of style that was the hallmark of the early mass-circulation dailies, the use of display and illustrated ads, photojournalism, and more recently, full-color printing, were derived and modified from magazines. Weekend supplements and entertainment guides packaged information with the chatty journalistic style of magazines. Color supplements and inserts have proved to be particularly useful; in Canada, these now account for 5.6 percent of all advertising revenue, about half the newspapers' total share of national advertising, reflecting the special importance attached by food and other retailers to attractive color layouts.

The Impact of Broadcasting

Newspapers and Radio

The newspaper competed for advertising with the periodical industry and a far more potent adversary—the broadcast media. In Britain, newspapers actively supported retention of the public domain monopoly of radio broadcasting and later fought the introduction of commercial television for obvious reasons. They were instrumental in the 1923 decision of the Sykes Committee that led to Britain's public broadcasting monopoly. The United States followed a different route. As commercial radio was being developed, a number of newspapers bought stations as a novel means of promoting their newspapers. By 1933, 28 percent of American radio stations were owned by newspapers—especially the big stations in large urban centers. Other newspapers protested the possible loss of revenue, but the pattern of cross-media ownership and the idea of radio as a commercial institution prevailed in public policy.

During the early Depression, newspaper advertising dropped 22 percent in North America while radio advertising rose slightly, due partly to the emergence of spot advertising to supplement network-based sponsored programming. Spot ads gave radio a regional and local reach in its advertising to supplement the national selling campaigns that came with networking. But the cost of radio advertising quickly rose as performers demanded a share of the benefits of their drawing abilities. At the same time, the proliferation of broadcasters resulting from radio's success meant that audiences, except for the most attractive network broadcasts, were little different in size from newspaper circulations in any given area.

Costs per thousand for local retailers remained satisfactory in newspapers, and it was mainly the national brand accounts, which were not in any event the mainstay of newspapers at this time, that shifted to radio during the 1930s. The actual range of products advertised on radio was limited. Food, drug, tobacco, and soap—the major product categories-formed "the backbone of American broadcast advertising, accounting for approximately two-thirds of the users in 1931." (Hettinger 1933, 128)

Radio began to compete in earnest with newspapers for the retail and local advertising trade after World War II, just at the time when newspapers were being forced to respond to the changes in the advertising market brought about by the introduction of television. However, the competitive pressures of television on newspapers were not as great as some have suggested. As Curran (1977) points out, the differences in the relationship of the two media to their audiences make them complementary. Television is a high quality display medium attractive for the mass marketing of consumer goods, while newspapers are a regional and local medium with excellent information properties. Television may have caused a shift of some types of consumer advertising away from newspapers, as it did in the case of mass-circulation magazines, but its real impact was in maintaining a competitive pressure on the rate structure for all media. It also increased the newspapers' reliance on retail and regional advertising, which has been increasing relative to the total market since the 1950s.

As we shall see, the degree of involvement by the advertising industry in the institutional development of the mass media was heightened enormously by the emergence of the broadcast media. But the ground had been thoroughly prepared by the industry's participation in the commercialization of the print media. Therefore, when radio came onto the scene, it turned out to be a fairly easy task to apply what had been learned to the new medium.

Magazines Narrow Their Focus

The 1920s witnessed the continued expansion of popular magazines, although nearly as many failed as were started. Total advertising expenditures were growing, but competition between media for the various markets was heating up. The national general-interest magazine was competing not so much with the newspaper, with its identifiable urban market very attractive to retailers, as with the new national radio networks. In some cases, national accounts were split between them or were shifted to the new sound medium as advertisers discovered spot advertising on a national basis.

Magazines responded to the challenge by offering new attractions to prospective advertisers. Women's magazines were at the forefront. A number of them set up departments with consumer panels and research services that they offered to interested advertisers. Thus, the magazines gradually became innovators of services desired by advertisers. The use of audience research as opposed to circulation data became a widely accepted defensive measure against the encroachment by radio as an advertising medium.

But adoption of audience research by magazines had effects far beyond that of raising circulation figures. Readership studies discovered overlaps in readership patterns and magazines with few multiple readers. This knowledge allowed advertisers more tactical leeway in placing their ads, and those magazines that did not meet the advertisers' needs simply faded away. Daniel Starch and others pioneered in researching audiences—that is, who was reading what publications—but they soon went beyond the mere counting of readers; they asked about the readers' backgrounds and interests, thus helping to define the appeal of a particular magazine in terms of its audience.

Research oriented around the activities of the mass media has been a major force in welding together the social institutions that make up the consumer culture. Beginning in the 1930s, "social research served to unify business, advertising, the mass media, and through them, the further development of American culture" (Hurvitz 1985). A continuous circle of mutual influence evolved, in which "researchers came to promote themselves to the media, the media promoted themselves to advertising agencies, agencies promoted themselves to business, business promoted itself to consumers, and consumers ultimately turned back to researchers for guidance" (Hurvitz 1985).

Magazines that survived the Great Depression began to use research to evaluate readers' reactions to features or new styles of presentation, and in many cases to measure response to and retention of ads themselves. The information gathered was important for setting editorial policy as well as for advertisers. Old formulas for success were cast aside and magazines developed new approaches. "Readership ratings came to be accepted as helpful 'feedback' which complemented readers' letters and editorial know how" (Barbour 1982, 134). This feedback helped editors to exploit their advantages in audience positioning, content, and style.

The introduction of television created frantic competition for the magazine industry during the 1950s, and the magazines both won and lost the battles. Many major national accounts, particularly branded foods and household goods, did shift to television. The product array advertised in a typical consumer magazine has narrowed dramatically over the last thirty years, with high concentrations of particular products in a few journals. A high proportion of the advertising space in *Maclean's,* a popular Canadian newsmagazine, is devoted to the alcohol industry. Many women's magazines have personal-care and clothing advertising and little else. Successful magazines accentuated a special feature of their audiences, such as age, sex, income, region, and lifestyle grouping, to provide them with a firm advertising base. Not all group interests were represented by the magazines that survived, but the mass-circulation magazines reoriented their relationship to national advertising by narrowing their focus in terms of the products they could attract to their pages.

The specialist magazine market today shows clearly the dynamic relationship between magazine format and content and advertising. However, special-interest journals first developed during the nineteenth century (without carrying ads) for markets ranging from high-class literary or news journals, to religious, farm, hobby, and business magazines. Most were secure in their relationships and only expanded their reliance on advertising slowly. Many of them still cover more of their production costs from subscription revenue than from ads. Special-interest and lifestyle magazines were not created by advertisers.

The newer special-interest magazine's editorial focus is on a particular activity and product array, for example *Skiing, Tennis, Photography,* and *Computers.* Advertisers tend to think of these as reflecting a certain lifestyle with a direct connection to a product range. The more traditional special-interest magazines such as religious, business, or glamor magazines are less explicitly an advertiser's medium. The lifestyle magazine uses its editorial content to attract a narrow range of potential advertisers. In many cases, readers use them as shopping guides to assess products; advice to beginners is a regular feature inducting the reader into the special knowledge and skills of the activity. The lifestyle magazine blends advertising and editorial content until they are almost indistinguishable.

This more focused relationship is noticeable also in the "advertorial" sections, which first started appearing in business magazines like *Fortune* and are now spreading throughout specialty magazines. The advertorial is really an adaptation by magazines of the topic-specific newspaper section (women, sports, science) in which advertising and content can be prepackaged and inserted as a unit. A recent research study has demonstrated that when these sections are based on a single theme they improve the recall of ads by 30 percent.

Finally, the controlled-circulation magazine is probably the best illustration of the influence of advertising. Controlled-circulation magazines—distributed on a national, regional, and local basis—are delivered free of charge to those on a highly selective mailing list usually confined to more affluent sections of the city. If demographic and readership surveys prove that this upscale market segment can be efficiently reached by the magazine, then enough advertising can be solicited to cover all production costs.

The success of a magazine is dependent not only upon its ability to cultivate an audience in competition with other magazines, but in competition with other media as well. The special character of that audience—its spending habits, disposable income, openness to approaches through other media—are crucial factors in determining whether advertisers will use a particular magazine. Under these conditions, magazines are under pressure to orient themselves to audiences that advertisers particularly want, and these tend to lie predominantly on the wealthier end of the scale.

Radio: Tuning in The Commercial Institution

The introduction of radio also marks an important point of departure for the advertising industries in North America and Britain. One of the most successful ventures ever undertaken by the advertising industry in North America was the selling of radio broadcasting as a commercial medium. Although the agencies and the commercial press were at similar stages of development, in Britain radio became initially a public sector monopoly. The agencies and advertisers had to wait beyond the introduction of television for the broadcasting industry to have a commercial component; in Britain, radio followed in television's footsteps. Among the forces responsible for this was the strong resistance of the well-established newspaper sector, which was functioning as a national advertising system and felt threatened by radio. In many ways, advertising methods and approaches in Britain remained oriented to print until well into the 1950s, whereas advertisers in the United States eagerly explored the possibilities offered by other media. This may help to explain why in North America the agency system emerged as an important cultural force early in this century, while in Britain a similar impact was delayed.

Even in the United States both government officials and major industry spokespersons were seemingly reluctant to allow radio to turn itself into a commercial medium. General Sarnoff, head of RCA and an early visionary of the "music box" concept for radio, spoke out strongly against the commercialization of radio as late as 1924. The radio industry magazine, *Radio Broadcast Monthly,* railed against the dash of advertising paprika, calling for governmental restrictions. Secretary of Commerce Herbert Hoover also wanted to preserve the dignity of radio, stating at the 1922 American Radio Conference that it was "inconceivable" to allow "so great a possibility for service ... to be drowned in advertising chatter" (Briggs 1961, 7). The commercialization of radio was not the first or most obvious choice.

Early entry into the broadcasting market by retailers and producers of electronic equipment—who controlled up to 40 percent of the licensed stations in 1923—meant that broadcasting itself was initially a kind of promotional service for the hardware. In 1922, station WEAF introduced the "toll" system for advertisers, enabling them to buy ten minutes of broadcasting time for one hundred dollars. But takers were few, even in New York; only $550 worth of radio time had been sold three months later.

Some early advertisers sponsored programs directly relevant to their products. Gillette hosted a talk on fashions in beards, and department stores backed programs on fashion, hoping to generate institutional goodwill and interest in their products. But for the most part, advertisers simply did not know what to do with radio. Only the development of regular weekly programs rather than one-time efforts led advertisers to see some merit in the new medium, although few programs—only 20 percent in 1927 and 36 percent by 1931—yet attracted sponsors.

The national advertisers and the agencies quickly became the best organized forces in the radio market, and their pressure helped NBC to emerge as the first national network of affiliated stations. Networks solved two major problems in broadcasting: they provided better quality programming, holding the interest of large audiences with the costs of production distributed across a number of stations; and their broader regional and national audiences helped to attract more advertisers into the medium, keeping rates down.

By the second half of the 1920s, national advertising on radio, although well mannered and institutional in nature, was catching on and becoming increasingly attractive to potential advertisers. As radio's audience grew, advertisers' interest followed. In the larger stations, the pattern typical today was already at work; programming was used to attract listeners who were then "sold" to advertisers (Barnouw 1978, 33). The Starch study of 18,024 radio homes for NBC did much to confirm the growing significance of radio listeners as potential markets for advertisers. Further audience research efforts detailed the rapid growth of the medium (17 million sets by 1932) and the interests and preferences of audiences to guide programming on the networks. The research shows how listening followed daily time curves, with evening audiences different in character and twice the size of daytime ones; how the programming mix of the networks was establishing different audience loyalties based on programming preferences; and, more importantly, how "program flow" from one show to the next could influence these loyalties.

Once programming sponsored by advertisers secured a firm foothold, and networking was a success, the full commercialization of the medium proceeded apace. Individual stations became dependent on the networks for material of sufficiently high quality to draw audiences, and on the fast-developing expertise of advertising agencies to secure a stable revenue base. National broadcasting and national advertisers nicely reinforced each other's interests. In 1922, only 6 percent of all radio stations were affiliated with networks; by 1937, this affiliation had risen to 46 percent, and by 1947 to 97 percent.

The growing evidence of radio's popularity and efficiency as an advertising medium persuaded some of the more adventurous advertisers and agencies to back it heavily. The Lord and Thomas agency helped Pepsodent to develop *Amos 'n' Andy*, which became the most popular show on radio and quickly helped to triple Pepsodent sales. Albert Lasker, the agency's president, was convinced that a more focused and forceful selling message than the usual sponsorship mention or well-mannered invocation for products could be used on radio. The Lord and Thomas agency developed such ads for the American Tobacco Company. In the hands of the agencies, the style of national advertising on radio was changing and radio programming was changing with it.

Cecil Widdifield, an executive at Schwimmer and Scott Advertising, developed the idea of transcription, which allowed programs and ads to be recorded and distributed to various stations for replaying. Since the cost of talent was a growing concern, not having to pay for every performance was a considerable advantage, especially in network efforts. Mistakes, hesitations, miscues, and flubs could be minimized and program quality controlled. With transcripted programs now precisely pre-timed, it was possible to sell commercial spots between programs on individual or specific groups of stations to accommodate regional needs. Spot advertising became an important alternative to sponsorship.

From the late 1920s until the start of World War II, advertisers and their agencies controlled programming directly. Sponsors did much more than sponsor. They actually produced the shows, hiring performers, writers, directors, and musicians and leasing the facilities for production from the networks. The networks had virtually no control over the programming, and there is no indication that they wanted it. The effect on programming was predictable: It became advertising by another name.

In the sponsor-controlled hours, the sponsor was king. He decided on pro-gramming. If he decided to change programs, network assent was considered pro forma. The sponsor was assumed to hold a "franchise" on his time pe-riod or periods. Many programs were ad agency creations, designed to fulfill specific sponsor objectives. The director was likely to be an advertising agency staff employee. During dress rehearsal an official of the sponsoring company was often on hand in the sponsor's booth, prepared to order last minute changes. In Radio City—completed in 1933—every studio had a sponsor's booth. (Barnouw 1978, 33)

Even though substantial parts of the networks' schedules remained un-sponsored, by 1935 7 percent of advertising expenditure was on radio, rising to a high of 15 percent during the wartime and postwar newsprint shortages.

During the war, government agencies in the United States requested net-work sponsors to encourage war services such as nursing campaigns and war bond announcements. Advertisers welcomed this opportunity to make their position more legitimate, since—with severe shortages of consumer durables due to war production—they had relatively little to sell. They formed the War Advertising Council to coordinate responses to requests for public-service messages and to produce these messages. Renamed the Advertising Council when the war ended, it determined the priority to be given to public-service announcements. General reputations and organizational images became an important aspect of advertising in postwar America. In other words, public relations and advertising began to merge.

Radio evolved differently in Britain, where government had controlled radio technology since its inception. Noting the unregulated situation in North America, and the rapid growth in the medium in the early 1920s, the British government appointed the Sykes Committee to recommend a radio broadcasting policy. The newspapers, which had not sought cross-media ties in owning and operating radio stations and were especially concerned about potential losses of advertising revenue, strongly lobbied both the Sykes Committee and its successor, the Crawford Committee, not to open up the airwaves to "advertising chatter."

The Crawford Committee's 1926 report led to the Broadcasting Act and the creation of a public monopoly—the British Broadcasting Corporation with a revenue base assured by an annual license fee on radio receivers. The BBC gave rise to an enormously influential tradition of public-interest broadcast-ing, but it soon became apparent that good intentions were not enough to elicit and retain audience interest; attractive and entertaining programming was required as well. In the 1930s, the BBC had to compete in many parts of the country with private commercial broadcasters beaming transmissions to Britain from the Continent. The corporation launched an additional network for popular light entertainment, and eventually, in the face of a new surge of competition from offshore pirate stations in the 1960s, expanded to four. However, the Sound Broadcasting Act of 1972 at last created a structure of mixed public and private ownership, and thereafter independent commercial radio stations have competed with the BBC's four networks in the major urban markets.

In Canada, the commercial and public-interest streams converged in another way. By 1923 there were sixty-two licensed, privately owned stations, including one that was for a while part of the NBC network. From the outset, spillover of programming and advertising content from the United States was a major concern. In 1928, the Aird Commission recommended a system of license fees and a public broadcast monopoly on the British model. No action was taken, however, largely as a result of the clash over jurisdiction between federal and provincial governments.

The next official report in 1932 made very different recommendations. It proposed a dual system including both public and private broadcasters with revenues raised through both advertising and license fees. The Broadcasting Act of 1932 established a commission to oversee the radio system and in 1936 this became a dual system of commercial (private) and public-interest sectors all regulated under the auspices of the Canadian Broadcasting Corporation. The CBC thus was in the anomalous position of operating a single network of public stations and private affiliates across the country to compete with signals coming not only from the United States (over 80 percent of Canadians could receive such signals) but also from Canadian commercial stations—over which, in the public interest, it had a certain amount of regulatory control.

Television: Solidifying the Commercial Vision

In 1936, the BBC undertook limited public broadcasting of television signals from Alexandra Palace as an extension of its public-service monopoly (Briggs 1961). This arrangement survived until the pressures of industry, advertising agencies, and a Conservative government majority in 1954 created a mixed broadcasting system with competing public and commercial elements. The new Independent Television Authority could allow spot advertising but not sponsored programming, so that advertisers could not gain a stranglehold on the production of programs, which the British authorities considered the major deficiency in the U.S. commercialized broadcasting system.

In Canada, the Massey Report on the arts, in spite of many complaints from private broadcasters, suggested that Canada should have a national TV network under the CBC before commercial television was permitted. This rather confused situation was perpetuated in the Broadcasting Act of 1958. By that time, over 60 percent of Canadians could tune in to border stations in the

United States; some Canadian advertisers preferred to use those facilities, and Canadian audiences had begun to develop their long infatuation with the products of American television. Finally, in 1968, although a new Act reaffirmed the concept of a single system made up of two different sectors, the public and private sectors in practice were split up and the responsibilities assigned to each were distinguished.

To the south there was little question that television would follow in the institutional mold of radio. American broadcasting began in 1939 on NBC from the New York World's Fair, with CBS soon following. By 1941, ten commercial television broadcast licenses had been issued. A moratorium on new station licenses was declared by the Federal Communication Commission (FCC) in 1948, so as to impose some order on the television sector, particularly with regard to channel allocation. The freeze lasted until 1952, by which time—although only sixty-three metropolitan areas were in the reception areas of television signals—television fever had been unleashed and the mass production of sets was underway. By 1957, television reached 97 percent of the continental United States and over 82 percent of homes owned a television set.

The prewar structure of radio programming was transplanted to television. Advertisers still controlled programs, usually with one sponsor per show. In the 1945–1955 period, two external factors influenced the relationships among broadcast organizations. First, the huge increase in available consumer goods led to commercials becoming an incessant part of the broadcast day. Second, the atmosphere of fear created by the cold war and McCarthyism made sponsors tread cautiously in producing programs.

By the mid-1950s, the networks were becoming more and more uneasy about the control they had ceded to advertisers thirty years earlier. Most important was a legal issue: The networks were legally responsible for what they broadcast, though they had little say it. Among other concerns was the lack of logic in programming; scheduling, in particular, was chaotic. The networks tried to implement the concept of "magazine programming," wherein they would take charge of content and offer spots separately to advertisers in order to gain flexibility in maintaining program flow, the holding of audiences from show to show. The advertiser was satisfied when the audience rating for his own program was high; the network wanted to maintain high ratings over as many programs as possible. But the idea fell flat. Advertisers obviously wanted to hold on to their considerable power. Why settle for a one-minute commercial when you already had a thirty-minute one?

Two things forced the situation to change: the discovery of fraud and deceit in the popular quiz shows, and the economics of program production. Production costs, even for soap operas and the game shows, were high, and talent was demanding a considerable payback on popular programs. It was difficult for one advertiser to produce an entire show and buy time for it from the networks as well. Production houses began to produce programs under contract to the networks or under network license, and then to sell spots on them to advertisers.

Although decision making seemed to be with the networks, advertisers still influenced programming as television was totally dependent on advertising for its operating revenue. What did advertisers buy with their dollars? The common-sense answer was that they bought time, either fifteen- or thirty- or sixty-second spots. But whose time did they buy? Advertisers did not purchase just abstract time: they bought the time of particular audiences. Audiences were the currency of the advertising business and they became the currency for television programmers as well.

This becomes clear when we examine how advertising rates are set. Two factors determine the amount that advertisers will pay broadcasters. One is the actual number of people watching the ads. This aspect of audiences is known as "cost-per-thousand," and it helps those who are paying to compare the audiences for particular media in numerical terms. In the past, before audiences were qualitatively differentiated, sheer size was the criterion. The larger the audience, the more the network could charge for advertising spots. The stress on numbers and audience share, which was what the polls reported, thus became essential to costing for the advertising industry. Its effect on programming was to create a conservative bias, with no risks and no controversy that would exclude, alienate, or miss parts of the audience. To appeal to larger numbers of people, programming, of course, must address itself to common denominators in cultural preferences—critics accused it of appealing to the lowest of common denominators. National network-sponsored programming simply could not afford to experiment with programming that only appealed to specialist or minority audience tastes.

The introduction of UHF (ultrahigh frequency), public sector educational broadcasting, cable, and then satellite began to fragment the audience. Moreover, as research into television audiences, their attitudes and preferences for products, lifestyles, and spending habits expanded it became clear to advertisers that there was a second important aspect of rates—the demographic characteristics of the audience. Advertisers became interested in buying audiences that consisted predominantly of people who were consumers, or potential consumers, of their products. Some kinds of audiences became more expensive than others. Programs had to be tailored to generate large numbers of the right viewers for the particular advertiser.

In the 1960s, for instance, CBS dropped a number of popular prime-time shows such as *The Beverly Hillbillies* and *Andy Griffith* because they attracted the wrong audience—elderly, low-income, and rural viewers. Advertisers had become keen on attracting young, affluent urbanites who would be willing to try new products and keep using them for a long time once they became loyal to a brand. By 1970, this new audience logic of the television marketplace was throwing the network schedulers into turmoil. Although advertisers made fewer decisions about which shows would be developed or cancelled, they continued to determine the criteria that programs had to satisfy: "They were helping create a dramaturgy reflecting the demographics of the supermarket.... The sponsor, from whom the money flowed, had left the sponsor's booth, but he had taken his influence along with him" (Barnouw 1978, 73). Far from freeing programming from advertiser control, the magazine format intensified it across the entire schedule.

> In practice, the networks, in their drive to sell every available advertising minute at the highest possible price, proved to be even less adventurous than the sponsors had....Advertisers, in short, had proven to be more responsible and innovative as programmers than the networks. Network-originated programming now was set on a course to become ever more rigid and standardized, enslaved to ratings....The magazine format programs turned out to be a formula designed first and last to accommodate advertising. At its worst the format amounted to little more than commercials in search of a program. (Bergreen 1978, 178)

Producers are also concerned with providing a conducive environment for the reception of commercials. Apparently this dictates a methodical blandness, so as not to upset or disturb the viewers as they are gently prepared for the ads.

Such was not always the case. In the early 1950s, the normal vehicle for drama presentation was the anthology series in which each week's show was different from the others. Many of television's finest moments were captured in the anthology series. However, because television was done live at this time, these self-contained plays featured indoor settings and tended to stress not physical confrontations but complex social and psychological issues without easy solutions. Meanwhile, the commercials offered happiness and salvation in one minute or less, which made them seem fraudulent.

The anthology series also often dealt with lower-class life and settings at odds with the sponsor's desire to encourage the audience to yearn for the glamorous, consumer-oriented lifestyles depicted in the ads. In the mid-1960s, the anthology series was replaced by a new format based on episodes. As the major Hollywood studios started to produce for television, the restrictions on live performance disappeared and drama moved outdoors into glamorous settings with handsome heroes and heroines. The episodic series relied less on the creativity of writers, or on dialogue, and more on the filling out of an already established formula that walked a few flatly developed characters through an action-packed dilemma. Alas, these dilemmas were all too often the familiar ones of modern consumer life, featuring troubled personal relationships being rescued by a timely application of standard social values (Barnouw 1978).

The content, form, and concerns of commercials mimicked each other as well as the surrounding shows. The game shows of the 1950s, such as *Queen for a Day* and *The Price Is Right*, explicitly emphasized consumerism; later, *Family Feud* and *The Dating Game* interwove social relations and the rewards of consumption more intricately. Soap operas moved to the nighttime schedule and up the class ladder from the middle-class setting of *As the World Turns* to the American aristocracy of *Dallas*, offering a new context for displaying the dramatization of consumption patterns and conventional status symbols.

The action adventures reflected ads more in terms of pace and excitement than thematic content. Once again, television blurred the distinction between programming and advertising, this time with respect to style—of character development, dialogue, music, and camera angles. Characters walked out of the programs and into the ads, even when the actors were left behind. Advertising uses television programming as a system of reference; returning the favor, programming uses advertising as its framework and, in some cases, its exemplar. *Sesame Street* adapted the pacing of advertising to the task of teaching preschoolers. Politicians took lessons from image counselors expert in flogging whatever was set in front of them before they ventured forth to debate the nation's fate. Shot framing or cutting techniques pioneered in advertising to condense storytelling became stock tools of television dramas.

Sharing the Market

Could the massive growth in print media circulations or the subsequent impact of radio and television on daily life have occurred without advertising? Advertising and the mass media marched hand in hand into the modern world. The massive increase in the number and technological sophistication of communication channels paralleled a similar expansion of messages directed toward consumers through advertisements.

Advertising expenditures grew steadily but slowly before the period of the commercial revolution in the press. The second half of the nineteenth century was a period of increasing numbers of new publications, and magazines and newspapers that previously had not accepted advertisements began to do so at this time. Also, a slow growth in new product types entered the advertising arena. The result was a moderate but steady growth in advertising volume up to the end of the century.

The beginning of the twentieth century was a major turning point for advertising. The revolution in the newspaper industry, which linked the increasing productivity of the press with income generated predominantly by advertising, coincided with a period of dramatic growth in advertising volume. The expansion of the magazine industry, too, in conjunction with a whole new range of products (especially branded consumer products), seemed to accentuate the growth of advertising. The first twenty-five years of this century was the period of advertising's most rapid growth.

Similar jumps in the volume of advertising can be connected with the introduction of radio in the late 1920s and of television in the early 1950s. The appearance of new media led inexorably to greater advertising volumes. The introduction of broadcasting media obviously produced competition for accounts among the media; but this competition only caused each medium to redouble its efforts to make its special qualities more attractive to advertisers by making the medium itself more attractive to audiences. The only period of declining investment in advertising came during the early Depression years of the 1930s when a number of major manufacturers reduced their volume irrespective of the availability of media.

Each new medium opened a new channel to audiences. Sometimes simply by adjusting the content and form of advertisements, audiences organized in a certain way by one medium could also be addressed by another. Advertisers, growing in number as nationally distributed branded products proliferated, faced an increasingly complex advertising environment. They shifted accounts from one medium to another as advantages presented themselves, creating competition among media for advertising revenue. Advertising did not cause the expansion of mediated communication. As Raymond Williams (1961) points out, one can notice a general increase in circulations for the daily press long before it developed into the commercial press. Neither the spread of literacy to the working classes nor advertising created the reading public; it was already well established when the commercialization of the mass media began.

But the reorganization of the press, linking profitability indissolubly to advertising revenue, did help to make the newspapers affordable for the new lower-middle-class reading public, which was becoming much more involved in social and political issues. The Crimean and Boer wars in Britain, the Civil and Spanish-American wars in America, and World War I everywhere had a dramatic impact on the daily reading of newspapers, giving advertisers access to new consumers and publishers increasing profits as per-issue costs decreased with the new printing technologies and economies of scale.

Similar arguments can be made about the growth of radio and television. In Britain, where radio was noncommercial, the number of receiving sets increased rapidly during the 1920s; and postwar austerity only partially moderated the demand for television sets in the early 1950s before commercial television was introduced. Advertising did not create demand for these media, nor did its invisible subsidies support their difficult early years.

Even in the United States, the surge of radio buying preceded any large-scale advertising efforts. In 1924, over 1.5 million sets were sold, with annual sales rising to over six million by the time the Radio Act of 1927 defined advertising as in the "public interest, convenience, and necessity." Whatever changes in programming were made to encourage listening in the early phase had little to do with advertising, though subsequent growth in audiences may have had something to do with the influence of advertising on programming. However, it is impossible to pin this down, since no one can say with assurance how noncommercial broadcasting would have developed. Yet evidence from countries with noncommercial or only partially commercial broadcasting supports the view that the growth of mediated communication responds primarily to general social change within which advertising plays only a small part.

This is not to say that powerful reciprocal forces were not exerted by the successive revolutions in media technologies and advertising. In creating an institutional context and rationale that supported advertising, the press laid the groundwork for the commercialization of other media. Although competing media threatened to detract from print's share of the advertising pie, in the long run, the careful studies by Hettinger (1933) and Curran (1977) on the introduction of radio and television, respectively, show that by and large the advertising revenue garnered by them is not won at the expense of older forms. There was always one clear beneficiary—the advertising industry (especially the agencies).

What was most affected by the emergence of new means of communication was the shape of advertising or the design strategy rather than the volume. As new media brought new styles and approaches to the tasks of mass communications, advertisers adapted them to the special requirements of persuasion. The selling message was altered by the communications environment.

The influence of advertising on communications media has received much attention, as we have seen. It is unlikely that any of the means of mass communication could exist as they do without the money they derive from advertising. Wherever television and radio are not funded by government grants, they are almost entirely dependent upon ad revenue; newspapers depend on advertising for two-thirds of their revenue and magazines for about 60 percent. What advertisers get in return for their money is the right to insert their message in the particular medium. But this is not a totally passive insertion, since it occurs in an environment where media compete for advertising revenue. In what follows we are particularly concerned with how advertising influences the non-advertising content and operations of the media—that is, with the relationship between advertising and programming.

One view, often put forward by advertisers and the media themselves, is that advertising revenues merely make the programs possible. Watching the ads is the price we pay for getting the programming, but there is no direct connection between the money derived from advertisers and the programming it pays for—or more broadly, between the media's business interests and its production and distribution of content. Another view stresses that because advertising guarantees the profitability of the media enterprise, programming has become geared to the interests of advertisers.

Attempting to reconcile or choose between these two opposing points of view presents an intractable problem. The interlocking interests of media and advertising were constructed step-by-step, through quite deliberate, marketplace transactions and public policy decisions, yet to most people this development seems as natural and inevitable as the succession of seasons. Opinion polls in Canada, for example, reveal that most viewers of television feel insulted and demeaned by advertising, but accept it as a necessary part of the media system. "Nearly forty years of the present broadcasting system has conditioned a generation of citizens to find it normal. Most people find it difficult to think of other kinds of broadcasting systems and uses" (Skornia 1965, 44).

It is certainly true that, in television at least, the economic power and decision making that control the processes of communication tend to be separated from the editorial and creative activities that develop the content and programming. In both public and private networks, programming policy and strategy is regarded as proprietary information. As viewers, we experience these institutions mainly as communication providers, not as business organizations. For example, our knowledge of program decision making is normally limited to statements by media executives on a particular show's slippage in the ratings; what we do not see directly are the processes that make ratings the primary desideratum in the show's success or failure.

The difficulty is compounded by the fact that advertising itself is a service industry in the sense that it is dependent upon the activities of producers and providers of services. Advertising's subsidy to the media comes from the industrial sector, which reclaims it from the consumer. There is no direct market in commercialized media, as there is, for example, in the movie industry; we only buy it indirectly through a value-added payment on the price of the goods we consume. We have no way of seeing how our choice of goods is translated into advertising support for particular programs, magazines, or newspapers. In earlier periods in our own society or in countries where political parties control media directly, the connection between politics and the content and form of messages seems reasonably clear. But it is far more difficult to spotlight the relationship between business and communication where advertising interests and the logic of buying audiences are involved.

Behind the people who appear to us on the box, whose voices ride with us in the car, or whose words seem as familiar as the morning toast they accompany, is a large organization making decisions that shape editorial and program content. And behind that organization is an invisible institutional structure supported by tradition, money, and power, establishing the framework within which those decisions are made. These relations are "remote and impersonal" (Curran 1981); analysis of the influence of advertising on communications is contingent upon being able to peer through the murky waters where the many-faceted institutional determinants of programming lie.

It is, therefore, essential for us to separate the various organizational factors that impinge upon programming. We follow Murdock (1982) in distinguishing between allocative and operational control of media organizations. Allocative control can be defined as "power to define the overall goals and scope of the corporation and determine the general way it deploys its productive resources"; operational control as "decisions about the effective use of resources already allocated and the implementation of policies already decided upon at the allocative level" (Murdock 1982, 122). Advertising's influence tends to be concentrated at the allocative level; programmers are likely to have a good deal of autonomy over immediate production. However, media operations are still limited by the range of options defined by the goals of the organization and the resources allocated. As new forms of ownership and control emerged in the modern commercial media organizations, agencies began to distinguish between management and programming decision making.

Another media historian, James Curran (1977), urges that we also distinguish between influences that affect a single media organization and those that change the system or institutional arrangements for the media as a whole. For example, in the mixed broadcasting environment of Britain, decisions made concerning programming in the private sector can influence actions taken in the public sector, because these organizations compete for a common audience.

Similarly, because of the competition within and among media for advertising finance, actions by one organization (for example, the decision to accept comparative ads, fifteen-second spots, or advocacy campaigns) can influence the system as a whole by attracting or drawing revenues to a particular medium. Such actions alter the entire system. The same can be said of government policy (for example, the ban on cigarette advertising on television or regulations for alcohol ads).

Finally, possibilities for the direct influence of content keep changing. In earlier times, newspapers depended on advertising for less than half of their income, and the opportunities for advertisers to exert major influence were limited simply by the nature of the accounts. Most ads were classifieds, and only a few national brands and newspaper chains existed. Most papers served a very diverse collection of advertisers with small accounts. If pressure were exerted, the editor was in a position to ignore it because he or she risked losing only a small portion of income to maintain journalistic integrity.

By the 1860s, the British firm of Thomas Holloway was spending almost £40,000 year on advertising; by 1890, Sunlight and Pears were spending up to £100,000 each. In America, Lydia Pinkham (home medicine remedies) was in the same league. It is reasonable to suppose that individual editors felt the presence of these large accounts in areas other than the balance sheet. Most of the magazines which at first refused all advertising, or just certain types, succumbed sooner or later.

The national branded products were generally produced by companies that also advertised other products. The potential threat of the angered advertiser was heightened when large advertising agencies started to work with several major accounts. At the same time, advertisers' interests were being diffused across a broader range of concerns. It was not the specific story that was a threat, but media editors' and programmers' preoccupation with issues that bore on advertisers' (and media owners') institutional interests—media and corporate regulation, news values, ideological issues in general, free enterprise and its prerogatives, and so forth. On such matters, business interests in the media and the rest of the corporate sector were in basic agreement. More directly, advertisers' interests lay less in specific contents and ideas than in the formats and stylistic techniques of media—layout, printing, program flow, orientation, and market strategy—which influenced the audiences gathered by the media and the markets that could be penetrated through them, their selling power, and the opportunities they gave to use advertising design and strategy to maximize advertising goals. Thus, the impact of advertising interests and practices spread generally through the whole media system.

CHAPTER **5**

Advertising and the Development of Agencies

As we have seen, the print media carved out a significant place in modern society before becoming dependent on advertising revenue. It is not unreasonable to suppose that they could have continued to develop with only a moderate dependence on advertising, relying upon mass circulation as the economic basis for expansion. Indeed, many of the mass-circulation print media were able to survive without any advertising well into the twentieth century (*Reader's Digest* is the best-known case).

Advertising did not create mass circulation, nor was the development of the broadcasting media inconceivable without advertising. Radio in America, after all, was initially conceived as a public service using public airwaves in the public interest; little thought was given to the role it could play in promoting consumer goods until well after the networks were established. Special-interest publishing and broadcasting based on specific loyal audiences (which continues to work well for many small magazines, radio stations, and religious and educational television) could have been the model for the development of the media. Today, with cable and pay television services proliferating, the return to the idea of paying for special communication services (rather than have them subsidized by advertising) is an important trend, but it did not prevail at the outset, when, at least in North America, the advertising subsidy took root and helped to shape the growth of the modern communications industries.

What actually happened was that advertising became the crucial bridge between the activities of selling products and communication as both spheres expanded rapidly—a simple, but much overlooked aspect of its significance in modern society. A bridge is useful to the extent that something crosses it; in the case of advertising, money, influence, and information crossed.

The flow of money, reasonably straightforward at first, became exceedingly complex. In the late nineteenth century, producers began to allocate a proportion of their income to advertising. At first, the money went directly to the media; later it was channeled through advertising agencies, which took a proportion of the billing as their sales commission. Consumers pay this advertising subsidy to the media as part of the price of a product. The proportion varies across industries—manufacturers of cosmetics, personal-care products, and household goods allocate a high proportion of all expenses to advertising. For example, up to 50 percent of the cost of a perfume may be attributed to expenditures on advertising. Advertising now accounts for almost all revenue for the broadcast media (except in public networks such as the BBC); 75 percent for the newspaper industry, and anywhere from 60 to 100 percent of income for magazines. Around 1913 just prior to the outbreak of the First World War, tax legislation was passed that made advertising a legitimate business expense. Producers were not required to pay taxes on their advertising. This tax exception remains in place and is justified upon the contribution advertising is thought to make to the economy and the media. Today this exception is considered a right of business, revealed in the few instances when individual U.S. states (Florida, Texas) have attempted to revoke the tax to raise state funds resulting in an outcry of protests by industry:

> The advertising tax deduction, which all businesses enjoy, is a fundamental principle of the free market. Advertising is part of the cost of doing business, and as such it can be written off against profits. It's as simple as that. Once the government starts interfering with that model, it finds itself in treacherous territory. (Anon. 2002)

Yet as the quote above illustrates, the loudest opposition to reconsidering the tax exception comes from the media and businesses which have the most to loose. Given the difficulties we have in measuring the exact contribution of advertising to the economy, it is a bit of a stretch to speak of "treachery" in this regard.

One of the major uses of this bridge, then, was to help allocate a proportion of the income accruing to industry from consumers to the development of media.. The media, in turn, adjusted to these new sources of revenue by setting up departments and services (such as market and circulation research) to accommodate their growing relationship with agencies and advertisers, thereby diverting funds from editorial, programming, and internal development efforts.

The history of advertising, therefore, is largely the history of the advertising agencies that served the needs of advertisers and media alike. In this chapter we explore the development and history of advertising agencies to 1980. In addition to the works cited, we have relied in our account on Sampson (1974), Presbrey (1968), Heighten and Cunningham (1976), Hotchkiss (1950), Seldin (1963), and Elliot (1962).

Advertising Agencies: Managing the Flow of Symbols

In the earlier phases, advertising agents received special rates and arrangements (or kickbacks) for bringing a high volume of business. This was, of course, a hidden subsidy to the agencies themselves. The early agencies, then, developed primarily as buyers in bulk of media space that they then divided into smaller pieces and retailed to manufacturers, especially to the makers of patent medicines. Part of their pitch to manufacturers was based on circulation figures, but the quality of their "data"—and hence the value of their "product"—was highly suspect. (In fact, they lied to both sides in order to maximize their spread as intermediaries.) Eventually this led to an effort, spearheaded by Rowells and Ayers, to establish reliable circulation data.

As the agencies developed new skills, such as copywriting and artwork, and expertise in the arts of advertising, they also began to sell these as a service to advertisers. Today, these creative aspects are often billed separately, implying that the portion of the advertising budget that is not a direct subsidy to the media may be growing—in terms of our metaphor, this is the portion devoted to "bridge-building." In this sense, the consumer has subsidized not only changes in communications media, but the development of the agency sector as well. As we pointed out earlier, it is very difficult to ascertain whether this has resulted in increased efficiency and lower costs for the consumer, or the opposite.

The flow of information also went both ways across the bridge. Information flowed from producers to consumers not only through the ideas and images of the advertisements themselves, but also through the more general influence of the commercialized media in shaping audiences and favoring types and styles of programming that maximized the effectiveness of advertising. Information also traveled in the other direction—from the communication sector, consumers, and culture in general back to the industrialists. The agencies, in some cases assisted by the media, pioneered investigations into consumers' responses to media and products, first in terms of ascertaining reliable circulation figures and later in terms of audience and marketing research (Hurvitz 1984b; 1984a, 205–15). Ultimately, the skills, sensitivity, and knowledge about consumers acquired in the process of media research were used to help manufacturers appreciate and cater to the idiosyncrasies of the consumer. Audience and market research gradually came to play an important part in business strategy. "Perhaps primary among the influences that have affected the advertising business is the transfer of the public's role from that of a recipient of goods and services to that of a shaping force" (Harper, Harper, and Young 1963, 45).

The expansion of advertising created an institution that supported the "intelligence" function of industry; producers increasingly became interested in contact with consumers, but they ended up making it largely through advertising agencies. Industry gradually adjusted its marketing practices to the novel situation created by the consumer culture, and by and large it was the agencies who taught them how to do it. As the agencies worked increasingly in and with the mass media, they developed a sensitivity to communications processes that few industrial managers could match. Advertising agencies thought about products in terms of symbolic and communicative activities and they parlayed their concern for audiences into an obsession with the consumer.

The agencies employed an increasingly complex array of symbols and images drawn from a storehouse of cultural references, matching the intentions of producers and consumers and opening up the communications channels between mass production and mass consumption. Figure 5.1 shows advertising situated strategically between the spheres of industrial and cultural production. Producers must identify and communicate to markets (buyers or potential buyers) the particular features of or motivations for buying their goods. Potential customers and the reasons they have for buying particular kinds of goods can be located and studied through market research, providing the producer with knowledge about consumption and consumers. The tendency has been for the agencies to become more and more knowledgeable about markets and more involved in strategic decision making about them. The commercial media must be able to spot the types of programs and schedules that will attract the most advertising revenue by drawing audiences that advertisers wish to reach. They need to prove that their audiences are of

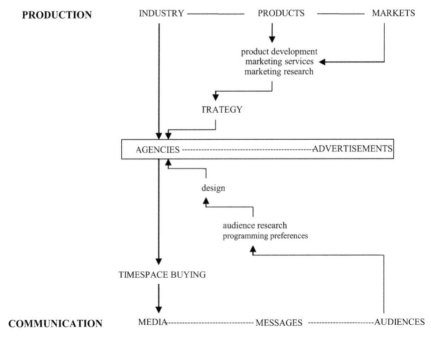

Figure 5.1 The Position of Advertising in Relation to Cultural and Industrial Production.

an attractive size and quality in order to promote them to time/space buyers in the agencies. They therefore expand the activities of their own advertising departments and bend programming decisions to attract the most appropriate audience to satisfy advertisers' demands.

Thus, programming and the production of culture become dominated by the needs of advertisers. Between these two spheres is the advertising sector, made up of the agencies and the service companies that support their activities. On the organizational level, the agencies make the link by taking industrial accounts and creating campaigns for them that require buying media time to gain access to audiences. The basic activity of agencies, namely the design and execution of advertising campaigns, always involves some equivocation. There is almost never a perfect match between the potential market defined by the producers' interests in selling and the audience for a program or the readership of a paper. Matching audiences and markets through communication design, therefore, has become the major mediation performed by the advertising sector, leading on a symbolic level to a communication output that fuses the meaning of products with the broader range of cultural references. The development of symbolic attributes for commodities was thus an outgrowth of this communication problem. The agencies discovered the ad campaign as the bridge to reconcile the different requirements of media audiences and consumer markets.

The first important activity of advertising was the reshaping of the institutional structure of media enterprises, the immediate effect of which was to change the relationship between media and their audiences. The buying and selling of audiences to advertisers became a dominant activity of the media. By the 1920s, print media were not only providing circulation guarantees or willingly submitting to circulation audits, but were actively devising ways to sell themselves to advertisers. Early on, they were touting their ostensible hold over their readers, as in this *McCall's* ad: "When a women shops...with imagination's aid she is looking far beyond the bright array of labels, the bins so neatly stacked, the price tags on the shelves. She has a picture in her mind, a tantalizing vision that guides her purchase. *McCall's* editors know how to implant these mental pictures" (Pollay, n.d., 24).

The advertisers' agents were successful in getting the media to adapt their formats to advertising needs. Organizing the right audience in terms of demographic compositions and size was critical, but having the right effect was no less essential. Attention holding, audience flow, impact and timing, layout, style, readability, and a hundred other audience-oriented details all become major considerations in media decision making. The agencies communicated to the media what advertisers wanted from their audiences by moving their accounts, by making demands and suggestions, and by the example of their own campaigns.

On behalf of the major corporations, the agencies explored and systematized the best approaches to selling goods; they created formats and styles, undertook research, and speculated about what made effective advertising communication that elicited a response from the consumer. Their work—selling-as-communication—necessitated a sound knowledge of the materials (consumers and symbols) and of the media that they were using, and they gained a sensitivity to the difficulties of eliciting a consumer's response.

In attempting to fuse selling and communicating, advertising reached out into the world of culture for its sources and references, acquiring a special sensitivity to social trends, to styles, and to the creative dimensions of selling. The agencies never accepted the notion that products could sell themselves. They mocked the industrialist's obsession with the product as such and remained acutely aware that they addressed consumers as audiences of media and were not sales representatives on the road or in the stores. They observed, altered, and transferred techniques, ideas, and images from one medium to another. They were soon leaders in specialized areas of communication, setting styles and patterns as well as reflecting them. As such, the trends, rhythms, and even the personnel of advertising had a wide influence on other forms of cultural production. Thus, advertising not only evolved as a unique cultural form with its own grammar and logic—where the relation between consumption and popular culture was always the central theme—but also as a pattern for the whole communication field, affecting cultural activities ranging from fashion to election campaigns.

Advertising's appreciation of the concept of the audience promoted creative explorations not only of popular culture, but also in the field of social research. In pioneering statistical research on audiences, advertising provided a new twist to the way in which institutions reflect the normative order; while their selling pitches were tied to accepted values and life images, they also began to explore and experiment with new variations, new "suggestive allusions," and new rhetorical styles as they tried to lace the motivation for purchase and the cultural context together.

Figuring out who the consumer was and how he or she could be best approached through media became a central facet of advertising practice. From the early writings of Professor Dill Scott, through the heyday of motivation research, right up to the current sophisticated statistical accounts of market segments, advertising agencies have attempted to use the understanding of consumers as a pragmatic feature of communicating with them. Social research helped advertising both to focus on a narrow range of normatively supported social imagery, and to make the connection between a valued image and its market relevance more precise, thus transforming the communicative activities of selling.

Although the agencies' personnel worked for producers of goods and services, they themselves came from the communication sector and brought with them different approaches and skills. Some early industrialists wrote and planned their own campaigns, seeing little advantage in hiring the skills of an agency or specialist; in many cases, their copy and promotional ideas were excellent. The agencies, however, grew out of the publishing world, first offering the service of evaluating publications' circulations and coordinating the purchase of space in regional journals. As they developed, the agencies persuaded industrialists that the task of campaign design and execution was too complex for amateurs, and they began to offer an ever-widening range of communication services. (On U.S. radio in the 1930s, they undertook not only the production of advertising, but of programming as well.) In many cases, agency personnel had moved to advertising from other communication activities, such as journalism, and later, radio or television production and direction. For them, the product was secondary to the task of selling it through their expertise in communication. In the constant dialogue with their clients, they brought their skills and concerns to the fore in marketing and advertising.

Debates have always raged in advertising about the best way to address the buyer; eventually it was agreed that this meant knowing about consumers and the media that were being used to reach them. In extending salesmanship, advertising had to change it. The army of drummers that the industry had used, mainly to persuade retailers to distribute their goods, was replaced with a barrage of messages designed to inform the consumer directly about the product (Joyce 1963, 21). Advertising changed the dynamic of selling by making it focus on the anticipation of purchase rather than on dialogue in the store. As the door-to-door sales representative was increasingly barred from the privacy of the home, the media were gaining access.

Advertising agents also learned that the relationship between an audience and a communication product was not like that between a consumer and most other products. Consumers treated buying a car as a long-term commitment, but their consumption of messages was different. Radios could be turned off and channels changed. Magazines could be browsed and dropped. Ideas and information disappeared or were forgotten. Attention had to be focused and held, and information had to be repeated. No upper limit existed to the pervasiveness of communication, but, likewise, there is no effective way to stop some very expensively produced information from being greeted with indifference.

The advertising profession was ever alert to the suspicion that its wares were a waste of money, since no one really knew whether advertisements had any effect. In this regard, the agencies played a crucial part. "By 1910, agencies and advertisers were already talking about 'marketing' and about integrating advertising with other marketing functions" (Joyce 1963, 22). Their chief tool was the marketing concept, a synthesis of what advertising agents were learning about communicative selling. The marketing concept is "a reaction to public needs and desires, sometimes even before those needs and desires have been stated.... It means listening to the public, primarily through research, and providing what it will buy, and buy again" (Harper, Harper, and Young 1963, 64). Advertising helped industry to integrate the marketing concept into its organization of production activities. Through research, strategy, and design the advertiser could take the consumers' everyday discourse about products and recycle it as the form, content, and logistics of communicative selling.

Indeed, in current American advertising practice it is not uncommon for typical consumers to speak directly to others like themselves. The marketing concept could not be more clearly demonstrated. Across the simulated backyard fence, a television actress advises her neighbor of the merits of a particular soap. The whole scene is reminiscent of an earlier era when people experimented with products, evaluated their merits, and shared their experiences directly with those close at hand. But the event is taking place on television during a specific type of programming designed to attract a specific audience segment (housewives). The script, actors, setting, even the color balance have all been carefully chosen, vetted by research, modified, and vetted again. The same is true of the product. Both product and ad, seemingly so simple and straightforward, is the outcome of a strategy devised by one of the largest agencies in the world for a major corporation with one of the largest advertising budgets. It was advertising that made businesspeople interested in what the consumer had to say.

> Within the business sphere, we have had the development of marketing as an essential technique founded on the needs and desires of the public rather than the plant capacity of the manufacturer. During the course of this changing relation between business and the buying public, the advertising agency has become a bridge between the two (Harper, Harper, and Young 1963, 70).

The two leading aspects of the historical mediation of advertising as a form of social communication are (1) the way it influenced cultural processes by shaping the generation of meaning in the consumer culture through its strategic position within the media, and (2) its impact on the production and distribution of goods through the marketing concept, which ultimately changed the nature of products and the way they appeared in the marketplace. These are illustrated in Figure 6.1. The link between goods and symbols is created by advertising as a commercial institution working in association with powerful firms in different industries, and as a system of messages that infuses every aspect of our popular culture.

Advertising in the Nineteenth Century

Until the latter part of the nineteenth century, manufacturers prepared their own advertising copy. Because publishers resisted requests for illustrations or alterations to the layout of the rigid, column-based format, the possibilities for creative expression lay only in the writing itself. Occasionally, a company might hire a writer or journalist to prepare the copy, but most often the task fell to the manufacturer.

Unlike newspapers, the picture magazines that abounded in the second half of the century could accept illustrations and graphic displays. Borrowing from the world of posters, illustrations began to creep into advertising, first showing the product's box or package and later demonstrating its qualities and uses. The well-known Pears bubbles poster was an innovation not just for using an academy artist to paint it, but also for the clever way it joined illustration and product (soap) with the title, showing that the illustration did not have to connect directly with the product's main selling point.

Indeed, many of the advertising styles and approaches that became the agencies' standard wares in the twentieth century had been explored earlier by individuals working alone. The agencies merely revised and systematized various practices, bringing the new psychology and statistics, as well as professional writers and artists, into the fold. Slogans, poetry, illustrations of enormous variety, layout, testimonials, coupons, contests, stars, naked women, and humor were already familiar ingredients in advertising. Once the volume of advertising began to expand and new formats won acceptance, the agencies assembled these basic materials into an integrated technical strategy using the new psychology and statistics, as well as professional writers and artists.

One of the first important services that agencies provided was the advertising directory listing newspapers that advertisers could use around the country, and, in some cases, in foreign countries. In the early nineteenth century, the firm of Lewis and Lowe published *The Advertiser's Guide to the Newspaper Press of the United Kingdom*, which was thirty-six pages long and included the average circulation, the average number of ads, the political character, and the price of each paper. Directories served the dual function of listing the agencies' wares as newspaper agents and providing circulation numbers for advertisers. One of the most comprehensive was the *Newspaper Press Directory* published in 1846 by Charles Mitchell, a thorough and well-organized man who had strong connections with regional newspaper editors. The directory was 474 pages long and included the usual list of newspapers and journals, circulations, affiliations, and price, but it also provided information for would-be advertisers "in their selection of journals as mediums more particularly suitable for their announcements" and other advice pertaining to the conduct of effective and legal advertising.

Mitchell's directory is the first instance of an agent attempting to justify his place in the scheme of publishing. Both publishers and advertisers suspected him of being an unnecessary parasite in the practice of advertising, but Mitchell argued that the provincial press would die without the agent. He attacked the notion that the advertising agent acted for the newspaper, stating that he rather assisted the advertiser to choose the best vehicle available. "The result of all this was important for the future—the advertising agent is a principal in his own independent line of business" (Hindley and Hindley 1972, 24).

Mitchell's directory shaped the practice of the slowly growing number of advertising agents. The 1856 edition included sections on libel laws, the changing newspaper, advertising taxes, and an essay on the philosophy of advertising dealing with copywriting, circulation, and market analysis. The directories reveal the extent to which the agencies were beginning to systematize the practice of advertising. Although only occasionally asked to provide copy or marketing advice, they were developing a full knowledge of their trade and offering advice in general terms. Mitchell, for example, noted that a lower-circulation paper read in the privacy of the home is a more useful advertising vehicle than a larger-circulation one read in pubs and beer shops, because the home reader browses and is more likely to return to the advertisements. By the 1890s, the shift from newspaper space sales to service in support of advertisers was well under way in England.

Volney Palmer, who set up his agency in Philadelphia in 1843, is generally considered to be the first independent advertising agent in North America. Like his British counterparts, he offered a list of selected journals in which he would arrange the placement of ads. His days were spent visiting businesses to persuade them of the benefits of his service. He offered free estimates, collecting a 25 percent commission on placements from the newspapers. An employee of Palmer's, S. M. Pettingill, left to open an office in Boston that became the largest of the thirty or so agencies operating during the 1860s. Pettingill offered his clients copywriting services in addition to the simple placement of their advertising inserts, which seems to have helped him to prosper.

The increasing number of newspapers was making the task of placing ads unaided too complex for the would-be advertiser. It was also changing the position of the agents. Newspapers lost interest in exclusive contracts with agents; in response, agents became independent brokers standing between the publishers and the advertisers, who bargained with the agents for the best deal on advertising space. As a space broker rather than a space seller, the agent's relationship with particular newspapers could be an advantage or a liability depending on the terms of the agreement.

George Rowell took space brokerage to its logical conclusion. He bought annual blocks of publishers' space, which he then resold to his clients at the rate of one hundred dollars for an inch per month in one hundred papers. Buying in bulk put Rowell in a position to bargain with the publishers for better prices, for he guaranteed payment irrespective of whether he collected his own payments. He also offered advertisers discounts for prompt payment.

Some agencies attempted to retain their special relationship with particular journals by brokering all the space in them on contract. J. Walter Thompson, for example, made breakthroughs in a number of literary magazines, including *Scribner's* and *Harper's*, which had refused to accept advertising until he persuaded the publishers that their journals would not be demeaned thereby. Thompson realized that such magazines, with their specialized and widespread circulations, would become an effective advertising medium to supplement the religious and farm newspapers and journals that he also serviced. By the end of the century, thirty important magazines were taking most of their advertising from him. "Thompson, more than any other agent, had developed the magazine field. This was a tremendous step forward for the entire advertising industry, because magazines were the first national medium" (Harper, Harper, and Young 1963, 79). The full significance of this step would be seen by the 1920s, when magazines became the major medium for national advertising, and the agency business itself a service predominantly for national branded and distributed products.

Rather than working in the interests of particular papers or journals, the major agents were directing advertisers to media suitable for their purposes and were thus beginning to have some influence over the press. But without information about actual circulations, they were in a precarious situation because they would always be perceived by the advertiser as favoring certain papers in their own interest. By the turn of the century, the untenable position of space broker had been abandoned for the more comfortable one of adviser to advertisers. Meanwhile, the American space broker was breaking the close attachment to the publisher by adopting the British idea of preparing directories with circulation and other information about each journal. In 1869, *Rowell's American Newspaper Directory* made many enemies among publishers who opined that his circulation figures and judgments were not up to scratch, but the importance to advertisers of such circulation estimates was drawing the agents closer to the advertisers. George Rowell was nothing if not enterprising; he sold ads in his directory to newspapers so that they could recommend themselves to potential advertisers. Another of Rowell's publishing endeavors blossomed eventually into the industry voice, *Printer's Ink*. As an entrepreneurial space broker, Rowell used his position between publishers and advertisers to advantage, but by 1895 there were four hundred like him in New York City alone.

With space brokering, the agent increased profits by buying space cheap and selling it dear. Another agent of the period, Ayer, took the final step away from the role of space broker. Ayer developed what he called the "open contract plus commission." This bound the agent and the advertiser for a period of time, usually a year, with the former taking a standard percentage of the billing as his commission; the agent no longer squeezed the advertiser to make a profit, but rather acted on the latter's behalf in finding the best group of journals for the advertiser's needs. The new arrangement helped to make Ayer the number one agency of the 1890s. The decision of the American newspaper publishers' association in 1893 to abide by their published rates and not to bargain with space brokers did much to make this system of billing work. The percentage commission tied the agencies' profits to the gross amount of billings they could win, and they would grow only to the degree that new sources of advertising could be channeled through the agencies rather than conducted directly with the newspapers. Local, retail, and classified advertising did not usually call for the use of an agency. For national advertising, however, working with an agency became a regular part of marketing. After the turn of the century, the policy of fixed commissions was gradually accepted by other agents and endorsed by the agencies' professional association.

Until the 1980s, in most cases the income to the agency from any particular client account was based upon the amount of money that the advertiser agreed to pay the media firms to display the finished message. Normally, this was 15 percent of the amount billed; if an advertiser, for example, paid $1 million to buy time or space, the income to the agency would be $150,000. In effect, therefore, hiring an agency cost an advertiser nothing, because, strictly speaking, this 15 percent came from the income of the media. If a company were to go directly to the media to buy space or time, it would have had to pay the full amount because the media save on clerical, administrative, and selling costs by dealing with a few agencies rather than with a plethora of advertisers, and find that the stable structure the agencies provide is well worth the commissions they are paid. In effect, therefore, there was no cost to the advertiser in hiring an agency.

The commission was, and has been, debated and criticized for many years, because the agency gets its cut regardless of the amount of creative work it does; if the same commercials are run for long periods of time, the agency will not have to do any additional work. Perhaps more important, because the agency's income is based upon media billings, it is in its interest to increase advertising expenditures and to push advertisers toward more expensive media. On the other hand, the commission system is one way to price a creative product. Since the advertiser does not pay the agency by the hour, it can continue to push for high quality material rather than settle for the agency's first offering. The commission system forces the agency to assume a share of the risk involved; if the campaign is ineffective, the agency must withdraw it and devise another strategy, committing more resources for the same income (or perhaps losing the account). The agency has to make sure that the resources it expends on the account are adequately compensated in the size of the billings, so effective and cost-efficient advertising is beneficial to both advertiser and agency.

The advertising agency was becoming a viable service industry for advertisers instead of an adjunct of the printing industry. But changes outside the publishing world were also beginning to shape advertising. The new range of household products to be sold in national markets—soap, tobacco, bicycles, bootblacking, bread, beer—needed the agencies' services. Many of these products were branded and intended to be distributed on a national or broad regional scale. By the 1890s, over four thousand entrepreneurs wanted to advertise their goods and services beyond their own localities. New retail outlets for these national branded goods created new relationships between retailers and consumers; "the rise of national advertising abridged the autonomy of local merchants," because the shift of consumer preferences to national brands weakened the older stores which traditionally sold un-branded and often un-packaged items—crackers, pickles, candies kept in jars or barrels (Pope 1983, 25). In the large urban areas, new department stores like Wanamaker's in the United States and Selfridge's in England engaged in a large amount of advertising and were developing large internal advertising departments and accounts, finding in many cases that they could deal with publishers on their own in buying space. These retailers had good reason to appreciate the new opportunities of display advertising. Thus, although they did not need the agencies' space-buying services, they did want other kinds of assistance to produce the constant flow of copy necessary for the newspapers. John E. Powers, who got his start as the first professional copywriter in North America for Wanamaker's in 1880, brought the simple and straightforward prose that became known as the "Powers style" to ad writing. He represented the new concern for communication skills being required by a whole new range of businesses entering into advertising without other connections to the communication industry. Ironically, although the department stores tended not to use the services of the agents, the new branded products they promoted depended on national campaigns devised and placed by the agencies.

Within the media, the cheap mail-order magazines for rural communities were being followed by national mass-circulation magazines largely dependent on the new nationally advertised products. These magazines, as Thompson realized, were perfectly suited to expand advertising's horizons. He was not alone. Ayer gave a $200,000 dollar line of credit against advertising space to Cyrus Curtis for the launching of his *Ladies' Home Journal*. Soon the agencies were able to supply a large amount of the advertising for such magazines. The most forward-thinking agencies were busy carving out strong relationships with the new media that were particularly suitable to their major clients, as well as encouraging media owners to develop new types of publications that could serve the agencies and the national products they represented. The agencies were to have a much more significant role in the development of consumer magazines (and, later, of radio and television programming) than they did in the earlier commercialization of the newspapers.

The Early Twentieth Century

Innovators in the print media and at the agencies realized the potential of systematic research. Curtis created a research department at *The Saturday Evening Post* around 1910. Probably the first example of an agency's market study demonstrating the relationship between circulations of particular journals and markets for particular products occurred in 1879. Ayer, attempting to challenge Rowell's hold on a threshing machine account, provided detailed market statistics on regional sales of threshing machines in order to make a case for a particular list of farm journals. Soon the agencies understood that knowledge of regional and sectoral fluctuations in markets and their relation to readerships for particular journals or papers was at the heart of advertising strategy.

With the rise of trade journals and consumer magazines as vehicles for national advertising, interest in marketing research among the agencies could only strengthen. Stanley Resor, who purchased the Thompson agency in 1916, was among the first to support research on consumer behavior as well as on media. In 1912, he commissioned an original study of consumer markets entitled *Population and its Distribution*, and hired a number of noted social scientists, including J. B. Watson, the "father of behaviorism," to bring systematic scientific study to the advertising world. In most cases, the research conducted not only provided proprietary information that could guide strategy, but like the copy, art, and planning facilities offered at this time it could be sold as a service separately from commissions for ad campaigns. The agencies were becoming a progressive voice in the development of standardized methods for researching audiences and consumer behavior.

The advertising business was being fundamentally reorganized. George Batten announced in 1891 that his agency would only take on service contracts that included all the functions of advertising for the firm. In 1899, Ayers undertook the whole process of designing advertising for the Uneeda Biscuit campaign, from choosing the name of the product to the supervision of merchandising promotions. At the Lord and Thomas agency, Albert Lasker hired the copywriter, J. E. Kennedy, to provide the full service that the new kind of inexperienced advertiser was likely to accept. Lasker and Kennedy devised the philosophy of "reason why" advertising and its fundamental rationale that "the way to sell was to build consumer demand" (Harper, Harper, and Young 1963, 79). Copywriting and marketing rather than familiarity with the regional press was becoming the central aspect of agency business, and agencies were being freed of their ties to the press. By 1917, 95 percent of national advertising in the United States was being handled by agencies.

The full service agency was set up around the work of four departments: creative, media, research, and account. Functional specialties (creative, media, copy, and so forth) rather than individual accounts are grouped together. It was the responsibility of the account department to coordinate activities within an agency and to manage the liaison between the agency and the client. The account department, therefore, had to become familiar with the client's business in order to be able to integrate business and market information with research and creative materials to ensure the success of the advertising campaign.

The founding in 1926, by advertisers, agencies, and media owners, of the Advertising Association with its mission to "promote public confidence in advertising and advertised goods through the correction or suppression of abuses" was itself a sign of the agencies' growing awareness of their key role in the marketing sphere. Industry-wide cooperation was essential to end the more outlandish and indefensible marketing practices if advertising were to achieve stability and promote business interests in general. This type of public interest advocacy proved how significant advertising was becoming in industry's overall strategies.

Of course, the harmony among agencies, media, and industry was ruptured at times, such as in the early 1920s when they parted company over the introduction of radio advertising, and again in the early 1950s over the beginnings of commercial television. But the unity was reestablished, and the Advertising Association continues as an umbrella group for media, advertisers, and agencies with a wide variety of informational, supervisory, and lobbying functions.

The entrenchment of the marketing concept in industry and the advent of new technologies in communication meant that the agencies' continued success depended on providing a wide range of design, copy, and marketing advice to advertisers, particularly for national branded household products, food, and automobiles, and that they were working increasingly in media other than newspapers. The professional association and the agents themselves opened up research and auditing methods for magazines, radio, and finally television, uncovering and specifying the potential audience. Representing the part of advertising that was closely tied to nationally branded products, the agencies became advocates of the new national media. As they defended and redefined their niche in the expanding advertising world, the agencies had to create the kind of knowledge, skills, and services that would promote the interests of advertisers. Their survival hinged on this; many of the earlier space-brokering agencies that could not adjust to the new requirements fell by the wayside. On the other hand, there was abundant reward for innovative agencies that began to develop the full-service agency model. By 1925, such agencies accounted for the major share of national accounts.

Communication Strategies

Probably the earliest impact of the new service agencies was to make copy the central consideration of advertising design. By the early 1900s, these agencies

realized that advertising of national brands was not just a matter of announcements, but rather of persuasion—using words to explain the advantages of
one particular product or brand as opposed to others, and making a specific
ad stand out from others in the increasingly cluttered columns of newspapers. Agencies had used those with literary talents before, but it now became
standard practice to hire writers as regular staff. Although earlier examples of
rhyme and rhythm abounded, the agency staff writers began to merge poetry
and selling in unique ways.

The first and most obvious was in the slogan, which departed from earlier
types of poetic writing in advertising by keeping the selling idea at the center
of the message. It borrowed heavily from newspaper headlines in striving for
a tightly compacted unifying idea, and from poster advertising in its dramatic
emphasis. Hardly literary, many were intriguing and innovative: "Good morning, have you used Pears soap today?" or "Don't be gulled by Yankee Bluff.
Support John Bull with every puff" (doggerel invented to repel the American
invasion of the British cigarette market at the turn of the century). Royal Baking
Powder's "Absolutely pure," or Kodak's "Press the button; we do the rest," reveal the compression and purposiveness of language that was emerging as
advertising's own signpost. Many of these slogans were developed for use with
poster ads or illustrated magazines. In retrospect, in their suggestiveness and
minimalist approach to language these slogans appear very modern.

The need for a carefully considered slogan at the core of an advertising campaign was becoming central to agency practice as a major factor in giving a clear
identity to a branded product. More than language styles were changing. The
concern for the stylistic integrity of branded products was leading to "personification" in the form of trade characters—Aunt Jemima, Lydia Pinkham,
the Quaker Oats Quaker.

One noted copywriter in this style was Earnest Elmo Calkins, originator
of some of the extraordinarily popular "Sunny Jim'" (character for a breakfast
cereal) verses. Calkins advocated the integration of design elements, artistic qualities, and literary features into "that combination of text with design
which produces a complete advertisement" (in Fox 1984, 63). In building
his consumer magazine empire, Cyrus Curtis came to Calkins, after failing to
find anyone else who could write the kind of copy he liked. Short and simple
sentences in the "Powers' style" were also ideally suited to sloganizing; effective copy became the heart and soul of advertising campaigns, culminating in
J. E. Kennedy's influential concept of advertising as "salesmanship in print,"
known as the "reason why" approach.

Getting the attention of the audience was just the first step in persuasion;
advertising had to appeal rather than just attract, for if no desire were evoked the
ad was not likely to be successful. An indispensable part of the "feedback loop"
for refining the system of persuasive communications was new gimmicks

that accompanied the novel copy styles such as coupons, one of the first ways in which advertisers could judge the effectiveness of their campaigns in terms of consumer response. The emergence of psychology as a scientific discipline was also influential. Rowell had predicted in the 1890s that advertising would eventually turn to psychology, and the publication in 1908 of the first systematic attempt by a social scientist to examine advertising, Professor Walter Dill Scott's *The Psychology of Advertising*, was to have a major impact on the profession.

Scott's operative concept was "the appeal," taking as his model hypnotic persuasion. Although he believed firmly in the appeal to rationality, he emphasized the importance of association. The product should be associated with pleasant experiences and ideas that the readers would associate with their own feelings and motives. He also stressed suggestion: "Man has been called the reasoning animal but he could with greater truthfulness be called the creature of suggestion" (cited in Pope 1982, 240–41). The two seemingly opposing tendencies of rationality and suggestiveness were not incompatible, for the whole point about reason-why advertising as a communicative strategy was that it was designed to persuade and to motivate.

The demand for reason-why advertising was closely connected with the needs of national advertisers to elicit demand for their new products. Especially in the realm of food, personal-care, and household products, the nature of the new item and the way it should be used were often unfamiliar. As we pointed out in chapter 4, one cannot assume a "natural affinity" between the wants of individuals and the characteristics of goods. Breakfast foods, toothpaste, canned foods, polishes, and an endless series of previously unknown products had to be carefully introduced into daily patterns of life, and the methods and reasons for using them explained in detail.

Furthermore, the manufacturer of a branded product had to attract customers not only to a new type of product but also to the firm's label, differentiating the special qualities of the brand from its competitors. This "educational" function of advertising became especially prominent in the period of dramatic social change after World War I, when rising affluence, upward mobility, a marked destabilization of traditional values, and, in the United States, the quick assimilation of a large immigrant population were creating a potential market for new products. Ads often had an explicitly educational theme, with self-improvement messages designed to help "socialize" consumers—pitches for personal-care products such as razors for men and toothpaste for women—being added to the earlier campaigns for soap.

Fundamentally different problems in selling arose as a result of this broader "social" approach in the message system. Envy, class relations, and authority were a matrix in which to ground motivation for purchase; anxiety and an awareness of peer group reactions, especially fear of ostracism or social failure (recall the

Brunswick toilet seat ad cited in chapter 3), became core elements in the rationale for adopting a new lifestyle or consumption practice. Two good examples of fear-appeal advertising come from Listerine: "Even your best friend won't tell you," and "Often a bridesmaid, never a bride." In order to ensure a "realistic" setting for such messages and define the selling idea with precision, advertisers had to take a careful look at the subtly changing social positions of consumers.

Research also dispelled the notions of the "single type" of consumer and the undifferentiated audience, and highlighted the fact that persuasion involved more than reciting the merits of the product. In consumer magazines, for example, readership studies were beginning to point out basic facts about readers. It became abundantly clear to the advertisers that different approaches were reaching different segments of the population, and that their message formats had to be tailored appropriately; advertising effectiveness was a matter of correctly understanding specific situations. For example, marketing research was revealing that women bought 80 to 90 percent of all household goods. Since advertisers believed that women were subject to irrational impulses and did not want too much reasoning in ads, copy styles were altered accordingly. Other researchers revealed that the reading ability and vocabulary of consumers were not very high; this, too, affected the design of messages.

Different concepts of human motivation were beginning to filter into the advertising arena from psychology. After about 1925, people began to be thought of as animals impelled by drives and instincts, motivated largely by petty emotions, sexuality, anxiety, and a desire for upward mobility. Placing irrationality at the heart of the consumption and marketing process heralded a major transition in the agencies' approach. They did not abandon reason-why advertising completely, but restricted it mostly to introducing new products, and even here they increasingly grounded the reason for purchase in one of the consumer's supposed psychological traits rather than in the characteristics of the product.

The non-publishing environment of radio represented a real challenge, and some of today's more successful agencies got their start as innovators in radio advertising. First, the audience and the effectiveness of advertising had to be proved to potential advertisers, entailing an expansion of the agency's research function into listener surveys. A. C. Neilson was hired to do the first listener study by the J. Walter Thompson agency; Hooper ratings became very popular.

A variety of services for both the radio and magazine trades was developed in this period. The use of scientific methods in advertising pioneered by Stanley Resor at J. Walter Thompson was expanding rapidly during the 1930s and 1940s. Magazines had initiated product testing by consumers. Product and copy testing became common practice in the agencies. Knowing the consumers' mind meant interacting with them in as many ways as possible. (The systematic study of consumer preferences and marketing research in general was developed largely by the agencies with help from the magazine industry.

Many of the women's magazines set up their own product-testing centers as consumption practice and decision making became a main feature of editorial concern; they also engaged in readership studies to establish their audiences, and created consumer panels to help advertisers, as well as to offer impartial advice to readers.)

A second relevant aspect of radio broadcasting was that advertisers stepped into the world of show business as producers of programming. Under the American network system, most of the major programs were produced by agencies that built studios, hired talent, and wrote scripts, thus broadening both their communication abilities and their understanding of the communications industry as they attempted to draw and hold an audience and to build a relationship between the advertisement and the program. People could not listen to selling messages all day, so the agencies began to explore styles of communication, the communication preferences of the audience, and the production values that would draw and hold them. Music, humor, stars, pathos, tragedy, excitement, and human relationships became familiar terrain for the advertising agency and opened up new ideas about how to improve advertising.

This much overlooked aspect was to have a dramatic and long-lasting effect on the skills and perspective that the agencies would apply thereafter in the service of their clients. Advertising on radio involved more than turning slogans into jingles. Radio was an enormously powerful communications medium, and its programming covered a wide range of human experiences. Probably the best illustration for the agencies' work in the 1930s is the development of soap opera. In the early years of radio, the major sponsored programs were clustered in the early evening prime-time period. Afternoon radio attracted few sponsored programs and consisted chiefly of music and household hints. Frank Hummert of the Blackett-Sample-Hummert agency decided to adapt the human interest appeal of the serial stories that ran in the daily newspapers to radio, inventing a drama called "Just Plain Bill," sponsored by Kolynos toothpaste, about a barber who had married out of his social class. Hummert pitched his appeal to the afternoon female audience. Its success created a deluge of imitators with far-reaching consequences.

The soap operas were written by the agencies and usually revolved around emotionally excruciating family dilemmas. The challenge was to develop product "tie-ins." (The term "soap opera" itself, of course, refers to the sponsorship of detergent manufacturers and testifies to the blending of advertising and programming.) A whole new domain of human interest and human interaction was being added to the agencies' repertoire as they experimented with story line, characterization, dramatic impact, and emotional tone and then applied what they had learned to the construction of ads. The close connection between programming and advertising not only implied that the programming was designed to suit advertisers' needs, but also—far more significant for the future–schooled the agencies in a whole new range of communication dynamics for ads. As a result, advertising became rooted in a distinctly human interest environment, and by 1938 radio had overtaken magazines in advertising revenue.

One important consequence was that products began to speak—to tell their own story. Although the full anthropomorphizing of goods had to await the use of animation on television (the Jolly Green Giant, the Michelin Man, the Pillsbury Dough Boy), radio took a preliminary step in dialogue; products, through advertisements, began to tell stories and the writing styles incorporated allusions to real social situations and a variety of settings.

The communicative impact of media advertising had its effects on other media. Improved techniques in art and the use of photography were important steps in the development of a new visual style. It was no longer sufficient merely to show the product; ads began to use pictures to illustrate abstract, scientific, or social qualities. Microphotography revealed germs in the sink; color shots emphasized the glamour of car ownership. An entire language of illustration was being developed, much of it borrowed and adapted from the film world. Magazine ads with comic-strip formats were soon followed by images arranged in sequence like the story board of a film. The expansion of the narrative in copy and illustration was fitting the product into lifelike dilemmas.

An example of the merging of entertainment and advertising worlds was the use of testimonials. Radio and magazines not only helped to create the star system, but used it effectively in advertisements. The stars of radio could introduce the product within the programs, and as spot advertisements gained in popularity, famous names (especially film stars) lent their prestige to goods ranging from cosmetics to cigarettes, grounding the appeal not in some kind of argument about use, but in the associational field of prestige. When scientists and doctors testified on behalf of yeast, household cleansers, or margarine, the appeal was rooted in the apparently more substantial domain of expert authority, but the persuasive format (an association with a human figure distant from the ordinary person) was, in fact, identical.

During the 1930s, these creative explorations of the possibilities inherent in new media developed side by side with increasing knowledge through research about the audience. For example, experiments with styles, formats, visual appeals, and media vehicles for selling goods more directly to women were undertaken when research indicated the primacy of the female consumer and identified her as the reader of particular magazines (depending on social background and interest) and as the listener to daytime radio. Whatever the degree of validity of agency assumptions about women, it is clear that these assumptions changed the way the agencies practiced advertising as they explored new forms for communicating with specific subpopulations of consumers.

After the heyday of radio advertising in the late 1940s, much of the experience and talent accumulated from radio production was turned to developing advertising modes suited for television in the 1950s and 1960s. Television was soon perceived as the "Cadillac" advertising medium for mass-marketed and branded national goods. It offered the display aspects of good graphics, the visual immediacy and excitement of film, music, and story lines, star testimonials, and the largest audiences ever drawn to a single medium. Its only limitation was the number of words one could squeeze into a thirty- or sixty-second segment. Television forced a further subdivision in the advertising market, and with its entrenchment as a national medium, both radio and mass consumer magazines would have to adapt to it.

As a medium of communication, television, like radio before it, offered new possibilities to advertising strategists. Encouraged by the agencies, early advertisers were enthusiastic about the size of its audiences and there was a vague but pervasive feeling that special powers resided in its visual representation and immediate attractiveness to most people. Products had been woven into a broad range of simulated and fictional settings since the turn of this century, but television simply could do everything so much better. Magazines had displayed goods amid Doric columns or Greek statues, thus positioning them within an associational matrix of images and styles; radio had opened up dialogue and social interaction as contexts within which appeals were made; television swept all earlier forms into its orbit and added others, ultimately offering the whole range of cultural reference systems to advertisers as aids in selling their wares.

Before the advent of edited videotape, television advertising consisted of two forms, either the filmed commercial or the "plug" for the sponsor by the host, a special advertising announcer, or a character within the show (Alfred Hitchcock and Johnny Carson found new sources of humor in this relation between media characters and advertising announcements). Filmed commercials were usually shot and edited by a camera crew and director borrowed from the cinema world, meaning the importation of a whole range of editing and cinematic techniques and concerns into the production of advertising. (Even today, there is a flow of personnel, ideas, and references between the cinema world and advertising, with some well-known directors working in both.) Shooting actors in ways that kept them credible, locating and arranging scenes, lighting effects, amusing story lines, and animation all became part of the advertising repertoire. Since television was best at simulating interpersonal communication either directly or as observed in drama, it seemed natural for television commercials to focus on these elements, and thus the testimonial and the minidrama became important elements of television advertising. Television offered a whole new range to the uses of people and dialogue that had been explored during the 1930s and 1940s. Visual and dramatic demonstrations—see-through toilets, the interiors of washing machines and stomachs, protective barriers on teeth and floors—all played an important part.

The early television years also led to refined research techniques within the agencies. Media research included circulation audits—specific viewer, listener, or readership studies—and early efforts to combine marketing and media research by establishing personal preferences in terms of products, pastimes, spending habits, and so forth; consumer research included demographic studies of users and product pre-testing; advertising research included consumer panels, copy-testing sessions, split-half comparisons, and so forth. Each proved useful in helping the agencies understand the problem of advertising design in the context of a more detailed and accurate knowledge of consumers and audiences for media.

Pioneered by radio and magazines, the audience survey or "the ratings" became the basis of television program decision making. Sponsors bought and retained shows so long as the mass audience share was retained; when the ratings slipped, sponsors moved on to more favorable ground. Research became the basis upon which the links between agencies and networks were forged for national-brand product advertising.

Motivation research, or in-depth studies of consumers, elicited criticism both within and outside the industry, because it represented a way of thinking about the consumer that seemed to violate many people's sense of propriety. To Ernest Dichter, the major advocate of motivation research, the criticism implied that advertising was seeking to exploit the consumer's presumed unconscious and often irrational attachments to particular things. In fact, it was a natural extension of the application of modern psychological theory and methods to advertising. Motivation research borrowed at least two major premises from Freudian psychology: that people's real motives are hidden, and that they can be elicited through conversation and free association. The advertiser who wants to sell must appeal not to the limited set of motives identified in the 1930s, but to the specific insecurities, delusions, and attachments of the consumer.

Motivation research was really the logical outcome of the pursuit of the marketing concept, for it started the selling activity with the consumer and the consumer's personal situation. Motivation research, unlike the earlier applications of scientific methodology or distribution statistics, rooted the selling act within the human personality by directly applying psychological constructs to advertising. Human psychology was to be the basis of commercial strategies. The advertiser started with the general theory that the consumer's psyche was ruled by an irrational insecurity and a strong erotic undertone and proceeded from there.

The model assumed that the consumer did not make rational choices and was easily persuaded by images. Products had to be fitted into the consumer's deepest sense of self, defending it and giving it greater expression. As a receiver of communications, the consumer was depicted as immature and more interested in *how* something was said than in what was said. Research showed that many ads were little remembered and that consumers came away from exposure to them with only vague impressions: to achieve impact, an ad had to strike deep by being superficial.

Motivation research gave advertising a bad name and brought to a head the criticisms of Madison Avenue manipulation. Many practitioners themselves doubted the usefulness of such techniques, and others found the research results almost impossible to translate into design and communicational terms. Steps were taken by the industry and eventually by governments to limit experiments with subliminal messages. Still, by the late 1950s most major agencies had undertaken campaigns based on such research. Some, such as the McKann-Erickson agency, rose to prominence on the achievements of its researchers. A number of agencies were also pioneering the use of semantic differentials, consumer panels, experimental designs, and sophisticated attitude measurement techniques.

In a reaction against the increasing use of research techniques and their application in advertising design and testing, which, some people claimed, limited the creativity and effectiveness of ads, smaller agencies and independent consultants thrived on the fringes of the large outfits. Shops like Ogilvy and Mather introduced some of the newer, softer-sell advertising. Ogilvy states that he was concerned with establishing "the most favorable image, the most sharply defined personality" through imaginative design—such as his famous Hathaway eyepatch ad. His point was that the creative mind could understand the psychological makeup of the consumer as well as, or indeed better than, the researchers could; it was the grasping of some ineffable quality which brought dynamic appeal to a campaign that could make the difference. Ogilvy and Mather were enormously successful, becoming the third-largest agency in the United States by 1980. Eventually the most successful agencies offered a combination of both strategies.

In the 1960s, advertisers were faced with a confusing array of media, claiming different types of strengths in audience and impact. The agencies' task was to devise a strategy that selected the best medium or the most appropriate blend of media for the promotion of a particular brand at the lowest cost. Each medium had its distinct advantages, and various types of campaigns could use the media all together, in sequence, or in some ordered combination. The objective was to define the goals of a campaign, to set advertising's position within the overall marketing mix (which might also include public relations, display, offers, coupons, distribution, and dealership arrangements), and to use the media to buy access to the right audience at the right time. Sophisticated research methods aided the competitive stances that media managers adopted in promoting the unique audience features of their particular medium.

Radio, having lost the big national campaigns, had redefined its audience appeal on a station-by-station basis. Each station was directed toward an age and demographic segment, and fancy brochures promised that rates were adjusted to the desirability of the audience segment they commanded.

The mid-1960s was also a changeover period for the magazine world, as many of the mass-consumer magazines ran into trouble and the survivors addressed smaller readerships with highly desirable characteristics for particular products. The new special-interest lifestyle journals flourished, advertising a highly selective range of products.

The new research techniques were starting to provide more information than size alone about television audiences. As sponsorship gave way to spot advertising, research helped to guide the spot advertiser to the right audience. Highly intensive monitoring revealed that the public did not relate to television as a mass audience. In some regions, demographic groups were shown to be related to preferences for networks, programs, and products. Advertisers became as interested in the qualities of the audiences drawn to their spots as in their size. Les Brown (1972) describes television's scramble for programming that would hold the audiences that advertisers wanted when the networks realized that even programs with large ratings but the wrong audiences would have to be dropped.

Consumer research also divided products into different types (durables, domestic consumables, personal consumables) with life cycles of their own fitted into cyclical usage practices. No one group of consumers could be seen as "typical"; consumers fell into market segments with clustered social practices. Some were innovators, tempted with new products and gadgets; others were facing major buying decisions such as a first bank account, a first car, or a first home. People over fifty were poor general consumers but subject to appeals based on prestige and tradition. Sports-oriented men were heavy consumers of particular kinds of alcoholic beverages.

Demographic variables are still measured, but the predominant focus of marketing and advertising research is on what we might call the "subjective" dimension of personal experience. The 1988 annual meeting of the Canadian Advertising Research Foundation featured a presentation by Dr. Jeffrey Durgee that gives a comprehensive account of what this focus on the subjective dimension of personal experience is all about. Durgee summarized his approach as follows: "The best advertising is based on consumers' subjective meanings." The key to understanding those meanings, Durgee said, is to be found in the notion of "structures," that is, "the ways consumers organize meaning to brands and products." He went on to describe these structures in the following way:

> *Life Context Structures* fit with the elements in life and can be determined by work questions, social questions and fantasy questions.... Products, like the

lead in a movie, gain meaning due to plot/implied (what role does it play); settings (where, when); relationship between people; opposition (relevant conflicts); symbols (aspects of people's experience); moods and sequence of events.

Product Component Structures—how people structure the components of a product. For example, with NyQuil, comment centered on the heavy dark liquid and the little cup, seen in terms of health and a communion cup or as narcosis and alcoholism.

Semiotic Structure. Qualitative researchers have a set of questions to determine what the product is a "signal" of (causally related). The product can be either a cause or an effect of the referent. A product is a "sign" of something if both product and referent belong to the same cultural context, and a "symbol" of something, if arbitrarily or metaphorically linked to it.

Latent Structures—found in consumer stories about first-time product use (causes of breakdown or performance beyond expectations); unusual, bizarre usage; odd ways of using; items that typify family, friends; exceptional events that the product was part of; and package/logo.

Semantic Structures. Using a list of descriptive words and applying them to a product category and competing brands, a distinctive difference can emerge in how a product is viewed (Marney 1988).

This approach has been given the name of "account planning" in England. According to one report, account planning "involves digging deep into the mind of the consumer in order to find a critical insight on which to build a powerful strategy." The key to this strategy is

> Listening and listening. Not just to what they [consumers] say, but to what they mean. Listening for the expressions of need, of dissatisfaction, uncovering attitudes and behavior patterns. The planner's job is to immerse him or herself in the world of the consumer until the point of view of the consumer permeates the planner's thinking, and leads to the discovery of a critical insight on which to build a powerful strategy (Bruce 1987).

This is an excellent statement of the two fundamental purposes of all advertising and marketing research: (1) to understand how consumers experience the meaning of products and how they formulate the intention to purchase; and (2) to construct persuasive communications strategies on the basis of that understanding that will reach the inner experiences of persons.

The flood of data that came to the agencies in the 1960s made advertisers think of consumers as organized collectivities that could be statistically described along two axes: media use and product preferences. Such revelations demanded a new orientation to advertising, and these research tools transformed the practice of advertising: "Such a conception calls for different communication and advertising objectives at different stages over time for a given product category and set of competing brands" (Sommers 1983, 8). Advertising was propelled beyond the marketing concept to the "marketing management concept." Effective advertising implied not only knowledge of the consumer, but also an organization that could coordinate media and marketing plans, accounting within this framework for the consumer's precise "social position" and the possibilities of using different media to reach her or him. Marketing management theory specifies the role of advertising's place within the current institutional context: to understand the market segment and the audience segment, and to transform this understanding into a convincing campaign strategy.

The adjustment to market segmentation has meant that agencies have had to incorporate a new range of research, design, and management skills and to reorganize their delivery to accounts. The advertising "problem" could not be solved simply by promising to place the agency's two hottest copywriters onto the account. In the late 1960s and the 1970s, there were a number of failures, buyouts, and consolidations as the large agencies adjusted to the new demands made on them: of the ninety-two largest agencies in 1966, forty-one no longer existed by 1979.

The industry today includes both large, full-service agencies and small "boutiques" offering highly specialized research, media buying, or creative work, a sensible division in the heyday of market segmentation, with its sensitivity both to general consumption patterns (such as the attachment to automobiles) and to distinctive subsidiary "behavioral zones" (such as sports or popular music). Daniel Pope, using Boorstin's concept of "consumption communities," stresses "the attractiveness of the community, not just the desirability of the product," wherein "context rather than the product becomes, in a sense, the object of the consumers' desires" (Pope 1982, 280).

The Bonding of Media and Advertising

As the preceding discussion indicates, we hold the view that an adequate appreciation of advertising's place in modern society arises out of a detailed examination of its historical evolution. This conviction is shared by others. Daniel Pope's *The Making of Modern Advertising* divides the history of advertising into three periods: the Gilded Age (about 1870–1890), the Progressive Era (1890–1920), and the Modern Era (1920–present).

The Gilded Age was the period of regional production and distribution when early industrial expansion led to increased advertising, largely in old-fashioned formats. The agencies acted as space brokers only, promoting the interest in advertising mainly on behalf of the print media. Growth in advertising was due to new products, proprietary medicines, department stores, and a very few national advertisers of branded goods; advertising played a very minor part in industrial production, and agency practice was in a rudimentary state of development.

The Progressive Era was the period of expanding mass production and the rise of national branded products. The broad institutional structure of advertising was established, with the service agencies moving to the centre of national campaigns. The business practices, ethics, and institutional structures of advertising were all put in place and regularized at this time, making it the formative period for the industry. Mass media advertising expanded dramatically and came to be regarded as a legitimate feature in the marketplace. Yet many remained unconvinced of either the necessity or desirability of product advertising on a large scale.

Pope's third phase, the Modern Era or "the era of market segmentation," stretches from the 1920s to the present. In this period, the marketplace began to move from production for mass consumption (that is, for an undifferentiated group of consumers) to one of production for consumption in a stratified marketplace increasingly defined by consumers organized into relatively well-defined subgroups. Pope suggests that by the end of the 1920s most of the important features of the modern advertising industry had already been established: the agencies' role in advertising, their strong links with various media, and their business practices (methods of payment and so forth). Thus, there remained only the need for advertisers to define market segments with increasing precision, and for agencies to learn how to address them. In this sense, the addition of new media and the changes in advertising approaches were of minimal consequence for the role of advertising or its eventual function in the contemporary marketplace.

Pope places comparatively little emphasis on the impact that agency practice, relations with the media, and marketing theory had on the evolution of the industry; however, he views its development as largely conditioned by the apparently irresistible wave of national product advertising itself. Once the agencies had responded to this wave by laying the foundations for their full-service capabilities, as they did in the 1920s, the institutional arrangements supporting modern advertising (according to this view) were in place. What happened thereafter was essentially the story of agency reaction to, and absorption of, the special features of later media revolutions.

However, there is more to the story of modern advertising than its institutional link to national manufacturing and the markets it developed. For us, no less important is the role that the agencies played in constructing the bridge between selling and communicating in contemporary society. Some other observers also have focused on a wider network of changes in seeking to assess advertising's social impact, among them Michael Schudson (1984). His interpretation isolates four important and interrelated dimensions: market forces, notably changes in the system of distribution; changes in methods of industrial production, especially the volume and types of goods; media forces and the way they adjust to advertising; the agencies and how they organize, promote, and redefine advertising practice.

Other authors—for example, Stephen Fox in *The Mirror Makers* (1984)—also identify innovations in advertising practice itself as the key factor in the industry's development. Fox argues that the influence of strong individuals within the business has taken advertising through periodic reconceptualizations of what constitutes good practice. He depicts its history as governed by alternating cycles of emphasis, shifting back and forth between "hard-sell" persuasive formats (reason why, unique selling point) and "soft-sell" suggestive ones (emotive or "creative," emphasizing design, lifestyles, and personal images). Although his biographical approach identifies the major advocates of these alternative positions and their arguments, it is less helpful in filtering out the essential differences between the creative approaches of the 1960s and those of the 1920s. Clearly both styles, the persuasive and the creative, have been a part of the repertoire of advertising for the past one hundred years, and they seem to come in and out of favor with different agencies at different times, for different classes of product, or with different types of audiences. But such cycles in themselves do not reveal the broader dimensions of change that make the two approaches so very compatible within the world of advertising. As one of our interviewees put the point:

> There has always been the distinction between two appeals: the rational and the emotional. They were separate. Either you had a rational product like a car or else you had an emotional one like cosmetics. We used to say, don't mix the two appeals. In the eighties you have to mix them.

The type of appeal used depends on circumstances. Fashion rules the industry, and approaches come in and out of fashion, with different agencies profiting depending on their orientation. But during the 1950s, for example, both heavily research-oriented agencies and those that stressed intuition and creativity thrived.

The idea that the industry just swings back and forth between two well-established poles leads to the belief that advertising has grown in sophistication over the years without really changing; for almost every type of ad today, there is some historical precedent. The alternation between persuasion and suggestion, so the story goes, is a struggle between the view of human beings as rational creatures and the view of them as emotional and creative.

Merle Curti found a smoother evolutionary development in the views of human nature held by advertisers, basing his study of changes in marketing outlook held by advertising practitioners on the contents of *Printer's Ink* for the period between 1890 and 1954. Curti sought to pinpoint the evolution of the dominant attitude in advertising thought. He divided the period into three phases.

During the first phase, The Rationalistic Image of Human Nature, advertisers tended to think of consumers essentially as rational and not easily persuaded by gimmicks. "Most experts who held to the informative purpose of advertising emphasized the basically rational, logical and sensible qualities of man without indicating further what these were" (Curti 1967, 338). They assumed that a person wanted to know first price, then function, craftsmanship, durability, and benefits—that is, all the reasons why one should buy—in order to make some estimation of the product's worth in terms of his or her own priorities. The rational view is reflected both by practitioners of reason-why advertising and by rationalistic academic psychology around the turn of the century.

In the second phase, The Irrational Conception of Human Nature, which lasted from about 1910 to 1930, "the dominant idea came to be that man is in actuality more irrational than rational. Merchandising techniques, techniques to appeal to various nonrational impulses, now received emphasis" (Curti 1967,347). Human nature was viewed as malleable, not fixed. Advertising operated by suggestion, pictures, attention-gathering stimuli, and playing on human sympathy to persuade the consumer to desire the product. Campaigns were based on "appeals" and imputed motives, and sales would depend on how well the advertiser could take advantage of people's competitiveness, shame, desire for approval, or need for reward for achievement. Appeals to personal appearance, prestige, family, and home also were featured.

In the third phase, which emphasized the behavioral sciences and originated during the Great Depression and extended through the postwar years, the rational and irrational views of human nature were merged and modified. Advertisers began to talk more of satisfying consumer wants as opposed to creating them, and social science became a major influence introducing new research methods and techniques to the industry. Psychological conceptions of human nature were very influential in this period; the tension between rationalist and irrationalist notions was dealt with by accepting both. Advertisers learned from psychologists "that whatever decision we make, however purely rational it may seem, is deeply influenced by emotional forces, conscious, subconscious, or unconscious. Of special importance was the increasing recognition of symbols in evoking emotional responses" (Curti 1967, 354). Personality traits such as self-esteem, impulses for creative expression, and concerns for social relations that had been highlighted in the behavioral sciences, were explored minutely by marketers as bases for selling.

Curti linked variations in thinking about advertising to social and institutional ones. His analysis does not cover the contemporary period, but this has been addressed by Monte Sommers (1983), who traces the transition from psychological approaches to a broader marketing management approach, which trickled down into advertising practice from marketing theory. This strategy integrated advertising into a "global" marketing framework, brought new statistical methods to bear on decision-making tasks (including the concepts of product and consumer life cycles and the hierarchy of needs), and generally defined new goals and purposes for advertising around the concept of market segmentation. In this strategy, the main concern shifts from the consumer to the market, specifically the description of, and access to, segments or groups of buyers.

Thus, the understanding of the advertising industry is based on changes in its structure and relationships in the larger business sphere, and on changes in advertising thought and practice within the industry itself. The advertising industry is depicted as responding to shifts in the market or to broader conceptions of man and society. For the most part, it is not regarded as a "transformative institution" in its own right, or as a factor of significant proportions in modern society.

A comment by one of our interviewees illustrates this outlook: "After factoring out TV and media change, I honestly believe that North American... commercial society has used advertising in 1910 the same as in 1980, except that advertising has adjusted as society has matured and the market has increased." However, we simply cannot discount variations in media when attempting to understand the changing qualities of advertising. For if we view advertising as primarily an extension of the industrial process of manufacture and distribution, and minimize its own interpretation of and contribution to mediated communication and its impact on modern popular culture, we run the risk of ignoring much of what happened in the twentieth century—the novel uses of visuals, dialogue, storytelling, film demonstration, characters, persuasive design, and marketing strategy.

Our own portrait places much greater emphasis than others on the close interconnections among advertising, the goods-producing sector, and media, and especially on advertising's connective or bridging function in relation to production and media. The advertising industry, led by its agencies, transferred knowledge about the media to producers, knowledge about audiences to media, and knowledge about consumers and how to reach them more effectively with marketing campaigns back and forth between producers and the media.

Advertising, especially the agencies, never responded just passively to changes in media, but in many cases became an active force in their development. Advertisers have been active lobbyists in the commercialization of the media and in reorganizing them to suit their own particular needs and orientations. It is impossible to write a history of the media in the modern world without giving significant attention to the role of advertising in shaping them, and at the heart of this story is the relationship between media and advertisers established by the agencies and the impact of this relationship on the concepts and practice of marketing thought. Advertising can never be thought of as simply an extension of what is happening in marketing or mass production or mass consumption; the key to its growing impact on society is what is happening in communications media.

Successive waves of innovation in magazine production, radio, and television are reflected in changes in advertising practices, from which resulted equally profound transformations in the way that advertisers thought about and approached consumers through the design of campaigns and marketing strategies. In order to map out these interconnections, we have constructed a historically based account that includes changes over time in the cultural determinants of consumption behavior, the system of industrial production and distribution, the organization of the advertising business, the communicative models brought into the practice of advertising, and media technologies. Our account draws on the earlier work of Pope (1983) and Curti (1967), but emphasizes a broader set of factors.

The bonding of media and advertising, which is the principal force in these varied dimensions, developed in four stages during the twentieth century. Of course, reality is not so neatly demarcated as the dating of the stages presents it, and the latter phases of each, representing times of realignment and transformation, shade into their successors. Most importantly, the characteristics of each period do not disappear, but rather become subordinate components in a newer and more complex environment. For example, rationalistic-informative approaches dominant in the early stage are not so much subverted by the development during the 1920s of new ideas about the consumer and new media as they are channeled to specific media and product categories; classified ads do not disappear but are gradually restricted to personal and small retail selling in the major newspapers. The development of advertising is a process of "layering" techniques and strategies, culminating in a versatile, multi-dimensional armory. Few ingredients have ever been simply discarded or forgotten; almost everything in the storeroom is subsequently dusted off, refitted, and returned to service in a more specialized niche.

Stage One: The Product-Oriented Approach (1890–1925)

The development of commercialized print media is closely related to our first stage, in which advertising is oriented toward the product. The service agencies, reaching beyond their earlier functions as space sellers, concentrate on copywriting and advertising design to sell the new national branded products. The agencies establish communication as the unifying element in the services they offer. They systematize and develop new styles of appeal, leaving behind the "announcements" of earlier periods in favor of a persuasive informational approach arguing the merits of the product (see Figure 5.2). The

Figure 5.2 Stage One: The Product-Oriented Approach.

appeals are predominantly rationalistic in the sense that "reason why" demands an explanation of the motivation for using a product. The written text is the core of this explanation, although new technologies, first in magazines and then in newspapers, allow the increasing use of illustration and visual layout elements in the development of arguments about the qualities of the product. The agencies focus mainly on national campaigns and become particularly important to the consumer magazine industry. They extend their explorations of the stylistic elements of campaign design, merging visual and rhetorical devices and codifying these in agency practice.

Stage Two: Product Symbols (1925–1945)

The professionalization of the agencies now makes advertising capable of influencing public policy on the development of radio, and responding positively and opportunistically to the national advertising possibilities of this new medium. Research into audiences for media broadens the marketing services offered by the agencies. The agencies move closer to the marketing concept, in which consumer disposition is a crucial element in advertising, even though knowledge about the consumer at this time is limited to very broad demographic or polling-based evidence. In this context, marketing thought begins to shift toward the nonrational or symbolic grounding of consumption based on the notion of appeals or motives, putting less emphasis on the product and its uses. More precisely, product-oriented advertising gradually is confined to particular media and types of goods.

The experience with media changes the practice of advertising. In magazines, photography and art allow for innovations in the associational dimension of argumentation. Products are presented less and less on the basis of a performance promise, and more on making them resonate with qualities desired by consumers—status, glamour, reduction of anxiety, happy families—as the social motivations for consumption. In radio, institutional association is the early basis for sponsorship of programming, but during the 1930s experience with the role of dialogue, stars, and the development of characters allows the advertiser to assimilate much more about the social context of consumption as the basis of advertising strategy. "Tie-ins" between product and program, attention-getting devices, consistent and strong brand images, and testimonials knit together goods with the social, rather than the functional, basis of consumption.

Stage Three: Personalization (1945–1965)

The agencies transfer their knowledge of and contacts with the entertainment world made through radio and magazines to the new medium of television. Television quickly becomes the major medium for national-branded product

Figure 5.3 Product Symbols: Freed from the burden of utility, products engage consumers with more abstract qualities of goods.

campaigns, and, in many cases, the major source of income for the agencies. The new medium can combine design and cultural symbolism with characterization, story line, and dialogue. The communicative potential of television offers many new avenues as the personnel, stylistics of imagery, patterns of attention, and programming format are bent to advertising purposes. The agencies are also major players in the realignment of context orientations in older media, as both radio and magazines adjust to the loss of certain types of major national accounts by tailoring their subject matter and editorial slants to new target audiences (see Figure 5.4).

Both creative and research oriented professionals believe that knowing more about the consumer is central to effective advertising. Agencies once more expand advertising practice so as to include new types of research, most notably the application of psychological concepts and techniques to studying consumers and what makes them buy. The advertiser seeks to gain access to the psychological makeup of consumers through personnel who are in tune with the times and who understand the ordinary consumer. Marketing strategy and advertising styles revolve around the idea of a prototypical mass consumer accessible through television—the quintessential mass medium—and characterized by a limited set of traits (interest in convenience, fascination with technology and science, desire for glamour).

Stage Four: Market Segmentation (1965–1985)

After about 1965, advertising practice adapts to the multi-media conditions of the present marketplace. Television itself is forced to target specific types of audiences desired by advertisers in order to compete with other media offering better access to local and specialized markets. Advertising is now seen as part of the marketing mix rather than as the main route to promoting consumption, and the agencies modify their routines accordingly, embracing marketing management, a philosophy that incorporates a whole new set of statistical and marketing research procedures into the preparation of advertising campaigns. These statistical packages concentrate not on personality but on activities of different subgroups of consumers, providing some analysis of their use of media, their consumption preferences, and their lifestyle attitudes. The breakouts of marketing research become the basis for decisions on design and media buying, allowing the agency to formulate marketing campaigns precisely targeted at particular groups of buyers (see Figure 5.5). There is no point in broadcasting expensive messages to those who, a bit of judicious investigation reveals, are bound and determined to remain indifferent to them.

CHEN YU

Figure 5.4 Stage Three—Personalization: Objects carried cues fitting and proper to guide the interior regions of the individual psyche.

Figure 5.5 Stage Four—Market Segmentation: Products are positioned within the web of collective activities resonating with implicit consumption styles.

Five (1985–Present)

As indicated in Table 1.1, we label the current phase of advertising strategy with the term "demassifying," and we identify the following metaphoric-emotive themes in the ads of this period: authenticity, creativity and play, self-reflexivity, diversity, and the transformation of the object. We devote the entirety of Part Two and Three, chapters 8 to 16, to a comprehensive analysis of what has been happening in Stage Five.

The Stages of Advertising Strategy: Conclusion

As we mentioned, no phase supplants the foregoing ones, but rather each complements the others, adding variations and new operations to the existing repertoire. Posters, signs, and flyers—the classic means of publicity in early times—still flourish. Classified and local advertising still provide up to one-third of newspaper revenue. "Rationalist," test-oriented ads still frequently appear in the pages of newspapers and magazines, especially for certain types of consumer goods (stereo equipment, personal computers, more expensive automobile lines). The status-envy appeal formats of the 1930s, the testimonial pitches, and the celebrity appearance all persist for specific uses.

This is an "articulated" communication system, a collection of distinct yet interconnected parts, composed of products, persuasive strategies, and media channels whose unity is forged by the accumulated experience of the advertising agencies. In the chapters that follow we explore how the shift toward market segmentation and growing interest in global markets, and the expansion of the commercial media were underwritten by changes to the advertising bridge and the transformation of the full service agency.

CHAPTER 6

The Structure of Advertisements

The proceeding chapters have illustrated some of the complex historical factors that occurred in Western societies and contributed to the formation of the mediated marketplace through the twentieth century. Specific marketplace contours were different depending upon region and politics, but all shared a preoccupation with the health of the economy and the process of commodification within everyday life. We sought to illustrate how media and advertising became key communication channels assuming a privileged role within the discourse in and through goods. Fatefully linked together, advertising supported the media, which assembled audiences for advertisers—both expanding and complexly transforming through the twentieth century.

Having sketched this institutional history, in this chapter we expand our analysis to the advertising content or "text" itself. The texts of advertisements provide insight into the changing strategies employed to communicate to audiences about goods. These designs sought to solve marketplace problems and to stimulate and maintain the importance of commodities within everyday life. In our study we adopted a historical perspective, which had been largely neglected in the advertising field, thus detracting from our ability to understand the development of the consumer culture.

Within oral language meaning remains dependant on the memory of speakers, whereas documentary texts provide a fixed account, or external record, of an attempt to create meaning (e.g., writing, images, maps, indexes, sound and audiovisual recordings). Advertising texts document the strategies employed by advertisers to negotiate the meaning of goods with audiences, and in this respect they represent a very important part of the discourse of consumption.

Promotional messages are typically informed by strategic goals, even if these goals are developed or revised after the creation of the design, but the articulation or encoding of strategic goals in messages is highly complex. Advertising texts recombine cultural symbols to create messages which speak to audiences about a variety of market problems (re-branding, product launch, brand distinction, reviving brand awareness, creating a buzz). The cultural symbols advertisers draw upon are not always easily disciplined to the promotional task. The types of messages communicated are shaped by changing practices and technology, and as well are subject to regulation and variations in business orientation and budgets. Advertising is the product of creative intuition, and inflicted by particular and historical styles and tastes.

Advertising texts are rarely the work of lone creatives; rather, they are scripted by committee, vetted, and redrafted: Advertising is the embodiment of compromise. Survey research and studies on how audiences are imagined also inform message design. From the perspective of decoding, or how messages are received by audiences, the text is complicated again: While advertising texts fix symbols or images they do not fix meaning, which requires reader's active interpretation.

The role of the audience in the making of meaning has garnered a great deal of academic attention. Some of the earliest academic interest in the advertising text emerged from literary studies which explored the formal properties of advertising—"poetic devices, structure, language"—using methods developed from the study of poetry and novels (Stern, 1999a). Compared to poems and great novels the advertising text was found to be not only different but inferior. The early critics F. R. Leavis and Thompson were particularly concerned that advertisers took little responsibility toward the education of their audiences and the advancement of culture. Poets, novelists, and their critics sought to enlighten their audiences and advance the beauty of written forms, whereas advertisers were concerned only with persuading people to buy something. Marshall McLuhan's *Mechanical Bride* (1951) saw advertising as part of a media system which was massifying culture and contributing to the debasing and vulgarizing of values. Leavis and Thompson felt that audiences should be educated in literary criticism to avoid falling victim to the persuasive techniques of advertisers.

These works are to be applauded as some of the first serious non-industry-based attempts to engage with advertising as a text, at a time when the vast majority of literary critics simply ignored or dismissed such texts. Yet, the positions of these critics were later exposed as being paternal and elitist by those who charged them with assuming that audiences lacked the critical faculties of critics, and with holding the position that popular pleasures were inferior to and debased high culture (Nava and Nava, 1992). The early text-based approach was plagued by a central blind spot, namely, a failure to investigate audience's psychology and mode of reading texts—something that became untenable in the 1960s as a new wave of literary criticism known as "reader-response" emerged, which did take into consideration the audience's approach to the text. The nature of the subjective experience of the reader now was of considerable interest to analysts.

Sociologists too began to take interest in the advertising text as they increasingly recognized it as playing a central role in the reproduction of capitalist social relationships (Ewen 1976). By way of contrast to literary analysis, social science methods tend to address large populations, and early methods were influenced by a scientific method that encouraged the rigorous, systematic explorations of representative samples. One of the most important methods was content analysis, where the primary concern was with the manifest content of messages and the objective was obtaining results that could be expressed in quantitative measurements.

Content analysis applies a protocol comprised of mutually exclusive categories to a sample of ads, typically a large sample of ads. To ensure validity this method typically employs large or representative samples, and care is taken to achieve inter- and intra-coder reliability, meaning that two or more people could agree with how the coding was done for any given advertisement. Researchers typically coordinate content analysis studies, rather than carrying out the research themselves. Informed by scientific procedures, content analysis attempts to eliminate bias by minimizing the role of the researcher's interpretation; hence content analysis typically focuses on the denotative, or clearly evident content: How many people are shown in the ad? Are they old or young, black or white?

These types of studies provide a credible picture of the denotative meanings within advertising and remain popular for monitoring advertising's representations of, for example, women, minorities, and the elderly. It also permitted researcher to document dominant themes within advertisements, and for those interested in uncovering the ideological intents of advertising this method remains important.

However, content analysis has a number of limitations. In breaking down meaning into categories, this method prevents the power and impact of the associational element of a single ad from being appreciated—and in advertising, the whole is often greater than the sum of the parts. While the denotative level of the advertisement provides important information, it does not address the connotative meanings invoked by the symbols in the advertisement. Few promotional messages can be fully appreciated literally, for the stock-in-trade of advertising is the process of invoking a chain of associations to enchant audiences. Finally, content analysis tends to average or universalize meaning, thus diminishing our appreciation for the complexity and intricate play of differences within advertising texts.

The second approach to studying the advertising text has addressed some of these limitations. Stemming largely from the humanities fields, qualitative or interpretive methods provide methodological guidance for exploring the layers of meaning within a given text. Arising out of disciplines other than science, these approaches are based upon the assumption that meaning does not simply exist "outside" of us, waiting to be objectively discovered; rather, it is constructed and necessarily apprehended through a process of interpretation. The researcher figures prominently, using his or her formal training and intuition to derive meaning from the text. Findings are presented, often discursively, in essay form. This method typically explores smaller samples of advertisements in great depth to uncover multiple layers of meaning. Unique interpretations are valued, and few efforts are made to produce "reliability" or inter-coder checks; rather the quality of a researcher's elucidations is assessed by peers.

Since the 1970s the study of advertising has been heavily influenced by semiotics, the "science of the sign," a branch of linguistics that originates in the work of Ferdinand Sassaure in Europe, as further developed in America by Charles S. Peirce. As a mode of analysis semiotics can enhance understanding of how meaning is constructed within an advertisements, and it is particularly instructive due to the way it draws attention to the "codes of advertising" the pool of cultural meaning that advertiser draw upon to communicate with their audience.

Semiotics can provide an answer to some very basic questions concerning meaning: How is meaning reconstituted both by advertisers and viewers of messages? More simply: How do ads work? It works with the concept of the sign, which may be separated into two components, "the signifier" and "the signified." The signifier is the material vehicle of meaning; the signified actually "is" the meaning. The signifier is its "concrete" dimension; the signified is its "abstract" side. While we can separate the two for analytical purposes, in reality they are inseparable. Meaning is derived not simply from the sign, but the signs relationship to others signs (Kristava, 1984), and signs not only communicate meaning, they also shadow other possible meanings.

Two seminal semiotic explorations of advertising have had a major impact on the field—Roland Barthes' *Mythologies* (1973) and Judith Williamson's *Decoding Advertisements* (1978). Barthes linked semiotic explorations to a critique of capitalist social relationships: In his work advertising was exposed as a myth which made ruling-class dominance appear natural, distorting the material relations of capital in a blanket of ideology. For Williamson advertising served a key cultural and economic role by providing commodities with the meanings they otherwise lacked. In her conception, the interpretive powers of audiences links them to a system of relations that simultaneously diminishes them as the very act of reading ads empowers the world of goods: Commodities become animated and powerful while human life is objectified and diminished. As audiences fuel their consumption-based identities through their readings of ads, they confuse their class position— hence Williamson's famous statement that advertising sells us ourselves as our identities become linked to the signification practices of advertisers.

Interpreting the coded messages embedded in advertising provides the means of understanding the broader system of culture. Semiotics highlights the way that we ourselves take part in the creation of meaning in messages, suggesting that we are not mere bystanders in the advertising process, but participants in creating a code that unites the designer and reader. If we are not adequately aware of the relevant referent system, we will not be able to decode the message. As audiences are fragmented into smaller and smaller market segments, the operative codes for each target group become more specialized. Advertisers generally like working with narrowly defined groups rather than with diffuse, broadly-based general audiences. The more narrowly one can define an audience and the more specialized the knowledge one can draw from, the more certain one can be of speaking to people in a language they will respond to.

While the notion of code is insightful and imaginative in its conceptual outline, the applications to specific cases too often lapse into vague generalities. For instance, Williamson's *Decoding Advertisements* starts promisingly by dissecting the codes of fashion that both embrace Catherine Deneuve and Margaux Hemingway as models and yet differentiate each from the other. Later on, however, when the content of these "referent systems" is presented, her discussion abandons the sensual codes of the fashion world for the more abstract and "deeper" codes of ancient cultural traditions. These deeper codes are explained in terms of complex anthropological notions, fashioned from the realm of magic and alchemy and from broad sweeps of time, narrative, and history.

Doubtless, Williamson's purpose here is to show how ads divorce these deeper sources of life and culture from the material and historical context that makes them truly meaningful. Yet what we are left with is a hollow notion of things such as "nature" and "history": Such analysis and criticism is not entirely incorrect, but it is just too broad to be of much use. All of modern culture crawls with references to archaic impulses concerning the animals we love or fear, the idiosyncrasies of dining and dressing, sex roles, puberty and adolescence, marriage and courtship, power and domination. And most of modern culture remains rooted in the old oppositions: good and evil, sacred and profane, life and death. Certainly, one finds all this ancient baggage dumped helter-skelter into advertisements; but one finds it just about everywhere else, too. Although it is fascinating to unpack it, doing so does not tell one all that much about advertising.

However, as method for the study of advertising, semiotics suffers from a number of related weaknesses. First, it is heavily dependent upon the skill of the individual analyst. Training for this type of analysis is a lengthy process, and because of the creative and intuitive powers of interpretation brought to bear in it, the extent to which this method can be replicated is questionable. Indeed, this genre has contributed to the construction of "celebrity" textual analysts. In the hands of someone like Roland Barthes or Judith Williamson, it is a creative tool that allows one to reach the deeper levels of meaning-construction in ads. A less skilful practitioner, however, can do little more than state the obvious in a complex and often pretentious manner. As a result, in these types of studies there is little chance to establish consistency or reliability—that is, a sufficient level of agreement among analysts on what is found in a message.

Second, because the semiotic approach stresses individual readings of messages, it does not lend itself to quantification of results; it is impossible to base an overall sense of constructed meanings on the examination of a large number of messages. What insights may be extracted from this approach must remain impressionistic. Third, semiology cannot be applied with equal success to all kinds of ads. For example, Williamson does not take a random sample of ads and then apply the semiological method to them, but seems to choose ads specifically to illustrate her points. Because such a procedure courts the danger of self-confirming results, the conclusions should, strictly speaking, be confined to those instances alone and not generalized to the entire range of advertising.

We have proposed a "middle range" methodology, adapting and combining what we regard as the major advantages of both semiology (sensitivity) and content analysis (systemization), while admittedly sacrificing some of the distinctive interpretive strengths of each. Moreover, we did not set out to study a general "system of signs" in advertising but rather the field of commercial signs within the specific framework developed in the preceding chapters, namely, the merger of advertising design and media practice as part of the internal development of the advertising industry.

The unit for analysis in both methods is identical—the single ad. Semiology by itself can arguably do a better job on the single ad in isolation, because it is explicitly concerned with the "movement" of meaning within the text and between the text and the outside world. By way of contrast, content analysis can do little more than "unpack" the surface meaning of an ad in a rather obvious way, on the other hand, its strength sterns from its ability to relate this information to the sample as a whole in a rigorous manner, and to detect patterns of similarities and differences.

The method we propose offers a way to specify and measure the different elements that make up the advertisers' codes as they are targeted to particular audience segments. If, indeed, advertisers do draw upon the frameworks of knowledge and expectations developed by their audiences, then advertisements directed at segmented audiences should reflect this differentiated appropriation. Values cannot be picked off the surface of the message and easily arranged into categories. Recognizing values depends on a process of interpretation and reintegration of the available information and requires a process of interpretation.

There are divergent codes operating in advertising because advertisers appeal to different audiences along different dimensions. The results give greater substance and concreteness to semiology's notion of code by blending its sophisticated interpretive sensitivity with the more specific, rigorous, and quantitatively-oriented strategies that one finds in content analysis. Instead of looking to culture or nature or "mind," as the semiologists do, we have searched for concrete marketplace codes that can be broken down into subsidiary categories and compared with each other in terms of relative significance. We have thus captured with one approach both the enormous range of the reference systems and the depth of meaning that the world of advertising so tellingly uses.

Dissatisfied by the limitation of the semiological approach alone (a richness of detail with respect to only a few "ideal types" of ads), our first study of advertising proposed a way to specify and measure quantitatively the different elements that make up the advertisers' codes as they are targeted to particular audience segments. If advertisers do draw upon the frameworks of knowledge and expectations developed by their audiences, then, we argued, advertisements directed at segmented audiences should reflect this differentiated appropriation.

While our study was centrally concerned with how the relationships between persons, products, and settings changed over time, we also argued that messages differ according to a variety of factors, including the target audience and the product advertised. One of the earlier studies on which this book is based (Jhally 1987) was able to represent quite concretely the differentiated codes used by advertisers in their messages directed at male and female audiences. The database for the study was television commercials broadcast during sports programming (male audience) and prime-time programming (regarded by advertisers as a female audience); one thousand network commercials were chosen as the sample (five hundred for each audience). This study found that advertisers were much more likely to encode the themes of beauty, family, and romance for female audience, and ruggedness and fraternity for men. The importance of audience code was the basis for the historical survey of magazine advertising.

Methodological Outline

The protocol for the study was devised over five years, and applied by trained coders whose work was subjected to inter coder liability measures. Two Canadian popular general-interest, mass-circulation magazines (*Maclean's* and *Chatelaine*) that spanned the seventy or so years of history in which we were interested. We chose successful and surviving magazines rather than ones that fell by the wayside. *Maclean's*, which started out with an almost exclusively male readership in 1908, still had a predominantly male readership (though far less so) in 1984. *Chatelaine* since 1928 has consistently been directed at a female audience, with approximately 80 percent of its readership currently women. This limitation assured us that the overall market was covered, and also enabled us to make some comparisons between magazines directed at the broadly differentiated male and female audiences. We believe that our sample cast a reasonably wide net in terms of capturing the most significant trends in advertising.

In order to minimize the effects of changes in the types of products that advertise in magazines, we selected products across a range that appeared consistently in magazines in significant proportions over the whole period. To make this selection, we constructed profiles of the frequency of advertisements by product type in both of our magazines by randomly examining two copies of each magazine for each year. We developed profiles for each magazine based upon examination of 15,000 advertisements, noting for each the size of ad and the product type. Using these product profiles, we limited the products that we included in the final sample to smoking, automobile, clothing, food, personal-care, alcoholic products, and corporate advertisements. All were present in reasonable proportions for most of the historical sample (alcohol was only introduced after the beginning of World War II). Based on these profiles, we were also able to estimate the proportion of all advertising in the magazines that our results reflected. In choosing these categories, we were assured of tapping more than 50 percent of the products advertised in magazines at any time (and, in most periods, much higher proportions).

A Historical Study of Advertising

The task of any content analysis is to "deconstruct" a set of ads into meaningful components or fields of representation and then to interpret the findings. In this study, we followed the course suggested by Leymore's semiological analysis (1975), distinguishing between person, product, setting, and text. We noted the presence of each of these fields and the proportion of the total display area devoted to it for each ad. The historical trends are shown in Figure 6.1.

It is clear that the text has been declining in importance throughout the period under study; a word count illustrated more precisely the steady overall decline in copy. The emphasis on copywriting in advertising's early years shifted gradually to one on display and illustration. In many cases, the contemporary ads contain nothing more than a brand name, a slogan, and a few explanatory words—demonstrating a crucial change in the way advertising ideas are expressed within the ads, most particularly in the relationship between language and visual elements, in the information they convey.

Changes in the proportion of textual and visual elements are not equally common in all ads. Advertisements for certain kinds of products, such as alcohol and tobacco, tended to use less text than others throughout the entire period, while automobile ads and corporate messages always used much more. Over time, product types became increasingly differentiated by the amount of text used. Detailed analysis revealed that the increasing "visualization"

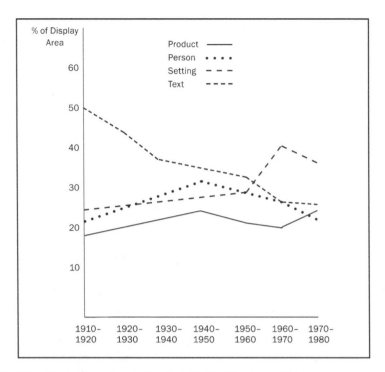

Figure 6.1 Display Area Devoted to Each Field of Representation.

of selling messages in advertising design was one facet of the specialization of appeals around product types. But the importance of the shift to visual representation in general cannot be underestimated. In the earlier period especially, the text explains the reasons for consuming, the identity of the user, the appropriate context for use, or the benefits of the product, thus acting as the predominant field for providing the overall interpretation of the relationship between person and product. As such, the text closes off any ambiguity that might emerge from the new kinds and qualities of information provided in the illustration.

By the 1950s setting information is more often conveyed by illustration that tends to combine physical and social settings rather than by description. Moreover, the setting code becomes the predominant field of representation during the 1960s and thereafter. Changes in advertising's use of the elemental codes (person, product, setting) are happening hand in hand with this transition in the mode (language/visual image) of representation. The development and expansion of visual forms of expression and communication prompted by artwork (some of the earlier inspirations were posters and period art styles) and photography has affected immensely the kinds of representations and information we find in advertising.

Advertising was not only "instructional" in the sense that it acquainted audiences with new kinds of products (processed foods, safety razors, deodorants) and the new social problems they were designed to solve, but also in that it taught the "grammatical skills" for decoding the ads themselves. In the 1920s and 1930s, many transitional ads use the text essentially to explain the image and its logic—to provide a key to the interpretation of the image. These transitional ads pave the way for forms that can leave out the explicit lesson by using the visual grammar with which ads are encoded and decoded. Thus they provide us with important clues to the interpretation of later ads.

The development of communication in advertising itself is, deeply intertwined with the more general communicative competences of the audience. Literacy and education were prerequisites for earlier forms of magazine advertising, decoding abilities are assumed in modern audiences who must make sense of modern articulations. The increased specificity and accessibility of advertising was underwritten by the successful adaptation of communicative techniques to the advertising genre. Figure 6.3 is an example of a transitional ad from the 1930s, in which microscopic inspection, foldaways, and image sequences accentuate the argument; Figure 6.4 uses a movie-like sequence of images to tell a story. These are but a few of the visual techniques that have expanded the communicative domains of advertising. One of the most important, and sometimes amusing, results of the application of these techniques is that it allows new points of view and forms of dialogue to emerge within the discourse of advertising. As seen in Figure 6.5, the introduction of the comic bubble even enables the product to "speak for itself."

Basic Advertising Formats

The above account provides the background for the interpretation of historical change in the general structure of representation in magazine advertising. In the following pages, we attempt to clarify the broad changes in advertising's patterns of representation through which people and products are brought into a "meaningful relationship." We will discuss representative ads that illustrate and highlight the framework for the interpretive task that all of us face when we try to make sense of ads. These ads are presented as ideal types to represent the prototypical formats within which the person-product relationship is constituted, and to help us chart the predominant patterns of meaning in various historical periods. The person-product relationship was forged within advertising's system of meaning into four basic communicative formats—crystallizations of the complex structure of advertising's multifaceted system of signs—which help us understand the basic patterns of integration between the semiological codes and the textual and visual modes of representation (Kline and Leiss, 1978).

Figure 6.2 Metaphoric Readings of Product Qualities: The text helps the audience form a metaphoric reading that links the product qualities with the visual sign.

Figure 6.5 Through the use of comic-book formats, objects not only come alive but are given a more influential role in solving the consumer's personal problems. *Source:* Courtesy of Lever Detergents Limited.

The Product-Information Format

In the product-information ad, the product is the center of attention and the focus of all elements in the ad is explaining the product and its utility. The brand name and frequently a picture of the package are prominent. The text is used primarily to describe the product and its benefits, characteristics, performance, or construction. Little other information is available and little reference is made to the user or the context of use of the product, except for instructions or special offers. The ad may contain visuals that emphasize the effectiveness of the product (for example, a microscopic view of a germ-free sink), or rational arguments pointing out the benefits of use, but it does not make extensive reference to the user. Those who believe that "rational" product information is what should be supplied to the modern economy often assume that this type of ad should constitute the whole field of advertising. An expansion of the earlier classified advertising format through more elaborate copywriting and illustration, the product-information ad was the dominant type around the turn of the century but has been declining steadily since then.

Several major variants of the product-information format differ primarily in the way they manifest the idea of the power of the product. The textually oriented ad (Figure 6.6) places greatest emphasis upon language—description of the product, promises, and argument. A second variant continues to rely heavily on text but also uses design and illustration to emphasize the features of the product and explain its advantages (Figure 6.7). In what might be called a demonstration ad, the ability of the product to achieve some end is visually illustrated, perhaps with the aid of scientific apparatus (Figure 6.8). Other variants and combinations exist, of course, and many modern ads give us elaborate visual representations of product benefits, but the central idea in this format remains the evaluation of a utilitarian matrix in which a product, its construction, its price, its utility, and its ability to perform certain deeds is considered.

The Product-Image Format

In the product-image ad, brand name and package again play an important part, but the product is given special qualities by means of a symbolic relationship that it has to some more abstract and less pragmatic domain of significance than mere utility. The product becomes embedded or "situated" in a symbolic *context* that imparts meaning to the product beyond its constituent elements or benefits. Product-image ads, therefore, work by fusing two composite systems of signs, or two codes within the framework of a single message—the product code and a setting code. (It is not surprising that semiologists have been most ardent in

Figure 6.6 The Product-Information Format: Heavy on text, illustration is primarily used to visualize the product and packaging.

Figure 6.7 The Product-Information Format: A more subtle blending of text and illustration also enabled advertisers to refer to abstract features of product characteristics and design.

Figure 6.8 The Product-Information Format: Visualization was used to help demonstrate the utilities of the product in new, more effective ways.

recognizing this structure for interpretation in the field of advertising.) In generating the overall meaning of the ad, these codes are not necessarily synthesized by causal or logical linkages, but by association and juxtaposition or some narrative device. The symbolic association thus established brings the product into a meaningful relationship with abstract values and ideas signified by a natural or social setting such as a landscape, the workplace, the household, a cluster of artifacts of daily life, a historic moment, or a recognizable tradition or myth.

In order for the setting to be understood as a code rather than a locus of use, it must provide a frame of reference for interpreting the product's qualities. Each code implies a system of classification to which we are referred as the basis for interpreting the product's qualities. The fusion of product code and setting code, which formulates the basis of the product-image, depends largely on narrative techniques like metaphor, implied use, allusion, allegory, story line, and simple juxtaposition to expand the symbolic dimension of the interpretation. Without these means for drawing together codes, product-image ads would remain impenetrable. Figure 1.3, the Packard ad from the 1930s, illustrates how a well-known myth can be the basis of a symbolic association in which the image of luxury and grandeur of the product is conjured. It is clear that the scene depicted is not the product in use. Moreover, without some knowledge of Cleopatra and her barge we could not make the required connection between the car and the abstract qualities being invoked.

The increasing use of art and photography encouraged the tendency to place the product within a symbolic rather than utilitarian setting because the communicative techniques involved in visual representation allowed for new ways of exploring the potentialities of products and their meaning in the human world. Visual representation, based on apprehended qualities, provides blurred and less clearly identifiable fields of reference. As depicted in advertising, settings are multidimensional and often provide ambiguous bases for the interpretation of the product image.

Typically, these settings are either "natural" or "social"; for example, in Figure 6.9 the superimposition of the cigarette package on a beautiful natural setting helps us not only to imagine a moment when we might use the product (the narrative), but, more importantly, to transfer the qualities of coolness and naturalness that we associate with this vista to the cigarette as well. In Figure 6.10, the name of the line of silverware takes on the connotation of social standing illustrated and stylized in the drawing; in Figure 6.11, the can of soup seems to emerge directly out of the natural ingredient itself. The same interpretive logic is involved whether the abstract value is placed in a natural or a social context.

The logic of associative transfer of value is also the basis of some ads in which the human element is used as the symbolic context. In Figure 6.12, the person

Figure 6.9 The Product-Image Format: In the fluid and swirling world of images, the transfer of natural qualities to products does not seem strange.

Figure 6.10 The Product-Image Format: Stylized illustration helps to crystallize the particular social qualities that can be transferred to products.

Figure 6.11 The Product-Image Format: In the magical world of commodities, products seemed to capture natural qualities and internalize them within the product image.
Source: Courtesy of Campbell's Soup Company Ltd.

Figure 6.12 The Product-Image Format: People appear, but as representations of abstract qualities such as "trust" rather than as living individuals.
Source: Courtesy of Coca-Cola Ltd.

literally steps to the foreground and brings with her the essence of "trust" and "quality" associated with her profession. The similarity of the human and bottle shape helps us to transfer the abstract qualities to the product, creating the fusion necessary for the product image. In all these cases, the predominant interpretation results from the transfer of the abstract symbolic quality or value associated with a particular context to the product.

The Personalized Format

The direct relationship between a product and the human personality defines the primary framework of the personalized ad. Here the person code takes on an importance quite different from its use in the product-image ads, in which people sometimes appear as part of a social setting that transfers abstract symbolic qualities to products. In personalized ads, people are explicitly and directly interpreted in their relationship to the world of the product. Social admiration, pride of ownership, anxiety about lack of use, or satisfaction in consumption become important humanizing dimensions of the interpretation of products, as we note from the gazes of the people in Figure 6.13.

The framework of interpretation in the personalized ad presumes that "the way an individual or a culture identifies similarities and differences between persons and groups in their milieu is the foundation on which everyday social intercourse is based" (Forgas 1981). As cognitive psychologists point out, this process of social judgment assumes an "identity matrix"—a frame of reference for personality categories. This matrix is appropriated in the personalized ad to embrace social interactions around and through the product. The product does more than refer to the world of human interaction; it enters and acts in that world and resonates with its qualities. Sometimes, the product itself speaks as if it were a person saying things that humans can't. To quote one jewelry ad, "Yes, falling in love was pretty easy. But our diamond says we're going to make it last." The distinction between person and product codes becomes obscured. Even the characters that speak to us from ads become confused about the distinction: Candice Bergen testifies about her perfume, "Cie goes with all the things I love to do. Cie is me."

The way the relationship between the product and person is constructed varies greatly depending upon whether, for example, the person is a user, a consumer, or a typical representative of some personality type (smart, sophisticated) or group (homemakers, businesspeople). People may be shown simply as models, presenters, or testifiers, or in the course of their daily life. In all cases, the meaning of the ad is conveyed by the link between the attributes associated with the people in the advertisement and the relationship they embody between themselves and the product.

Figure 6.13 The Personalized Format: Pride in ownership and social admiration speak of a direct personal relationship to products.
Source: Courtesy of Ford Motor Co. of Canda Ltd.

As the significance of the product becomes mediated by direct and personalized relationships, the separate worlds of people and products also merge. The cycle of consumption and satisfaction becomes an important thematic focus for exploring the relationship between people and products. Social interaction and judgment extends to and flows through the products people have or use. The product may even be personified, taking on human characteristics. In consequence, the dimensions of meaning that connect people and products are affective rather than associative or pragmatic. The emotions that engage people in human intercourse (love, anxiety, pride, belonging, friendship) also engage them with products.

The personalized format has a number of important variants. One is the testimonial in which the person's relationship to the product is based on experience with use or consumption (see Figure 6.14). Often, narrative devices are used to explicate the human dimension of the relationship between the persons testifying and the product in order to let them enter the scene with their particular qualities of credibility (see Figure 6.15). At other times, a person's role, or even just fame, provides the connection between the product and its recommendation. The scientist recommends the effectiveness of a cleanser, the starlet certifies her satisfaction with a soap, and the typical housewife tells us how pleased her husband is to have clean collars. A throng of characters display and tell us about their reactions to products. Early versions of this format often stressed the utility and effectiveness of the product, but more modern versions—which rely primarily on the visual image—stress the emotional experience of responding to products and being satisfied by them.

In a second variant, the person is not present to "stand behind" the product so much as to "stand for" it (see Figure 6.16). The connection is made on symbolic grounds rather than through use or consumption. This is the basis of an ad image that has become famous all over the world, namely the Marlboro Man; in this imagery the associative symbolic logic is very like the product-image ad, except that the symbolic reference stops at the world of social interactions and personality rather than referring onward to abstract values. The Marlboro Man *is* the product; in ads of this type, the person does not testify to or explain use, but conveys a range of attributes (here ruggedness, masculinity) to be associated with the product according to the personal prototype he or she represents. The person in these ads embodies a typified field of personal and psychological reference whose attributes can be transferred to the product by the convergence of these two fields of signification.

In the self-transformation ad, people change—make themselves better—through the possession or use of the product. In the most common self-transformation ad, consumers are invited to imagine themselves in some

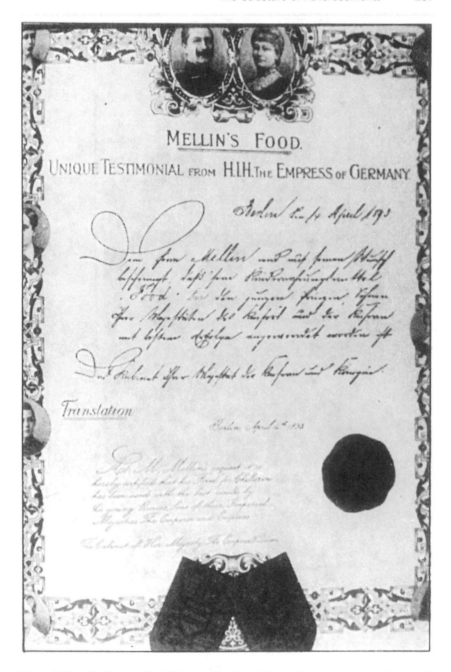

Figure 6.14 The Personalized Format: Testimonials are based upon experience with and use of products, often by celebrities.

Figure 6.15 The Personalized Format: Narratives help introduce expert testimonial while personalizing the use.

Figure 6.16 The Personalized Format: Models stand for products and the connection between the two is so complete that they become interchangeable.

more idealized state (see Figure 1.4, the Nice 'n Easy ad). Figure 6.17 is an elaboration in the form of a "makeover" ad, typically associated with cosmetics and clothes. More subtle visual cues, like the mirror in Figure 6.18, are often used to imply the psychological nature of the transformation. The mirror helps to remind us of the relationship between the "antecedent" and "idealized" representations of human personalities that are at play in these ads. As the texts explain it: "Reflections of you. The way you want to be. To feel this season. Alive. Rejuvenated."

A fourth variant places the product at the very center of social interaction—that is, within the stream of human relations. As Chevrolet once told us, its vehicle was, "More than a car—a member of the family." We see the product bring people into greater intimacy in Figure 6.19. In other advertisements, women get together to solve a personal problem, mother and father are in conflict over their son, or a person uses the power of a product to increase his or her own sexual attractiveness; in all ads of this type, the product is woven firmly into the web of human social interaction. Romance, friendship, social status, and the family provide the main social contexts for product use and association, although advertising draws on the whole gamut of social situations.

The common ground in all these variants is the "personalization" of the product image. The framework of interpretation is built specifically and directly around a relationship between people and products. The product no longer stands as an autonomous object independent of the human world, but rather is displayed as an integral part of the codification of human existence and interaction.

The Lifestyle Format

In lifestyle ads, a more balanced relationship is established between the elemental codes of person, product, and setting by combining aspects of the product-image and personalized formats. The lifestyle format expands the identity matrix of the individual into a framework of judgment for social beings in a social context.

In most lifestyle advertising, the setting serves in the interpretation of the person code. Social psychology describes this as the use of "stereotypes" rather than "prototypes." A prototype is based on attributions about the personality or characteristics of a person (friendly, warm, intelligent). A stereotype is based on inferences about the relationship of the individual to the group or social context (class, status, race, ethnicity, role relations, group membership), and the notion of group identity is implicit in judgments about the individual. The lifestyle format, like the stereotype, implies that "situations

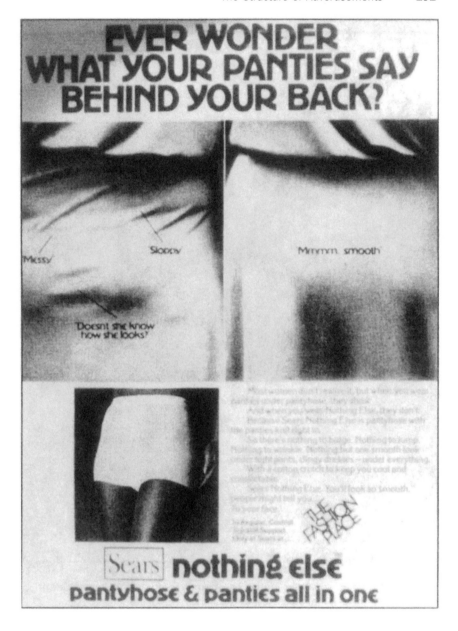

Figure 6.17 The Personalized Format: Showing consumers before and after use emphasizes the role products play in self-improvement.
Source: Courtesy of Sears Canada Ltd.

Figure 6.18 The Personalized Format: The mirror accentuates the fantasized completion of the self made possible by the world of products.
Source: Courtesy of Eaton's.

Figure 6.19 The Personalized Format: Situated at the center of social interaction, products become intimate partners with use.

are susceptive to classification in terms of different kinds of effects which they exert on the subject, that is, in terms of their significance for his well-being" (Forgas 1981). In one variant of lifestyle advertising, the idea of social identity is conveyed primarily through the display of the product in a social context; the people who are inserted into the scene remain undefined, providing only a vague reference to the person code (and therefore implicitly to use or consumption style). Often the occasion provides the unifying idea; more commonly, people, products, and settings of consumption are harmonized around a unified impression, as in the Dubonnet ad (Figure 1.5); no other information is really necessary because the ad provides a direct vision of a consumption style.

Early references to consumption style help to reveal the important dimensions of the lifestyle format. In Figure 6.20, a post-World War II ad for Coca-Cola, the text cues our understanding that consumption hinges around appropriate settings and occasions rather than strictly on satisfaction. Coke is being integrated into a consumption style, connoted by recognizable people in a known social situation, without emphasizing the act of consumption.

The other major variant of the lifestyle format synthesizes the component codes through a primary reference to an activity rather than directly to a consumption style. Here the activity invoked in text or image becomes the central cue for relating the person, product, and setting codes. In Figure 6.21 (cleverly captured within the shape of the product), sharing a friendly sporting activity is the basis of the connection with common use of the product. Lifestyle ads commonly depict a variety of leisure activities (entertaining, going out, holidaying, relaxing). Implicit in each of these activities, however, is the placing of the product within a consumption style by its link to an activity.

In modern advertising, the allusion to consumption style is often very subtle. A romantic photograph can provide the basis of a story, however condensed and simplified. The minimal reference, "Last night," in Figure 6.22 suggests both product use and a significant moment in the story to help us interpret the photograph, which resonates with implied social dynamics. Such simple narratives are typical of the sophisticated way contemporary advertising blends visuals with text or "dialogue" to express consumption styles. For all the ambiguity and condensation we see in lifestyle ads, the modern reader seems to have little trouble understanding the implications of these scenes.

In the lifestyle ad, the dimension of consumption that provides the unifying framework of interpretation is action or behavior appropriate to (or typical of) a social group or situation, rather than use, satisfaction, or utility. Lifestyle ads become most prominent after the 1950s, and, in part, reveal the accommodation of magazine advertising to television's powerful visual

Figure 6.20 The Lifestyle Format: Immortalizing the trivial moments brings into relief the appropriate social occasions for consumption.
Source: Courtesy of Coca-Cola Ltd.

Figure 6.21 The Lifestyle Format: Reference to particular lifestyles is internalized within the essential meaning of the product and reflected in its use.
Source: Courtesy of Anheuser-Busch, Inc.

Figure 6.22 The Lifestyle Format: The allusion to consumption style can be subtly nested in personal narratives even in the breaking of social conventions.
Source: Courtesy of Max Factor & Co.

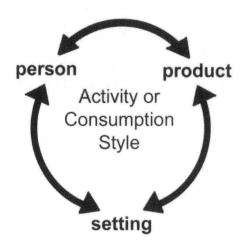

Figure 6.23 Activity or Consumption Style.

methods of storytelling and the matrix of consumption styles it portrays. We use the interpretive framework to synthesize the person, product, and setting codes in the lifestyle ad as shown in Figure 6.23.

Toward an Integrated Historical Framework

In each culture there exists a main operator by which its representations are transformed into reality. At times individuals and at times animals were elevated to this role. In our culture, the mathematical-physical sciences, that is the sciences of quantifiable and measurable objects, serve as the paradigm for all knowledge. We are spellbound by reverse animism which populates our universe with inanimate machines in the place of animated beings (Moscovici 1981).

In advertising, we may indeed be spellbound by things, but we do not seem to be transfixed by the scientific world view. This century opened with rationalism and the objective characteristics of goods at the center of advertising, implying a predominantly pragmatic relationship between persons and objects; but this mode of representation has systematically been eroded and replaced by one in which products have been "re-animized" and given meaning, transporting them from the rational-physical universe of things to the world of human social interaction. Perhaps the world of advertising has provided the counterweight to the scientific rationalism that rules elsewhere in modern culture.

The changes that we have described in advertising design took place in the practice of marketing and advertising (discussed in chapter 5). The marketing concept was helping to draw attention away from the notion of "utility," which had emphasized the product and its effectiveness, toward that of "use," which was concerned primarily with the way the product enhanced the experience of satisfaction achieved through the act of consumption. The shift from informational to symbolic presentation, typical of the product-image format, was no doubt enhanced by new communication technology. The introduction of photography facilitated a greater emphasis on people and settings. Demonstrating the utility, construction, or effectiveness of a product is difficult to express visually. Use, on the other hand, seems to adapt well to illustration, especially when it is merely implied.

As the emphasis moves from the efficacy of the product to the personal consequences of consumption, the advertising designer can explore the drama of consumer satisfaction rather than the prosaic facts of product effectiveness. Communication design became more than a passive reflection of the environment—it became a transformative activity. The door is opened to more symbolic rather than rationalistic approaches to communication. The shift to product-image formats opens up advertising's discourse about products to include images of status, glamour, beauty, health, and respectable middle-class mores among the images of product quality.

The proliferation of representations of people in advertising creates its own problems. Changes in orientation are, of course, in part reactions to problems and conditions created within the institutional structures and the practice of advertising itself. During the 1940s, advertising becomes so cluttered with pictures of typical people and beautiful people that the distinctive product image is almost lost. In the 1950s, some advertisers add distinctive features to their characterizations (the famous Hathaway eyepatch, for instance), or attempt to sharpen the product image through greater attention to the setting. The problems of clutter and the need to develop strategies to seize audience attention was to become a major thrust of advertising design

The following description of the development of advertising as a series of emergent phases is our attempt to summarize the major adjustments in communicative formats in response to a multiplicity of problems facing the advertiser on the cultural, institutional, and practical levels.

Until the 1920s, the concern with the function, benefits, price, and construction of products dominated magazine advertising. In this utility format the product was the central feature and advertisers sought to address the question: What does this product do? In the 1880s, advertisers were highly restricted by the types of illustrations that were possible, but the commercialization of the media led to new possibilities in display and illustration, especially in magazine ads. The ads of the early twentieth century explored the nature of the product within these physical confines, as well as within the societal confines of the late industrial era. Now a much better representation of the concrete "being" of the product was possible. John Berger (1972) has commented generally on how oil painting increased the "tangibility" of artistic imagery, and on how photography extends this feature of visual representation in advertising.

The continuing development of the visual dimension of advertising and changes in advertising copy sped the transition to symbolic representations in the 1920s. Under the influence of the new media of film and radio, emphasis on what the product *did* diminished while the visuals increasingly explored what the product could *mean* for consumers—where it fitted within a world view expanded to encompass the whole of society and nature. This signaled a second phase in the developing relationship between people and products in which the product itself became more abstract—a value achieved in use rather than a thing valued in its own right. The product seemed to demand an answer to the question: What does it mean to use this product? The explicit depiction of the relationship between people and products became central; use began to replace utility as the most frequent means of showing the connections between people and goods.

Advertising in the period after 1945 faced a new challenge: the enterprise of turning war productivity to the purposes of the consumer market. New dimensions were added to discourses about uses. The key question became: What emotional reactions are consumers supposed to experience in consumption? Product quality and general consumer satisfaction were no longer sufficient. The product was being registered within a complex matrix of human emotional responses. The people in advertisements were not just experienced users of products; they had to convey an impression of the *nature* of the satisfaction they achieved. Advertising increasingly addressed questions such as: How can I become happy through consumption?

From the late 1960s onward market segmentation became the operational matrix of advertising strategy. The concern has shifted to the identification of the consumer and the nature of the act of consumption within a social situation. The product has become a totem, a representation of a clan or group that we recognize by its activities and its members' shared enjoyment of the product. The response to consumption seems to be less concerned with the nature of satisfaction than with its social meaning—the way it integrates the individual into a consumption tribe. Meaning here focuses on questions such as: Who is the person I become in the process of consumption? Who are the other consumers like me? What does the product mean in terms of the type of person I am and how I relate to others?

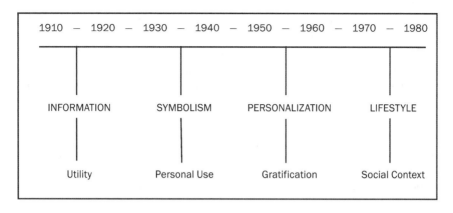

Figure 6.24 Phases in the Development of Communicative Formats: A Historical Model.

Figure 6.24 illustrates phases in the development of advertising's communicative formats. The sequence in this model is a broad interpretation of patterns in the development of advertising's communicative dimensions in a theoretically stable field in which data have been corrected for product and magazine type.

In fact, a more detailed analysis of codes found that both the type of product and magazine are related to changing qualities of advertising format. Certain products are sold consistently over long periods with the same approaches, as indicated by their orchestration of codes. For instance, across all periods we found that personal-care products were predominantly personalized, automobiles were given product-information treatments, and alcohol ads tended to be symbolic (concentrating on product image) or lifestyle in form (Kline 1983; Jhally, Kline, and Leiss 1985). The variation in advertising format for a product type seems to bear an inverse relationship to the increasing segmentation in marketing and media practice. F or example, there was less variation in advertising presentations for particular product types in the 1960s than there was in the 1930s.

Advertising formats gradually narrowed as well, within the two magazines used in our study, in part because of the reduced range of products that advertise in their pages. But we also find that the advertising formats for the same product range differ noticeably between the two magazines, showing audience segmentation as well as market segmentation at work. Although in both magazines the product appears with identical emphasis, in the male-oriented magazine greater emphasis is put on the use of text and on the person code, while the female-oriented magazine shows greater stress on setting codes typical of the product image and lifestyle formats.

Segmentation—noted in our review of advertising thought and practice— manifests itself in general trends in advertising formats as the constraint imposed by product type and audience orientation. This segmentation reached its highest level during the last twenty-five years, coincidental with the increasing emphasis on settings for consumption typical of lifestyle advertising. In this respect, the historical sequence of advertising formats is more like the overlaying process depicted in Figure 6.25, in which a new communicative approach or emphasis does not eliminate previous ones but rather allows more specific responses by the audience to the type of product. The accumulated experience and knowledge of the advertising industry as a whole, as distinct from trends within particular agencies, is reflected here. As advertisers come to believe that people buy cars based on their performance, cosmetics based on their image, and cigarettes based on how they feel about other cigarette smokers, these theories about consumers and how to persuade them become part of advertising communication.

If advertisers also believe (and they do) that women are less rational consumers than men, this will be revealed in the fact that the more rational forms of advertising occur less often for women's products and in women's magazines. Once again, careful analysis by product type and by magazine revealed that these results are "segmented." For example, analysis indicated that self-transformation ads, originally developed for the female audience, have been steadily gaining favor in the male-oriented magazine, whereas the "white

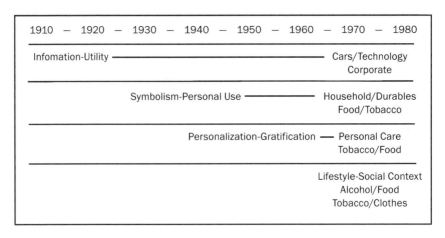

Figure 6.25 Phases in the Segmentation of Advertising Form: A Stratified Model.

magic" theme (imparting the virtues of nature to the product) and "black magic" (the product's power to captivate and allure) are highly concentrated in the female-oriented magazine. These differences are due, in part, to the concentration of these themes around personal-care products such as cosmetics, and, in part, to the increasing tendency of advertisers to address the male and female audiences differently (Jhally, Kline, and Leiss 1985, Table 1). The attempt to subsume audience and market segmentation into advertising's communicative strategy and design is an important part of the advertising system today.

Our study of advertising imagery shows a richly textured and artfully constructed set of messages whose common purpose is to bind together persons and products. The message formats evolve in a series of stages, as advertising practice is shaped by, and helps to shape, new possibilities provided by communications technologies. But society and culture are evolving as well, and we will now turn to the task of integrating the historical schemas presented above into the larger supporting framework.

Cultural Frames for Goods

In earlier societies, individuals became acquainted with the meanings carried by objects through culture and customs. In a consumer society, needs and commodities must be introduced by some other means. Marketing and advertising become the chief matchmakers. Toward the end of the nineteenth century, the burgeoning array of new goods that began to emerge from mass-production techniques presented businesses with the challenge of "binding" products to culturally sanctioned formats for the satisfaction of needs. Marketers and advertisers had to start constructing props for the ball—sets of masks for goods—using whatever media technologies and persuasive or "appeal" formats were available to them. But partners at the masked ball need melodies, not words, for dancing; they also need instruction in the new steps. The music and the choreography for any dance come from its cultural frame of reference.

First, the ground had to be cleared, ground that had been occupied by traditional social collectivities rooted in pre-modern economic conditions and formed by regional, religious, ethnic, linguistic, craft, and other local customs. The objects that circulated therein reflected these determinations: the distinctive dress and cuisine of ethnic communities, the closed associations of skilled craftsmen, the special kinds of things provided for feasts and celebrations. The coming of the market-industrial system changed all this.

Where the division of labor, mass migrations from rural to urban areas, sustained technological innovation, and the erosion of traditional customs had rent the fabric of social collectivities, mass marketing began to feel its way, gradually stitching together a new type of human association. In the first phase of mass marketing, before the emergence of the consumer society, familiar objects were replaced by industrial articles promoted largely on the basis of their own "abstract" qualities: their utility, advanced technology, low cost, and efficiency. Thereafter, marketing and advertising strategies sought with ever greater self-awareness to fill the void left by the disappearance of traditional cultures by creating a sense of social solidarity in messages about the relations between persons and things. Whereas the new system of commodity production emptied the world of the traditional material elements in the lives of groups, the new system of mass marketing sought to refill that world with its own form and content.

The consumer society brings into being a distinctive way of life based on a notion that individuals can regard their affiliation with social groups as a fluid milieu of temporary associations that are based on styles of appearance and behavior as well as on choices of activities. No one is bound permanently to particular circumstances originating in accidents of birth or fortune; on the contrary, everyone can participate in an eternal process whereby groupings are dissolved and regenerated.

The distinctive content of the consumer society is that these temporary associations, based purely on the arbitrary wills of their members, revolve around structured sets of products and messages about them. "Flapper," "zoot suiter," "soul," "hippy," and "punk" are just a few of the exhibitionist styles that the more cautious majority have skirted apprehensively on their way to department stores and supermarkets; after a decent interval, fragments of such styles, suitably muted and sanitized, filter unrecognized into the consumption practices of more respectable folk. Marketers and advertisers are responsible not for imposing behavior patterns on unsuspecting people, but rather for ensuring that (lest the audience fall asleep) sufficiently entertaining new productions are mounted in the theater of consumption, that (lest the audience stay away) the program is changed often, and that (lest the audience be offended) the theatergoers become broad-minded enough at least to tolerate, if they cannot enjoy, the extravagances that are paraded before their senses.

In much national product advertising, goods stand in an indeterminate relation to the personal activities, interactions, and self-transformations associated with them. There are no "causal" connections between the persons and the things represented; rather, the product simply is associated with a highly stylized set of visual images. The product image serves as an emblem for a social grouping; consider the Coca-Cola ad that portrayed a multi-racial, multi-ethnic group of young people singing sweetly about "harmony" in the world. We call this the magical representation of social collectivities.

In such a format, the product appears as a sign or indicator for a collectivity that is defined by its appearance and activities—the devotees of punk music and rock video, the beer-drinking sports fans, the fitness and healthy living set—and constituted as a social series by means of the various products with which it is associated. This mode of presentation represents another framing of goods, part of the story of advertising that began about a hundred years ago. The principal stages of development are sketched in Table 6.1, which is based on the stages in advertising practice we developed in chapter 5 and illustrated by our historical study of magazine advertising above.

The cultural frame for goods supplies the general design principles for fashioning the masks for goods that highlight what is distinctive and unique about each period. This does not mean that a single cultural frame overshadows everything else that is happening at that time, or supplants completely what came before. Different marketing/advertising strategies overlie one another, and all continue to play some part in the total sales effort down to the present day. In other words, we cannot segregate events neatly into separate piles, since human action is not a well-ordered phenomenon. But using cultural frames of reference can help us to mark where the edges of behavioral patterns (that in themselves remain rather indistinct) rub up against one another. We have called the four cultural frames for goods idolatry, iconology, narcissism, and totemism.

Phase One: Idolatry

We name the period 1890–1925 the idolatrous phase of the market-industrial society because advertising messages at this time carried a strong tone of veneration about products. What generated this tone was the industrial system's newly discovered sense of power and accomplishment, dating from about 1875, when it recognized that its great capacities could be applied to the mass production of consumer goods. There followed a great outpouring of mechanical devices, cleverly answering or anticipating the requirements of every conceivable task and occasion in domestic life, so bountiful that some people surely must have feared being buried under an avalanche of objects.

The overt selling strategy can be described as "rational" because its discourse was saturated with descriptive narratives about products and their many qualities, about the great range of their potential uses and benefits, about their common-sense advantages in saving time, energy, and money. But it must also be characterized as a quasi-logical discourse because the surface appearance of the text—dispassionate, informative, elaborately reasoned—concealed vital qualitative differences between quite sensible products and uses on the one hand, and simply fraudulent and sometimes even dangerous ones on the other. The patent-medicine advertising of earlier times was notorious for systematically confusing real and imaginary ailments, and even

Table 6.1 Evolution of Cultural Frames for Goods in Relation to the Development of Media, Marketing, and Advertising

Media for Advertising	Newspapers/ Magazines	Radio	Television	Television
Marketing Strategy	Rational	Non-rational	Behaviorist	Segmentation
Advertising Strategy	Utility[a]	Product Symbols[b]	Personification[c]	Lifestyle[d]
Period	1890 1910	1920 1940	1950 1960	1970 1980
Elements in Ads	Product qualities/price/use	Product qualities	Product	Product
		Symbolic attributes	Person prototype	Activity: person-setting
Metaphoric-Emotive Themes in Ads	Quality, useful, descriptive	Status, family, health; white magic; social authority	Glamor, romance; sensuality; black magic; self-transformation	Leisure, health; groups, friendship
Cultural Frames for Goods	Idolatry: Products are abstracted from process of production, presented as pure use-values	Iconology: Products are embodiments of attributes, configured in social judgment	Narcissism: Products are personalized and satisfaction is judged in interpersonal terms	Totemism: Products are emblems of group-related consumption practices

* Pre-1890: Posters and billboards.
[a] See Figure 1.2. [b] See Figure 1.3. [c] See Figure 1.4. [d] See Figure 1.5.

more so for making utterly unfounded claims about the efficacy of products. Until about 1905, narcotic-based elixirs containing opium and cocaine were widely touted in baby products such as colic cures and teething remedies and in products said to relieve " female distress"; this may remind us why some restrictions on the creative imaginations of producers and marketers are thought to be necessary.

Whether the uses were exotic or prosaic, the discourse through and about objects was anchored in the object itself and its image. By calling this "the idolatrous phase," we do not mean to suggest that the discourse was generally false or misleading, for the great majority of goods had some sensible quotient of genuine utility, and the lavish descriptions of their qualities contained an unmistakable undertone of equally genuine pride in their manufacture; rather, we wish to highlight the fact that the "veneration of the object" has inherent limitations.

While offering a coherent design principle for messages about the relationships between persons and things, and while celebrating enthusiastically the technological innovations of the day, the focus on the object was a backward-looking practice in many respects and thus an inadequate medium for the newly emerging consumer society. The uses with which products were largely associated originated in traditional patterns of activity, artisanal values, and established stereotypes for personal roles. The messages about the new products extolled their capacity for helping people do better and more quickly the tasks they were accustomed to doing. By and large, they did not seek to upset the culturally grounded interpretations (for example, sex-role distinctions) either for familiar undertakings or for the types of objects ordinarily associated with them. This severely limited the scope of the consumer market with respect not only to the range of goods supplied, but more importantly to the far richer range of meanings that could be attached to goods once traditional roles and activity patterns were challenged.

Phase Two: Iconology

Icons are symbols, and between 1925 and 1945—the initial phase of the consumer society—the utilitarian aspects of goods were increasingly subordinated to a network of abstract, or symbolic, qualities and values. The masks for goods were no longer copied directly from the manifest appearances of product characteristics or from allegations about pressing personal needs. This marked the transition point at which the earlier denotative discourse, reflecting the quite specific attributions of qualities to things, became subordinated to a far more expansive connotative discourse, rooted in suggestion, metaphor, analogy, and inference.

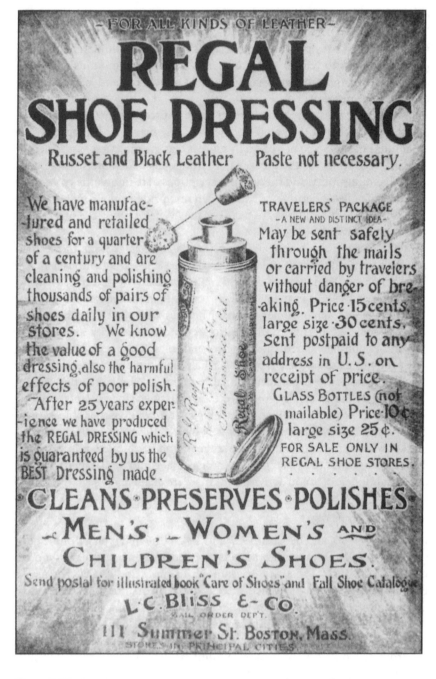

Figure 6.26 The industrial system's newly discovered sense of power was manifested in a strong tone of veneration of the product.

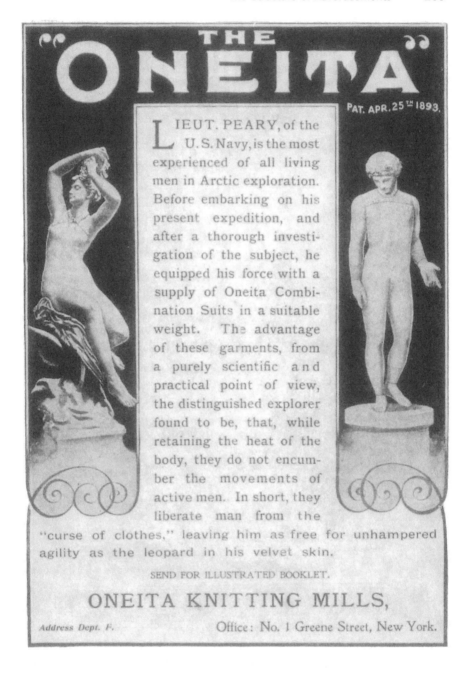

Figure 6.27   The overt selling strategy was rational because its discourse was saturated with descriptive narratives about products and their many qualities.

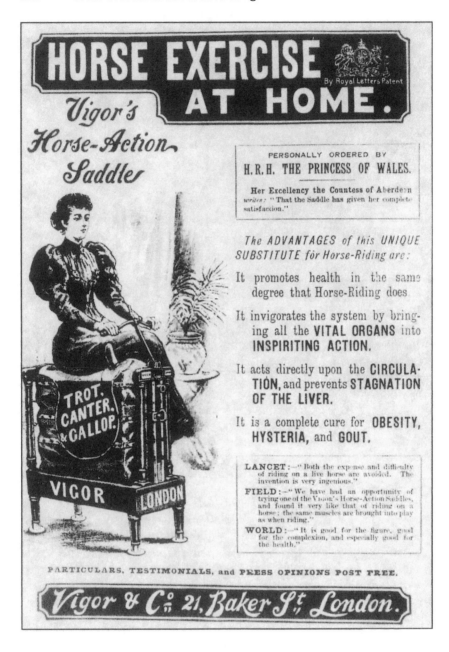

Figure 6.28 Advertising manifested a quasi-logical discourse that systematically confused real and imaginary claims.

In the iconistic phase, the focal point swung away from the object as an independent entity and toward the person as the intended user, but the process stopped halfway. Although the qualities of goods referred to in advertisements were generally cast in more abstract and suggestive terms, these qualities were still bound tightly to the things themselves: automobiles were expressions of a modern outlook, soaps of family integrity and caring, shoes of sobriety or status. (This theme is epitomized in the mode of representation that we have named "white magic," wherein the product appears to capture or control some potent but largely unspecified force of nature.) On the other hand, the persons who appeared in ads were not yet autonomous individuals; they were often mere exemplars of reigning social values carrying the burden of society's commitment to family structure, status differentiation, and hierarchical authority.

Iconology was a system of meanings, not a representation of feelings. Its inherent limitation was that the reigning social values that were supposed to link the attributes of things (freshness, goodness) with the interests of persons as consumers were too domineering and overwhelmed all other elements in the message format, causing both products and persons to appear "frozen" in space and time. The advertisement's communicative power was checked and held in equilibrium, hovering uncertainly between the poles of person and product.

Phase Three: Narcissism

Whatever its ultimate shortcomings, the iconic era opened the way toward cultural frames for goods that were more satisfactory in the consumer society. As the focal point shifted closer to the person, it brought emotion, which had been absent earlier, clearly into view. To make the discourse through and about objects truly come alive required greater psychological depth in the portrayal of the person, the creation of a domain where the meaning of things could resonate in response to an individual's changing emotional states. Having been admitted to the innermost recesses of the psyche, the product reciprocated by placing its powers at the individual's disposal. In the narcissistic phase (from about 1945 to 1965), consumers were encouraged to consider what the product could do for them, personally and selfishly. A prominent theme in advertisements in this phase is images of control over other people's judgments exerted with the product's assistance; we have labeled this "black magic."

During this period, objects were released from bondage to authoritative symbols. For the first time in the consumer society, things entered the sphere of ordinary human experience, and the means of entry was the metaphor of

Figure 6.29 Utilitarian aspects were subordinated to symbolic qualities and values.

Figure 6.30 The persons who appeared in ads were mere exemplars of reigning social values.

Figure 6.31 Products and persons were abstract, appearing "frozen" in space and time.

"personality." The most striking example is what has been called the "mirror ad," wherein the human face (almost always a woman's face) dominates the scene and stares out from the medium at the viewer-consumer. Like the product-symbol ad of the preceding era, this format too has a domineering tone; the difference is that this tone is carried not by abstract values but by the authoritative gaze of the human persona. (The literal meaning of the word "persona" is "actor's mask.") Despite the fact that the model in the ads is stylized, rather distant, not easily recognized as a "real" person—appearing as a kind of "imaginary other"—there is enough emotional force in the gaze to create a bond of identification between the viewer and the ad persona.

Persons were shown in social interactions as well. Romance was for the 1950s an effective way of communicating suggestions about erotic relationships without giving too much offense; images of warm family relationships were also prominent. Products seemed to bask in the glow of interpersonal attachments, as it were, showing for the first time in a market-oriented system that objects not only carried cues for public behavior, but also were fitting and proper as guides in the interior regions of individual psychology.

The personalization format, too, had its own limitation, but one that was easily overcome. The range of imagery used for displaying the product in relation to interpersonal dynamics was too narrow, too conventional. But meanwhile industrial society had been changing rapidly; steadily rising real incomes during this phase opened the way to the far freer experimentation with "styles" of life and consumption that was to become a hallmark of the succeeding period.

Phase Four: Totemism

In primitive societies, totems are representations of animals or other natural objects identified with a particular subgroup, such as a clan. Totemic artifacts as a whole constitute a code, that is, a system of social meanings. The things represented as totems are thought to stand in some intrinsic relation to each other, and, as emblems for interrelationships, they can be read for what they signify about social interactions among those who are divided by and grouped under them.

Marshall Sahlins has applied the concept of totemism to contemporary society. Traditional totemism constructs a "vast and dynamic scheme of thought" by its "systematic arrangement of meaningful differences" in representations of natural objects. The market-industrial society seeks to do something similar using manufactured goods: "The goods stand as an object code for the signification and valuation of persons and occasions, functions, and situations"

Figure 6.32 Released from the bondage of symbols, things entered more intimately into the spheres of ordinary human experience.

(Sahlins 1976, 178). Earlier in this chapter, we illustrated this point with examples of how choices among types of clothing and food are made.

During the present totemistic phase, the identifying features of the three preceding periods are recalled and synthesized. The product-related images are gradually freed from serving only the narrowly utilitarian qualities of the thing itself (idolatry), abstract and authoritative symbols (iconology), or a too restrictive array of interpersonal relations (narcissism). Here utility, symbolism, and personalization are mixed and remixed under the sign of the group. Consumption is meant to be a spectacle, a public enterprise. Product-related images fulfill their totemic potential in becoming emblems for social collectivities, principally by means of their associations with lifestyles.

Lifestyle patterns, like the older "totemic operators," incorporate social differentiation and testify to the existence of subgroups through symbolic displays. Today's totems (product images) themselves are the badges of group membership, which also entails self-administered codes of authority for dress, appearance, popular entertainment, customary places of assembly, behavior rituals, and role stereotyping (for example, "macho" versus "non-macho" subgroups).

With this fourth stage in the sequence of cultural frames for goods, we are able to pull together the principal strands of argument from earlier chapters. Earlier we tracked issues about the formation of the sense of satisfaction and well-being in the consumer society, and arrived by diverse paths at the concept of lifestyle; however, our discussion remained largely at the level of general notions, such as relative standing. We noted that the concept of lifestyle had begun to play a prominent role in marketing and advertising forums.

The present chapter led us to the same place by far different routes. Here we paid close attention to the tangible features in the landscape of the consumer society, namely, goods themselves. The masks they now wear, reflecting design techniques perfected over almost a century of marketing/advertising strategies, bear the emblems of ever-shifting lifestyle patterns. The existence of such patterns means that there is a wonderfully orchestrated play of social behavior oriented around consumption practices today—our masked ball. Given its prominence in our lives, we should concern ourselves with how the spectacle is staged.

We may think of marketing as the host, and advertising as the master of ceremonies and conductor. Their staging for the spectacle of consumption often is brilliant, so much so that it can distract us from our duty to ensure that we do not sacrifice or neglect other important values and goals just because we have become enraptured by the dance.

Figure 6.33 Tone was sometimes carried through a persona—stylized, rather distant-appearing as a kind of "imaginary other."
Source: Courtesy of Crane Canada Ltd.

Figure 6.33   Continued.

Figure 6.34 The meaning of things could resonate in response to an individual's changing emotional state.

Figure 6.35 Objects secretly promise mystical powers of control and enchantment.

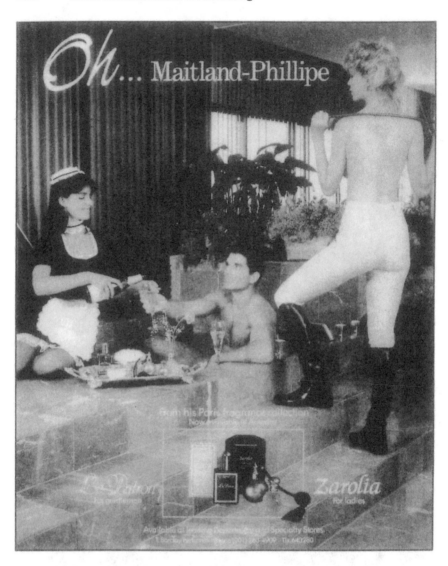

Figure 6.36 Things must be read for what they signify about social interactions among those who are divided by and grouped under them.

Figure 6.37 Utility, symbolism, and personalization mix. Consumption is a public spectacle as product images fulfill their totemic potential by means of their association with lifestyles.

Figure 6.38 Totemic distinctions can be conveyed through the abstracted stylizations associated with patterns of modern life.

CHAPTER 7

Goods as Communicators and Satisfiers

- Think up the object according to its image, not to its function
- Render the reading of function ambiguous
- Tend toward a contradictory image: both HARD AND SOFT
- Put dissimilar parts together
- Introduce an unexpected element (give a feeling of suspense)
- Make calm, poetic, introverted, mildly self-mocking objects
- Think of objects that are always different from each other (differentiated series)
- Give products mixed craft and computer-world characteristics

("Rules of Design," Domus Design Magazine, 1984)

Image and Metaphor

At first glance, what appears to distinguish the economies of modern, Western, industrialized countries from others is the sheer number and variety of products. While this provides a convenient yardstick for those who like to measure the superiority of our standard of living by counting telephones, toilets, and television sets, another great difference, no less dramatic in scale, often goes unnoticed—the layers of images and symbols that surround us relating these products to our personal happiness and social success. Just because it fits so snugly and comfortably, our thick cloak of symbols seems to be a natural part of our being. The consumer society constructed this field of symbols and implanted it at the center of marketplace activity, causing a profound transformation in social life. The nature of this transformation, the change in the social function of goods from being primarily satisfiers of wants to being primarily communicators of meanings, will be explored in this and the succeeding chapter.

Three forces are largely responsible: (1) the recognition of consumption as a legitimate sphere for individual self-realization; (2) the discovery by marketers and advertisers that the personal or psychological and interpersonal (or social) domains of the consumer, rather than the characteristics of goods, were the vital core of merchandising; (3) the revolutions in communications and mass-media technologies that made possible the rapid evolution of advertising formats, including the special significance of visual or iconic imagery.

225

Such developments became united in a social process that can be summarized in the following propositions. First, individuals should expect to achieve a significant measure of personal happiness and evidence of social success as a result of their involvement in consumption. Second, messages about achieving happiness and success will use "open-ended interpretive codes"—social cues for indicating to people how to decide what is socially acceptable at any given time, which do not rely on fixed or traditional cultural norms but rather encourage experimentation in achieving satisfaction. Third, the ability to transmit live visual representations of group action into domains of private life (especially the home) will offer guidance to people on how to integrate these particular commercial messages about goods into general patterns of behavior.

These three propositions, in turn, are bound together by a single underlying theme: The most important feature of consumption activity is the *interpretation* of what "satisfaction" means in the lives of individuals. In the present chapter, we follow up the discussion of advertising formats in chapter 6 in order to see how advertisers have integrated the psychological or subjective dimension into their portrayals of products. We seek to show that this innovation is rooted firmly in the understanding that, in the consumer marketplace, one's sense of satisfaction and well-being is based not on accumulated possessions but on subjective, shifting estimates of where one stands in relation to others and what values are most important.

Before turning to the structure of imagery in advertising, let us say a few words about the key terms used throughout this examination, namely image, icon, and symbol. *Image* (the root of the word "imagination") is the richest of the three, meaning either a verbal or visible representation, especially of a vivid or graphic character, suggestive of some thing, idea, or concept. Thus, imagery may be verbal—as it is most powerfully in poetry—or pictorial in nature. Modern advertising, of course, frequently utilizes pictorial and verbal forms simultaneously, and when we discuss the imagistic mode of communication in advertising, we are referring to printed messages or electronically transmitted audio and visual signals with both a verbal and a pictorial element.

Icon is interchangeable with the pictorial aspects of image; in common use it means a picture of a venerated figure in a religious setting. We use it to refer to pictorial representations of those secular values that have a special place or high status in our culture ("mother" and "father" in older times, "being modern" and "being cool" today). Thus, the iconic mode of communication refers to ads wherein the pictorial or visual element is clearly predominant in the message as a whole, incorporating only a few words of written or spoken text in association with dramatic visual imagery.

By its very nature, verbal imagery is discursive while visual imagery is non-discursive. Implicit in the former is an argument or a case for the association of the image with what it refers to, so that one could, if asked, spell out the relationship in a more extensive written text. In visual imagery, there is often an abrupt "imaginative leap" and a freer play of associations that is difficult to put into words. This is not a hard-and-fast rule, however, and many exceptions can be noted.

A *symbol* is a visible sign of something that is itself not apparent to the senses—it "stands for" something else. It invites comparison between the representation (the sign) and what it stands for. For example, an animal used as a brand symbol for a certain automobile model sets up a field of mental associations and possible analogies between the characteristics of the animal (both real and mythic) and those of the automobile (both physical and imputed).

Although symbolism can be expressed in verbal as well as iconic forms, modern advertising has strongly favored the iconic. Among the reasons for this is that successful verbal imagery requires a reasonable degree of language skill in the reader or listener and a high level of attentiveness to subtleties in the message. But readers scan advertisements quickly and are therefore likely to miss sophisticated plays with words. Verbal imagery may thus be employed advantageously in short slogans, but in longer texts the result is unlikely to repay the creative effort. Also, the newer communications media—improved photography, film, and television—overwhelmingly favored the iconic; radio, of course, is the exception, but even it contributed to the general trend by lessening the share of popular attention enjoyed by print media and by emphasizing brief, pithy slogans in its advertising style.

We suggested in chapter 2 that the consumer society arises out of the ashes of traditional cultures, which are characterized by relatively fixed forms for the satisfaction of needs, and unleashes a grand experimentation with the individual's experience of both needs and the ways of satisfying them. The consumer society does not set up its own fixed models of behavior to replace traditional ones but rather constructs, through marketing and advertising, successive waves of associations between persons, products, and images of well-being in an endless series of suggestions about the possible routes to happiness and success.

Marketing is so fascinated with the communicative tools of symbol, image, and icon because they are ideal for such constructions. They work by allusion, free association, suggestion, and analogy rather than by literal and logical rule. One possible interpretive scheme or specific instance of a correspondence between a product, a setting, and a type of person does not exclude another, or indeed many others. And this is the precise intention: that the whole ensemble of goods and messages should be as versatile as possible, should appeal simultaneously to the entire spectrum of personality types and lawful urges, including those half-formed, inarticulate yearnings that individuals can be brought to recognize and express only through the very play of such images.

As the message structures in ads become more subtle, a variety of techniques connect the various dimensions—text, visuals, slogan or headline, and, ideally, ad design itself—without calling attention to the "connective" techniques. Pollay and Mainprize (1984) have described some of these techniques, for example, presenting "puzzles" that require viewers or readers themselves to "construct the message and constitute the selling proposition." They also demonstrate how metaphor works in the composition of advertisements by putting people, activities, and scenes side by side with products and seeking to convert this contiguity into a meaningful relationship.

Paul Ricoeur (1977, 7) writes that "metaphor is the rhetorical process by which discourse unleashes the power that certain fictions have to redescribe reality." We would modify this superb statement only by emphasizing that the term "discourse" should refer to both verbal and pictorial communicative modes. Advertisements certainly are fictions, that is, imaginative creations or artful representations of possible worlds, and they strive mightily to redescribe reality, by taking familiar components of everyday life—recognizable people, indoor and outdoor settings, and social situations—and conjuring up scene after scene full of hypothetical interactions between these components and a product.

A double symbolic process is at work in the consumer society. One facet of this process is the symbolism consciously employed by businesses in the manufacture and sale of products, including the imagery used in advertising. Especially since the advent of market segmentation, marketers have through demographic statistics some prior idea of the target audience for their messages, and know that a well-conceived sales campaign drawing upon an almost unlimited stock of traditional and innovative imagery can elicit new wants and consumption styles. The other facet is the symbolic associations selectively employed by consumers in admitting new wants and in constructing new lifestyles. Up to 80 percent of new products introduced into the marketplace fail to reach their profit objectives, with a high proportion of these then being withdrawn from the market—a pointed lesson not only for entrepreneurs, but also for social commentators who agonize over the "manipulation" of popular consciousness by advertisers. One should not underestimate the elementary common sense of the general population, just as one should not underestimate the degree to which individuals are dependent upon social cues for guidance in how to consume things.

The Icons of the Marketplace

Goods in the marketplace today appear cloaked in layers of symbols and images conveyed by many means, including product design, packaging, store displays, fashion-trend changes, peer-group pressures, and media-based advertising. Sometimes the schemas of association are complex and exquisitely composed, so that the idea of an intended "message" is simply irrelevant. Around 1985, a window display at Tiffany's in New York mounted a scene of urban decay in which two mannequins—a male Bowery bum and a tattered bag lady—were posed as the setting for a $50,000 gold-and-diamond necklace, which was placed at the bag lady's feet. In this case, the window display, through the incongruity of its elements, calls attention to itself by reversing our normal associational fields.

Goods appear as mere receptacles for the generalized play of meanings, as "fields" for human states of feeling that are projected onto the physical and sensual substance of the object. The goods themselves almost seem to be mirrors that reflect back to us the blurry and fleeting set of images cast over them.

"Modern goods are recognized as psychological things, as symbolic of personal attributes and goals, as symbolic of social patterns and strivings. In this sense, all commercial objects have a symbolic character..." (Levy 1969, 410). On the immediate level, the introduction of symbolism in presenting goods helped to influence specific consumer choices. On a deeper level, another process was at work. Paradoxically, when utility is rooted in the product's own characteristics satisfaction, too, is circumscribed since it is derived from allowing the product to carry out functions for which it was designed. When use is rooted in the consumer's psychological state, however, anything goes, for then something is useful only insofar as and so long as one believes this to be the case. But belief in the modern world is a flimsy affair, readily convertible as newer promises circulate. As goods are enveloped in symbols, the requirement to enlarge the scope and intensity of the total commercial effort in everyday life accompanies this transition in focal point from the object to the person.

The marketers' designs are not acts of unaided imagination. A considerable amount of consumer research established the importance of the symbolic attributes of goods in purchasing choices, both in general and with respect to specific frames of reference such as status, gender, and social class. Marketers seek to base the product image on a prior analysis of the interpretive predilections of the target audience. They may construct the image either for mass markets by using open codes of interpretation (symbols recognized by the average person everywhere), or for specific subgroups (such as teenagers) by using restricted codes.

Since consumption is, in part, a form of popular entertainment, the play of symbols in advertising generally is confined to the more superficial levels of psychological processes. But the price of superficiality is that the attention-getting power of most pitches decays rapidly and the turnover time gets shorter and shorter. Visual imagery is inherently better equipped than verbal expression—especially where vocabulary cannot be allowed to become too extensive or concept too subtle—to map and explore the surface features of changing events and to relate them quite arbitrarily to products through analogy and association, the potent inferential capacities of metaphor.

What results is a situation in which people are surrounded by things that are themselves "alive." The intensely personalized focus of the message and the incorporation of references to social settings and events provide the backdrop for the advertiser's imaginative task, which is to design the "package of stimuli so that it resonates with information already stored within an individual, and thereby induces the desired learning or behavioral effect" (Schwartz 1974, 24). Such information is not, except incidentally, the economist's information, which is composed of the product's characteristics, but rather the imagistic associations between the product and what is known about individuals and their expectations in life, including their feelings about status, peer-group influence, roles, social mobility, and changing lifestyles. This resonance between persons and things circulates freely through all of society's information channels, both interpersonal and institutional, including, of course, the mass media. In this context, the realm of needing becomes immersed within the domain of communication. As a result, goods play a distinctive role in the human dialogue.

Considered as repositories of stored information in the broader sense, goods are an important means whereby consumers can communicate to others their relationships to complex sets of otherwise abstract social attributes (such as status), thus identifying themselves within social structures. This is the most general significance the "transformational" mode in marketing and advertising. The most important function of product-related imagery is not to increase levels of consumer spending, but to transform the personal meaning of the everyday use of products as a whole.

"Corporate image"—and, at least in some countries, "national image"—advertising has become increasingly prominent in recent years, doubtless trading on the success of the product-image ad. Quasi-political messages promulgate the self-proclaimed qualities of the business or government entity itself, or its reflections on what is happening in society and politics. The major oil companies have spent considerable amounts of time and money on corporate-image advertising since 1973. Nationwide department-store chains have engaged in highly stylized "generic" campaigns, in part to protect their market share against invasion by specialized boutiques trading on the wave of market segmentation. Imagistic advertising is now also used by governments with broad political purposes in mind. Governments routinely use media advertising to promote "government policy," which is widely regarded as a poorly disguised exercise in self-promotion for the party in power.

Having discussed the growing preponderance of imagistic modes of communication in advertising that favor visual over verbal forms of expression, and having looked at some actual types, we wish to explore the special importance of iconic representation in presenting product-related imagery. Iconic representation, used alone or in conjunction with verbal text, is far more effective than text alone. Relative costs for advertising time and space reflect not only the potential reach of the mass media in the marketplace (the size and demographic features of the audience), but also the potential effectiveness of communications through these media in influencing consumption patterns. Among the various media, magazines and television emerged as prestige advertising vehicles because they are well-suited for transmitting both verbal and pictorial information. The intuitive understanding by advertisers that these two forms of communication could be highly effective was corroborated by findings reported in the psychological literature on the way people process information.

Given the highly selective way persons are known to survey their environments, it is the task of advertisements to break through the barriers to attention that people normally build. Design, layout, contrast, color, striking and unusual imagery have all been shown to increase the likelihood and duration of visual scanning. Television has the special advantage of combining the dimensions of sound and picture together with movement and editing techniques to secure and enhance attention. Furthermore, research shows that iconic representation has a relatively greater impact on the "affective-opinion" components of attitude, that is, those aspects related to making decisions (Kline 1977). Iconic representation can be absorbed in a sort of "parallel process" without full conscious awareness, and thus it can register an impact without being translated into explicit verbal formulations.

Above and beyond the concern with attitudinal barriers, the advertiser's objective is to clearly differentiate its product's image from others by soldering the associational links between brand and image as fully as possible. The ad's impact, of course, will depend upon the degree of retention of these particular associations by the audience. When a visual image is used as a "memory peg" for the message, a person's retention of the ideas associated with the visual is significantly higher than it is if the verbal information is presented alone (Segall 1971; Sheehan 1972). A catchy tune or jingle has been employed as a memory peg for many years, but it appears that a visual image works even better.

Several other processes are also worth noting here. First, unusual or absurd images seem to enhance retention. Second, joining otherwise separate elements in a visual presentation appears to be advantageous; a complex of attributes is more easily recognized and remembered than a single one. Third, pictures elicit a greater number of free associations than do words.

The implications are obvious. Not only does visual imagery increase the attention paid to an ad, but it also can build strong associational links to a greater number of qualities, while at the same time retaining a high degree of ambiguity. The ambiguity that can be supported by visual imagery is significant, both for the ease with which symbolic qualities can be dispersed over a

wide variety of product categories and types, and for the resultant indetermi-
nancy of the associations. "Convenience" can be combined symbolically with
images of "gourmet skill" for foods, "neatness" for household cleansers, and
"casual lifestyle" for clothing. The openness of the product image to varying
permutations and interpretations means that both advertisers and consumers
can experiment freely with the meanings—which may be constructed differently by each, to be sure—in a particular ad campaign.

The consumer culture grants both marketers and shoppers wide latitude
for such experimentation. The general tendency has been an almost uniform
expansion of the boundaries of permissible symbolic reference. There are still
forbidden zones established by legislation (restrictions on tobacco and alcohol
ads), social taboos (forms of sexual expression), "good taste" (governed by industry codes), and unsuitable themes (those that are intrinsically inappropriate for selling goods, such as prejudice). Still, the borders of these zones are
being scouted constantly for new material (as Tiffany's did with its bag lady
image), and the prevailing rules are tested regularly by indirect or oblique references to currently prohibited images. Advertising's special love of humor
comes in handy here, since humor defuses tension and serious disagreement;
the waters can be tested, so to speak, by humorous or allegorical treatments
when "straight" depictions would not do. A slightly ominous Russian com-
missar in a vodka ad, it is hoped, will add some allure to what is otherwise
just another colorless liquid distilled from ordinary grain at a factory in the
suburbs.

Thus, we take for granted the existence of an "image pool," without being
able to specify how capacious it is or how varied are the entities it holds. From
it, the advertiser must fish out something that will differentiate one brand from
other products in the same use-type or the same subgroup of a use-type (such
as a specific "class" of automobiles). Shampoos will be distinguished from con-
ditioners, and Shampoo X-1 will be associated with "luxuriant beauty," X-2
with "youth and excitement," X-3 with "the natural look," and so forth. The
effect is a broad range of divergent qualities associated with a certain product
use-type. Uncertainty, defined as the range of possible alternative associations
for a single product type, becomes a feature of the product image (as opposed
to the brand image).

There are three key characteristics of the image pool. The first and most
important is that it *redescribes reality*, stemming from its basic function in
the service of marketing: the selling of well-being and happiness through the
selling of goods. Since this is accomplished by selecting scenes from everyday
life, the social reality in which we actually live is systematically redescribed
to provide a suitable canvas on which the advertiser can work. This canvas
is the basic level of redescription; on it is sketched a higher level, created by
the nature of advertising's predominant communicative mode—metaphorical

expression—wherein occurs the free play of associations drawn from the common image pool. The basic level is a function of advertising's commercial nature; the expressive aspect (the higher level) is not determined in detail by commercial considerations. The second element is *ambiguity*, which arises in the shift in emphasis from textual to pictorial information, the carefully constructed indeterminacy of the advertisement's open codes of interpretation, and the abstract quality of the product's symbolic attributes. The third is what we might call *fluidity*. Given the sheer number and variety of imagistic plays, we have no simple or straightforward paradigms for finally arriving at contentment or well-being. All that is certain is that new shows will be mounted, and that they will be preoccupied with involving our psychological energies in the theater of consumption.

People must interpret both their needs and their experiences within the context of this elaborate and subtle message system. We can assume that they encounter much frustration and some anxiety in all this, but we also know that people find enjoyment in the stimulation of their desires by marketing techniques. There is a strong affinity between modern advertising's communicative modes and the social framework for the personal experience of satisfaction and well-being in a consumer culture. It is just this affinity that gives advertising its broad cultural and social significance.

Earlier in the chapter, we suggested that the predominant communicative forms in advertising—symbol, icon, and image, all unified in metaphorical expression—were oriented toward a single mode in human thinking and sensitivity: comparative judgment. Now we shall turn from individual to social judgment, that is, to how persons in social interactions form opinions about their economic well-being and "success," and how goods fulfill their role as "satisfiers" in this process; there, too, comparative judgment is the very heart of the matter.

Relative Standing

We have seen that in the consumer society the consumer, not the product, is the core of the message system about the sphere of consumption. Not the consumer as isolated individual, however; the act of consumption is always a social process. In selecting, using, and enjoying things, people look around to find out what others are doing. We can call this need for individuals to relate their tastes and choices to those of others the "intersubjective" aspect of consumption activity. It is bound up with a more general behavioral pattern that appears to be deeply rooted in the human personality—namely, the concern with "relative standing," the continual scanning of the social landscape to ascertain how others are doing and to compare one's own condition with theirs.

Traditional cultures established quite firm guidelines for intersubjective comparisons, presenting a limited set of role and behavioral models to guide tastes. The consumer society abolishes all such limits and creates an "open set" of intersubjective comparisons; advertising is one of the most important vehicles for presenting, suggesting, and reflecting an unending series of possible comparative judgments.

A famous study of the processes of social comparisons is Thorstein Veblen's *The Theory of the Leisure Class*, first published in 1899. Veblen writes: "With the exception of the instinct of self-preservation, the propensity for emulation is probably the strongest and most alert and persistent of the economic motives proper." Ownership of possessions—and the more the better—is commonly regarded as the basis for the drive to succeed, but Veblen contends that this view is superficial. It is not so much what one has as the relationship between what one has and what others (the more successful) have that is most relevant: "The motive that lies at the root of ownership is emulation. . . . The possession of wealth confers honor; it is an invidious distinction."

The fact that, in a developed market economy, all specific forms of wealth can be represented by a single standard—money, or what Veblen calls "the pecuniary standard"—dictates how the propensity for emulation is expressed in modern society. All tangible forms of wealth (grand houses, yachts, servants) are merely momentary signs of relative success and do not have any lasting significance. Unlike traditional societies where forms of wealth and social success, like the forms of satisfaction, tend to remain the same over long periods, a market society undermines fixed standards. Competition for social honor is freer, but victory is fleeting, since the criteria for success are always subject to redefinition.

An individual's striving for a permanent place of distinction is like the pursuit of a mirage across the desert. The horizon of social honor recedes as one approaches it:

> But as fast as a person makes new acquisitions, and becomes accustomed to the resulting new standard of wealth, the new standard forthwith ceases to afford appreciably greater satisfaction than the earlier standard did. . . . So long as the comparison [with others] is distinctly unfavorable to himself the normal, average individual will live in chronic dissatisfaction with his present lot; and when he has reached what may be called the normal pecuniary standard of the community, or of his class in the community, this chronic dissatisfaction will give place to a restless striving to place a wider and everwidening pecuniary interval between himself and this average standard. (Veblen [1899] 1953, 38–39)

The need for conspicuous consumption is not confined to those at the higher income levels; its traces are found universally in the ordinary life patterns of almost everyone, excluding only the very poorest (who display it as soon as they cease to be very poor). And it does not refer only to luxury goods, for the drive to consume is embedded in the very search for satisfaction itself, including the acquisition of what are commonly referred to as the necessities of life. Virtually everything we use has what Veblen calls a "ceremonial character": While what we consume serves the physiological maintenance of life, even at the level of immediate needs, it also places us at some known point in the set of social interactions whereby persons are judged as being more or less "successful."

In *The Joyless Economy* (1976), Tibor Scitovsky took up these themes in discussing people's changing preferences in consumption patterns. He sees a reciprocal relationship between changing preferences and changes in the sense of satisfaction stemming from particular activities. The dominant economic theory in his view "overlooks the possibility that the same influences that modify our tastes might also modify our ability to derive satisfaction from the things that cater to our tastes."

Were we to assume that our tastes—the kinds of things we choose to spend our money on—remained constant throughout our lives and were unaffected by the social changes (such as the images of new lifestyles) occurring around us, then we would become progressively more contented if our real income increased and we could afford to acquire more and more of the things we desired. In fact, when asked to rate themselves in attitudinal surveys—as "very happy," "fairly happy," "or not very happy"—proportions of the population in each category changed very little between 1946 and 1970 despite the dramatic and steady rise in real incomes in Western nations after World War II (in the United States, average per capita real income rose by 62 percent between 1946 and 1970).

Why? Scitovsky sees four aspects to the answer. First, a significant proportion of the satisfaction in life that people experience is derived from status itself, that is, from the relative social rankings or interpersonal comparisons that are made at all income levels. Second, much satisfaction is derived from employment, but, once again, the degree of satisfaction is closely correlated to the income level and prestige of some jobs (especially the professions) as compared with others. Third, there is a strong correlation between satisfaction and genuine novelty; although we are accustomed to a steady stream of "new" goods, most of them are variations on the "collections of characteristics" that already exist, and, Scitovsky contends, the consumer society progressively reduces the amount of genuine novelty in our lives. Fourth, the admirable advantages in material comfort we have gained in the last generation—better housing, food, clothing, heating, and air conditioning—does not yield an enduring sense of satisfaction for us because comfort is like addiction: We quickly become accustomed to what is provided, take it for granted, and seek more; only when we are deprived of our customary gratifications do we even notice that we have them and are dependent on them. For example, those who grew up with outdoor toilets and at some point in their lives acquired indoor facilities appreciated the new comforts and valued them highly, whereas those who have had the indoor facilities all their lives regard them as nothing special. Central heating and air conditioning quickly become "normal" for indoor environments; most people are aware of them today only when the machinery breaks down.

Taken together, these four aspects of material progress "well explain why happiness should depend so much on one's ranking in society and so little on the absolute level of one's income" (Scitovsky 1976, 139). *In Social Limits to Growth* (1976), Fred Hirsch explores these themes further, arguing that a market economy produces two basic types of goods: those that provide for basic material necessities, and "positional goods." As the general wealth increases, the proportion of positional goods in total production becomes progressively larger.

Positional goods are the things that allow us to detect social status differences among individuals; their chief value lies in the fact that some persons have them and others do not. As we mentioned earlier, the valuations of things and activities are quite arbitrary. At one time, moving from central urban areas to the suburbs represented a positive status change for those who could afford it; at another, moving back from the suburbs to the center of the city allowed the status rewards to be garnered.

Timing, degree of selectivity, and appropriate reference groups are what create positional goods in a consumer society. When only a relatively few persons have access to goods that are generally desired, such as country estates, the status benefits to them and the "social distance" between them and the rest of the population are enormous. A rising level of general affluence means that more people can strive for these symbols of success, and a few new entrants will be admitted to the select circles. The marketplace, however, also responds by subtly debasing and reinterpreting the success symbols; suburban housing developments where a few large trees have been left standing for the publicity pictures will be marketed as "country estates that everyone can afford." Meanwhile, the social elite has conjured up a new set of restricted-access status symbols for itself.

Hirsch is concerned, however, that this elaborate charade, which is something like an animal chasing its tail, requires considerable amounts of material resources to sustain it. A good example is the relationship between employment opportunities and educational qualifications. When relatively few people finished high school and even fewer went to university, higher education was widely perceived as the gateway to the professional careers monopolized by the elite, since entry to such professions required university degrees. Responding to popular demand, governments created more universities and more opportunities for entry, and more people now hold advanced degrees. Yet there remains in society as a whole roughly the same proportion of elite positions as before. What happened was that the social significance of advanced university degrees was diluted, with many who hold such degrees now filling low-status occupations while educational requirements for occupations shifted upward across the board. Society responded to the demand for fairer access to elite positions through university education with a shell-game trick.

In different ways, Scitovsky and Hirsch are both concerned with a similar feature of a competitive, market-oriented society that has generally reached a level of material affluence—namely, the great importance placed on the symbolic attributes of goods and the myriad ways in which rank and status are attached to them. Goods are not scarce in an affluent society; but the *status attributes of goods* are socially created scarcities, as they always have been. Status or prestige is inherently scarce. There can never be enough for everyone because the whole point about attributes like prestige is that by their nature they must be distributed unevenly; only a few persons can be famous.

Traditional societies customarily solve the issue by assigning prestige arbitrarily to those who inherit certain bloodlines or who do well in certain well-established forms of competition. The consumer society, in contrast, recognizes an open-ended set of competitive situations, but its need for status differentiation is no less acute. Therefore, to keep alive the game of relative standing it must fashion new socially created scarcities at every turn, new symbols of success to be striven for. It matters not at all *what* is chosen to mark status differences. The important point is that in the consumer society there can be no end to the process.

Quality of Life

During the past twenty years, both single-item and multi-item scales have been used in extensive survey research on "subjective well-being" (Diener 1984, 542–75). For example, Dupuy's "General Well-Being Schedule" is a multi-item scale that seeks to assess seven different aspects: life satisfaction, health concerns, depressed mood, person-environment fit, coping, energy level, and stress.

Robert E. Lane (1978) looked at the findings of various studies to identify the most important elements in the composition of happiness: autonomy, or the feeling of having some control over the events affecting one's life; self-esteem, or the feeling of being respected for one's personal qualities; friendships; warm family relationships; and sufficient leisure time that is insulated from tension and stress. Other studies have grouped the elements of satisfaction into "social values" (love, family, friendships) and "material values" (economic security, success), reporting that the former outrank the latter by considerable margins. Certainly, no one claims that interpersonal factors are or can be the sole determinants of happiness; and it is also the case that, in our society, marketplace transactions and material values contribute a great deal to the life-satisfaction of many persons. Neither aspect should be ignored. The fascinating question is how they interact.

Norman Bradburn's (1969) investigation of national norms for mental health in the United States through periodic national surveys led to his interest in more general aspects of happiness and well-being. In his view of the psychology of well-being, two independent dimensions, one of "positive" feelings and one of "negative" feelings, react independently. In other words, most of us are at the same time satisfied by some aspects of our lives and dissatisfied by others; the two domains exist side by side, without balancing or canceling each other out. Although the hypothesis is still controversial, subsequent research has added considerable support to it, as well as further refinements to the measures used in the surveys (Diener 1984, 547–49). It also appears to fit well with our own basic concept of the "fragmentation" that occurs in both the expressions of needs and the forms of satisfaction in a consumer society. Out of the attempt to match the dissociated "bits" of needs and satisfactions arise two parallel and disconnected series of feelings, one generally characterized by content and the other by discontent.

One of the earliest cross-national studies to use a self-evaluation approach was Hadley Cantril's *The Patterns of Human Concerns* (1965). Cantril developed a single-item "self-anchoring striving scale" and individuals were asked to define, on the basis of their own assumptions, perceptions, goals, and values, where they believed they stood in relation to the two extreme points on the scale, which represented the "best possible" and the "worst possible" conditions of life. This study presents data from thirteen nations, including both rich and poor in terms of material conditions, and concludes that in all societies the sense of well-being is most strongly correlated with one's place in relation to the expectations generated by the social norms of the culture in which one lives.

Richard Easterlin (1974) re-analyzed Bradburn's and Cantril's data with a specific issue in mind: What can we conclude about the relation between income and happiness? In almost every case studied, and notwithstanding marked differences among types of societies, there is a very strong correlation between relative income and happiness within a particular country at a particular time. In other words, those with more income are, according to their own reports, more satisfied than those with less. But this correlation does not hold over a period of time in that increases (no matter how large or over what period) in real incomes spread throughout a population do not cause any greater proportion of that population to report themselves as being happier than they were earlier. Comparisons among countries also show a poor correlation between income and happiness in that no significantly higher proportion of people report themselves as being happy in countries with a relatively high material standard of living than in those with a lower standard. "In judging their happiness, people tend to compare their actual situation with a reference standard or norm, derived from their prior and ongoing social experience.... Over time, however, as economic conditions advance, so too does the social norm, since this is formed by the changing economic socialization experience of people'" (Easterlin 1974, 118–19). The horizon of satisfaction is a moving line, as Thorstein Veblen suggested long ago. Contentment is not measured by what one has, but by the ratio between what one has and what one thinks one ought to have in order to maintain self-esteem in the face of the normal consumption standards accepted by one's peers.

These cross-national and cross-cultural studies lend support to our premise of the strong interdependence among individuals in forming the sense of life-satisfaction associated with consumption behavior. Whereas anthropological researches on primitive human societies had shown us just how important this interdependence was, its significance in modern society has long been downplayed, especially in economic theory.

Finally, some of the research in this area has a direct bearing on the factor we have isolated as the heart of advertising's preoccupation with metaphorical expression, namely, comparative judgment: "A number of theories postulate that happiness results from a comparison between some standard and actual conditions." Such comparisons may occur either consciously or unconsciously, and the standard may be represented by one's contemporaries, one's past life, or one's aspirations. "Social comparison was the strongest predictor of satisfaction in most domains" (Diener 1984, 566–67).

Consumers in a developed market society are not left to wander alone and unaided amid heaps of goods, computing and recomputing to some decimal place the most advantageous fit between their yearnings and their purses. They do not—nor do they wish to—form their tastes and preferences in the private bliss of ratiocination and then descend upon innocent merchants to scrutinize their shelves with cold and wary eyes. Except when (as is too often the case even today) groups are pressed hard against the limit of deprivation by exploitation or an inhospitable environment, consuming is an elaborate social game, as it has always been in human cultures.

Lifestyles

In the late 1960s, sociologists started to write about "taste cultures," subgroups within a larger social setting formed by some well-defined features of their preferences as consumers. This was, in part, a reaction against the theory that modern industrial societies and the mass media of communication within them were responsible for creating "mass culture," a bland uniformity of popular taste that inevitably reduced all cultural domains (music, film, plastic arts, and so forth) to a lowest common denominator of quality. That theory is unfounded; although many of the attractive elements in traditional popular cultures had indeed been eroded, new syntheses continue to arise whereby different segments in the population affirm their commitment to distinctiveness and quality in contemporary popular culture.

In the 1970s, other sociologists developed a more wide-ranging theory—that of "cultural class" (Peterson and DiMaggio 1975; Lewis 1977). A cultural class is simply a component group within a modern society that has a "shared pattern of consumption." "Memberships" in cultural classes are voluntary and discretionary, based only on free choices made in everyday situations, and members may switch their allegiances from one class to another at any time. Taste cultures and cultural class are well illustrated in the phenomenon of popular music.

These new concepts were combined with ideas growing out of personality theory and attitude/opinion research, and given a more systematic expression in the notion of "lifestyles." Research teams based in advertising agencies, universities, and institutes created a series of "cluster analyses" to identify consumer typologies and to characterize different patterns of tastes and buying behavior. Potential consumer markets are stratified according to a number of characteristics: (1) demographic—age, sex, income; (2) geographic—region, urban, rural; (3) psychographic—personality traits; (4) type of preferred benefit—taste, feel; (5) volume —heavy versus light user. Marketers then combine this sophisticated approach to market segmentation with product differentiation, and product positioning and repositioning, in order to fit their product type and characteristics, and its relation to competing products, as closely as possible with the nature of the target market (McDaniel 1982, ch. 4). Various industries have adapted these general typologies to highly specific marketing domains, such as eating out, grocery shopping, and entertainment.

Among the more general studies, the one by Arnold Mitchell and his colleagues, sponsored by SRI International (formerly the Stanford Research Institute) and reported in Mitchell's *The Nine American Lifestyles* (1983), is perhaps the best known. They used the term "lifestyle" to describe "a unique way of life defined by its distinctive array of values, drives, beliefs, needs, dreams, and special points of view." They were looking for a scheme that would encompass individual, social, and marketplace dimensions of life, and that would be successful in predicting how a change in one dimension would affect the others, and also how the size and composition of social groups would change over time. To do this, they devised what they called the "VALS" (values and lifestyles) typology and arrived at a scheme made up of nine identifiable lifestyles (Mitchell 1983, 4).

Need-Driven Groups (11%)
Survivor lifestyle (4%)
Sustainer lifestyle (7%)
Outer-Directed Groups (67%)

Belonger lifestyle (35%)
Emulator lifestyle (10%)
Achiever lifestyle (22%)
Inner-Directed Groups (20%)
I-Am-Me lifestyle (5%)
Experiential lifestyle (7%)
Societally conscious lifestyle (8%)
Combined Outer- and Inner-Directed Group Integrated lifestyle (2%)

The figures in parentheses give the proportion of the adult population in the United States that, it is claimed, falls into each of these categories on the basis of the responses to the survey questionnaire completed by respondents in 1980. A rudimentary application of the typology was also made for France, Italy, Sweden, the United Kingdom, and West Germany.

The nature of each lifestyle is, for our purposes, sufficiently indicated by its name. As Mitchell indicates, the scheme combines elements from familiar conceptions of need- or drive-hierarchies (the most famous of which is Abraham Maslow's, 1987) and David Riesman's (1950) inner/outer-directed distinction. Its most challenging feature is that it attempts to describe both actual social groupings and a hierarchy of stages in personal self-development that culminates in psychological maturity. Except for those literally trapped in the most impoverished need-driven circumstances (such as poverty-stricken older persons), and for whom social constraints such as racial discrimination impose serious practical barriers, movement "upward" toward the integrated lifestyle is thought to be possible for anyone, and desirable from the viewpoint of developmental psychology.

The one most relevant application for us is stated concisely by Mitchell himself: "Perhaps the most fundamental business use of lifestyle research lies in market segmentation." The typology can, it is claimed, assist business in the great task of "matching product to consumer" through precise design and targeting in advertising, as well as in product development, design, and packaging, not to mention its possible virtues in long-range strategic planning by businesses (Mitchell 1983, 165–72).

The application of lifestyle research to marketing is well-developed in Japan. The Hakuhodo Institute of Life and Living (1982) uses the following market-segment categories:

Crystal Tribe (attracted to famous brands)
My Home Tribe (family-oriented)
Leisure Life Tribe
Gourmandism Tribe
Ordinary People Tribe
Impulse Buyer Tribe

The preface to the research report notes that the term "consumer" in Japan is being replaced by the phrase "life designer," a change intended to take into account the high proportion of the population who formulate and express their wants autonomously, rather than merely by reacting to what happens to be featured in the marketplace at any time. This report is concerned especially with what is called "*hitonami* consciousness."

Hitonami translates literally as "aligning oneself with other people" and thus is roughly equivalent to "other-directed." Hitonami, the internalization of the immensely powerful pressures enforcing social conformity in attitudes and behavior, was deeply rooted in traditional Japanese society. After World War II, however, the social upheaval of the war and the postwar economic prosperity encouraged a new form of hitonami consciousness: "keeping up with the Satos," the social conformity of upward mobility and changing circumstances. Dominating Japanese society until the late 1970s, it is now giving way to newer trends.

The Hakuhodo survey sought responses to a questionnaire on ten major aspects of daily life.

The survey found most Japanese in the 1980s rejected "keeping up with the Satos" in the sense of using material possessions to indicate social status. They buy products that "suit them in their style of life," and they place the highest value on "cultivating themselves and seeking self-fulfillment." Although the attitudes are represented by only a small proportion of the total population who have "sufficient confidence in themselves to act as innovators and trend setters in many aspects of Japanese daily life" (Hakuhodo Institute of Life and Living 1982). Their approach to consumption is similar to the styles of consumption recognized by Galbraith in the United States and Baudrillard in France. What lifestyle research adds is evidence that many persons appear to express or communicate publicly both their value-orientations and their consumption preferences in discernible patterns.

Things Come Alive

Goods have meanings. Goods convey meanings. These elementary propositions help us to understand the consumer society and the role of advertising within it. A book entitled *The Meaning of Things* calls attention to "the ability of an object to convey meaning through its own inherent qualities" (Csikszentmihalyi and Rochberg-Halton 1981, 43). We have shown that, in a consumer culture, an object's qualities are a complex unity of two broad categories of characteristics—material and symbolic, or imputed. The communicative function nestles inside consumption behavior in all human cultures at all times; objects serve the twin purposes of satisfying needs and conveying meanings.

In general, we agree with Mary Douglas and Baron Isherwood that "the essential function of consumption is its capacity to make sense.... Forget that commodities are good for eating, clothing, and shelter; forget their usefulness and try instead the idea that commodities are good for thinking; treat them as a nonverbal medium for the human creative faculty" (Douglas and Isherwood 1978, 62). We need only add that the role of advertising in modern industrial societies is to verbalize and to image the possible meanings of things, and to facilitate the exchanges of meanings occurring in social interactions.

Every aspect of contemporary life in market-industrial societies is permeated by the presence of objects, and it is extraordinary how quickly this situation arose and how easily humans adapted to it and learned to take it for granted, almost as if it were the "natural" condition of the species. One has to look back only two hundred years at the most to pre-industrial societies to realize the narrow range of things that were used in the normal routines of life, even for privileged classes, in comparison with the present day. Although the operative mechanisms in many devices are a mystery to most of us, they do not seem to inspire awe or terror, but rather indifference. After all, one cannot get too excited about the newest video game or electronic gadget, for one expects that next month or next year there will be something else yet more titillating.

We should not be misled by the sheer quantity of things around us and suppose that little remains to link us with older societies. The sphere of consumption in general, and how we use goods therein as communicators of meanings, are among the most dramatic instances of fundamental continuities and similarities among human cultures, from what we call "primitive societies" to our own. So common is the practice of investing material objects with richly textured layers of interpretive significance that it must be regarded as a basic feature of the human personality. Things are not merely passive adjuncts or decorative accompaniments, rather they "come alive" in the context of social interactions.

In an analysis of gift exchange and reciprocity among the New Zealand Maori, the anthropologist Marcel Mauss claimed that the very basis of exchanges of objects among persons was the idea that the object contains the "life-force" both of the person who made it and the natural materials used in its construction, as if the exchange of things were conceived by the Maori as the exchange of persons (Sahlins 1976, 215). In contrast, our modern industrial society fashions its objects through applications of its very rationalist science and technology, and it admits no obscurantist notions like life-force when it applies its rationalist technology to fashioning objects. Yet, at the same time, our marketing and advertising enterprise represents these products to us as if they were magically endowed with life; in television advertising products speak, move about spontaneously, and bring persons together. So much for rationality.

Human relations are mediated by things, which express, conceal, shield, or distort our motives and objectives. To have things serve us in this way we must make them seem as if they are alive or endowed with life-force. They serve thus as a "protective medium" into which we transfer the intricate webs of personal and social interactions.

We name our collective enterprise for producing things "the economy" and we often speak of it, too, as a living force. In times of business slowdown, we call for actions to "get the economy moving again," as if it were some huge, sluggish beast that inexplicably has stopped to rest. High government officials say that the purpose of public policy is to "stimulate the private sector," a phrase that perhaps ought to be dropped from the bureaucratic vocabulary on account of its non-economic undertones. A constant refrain is the admonition to "let the market decide" among various options. Investors are said to "lack confidence" in the economy, as if it were some ne'er-do-well relative seeking a loan. Every commentator has a favorite nostrum for restoring the economy's "health."

Goods can act as communicators in social interactions because we breathe life into them. "Man needs goods for communicating with others and for making sense of what is going on around him. The two needs are but one, for communication can only be formed in a structured system of meanings. His overriding objective as a consumer, put at its most general, is a concern for information about the changing cultural scene." Goods are part of a "live information system"—not merely the messages or messengers in the system, but, in fact, the very structure of the message system itself. What is important is not the meanings attached to a particular thing or type of thing at any moment, but rather the relationships among an ensemble of goods (Douglas and Isherwood 1978, 95).

The above anthropological perspective on the function of goods in human cultures is significant for our understanding of contemporary life and helps us to appreciate the full extent of advertising's role in the consumer society. Note immediately that the phrase "live information system" denotes not bits and pieces of data about products, but rather the very activity of "making sense out of the cultural world around one," which, in turn, depends upon discovering a structured or patterned system of meanings in relation to which one can form one's tastes.

In the consumer society, we maintain, no institutions are more directly concerned with providing patterned systems of meaning for consumption activity than marketing and advertising. In the twentieth century, the evolution of cultural frames for goods (presented later in this chapter) reveals the broad outline of these patterns, and the influence of the "lifestyle" concept in the most recent period simply shows how explicit the patterning has become. Yet institutional strategies, no matter how influential, do not create or manipulate the patterns unilaterally: marketers and advertisers canvass the whole range of cultural symbols, past and present, and blend their borrowings with the characteristics of current goods and services in which, they hope, the symbolic meanings can be made to resonate. The resulting set designs are by no means always pleasing to us as consumers, but we do seem to be willing to return regularly to the theater of consumption for the latest performances.

Advertising should be understood as a major cultural institution, not merely as just another of businesses' tax-deductible expenditures, because the world of goods that composes the manifest or surface level of its productions is itself one of the principal channels of social communication. Anthropological researches show us that this has always been so; what is new is the way we use this channel today. Sidney J. Levy contends that the anthropologist's perspective can "lead to a fuller understanding of why marketing managers do what they do and why consumers buy and consume as they do," because it interprets goods and services "not in themselves alone, but in their social symbolic role, as means of exchanging communications and furthering social processes" (Levy 1978, 568).

The market-industrial society is unique not for its obsession with material objects, but for its capacity to transform the mix and characteristics in the world of objects quickly and regularly, opens new channels through which this discourse can flow. Yet goods themselves remain the communicators, and it is through them that the discourse flows.

Marketing and advertising are the major channels in the technological infrastructure for this communication process in the consumer society; other components are the residue of traditional cultures (especially outside North America), youth subcultures, the celebrity or "star" system, and the corporate business style as the preeminent model for career progress. In these and other components runs the "discourse through and about things" for the consumer society. Were marketing and advertising to be banned outright, for example, these other channels, or some newly designed ones, would have to be pressed into service to take up the slack. For, like our ancestors, we appear to be compelled to fashion our social interactions through goods.

The construction of social relations through goods is one of the strongest threads binding together human development from the earliest times to our own; all cultures shape into symbolic forms the materials of nature extracted from the environment. Marshall Sahlins emphasizes this theme in contrasting consumption practices of primitive societies with our own (Sahlins, 1976; 1972). He sees the most important difference not in levels of technology or types of objects but in the "site of symbolic production." He uses this term to refer to the social institutions most influential in reproducing and transmitting the behavioral norms that guide individuals in everyday life (for example, knowing what to eat and how to dress). In primitive societies, kinship is the privileged institution in this regard—today, it is the economy. Therefore, we should look upon the marketplace not just as a decision-making forum for employment, consumer expenditures, and capital formation, but much more broadly as a cultural system, as, in fact, the privileged institution for the re-working and transmission of the cultural symbols that shape our lives.

Now we can combine the theme of relative standing with the idea of goods as communicators into a unified conception of the marketplace as a cultural system. For the market-oriented discourse through and about things creates a powerful set of symbolic processes founded on an internal tension that si-multaneously unifies and differentiates between persons. On the one hand, this discourse is a unifying force in society because it is anchored in one of the cornerstones of the human personality, namely, the propensity for using ma-terial objects as intermediaries in social interactions. The ensemble of goods thus serves as a general communication system in which everyone, at least potentially, can participate. On the other hand, the ensemble of goods is not a random assortment but a highly structured collection; material objects, having a certain permanence and being easily distinguishable from each other, serve ideally to mark social distinctions according to who possesses or controls any particular thing and who does not.

Such discriminations about social rank are grounded in what Thorstein Veblen ([1899] 1953) called an "invidious distinction," a judgment on a per-son's worth made largely in terms of whether or not that person appears to be willing to accept a given consumption standard as a behavioral norm. Even a casual glance will persuade us that the consumer society throws up invidious distinctions everywhere. We are constantly urged to compare the advantages of one brand over another, one class of goods over another, one marginal in-crement of satisfaction over another, one set of values over another, indeed one "lifestyle package" over another. Yet it is exceedingly difficult to pinpoint a rational basis for opting this way or that, which leaves most people with only a cheerful proclivity to play the game for its own sake.

And in truth, it is a fascinating, subtle, and exceedingly complex game, one that is hard to see clearly in our consumer society because of the sheer num-ber and variety of goods and the worldwide scope of market transactions. We propose, therefore, to step back and examine how some earlier societies used goods as communicators in more tightly structured exchange relations, there-by glimpsing today's game better from a distance.

The Consumer Society as an Anthropological Type

In a market society, all goods and services are "equivalent" in the sense that a common currency guarantees access to each of them on the same terms. In principle, no one who has the money to pay the asking price for anything is denied the right to acquire it, and distinctions among things are marked on the surface only by their relative prices. However, we do not normally carry our possessions around with price tags dangling from them, but instead rely upon the characteristics of the goods themselves—both their physical properties and the symbolic meanings imputed or ascribed to them—to say things about ourselves to others.

Communication is made possible, as Douglas and Isherwood have explained, by embedding behavioral signals within a structured or patterned system of meaning. We understand these signals because they are part of a set of events that has an internal coherence; a designer label on an article of clothing must conform to certain rules (for example, only certain names on the label will make sense) in order to communicate the desired signals. As individuals, we are dependent upon social institutions—such as, in a consumer society, marketing and advertising—to construct those patterns of meaning.

The formation and operation of such institutional patterning can be seen with great clarity in earlier societies because the markers for the patterns were specific physical objects, and because the rules of the game for consumption behavior segregated activities on the basis of the objects involved. Earlier societies can show us not only dramatic instances of how goods serve as communicators, but also how ways of investing consumption activity with meaning persist to the present day.

Anthropologists have presented some primitive societies as made up of two dissimilar but related domains: the "subsistence economy" and the "prestige economy" (the latter is sometimes further subdivided, as we shall see). The subsistence economy produces—usually by the collective labor of extended family groups—all the basic necessities of existence for everyone, which make up the "consumption norm" for a particular society. An established redistribution mechanism for the goods produced in this domain is gift-giving managed by the tribal chief, and this "welfare" activity ensures that no constituent group's consumption level falls below an acceptable minimum.

The "prestige economy" is based in transactions within an entirely separate class of goods using specific media of exchange and often elaborate rules of conduct. It involves a restricted group of participants (usually only males). Possession or disposition of valued goods confers honor and prestige upon an individual and his kin group. The propensity for emulation, to use Veblen's phrase, that is embodied in the prestige economy is, in many cases, no trivial sideline in social affairs, but rather the very core of everyday life.

A dramatic instance of prestige competitions occurred among the Kwakiutl of British Columbia, who lived in a region of great natural abundance. "The Kwakiutl, even more than most peoples in the world, were obsessed with rank—indeed, in the midst of such plenty they created artificial shortages in the social system and their striving for high social position was an integral part of the economy" (Bohannan 1963, 254). Prestige was won by giving away vast quantities of ceremonial goods at potlatches. Competition was confined to two kinds of things: blankets and large pieces of engraved copper. The contest required potlatch rivals to offer up increasing numbers of blankets, until one participant ended this phase by tendering a copper piece; the competition ended in the destruction of copper pieces, the victory going to the person deemed to have destroyed the piece of greatest value. The rivalry was structured as a ritualized series of exchanges among designated objects which culminated in translating material values "into the purest value: reputation."

Related research on the economy of the Tiv, in what is now Nigeria, offers one of the best illustrations of how ranked and discontinuous spheres of exchange worked. The subsistence economy included food (yams, cereals, vegetables, seasonings, chickens, goats, sheep), household utensils (mortars, grindstones, calabashes, baskets, pots), and some tools. Exchange of these goods involved gift-giving and bartering. The prestige economy was complex, made up of two tiers.

One segregated category of goods embraced slaves, cattle, ritual offices, a special type of cloth, medicines, and brass rods; exchanges took place only at ceremonial occasions, and within this category brass rods served as a medium of exchange. Above it stood another tier with a single "good": the exchange of rights in women.

Transactions that crossed the various domains were sometimes necessary, such as when a large amount of food was required for a feast and had to be paid for with brass rods, or when rods were used to purchase a wife. But the ranking of the three domains was all-important. The whole point was to avoid, so far as possible, exchanging high-category goods for lower-category ones; he who had to do so in order to fulfill a social obligation inevitably suffered a loss of prestige. Conversely, one strove to take advantage of another's social needs by converting lower-status goods into higher-status ones (Bohannan 1963, 248–53).

Richard Salisbury (1962) found that the Siane people in the New Guinea highlands also had three spheres of exchange and that each dealt with a distinct assortment of goods. Goods in the subsistence sphere included everyday food items (sweet potatoes and other vegetables), tools, clothing, and housing. These goods were produced within each clan, maintaining both kinship relations and the basic consumption level enjoyed by everyone. Luxury goods encompassed tobacco, palm oil, pandanus nuts, salt, snakeskins for drums, stone for axe-blades, and palm wood for spears. These were produced or acquired through individual initiative, and exchanged on a reciprocal basis. They could be enjoyed privately or supplied to entertain visitors, for generosity toward one's guests was admired. Luxury goods formed an intermediary class allowing for the expression of individual differences in consumption style, unlike the subsistence goods, which exhibited little or no variation. Ceremonial goods were valuables exchanged by barter at public events, and included shells, ornamental axes, necklaces, plumes, headdresses, and pigs. Ceremonial exchanges occurred both within and between clans and a detailed accounting of comparative value was kept. An individual created strict return obligations to himself (and by association to his clan) by presenting ceremonial goods to others, and thereby gained a certain measure of prestige. Presenting such goods was also a vehicle of social mobility within the clan.

Very few transactions violated the boundaries set up between the three different types of goods, because they existed to supply a structured setting for social relations. The type of object clearly identified the sphere of activity and the accepted behavioral norms associated with it. "The more general rule is that commodities are used only in situations where the nexus of activity is clearly one of intra-clan help, inter-clan presentation, or exchange between trade friends; no commodity can be used in an ambiguous situation" (Salisbury 1962, 103). Not only were ceremonial goods never exchanged for food or luxuries, but persons who bartered between the subsistence and luxury spheres were banned from the trading for ceremonial goods.

The impact of the introduction of a new technology (steel rather than stone for axe-blades) on the closed, hierarchical spheres of exchange is of special interest. Production patterns in the subsistence domain remained the same, since women tended the crops and only men owned and used axes. The far greater efficiency and durability of the steel blades meant men had to spend significantly less time clearing the planting areas and building houses. The newly available time was absorbed exclusively into extending the domain of prestige competition, which was carried out both by fighting and by the peaceful exchange of the appropriate ceremonial objects.

Our primary motive in reviewing this anthropological literature is to emphasize the point made by Douglas and Isherwood that networks of social communication—including the world of goods as an information system— rely for their efficacy on structured situations. The discrete and hierarchically ordered spheres of exchanges in primitive societies show with great clarity the connection between social institutions (sex roles, group relations, relative standing, and so forth) and the use of goods as communicators. Richard Salisbury summarizes:

> The presence in non-monetary societies of discrete scales of value … is a simple mechanism insuring that subsistence goods are used to maintain a basic standard of life below which no one falls; that free-flowing power [prestige] is allocated peacefully, with a minimum of exploitation (or disturbance of the individual's right to subsistence) and in accordance with accepted standards; that the means for insuring flexibility in the society do not disrupt the formal allocation of statuses in the society or the means of gaining power. (Salisbury 1962, 204)

These discontinuous spheres of goods are a visible manifestation of the "deep structure" of human needs, showing that needs develop and emerge not haphazardly one after another in an undifferentiated series, but in clusters that reflect our efforts to delineate meaningful spheres of activity. The number of our wants and the number of objects available to minister to them is far less important than the nature of the boundaries erected to discriminate between the clusters and to create "structured situations" in society.

The physical and symbolic characteristics of the material tokens of prestige used to mark a person's standing relative to others must be capable of being clearly recognized as such, and they must be sufficiently complex to portray the necessary range of discriminations. So long as these conditions are satisfied, it matters little what is chosen; broken bits of seashells or beads of colored glass will serve as well as mansions, antiques, or the top floors of downtown high-rise buildings.

Which brings us back to the consumer society. After studying the social behavior of the Siane, Richard Salisbury thought he discerned analogies between their three domains of activity and goods and the ways in which we regard at least some of the commodities we produce today. The one notable qualification is that we mix together what they strive so arduously to keep apart. In our range of automobile models, for example, one can discern a "subsistence nexus" in that all will convey passengers from place to place; a "luxury nexus" in all the available options and sophisticated gadgetry for greater comfort that most purchasers cannot resist; and a "ceremonial nexus" in the relative standing or prestige that certain makes and models signal.

In a consumer society, the most influential determinant of the status value of a commodity is its price, but marketing techniques allow many other factors to mitigate its impact. In automobile models, a "sporty" or "racing" package of imagery may be acquired at various points on the price scale. The terms "luxury" and "luxurious" often are employed indiscriminately in advertising copy for goods of undistinguished quality, in an attempt to persuade the consumer of modest means that even he or she can acquire something special and need not rest content with the ordinary things of life. Marketing strategies attempt to "punctuate" consumption activity by seeking to distinguish ordinary and special occasions, mimicking the spheres of goods in earlier societies.

Other ancient practices permeate consumption practices in modern society. The most noticeable is sex stereotyping. Many studies have documented its presence in advertisements and have raised questions about its impact on behavior. In the context of our discussion here, sex stereotyping illustrates a basic point—that goods can serve as important communicators in human interactions when they are embedded in what we have called structured situations.

How goods communicate meaning through the structured situation created by sex stereotyping is shown clearly in Erving Goffman's *Gender Advertisements* (1979). Advertisements portray the physical carriage and gestures of male and female models and of specific parts of the body, such as hands, in ways that reflect and reinforce traditional patterns of sex-role expectations.

Our food preferences also continue to carry cultural baggage. In North America, we not only separate animals generally deemed fit to eat (cows and pigs) from those that are not (dogs and horses), but also construct a status hierarchy placing beef above pork and, within this, some flesh parts (steak) above others (organs). Sidney J. Levy conducted in-depth interviews with six consumers concerning their attitudes toward cooking and eating—which he called their "stories" or "myths":

> The little myths show how the basic vocabulary of cooking and eating is used to express identities by males and females, the young and the mature, and people in low, middle, and high status positions. General modeling by age, sex, and social status is a familiar one to marketers; here the analysis observes how specific symbolic distinctions are being made among specific foods, ways of preparing them, and in some of the ideas they represent, such as family unity/dispersion, naivete/sophistication, routine/festivity, sickness/ health, grossness/subtlety, conformity/deviation, sacred/profane, etc. (Levy 1981, 60)

Levy thinks that structured differentiations like these condition personal experience in the consumption process, and that marketers can facilitate what he calls the "dialogue" between marketers and consumers if they are aware of this.

Finally, the economist Albert O. Hirschman (1982) has identified some discrete domains in today's world of goods by analyzing how we ordinarily derive benefits from them. He distinguishes between the goods we consume (consumer nondurables) and the goods we use (consumer durables). The goods we consume include all those things whose composition we destroy or alter in deriving benefits from them (food and drink, fuel, personal-care products, and most clothing). Other things we use over long periods without greatly changing their material composition; Hirschman further subdivides this category into things in continuous use (housing, refrigerators), in sporadic use (cars, dishwashers), and occasional use (pianos, cameras). We derive immediate, sensuous, and clearly identifiable pleasure from nondurables—the taste and smell of food, the feel of clothing, and so forth. But we find most durables, although largely indispensable, provide little lasting satisfaction; after our initial pleasure when we acquire them, they become part of the taken-for-granted routine of everyday life. As Tibor Scitovsky pointed out they are the comforts we depend on and assume will be supplied one way or another, but usually we are aware of them only when they are absent.

Hirschman's contribution to explaining why surveys fail to show a rising proportion of general happiness in contemporary society suggests that disappointment "arises typically because new types of purchases are undertaken with the kinds of expectations that consumers have come to associate with more traditional purchases" (Hirschman 1982, 45). The suggestion is a "lag effect" in the individual's search for satisfaction. People tend to compartmentalize their positive and negative feelings, and we surmise that there must be a deeply rooted ambiguity in personal experience in the marketplace. In part, then, this ambiguity is a response to changes in the types of goods themselves; different types of goods reflect different structures of meaning, and changes in them affect the kinds of gratifications that can be derived from consumption.

The issue of consumer disappointment forces us to ask: Are persons misled in any significant measure by the symbolic meanings woven into the world of goods? We have offered numerous illustrations, drawn both from earlier societies and our own, of situations in which material objects are the prestige tokens that "stand for" social distinctions and that facilitate the flow of messages between persons. Do these communications processes always serve worthy purposes? Or do they also distort and blur our perceptions of social events?

Fetishism: Distorted Communication in the World of Goods

The objects we acquire, display, or simply admire are a powerful medium for the circulation of messages about ourselves to others, and for learning the forms of expression for social interactions (the status symbols, clothing styles, and so forth) that appear to be sanctioned at any one time. This ensemble can be said to represent, in Marshall Sahlins's (1976) words, "man speaking to man through the medium of things." Presumably, most of us, most of the time, strive to convey our intentions and perceptions truthfully; but evasions, outright lies, and honest mistakes are not unknown. More important, the subjective bias with which we all operate inevitably colors our reading of events. So we must ask: Is the discourse through and about things spoken with forked tongues?

In considering this question, we will continue to look chiefly at the place of objects in social interactions, and pay little attention to the role they might play in the psychological development of individuals. (For an excellent discussion of this point, see Part I of *The Meaning of Things* by Csikszentmihalyi and Rochberg-Halton [1981].) There are stages in childhood where a fixation on particular objects seems to be both a necessary and a normal process that, so far as we know, occurs universally. However, in some cases, an abnormal fixation on objects can occur in which, for example, a male cannot perform sexually under normal conditions, and seeks to use what psychoanalytic theory terms a "fetish object," such as a woman's shoe, as a catalyst to reaching orgasm.

The notion of fetish, as we shall see, is helpful for investigating to what extent the discourse through and about objects contains elements of distortion and misrepresentation. The Portuguese coined the terms "fetish" and "fetishism" as a result of the European encounter with African societies beginning in the fifteenth century. They were describing the widespread practice they observed of addressing or employing material objects in order to effect a change in the condition or behavior of another. Traditional ceremonies involving fetishes persist to the present. Of special interest are practices that blend old fetishisms with other elements in response to pressures exerted by twentieth-century market forces operating on a global scale. The anthropologist Michael Taussig tells of Bolivian tin miners who have called upon a mixture of folklore and Christian doctrine to construct a representation of what has happened to traditional ways of life, particularly in the domain of producing goods. The tin miners' mythic structure explains that the people have been seduced away from their traditional agricultural pursuits by the promise of great wealth in the mines. But the mine owner is actually the devil who has deluded the workers. To protect themselves from the dangers of the mines, the miners adapted peasant sacrifice rituals to their new situation, seeking to propitiate the devil-owner with gifts and ceremonies, chewing coca together and offering it to the icon that represents the devil-owner.

> His body is sculptured from mineral. The hands, face, and legs are made from clay. Often, bright pieces of metal or light bulbs from the miners' helmets form his eyes. The teeth may be of glass or crystal sharpened like nails, and the mouth gapes, awaiting offerings of coca and cigarettes. The hands stretch out for liquor. In the Siglo XX mine the icon has an enormous erect penis. The spirit can also appear as an apparition: a blond, bearded, red-faced gringo wearing a cowboy hat, resembling the technicians and administrators.... He can also take the form of a succubus, offering riches in exchange for one's soul or life. (Taussig 1980, 143)

Thus, materials from older fetishistic practices were adapted and transformed to provide a workable representation of what the introduction of wage labor meant for the relationship between humans and the material world. The personification (the devil) of the agent behind these changes is anchored in the concept of "seduction" when, lured by material wealth, people accept the rules of the game in a market economy founded on working for wages and producing tin for world markets.

What prompts cultures to create such representations is the need to supply a coherent account (however implausible it may appear to outside observers) of changes that have a major impact on established ways. Social relations oriented around longstanding modes of production and exchange—subsistence agriculture, extended family or kinship groups, barter—began to dissolve as private capitalists and market economics took control. But what is *visible and tangible* about these changes? It is not capital-investment decisions, international stock-exchange fluctuations, or profit targets set by multinational corporations for their operations in foreign countries. It is loss of access to land, cash wages determined and paid by strangers, radically different types and conditions of work, and the breakdown of kinship groups. For the indigenous peoples of Bolivia, just as for the peoples of Europe a century earlier, structures of life and experience familiar to countless generations suddenly disintegrated before their very eyes. It is hardly surprising that they should suspect the devil of having a hand in it.

The objects of the material world and the activities needed to sustain life no longer make sense by the accepted standards of judgment. The establishment of a market economy unravels and discards not only specific things, habitual routines, and norms but also the integument holding them together, the sense of a collective identity and fate. At first, no new means for binding together the experience of the material world is proffered. It appears only as an "immense and astonishing collection of goods."

The preceding phrase is from the opening sentence of Karl Marx's *Capital*. In reading the many tomes on political economy published in his day, Marx noticed something peculiar about how social commentators described the emerging market society and its advantages. They seemed to regard the domain of material production, when governed exclusively by the rules of "free markets," as something beyond human control, obeying only its own inherent principles, almost as if the economy possessed a "life of its own." (The reader may recall our own examples of this in contemporary discourse earlier in this chapter.) Marx saw in this philosophy an analogy between the propensities of religion and the new way of thinking about a market economy that had been developing since the eighteenth century. In religious thought,

> the products of the human brain appear as autonomous figures endowed with a life of their own, which enter into relations both with each other and with the human race.... [So] it is in the world of commodities or goods with the products of men's hands. I call this the fetishism which attaches itself to the products of labor as soon as they are produced as commodities, and is therefore inseparable from the production of commodities. (Marx [1867] 1976, 165)

This is a remarkable statement, especially considering when it was penned; except for some perceptive comments on related topics made around the turn of the twentieth century by Thorstein Veblen and Georg Simmel, two of the founders of modern sociology, about a hundred years passed before the fetishism/market economy theme was seriously taken up again. What connects Marx's notion with our earlier discussion of fetishism is that he, too, encountered the idea by reading a book (in his case, one published in the eighteenth century) about European voyages to then unfamiliar places. He detected a similarity between the fetishistic practices in African societies, where certain material objects were regarded as embodying forces that could affect human behavior, and the way the political economists of his own day described the operations of a market economy as an independent force in society, steered by its own mechanisms (the so-called laws of supply and demand) that compelled all sensible men and women to act in accordance with its dictates. Those who protested against poverty or degraded working conditions were told that there was a "natural" level for wages, determined by the marketplace itself, and that neither labor unions nor legislation could interfere with its mysterious ways. Any notion of tampering with the wild, roller-coaster ride of the business cycle in the nineteenth century was resisted just as strenuously.

Marx contended that this conception of the economy and its "laws" was regressive, because it left most people at the mercy of unmastered forces. But his argument also contains a particular point of special relevance for this chapter, namely that the misrepresentation about production and consumption in a market economy is embodied in material objects themselves. And should such a fundamental misrepresentation be found to exist, it necessarily would call into question the power of goods to serve as meaningful communicators of personal intentions, motives, and objectives.

To live according to the principles of a market economy is to be immersed in buying and selling transactions every day, where everything one has (especially one's mental skills and physical energies) and everything one wants or needs has a price. In other words, as a market-industrial economy expands, more and more elements of both the natural environment and human qualities are drawn into the orbit of exchanged things, into the realm of commodities. Everything has some use to someone (or so it is hoped), and likewise everything has a price at which it can be acquired.

When elements of nature and humanity are ever-increasingly absorbed into the market's orbit, becoming exchanged things, they begin to appear to us as objects, or at least as *objectified forms*. Fewer and fewer aspects of our environment and ourselves remain "outside" the domain of buying and selling. By and large, in earlier times individuals were expected to adjust their behavior to role requirements, and, in the early phases of our modern economy, occupational structures dictated the behavioral standards to which people were expected to conform. More recently, however, we are commonly told to "market" ourselves, to regard our qualifications and experiences as components that we can "repackage" in various ways to suit the demands of changing employment patterns.

The process of converting more and more elements of natural environments and human qualities into objectified forms—commodities constitutes the very essence of an expanding market-industrial economy. This busy enterprise has yielded abundant fruit, which is why the social wealth produced by it appears, in Marx's words, as an "immense and astonishing collection of goods." This is what strikes us immediately, overwhelmingly, as we look about us and consider just how much *more* there is now than at any other time. So strong is this impression that it is easy not to notice that what is missing, what does not appear immediately to us, what remains hidden beneath the surface in the vast world of goods, is any adequate representation of the *social* character of production and consumption activity.

With the progressive specialization of labor, most of us work at a narrow range of tasks, and in industrialized nations today the majority of the labor force has no direct involvement in the production of any material objects, although upon reflection we know that we work in an integrated production system and that what we do is connected somehow with the overall economic result. For the most part, we encounter objects as users and consumers; since in these settings we usually have specific aims in mind (the accomplishment of certain tasks or the gratification of particular wants), the social processes through which these objects came to be produced as appropriate for consumption remain in the background.

In our political rhetoric, we worry a good deal about the condition of our economy as a whole, but this is a rather abstract and distant concern. The point is that we tend to allow the economy itself, as the sphere in which the world of goods is produced and consumed, to represent what binds us together as a society. Goods themselves do provide some of the major lines of communication for our system of social relations. But the lines are buried, so that we sometimes run the risk of focusing too much interest on the surface attractions of things and too little on their more important communicative functions: "If things attract our attention excessively, there is not enough psychic energy left to cultivate the interaction with the rest of the world" (Csikszentmihalyi and Rochberg-Halton 1981, 53).

This point may become clearer if we recall the "double symbolic process." On one side, businesses incorporate their understanding of consumer preferences (and how they might be changed) into the physical and symbolic characteristics of the product, though the design and marketing strategies are not necessarily visible or obvious to consumers (nor are they meant to be). Meanwhile, consumers construct their own self-images and preference patterns out of an enormous array of symbolic associations and behavioral codes that manufacturers are not always able to anticipate or decode. Thus, what we get is not the whole story.

Marx did not see the consumer society emerge, but he did spot the first forms of this peculiar feature in a market economy, remarking that the objectified forms for what is produced and consumed there have an "enigmatic" or "mysterious" character; although marketed goods have a richly textured social composition, involving coordinated production, distribution, and consumption on a global scale, their social character is not immediately apparent. Thus, commodities are "sensuous things which are at the same time supra-sensible or social"—a combination of features that we can see, touch, and smell, on the one hand, and of the complex but hidden social relations orchestrated by the market economy on the other.

Commodities are, therefore, a unity of what is revealed and what is concealed in the processes of production and consumption. Goods reveal or "show" to our senses their capacities to be satisfiers or stimulators of particular wants and communicators of behavioral codes. At the same time, they draw a veil across their own origins: Products appear and disappear before consumers' eyes as if by spontaneous generation, and it is an astute shopper indeed who has much idea about what most things are composed of and what kinds of people made them.

Marx called the fetishism of commodities a disguise whereby the appearance of things in the marketplace masks the story of who fashioned them, and under what conditions. Is it important for us to hear this story? Are we, in being deprived of it, experiencing a systematic distortion of communication within the world of goods itself?

The story matters not because we would necessarily act differently once we heard it, but because it draws attention to some otherwise unnoticed aspects of a market economy, including the role of advertising in it. Although goods serve as communicators of social meanings, they do not do so in straightforward or unambiguous ways. Goods are communicators in a market-industrial society, just as they have always been in human cultures; but precisely what they communicate—and, equally as noteworthy, fail to communicate—is something that can be determined only by close analysis.

Commodities tell us a great deal about themselves, at least insofar as their surface features are concerned, especially in advertisements. But, unlike goods in earlier societies, they do not bear the signatures of their makers whose motives we might assess because we know who they are, nor do they tell us how we should behave with them as they do in societies with closed spheres of exchange. Recall that among the Siane people in New Guinea "no commodity can be used in an ambiguous situation" (Salisbury 1962, 103). In contrast, a market economy revels in ambiguities that flow from the double symbolic process, and under their sway the discourse through and about objects must be, in some important measure, systematically distorted—a passage through a carnival hall of mirrors.

The distortion arises primarily on account of what is omitted at the surface level of representations about needs and commodities. Neither the conditions of production, nor the manufacturer's marketing strategies, nor the subtle ploys of the ad agency's creative department are meant to attract our attention as the object presents itself to us. On the other hand, although most people seem willing at least on occasion to indulge their fantasies in stores, market researchers can find no simple correlations between personality traits and ordered arrays of consumer preferences. Like producers, consumers too draw a veil across the sources of their enterprise.

A market society is a masked ball. Here we bring our needs to dance with their satisfiers (goods) in close embrace to the melodies of an unseen orchestra. The costumes serve products well, for they hide the fact that so many of them are just ordinary chemical compounds tarted up in fancy packages; our disguises are equally advantageous, shielding from others' gaze our many disappointments—as consumers—in our partners' performances.

There are distorted patterns of communication imprinted on the collection of goods circulating in a market-industrial society because some important aspects of producing and consuming activities generally remain out of view. The discourse through and about objects is carried on from behind elaborate masks; advertisers and marketers fashion huge numbers of masks, and in selecting some, consumers allow themselves to be persuaded that they can serve their needs. At social events, conversations are customarily limited to polite remarks about superficial matters, and discourse in the marketplace generally confines itself to the surface qualities of objects and our possible reasons for being interested in them.

In fashioning masks for goods, marketers and advertisers use all the available media of communication to move back and forth across the interface between the production and consumption spheres, restlessly creating and refurbishing zones of encounter between needs and products. As we indicated earlier, advertising mirrors the identifying sign of the consumer society—the unending play with new possibilities for satisfaction. This sign is reflected concretely in the general characteristics of goods themselves—changing qualities, styles, materials, and modes of appeal. As represented in advertisements, goods are active, potent ingredients in social interactions; they are bearers of powers that can affect us and assist us in affecting others. In advertising, we encounter a lush and entertaining realm of fetishes.

Certainly our fetishes do not serve us in the same way as those used in primitive societies. Another important point is that in modern society goods themselves are not fetishes, except in unusual or abnormal circumstances. Rather, through marketing and advertising goods are fitted with masks that "show" the possible relations between things on the one hand and human wants and emotions on the other. These masks are our fetishes. They make things come alive, make them able to act—almost literally—as participants in social interactions. They encipher goods in codes that we can read and act upon.

This perspective enables us to understand two interrelated features of the consumer society: the ambiguous sense of satisfaction experienced by individuals, and the role that marketing and advertising plays in its formation.

Distorted communication is a structural component of the world of goods itself. In a market-industrial society, the domain of communication is indeed systematically misleading because it makes so few direct references to many essential aspects of our producing and consuming activities. Any direct connection between goods and the enduring sources of contentment in life is concealed; the happiness surveys report that people regard earlier generations (which had a noticeably lower material standard of living) as being more contented, but also that most would not wish to live as people did in those times.

Certainly, advertising seeks to link goods with images of happiness and content by designing masks for things that display such linkages. Sometimes the designs are actually false or misleading, but this is not one of their inherent features. Legislation and industry guidelines (at least in Western societies) have tended to considerably reduce the extent of overtly untruthful or deceptive practices. While the masks are meant to influence consumer behavior, it is certain that they do not and cannot control it. Thus, we do not contend that modern society's realm of fetishes is generally harmful or manipulative in general. The vital issues about advertising today are specific ones, such as the wisdom of promoting alcohol and tobacco products, stereotyping, and directing messages at children. We shall return to these points in chapter 16.

PART **II**
1985–2000

CHAPTER 8

Consumer Cultures and Mediated Markets

Introduction to Part II

When this book was first published in 1986 we were concerned with the lack of historical studies of advertising texts and industry practices. We also felt that advertising's contribution to culture as a privileged form of social communication was under studied and theorized. Since the initial publication of this work, however, many authors have filled these blind spots. For example, our understanding of advertising history has been enhanced by new historical work (Marchand 1986; Lears 1994; Applegate 1998; McFall 2004; Arvidsson 2003; Pinkus 1995). In addition, advertising's relationship to culture has become a topic of considerable interest and the subject of many new works (Goldman and Papson 1994; Wernick 1990; Twitchell 1995; Cross 1996, McAllister 1995/1996).

Second, other researchers have built upon the findings and methodology of our historical content analysis. For example, Richards et al. (2000) drew upon aspects of the method to develop a protocol to explore the changing psychosocial dynamics of post-1950 British advertisements. And our concept of cultural frames for goods has been applied to explore the stages of advertising development in non-Western cultures.

In Part II, we seek a method for examining advertising and for reading in and through them the meaning of modern society's grand spectacle of people and products. In analysing the fifth phase of advertising we continue the cultural frames approach, studying advertising texts from the context of the cultural and institutional change of a given historical moment. In the preceding historical chapters we have argued that advertising never was a monolithic institution with a single *modus operandi*, primarily because social and cultural changes and competition between brands, agencies, media and consumers brought a competitive dynamism to the consumer marketplace. Brand appeals and marketing strategies favored in one sector or at a given moment in time, constantly give way to other ways of seeing and valuing the world, of doing business, of using the media, of thinking about and addressing the consumer.

Moreover, the strategic work of advertising is based on a constant surveillance of our changing culture. Fads, fashions, trends, and individual behaviors are being monitored and diagnosed through a constant stream of market intelligence tools, which helps industry adjust to social change. Because of their research, agencies are constantly thinking about consumer trends, diagnosing the social structure of markets, assessing the patterns of fluid audiences for various media, and distilling all this information into communication strategies targeted toward specific segments of the population. The constant oscillation between communication design and market surveillance leads us to characterize the transactions which take place between producers and consumers via the agency system as a dynamic negotiation taking place in time—although not necessarily one conducted on an equitable basis.

Mercifully, few commentators now use the term "manipulation" to describe the part played by agencies in the market's communication system. It is with the new circuitry of the mediated marketplace in mind that many social theorists have been rethinking the part played by advertising in the consumer culture. We will review in a moment some recent attempts to assess the emergence of a consumer culture over the last quarter-century, which have contributed to a more complex picture of the mediated marketplace. But unlike some commentators, we continue to see advertising as a constitutive part of the cultural transformations that have taken place during the last century.

It is important, we believe, to remember that despite all their research, agency personnel still contribute creatively to the formulation of branding and targeting strategies, and also negotiate placements within the media channels and niches through which marketers can address their targeted consumers as audiences. Advertisers continue to practice strategic social communication, which is orchestrated on behalf of goods and service marketers to influence consumption practices. It is the evolving strategic interplay between creative communication design and perpetual cultural diagnosis that makes the advertising agency's role in what we have labeled its "demassified" phase so hard to pin down. These same characteristics make its practices so interesting to examine.

Social Communication in Demassified Markets

During the advertising's fifth phase, the newer forms of market segmentation and lifestyle targeting (based on style, values, and attitudinal preferences) continued to augment the older forms of targeting by age, income, or other demographic classifications. Adding another historical component to our content analysis, therefore, promised to offer few insights to those already uncovered by others and ourselves. What we found striking about the last quarter-century is that the information and influence flowing between marketers and consumers in the mediated marketplace became even more elaborate, diversified and complex, related we believe in large part to a process we call "demassification" within consumer culture. Demassification further secured the industry's reliance on lifestyle targeting and, along with the expansion of globalization, changed the strategies of advertisers.

It was in the 1950s that what was sometimes referred to as "faceless" mass consumers first began to reveal their more distinctive and variegated consumption profiles to market researchers. The so-called "baby boom" was the prized market segment, due to its large numbers, financial clout, influence on parental spending, and, eventually, its destiny to be the future big-ticket-item consumers. This cohort proved to be a rich training ground where marketers could perfect segmentation, lifestyle, and lifecycle marketing techniques. New modes of address and marketing practices were developed to woo the young boomers. Over time, these strategies biased marketers into accepting the boomer's life experience and orientation to consumption as synonymous with the model customer.

In his detailed study of the men's fashion and automobile sectors Thomas Frank concluded that it was during the 1960s when advertisers began so realize the importance of the youth market. Lifestyle—one's taste, political persuasion, affinity with materialist values—was particularly important to young people, and fashion and taste in music enabled marketers to distinguish among individuals, even those of similar demographic backgrounds. To better address the changes in the marketplace, business historian Richard Teldow draws attention to the way in which marketers began to merge demographic and psychographic data "to create divisions in markets that [marketers] can exploit with competitive advantages" (Frank 1997, 23). This type of segmentation was one of the most novel inventions of the late twentieth century, transforming how we map culture, and instigated fundamental changes in the marketplace:

> The fragmentation was based on realities [primarily geographic], but this new segmentation springs wholly from the imagination of the marketer. Pepsi and other such companies have been more interested in the term segmentation as verb than as a noun. They have segmented markets, rather than merely responded to a market segment that already existed. There was no such thing as the Pepsi Generation until Pepsi created it. (Frank 1997, 24)

The shift to segmentation involved the construction of consumer subjectivity, as manufacturers and advertisers attempt to call group identities into existence where before there had been nothing but inchoate feelings and common responses to pollsters' questions.

As we shall see, our world has continued to change since the 1970s in ways that have impacted commercial media and the practices of advertising agencies—including diversifying social values and lifestyles, globalizing markets, new media technologies, environmental crises transforming the marketplace into juggernaut of changing consumer styles, fads and fashions. Although much of their research was used merely to assuage clients, it provoked marketers to think more seriously about listening to consumers—not just as users of products, but now as "lifestyle managers" lodged in the flux of fashion cycles and fads. Consumer researchers began to track social trends, hunt for "cool," time the shortening fashion cycles, and think more carefully about the emotional life of consumers in the constantly changing consumer culture. Moreover, in a media-saturated marketplace it became crucial for media planners to not only have a snapshot of who was watching what, but also to understand how audiences migrated across new media (mobile phones, videogames), zapped ads or processed multiple channels (young people often engaged with three media at once).

Lifestyle niches were recognized as having a more broad influence within the mediated marketplace. In their work *Economies of Sign and Space* (1994), Lash and Urry contend that the erosion of older social bonds meant that individuals now live less in stable community or kinship networks and more in fluid lifestyle niches. Mobility, constant change, and popular culture's disdain towards orthodox rules have become increasingly characteristic of this period. Social roles that were once fairly stable have been subject to challenge and reversal: Even the family, once the core site of self and social definition, has become subject to flux.

Within this context, where personal aspirations and expectations have been set in motion, Lash (2002) sees the maintenance of self and continual revision of ones everyday life via the process of reflexivity as core activities. For Giddens (1991) lifestyle has emerged as the central means by which individuals now seek to find meaning, identity and stability. Yet, surprisingly, Giddens adamantly separates his definition of lifestyle from that provided by marketers and advertisers—who are the acknowledged masters of their trade:

> The notion of lifestyle sounds somewhat trivial because it is so often thought of solely in terms of a superficial consumerism: lifestyles as suggested by glossy magazines and advertising images. But there is something much more fundamental going on than such a conception suggests: in conditions of high modernity, we all not only follow lifestyles, but in an important sense are forced to do so—we have no choice but to choose. (Giddens 1991, 81)

We do not believe at all that the lifestyle categories developed by advertisers are so easily separated from the "lifestyle narratives of self" that Giddens theorizes. Much of the work that follows explores how the marketers' lifestyle categories have become important resources by which individuals understand themselves and their culture. And, while the analogous theoretical ideas of Lash and Urry are intriguing, like Nixon (2003) we think that their theoretical assumptions would benefit from a more detailed historical exploration of the research, marketing, and advertising techniques used to target lifestyle niches.

Our study reveals that marketers, product designers, advertisers and media play a considerable role articulating lifestyle orientations. But we also argue that the output of these institutions is powerful not because audiences are passively overcome by it, but because individuals actively invest themselves in defining, maintaining, defending, and critiquing the lifestyle constructions offered up by the mediated marketplace. We find that allegiance to particular lifestyles is based less on choice than on *critique*—meaning that individuals often define themselves through a rejection of certain lifestyle options. The spectacle of people and products involves a negotiation over styles of life.

Within these negotiations consumers are less likely to be recognized as a mass phenomenon, leading marketers to emphasize trends toward the customization of products and the segmentation of consumers and audiences. Consumers and audiences expected their diversity to be acknowledged, because these audiences, in fact, have become increasingly diverse: For example, the baby-boom generation was peopled with 24 percent of non-Caucasian descent, whereas Generation X had 34 percent. This diversity in the popular marketplace brought with it differences of language and the use of goods; the peculiarities and practices associated with minority groups, formerly a set of isolated cultural subsystems, went through a process of being absorbed into the mainstream popular culture.

Computers increased the ability of organizations to track and monitor the consumption of their products. Many found that a small minority of consumers accounted for a great deal of their business. Others with new products sought out lucrative markets, particularly urban elites and youth. Each market segment required to be spoken to in an agreeable tone. Advertisers had to find the correct tone for the first-time homebuyer, the young skateboarder, and the pensioner, as each one of these consumers had a different values structure and set of needs due to its place within the lifecycle. Although some products continued to find the means to sell to a mass audience, the new splintering of culture, in which people sought to form individual lifestyles, challenged this approach. New techniques in research constructed a greater array of marketing targets. Likewise, appreciation of the distinctions consumers drew around different product categories grew. Market researchers developed new terms such as high involvement, low involvement goods; those that, due to price or status value, invoked considerable thought and reflection on the part of the buyer, and those in which the self and the pocketbook had less at stake, making the purchase slightly less risky.

As careful histories of twentieth century marketing have revealed, interest in refined target markets is not a particularly new phenomenon, of course (Turow 1997; Strasser 1995). As early as the 1920s, advertisers had been developing important distinctions between consumers (Marchand 1985). For example, in the 1930s Britain's Lloyds Bank sought to distinguish itself by foregoing the mass market trend favored by its competitors, by targeting affluent consumers (Botterill 2001). What did change during the fifth phase was the increased willingness—often driven out of necessity as the old marketing efforts no longer worked—of advertisers to open new forums of negotiations with their consumer. It is also clear that, if possible, business would continue to try to target a "mass consumer," for this technique is easier and continues to work well for some fast-moving packaged goods and domestic products such as laundry detergent.

Advertising came to focus its address to play such overarching and complex roles for an every expanding number of consumer segments (business class air traveler, minorities, teenage girls, children, retired office workers, the aspiring and the anti-materialists) that the bridge of advertising shot off into a maze of capillaries. In offering potential cues about how to manage anxiety, excuses for indulgence, fantasies for escape, and messages about how to live a good and true life advertising was a polyglot of lifestyle possibilities.

Approach

In charting these socio-cultural changes, which advertisers articulate back to us in the media, the advertising sector also contributes to the public's understanding of the dynamics of the mediated market economy. It is this aspect of reflexivity to which we now turn, in order to discuss the new cultural frame added over the last quarter century to the discourse through and about goods. This frame leads us to a new understanding of the advertiser's role in the formation of, and communication to, target markets. We concentrate on case studies of two key target markets—youth and the urban professionals we call "the culturati"—who both received an inordinate amount of advertiser's attention in the post-1985 period.

This type of focused approach to the study of advertising has been used in several other new marketplace histories—for example by Frank Mort, and in Sean Nixon's work on the formation of the "new male" market in 1980s Britain, in Stephen Kline's (1993) work on the construction of the children's market, and in Lori Anne Leob's *Consuming Angels* (1994), an exploration of how early advertisers addressed Victorian women to great effect.

As we hope to show, agencies hold in dynamic tension a dual task of creative design and strategic market analysis, but do so with increasingly sophisticated panoply of research techniques, and an aesthetically diversified palette of communication forms, within a multi-channel communication environment. One of the most important consequences of this growing interest in the cultural dimensions of consumer experience was the idea of the "cohort" (first applied to the baby boom): the first TV generation. This concept integrated the lifestyle and lifecycle concepts with an attempt to understand their common media experiences, all of which helped marketers to understand this group's unique progress through the lifecycle.

To sell to boomers, marketers had to understand the interior spaces of those who were living out their days within this cohort—whether it was selling cars based on their anxieties about child safety, or on their nostalgia for their youthful freedom. And to do so marketers have required more market intelligence. Faced with a constantly fluid marketplace, "strategies, communications, packaging and brand portfolios need to be revisited, evaluated and continually refined to remain relevant and impactful" (Morrison 1997, 23). It is this reconfiguration of the advertising nexus over the last quarter-century that will preoccupy us in this second section of the book.

Acknowledging the importance of these multiple feedback loops that circle back through the advertising design process, perhaps the contemporary advertising sector can be better characterized as "multiplexing" forum which coordinates, absorbs and fuses a variety of social practices in competing cultural sites—making agencies into the hub in the oscillating feedback loops built into our market culture.

Figure 8.1 offers a view of the agency's central role at the hub of the mediated marketplace system. Agencies no longer maintain the same holistic "full service" structure as in previous eras; rather, services were unbundled, with component parts (research, media planning and buying) often operating independently, as either niche businesses or—addressing the management of global brands—brought under the umbrella of brand managers and/or the massive communications corporations that emerged during this period. Promotional tactics merged with advertising, as commodity messaging infused popular

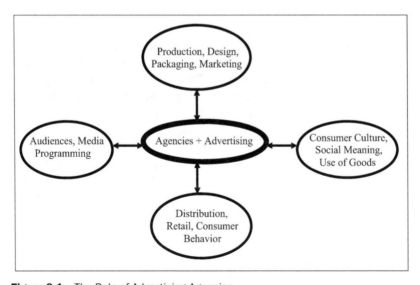

Figure 8.1 The Role of Advertising Agencies.

culture, word of mouth channels, and cultural events, and as the integrity of the distinction between "above the line" (advertising through traditional paid for media channels) and "below the line" (promotion, public relations, events sponsorship) was effaced. Thus, although we continue to use the term agency, we recognize a significant realignment within marketing communication systems where agencies function as multi-tasking players, coordinating brand strategies within globally segmented markets.

Although there are many factors contributing to the profound changes taking place in market society, agencies occupy a privileged position within the market because they are constantly monitoring, interpreting, and rearticulating the underlying social and economic trends in the market economy. Situated between producers and consumers in the ever-changing marketplace, and between media and audiences in the fragmenting mass media system, advertising agencies became a key site of negotiation between the marketers, strategizing of their brand sales, and consumers managing their lifestyles.

But as marketing emerged as the preeminent model of social influence in the capitalist economy, the advertising tactics and media channels forged by agencies did not remain the exclusive purview of merchandisers touting the benefits of their products. Since the time of the American Civil War, advertising agencies became increasingly involved in applying their communication expertise to the general task of public communication by governmental agencies (such as the military), corporations, political parties, and, eventually, advocacy groups. Throughout the twentieth century we have witnessed advertising becoming as much a part of electing presidents and saving the rainforest as it has been in selling cars, snacks, and credit cards.

The diffusion of the marketing model into the general field of public communication began in earnest during World War I with the employment of advertising agencies to prepare poster campaigns to recruit soldiers and sell war bonds. Many advertisers also incorporated nationalistic themes into their messages. After the war, corporations continued to attempt to convince the public that capitalism had a "soul" (Marchand 2000). Increasingly public and community relations, and the legitimizing of the corporation's growing place within the ever-expanding economy, required meeting the public's expectations of corporate responsibility. To assuage public unease, particularly during times of labor unrest, or bad publicity, corporate image ads were intertwined with brand promotion to remind the public that, despite some missteps, corporations were still "good citizens." In this sense advertising was just the much criticized front-end of a more broadly based marketing model that was transforming the cultural and economic dynamics of our mass society.

During the first half of the twentieth century, therefore, we think it is fair to say that the agencies' role began expanding well beyond the narrow confines of providing services to corporations seeking to promote product sales to consumers.

First, advertising was used by a wider array of organizations large and small—including governments, corporations, and political and advocacy groups—to manage relationships with the public. And second, as advertising emerged as the preeminent way to organize and manage social influence through public communication, the marketing concept itself evolved into a strategic communication problem-solving practice that could be applied to very different tasks of social mobilization and adjustment. Agencies were no longer simply experts in communicating about product benefits and lifestyles but in communicating about the ways that individuals could manage their lifestyle choices in a risky world (Giddens 1991)—whether this meant acknowledging the energy crisis to sell cars, reducing older people's fears of bank machines, or getting young gay men to use condoms.

Advertising's social-therapeutic contribution to the consumer culture became especially apparent during the Second World War, as corporations whose products were rationed undertook responsibility campaigns, reminding consumers they were doing their patriotic duty. So too government information bureaus turned to advertisers and communications and public relations specialists to research, design, and manage their propaganda campaigns, whether they were food rationing, morale issues, or labor-force shortages.

In her well documented history, Inger Stole traces how, in the early 1940s, under the threat of the removal of business taxation deductions for advertising, the advertising trade associations banded together to form a public relations arm called the Advertising Council. This body, according to Stole, "neutralized the threat of hostile government actions towards advertising... [and] helped create a public impression of the industry as civic-minded and patriotic." The Advertising Council coordinated the activities of over four hundred advertising agencies, who volunteered the time of their employees to create campaigns to fulfill the government's wartime objectives. This arrangement was responsible for the successful war bond advertising campaign which convinced the public to give money to the government because "Uncle Sam" needed the funds to prosecute the war. A study of weekly and monthly magazines revealed that by 1942, 40 percent of ads contained some sort of war appeal (Shepard 1942). So successful was the Advertising Council in promoting the industry that it continued its work after the war, endeavoring to "promote an image of advertising as a responsible and civic-spirited industry, of the U.S. economy as a uniquely productive system of free enterprise, and of America as a dynamic, classless and consensual society" (Griffith, in Stole 2001).

After the war, agencies continued to be called on for their knowledge as health and safety agencies attempted to deploy the same media channels, research techniques, and persuasion tactics to stop smoking, to prevent drunken driving, and to promote energy conservation. In many cases governmental offices and health advocacy groups teamed up to launch "public service" advertising or social marketing campaigns (Goldberg et al. 1997). By the 1980s the airwaves were filled with ads promoting national pride, energy conservation, environmental conservation, healthy lifestyles, condom use, and a host of other do-good objectives. The French government, lacking the burden of a Puritan ethic, enlisted French cinema icons to strip down and provide the public with a precise condom product demonstration (Faircloth, 1998). UK Prime Minister Tony Blair pledged £50 million for a three-year anti-tobacco advertising blitz (Tylee 1999). In 1998 the U.S. government spent $1 billion on a four-year anti-drug advertising campaign (FitzGerald 1998).

While this sum is impressive, the bulk of U.S. government advertising expenditure is still devoted to promoting the military; some top-rank advertising agencies are enlisted to carry out the job.

> Currently, WPP Group's J. Walter Thompson, Atlanta, creates ads for the U.S. Marine Corps; Publicis Groupe's Leo Burnett USA handles the Army; Interpublic Group's Campbell-Ewald, Warren, Mich., is agency of record for the Navy, while sibling Foote, Cone & Belding, New York, handles the Postal Service. WPP Group's Ogilvy & Mather, New York, handles the Office of National Drug Control Policy or ONDCP. (Sanders, 2004)

To combat the hysteria whipped up by the tabloids about refugees and asylum seekers, the United Nations invested in a pan-European advertising campaign to promote tolerance (Wheeler 2000).

In Canada, the Government of Canada remains the biggest single advertising spender—especially in a year before elections. In 2002 the UK government's advertising unit, COI Communication, spent £121.5 million, making it the second most advertised brand that year. This represented a bit of a slide, as the government has consistently held the top spot, but it had deliberately reduced its advertising spends by 15 percent that year after a spate of public criticism. Even those who critiqued consumerism turned to media advertising channels to get their messages to a wider audience (e.g., Adbusters, Greenpeace, PETA).

Beginning in the 1970's corporations too—led by oil and chemical giants like Shell, Exxon, and Mobil—began to fund major corporate advertising campaigns as the main thrust of their public relations efforts, repositioning themselves as socially responsible and responsive organizations adjusting to the environmental crisis, community crises, and economic slow-downs that periodically disturb the complacent surface of society. So, by the 1980s it was not uncommon to find global corporations as outspoken critics of the status quo on issues ranging from deforestation to sexism in their ads.

From the 1980s onward, then, four broad social groups became the most frequent users of advertising in most market democracies. The first, product, brand, and corporate advertising, emerged out of the interest of merchandisers to promote their products and services by paid commercials intended to inform consumers of product or brand attributes, values, or "stories" (e.g.,

Saturn cars, Tide laundry detergent). This most familiar of advertising categories now includes corporate advocacy, social marketing, and responsibility themes (such as Nike's attempt to deal with the issue of worker exploitation by its foreign suppliers). Second, there is government advertising, in which information is provided about services and programs (e.g., availability, access) and government program objectives (e.g., anti-smoking and anti-drinking-driving campaigns) are promoted by using risk communication and social marketing campaigns. Third, there are campaigns by public interest groups, charities, or non-governmental agencies which advocate on behalf of their organizations' positions on social issues, health and environmental problems, preventative programs, and broad social values (e.g., Mothers Against Drunk Drivers' anti-drinking-and-driving campaign; Shell Oil's environmental protection messages; Greenpeace's anti-sealing campaign). Fourth, official political parties and "third-parties" with an interest in public issues seek to support (or campaign against) a particular party and its policies—mostly during, but not necessarily confined to, election campaigns (including image, issue, and attack strategies).

In the following chapters we will attempt to elaborate further on the evolution of the unique institutional location which agencies occupy at the heart of an evolving mediated market system. Because they superintend the strategic design and distribution of information about the use and social meaning of goods, advertising agencies are responsible for the creation of a privileged discursive practice in our consumer culture. By virtue of the media's saturation of everyday life and the broadening sophistication of marketing as a strategic enterprise, advertising agencies have become recognized as a special (and uniquely problematic) cultural sector at the intersection of merchants plans and consumers desires.

But for now we need to note that these new agency practices evolved in a context where advertising was understood not as a matter of salesmanship in print but rather as a strategic communication practice, orchestrated within the context of the multi-dimensional and flexible agency system, where personnel who worked on a car campaign one minute could work on an anti-smoking one the next—and on a primary campaign for a politician on the following day. Budding creatives often cut their teeth on low-budget public service announcements or charity ads, only to go on to handle accounts as large a Burger King and Morris Mini cars (especially at innovative agencies such as Crispin Porter Bogusky).

The ever-evolving development of promotional strategy does not simply flow from product sectors to non-profit and advocacy groups, but also in the reverse direction. Bank advertisers use the songs and images of social protest to sell their services; fashion designers buy space to raise consciousness for issues such as AIDS; videogame and soft drink manufacturers host hoaxes, happenings, and Internet buzz tactics with overtones of social movements created by the Situationists, Zapatistas, and Greenpeace. So too there has been a blurring of the supposedly sharp distinction between political, public service and commercial speech in our market society—and between social change and promotional advocacy as well. That Western governments increasingly understand and address their constituents as consumers instead of as citizens can be considered an expected outcome of the longstanding association between advertising agencies and the larger context of communication about political and social issues.

Debating Advertising

To situate our new study, in this section, we briefly review some of the key theoretical and methodological currents that have influenced advertising debates. Advertising became a very popular area of study explored from a multitude of disciplinary and interdisciplinary perspectives (Nava 1997)—history, art, literature, sociology, anthropology, philosophy, political science, to mention a few. In our minds, however, the most influential perspectives towards advertising study (the questions asked, the themes focused upon) have emerged from long standing academic debates about the links between texts, social relationships and power. This period of study has been marked by considerable contradiction, as authors drew attention to the powerful biases of marketplace communication, at the same time, audiences were seen as more media literate and empowered in marketplace dynamics.

To appreciate the uniqueness of contemporary critiques it is useful to begin with some of the early debates of advertising. We saw how the first critics of advertising were concerned with its cultural contribution (Leavis and Thompson [1933] 1977; McLuhan [1951] 2002). Early social movements objected to how advertising polluted public space. But confronting the rapid diffusion of commercial television after the Second World War, social critics began to question the classical economic account of the consumer marketplace and advertising's role within it.

The economic concept of advertising as a business practice is rooted in classical liberal economic theory. Its starting point is the rational consumer who chooses among goods offered in the capitalist marketplace to satisfy his or her needs based on the product information provided by advertising. Yet the intrusive presence of advertising provoked many within business and academic circles to rethink advertising as symptomatic of a growing malaise in mass markets. The prime objects of their critical inquiry were the twin assumptions of fair competition and the free circulation of product information, which allowed autonomous consumers to make rational choices.

Social commentators began to challenge the classical economist's version of advertisings limited communicational role in the marketing concept arguing that mass advertising was a persuasive force, which shifts the very balance of power between producers and consumers. Galbraith's analysis feared that granting merchants unfettered use of media allowed them to gain control over consumer demand. The economic models twin assumptions of fair competition and the free circulation of product information, which allowed autonomous consumers to make rational choices he argued, were no longer valid given the pervasiveness of advertising.

Stuart Ewen points to the transitional period in the 1920s when advertising messages shifted from focusing on products and their qualities to defining consumers and their social aspirations as an integral part of the social meaning of goods. He claims that at this moment that marketers realized their task was to create demand in consumers rather than simply to reflect their innate desires. Advertisers, therefore, contributed to the "self-conscious change in the psychic economy" (Ewen 1976) by flooding the marketplace with the hope that consumers could encounter something grander in the realm of social or psychological experience than previously had been unavailable to them. Material objects thus came to play an increasingly important role in social interaction and everyday life as symbols of prestige and status—for the masses.

Advertising caused unease because it seemed to have broken free from its original product information mandate to become a highly persuasive and seductive form of communication. In their study of the rhetoric of advertising, Gunnar Andren and his collaborators distinguish between non-rational influences, or persuasion, and rational influences, or argument. The latter operates in the public or consumer interest whereas the former does not. The rhetoric of advertising (the form of presentation) would have to conform to a particular set of criteria if the communication were to qualify as sensible guidance to the consumer. Andren et al. (1978, 112) conclude, not surprisingly, that advertising does not contain sufficient information to be the basis of reflective choice among products, and that "advertising does not serve the consumer or the public interest."

Philip Nelson (1974b) sought to explain the role of advertising by giving a more complete account of the consumer's various sources of information. Because consumers do not have perfect information about goods, he writes that they have to rely on past consumption experiences, the advice of friends and relatives, consumer reports, and, of course, advertising. Nelson is aware that the information argument appears to be weakest in the case of national television advertising, but he attempts to construct a model that will accept this as a form of information as well. Conceding the point that much national advertising offers no help in ranking competing brands on any "informational" criteria (because all claim to be the best and only experience can differentiate them), he still believes that it conveys some vital information-namely, that a brand advertises. The more a brand advertises the more the consumer is likely to believe it is a better buy. The mere existence of the commercial is its total informational role.

> The consumer is right in his belief that advertised brands are better. The better brands have more incentive to advertise than the poorer brands.... Simply put, it pays to advertise winners rather than losers. In consequence, the amount of advertising gives consumers a clue as to which brands are winners and which brands are losers. (Nelson 1974b, 50)

In effect, Nelson meets the controversy over the irrational nature of national advertising by ignoring it.

Charles Lindblom (1977) and Morris Janowitz (1978) believe that advertising's main purpose is not to sell us particular goods, but rather to persuade us that *only* in consumption can we find satisfaction and happiness. In a similar vein, the French writer Guy Debord suggested that the whole enterprise of the consumer society is simply a fraudulent spectacle.

> When economic necessity is replaced by the necessity for boundless economic development, the satisfaction of primary needs is replaced by an uninterrupted fabrication of pseudo-needs which are reduced to the single pseudo-need of maintaining the reign of the autonomous economy. (Debord 1970, 51)

According to Christopher Lasch in *The Culture of Narcissism* (1979), in its new role as persuader advertising contributed to "the propaganda of commodities" by which "advertising serves not so much to advertise products as to promote consumption as a way of life." This propaganda has two functions: to offer consumption as an alternative to rebellion or protest, and to turn alienation or reification itself into a commodity. While Lasch acknowledges the liberal values and emancipatory promises promoted by advertising's social promises has helped to change social aspirations and relations, he fears it has generally been within the spectrum of social relations promoted by capitalism.

> The "education" of the masses has altered the balance of forces within the family, weakening the authority of the husband in relation to the wife and parents in relation to their children. It emancipates women and children from patriarchal authority, however, only to subject them to the new paternalism of the advertising industry, the industrial corporation and the state. (Lasch 1979, 140)

As we have seen, post-war advertising did not confine itself to describing goods and their utility. The world of goods it portrays is a cornucopia offering endlessly varied possibilities of improving our lives. Commercials promise all kinds of things: goods can make us stunningly attractive in an instant, give us power over other people's affections, cure us of all illness, capture and package nature for our use, lift our emotions, act as a passport into a fantastic community of desirable persons. Howard Luck Gossage, ad-man turned social critic, comments that magical stewardship in any society is associated with its most important domain; in western capitalism, this is the consumption of goods. Further, because advertisements must have wide appeal, they have to play on very basic human emotions: "They go beyond reason into something even more basic, the most common denominator of all, magic" (Gossage 1967, 364). Advertisements draw upon the entire magical repertoire, including contagious magic, charms to avoid dire consequences, taboos, command over the supernatural, incantations (jingles), and even the devil's blandishments.

> Mephistopheles grants a boon: eternal life, youth, prowess, togetherness, unfulfilled dreams. His price is always something. When it is such a small thing as a pack of cigarettes, or a soft drink, or a lipstick, why should we not take a chance? (Gossage 1967, 367)

He worried therefore that consumers are influenced by advertisings false promises that the product will do something special for them—something magical that will transform their lives.

In an essay appropriately entitled "The Magic System," Raymond Williams (1980 [1962]) refers to this aspect of advertising as a "highly organized and professional system of magical inducements and satisfactions" that coexist strangely with the rest of a highly developed technological society. Yet Williams wrote that the magical social properties conferred upon goods by advertising shows us that it is wrong to regard modern society as being too materialistic—as putting too much emphasis on the possession of goods. Rather, we are *not materialistic enough.*

> If we were sensibly materialist, in that part of our living in which we use things, we should find most advertising to be of insane irrelevance. Beer would be enough for us, without the additional promise that in drinking it we show ourselves to be manly, young at heart, or neighbourly. A washing machine would be a useful machine to wash clothes, rather than an indication that we are forward-looking or an object of envy to our neighbours. But if these associations sell beer and washing machines, as some of the evidence suggests, it is clear that we have a cultural pattern in which the objects are not enough but must be validated, if only in fantasy, by association with social and personal meanings which in a different cultural pattern might be more directly available. (Williams [1962] 1980, 185)

Williams then returns to the economists arguments distinguishes between a rational use of goods, based on their utility alone (what they can do for us), and an irrational use of goods, based on what they symbolize (what they mean to us)—a distinction between use and symbol.

Thus, capitalist consumption is characterized by irrationality because of the symbolic system of meaning within which goods are located. But note that for Williams *any* symbolic system is irrational, for rationality is based only on utility, only on the objective performance features of the product. For goods to take on any other meaning is unhealthy. Fred Inglis also sees the consumption of objects based on such arbitrary characteristics as socially harmful.

> Attainment of the values is signalled by acquiring the appropriate objects, using them, throwing them away and acquiring replacements. Continuous and conspicuous consumption is the driving energy of this fiction.... The objects advertised are drenched in a certain light and smell. They give off the powerful fragrance of the very rich and instead of leaving the object in an intelligible domestic world, remove it to a fantastic one. (Inglis 1972, 17)

Once again, the contrast is between an "intelligible domestic world" and a "fantastic one," one of consumption—that is between use and symbol. One of the cornerstones of these critics then, that is that goods should be represented in advertising with no meaning over and above their functions as conceived in strictly utilitarian terms, because any additional meaning is false.

Criticisms of advertising often are based on the opposing presumptions, namely, that it has distorted our economy and flattened our culture. Critics of advertising usually compare advertising to propaganda, portraying marketing communication as a persuasive, powerful, and manipulative force exerted on consumers. They claim that advertising distracts people from paying attention to their own inner needs, gets them to focus on the banality of mass-produced objects, and leaves them unable to decide rationally what exactly their real needs are or how best to satisfy them.

Many of these critics assert that advertising actually destroys the competitive and rational nature of the free market economy by handing corporations a powerful means of shaping consumers' choices and making them desire what they don't really need. Even classical economists worried that advertising could distort fair competition by becoming an high priced entrance barrier for small upstart companies with new products, thus reducing competitive relations and product innovation contributing to oligopolistic markets. The consumer is seen, from this perspective, as the confused and hapless economic victim of the advertising industry's clever machinations. Yet all of these critics converged on one major point: marketers' constitutive role in the formation of social consumption patterns within the market economy.

Since critics feared that the advertising industry might play a distorting role in the social relations of mass-market researchers set out to study the influence of advertising on the level of consumption in our society. The classic work in this field, Neil Borden's *Advertising in our Economy* (1945), concluded that, while advertising may accelerate trends in consumption patterns, it cannot by itself create these patterns. Twenty-four years later, Julian Simon stated that advertisements for products such as alcohol, soap, and drugs—some of the products at the heart of the controversy about advertising—do not seem to have much effect on the economy and "hence from an economic point of view, it is immaterial whether they are present or absent.... All this implies that the economic study of advertising is not deserving of great attention" (1970, 285).

Downplaying advertising's economic influence became an increasingly familiar refrain of the industry's explanation of advertising's role. Advertisers contend that there is little evidence to show that advertising has any affect on aggregate sales—in other words, it does nothing to increase the overall level of consumption. Advertisers claim they simply do not have the knowledge or tools required for manipulating people (no matter how much they might want to do so). Indeed, after reviewing the literature one is tempted to conclude that in no other domain has so much effort yielded so little insight. Market research has provided remarkably little reliable information on the kind of advertising that works with various market segments, or why consumers react to commercials as they do. Testifying before the Federal Trade Commission in 1971, Alfred Seeman summarized this position:

> I can see why people outside the advertising business think we have an unlimited supply of scientific tools and techniques so magical that we can manipulate almost anything. The fact of the matter is that we are successful in selling good products and unsuccessful in selling poor ones. In the end consumer satisfaction—or lack of it—is more powerful than all our tools and ingenuity put together. The economics of the marketplace insist that an advertiser must satisfy the consumer—that is, get repeat purchases—or fail. Often we think, after using all our techniques, we have a sure bet in a new product, for instance, only to find that it fails in the marketplace. You know the story: We had the perfect dog food except for one thing—the dogs wouldn't eat it.... The use of language is not a science, it is an art. (quoted in Moskin 1973, 44)

People who work in the advertising industry certainly do not feel that they are all-powerful manipulators, as these representative comments indicate:

> The recipients think that advertising is a powerful tool, capable of great things. We in the business see it as a fragile tool—if we could sell everything there would not be so many failures. The thing that intrigues me is that everyone thinks the advertising business is so sophisticated and that we have all sorts of research. We always laugh at that. We're working on something and come up with a dumb idea and laugh. Things happen so simply. In a lot of cases you don't need years of experience. If you are a good lateral thinker and approach it from a different way then you can present it to the consumer. Manipulating wizards? It's one of the misconceptions and I wish it were true—we'd be running the country and sitting in the sun somewhere if I knew absolutely how

to manipulate people. The fact of the matter is that human beings can't be thus manipulated—if they could we could banish war and apply the same techniques to larger theaters of life and control whole populations. We can't because fundamentally human beings refuse to be categorized and are finally unpredictable. (Interviews)

Seldom does one find an industry so strenuously arguing the ineffectiveness of its own product! Given agencies insistent claims about their winning of brand share for their clients, was it credible to believe that producers would respond to consumer's desires for better and cheaper products. The overall impression one derives from this self-deprecating view is that advertisers do not know how to manipulate. Advertising is an art form. It is incapable of steering audience responses reliably in one direction or another.

Advertiser's grew tired of being blamed for all the ills that existed in the modern world—whether sexist attitudes or environmental pollution. The industry's public relations flacks have always protested that advertising was not as powerful as these critics claim. The only persuasive intent they would admit was the desire to shift brand preferences within product sectors—to win market share in a competitive and every changing marketplace. Advertisers cannot risk not advertising, even though they can never be entirely sure it is worth the money. Second, while advertising may not influence aggregate demand for a particular product group, it influences substantially the market share commanded by any company at a given time. As advertising executive Frank Convery says: "The task of most advertising is to keep the product on the market or increase its share from someone else. This is share-oriented advertising, pushing brands. Most, even for tobacco, is brand oriented—it doesn't make people smoke" (Interview).

Yet as advertising expenditure grew the debates about it grew more vociferous. Other writers did claim to find a clear economic role in expanding the size of markets. For example, Mark Albion and Paul Farris write:

> We believe strongly that advertising, as an efficient form of mass communication, can accelerate the growth of new markets and new entries into markets. We doubt that advertising significantly determines the ultimate size of a market...Other factors appear to be much more important in increasing demand. The effectiveness of advertising is severely limited, relegated mostly to new products and new services. (1981, 179)

Studies on the economic effect of marketing communication have focused on advertising's role in developed Western economies, particularly the American economy. Some researchers have sought to measure the claims of manipulation and the creation of artificial demand in cross-national terms. In a 1980 paper, Rachael Querles and her colleagues sought to test whether advertising creates demand by asking a wider question: What factors determine how much we buy? Two broad answers are usually given. Critics think that advertising (and specifically television advertising) is a persuasive force, a contributing factor governing how much a society consumes. Classical liberal economic theorists believe that the level of consumption is based more on how much people have to spend that it is on advertising; the level of affluence, in other words, is the dominant factor in explaining how much a society consumes.

Querles and her co-workers quantified the subsidiary elements of these two explanations. They measured the level of consumption in each society in terms of consumption per household; the level of advertising as the amount spent on advertising; and affluence in terms of a society's per capita gross national product (GNP). By comparing different societies along these dimensions, they hoped to be able to see the relative influences of advertising and affluence on the level of consumption in general; that is, whether high levels of consumption are more dependent on advertising or on wealth. Using data from forty-two nations representing the industrialized nations of Western Europe and North America, as well as the developing nations of Latin America, Africa, and Asia, they performed a regression analysis to determine which of the factors was more significant.

The results were far from clear-cut. When total advertising expenditures (both broadcast and print) were included in the calculations, it seemed that claim that advertising fuels demand was upheld, because consumption seemed to correlate more closely to it than to the relative level of affluence. However, when advertising expenditures were broken down into broadcast and print expenditures and treated separately, a curious result appeared. Broadcast advertising, which according to most critics is the most persuasive tool in the creation of demand, was much less of an influence upon the level of consumption than was print advertising. Curiously, the findings of the Querles study indicate that the rational information of print is more influential than television's persuasive formats.

If the Querles study is assumed to be valid, what conclusions follow? The authors suggest that "it is possible that consumers are not really manipulated by advertising but are instead beneficiaries of a more efficient distribution system made possible by advertising" (Querles, Jeffres, and Schnuerer 1980, 11). Advertising may actually increase the level of consumption, not because it is persuading us to do things we would not otherwise do, but by making the system work more efficiently for the benefit of both consumers and producers. In the light of such empirical evidence and the plausible protestations of innocence from the advertising industry, the notion of the malleable consumer appears more and more implausible. Consumers may well be bewildered and confused, but, if they are, it is not because advertising is manipulating them. The relationship between advertisers and their audiences was more complex.

Advertising and the Economy: Cultural Criticisms

Many of the early economic critiques of advertising rested on a clear separation between economic and cultural spheres, a divide, which through the 1980s critics increasingly drew into question. A new political economic situation was outlined in which economy and culture, work and leisure were merged (Slater 1997; Callon 1998; du Gay 2002). The cultural and service industries were recognized as major engines of economic grown, particularly in the United States and Britain. The expanding cultural and knowledge industries sector (videogames, fashion, media, education) demanded innovation, creativity and play. Software manufacturers at Microsoft, advertising agencies, and a host of top-100 corporations encouraged employees to play games and puzzles to enhance their productivity. Entertainment became a major industry and experience a major commodity. Companies grew rich not only on the "things" they produced but the feelings and affections they stimulated and channelled. This had important consequences for the study of advertising, which promoted not just objects but services or experiences.

Consumption traditionally registered with economists as the destructive, if rational act of the lone individual meeting their needs in the marketplace, catalogued under the ill-defined heading of "demand." Within social theory, according to Daniel Miller, consumption had long remained an unacknowledged area of study. This situation changed drastically during the 1980s as consumption was recognized as central to economic growth cycles. Economists carefully tallied consumer spending and confidence factoring it into their "health" reports of the economy. Consumption was redefined as a productive and social force.

The economist's view of the consumer as an anatomized individual rationally satisfying their needs unfettered in the marketplace was deconstructed exposing a socialized consumer, driven by their desire and body as much as their mind. Consumption is a very social act wherein symbolic meanings, social codes, relationships and political ideologies are produced and reproduced. Baudrillard pressed this point with the argument that capitalism was no longer driven simply by a work ethic, but a "pleasure ethic"—personal consumption had become a systemic compulsion. As culture and economy blurred consumerism became our culture, the arena where we knit together our sense of social belonging. In this new political economy, Davidson (1992) noted, the older critiques of advertising and consumption—making an argument for the return to a rational, utilitarian relationship to goods—appeared elitist and inconsiderate of people's everyday life and interests, at once romantic and paternal.

Criticism turned toward exploring advertising's cultural contribution, particularly in relation to gender and race. New post-modern epistomologies challenged modernism's faith in science, knowledge, and universalism. The vast expansion of knowledge in the modern period had neither delivered society from superstition or oppression (Giddens 1991). Michel Foucault argued that knowledge was less of a tool for utopia than a form of "power," a productive force within society.

The legacy of science in modern societies, according to Giddens, popularized a general sense of scepticism and doubt, and anxiety. Scientific practices were argued to be neither benign nor exacting. The role of science and rationality in war, the holocaust, and environmental and cultural destruction were highlighted in these critiques (Berman 1981; Shiva 1992; Shiva 1997). Because individuals in late modern society were subject to conflicting health risk information (fish is good for your heart; fish is full of PCBs), they are encouraged to become reflexive or skilled at constantly reviewing their attitudes and behavior in light of new information. Giddens understood the contemporary rise of fundamentalist religion and nostalgia as attempts to construct certainties under social conditions of constant flux that provided considerable anxiety.

Positivism and objectivity asserted that universal "facts" about the world could be revealed through the scientific method, but new post-modern arguements rejected approaches to knowledge that totalized and universalized. Science, based upon laws and averages, not only totalized particularities, but also silenced and left unstudied the multiplicity of voices and experiences teeming beneath the universalizing labels. Feminists rejected the "Cartesian subject" as universalizing a masculine approach to the world that marginalized the experience of women. For feminists the cloak of scientism, despite its best intentions, was less about the production of knowledge than the enactment of power over the subjects it silenced (May 2001). The idea that researchers could distance themselves from their objects of study by the scientific method was shown to be an impossibility. In place of positivist procedures qualitative and interpretive methods emerged claiming to be more sensitive to the constructed and subjective nature of knowledge. Saussurian semiotics lodged a devastating blow to positivism by positing that the link between the sign and referent was arbitrary: The material world was not transparent, but rather "constructed" through language and symbols. The meaning of the world was the product of relations between one sign and the next. There was no neutral relationship between the word and the object. The role of meaning and language played in the construction of lifestyles and identity became the subject of considerable study. The semiotic study of advertising flourished through the 1980s and 1990s, as authors built upon the seminal studies of Judith Williamson and Roland Barthes. Semiotics became a popular topic of study in university courses, was used within the advertising industry, and was the subject of many new advertising books (Beasley and Danesi 2002; Danesi and Perron 1999; Cook 1992).

The approach known as "deconstruction," developed in the late 1970s by French philosopher Jacques Derrida, also had a profound influence on the direction of advertising study. Whereas traditional studies had focused on the signs present in the text, Derrida encouraged readers to look for what was absent, the "unperceived, the nonpresent, and the nonconscious" (quoted in Stern 1993). This methodological perspective drew attention not simply to the "sense" the advertisement made but its "gaps, inconsistencies, and contradictions." The challenge of interpreting a text is to recognize what is central to meaning and what is more superfluous, Derrida argued: For example, binary relations (man/woman; white/black; nature/culture) were key to meaning generation, thus central to analysis. Deconstructing the text made researchers more sensitive to the absent halves of the binary terms. Through deconstructing texts Derrida noted that language was not neutral, but rather projected male dominance. Advertising had privileged white Western males while keeping others (women, blacks, Eastern cultures) in the shadows. The role of the critic was to expose this dominance and to illustrate how it subordinated female forms of power, knowing, and reading. Deconstruction challenged the legitimacy of the biased representations in advertising.

Of course, feminists had been deconstructing texts for sometime being the first to challenge the "universal code" of "mankind." most easily done by simply changing or reversing the gender roles performed within advertisement (Stern 1999). Early advertising studies emphasised the "generic" woman, her gender displays, stereotypes, and products targeted towards her. Erving Goffman's classic study (1979) of gender displays, for example, explored the positioning, relative size, gaze, head tilt, and posturing of advertising's female characters, revealing how women often appeared childlike, smaller, less functional and focused in the world than men did. Reader response studies also revealed that men and women interpreted texts differently:

> Men tended to read for authorial intent, were motivated to acquire information from a story, were less likely to draw inferences, and were more likely to make evaluative judgments. Women in contrast tended not to search for authorial intent, were motivated to experience a story's personal relationships rather than to get its 'point,' were more likely to draw inferences and were more likely to empathize than to judge the characters. (Stern 1993, 194)

The role of race in advertising and the black/white binary received much study. Like women, blacks were under-represented in advertising, and were often cast as "menial workers, poor recipients of charity, and social problems; while others were athletes, musicians and entertainers" (Stern 1993). Marilyn Kern-Foxworth (1994) illustrated how black characters in early advertisements from Aunt Jemima to Uncle Ben conformed to dominant stereotypes: Blacks were represented in slave and servant roles and characterized as sociable and deferential. Finding texts heavily biased toward the depiction of white, educated, heterosexual males in favorable terms, advertising was denounced by feminists and civil rights campaigners, not because of its relationship to consumption or the economy, but because it was understood to be a powerful social discourse that projected negative representations which contributed to the devaluing of some sectors of the population.

Whether it was a matter of textual analysis or reader response, the central interest of early studies was to reveal the differences between men and women. But this approach also became diversified. Within feminist social movements some women began to complain that their experience was not being addressed by the dominant liberal feminist position. Critics asked whether feminists were simply reproducing masculine approaches by lumping all women into one category. The emphasis on the universal woman in opposition to man had shadowed the multiplicity of women and their different experiences—black women, old women, religious women, Western women. Within these complex discussions the biologic definition of gender was attacked. Judith Butler's 1989 *Gender Trouble* radically separated sex from gender: Privileging the subjective domain of gender, Butler argued that gender was neither essential nor innate but enacted, performed. Attention shifted to the social construction of gender. The discipline of women studies was reframed as gender studies in order to provide a place for the study of homosexual and transsexual subjectivities, whereupon the contribution of advertisers to the maintenance of "heterosexism" was added to the agenda of research.

Likewise the early-1970s studies of how advertising portrayed African Americans had lumped all blacks together regardless of gender, age, or nationality, thus failing to register the plurality of multiculturalism. The emphasis on "black" had displaced the study of Asians, Hispanics, and a host of other minority groups. But new work rendered the understandings of race much more complex. Post-colonialist writers like Edward Said developed theories that placed greater attention onto how race was represented in the advertising text. The idea of the "other," that is, how the construction of self and meaning occurs through a process by which one makes appeals to what one is not, opened up an entirely new line of study. For Stuart Hall this construction of "otherness" is central to meaning making. Finally, the biological basis of race was also challenged, as 1990s scholarship rejected "the category of race as a biological fact, even questioning its position as a physical attribute of individuals immediately obvious to observers" (Stern 1993, 5).

Researchers also began to explore more carefully the differences in groups previously represented as being quite homogenous. Critics began to explore the differences within (as opposed to between) genders. Attention turned from the study of white, European, heterosexual, educated men, to multicultural research that sought to traced the complex intersections of race, class and sexual orientation (O'Barr 1994; Kemper 2001).

The interpretive powers of the individual to defy, critique, and rework the set of socially constructed categories became of great importance. Within mass audiences considerable divergence emerged in the readings of the individuals who together formed those audiences. The growing interest in the "reader" or "subject" of the text provided a prominent place for psychoanalytic readings of advertising (Haineault and Roy 1993; Richards et al. 2000). Advertising was becoming a resource not simply for information, gauging relative standing, or exploring the good life, but a source of symbolic material that reflected psychic tensions, resolutions, and repressions, and provided resources for the reader's identity work. Fish argued that readers existed in "interpretive communities" where social-cultural histories patterned approaches to the text (Fish 1980, 4). There was no one universal reader but subcultures of readers with "different cultural expectations, life experiences, and interpretive habits" that shaped how they construed meanings of incoming media messages. Readers came to the text with a variety of literary competences and tastes, or cultural capital. The unique literacy that individuals brought to bear on a text were highlighted as the "active" nature of audiences was asserted.

The End of Semiotics?

Matthew McAllister uncovered several broad ideologies identified by contemporary researchers. The advertising text was said, for example, to "purify" messages, presenting elements that support the sale of goods while ignoring those that downgraded the world of goods. In using new and old symbols to appeal to audiences, others believe that advertising continues to co-opt meaning, subverting more authentic meaning to the promotional cause. Another view saw advertising as "infecting" other realms of meaning, making it impossible, for example, to separate the sports stars from the brand that they sponsor. Others have argued that bringing cultural referents into the frame of advertising devalues and trivializes important issues. According to some critics, the Italian sweater maker, Benneton, does not raise awareness of AIDS by depicting dying patients in their advertisements; rather, it profits from a prurient interest in disease and thus trivializes a very serious calamity for affected individuals. And Thomas Frank illustrated how advertisers co-opted cultural rebellion, converting critique into a handmaiden of commerce (McAllister 1997, 55–58).

But the idea that advertising "permeates," "invades," or "co-opts" an allegedly "pure" cultural realm was challenged by the argument that there is not longer a separation between advertising and culture, culture and commerce, culture and politics. Wernick (1990) argued that all meaning had become impregnated with the promotional impulse, which complicated the idea that there exist "authentic" realms of speech or actions separate from commercialism. According to Sut Jhally, advertising is powerful because it provides very palpable images of what people desperately seek, "the things that make people human: *love, friendship, security, some kind of autonomy.*" These dreams of humanity are not what should concern us, according to Jhally; what troubles him is that they are not embedded within a collective political body, but rather incorporate interests that continually link them back to commodification and economic growth, where they threaten the survival of the planet (Jhally 1997).

The critique that advertising is a myth which "naturalizes" particular ways of viewing the world was challenged by Foucault, who argued that liberal democracies were not governed simply by ideology or coercion, but through bodies, a process he referred to as "biopolitics." Drawing upon these ideas McFall (2004) counters the proposition that advertising obscures "real" material conditions, contending that this is not a plausible idea, simply because there is no such real material condition separate from language. Rather language and culture are always bound to material practices. McFall thus questioned the emphasis on textual analysis within advertising studies.

Foucault, she says, displaced the role of the semiotician or critic, in order to refocus study on the discourse itself and its struggles over meaning and truth. Discourses "are transparent, they need no interpretation, no one to assign them a meaning. If one reads texts in a particular way one perceives that they speak clearly to us and require no further supplementary sense or interpretation" (Foucault 1980, 115). Meaning, for Foucault, is the plural outcome of ongoing, active process and negotiation, and therefore has no single, essential core accessible only to the skilled analyst or semiotician. While textual analysis may be interesting it adds little to historical understandings of discourse. It is thus that Liz McFall (2004) argues that textual analysis has not helped illuminate understandings of advertising, rather diverted attention from the study of industry practices, where the meaning of advertising is more clearly revealed. Her study sought

> to make a case for an approach to the study of advertising less centred upon the problematic of meaning. The simple reason for this is that while debates about the nature of meaning provide a fertile and fascinating philosophical challenge, in the end they reveal little about advertising…critical debates about advertising are hampered by their focus on meanings of texts and products, at the expense of the practices of the industry. (McFall, 2004, 10)

McFall is one among several new historians who have abandoned the emphasis in modern history on the idea of progress. Modern social and technological change had been supported by the idea that these changes were leading to a "better day," that life within contemporary society was superior to life in the past and that history was linear. Michel Foucault convinced a new generation of scholars that history was better studied as "genealogy," and that the views on modern history had betrayed the plurality, chaos, change and fluidity of everyday practice. Contradiction, paradoxes, and contingency seemed more powerful explanatory factors of the human condition than did seamless grand narratives (Firat and Venkatesh 1995).

Thus, McFall is critical of historical advertising studies which, she believes, have forestalled the appreciation of past practices in an effort to reveal the "wonders" of the contemporary world through advertising. She advocates instead a genealogical study of advertising, which accepts that the codes of adverting evolve in a "piecemeal fashion," shaped by a "patchwork of historical conditions and accidents" (McFall, 2004, 33). In her study of early twentieth century British advertising practices, McFall discovered that early advertisers were highly innovative in their approaches, interested in target markets, understood their audiences as "savvy" and sought to persuade them by emotional appeals. In short, many of the factors deemed as unique to the contemporary period of advertising were not very new at all. McFall's study of advertising stresses the themes of reversals and accidents, telling a non-progressive and non-linear narrative of advertising.

Foucault's ideas also informed Anne Cronin's (2004) study of advertising, which rejected the semiotic question: How do ads work, in favor of a different one: What work does advertising do? Her answer to this question is that advertising has emerged as a key social "discourse," a site of struggle over the truth about human-object relationships. According to Cronin, nineteenth-century discussions of unhealthy consumption habits located the cause in a multitude of arenas: seduction of the commodity itself, the easy access to goods in the new department store, and the weak will of the individual. By way of contrast, in the twentieth century advertising emerged as a lightening-rod for social concerns, raising fears about the unhealthy side of our relationships to goods, becoming the arena in which we worked through our collective relationships to goods. Thus, Cronin asserts that advertising is a discourse in the Foucaultian sense, meaning a site of struggle over the construction and legitimation of "truth." Specifically, the advertising industry serves to adjudicate a social discussion about people and things. Unlike McFall, who rejects Barthes notion of myth, Cronin reworks it:

> In my analysis, I am using myth to reference advertising as an entire institution not merely the textual end-products of its processes, and I am also departing from the classic sense that myth functions through naturalization. Instead, I argue that the complex circulation of beliefs and commercial imperatives acts to constitute the institution that is advertising. In parallel, I argue that advertising is used as a trope (by academics, by regulators, by advertising practitioners) for rehearsing understandings of the social and social relationships. In this sense, advertising itself functions as a myth that circulates through multiple sites and articulates diverse commercial and political interests. (Cronin 2004, 3)

The power of advertising is "productive" not simply because it encourages consumption, or that as a social discourse it creates cultural bias. Rather, as an institution advertising creates classifications that frame what can be legitimately thought about goods. Advertisers are self-promotional, but regulators and academics have uncritically agreed with the sales pitch that advertising is all-powerful. Together advertisers, regulators, and academics circulate a distorted view of advertising. In light of the non-conclusive evidence about advertising's impact on consumption choices, it is deemed either all-powerful or utterly benign. The "myths of advertising are not falsehoods or misrepresentations in any straightforward sense: they function as mobile power-knowledge formations that allow for the rehearsal of understandings of social relations (including advertising's own influence in the social realm) and produce classificatory structures" (Cronin 2004, 113).

Social Change and Agency

We are struck by the extent to which both McFall and Cronin, in selectively using certain of Foucault's ideas and ignoring others, downplay the role of the consumer within the social construction of the mediated marketplace. The agency of the consumer in contemporary market dynamics has been consistently highlighted in the consumer culture literature (Abercombie 1994). And this focus on the agency of the consumer is consistent with one of Foucault's greatest insights into liberal society, namely, his argument that power is not enacted "over" or down," but in and through individuals: "Governing people, in the broad meaning of the word, governing people is not a way to force people to do what the governor wants; it is always a versatile equilibrium, with complementarily and conflicts between techniques which assure coercion and processes through which the self is constructed the modified by oneself" (Foucault 1999, 162).

In the account of advertising that follows, considerable emphasis is placed on the "reflexivity" of the consumer and the negotiations that take place between target audiences and advertisers. This negotiation is enacted both formally, through the research cycle, and tacitly, through advertisers' conceptions of their audiences. In this context we have found the conception of the consumer advanced by Miller and Rose (1994) invaluable. They offer a thoughtful perspective on the importance of market research which offers a welcome corrective to the way business ideologues defended these activities. Their argument is based on empirical evidence culled by Tavistock psychoanalysts, who undertook work for prominent advertisers in the fast moving goods sector (ice cream, beer) in the 1960s. Miller and Rose are struck by the seriousness with which these analysts applied their psychological techniques to the study of everyday consumption:

the process, what was entailed was an unprecedented and meticulous charting of the minutiae of the consuming passions by new techniques of group
discussions, interviewing and testing. This charting does not merely uncover pre-existing desires or anxieties: it forces them into existence by new
experimental situations such as the psycho-dynamically interpreted group
discussion that enable them to be observed, it renders them thinkable by
new techniques of calculation, classification and inscription such as 'flavour
profiling' and hence makes them amenable to action and instrumentalisation
in the service of sales of goods. (Miller and Rose, 1994, 9)

They believe that researchers clearly played a vital role in bringing the seemingly banal and unacknowledged act of everyday consumption to the surface.
Yet they were also struck by how enthusiastically consumers engaged in these
sessions and how candidly they confessed to their often troubled relation to
goods. Consumers appear to enter the research process as representative volunteers in the complex negotiations between corporations and their potential
customers.

Miller and Rose note that the diagnosis and categorizing of consumer experiences is neither simple nor neutral. Nor do they deny that the typologies
generated often contribute to market segmentation strategies. But, following
Foucault, Miller and Rose argue that market research must also be understood
as one of the generative channels through which marketers "mobilize the consumer" as participants in their decision-making. This idea of mobilization implies that consumers are not simply passive victims who allow researchers to
objectively document them; rather, they enter the research enterprise as consumer citizens who honestly want to articulate their consumption practices
so that the marketplace can better respond to them. Consumers at previous
moments in marketing history had perhaps accepted their role more passively.
But by the 1970s, both marketers and their research subjects acknowledged
the need to establish new civic forums for negotiating the meaning and use of
goods.

The Research Cycle and the Incorporation of the Consumer

Historically, as we have seen, most major marketing campaigns were crafted
within the marketing concept's three idioms of marketplace surveillance—consumer, audience, and advertising research—often used iteratively or in combination by agencies in campaign planning and execution. Although research
has long been their calling card, by the 1960s it had become a key tool guiding
agency communication design: by giving them insight into the changing consumer culture, by helping them to formulate brand strategy, by informing the design of
the appeal and content of advertising, and ultimately by charting the best routes
through the increasingly diversified and ever expanding media channels.

Consumer research refers generally to the many ways advertisers track the spending and product choices of different individuals or groups within market. Although initially quite narrow, focusing on the demographics of purchase behaviour, willingness to buy, and obsolescence; the growing sophistication of psychology has made consumer intelligence an integral part of the advertising brief by identifying the prime market segments who are interested in your product and targeting their particular personality, desires, aspirations or use patterns.

Two conceptions of consumer research have been particularly important in directing advertisers to those most predisposed segments of the population—lifecycle and lifestyle. "Lifecycle" refers to the notion that consumption behaviour changes with the maturation of the individual. As people go through life they develop different interests, confront new challenges, see and value the world differently, and ultimately establish different consumption patterns. For example, those entering their childbearing years not only wrestle with their new status, but also must provision their nest. They tend to move into larger living spaces, buy different foods, and spend up to $2,500 in accessories for each child. So it makes sense to advertise your baby bouncer in those media venues that have strong ratings among the twenty-five to thirty-five-year-olds. Lifestyle research also offered important advantages to advertising strategists by taking market segmentation analysis beyond demographics. Through the clustering of responses on questionnaires, advertisers became better able to appreciate the underlying patterns of consumer values and activities finding that consumers can be understood to diverse quit distinctly along the lines of values.

But as we have seen, lifestyle research would be of little practical value without media research. Media research, mostly carried out by arms length media organizations (Neilson, BBM, BARB) measures the audiences that the media organizations assembled, providing essential feedback on audiences for both programmers and media buyers working on behalf of advertisers. At first satisfied with circulation and gross rating points, audience research has become a complex science which charts the shifting psychographics of media use patterns of various audience demographics—for example seniors who watch the most TV, or teens who listen to heavy metal rock music on the radio. The combined analyses of the segmentation of markets, and the fragmentation of media audiences that guided the targeting of most campaigns since the 1960s, began to carve out niches within the mass marketplace. Perhaps the most obvious was the Saturday morning blitz of children's toy advertising based on the growing knowledge of the patterns of family life (Kline 1993).

But since campaigns are costly, advertising researchers also wanted to understand their audience's responses to advertising messages. Indeed, since the 1920s a range of research tools —from Starch scores to eye-tracking—had been developed to provide crucial intelligence for agencies about the communication process itself (Pollay 1979). Advertising research was often undertaken within the agencies to immerse the creatives in the life-worlds of potential customers. Campaign ideas are often then pre-tested on targets within focus groups for comprehension, acceptability, and retention providing clients with some measure of advertising effectiveness. Advertisers also undertook independent studies of effectiveness: Versions of their creative work can be compared in test markets and sales-tracked, and the long-term awareness of the brand positioning and willingness to purchase related to campaign goals and investment can be documented. These various types of evaluation research helped the agency to acquire legitimacy in the post-war years, for clients were soothed by the thought that their campaigns had been based on marketing surveys and their impact on brand positioning and share evaluated carefully.

Market Power

Armed with reams of market intelligence and fronting their creativity, full-service advertising agencies became the visible manifestations of the promotional communication system, providing a constant reminder of the new dialogic relationships between producers and consumers, creatives and audiences. As the public relied more on the products of the market to construct their lifestyles, so too grew their concern about how those products were conceived, defined, marketed and modified. These marketplace practices were now recognized as a feature of public discourse. Sometimes this was overtly stated in ads themselves, the ones that show people in focus groups, test markets, advertising pitching sessions, or in consumer trials. In some ads we have even witnessed consumers complaining, zapping, or ignoring the failed rhetoric of "un-hip" competitors.

In the fifth phase, therefore, consumers are not so much depicted as ignorant of advertising; more commonly, they are savvy and demanding, having input into the market as "vigilant" customers. Understanding the consumer was integral to modern marketing practices but in the mediated marketplace consumers also increasingly sought to understand the interests, strategies and practices of marketers and advertisers.

Just as popular culture had assimilated much of the therapeutic language of psychology (passive aggression, anality, masking true feelings), so too did popular culture assimilate aspects of the specialized discourse of the marketing fields. In everyday discussions consumers *understand themselves and others as "targets,"* using the marketers' construction of the consumer's mind to map their own social worlds (as housewives, "tweens," yuppies)—often deconstructing the motivations of an advertising strategy as skillfully as experts. Consumers were aided in their understanding of marketplace promotion techniques by the media, who had learned that many advertising and marketing stories could cross over from the business pages to a general readership.

Recognizing the market as a key institution of social exchange, the media celebrated its innovations and sought to play its watchdog function in exposing its weaknesses. Product launches and business scandals could become front-page stories in newspapers. Advertising campaigns were analyzed and deconstructed by industry experts for entertainment. Consumer research was as likely to be published as scientific research. Marketplace practices also became subject to serious study. Advertising content was accepted in the university setting as a "text" worthy of serious contemplation. Schools sought to teach children to be media-literate and aware of promotional hype. Some pupils found these lessons to be sophomoric, for their years of media consumption had made them key readers not only of advertising images, but also of the motivations behind them. The increased penetration of the Internet provided consumers with a new means of obtaining information about goods.

The bridge of advertising was no longer a submerged aspect of the marketplace, but rose into popular consciousness to become itself a site of struggle and self-expression. Consumers realized that they were locked into a negotiation with producers and advertisers over the management of their lifestyles. In the highly competitive marketplace of the fifth phase, failure to recognize the diverse interests of consumers and permit at least a modicum of negotiation could prove to be disastrous. Again and again what we find in our examination of the practices of marketers and advertisers are examples in which industry practitioners sought to address and contain some of the demands of consumers. For their own part, marketers and advertisers acknowledge the growing attentiveness of consumers and audiences to their practices. They recognize that they are speaking to more media- and marketing-savvy individuals who expect their interests to be reflected within the dynamics of the marketplace. Does this imply that we had moved into a new phase of consumer empowerment? Not necessarily. Rather, this period is better thought of as a phase of marketplace development predicated upon the self-conscious inputs of consumers and audiences.

CHAPTER 9

Late Modern Consumer Society

Introduction

In this chapter we explore the work of some authors who have sought to characterize the changes taking place in consumer society since the 1980s, as governments gave greater freedom to business, loosened market regulations and eased taxes, to maximize productivity, promote consumer spending, and develop a more flexible and responsive industrial infrastructure (Bell 1976/1996; Harvey 1989; Lash and Urry 1993). Postmodernism became a catchall phrase for the many cultural transformations of this period, and we focus on two debates in this literature that closely relate to the discourse through and about goods.

The first postmodernist thesis asserts that flexible stylization and the vast expansion of the cultural industries signaled a transition from a "material" to "dematerialized" culture. The profusion of media and commodity signs are understood to have become dominant structuring agents in society, and consumption an elaborate game of culture where the materiality and usefulness of goods has become secondary to their communicational aspects. In the onslaught of signs, modernist notions such as truth, morality, and patriarchy no longer inform people's world view, as they now looked for guidance to the mediated world of commodity signs.

One view saw culture break from the container of political economy: People undertake lifestyle construction to express their identity and compete with others in this expanded field of cultural consumption. As second view saw consumer culture in the process of "demassifing," as social relations rooted in class, family, and work were challenged by the fashioning of individual lifestyles in the expanded domain of consumer culture. Counter-culture movements are recognized as playing a considerable role in popularizing lifestyle experimentation, and their fusion with commodities contributed to the union of culture and economy. Many authors implicated advertising in both of the trends toward demassification and dematerialization. These transformations are said by some to have liberated individuals from modernity, creating space for new truths, new freedoms, diversity, and the expansion of desire. On the other hand, others think that these processes signaled a new level of capital domination, namely, the deepened commodification of everyday life, the promotion of historical ignorance (Jameson 1984), and a morality based on empty play, style and image (Lash and Urry 1993).

Political Economy

During the 1980s and 1990s politicians began to be packaged and promoted through media images as just another form of goods in the marketplace, illustrating Wernick's (1990) point that promotional dynamics had seeped into all areas of social life and civil society. America had perfected the promotional politician, but Britain borrowed these tricks. Tony Blair's "new Labour" party spun its way to victory in a blaze of focus groups. Blair invited popular cultural artists to Downing Street, to illustrate that he was "hip" with the network of culture. But this emphasis on image did not divert politicians' attention from the management of national economies, for indeed all Western leaders, no matter how arrogant, realized their place in history books was subject to the health of the economy during their reign. Thus politicians carefully inspect the quarterly and monthly economic performance reports for signs that all is well, reminding us of the ancient soothsayers who sought similar assurances in the entrails of animals. Sometimes it seems that as far as public policy debates are concerned, our leaders have time for little save nursing the Gross National Product. How well we manage to produce things, encourage investment, or the rate of inflation was a matter of public concern.

The policies of two leaders, Margaret Thatcher and Ronald Reagan, have been identified as playing a key role in the socio-economic changes of the 1980s and 1990s (Hall 1988). Reagan and Thatcher were less interested in making government competent and compassionate, than in dismantling it. Both believed in the microeconomic policies of Milton Friedman, who argued that Keynesian macroeconomic policies, which sought to redistribute wealth through government spending, were not the solution to the economy's problems, but the problem itself. Too much regulation of the economy, Friedman argued, funneled through a bloated and inefficient state government, was crippling productivity. He thus advocated policies that privileged business expansion and consumer spending.

In the first half of the twentieth century government had expanded to provide the public a buffer from market forces, which were thought to produce systemic inequality and to neglect collective resources. However, beginning in the 1980s the public sector was recast as wasteful, inefficient, dictatorial, and in need of private sector input. The economy was jumpstarted by a radical deregulation policy meant to free businesses from their national responsibilities. Lower corporate and personal income taxes directed funds out of the hands of government to consumers and business. Finance, not regulation, was seen as the best means to encourage government and business to be more accountable and efficient. Because interest rates indirectly encourage or discourage investment, thereby turn on and off the tap of growth, their adjustment was a means of controlling inflation and the whole economy. In 1981 President Reagan signed the Omnibus Reconciliation Act and the Economic Recovery

Act which turned the reduction of government spending and tax cuts into law. Publicly-held sectors of the economy were subject to private sector takeovers. In Britain Margaret Thatcher privatized such key public arenas as the railways, water, and social housing. The changes eased individuals' social responsibilities to one another, and at the same time made them more subject to market forces.

Politicians were hardly vanguards of the many political economic changes, but rather followed the interests of business. Since the 1970s big business had rattled the gates of government, demanding to be released from national responsibilities, promising in turn that it would increase productivity and profit within globe markets where there was a bounty of consumers, cheap labor, and less stringent environmental requirements. Globalization, the drive of businesses to expand markets outside of national boundaries, was hardly new, having played a prominent role in imperial and mercantile economies, but new communication and transport technology, combined with new management practices and the liberalization of trade barriers, brought a new intensity to globalization (Bauman 1998; Harvey 1989; Castells 1996, 1997). Britain, America, and Canada supported the global expansion of domestic business. Released from regulations, corporations became multinational consolidating globally. Like a genie let out of the bottle, these global giants assumed considerable influence over the national and global politicians who had given them vastly increased freedom to operate.

Globalized markets and new communication and transport networks more rapidly cycled objects, ideas, and people across the earth (Appadurai 1988). Global corporations negotiated their businesses across time zones and stayed open twenty-four hours a day. Time and space were compressed and the pace of work accelerated. People moved not just to the urban centers in their own countries, but also to other countries to find work. Globalization was not simply about powerful economies expanding outward, but also about transformation within and between national boundaries. In the United States the Hispanic population topped 13 percent, larger than the African American population (10 percent).

Neo-liberal policies did stimulate the economy, and inflation began to decline in 1981. During that year a new one-day record was set on the New York Stock exchange, with 147,070,000 shares traded, signaling a vast increase in financial speculation. Global monetary flows, which had once been a few hundred million dollars daily, reached $2 trillion a day. According to Don Slater, "turnover time reinvestment and capital reach high velocity in this period" (Jameson 1984; Lash and Urry 1987, 1993; Mandel 1976). Businesses reconsolidated in the new environment, and the 1980s unfolded as a period of merger mania, aided by deregulation policies. The lowering of labor costs helped to increase stock prices, as well as the salaries and stock options of corporate

CEOs. Billionaires replaced millionaires. Although global marketplace competition was great, the stakes of winning in this game were immense.

This period also witnessed a scaling up in consumption patterns particularly in the U.S. New flexible manufacturing processes were associated with a more rapid cycling of a diverse array of goods. Consumer spending became the central areas of economic expansion (over 65 percent of the GDP). By the 1990s, according to James Twitchell (2000): "Americans spend three to four times as many hours shopping than Europeans, and have four times as many 'things,' and vastly the number of things of developing countries" (p. 283). Britain was close behind: Surveying the patterns in Britain during this period, Martin Lee noted a vast increase in commodity consumption and announced "consumer culture reborn" (Lee 1993). Cappuccino machines, mobile phones, SUVs, and loft apartments became essentials as the discourse in and through goods took on a new dialect. Consumers assumed increased levels of debt to finance their lifestyles. Undaunted by a mini stock market crash in 1987 and a recession in the early 1990s, the twentieth century ended on an economic boom.

Dematerialization

For some these mature marketplaces seemed to be dematerializing under a thick layer of information and symbolic processes. Surveying changes in America in 1976, Daniel Bell argued that there had been a massive transition from an industrial society, focused upon making material goods, to a "post-industrial society," where science, innovation, information and services accounted for over 50 percent of the Gross National Product. The service economy was layered on top of the manufacturing sector, just as industrialization had been layered atop agricultural society. An increased dependence on science expanded the role and power of technicians and professionals and the importance of information and knowledge. The white-collar service sector expanded, and contributed to a changed role for women, as they filled many of the jobs in that sector.

A global division of labor was being born, wherein developing countries would provide agriculture and manufacturing while developed countries assumed control of services. "In 1970, manufacturing employed 69.7 million people in the ten major developed economies. In 1992, the last year when data on all ten countries is available, only 63.7 million had their employment in this sector." (International Labour Office, 2004) There occurred a great decline in the agriculture sector in all ten major developed countries between 1970–1996, according to data from the *Comparative Civilian Labor Force Statistics* compiled by the U.S. Bureau of Labor Statistics, while the service sector in these same countries rose from employing 127.4 million in 1970 and 216 million in 1994. Both in percentage and absolute terms, the increase in service employment has been the largest in United States and Japan.

In their *Economies of Signs and Space* (1993), Lash and Urry argued that modern economies had moved through three phases. Nineteenth century industrial capitalism focused upon building industry and extending the money economy. In the twentieth century the state assumed a larger role in shaping society while businesses concentrated on mass production and implemented marketing and advertising into their business cycles. Toward the end of the twentieth century, the fixed production lines and the state interventions which informed organized capitalism were disassembled, as capitalism moved into a disorganized phase characterized by globalization and the flow of money, work, goods, information and images across time and space. Lash and Urry's book supported others who had similarly argued that work had become increasingly "dematerialized" and abstract over the course of this historical development:

> A long and exceptionally disparate line of thinkers (for example Bell, Toffler, Tourraine, Mills, Riesman, Lyotard) argue that regardless of the materiality of the final production, the process of production is increasingly governed by non-material functions involving knowledge, science, expertise, systems, planning and cybernetic skills. The raw material of much industry is increasingly non-material, as a result of technological developments, the rationalization of corporate management and the increasing abstraction of international and financial and investment networks. (Slater 1997, 194)

Networks replaced production lines, and new technology and information systems were used to create more customized products. Point of sale computers at checkouts gathered more accurate records of consumer purchases. Information was instantly relayed to distribution and production centers, which replenished stock. New technologies permitted greater customization of goods 'just in time' doing away with the problems of stockpiling. Batch production supported continual change and diversity of design. For example, the Italian sweater designer, Benneton, includes tags on all of its sweaters. When a sweater is purchased at any one of their stores around the world the purchase is recorded and through global communication technology fed back to the Benneton home office, which either replaces the sweater that is purchased or makes the decision to replace it with a new line. Cars parts are produced all over the world and reassembled at branch plants where the product is needed. Lash and Urry contend that corporation's have become more "reflexive" due to the continual adjustments they make based upon a nonstop stream of information. The new relations of work require professionals who can manipulate social and technological systems (finance, health, retail, high tech, promotion and marketing), and these types of work demand increased levels of education and mobility (Zukin 2004).

In these studies much attention was paid to the expanded role of the marketer, advertiser, designer, and other "cultural intermediaries" for, as Lash and

Urry (1993) noted, dematerialization was not simply an information and service revolution, but a cultural revolution as well. The growth in facts, figures, and cognitive information was bound up with an expansion of aesthetic and cultural information and the formation of a thriving visual culture in advertising, movies, art, style, and fashion. The expansion of media and advertising extended audiovisual material and was understood to add depth and breadth to visual culture. Lash and Urry remarked on the phenomenal growth in the health and therapeutic, personal service, and entertainment sectors.

Wolf (2003) announced the arrival of the entertainment economy, noting that the driving force behind the American economy were no longer the manufacturing Rust Belt of Detroit and Chicago, but rather Hollywood and Las Vegas. Although there were material elements, in the main workers in cultural sectors produced non-material commodities—fitness regimes, therapy sessions, acupuncture, and movies. Lash and Urry labeled these aesthetic commodities "postmodern goods," and noted that "the aesthetic component in manufactured products (and services) has in particular come to the fore in recent times" (1993, 123). So too did Celia Lury argue that contemporary Western material cultures could be distinguished from others due to their intensive emphasis on stylization.

Richard Pollay observed that the role of advertisers had changed. In the early twentieth century, when goods were largely unfamiliar to consumers, advertisers were taken up with the task of announcing and explaining products. By the 1970s goods became all too familiar. Most of us still did not understand their chemical properties, or the complex labor relations that make up the commodities we consume, but we are fully accustomed to product lines and media genres. It became increasingly difficult to distinguish products as new, for techniques of production and communication allowed competitors to replicate innovations with ease. Advertisers argued that symbolic distinction was the key savior for businesses who did not want to complete on the basis of price. The brand became increasingly important. As a contemporary advertising critic notes: "In a world of increasingly commoditized products and services, the only sustainable differentiation lies in the values, esthetics and information content of the brand, and the originality with which they are communicated to consumers" (Pollay 2002, 32).

Under conditions of "disorganized" capitalism corporations placed increased emphasis on their brands and images. Marketing and advertising became the key forces within production cycles, as achieving volume sales was thought to be impossible without advertising. The customized expansion of and diverse goods was matched by an equally wide, and diverse array of commodity symbolism, leading commentators to speak of consumer society as "saturated with meaning." According to Klein (2001), first-world companies coordinated production on "global assembly lines," offloading manufacturing onto the third world and devoting their full attention to promoting their brands, which colonized space in an expanded global media network.

The Triumph of Culture

The work of Jean Bauldrillard was endlessly debated during this period, due to the bold statements he had made about consumer culture and the role of symbolic processes in socialization and political economy. He had argued that media and advertising systems were key structuring agents, that is, institutions of socialization. Media no longer reflected society, but constituted it. Representations, simulacra and hyper-real experiences were the connective tissue that knit together people's understanding of the world. This ecstasy of communication or semiotics of meaning had disrupted and the line between reality and simulation: Older distinctions such as high and low culture, or the real and the fake, imploded under this play of signs. To illustrate his point graphically, Bauldrillard argued that the 1991 Gulf War was nothing more than the images that flooded through people's television sets, and in this sense, for them at least, "it did not happen."

Media and advertising severed the link between the sign and the referent, the object and its traditional meaning. Advertisers constantly wed ill-matched signifiers and signified to promote products—baked beans were exotic; hair gel represented love; and mobile phones, social progress. The result was an erosion of traditional meaning structures, increased attention to sign values, and allegiance to a constantly changing cultural code. Consumers no longer consumed things or sought to satisfy their needs per se, for there was only one need, namely status competition, which was undertaken through a complex game of assembling and disassembling the signs of the marketplace (Slater 1997).

In other words, Bauldrillard (1981; 1988) argued that cultural processes had overthrown the container of political economy. One's relationship to the modes of production mattered less than one's standing within the modes of consumption. Social class was overturned by a fixation on the arrangement of signs. Following Reisman, Bauldrillard saw advertising replacing social manners and etiquette, as the moral tales and social norms of commercial culture took on more importance than neighbors, peers, teachers, or workmates. Truth did not so much disappear as become irrelevant: "Where there is only signs there is only difference, but differences that cannot be differentially valued or hierarchies; only different signs that are all equivalent to each other (Slater 1997, 196). What was truth compared to fashion, style, and the sign? A fashion world is a relative world where personal taste, not appeals to higher moral distinctions, prevails. The sign economy privileges spectacle and affect over rational thought and, according to Bauldrillard and Jameson, renders audiences "schizophrenic" and passive. Mary Cross, too, saw these processes at work in her theorization of advertising. She noted how on the "glossy skin" of advertising we are asked "not to think, closing off the universe of discourse through one-dimensional words and a one-way communication that leave us panting, but passive, allowed to participate in the system only as consumers" (Cross 1996). Cross maintains that "advertising's game is to turn language into logo, not logos, into glamour, not grammar, moving it out of the rational to the non-proposition of the figural, the visual, where images like those of our dreams can take command of consciousness to promote that great big market-place dream of material happiness, the American one." As for Bauldrillard, the cultural field had challenged the patterning of industrial society and reigned victorious; culture had superseded political economy and class.

These ideas set off considerable debates. Returning to the work of Marx, Sut Jhally replied that Bauldrillard had constructed a straw man in asserting that Marx had allegedly neglected use-value. He illustrated how Marx's concept of use-value was conceived as shaped by social processes. The transformations that had occurred in the historical development of the market economy re-mained fully rooted within the capitalist form, he argued. For Lash and Urry the transitions of this period represented a merger of cultural and economy:

> Production cycles are taken up with reflexive accumulation in which eco-nomic and symbolic processes are more than ever interlaced and inter-ar-ticulated; that is, that the economy is increasingly culturally inflected and that culture is more and more economically inflected. Thus, the boundaries between the two become more and more blurred and the economy and cul-ture no longer function in regard to one another as system and environment. (1994, 64)

Daniel Miller proposed that to appreciate the changes of this period one "must grasp cultural and economic action as internally related to one another.... Economic and cultural categories are logically and practically in-terdependent: neither can be reduced to or separated from the other." It is as wrong to reduce market features to cultural "sign values" as it is to "bracket qualitative features for the purpose of micro-economic analysis". The "cultural turn" and the degree of emphasis on "symbolic systems and systems of mean-ing" lead to neglect of "the unintended consequences of intentional actions of structural conjunctions" (Miller, 2002 40).

As we suggested earlier, goods have always had imputed meanings, and all cultures have carried on a "discourse in and through" objects. In this con-text Andrew Wernick offers a useful way of understanding the changes of the period we are discussing. Acknowledging that goods have always circulated through the marketplace with imputed meanings, Wernick (1990) noted that it was not the profusion of signs that was so distinctive, but the expansion of institutions—the systematic and concentrated efforts devoted to aid the circulation of goods through the marketplace and culture, not only by advertisers, but the entire social system. Not just politicians, but all of us, have become promotional subjects. He too confirmed the merger of culture and economy.

The institutionalization of the discourse in and through goods has been successful because audiences are accorded a role in the creation of meaning. Bauldrillard's depiction of audiences and his bleak prognosis for consumer society neglects to acknowledge the active role played by audiences. Although in early work Bauldrillard saw consumers as active participants in meaning-making, this emphasis was later lost as audiences became for him a "silent majority" awed by the spectacle of the code, fixated upon the kaleidoscope of the consumer society, and unable to make meaning in their so-called "schizophrenic" state. Against this media-centric view, Andre Jannson pointed to empirical studies that consistently revealed the healthy interpretive schemata maintained by audiences.

> In empirical studies of consumption researchers find that individuals continue to make a great deal of sense through their consumption patterns. Consumption is not just imposed upon them from some code enacted by the media but is a form of negotiation between the individual reader and the producer and advertiser. (Jannson 2001, 67)

Lifestyle Diversity

Another strand of debate concerning the changing contours of consumer culture focused on the idea of lifestyle construction. In older traditional cultures, where the market played less of a role in creating identity formation, lifestyle was more bound to group processes. But since the early twentieth century sociologists had noted how under conditions of modernity some individuals and groups secured status not because of their income or family pedigree, but through their "style of life." Max Weber distinguished power from status, power being the domain of the legitimation of leadership, linked to class and access to the modes of production.

Social status, on the other hand, was predicated on the patterning of fashion and leisure practices read by others and used as a basis for whether social honor was bestowed or denied. Money did not dictate cultural honorifics, socio-cultural judgment did. Weber had thus suggested that consumption, in contributing to social esteem and group prestige, divided people in quite distinctive ways from class: "Classes can be divided according to their relationships to production how they acquire goods, 'status' according to the principle in which goods in the form of specific types of life styles are consumed" (Weber 1972, 538).

In 1899 Thorstein Veblen drew attention to how some sectors of society used goods strategically to mark their uniqueness. Elites engaged in conspicuous consumption, and flaunted their aesthetic knowledge in consumption acts. Georg Simmel (1910/1990) also recognized a growing multiplicity of cultural styles in constant change as lying at the very core of the modern experience. Simmel, however, had a distinctive view some from contemporary critics about the relationships between style and emotion. Style was understood to mediate feelings that had once emerged in less ambiguous disguise, and, he argued, created a wedge between individuals.

> Indeed, the mere existence of style is in itself one of the most significant instances of distancing. Style, as the manifestation of our inner feelings, indicates that these feelings no longer immediately gush out but take on a disguise the moment they are revealed. Style, as the general form of the particular, is a veil that imposes a barrier and a distance in relation to the recipient of the expression of these feelings. (1978, 473)

This evidence suggests that the processes of lifestyle formation are not peculiar to the postmodern period; however, many social theorists regarded its importance in social life to have been greatly expanded. In a late 1960s study of French cultural consumption patterns that built upon the ideas of Weber, Bourdieu argued the field of culture had become an expanded domain of status competition. Although money flowed in and through the cultural field, the true prizes were publications, recognized art work, the acknowledgement of peers. In a profoundly original turn, Bourdieu altered Weber's dichotomization of status and class, as well as Bauldrillard's assertion that style and sign had eroded class, arguing that class continued to be complexly mapped in and through cultural consumption. Classes, he noted, were defined as much by their consumption as their relationship to production.

Consumer society was understood by Bourdieu to be made up of interdependent fields, each with their own rules and forms of capital. People compete in fields for interest and resources. The two most important fields are the economic and cultural. Money is the capital of the economic field, the game is to maximize profit, buy low and sell high. Within an economic field goods are viewed in terms of price, quantity, and availability (scarcity). In the cultural field, individuals struggle for "recognition, consecration, and prestige," which are purely symbolic. Activities in the cultural field do not disrupt but add to the economic field. What was most pertinent for playing the game of culture was cultural capital acquired through education, the profession of one's parents, and access to cultural knowledge, all of which bestowed cultural resources. Unlike Bauldrillard, Boudieu does not radically separate the symbolic from the social, but rather attempts to show a "correspondence between social and symbolic structures based on the systematic unity of social life and the existence of structural and functional homologies along all fields of social activity" (Bourdieu). The types of cultural capital that one acquires relate to one's "feel for the game."

Because cultural resources are arbitrary, what is important to study are the processes by which particular goods or tastes come to be honored above others. Artistry is most important, where prestige is acquired by marks of distinction that are awarded for the expression of a "specialty, unique manner, or style." Uniqueness is judged against the history of cultural classification. The ability to recognize and produce innovative expressions requires high levels of knowledge; hence those with education, professional family backgrounds, and access to cultural knowledge are at an advantage, having been exposed to a wider range of aesthetic objects.

Taste identifies the individual and their choices in relationship to the diverse and changing cultural field, and those with considerable cultural capital utilize its power to assure that their tastes are recognized as being superior. Those with high levels of cultural capital assume a "disinterested" attitude toward cultural relations and artifacts, appreciating and evaluating goods but not displaying a passion for them or a dependence on them. Taste leaders look at cultural good analytically, more as a scientist or anthropologist might.

The paradigm within which consumers were understood had shifted, noted Slater. Whereas, for the social analyst of the 1960s "the modern consume was suckered, was conformist, really wanted things, was really in the game…, the postmodern consumer is hyper aware of the game itself (the only way to play). Cultural capital allows this consumer to make sense of the detached signs and treat them just as signs; obtains pleasure not from the things themselves but from the experience of assembling and deconstructing images; must be free of obligations of finalities in order to keep in view the play of signs and keep up with it" (Slater 1997, 197).

Those with high cultural capital asserted a sense of innate "good taste." Bourdieu found they were more likely to appreciate abstraction, refer to a work by the producer's name, or discuss the style or school associated with the cultural object, using this knowledge to assert superiority. Products that were highly promotional or trendy, or were ordinary commodities masquerading as works of art, were generally considered less worthy of honor. Those with less cultural capital were drawn to realist art that directly moved them, were more likely to discuss what they liked without reference to formal qualifications, and were more likely to see an object as novel. Thus, their tastes could be dismissed.

Micheal Featherstone (1991) maintains that the new cultural intermediaries were particularly influential in contributing to the character of contemporary consumption. Cultural intermediaries played "an important role in educating the public into new style and taste." The unique social position of the petite bourgeoisie, or what Featherstone called the "new middle class," left them particularly aspirant and interested in achieving status. They were fascinated with the lifestyles of intellectuals and artists, and in the aesthetic realm: "It can be argued that sectors of the new middle class, the cultural intermediaries, and the helping professions will have the necessary dispositions and sensibilities that would make them more open to emotional exploration, aesthetic experience, and the aestheticization of life" (Featherstone 1991, 45–46).

Unlike privileged classes who seek to protect established tastes to defend their status, the new middle class were aspirant, open to continual self-improvement. They embraced the growing fluidity of relations, and celebrated the breakdown of traditional social relationships. Lash and Urry (1994) saw the "new cultural intermediary" as playing a pivotal role in the "production, codification and diffusion of symbolic goods; such intermediaries would include people working in fashion, the media, marketing and design." Linked to production and media channels, these symbolic workers popularized art through commercial design and were thought to contribute to the "aesthetization of contemporary everyday life." They popularized art outside the museum and gallery, expanding the creative project of mixing and matching commodity signs to fashion their diverse lifestyles.

The rapid exchange and fragmentation of signs in postmodern culture dissolves the hierarchies of older social and cultural categories. Cultural intermediaries celebrated the inclusion of those previously excluded from cultural participation by the gatekeepers of high culture. The contributions of non-Western authors and musicians were recognized and celebrated. The moral distain toward consumption was broken and popular pleasures were embraced and subjected to more serious study. For example, Featherstone suggested that researchers should attempt to understand consumer culture instead of condemning it out of hand, as he believed critical theorists once had:

> The theories of Adorno, Horkheimer, Marcuse and other critical theorists are no longer accorded great significance. Their approach is often presented as an elitist critique of mass culture, which draws upon what are now, regarded as dubious distinctions between real and pseudo individuality, and true and false needs. They are generally regarded as looking down on the debased mass culture and as having little sympathy for the integrity of the popular classes' pleasures. The latter position has been strongly endorsed by the swing to postmodernism. (Featherstone 1991, vii–viii)

Bourdieu's study of cultural consumption inspired others to argue that the marketplace could be understood as a cultural field. Mica Nava (1997, 66) wrote that the Edwardian department store with its lavish display of goods schooled women in the acquisition of cultural capital: "Stores offered a resource for understanding how others dressed," and as such became an important resource for women's pleasure and status. Women enjoyed fashion without being derailed by males—indeed men increasingly opened themselves to the pleasures of fashion. Culture was demassified as the number of goods and individuals striving to create competing styles grew in the modern marketplace.

In her study of shopping habits Sharon Zukin (2004) drew attention to a turn within New Yorkers' dinner conversations, where through the 1980s and 1990s discussion turned from politics to the aesthetics of food and shopping, leading to heated debates over where to find the best raw buffalo mozzarella cheese in town. North Americans, she maintained, were becoming Parisians, who for centuries have "waxed philosophically about cuisine and fashion, and interior design." This turn to "foodie culture," according to Zukin, is just part of a larger trend in which shopping has become a key site of the acquisition and display of cultural capital. Referring to the work of Bourdieu, Zukin (2004, 38) notes that shopping is much more than the purchase of commodities: "Shopping isn't just a process of acquiring goods and services—it's a lifelong process of learning about them. And the faster these products change, the more we have to keep up with the changes by shopping."

Advertising provided a means for acquiring cultural capital without entering the store. The lifestyles of the urban American, as we shall see were fatefully integrated with media and advertising cycles. Individuals turned to the expanded field of the sign economy to secure status. Lash and Urry noted how commodity representations had become the cultural artifacts individuals used to categorize the world. The expanded field of signs also became a rich resource for identity projects, and consumers became increasingly visually literate due to their exposure and interest in the vast sea of commodity signs and a diversity of styles. The meaning of the goods had become essential to their circulation within the economy, and key aspects of the person's sense of self. Knowledge of goods became essential for participation within the expanded cultural domain, and as Jansson (2001, 31) writes, "conspicuous patterns of consumption take the place of continuous interpersonal contacts within an individual's biography." Lives were marked not only by the birth of children, the death of relatives, obtaining graduation, but also by the best bottle of wine, the most fantastic shirt, and the life-changing trip.

Juliet Schor saw social comparison as the key driving force of consumption in American in the 1980s and 1990s. The fragmentation and mobility of modern lifestyles (30 percent of all people living in London are single, for example) changed the character of the neighborhood. Instead of spending time with family, neighbors, and friends, people spend more time with the television and other forms of media. The lifestyles on television, says Schor, became a key resource of self and social understanding. Characters in soap operas and sitcoms were the new advice-givers in the global village, offering personal counsel and displaying potential styles. People no longer compared themselves to the Joneses next door. The problem with this situation was that there is a vast inequality between those in the media and those watching: "Because television shows are so heavily skewed to the lifestyles of the rich and upper middle class, they inflate the viewer's perceptions of what others have, and by extension what is worth acquiring—what one must have in order to avoid being left behind" (Schor 2000, 449).

This period seems to have been accompanied by a general interest in celebrities, but relationships to the mediated world are very complex. Silent film stars were very influential in the 1920s, but the contemporary period brought a diverse range of celebrities who cycled through the mediated marketplace in full color. Unlike politicians and business leaders, these individuals did not try to tell us what to do, or how to be. If we chose to follow them, we do so voluntarily. Part of the pleasure of the celebrity is not that they possess a great deal of cultural capital, for indeed they did not (they are more endowed with fame and social capital), but they do offer a dazzling array of stories, images, and lifestyle motifs out of which popular cultural capital could be acquired. Celebrities are important fashion and lifestyle setters; they also embody a new dream of social mobility, having achieved their success not through financial acumen, like financial tycoons, but by their creative talents. Youth dream less about becoming a captain of industry and more about becoming a member of the cultural elite—joining the ranks of sports stars, musicians, filmmakers, or general celebrities. Thousands lined up to compete on *Pop Star*, where hopefuls seek to get their big break into show business.

The expanded influence of the cultural industries and consumption, Lash and Urry contend, could only occur in a society in which the traditional institutions of workplace, community, and family had lost their power over shaping one's life. In this sense consumer society was a de-traditionalized society, where experimentation in self-exploration and new social affiliations were required. Giddens (1991) argues that in conditions of post-traditional society individuals have no choice but to forge a unique lifestyle in order to create, in a culture of constant change, personal stability in their own domains. The traditional guide posts available for identity construction have disappeared, to be replaced by an ever-changing array of signs, styles, experts, and advice through which we must continually sift and make choices.

To stabilize themselves individuals construct lifestyles, habits, and routines of day-to-day existence, scripting a narrative of self. In traditional culture, where social place and identity were more circumscribed, there was less latitude for self-selection. But survival in a post-traditional society calls for higher levels of self-reflexive self-monitoring, and a willingness to adjust in light of new information. From the breakfast we choose, to the type of job we have, to those we affiliate with, to what we wear, we have both more latitude to choose and greater responsibility for our choices. Giddens links the vast expansion of the therapeutic and self-help industry to the project of self-reflexivity. This sector counsels individuals on how to successfully engage in continual self-transformation. But whereas traditional institutions sought to stabilize identity, therapeutic institutions encourage one to work continuously on one's self.

Unlike many other writers, Giddens sees the potential for more authentic and meaningful social relationships emerging in post-traditional society. Traditional relationships held together out of social obligations often diminished individuals, whereas contemporary relationships are "purer" in the sense that people come together out of interest and the mutual pleasure and support they offer. For example, traditionally women were obliged to stay in marriages to men not out of choice but because the arrangements suited the needs of the wider family. Today women select their partners out of love and are free to leave marriages that do not bring them personal happiness.

Demassification: Romanticism, Countercultures, and the Drift Toward Distinction

Cultural change in the post-1980s period was also linked to counter-culture movements and the cultural impulse towards individuation and distinction that brought a reworking of middle-class ethics and mass cultural values. In *The Cultural Contradictions of Capitalism*, Daniel Bell (1979) suggested that the sentiments of contemporary consumption were linked to the wane of the bourgeois ethos and the rise of an anti-bourgeoisie one. The Protestant Ethic "was one of piety, frugality, discipline, prudence, the strenuous devotion to work, and delayed gratification," which had focused attention on the accumulation of wealth. Success in the accumulation of capital introduced a notion of boundlessness, and according to Bell this sense of boundlessness "spilled over into the cultural field and informed ideas about the self."

Artists were to play a key cultural role in the construction of new subjective positions. Art was increasingly put in the service of subjectivism, romantic self-exploration, innovation, distinction, and subversion. Creative artists dedicated themselves to self-expression, blatantly disregarding traditional mores and social sanctions. Sentiments in artistic circles were decidedly anti- bourgeois, prizing romantic self exploration, mysticism, and magic, and promoting the idea of boundless experiment, of unfettered freedom, of unconstrained sensibility, of being superior to order, of the imagination being immune to merely rational criticism. The axial principle of modern culture is not restraint but rather "the expression and remaking of the self" in order to achieve self-realization and self-fulfillment. And in its search, there is a denial of any limits or boundaries to experience. It is a reaching out for all experience; nothing is forbidden, all is to be explored (Bell 1979).

Bell pointed to the 1960s as the moment during which the avant-garde cultural movement were evermore linked to economic expansion: "A society given over entirely to innovation, in a joyful acceptance of change, has in fact institutionalized an avant-garde and charged it—perhaps to its own eventual dismay—with constantly turning up something new. In effect, 'culture' has been given a blank check, and its primacy in generating social change has been firmly acknowledged" (Bell 1979, 432).

In this transition, Bell argued, art was popularized through the entire social structure, challenging the traditional monopoly that cultural elites have over defining what art was acceptable. People on the street became the arbiters of artistic taste as art was liberated from the control exercised by high cultural circles. The fences that surrounded art were burst by the forces of postmodernism: "The postmodern overflows the vessels of art. It tears down the boundaries and insists that acting out, rather than making distinctions is the way to gain knowledge. The 'happening' and the 'environment', the 'street', and the 'scene' are the proper arena for life" (Bell, 1996, 52). Bell celebrated the democratization of creativity unleashed in consumer society, but was also wary of how the new values might destabilize social relationships.

Pleasures and Desires

Colin Campbell (1987) also contended that contemporary consumption was driven by an anti-bourgeois ethic. Campbell set out to explain how new wants were continually generated in a consumer culture. Unsatisfied with theories that saw the captains of industry, advertisers, and marketers as the fuel propelling consumers' insatiable interest in novel goods, and unimpressed with the theory that posited status competition as the drive of contemporary consumption, Campbell presented the engine of consumption as the private and elective pursuit of pleasure. He acknowledged that "there are elements of imitation in all forms of social conduct, but in so far as middle-class character ideals are concerned, orientation to the approval of others is likely to be less important than self-esteem" (Campbell 1987, 14). Campbell traced the interest in self-esteem and self-development to the romantic movements that emerged first around 1750, which prized self-exploration, novelty, fashion, and art, and to the nineteenth century bohemian artists and poets who expanded romantic attitudes further, defining life as an evolving work of art.

Campbell noted that the role of pleasure in consumption was neglected due to an overemphasis on needs and satisfaction. Happiness, not pleasure, was the dominant frame within the study of consumption. He argued that there was a significant conceptual distinction between pleasure and satisfaction. To be satisfied requires manipulation of real things: "Food can relieve hunger, clothes provide warmth, houses shelter, people affection." Pleasure, on the other hand, does not exist in the object but "is a type of reaction which humans commonly have when encountering certain stimuli." Whereas satisfaction indicates a state of being, a drive from within the individual, which pushes one to the act "so as to restore a disturbed equilibrium," pleasure is a "pulling from without in order to experience greater stimulation." Satisfaction is a state of being, whereas pleasure is "a quality of experience." Pleasure can also be simulated through dreaming and thinking in a way that satisfaction cannot.

> Hence, whilst one typically needs to make use of objects in order to discover their potential for satisfaction, it is only necessary to employ one's senses in order to experience pleasure, and, what is more, whereas an object's utility is dependent upon what it is, an object's pleasurable significance is a function of what it can be taken to be. Thus whilst only reality can provide satisfaction, both illusions and delusions can supply pleasure. (Campbell 1987, 61)

People developed a new skill of pleasure, which was associated with literacy and cultural cultivation. But, noted Campbell, pleasure is bittersweet, because we seek to "experience in reality those pleasures created and enjoyed in imagination," which "results in the ceaseless consumption of novelty." This explains why "the individual's interest is primarily focused on the meanings and images which can be imputed to a product, something which requires novelty to be present."

Others also saw novelty and aesthetics and a new structure of feeling as key dynamics of contemporary consumerism. Attempting to distinguish postmodern consumption from that that preceded it, Featherstone (1991) noted the lengths consumers went to fashion their lives as works of art. A great deal of attention was paid to the active participation of consumers in marketers and advertising offerings. Featherstone argued that the profusion of media and commodity symbolism supported the "aestheticization of everyday life." Consumer orientations were seen as shifting from utility toward style.

> Consumer culture through advertising, the media, and techniques of display of goods, is able to destabilize the original notion of the use or meaning of goods and attach to them new images and signs which can summon up a whole range of associated feelings and desires.... [This] points to the significance of the active cultivation of lifestyle within the imagery of consumer culture. That is, individuals are encouraged to adopt a non-utilitarian attitude towards commodities and carefully choose, arrange, adapt and display goods—whether furnishings, house, car, clothing, the body or leisure pursuits—to make a particular stylistic statement which expresses the individuality of the owner. (Featherstone 1991, 114)

Consumers embraced novelty and eclectic consumption patterns, assembling an ever-changing array of signs, displaying omnivorous consumption. They were as open to opera as the rodeo and were drawn to emotionally-rich and cosmopolitan experiences. Jean-François Lyotard noted that the unlinking of signs from referents and the dismantling of the influence of older social norms permitted greater the emergence of greater eclecticism. Unleashed from "intrinsic meaning or anchorage in the world, they simply constitute a selection of signs from which to pick and mix": "Eclecticism is the degree zero of contemporary general consumption: one listens to reggae, watches a western, eats McDonald's food for lunch and local cuisine for dinner, wears Paris perfume in Tokyo and "retro" clothes in Hong Kong; knowledge is a matter of TV games." (quoted in Slater 1997, 196)

The profusion of aesthetic images was also linked to new feeling-states. Desires previously hidden emerged in the geyser of signs. For Featherstone this was to be celebrated, for it served a therapeutic role, bringing previously repressed feelings to the surface for examination. The stiff upper lip of the work ethnic and the sentiments that privileged reason and stoicism suppressed the exploration of feelings. The aestheticization of everyday life opened the floodgates, as postmodern consumer culture offered new emotional and bodily pleasures, "the question of the emotional pleasures of consumption, the dreams and desires which become celebrated in consumer culture imagery and particular sites of consumption which variously generate direct bodily excitement and aesthetic pleasures" (Featherstone 1991, 13).

The new middle class undertook consumption patterns which sought to maximize emotional experience, such as body-tattooing and piercing. They embraced the general relaxation in culture, taking pleasure in experimenting in a field that no longer upheld a strict clothing, relationship or manner codes. They could freely express their feelings, and enjoy the pleasures offered by the play of signs in the market place.

> Representations became increasingly played with and manipulated by a knowing and educated public who learned to take please from the aesthetic games, which the consumer culture endlessly offered... To play the game of consumption requires a savvy knowingness of signs, the ability to be critical of them and take pleasure from their readings." (Featherstone 1991, 13)

For Featherstone contemporary consumers display a higher level of emotional expression than before: Whereas the older culture encouraged the repression of emotion, contemporary culture encourages people to display their feelings and experiences. Talk shows, self-help books, magazines, and advertising all link self-fulfillment to a process of working through emotional issues in order to experience pleasure. Yet to maximize pleasure requires what Featherstone called the "de-controlled control of the emotion," the undertaking of calculated periods of abandon to achieve maximum pleasure. Careful calculations were made to maintain one's work commitments and fitness regimes, in addition to indulgences in leisure activities and mass media consumption. High levels of discipline are required to modulate between control and freedom in the new marketplace.

Counter Culture Movements and Contemporary Consumption

Campbell (1987) noted how bohemian values had been linked in the past to new styles of consumption, accompanying the consumer booms of 1890 and

1920 and the counter-culture movement of the late 1960s. It is only recently, however, that careful historical work has been undertaken to explore the role played by of late-1960s counter-culture movement on the character of contemporary consumption practices. Two recent histories, by Thomas Frank (1997) and Hazel Warlaumont (2000), offer detailed accounts of how various anti-mass sentiments which had first emerged in academic and artistic circles in the 1950s—the beats and hipsters in America, and the angry young men in Britain—were popularized a decade later by the baby boomer generation.

Youth acted out against the forces of mass society that they felt were repressing them. In the late 1960s and early 1970s diverse resistance movements in the United States, Britain, Eastern and Western Europe, and Japan grew up, sharing two common threads: a deep sense of alienation and contempt for mainstream values. In 1968, as the Beatles sang "Revolution," protests erupted around the world, the most spectacular of which occurred in Paris in May of 1968, when students and public workers engaged in acts of civil disobedience. In a country with a history of protest, this rebellion was unique as the ringleaders were neither republicans nor workers but philosophers and students. Bureaucracy was as much the enemy as capitalism was. The drive was to rebuild society completely, breaking free of alienation by mounting a creative revolution. A poster attached to the main entrance of the Sorbonne on May 13, 1968 announced the vision of the movement: "The revolution, which is beginning, will call in question not only capitalist society but industrial society. The consumer society is bound for a violent death. Social alienation must vanish from history. We are inventing a new and original world. Imagination is seizing power."

Universities became hotbeds of protest, for they both harbored the movement's key intellectual spokespeople and were also part of the establishment, teaching the trades of mass society in their business, law, and science departments. Administrative offices were occupied at Berkeley in California, in Britain at the London School of Economics, and in Vancouver at Simon Fraser University. Protests occurred in New York City and tanks rolled into Prague to break up youth protests in what came to be known as the "Prague Spring." In Italy Radio Alice and its linguistically-charged political messages excited youth and so threatened politicians that it was shut down by the military. In the United States protest coalesced around the Vietnam War. Young people facing the draft refused to bear witness to a war they saw as unjust. Television revealed the atrocities of the American military intervention in new graphic and gory detail. The My Lai massacre saw women, children, and elderly Vietnamese citizens brutally attacked by U.S. soldiers. Respect for politicians dropped. Members of the counter culture movement rejected other authority figures, including professionals and big business leaders. The mass market, once associated with abundance and classlessness, was seen through the eyes of the counter culture as a place of stifling conformity and homogeneity.

The ideas of European existential philosophies, particularly the concept of alienation seemed perfect metaphors to many youths for describing their suburban experience. Counter-culture youths rejected what had been acceptable to the preceding generation. Indeed, they felt the previous generation was complicit in perpetuating an inhuman system. They could not derive meaning from their parents' values and experienced an internal civil war, rejecting their white middle-class heritage. Some youth shunned their parents' middle-class suburban lifestyles and moved to warehouse lofts in the seedier parts of the city's downtown core, and to communes "out on the land"; mass society was rejected, individualism and self-expression ruled.

As we have seen, Bell and Campbell described the emotional opening of this period as part of the transformation of ethics. For Featherstone it was a transformation of sign systems and the force of new cultural intermediaries. Very few acknowledged the profound gender transformation that also had occurred at this moment, and its lasting consequences. The role of women in this movement and as a shaping force in the emergent consumer culture has, in Nava's (1997) memorable phrase, been largely "disavoweled." Feminism played a significant role in the counter-culture movements of the 1960s and 1970s. Women rejected traditional gender politics and sexual mores, demanding equal pay, acknowledgement of their domestic labor, and more support from their husbands. They won a series of court victories (divorce, abortion), which empowered women in ways we now take for granted. The introduction of the birth-control pill helped support experimentation in "free love," and women could control sexual reproduction. More open attitudes toward sex also chipped away at the historical sanctions against homosexuality. Women were the emotional revolutionaries of this period, promoting eroticism, peace, and a fuller expression of feelings. One woman described her transformation during this period:

> It was as if we were encased in plastic. Girls were expected to wear stockings—not panty hose, but stockings—and girdles with garters that made holes in your legs. We wore stiff petticoats and brassieres that pushed you up and out in a very unnatural way. And we used to tease our hair and then spray it, and when we walked out in the morning on the way to school, it looked as if we were surrounded by plastic. Everything was artificial. . . . And then in 1964 it was as if I had stepped onto another planet. Everything was so free and loose. . . . I wore jeans everywhere and let my hair grow the way it naturally wanted to. It was as if I had become another person. I felt as though I was myself for the first time. (Warlaumont 2000, 94)

Building upon the ideas of the 1950s beats and hipsters, hippies fashioned a unique lifestyle, encouraging self-experimentation. They embraced symbols and practices to distinguish themselves from their parents. Middle-class kids rejected formal dress, refusing the suit and tie of the company man in favor of collarless shirts and Nehru jackets. In solidarity with the honest, simple, authentic values of the working person which were threatened by mass society, many youth embraced the durability and looseness of peasant skirts and jeans.

Influenced by existentialism, counter-culture movements were mistrustful of the traditional classifications, and sought to erode the Western dichotomies believed to separate men from women, blacks from whites, spiritualism from secularism. Unisex fashion was prized (men grew their hair long, women wore jeans); whites fought alongside blacks in the civil rights movement. Inspiration was drawn from Eastern philosophies and religions with less bifurcated worldviews. Rituals from pre-industrial society, primitivism, radical politics, and drugs were all invoked in the service of escaping mass society. In this sense the counter-culture shared much with the romantic movements that preceded them.

And the counter-culture represented a serious critique of consumerism. Some chose spiritual and artistic pursuits and transcendentalism over materialism. The empty surface of goods, slavish pursuit of fashion, and identical mass-produced commodities were loathed in equal measure. Quality of life was valued above the flaunting of paychecks. Hippies rejected the 9 to 5 timetable of traditional work and some sought to "tune in, turn on and drop out," an attitude that stood in stark opposition to the work ethic. Although the movement was profoundly diverse, the basic message was clear: Be real; be authentic; be creative; be yourself—avoid the mass. Thus, the processes of demassification appear to lie not only in changes in production processes, but also in the cultural impulse for identity and distinction felt around the world.

Advertisers Get Hip

The advertisers, product designers, and marketers who had celebrated mass society were some of the first to awaken to the idea that this motif no longer resonated well in popular culture. To address the anti-consumerist challenge advertisers moved away from hard selling and began to adjust to the more variegated palates of their emergent target audiences, enchanting them with self-aware designs that factored in audience intelligence and entertained them with more novel and creative formats. Product designers focused on stylization and customization instead of on utility, as advertisers and marketers began to demassify the mass market, breaking consumers into ever-finer market segments and targeting them through an expanded and more refined media system. No longer was fashion dictated to by a single idiom, as there was not a vast array of styles to suit every taste.

Advertisers registered that young audiences were rejecting their traditional mass society formats and the happy, bland world of consumption which for the counter-culture was the epitome of inauthentic values. Audiences were undertaking sophisticated and critical readings. Unlike Featherstone, who implies a blanket embrace of new values by cultural intermediaries, Frank's study argues that innovation occurred in the minds of a few young creatives, who were particularly sensitive to the sentiments of their generation. One of these was Bill Bernbach of Doyle Dane Bernbach agency (DDB), who introduced designs that placed an emphasis on creativity, individuality, irreverence, and humor. The new style can be seen in his Volkswagen ads of the period (Figure 9.1). So powerful was the new format that it transformed a quintessential mass-produced vehicle into a product coveted as unique by those who otherwise loathed mass society. Such is the power of advertising to transform the "sign" and "referent." Bernbach broke tried and true rules in order to create more authentic advertising:

> What made the Volkswagen ads seem 'honest' are the curious admissions of (what appear to be) errors with which the ads are peppered. The sedan is "ugly" and "looks like a beetle"; the Volkswagen station wagon is "a monster" that "looked like a shoe box" with "a flat face and square shape".... To make such admissions, even counterbalanced as they were with humor ("Could it be that ours aren't the funny looking cars, after all?") was a violation of fundamental principles of salesmanship. (Frank 1997, 63)

The anxieties addressed in advertisements began to shift from a concern with status to a concern about maintaining individuality in the face of a homogenizing culture. Advertisers learned important lessons about new cultural dynamics, such as the declining interest in the old markers of status, and new dynamic of "cool" and authenticity. Advertisers did not create these sentiments, but they would circulate them widely. The shift in advertising for Frank had profound consequence: Social opposition was redirected to consumption. The search for authenticity did not disrupt commerce, but instead fueled it anew. The cultural drive for authenticity, creativity and identity was directed by advertisers into the world of goods.

> The sixties are more than merely the homeland of hip, they are a commercial template for our times, a historical prototype for the construction of cultural machines that transform alienation and despair into consent. Co-optation is something much more complex than the struggle back and forth between capital and youth revolution; it's also something larger than a mere questions of demographics and exploitation. Every few years, it seems, the cycles of the sixties repeat themselves on a smaller scale. With new rebel youth cultures bubbling their way to a happy replenishing of the various culture industries' depleted arsenal of cool. (Frank 1997, 235)

Traditional models of capital expansion emphasized how corporations seek to homogenize and stabilize cultural distinctions and disruptions. Frank's model suggests that corporate expansion is not disrupted but fuelled by cultural discontent and diversity.

But it would be wrong to view Bernbach's work as a strategic plot designed to assimilate counter-culture opposition, for it emerged out of a creative who shared an affinity with the values of the youth movements and a trial and error process to find images and symbols that engaged disaffected audiences. The success of the new formats of the late 1960s led to their widespread adoption, and this period was recognized as a moment of creative flowering in the advertising industry. According to Frank, advertisers went from being just another cog in the big business machinery to promoters of counter-culture values, transformed from gray-suited business folk aligned with the oppressive establishment, to "cool" creative artists.

Warlaumont, however, reaches different conclusions based on the same evidence. She argues that the creative revolution in 1960s advertising, celebrated in the industry and documented by historians, was more than a creative burst from the "great men" of advertising; it also represented a restructuring of the industry and a structural adjustment of the marketplace to new cultural sentiments. Those sentiments were larger than the male creatives who recognized them, and although Warlamount does not make this explicit, they were in fact informed by changing gender dynamics.

Holt drew attention to the lighter touch advertisers assumed in their designs post-1960s as they adjusted to new consumer sentiments. Holt agrees with Frank that the experimentation of the 1960s counter-culture "reflected a passionate, reflexive concern with existential freedom," in which one's life became not only a work in progress, but also a work of art. But a significant problem then emerged: The project of self-construction was necessarily linked to the marketplace, but to be successful consumers individuals had to feel that they, and not the corporations, were the ones scripting their lifestyles. The 1960s had created a legacy of consumer resistant to hard sells and messages that dictated what people should want. Now audiences wanted their individuality to be acknowledged, and they sought novelty and authenticity from the marketplace, not homogenization.

The advertisers' mode of address to consumers had to make them believe they were "freely constructing their own ideas through their consumption." To get past the radar of savvy consumers, brands had to appear as something consumers themselves had invented and "disseminated at parties without an instrumental economic agenda, intrinsically motivated by their inherent value" (Holt 2003, 83). The branding paradigm shifted from brands as "cultural blueprints" to brands as personal "resources." Holt notes three ways in which advertisers achieved their goals. First, they assumed an ironic and reflexive form of address which acknowledged the consumer's savviness with a knowing wink and nod (Diesel, Sprite). Second, they rode the coattails of "cultural epicenters," associating brands with people and places that innovated new cultural expressions (Adidas and ghetto cool). Great care was taken to uphold the appearance of being a part of the subculture and not being labeled as a parasite. And third, agencies also anchored brands in authenticity by capitalizing on brand heritage. Levis, for example, had been in the market so long it had considerable "heritage cachet."

In their content analysis of post-1950s British advertising, Richards et al. found that in the 1980s and 1990s references to status had dropped off dramatically. Individualized and customized messages grew more prevalent. These new addressees contributed to the paradox of brand communities "in which consumers claim to be doing their own thing while doing it with thousands of like minded others" (Holt 2002, 83). Gap is the quintessential brand for this strategy, promoting mass fashion through the values of authenticity and individuality. Holt has suggested that, although consumers felt they were constructing individual styles, there are no sovereign identities: "As symbolic integrationists tell us, even sovereign identities require the interpretive support of others to give them ballast" (Holt 2002, 88).

The Trickle Begins to Bubble

Counter-cultural values legitimated new areas of cool, expanding the field of social comparison. The traditional fashion road map that cycled from Paris, New York, London, and Italy was well established by the *haute-bourgeoisie*, but romantic values, popularized throughout culture, reworked old hierarchies, adding new branches to the dominant roadmap of style. The raw, authentic feel and look of the street and the margins became new sources of style innovation. While sophistication continued to bubble down from the runway and cultural elite, the counter-culture movement legitimated the "street" as a source of authenticity, sexiness, and coolness.

The styles of the traditional economic elite surrendered to the conquest of cool. The fashion label St. John offers a good example. This brand consistently targeted wealthy middle-aged women with a message of old bourgeois respectability. A well-groomed, well-turned-out middle-age model was the face of this fashion line. The model was typically shown in Chanel-type suits against a backdrop of old Europe cobbled streets, or in evening dress surrounded by tuxedo-clad men, or in the desert holding the reins of a camel. All these motifs invoked a sense of old-world respectability and cosmopolitanism. St. John was stalwart, holding on to diamonds and caviar to the bitter end. But at the turn of the twentieth century even St. John acknowledged the rising status of the cultural intermediary and the changing symbolic arena. The familiar model began to appear in leather pants, in the back of pick-up truck driving down the streets of Las Vegas, or in a mini-skirt surrounded by surly young men holding electric guitars.

Fashion magazines such as *Vogue* offer not only the latest trends from the fashion houses but also those from the street. Mundane objects of trailer-trash culture, such as retro "sneakers," become the objects of cool fascination. High fashion designers like Dior cover their models in dirt and mud.

The 1960s had taught advertisers and designers that youth played a key role in fueling cultural dynamics. Marketers saw youth as a central target market because they were thought to be forming brand preferences, had increased amounts of disposable incomes and influence over their families spending, and were more willing to experiment with new consumer goods and electronics. Youth, the factory of cool, not only moved by cool, but also most likely to undertake cultural innovation to produce it. Harnessing cool became a preoccupation of many businesses during this period. Through the 1980s businesses sought to systematize cool trends through "cool hunting"—finding, test marketing, and learning about cool. Malcolm Gladwell (1997, 373) spent time with two professional cool hunters and sought to reveal some of the ticks of their trade. He noted there were key rules of cool: "Cool cannot be manufactured only observed…it can only be observed by those who are themselves cool…it cannot accurately be observed at all, because the act of discovering cool causes cool to take flight."

Marketers understand the central anthropological principle of the discourse in and through goods: It is not the object, but people, who make being cool what it is. Cool hunters don't look for cool objects, but cool people. Goods take on different social meanings in relation to the contexts in which they are circulated and the spheres of influence in which they operate. Cool hunters describe cool people as essentially the aristocratic romantic individual. They look for a character that is the polar opposite of David Riesman's outer-directed individual. As a cool hunter notes, "I'm looking for someone who is an individual, who has definitely set himself apart from everybody else, who doesn't look like his peers" (Gladwell 1997, 372).

Gladstone notes the processes of cool hunting are most closely associated with youth, where the project of identity formation is particularly acute. He writes, "Cool hunting represents the ascendancy, in the marketplace, of high school." Celia Lury noted that youth has ceased to be a description of age and had become a general style and structure of feeling that dominates media and is associated with freshness and novelty. In his historical study of the "Pepsi Generation" Hollander (1992, 97) observed: Youthfulness, or what might be labeled youngness—a nostalgic and fantasized state of looking and feeling young without having any of the cares and concerns that youth actually face—has a strong appeal for many younger and older individuals. It is the basis for the youth appeal that has been used in much promotion to those markets. It is part of the "Pepsi Generation" campaign.

In 1958, when Norman Mailer wrote *The White Negro*, he reminded a generation of white kids that the males of the African American population were where the cool hipsters should draw their reference. This legacy played itself out within the dynamics of post-1980 consumption, as black and other ethnic communities became hotbeds of cool. Ethnicity, Lury says, became a potent site of distinction, used by marketers to signal novelty and exoticism. Klein (2001) noted how the connection between blackness and cool had long roots within American culture and that contemporary advertisers had grown very adept at harnessing this fact in their marketing and promotional designs:

> As designer Christian Lacroix remarked in *Vogue*, "It's terrible to say, very often the most exciting outfits are from the poorest people." Over the past decade, young black men in American inner cities have been the market most aggressively mined by brandmasters as a source of borrowed "meaning" and identity.... The truth is that the "got to be cool" rhetoric of the global brands is, more often than not, an indirect way of saying "got to be black." Just as the history of cool in America is really (as many have argued) a history of African American culture...for many of the superbrands, cool hunting simply means black culture. (Klein 2002, 74)

Black music had been the backbone of the counter-culture's own rock music. Musicians were cultural heroes of the counter-culture movement, popularizing not just particular riffs but the fashions and lifestyles that accompanied them. From the 1980s onward, MTV provided "musician porn" to kids who no longer had to go to live gigs to hear their heroes or to see their hair and clothing styles. One of the most important musical developments was urban music, rap, and assorted hip-hop genres. Rappers are steeped in a particular "street cred [credibility]," reflecting a tough machismo (time in prison, tattoos, scares, guns) and risky romanticism. Rap has been particularly popular with privileged white males searching for a cultural meaning beyond video games and horror films in which to assert their manhood. Some of the hottest arbiters of culture emerged from the ghettos of New York and the gangs of Los Angeles. Alex Kotlowitz quotes Sarah Young, a consultant who specializes in the urban market, who states, "Inner-city kids will embrace a fashion item as their own that shows they have a connection, and then you'll see the prep school kids reinvent it, trying to look hip-hop. It's a cycle" (Schor 2000, 255).

Kotlowitz drew attention in his work to the cycling of styles in the mediated marketplace. At the same time as the privileged middle-class whites were engaged in romantic fantasies of life in the ghetto, wearing baggy trousers with no belts (thought to be inspired by prison garb, where belts are removed to prevent suicide), the black rap artists embraced the conspicuous consumption of the yesteryear rich, such as expensive Mafia-style suits and ties. While brands like St. Johns sought to get hip, rappers popularized French brandy, Krystal champagne, Hush-Puppy shoes, and Tommy Hilfinger's preppy clothes, while also swaddling themselves in hip hop jewelry known as "bling bling." The older markers of the elite became boring, pretentious, and conservative within new values systems which prized authenticity, individuality, and experimentation of style; but the middle classes could re-appropriate them with a sense of irony. Alex Kotlowitz remarks that young disadvantaged black youth "are as much consumers as they are consumed; that is, they mimic white America while white America mimics them" (quoted in Schor 2000, 255).

Surveying these changes, Holt noted the vast outpouring of symbolic products, the mass production of luxury goods, the continual cycling of style, and increased mobility made it more difficult for style leaders to form and secure a dominant influence. Within the mediated marketplace traditional hierarchies became more fluid. The meanings of goods multiplied and luxury goods became more widely available. Clearly articulated status groups have trouble "jelling" because of the great amount of mobility and travel, in which one's referents increasingly become an impersonalized other.

> Although status judgments based on the goods one owns and the activities in which one participates have merit for describing small, isolated, relatively immobile populations, they are of little value for most of the populations in an era of transnational consumer capitalism. Status construction now must contend with the tremendous geographic mobility of American professionals and managers, the privatization of social life, the proliferation of media and travel, and the anonymity of urban environment, all of which have impersonalized the "other" whom one views as social references. (Holt 2003, 215)

This bubbling forth of style influences from many different spheres was accompanied by an increase in the speed in which styles are turned over: "Indeed, one of the most oft cited reasons for the high street's success is its strength at 'translating fashion trends', which seems to happen faster every season" (Freeman 2003). The new flexible production processes and emphasis on the symbolic aspect of goods has increased the speed with which goods are turned over. Fashion seasons, which once reflected natural cycles, revolve around fashion weeks, the Oscars, and cycles of promotion in the media. Fashion cycles get shorter and shorter and styles are endlessly changed. Disposable commodities make more sense than durable items because objects are being rendered out of style almost as soon as they are purchased. Yet this trend also has fuelled an opposition movement, a blossoming of the second-hand and vintage clothing market and a search for enduring objects. Many of the new goods are non-material, including movies, images, and information and can be channeled through the new communication lines. The result is both an increased intensification in the turnover of goods, as well as a vast pluralization of the styles that are available (Lee 1993; Harvey 1989). Marketers have turned their attention away from long-term purchase patterns to short-term ones.

Demassifying Modes of Consumption

Jannson (2001, 67) agrees that in the mature consumer culture "the circulation, purchase, sale, appropriation of differentiated goods and signs/objects today constitute our language, our code, the code by which the entire society communicates and converses." Commodities and their signs are seen in his work as the means through which culture is enacted. However, he has also argued that there is no longer "one type of consumer" or "one process of cultural circulation," for meaning circulates in and through many domains, including advertising, celebrity culture, youth movements, word of mouth channels, street fashion, Paris designers, and animal rights movements. Consumers have been demassified and a wide variety of factors guide them in their consumption patterns.

Jansson suggests it is possible to find several "overarching value principle[s] governing not only consumption practices, but also the lifestyle formation in general." These principles govern "how the individual applies different modes of consumption in different contexts." He outlines seven different forms of consumption ethos. The instrumental ethos seeks gratification of physical and material need through "fictional solutions" and is attentive to the "functional use-value and exchange value of goods." The work ethic dominates over consumption, and in its most extreme forms individuals guided by this ethos strive towards an ascetic lifestyle. In contrast, the consumption ethos of the realistic hedonist is driven to maximizing bodily pleasures. The preferred methods of obtaining bodily pleasures are to repeat continually and escalate a consumption ritual that had provided pleasure in the past. This ethos is not guided by an interest in experimentation, for there is a fear of failure. In its extreme form, this ethos is similar to addiction. A third consumer ethos seeks to find pleasure not through the body and the senses but through emotional and spiritual stimulation: Consumption here is driven by a quest for a higher spiritual joy and aesthetic pleasures. The image and style of the goods are more important than their materiality.

The reproductive consumption ethos is preoccupied with inner-directed consumption that seeks to reproduce one's socio-cultural standing via conspicuous over- or under-consumption. The pretentious ethos, in contrast, does not consume to mark who one is, but rather represents a quest to express who one wants to be. Considerable anxiety accompanies this approach to consumption, as there is a concern that others might see oneself as someone else than one actually experiences oneself to be. Driven by ambition and desire for social mobility, this ethos can be subject to the frustration of social failure and promotes the development of narcissism. Progressive consumption is lodged within an anti- or pre- consumerist orientation: Consumption is guided by ideological concerns and anti-materialist values, such as environmentalism, feminism, veganism, and global solidarity. As consumer culture expands, argues Jannson, this mode of oppositional consumption pattern has become increasingly prevalent. Jannson suggests that the processes of consumption have become so complicated that they must be understood within this typology.

Social arrangements in which media images and media influence commodity-signs to an increasing extent are used as sources for the expressions of identity. Through the operation of commercial intertextuality, these expressions, in turn, contribute to the reproduction of cultural categorization, which in a specific period of time are shared within a certain (although often vaguely demarcated) cultural community, and relevant within certain situational context of consumption.

Symbolic and Material Inequalities

It is important to celebrate the new freedoms the sign economy has brought without loosing sight of the persistence of old forms of inequalities and the development of new ones. Scant attention within the consumer culture literature has been paid to the worsening of economic inequalities through the 1980s and 1990s. The new means of raising social funds—taxing smoking and alcohol and lotteries—have proved to be regressive support mechanisms for government budgets, and in general the gap between the rich and the poor has expanded. In 1979 the top 5 percent of income earners made 10 times more than the bottom 5 percent; in 1993 the difference was 25-fold. Social mobility was stunted. In Britain a child born into a working class family in 1999 was less likely to experience social mobility then a child born into the same situation in 1946 (Aldridge 2004). The American sociologists Sheldon Danziger and Peter Gottchalk (1997) undertook a study that tracked a diverse group of children for twenty years and found that nine out of ten remained in the lowest two economic brackets despite the 1980s boom (Macarthur 2003). The Federal Reserve, the central bank of the United States, reported in 1990 the top 1 percent own 40 percent of the country's wealth, making the United States the most unequal country of all wealthy nations, representing the greatest degree of social inequality since the 1920s: "About 90 percent of the total value of stocks, bonds, trusts, and business equity were held by the top 10 percent. Despite the widening ownership of stock (48 percent of households owned stock shares either directly or indirectly in 1998), the richest 10 percent still accounted for 78 percent of their total value" (Wolff 2000, 1).

According to Gary Cross (2003) the tax cuts disproportionately privileged the rich. The top wage bracket paid 70 percent in income tax in 1980, but just 28 percent by the end of the century. Real wages have declined steadily since 1973. People work on average one more month per year than they did in the 1970s. Over half of all the new full-time jobs created in the 1980s paid less than

$250 a week, or $13,000 a year, below the poverty line for a family of four. "The real after-tax income for families headed by a person aged 25 to 34 declined 2.3% between 1961 and 1982," which is not much until one considers that most families now have two incomes, and that their combined earnings often are less (in adjusted terms) than what one of their parents earned alone. While many women wanted to enter the workforce, they increasingly had little choice as it was difficult for families to maintain themselves with a single wage earner. The participation of married women between 25 and 34 in the work force doubled from 29 percent in 1961 to 62 percent in 1985 (Longman 1985).

The inequalities of wealth created at the national level within the sign economy were even grosser at the global level. Zygmunt Bauman (1998, 70–71) provides a summary of some of the reports which have tracked the disparity between nations:

> the total wealth of the top 358 "global billionaires" equals the combined income of 2.3 billion poorest people (45 percent of the world's population)....Only 22 percent of global wealth belongs to the so-called "developing countries," which account for about 80 percent of the world population....Unfortunately, the technology makes no impact on the lives of the world poor. In fact, globalization is a paradox: while it is very beneficial to a very few, it leaves out or marginalizes two-thirds of the world's population.

If the organized economy of the immediate post-WWII period created haves and have-nots, globalization has created a new divide between people: the mobile, able to move with the times and take advantage of the opportunities, and those who either remain stuck in declining agricultural and rural industrial rust belts, or become landless refugees, mobilized not by their own choosing, but by war. The United States dominates the globalized economy. The cold war and the challenge from Japanese companies provided some restraint on American industry, but after the fall of the Soviet Union, the end of the cold war in the late 1980s, and the meltdown of the Japanese economy in the 1990s, the United States was left as the biggest kid on the global block, economically and militarily. A recent study of global corporations revealed that eight spots out of the top 10, and 62 out of the top 100 global companies, are of American origin (*Globe and Mail*, Toronto, July 25, 2004, B9).

Some writers maintain that the post-1980 period has instilled new types of "symbolic inequalities." Those with more aesthetic knowledge could appreciate aspects of consumer society that evaded others. The development of cultural capital takes time, often requires considerable education, and is enhanced by exposure to many different experiences and people in the arts. Critics began to speak of a divide between those rich in symbolic knowledge and others who were not. Lash and Urry (1993) discuss "information ghettos," social spaces which are disconnected from society's main networks, enduring "a vicious spiral of economic, social and cultural poverty." The lines of the information network do not reach Africa, nor most of South America. The cultural divide expresses itself in the 1990s with the growth of an information economy where access to computers and the internet marketplace become necessary to compete.

Turow (1998) draws attention to the refined targeting strategies of marketers and advertisers during this period. More comprehensive research reveled to businesses that the vast majority of their profits were often made by a few elite segments of their consumer base. Some consumers became more important than others and it made sense to cater to their tastes. Businesses targeted niche markets with customized goods, and advertisers and media targeted finer audience segments. Turow argues that this refined targeting is dividing American's common culture and drives a wedge between people, making it difficult to find shared cultural meaning. "Niching" is considered a worrying trend that "will allow, even encourage, individuals to live in their own personally constructed worlds, separated from people and issues that they don't care about or don't want to be bothered with" (quoted in Cross 2000, 226).

Cultural Intermediaries and New Work Anxieties

Angela McRobbie's sociological exploration of work in the new cultural industries has demystified some of the awe that surrounds these professions. Young people were drawn to the romance of the cultural industries, with its promise of a blur between work and leisure, a world in which one's job was so fascinating, socially enriching, and prestigious that one could forget it was work at all. Film, media, and cultural studies departments began to recruit higher levels of students as dentistry, law, engineering, and accounting. McRobbie argues (2002, 109) that work in the cultural industries became synonymous with self-actualization:

> The couplet "creativity/talent" has recently come to represent the most desired of human qualities, expressive of, indeed synonymous with, an "inner self," and hence a market of uniqueness, and particularly resonant for young people poised to enter the labor market. Creativity is not unlike what 'soul' used to be, a mark of the inner, meaningful self. But these resources are not simply there, on top. They have to be worked at.

This deep commitment to the idea of creative labor, according to McRobbie, has left many cultural workers in a vulnerable position. The entrepreneurial nature of the work, high competition, and lack of wide distribution channels for creative products, mean workers are very dependant on large monopolies, who demand a great deal from workers desperate to "make it." The chosen few enjoy a lucrative career, but the majority of others worked part time, for little or not money waiting in anticipation for their day to arrive—often it did not. The jobs of cultural works are arrayed in a way that makes it difficult, if not impossible, for them to fight for their collective interests as blue-collar workers once had with great success. The cultural industry is like a casino, which pays very well for the few winners but takes much from the masses that continue to play for payday. Studies revealed that workers feel increased time pressures; one reported that 65 percent of Americans felt that their pressures of work left them with little time to enjoy leisure or consumption (Cross 2003).

For many new social movements, youth, and sectors of the general public the idea that government could act as a tool of social betterment was increasingly drawn into question. According to Giddens (2003) the media broke the cultural of deference, as reporters revealed the soft and often scandalous underbelly of political life and new technologies helped to circulate the information widely. Concerns grew over the lack of political participation, particularly of the young and underprivileged. Skilled at utilizing the media, new social movements brought topics onto the political agenda, including feminism, environmentalism, racism, and globalization. Some of the most ardent critics of power and the neo-liberal agenda are no longer the working class, but students, educated elites, NGOs, individuals from the nonprofit sectors, and a smattering of journalists and popular writers. Despite their newly-acquired counterculture credentials, advertising and global brands continued to be the objects of protest from a new generation who demanded "no logo" (Klein 2001).

Blinded by the Light:
The Limits to the Aestheticization of Everyday Life

As we have seen, many of the theories about contemporary cultural change linked consumption to aestheticization, identity formation, and status. A smaller but no less significant group of theorists have argued against this framing. For example, those who undertook empirical studies of shoppers' habits often found that aestheticization played a more minor role in consumer decisions than the theorists had allowed. While Zukin (2004) found many consumers who were interested in the aesthetics of the table, she also observed they were focused far more on locating 2-for-1 sales. Lunt and Livingston (1992), too, found that consumers were taken up not simply with aesthetic interests, but rather with complex financial calculations.

Alan Warde maintained that academics had overemphasized some of the flamboyant aspects of consumer behavior among various subcultures, thus neglecting ordinary consumption patterns. He cautioned that this emphasis overlooked the many studies that illustrate how thrift and economizing remain essential components of consumption, at the forefront of many consumers' minds, above aesthetic manipulation and appreciation. Very few consumers indicate that they find consumption "a pleasurable leisure pursuit." While aesthetics might be important for sectors of the middle class and youth cultures, he notes, the majority of consumers prefer comfort to beauty. Indeed, he argued, people's pleasure at eating out is not just for aesthetic enjoyment; a great deal of their discourse about such practices involve getting "value for money." Warde also suggested that individuals consume to fit in with others, not to stand out as consumer leaders: "The extent of aestheticization might be assessed by the frequency with which an aesthetic orientation to practice is adopted. I think it is limited. In the end, my guess would be that most people prefer a comfortable to a beautiful life, and that the heroic consumers of Featherstone's account are indeed restricted to a fraction of the middle class and some youth sub-cultural groupings" (Warde 2002, 193).

Daniel Miller's account of North London shoppers found that the mostly female participants shopped for "love"—one of their primary concerns was that others would appreciate what was purchased. Even single women, he observed, purchased goods with imagined social relations in mind. Similarly Lodziak (2002, 43) noted the many areas of consumption that have been neglected due to the focus on the aestheticization of everyday life, such as the pleasure of "replacing old, inefficient products with more reliable and efficient ones," or for "getting a bargain," or for purchasing a gift for a loved one, or from just having fun with the kids at a theme park, and so on.

Unstable Satisfiers

Marketers in the consumer society play endlessly with new ways of expressing wants, combining them in different ensembles (lifestyles), and appear to be confident that most people will continue to participate—with varying degrees of intensity and resources—in the game. But what is likely to happen to the individual's sense of satisfaction and well-being in this setting? When the characteristics of goods change quickly and continuously, the needs through which individuals relate to them must also be in a state of permanent fluidity. When goods are little more than changing collections of characteristics, judgments about the suitability of particular goods for particular needs are, so to speak, destabilized. It becomes more difficult to match a specific personal need with the qualities of the things that maybe touted as suitable satisfiers for it.

Characteristics are distributed and redistributed across previously distinct categories of needs, experiences, and objects: The taste of menthol in a cigarette is said to be "like" the feeling of springtime, and the ownership of a new automobile model "like" gaining a new personality. The expression of needs is progressively fragmented into smaller and smaller discrete "bits," which are then recombined in response to marketplace cues into temporary patterns. For example, a generation ago, a teenager, in order to appear "presentable" at school, had to respect certain very broad behavioral determinants—neatness and cleanliness, gender identity, and provision of basic supplies (book bag, notebooks, and pencils). Now the presentation of self in this setting requires minute attention to aspects of dress, ornamentation, hairstyles, and accoutrements that are determined by heavily marketed popular music subcultures. Each facet of self-presentation has been broken down into component parts, and related in astonishingly varied ways to changing assortments of products and consumption styles.

The consumer society tends to abandon the fixed forms of need-satisfaction typical of traditional cultures and to experiment continuously with newly constructed formats. However, it is often hard to predict how audiences will respond to new formats. We find that advertisements preserve traces of the more stable formats inherited from the past, linking new goods and styles with traditional images of well-being: the slower pace, quiet and serenity, open space, and closeness to nature of rural life; happiness of loved ones in a close family setting that includes multiple generations; the attainment of goals set in accordance with personal, rather than institutional, demands; the concern for quality and good taste in judging fine foods, wine, and clothing—in short, all of the aspects of social life that at one time were not derived from the marketplace.

An advertisement's composition often connects background imagery with products having not the slightest intrinsic relation to it—the automobile or cigarette package displayed against a stunning picture of unspoiled wilderness, the liquor bottle set in a farmhouse room full of hand-crafted furniture—in a straightforward attempt to effect a transfer of the positive feelings evoked by the imagery to the product. The message structure as a whole plays upon ambiguous feelings for the well-established, traditional formats for satisfying needs on the one hand and for the attractions of new products on the other; the undertone of nostalgia reflects our awareness that our commitment to "newness" means that those older formats must become ever more remote.

Advertising has a unique capacity for sustaining a productive tension and ambiguity in its juxtaposing of images and symbols. Images from quite different contexts can coexist without contradiction because the message is not being communicated as a "rational argument." Rather, they are meant to evoke the realm of "meaning" and, since the symbols are only "suggestive" (of whatever meaning may occur to the viewer), the ordinary rules of logical inference simply do not apply. The essence of modern advertising is not truth but "believability" (Boorstin 1962, 226).

If personal satisfaction results from successfully matching the qualities of needs with the characteristics of goods, consumer experiences today must be very curious. There cannot be direct correlations between the properties of individual wants and the properties of goods. Individuals experiment with their wants, producers shuffle the characteristics and assortment of goods, and marketers try various strategies in market segmentation, message formats, lifestyle imagery, and media technologies. This is indeed a fluid and unstable setting for the satisfaction of needs.

We should therefore expect to find not a clear, overall sense of satisfaction or its opposite, but rather an indistinct grouping of particular satisfactions and dissatisfactions existing uneasily together. In personal reports about happiness and unhappiness with respect to such things as jobs and marital relations, researchers found analogous configurations, with no unified feelings but rather with two independent dimensions of negative and positive feelings, with the two sets failing to interact or cancel each other out (Bradburn and Caplovitz 1965). Finding oneself upon the field of expanded lifestyle representations, required hard work and there was evidence that it might be littered with disappointment. Increased numbers delayed having children and marrying to enable them to establish their careers. People worked harder and longer to maintain, and seek to develop their desired lifestyles. Yet, satisfaction in consumption appeared to continue to evade many. A study showed that 27 percent of people earning $100,000 annually felt that they could not afford the basic necessities of life, as the amount of money people felt they required to be happy was ratcheted up to a great extent (Cross 2003, 223). According to Andrew Oswald, professor of economics at Warwick University, "The improvements in prosperity over the last 30 year has had no effect on reported levels of life satisfaction or happiness in the UK and that is quite remarkable" (quoted in Seager 2004).

In the consumer society, where marketing has penetrated every domain of needs and the forms of satisfaction, advertising carries a double message in its "deep" structure, not visible in the actual text or images, into every nook and cranny of personal experience: One should search diligently and ceaselessly among the product-centered formats to satisfy one's needs, and, at the same time, one should be at least somewhat dissatisfied with what one has or is doing now. Thus, there is a double ambiguity in the individual person's experience of needs and satisfactions that corresponds to this double message. Needs no longer have an integrated form of expression running in well-defined channels maintained by cultural traditions. Instead, they are fragmented into an unordered array of ever-smaller bits of desire that may be assembled in many different ways. The ambiguity in personal experience, wherein individuals maintain separate domains of happiness and unhappiness, is rooted in this fragmented state of needs; elements of different types of desire exist side by side to be combined temporarily and then rearranged as the latest opportunity for satisfaction is presented.

This fragmentation of needs stands in reciprocal relation to the disintegration of goods as determinate objects. Many goods are now temporary associations of physical and imputed characteristics, unlike the products of traditional crafts, which changed slowly in shape and composition over long periods. So there is an ambiguity implanted in goods themselves; identical chemical substances used to manufacture various brands of soft drinks may be combined with sharply differing images of social group dynamics in sports or rock music settings. Advertising stands at the crossroads where the two sets of ambiguities meet and interact.

Loss of Social Consumption or a Celebration of Materialism

In his recent history of consumer culture, Gary Cross (2003) documents the expanding zones of leisure and cultural consumption throughout the twentieth century in America. He acknowledges the increased freedom afforded to the individual in the expanded field of leisure and consumption. Cultural goods offer the potential for a deeper exploration of self than was possible in industrial society. However, Cross notes, the increases in standards of living had not encouraged "introspection and self cultivation" but rather an insatiable quest to find ones self in "personal stuff." Consumption has become more diverse, but also less social. The high sociality of traditional consumption bound communities, groups, and families, but modern consumers are not required to consider others in their consumption decisions. People now fashion their own unique spaces of consumption apart from, and to distinguish themselves from, others. Instead of linking people together, postmodern consumption encourages a vast expansion of status competition. Cross (2003, 244) concludes that the expansion of popular culture contributes to the divisions between people, "In a society that had sacrificed the rituals of social stability for the commodities of personal mobility, it made sense for the individual to compete through goods." Within the field of consumption individuals are not burdened by morality of others, they need not concern themselves with their community, neighbors, democracy, family or children. They are free to engage in unfettered self-fulfillment.

But James Twitchell bemoans critics like Cross who pine for communal values, arguing instead that American culture has clearly chosen individualism over the group. While social critics romanticize about a society of tight knit families and communities, Americans wanted a society that supported their individual lifestyles. Twitchell (1995) contends that the key reason why Americans have embraced the marketplace is precisely because it frees them from social relations. The central appeal of the "American way of life" is that individuals are not burdened by the dictates of others, but rather are free to pursue their personal dreams: "Mallcondo [sic] culture is so powerful in part because it frees us from the strictures of social class. The outcome of material life is no longer preordained by coat of arms, pew seat, or trust fund. Instead, it evolves from a never ending shifting of individual choice" (Twitchell 1995, 289).

For Twitchell contemporary consumption has been less about "keeping up with the Joneses" than "keeping away from the Joneses." America long been considered the land of milk and honey because of its large middle class, but it is now made up of people who no longer want to be middle class; they seek to be "cool, hip, with it, with the 'in' crowd, instead." This emphasis has lead to a pluralization of lifestyles, defined as the secular religions, or "coherent patterns of valued things," signaling not what people do but what they buy.

> One of the reasons terms like yuppie, baby boomer, and Gen X have elbowed aside such older designations as "upper middle class" is that we no longer understand social class as well as we do lifestyle, or what marketing firms call "consumption communities." Observing stuff is the way we understand each other. Even if no one knows exactly how much money it take to be a yuppie, or how young you have to be, or how upwardly aspiring, everyone knows where yuppie gather, how they dress, what they play, what they drive, what they eat, and why they hate to be called yuppies. (Twitchell 1995, 289)

Postmodernism for Twitchell does not signal a "dematerialization" so much as an unleashing of materialism. The demise of the old morals of consumption permitted a vast expansion of material consumption in the post-1970s period. People did not just dream about goods or read their surfaces, they acquired them: "The average American consumes twice as many goods and services as in 1950; in fact, the poorest of the current populations buys more than the average fifth did in 1955." People drive massive SUVs, and house sizes in America have doubled and sometimes tripled in size to make way, not for more children, but more stuff brought home every Saturday from the shopping trips to Wal-Mart. Twitchell argues that the reaction to the dismantling of the Berlin wall in 1989 showed that many other countries are eager to join the American way of consumption. The impulse for individuality achieved through consumption of goods is global in its scope.

Although Twitchell acknowledges that the worship and practice of materialism delivers bads (waste, permissive child-raising) as well as goods, people have chosen it over all other social systems. The marketplace provides people with what they want. Twitchell maintains that it is difficult for today's middle-aged academic critics to offer intelligent commentary on contemporary consumption because they refuse to see that Americans consume in high levels because they simply want goods and hold onto materialism as a dominant ethos of life. Individuals are liberated and freely express their desires in the marketplace. Those who remain in poverty, notes Twitchell, do so because they lack the ability to change their situation.

> We have not been led into this world of material closeness against our better judgment. For many of us, especially when young, consumerism is our better judgment. We have not just asked to go this way we have demanded. Now most of the world is lining up, pushing and shoving, eager to elbow into the

mall. Getting and spending has become the most passionate, and often the most imaginative, endeavor of modern live. While this is dreary and depressing to some, as doubtless is should be, it is liberating and democratic to many more. (Twitchell 1995, 290)

Twitchell's analysis presents American consumption patterns as vanguard within the late modern consumer society. America has been seen as one of the key innovators of consumer culture and the spread of the American way of life globally have occupied a great deal of attention (Tomlinson 1990; Ritzer 1993). Twitchell is correct in stressing that consumption is a cultural practice and interest in materialism has not been fabricated and foisted on an unsuspecting public. But the idea that consumer's choices are completely unfettered is as extreme as is the contrary notion that advertising manipulates needs. Culture is not simply an objective expression of consumers; rather, it is filtered through a marketplace, and through advertising and a mediated popular culture. While institutions do not produce values, they do filter, distribute, and amplify them.

Twitchell neglects to remind his reader that America also spends five times more on advertising than any other country in the world. Any analysis of consumption must account for not only the force of cultural values and individual agency, but also the influence of institutions, particularly market institutions like advertising and media, have come to play an increasing role in cultural dynamics. We believe that the way to understand the situation is to see it as a highly contingent and complex negotiation of meaning and practice, and in the chapters that follow we explore these negotiations.

CHAPTER **10**

Media in the Mediated Marketplace

As we have seen, media have attracted considerable attention within debates about consumer culture. The last chapter showed that the processes of dematerialization and demassification have uniquely animated social relationships within the consumer culture during this time period. In this chapter we explore how changes in the media market during the 1980s and 1990s provided new tools for dissemination, enabling agencies to communicate their messages to broader and more targeted audiences. As our metaphor about the bridge suggests, the relationship between advertisers and media goes both ways. The history of the commercial media in western industrial societies is, in a sense, the playing out of this interaction between audience and marketplace. Commercial media do not passively respond to advertisers' desire to purchase space, but instead actively seek advertising funds for their own profit and expansion.

In this process we note that, by and large, agencies have not encouraged their clients to change the market segment to match the audience segment available to them, but rather have tried to persuade the commercial media to change the audience segment to match the desired market segment. Responding to the broader change wrought by demassification, the media system fragmented, designing itself for penetrating finer niche audiences. In the pages ahead, we will suggest that demassification has been animated by three major trends in the commercial media system, namely, new technology, globalization, and "niching."

The first trend was the assimilation of new technologies into the mass marketing system. Up until the 1980s, network television was the privileged mass medium: It best assembled national audiences, becoming the place where the branded dreams of advertisers and agency cultural capital became fixated. However, network television became increasingly challenged by the home video market, and the proliferation of thousands of alternate channels on cable, satellite and digital television. During this time, audiences could also choose among a burgeoning array of lifestyle magazines and radio stations catering to a variety of niche tastes. In their influential book *The Third Wave* (1980) Alvin and Heidi Toffler saw computer technology as galvanizing the growing cultural impulse for diversity and individuation by further demassifying the mass market system. Computers, robotics, and telecommunication "smart" technologies, they argued, permitted greater customization of production, leading to a more diverse array of goods and an expanding domain of consumer choice. With the Tofflers' prophesies ringing in their ears, marketers heralded the Internet as *the* watershed technology, promising a new era of one-to-one marketing and instant shopping with a click of a button. Realizing that consumers were increasingly mobile and no longer constrained by the old 9-to-5 routine, the industry expanded their offering of media formats and genres "24/7."

The second trend has been globalization. In 1967 the first commercial satellite was launched into space by the United States, signaling a new era of global communication. In particular, the last twenty years have seen tremendous expansion in the global media sector, as the commercialization of television channels spread from Krakow to Beijing. *Glamour* and *Cosmopolitan* magazines, which had long circulated between New York, Paris, and London, now offered fashion advice to women from Rio to Singapore. Meanwhile, corporate Web sites allowed consumers to access information about their products from anywhere around the world. In this newly networked world, global media conglomerates sought to exploit their ability to straddle world markets by creating synergies across their media holdings, syndicating programs, program formats, celebrities, and merchandising for global distribution.

The third trend is a growing tendency to carve out new niches in the media marketplace. Although advertisers have long used research to target specific market segments, during the 1980s and 1990s they became increasingly convinced that the world's population was splintering into a wide variety of interest groups (including gays, blacks, feminists, and environmentalists). Joseph Turow (1997) noted a particular shift in agencies' thinking during the 1980s, as they entered into serious discussion about the changing nature of North American society. The all-important "baby boom" cohort had reached maturity and had begun to have children; however, the worrying discovery was that they were not following the consumption patterns of their parents' generation. Instead, boomers tended toward more individualistic forms of consumption. Accordingly, advertisers determined that reaching this massive cohort would require media that reflected that spirit of individualism. And so, an assault began on traditional media regulation—the force that industry members perceived to stand in the way of a more diverse media system.

De-Regulation and Convergence

Since 1934 the United States' *Communication Act* had laid down clear regulatory demarcations between those who produce programs and those who carry them, in order to prevent broadcasters from distributing their own content (a practice considered detrimental to fostering the type of diverse content required by a democracy). At the same time, Britain, other European countries, Canada, and Japan had taken a different path to secure diversity with the construction of public broadcasting systems. Unlike the United

States, these countries believed that private interests and profit motives could not produce diverse quality national programming.

While advertisers and media producers generally work together to secure one another's interests, historical analysis reveals that the division of labor between these parties has long been subject to negotiation and re-articulation. In the United States, early television was produced by advertisers. Popular 1950s sitcoms like *I Love Lucy* were produced by Phillip Morris tobacco, explaining why characters smoked in each episode. This relationship between advertisers and popular cultural programming was not considered a problem until the 1960s, during which time the major television networks convinced advertisers that it would be more beneficial for them to purchase the spaces between network-produced programs than make their own. In exchange for program control, networks created a special "prime time" (6:00 p.m.–10:00 p.m.) slot and informally promised to limit the number of ads, so that those shown would be properly showcased for the large viewing audiences; in exchange, advertisers paid a premium price for prime-time slots. In time, regulators created a clear division between programming and advertising, discouraging any promotions that were not clearly labeled and which were longer than sixty seconds. Such regulation was considered necessary to protect vulnerable audiences, such as children, from potentially harmful effects of promotion.

Early regulation was supported by a number of strong anti-trust law precedent cases. One example is found in the treatment of the American Broadcasting Corporation (ABC) by the courts. This network was originally conceived in the 1930s by the radio giant RCA, which wanted to parlay its radio profits into launching the new television medium. RCA created two television networks in the 1930s, one called Red, the other Blue. Concerns about monopoly practices lead to an anti-trust court case in 1936 that forced RCA to divest one of these television networks. RCA decided to divest the Red network (which became known as ABC), retaining the blue (which became known as NBC). During the 1960s, the network again found itself embroiled in controversy, as the information giant ITT's bid to purchase ABC was denied. The court decision was influenced by a concern that the network would become a wasteland of corporate promotion. Courts had adopted a role of limiting media monopolies in order to protect audiences and foster diversity.

In the 1980s a new commercial ethos emerged, and regulation (once considered a public good and an enabler of programming diversity) became known as "red tape" that prevented diversity in programming and audience choice. One of the first acts Ronald Reagan undertook upon being sworn in as President of the United States in 1980 was to change communication policy, appointing new judges and a new head of the Federal Communication Commission (FCC). The new regulators viewed the older regulatory framework as a barrier to the advancement of American technology, commerce, and consumer satisfaction, and together they initiated a process of deregulation. This ideology still rules in Washington, D.C. In the words of FCC Commissioner, Michael Powell: "The oppressor here is regulation" and the best approach towards media regulation is to "let markets pick winners and losers" (Jackson, 2001). In 1984 the United States Justice Department had struck down the informal relationships between media and advertisers. Now there would be no limits to the number of advertising minutes that networks could sell (Freeman et al. 2000).

That same year the FCC had lifted its restriction on promotional material longer than sixty seconds, permitting program-length "infomercials" (based on the argument that contemporary audiences wanted product information and could easily tell the difference between advertisement and program content). Shopping channels emerged, enabling consumers to purchase merchandise on display by phone. Advertising also entered into previously protected broadcasting spaces. In 1992 a bill was passed allowing children's advertising on commercial television. Again, regulators defended their position, arguing that advertising funds could assist the production of high-quality, diverse children's programming and that even very young children could tell the difference between a program and an ad.

Through the 1990s a second wave of deregulation dismantled the earlier controls drawn around media function—content, communication, carrier—to support the expansion of the Internet. The Internet rendered the distinction between cable and telephone; or carrier and provider, moot. Companies argued that their global expansion was hampered by the added expense they incurred through the regulated practice of subsidizing local telephone with profits from the higher rates changed for long distance calls. The 1996 *Telecommunication Act*, written with these matters in mind, dismantled local call subsidies, increasing competition between long distance and local telephone providers and cable companies to create a favorable environment for the development of the Internet and new wireless technologies.

The courts supported the FCC's interest in "convergence"—equalizing treatment and encouraging competition between various media providers—particularly broadcasters, cable, and telephone companies. Old media distinctions blurred as cable providers won the right to become content providers, while broadcasters won the right to have their licenses extended to eight years and "a completely free and guaranteed entry into HDTV/digital broadcasting" (Tunstall and Machin 1999, 50). Telephone companies began providing entertainment content, and cable companies began supporting telephony. Not to be left out, computer providers like Microsoft entered show business, delivering entertainment to consumers direct to their computer screens.

In 2000 the FCC passed by majority vote a decision to allow networks to purchase other networks. The courts also overturned regulation that had barred horizontal integration between television stations, newspapers, and radio stations in the same market. Also in 2002 the courts struck down the law barring cable companies from merging with broadcast networks. In its ruling the court challenged the FCC to explain why a television station was forbidden to reach more than 35 percent of American homes. FCC Commissioner, Michael Powell argued that denying television stations a right to growth amounted to hampering their freedom of speech.

Media Monopolies

Deregulation opened the flood gates for media consolidation, creating vast new media monopolies. Perhaps nothing announced the new era of media monopoly more clearly than Disney's 1995 purchase of ABC and its cable holdings. In this $19 billion deal Disney became the second largest media corporation in the world, with $22 billion in profits (Croteau and Hoynes 2001). However, this merger was soon shadowed by the AOL–Time Warner combination that brought together the Internet interest of America On Line, the Time Inc. publishing empire, Warner Brothers' film and television holdings, and Turner Broadcasting (CNN) to form the largest media company in the world, with revenues of $26.8 billion. Another sizeable merger included CBS–Viacom, with 1998 combined revenues of $18.9 billion. By 1999, nine media monopolies (Disney, AOL–Time Warner, Bertelsmann, Viacom, News Corporation, Sony, TCI, Universal, and NBC) controlled the majority of the global media system (see Figure 10.1).

Herman and McChesney have noted these media companies entered global markets rapidly: "Time Warner and Disney, generated around 15 percent of their income outside of the United States in 1990. By 1997, that figure was in the 30–35 percent range." Profit came both from lucrative syndication deals and advertisers seeking global audiences; in one decade "Disney and Time Warner…almost tripled in size" (McChesney 1997; see also Herman and McChesney 1998). Today, the global media business is dominated by companies from the United States; however, consolidation has also occurred in European, Asian, and Latin American media companies.

As publicly traded companies who had acquired considerable debt, the media giants placed the bottom line at the top of their agenda. Labor costs were kept down through the implementation of new technology. A 1986 British newspaper industry incident offers an illustration of the lengths global media monopolies will go to cut costs. Rupert Murdoch's News Corporation implemented cost savings digital technology to produce its newspapers, effectively wiping out an entire workforce overnight. In what became known as "the Wapping dispute," unions fought to save these jobs, but, as miners had learned earlier, the British government now sided with business, not workers. Following general management trends, media monopolies supplemented their full time labor force, and its costly benefit packages, with part time and

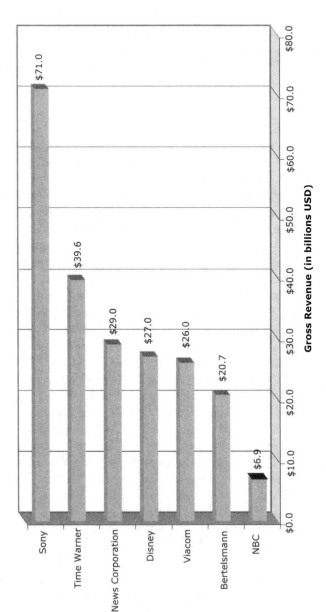

Figure 10.1 Top 7 Global Media Corporations Gross Revenue for 2003.

contract employees. Boutique media companies blossomed in niches where the monopolies were either too large to maneuver, or too risk-averse to enter. In time, successful boutique businesses were often purchased by larger holding companies. CEOs who orchestrated these media deals and oversaw these media behemoths were awarded astronomical wages, benefits, and stock option packages. Now, the most important employees in media were not the people who produced the copy, program, or Web page, but the executives, accountants, and lawyers who worked out specialized contracts and provided sales teams with projections upon which they were to rank their success. To manage their massive size, media monopolies unbundled specialized components of the business, pitting departments against one another in the belief that competition instilled productivity and innovation. Next to the military and pharmaceutical industries, the entertainment economy became one of the major engines of economic growth in the United States.

Media companies became enchanted by the idea of "synergy," a business logic holding that funds could be saved by maximizing cross-promotional efforts across media holdings. In Disney's case the company used its merchandizing division to make T-shirts promoting its sports clubs, its television division to promote the games, and the characters in its theme parks to enliven a new generation of fans. Janet Wasko (2001, 80) noted, "All components of the Disney corporation point back to the Disney corporation." Synergies expanded media promotion as media increased branding and promotional efforts, leading to an increasingly-familiar sight: logos at the bottom of the TV screen.

Today, media networks have no economic incentive to produce good quality programming that challenges and excites the audience. It is enough to produce material that is simply attention-getting, rather than communicating interesting or thought-provoking ideas. Networks occasionally adjust particular programs and rejuggle the same elements—sex, adventure, violence, and celebrity—creating commercial television that Todd Gitlin (1983) has called "recombinant culture." Today's total television audience remains remarkably stable in size, since watching television has become a habitual activity, regardless of what is being broadcast. Knowing that they can do little to affect the overall size of the total television audience, each network concentrates on making sure people watched their shows and not somebody else's—as cheaply as possible.

Media buyers have complained about the poor quality of content offered by the media because of synergies, wherein privileged repeats and reruns have become an inexpensive means of filling the insatiable need for programming on the flow media (i.e., television and radio). Donna Speciale, Executive Vice President of National and Local Broadcasting for Grey Global Group's Media Com (New York) has voiced her complaint that American networks no longer invest in quality programming.

> The broadcast networks took the easy way out with news shows, and more recently, reality and game shows. But this is not sticking. There has not been a hit in a year and a half. [Networks] are going backwards. Airing Mary Tyler Moore and Carol Burnett [specials] is pretty sad. (quoted in Ephron 2002, 36)

It is worth pointing out that the growing concentration of media companies did not go entirely unchecked in the United States. Two very significant court cases during this period sought to prevent monopoly control. The first was the break up of the massive AT&T telephony holdings into seven "Baby Bell" companies. However, courts were unable to prevent financial speculators from cross-media investing, and the Baby Bells were simply recombined through various investments. Another anti-trust suit was launched in 1995 by Netscape, an Internet browser seeking to defend its 80 percent share of the market by challenging Microsoft's plan to bundle its new browser "Explorer" with the "Windows" operating system that dominated 90 percent of the personal computer market. The court ruled that Microsoft's dominance, while not illegally acquired, was illegally maintained, by methods like strong-arming computer manufacturers to make Explorer the default browser when consumers turned on their computers.

This case was settled in 2003 when AOL–Time Warner purchased Netscape. Microsoft provided AOL–Time Warner $750 million to settle outstanding litigation, and free use of Explorer for the next seven years, which will effectively kill Netscape's market presence (*Guardian*, May 31, 2003). Hence, despite the AT&T and Microsoft anti-trust cases, the media conglomerates' immense economic clout and deal-making skills have enabled them to skirt court rulings and regulation.

Extending the Mediated Marketplace: Changes in Media Post-1980

Having explored some of the broader regulatory changes that shaped the media environment in the 1980s and 1990s, in this section we discuss some of the major commercial media changes pertaining to each major advertising medium. Featured below are four charts showing trends in global advertising expenditures (Table 10.1 and Figures 10.2–10.4).

We note that the press continued to collect the lion's share of the global advertising spend. However, the fortunes of the press showed steady decline, with television sales rising slightly to garner 38 percent of the total global advertising dollar spent by 1997. Disbursements on radio remained fairly consistent at 7–8 percent, as did outdoor advertising, capturing roughly 4 percent of the total global amount. Cinema remained a negligible commercial medium.

Table 10.1 Global Advertising Expenditure on Major Commercial Media (1987 to 1997)

	Press	Television	Radio	Cinema	Outdoor
1987	57.7	30.1	7.6	0.3	4.4
1988	56.5	31.1	7.6	0.3	4.6
1989	56.3	31.2	7.6	0.3	4.6
1990	55.7	31.8	7.6	0.3	4.7
1991	54.6	32.7	7.6	0.3	4.9
1992	50.6	37.5	7.1	0.3	4.6
1993	51.3	35.8	7.9	0.2	4.7
1994	50.4	36.7	8.0	0.2	4.7
1995	50.5	36.8	7.7	0.2	4.7
1996	49.0	38.2	7.9	0.2	4.6
1997	49.0	38.2	8.2	0.2	4.4

Source: *World Advertising Trends 1999*, published by NTC Publications Ltd.

The Internet

Despite all the hype that has accompanied Internet advertising it is noteworthy that its impact on advertising spends to date has been minimal. While we could assume that perhaps it takes time for a new medium to establish itself with advertisers, all other media, particularly television, established a relation-

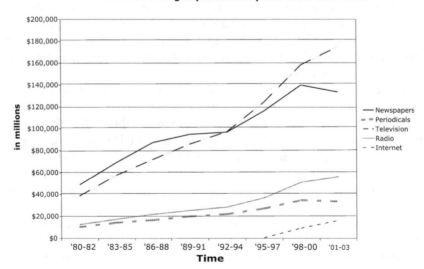

Figure 10.2 Historical Trends in Advertising Expenditure by Medium: United States.

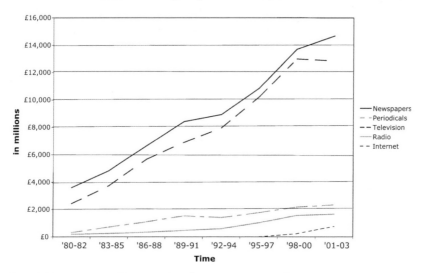

Figure 10.3 Historical Trends in Advertising Expenditure by Medium: United Kingdom.

ship with advertisers much quicker than the Internet has. This should not lead us to discount the impact of the Internet on the marketplace, however.

To understand the impact of this new medium we have to explore it from another angle. Like all new technologies, the Internet fostered not only new media practices but new technological dreams: For some the Internet became the answer to the age-old riddle of how to close the gap between audiences and consumption practices. The expansion of the Internet and computer technology into people's homes was less rapid than the adoption of television, but their impact on how advertisers conceived of their practices, audiences, and distribution systems was phenomenal.

In the 1970s the Internet was a network of computers linked to one another via telecommunication, to enable research scientists to communicate and share information, while protecting that information from military attack by spreading it throughout the network instead of one centralized location. Numbers of Internet users increased quickly in the 1980s, as universities throughout the world linked up to join the network. Since that time, the Internet has transformed the stand-alone computer into a communication tool, allowing individuals to connect to others effortlessly. Users can self-publish, share favorite Web sites, find facts, trade gags, and meet strangers with like affinities and hobbies. The volume of information, self- guided search capacity, interactivity, and the ability to connect people through e-mail, chat rooms, and games set the Internet apart from all other media.

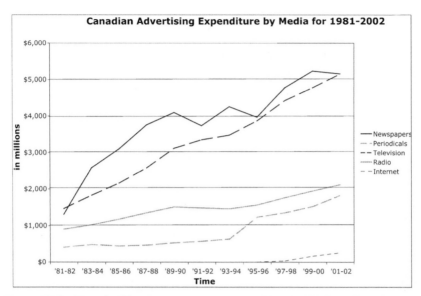

Figure 10.4 Historical Trends in Advertising Expenditure by Medium: Canada.

By 1992 the volume of activity on the Internet convinced entrepreneurs to consider the medium's commercial potential. Speculators found it relatively easy to sell interest in the medium by promoting it as a powerful new marketing tool that provided the means to speak directly to consumers and permit them to order goods online. And as they interacted with Web sites, consumers left data footprints that could be interpreted and acted upon by intelligent database systems, enabling unprecedented automatic one-to-one target marketing. Since the Internet appeared to solve many marketing problems, existing companies constructed corporate or product websites, and for seven years investors poured trillions of dollars into the development of new Internet companies, or "dot.coms."

Among the ways the Internet distinguished itself from other mass media was its audience base. Television had been embraced by those of all ages, but the Internet forged a digital divide, as the young, the wealthy, and the West were among its early adopters. The young were more likely to get their news from the Internet than traditional media sources, and to use it in conjunction with other media (multi-tasking). Some young people became so proficient in computer skills that they parlayed them into income-producing Web sites for businesses. Others became killer application entrepreneurs (i.e., Shawn Fanning, founder of Napster). The computer nerd had become cool, as horn-rimmed glasses became a high fashion statement. The promise of cyber-commerce fueled Internet speculation, which, not unlike the tulip bulb craze in

Europe centuries earlier, blew air into an economic bubble which inflated the United States' economy through most of the 1990s.

During that decade, corporations became excited about the Internet's advertising potential. Media consultant Paul Allen (2000) reported the Internet industry's claim that its presence in the advertising market promised to "put NBC out of business." Many of the ad formats designed for the Internet sought to overcome viewers' impulse to avoid advertisements. Like the television channel changer, the computer mouse enabled viewers to click themselves away from advertising. In response, pop-up advertising boxes opened when a Web site was chosen. Others lingered behind windows, unnoticed, until users closed the main windows. Some pop-up boxes were designed not to close, and many of them invited the viewer to click to find out more. Some Web sites required viewers to watch advertisements before they were allowed to obtain the information they wanted. In a period when television advertisers were perfecting their soft sell, many Internet advertisers took advertising back to the Wild West days of hard-selling barkers. Over time subtle methods of promotion emerged, such as product placement in popular gaming or chat room sites and downloadable images of pleasure, such as the BMW films. Personal e-mail accounts were bombarded with spam, unsolicited advertising messages. Offline, the rights to insert advertising messages on screen savers on computers in cafes and educational institutions were sold to advertisers. However, although businesses have found some success providing consumers with greater information about products, the Internet, to date, has been a disappointment as an advertising medium. Investment in digital media today falls far short of early expectations.

> Digital media buys remain a minuscule percentage of the overall ad budgets for all but technology, telecom, and financial services marketers. Even automotive marketers, widely regarded among the savviest about investing in online programs, are only putting 2% to 3% of their media dollars toward online media, according to media agency executives. (Elkin 2001, 8)

Predictions that the Internet would put television out of business have not come to pass. Indeed, the Internet did not lure advertisers away from conventional media, but instead increased advertising profits as Internet companies heavily promoted their dot.com businesses through television, magazines, and newspapers.

Despite heavy promotion, consumers' patronage of Internet businesses did not grow fast enough for investors, who in 1999 grew increasingly nervous that the vast sums of money they had invested in Internet businesses had produced no return. This worry began a run to shift money out of high tech stocks, resulting in a crash in the high tech industry. Since its peak in 2000, 40 percent, or some $7 trillion, has been wiped off the value of U.S. shares (Henley Centre

2004). In the aftermath, the Internet's reputation as an economic miracle tool has been tarnished, but not beyond repair.

While the Internet has yet to establish itself as a traditional commercial media space, it had by 1998 attracted over 79 million individuals over the age of sixteen in North America to purchase goods and obtain services online, and the numbers joining these early cybershopper continues to grow (Nielsen Media Research 1999). We believe the Internet's significance for advertising was not that it introduced a new commercial media, but rather that it instilled a new way of thinking about accessing consumers and distributing information and products in a more fragmented and individualized way. Marketers developed a new lexicon as they thought of the possibilities of the Internet which included such terms as "one to one marketing," "data base marketing," and "pull instead of push marketing."

Internet or on-line advertising now appears to be going through a period of transformation. After over a decade of effort, the internet has failed to capture more than 1 to 4 percent of the advertising spend. The first philosophy to guide on-line advertising emphasized "push," or focusing upon how to get the messages in front of audience's eyes, even if those eyes were resistant. Push formats included banners and pop-up ads as well as junk e-mail. Perhaps the greatest reason for advertisers' disinterest in these formats was their failure to consistently deliver targeted or large audiences. Many people find these formats highly intrusive, and associate them with the thriving online pornography business that has extensively exploited these techniques. Thus while push formats might get the message in front of viewers, the format often angers viewers, making them unreceptive to the sales pitch, and encourages them to click away quickly. Even Microsoft has criticized spamming, for it hogs an inordinate share of bandwidth, which they would rather use to pump their interactive technologies through to consumers. Programmer jockies have become heroes of the people by creating publicly available shareware to block these intrusive sales.

Since the turn of the twenty-first century, however, a new guiding philosophy has emerged to compete for on-line attention. The new emphasis is on "pull" and creativity, as audiences are provided the opportunity to engage with the message instead of simply enduring it. A highly diverse list of pull online techniques has emerged. As Turow has noted, these techniques represent a new arsenal in the war for audience attention, which are currently being deployed and tested. Formats include, for example, more thoughtful pop-up ads and icon buttons strategically placed within Internet communities, particular video gaming, comic and chat rooms that dance, move or represent a well-liked character. The viewer chooses to click on the icon, whereupon a targeted message for a product associated with the site is delivered, such as the latest video game or comic. Other formats include short downloadable films devoted to showcasing brand name cars; an interactive chicken that dances for a fast-food outlet, allowing audiences to type in a command for the chicken to execute; and games allowing the viewer to play with a ball and paddle or to paint a virtual picture, under the glow of a brand name. Other techniques attempt to link online promotional effort to offline media and cultural events. For example, a major Japanese electronic firm offers viewers a picture of the trunk of a virtual tree, and if one hundred people take the time to visit the site on a particular day and type a message on a virtual leaf, the corporation pledges to plant a real tree in Australia.

A video game corporation created a four month long advertisement which it refers to as an "interactive theater piece." The campaign included three Web sites, videos, voicemails, direct mail, e-mail, "blogs" (weblogs), traditional print and television, Internet TV, live stunting, package design, and small-space newspaper media purchases. The campaign followed the plight of a young man who took part in a focus group testing of a new video game, during which he became infected by a virus that caused him to tackle people to the point of injury. He uses the Internet to seek out others who were exposed to the game. They too have the same symptoms. The drama follows his fight to prevent the corporation from releasing the video game, a saga carried out through a host of media and "viral" marketing techniques.

Our protagonist notes that the corporation tries to throw him off the case by leading others online to believe that he is being paid by the corporation to undertake this stunt. Overcome by corporate power, the young man goes on the run, but he leaves by warning (daring?) others to use to the new game to see for themselves the authenticity of his tale. The promotional video made to document the event is fashioned in the style of the movie *Fight Club*, a biting critical commentary on modern consumption and masculinity that made a significant impact, particularly on young males—also the most likely segment to purchase a video game. This type of advertising takes postmodern irony and synergistic media marketing to the level of grand opera, using the themes of anti-advertising and corporate advertising as the platform for promotion.

The effectiveness of these types of messages on sales is still a question, but granted that this can be said of most advertising, this may not be an issue. Perhaps more important is whether advertising agencies and creatives are excited by these formats, and in view of the fact that a "cyber jury" has recently been added to many of the major advertising design awards, including Cannes, there is a good reason to believe that they are. Finally, the implication of interactive and digital television which would allow viewers to touch the screen and purchase the shirt that the celebrity on the screen is wearing, is a dream that computer manufacturers are currently working very hard to turn into reality. The role of these messages as a form of social communication, however, is just beginning to be researched and critiqued.

Television

During the 1980s and 1990s television remained the linchpin of the commercial system, but it was also transformed. In the new media environment, technology and programming permits audiences to register their unique viewing preferences more easily. The remote control and VCR allow viewers to zap commercials and change channels without leaving the comfort of their chairs; and researchers realized that, given the chance, audiences will choose distinctive programming according to their age, sex, education, income, and occupation. Researchers also revealed that the control of the channel changer was an issue for families (males most often took command of it), but this problem appeared to have been resolved with the purchase of additional television sets. Increasingly cheap to purchase, television sets entered kitchens (for mom), bedrooms (for kids), and family rooms. By 2000 the average home had three television sets; family viewing did not disappear, but became one option among several. The number of VCRs in U.S. homes jumped from 5.5 percent in 1983 to 58 percent in 1988 (Turnstall and Machin 1999, 45). The adoption of VCRs in Europe was even greater. The key attraction of this technology was that it allowed audiences to view movies at home, liberating them from advertising shown in the theaters (although not the long list of movie trailers at the start of each reel), as well as from the television executives' control over the movies they watched. The VCR also enabled people to "timeshift," recording their favorite television shows in order to watch them at personally convenient times.

Freed from regulation that restricted their distribution of content, cable companies expanded. Like radio, cable companies chose to package their programs into specialized types or genres to distinguish themselves from broadcasters. This approach also delivered the niche audiences advertisers wanted to reach. Content services began in 1979 with ESPN, a dedicated sports channel, followed by C-SPAN, specializing in current events. In the 1980s cable added CNN (twenty-hour news), then MTV (Music Television) in 1981. Through the 1990s a variety of specialty programs were licensed, including Arts and Entertainment (A&E), the Discovery Channel, the History Channel, and the Cartoon Channel. By 2000 this trend included lifestyle programming (e.g. channels dedicated to fashion, celebrity gossip, music, home decor, gardening, and cooking). MTV spawned a range of specialty music channels catering to ever more refined music niches (urban, black). Providing both local and network services, cable television's subscriber base grew significantly (*Advertising Age*, 27 March 1995; Mandese 1995). In 1975, 16 percent of homes had cable; by the mid-1990s that figure had climbed to 65 percent (Lloyd 1998, 91). As the number of channels available on cable in the United States expanded, so too did the number of homes subscribing to cable.

The growth of channels was slower in Europe because many countries remained loyal to the public broadcast models; for example, until the late 1980s Sweden had only two public television stations (Jansson 1999). The expansion of channels was limited for good reason. Public broadcasters had little incentive to offer more channels, because they required additional investments and did not necessarily guarantee more funding in climates where raising taxes for public resources had become anathema. The British Broadcasting Corporation (BBC) sought to use satellite to expand the range of available programs, since cable penetration was limited. To fulfill its duty to protect cultural and national sovereignty, the BBC initially insisted that British satellite technology be used and that programming be directed to UK audiences alone (Negrine 1988). But principles cost money, and the government was unwilling to provide additional funds to permit the BBC to fulfill this mandate.

To circumvent this obstacle, a compromise was struck. A consortium of British companies (Granada Television and Virgin) banded together with the BBC to form British Satellite Broadcasting (BSB). BSB began transmitting in the 1990s through leased U.S. satellites; however, this national satellite service found it difficult to compete with Sky Channel, which since 1991 had beamed programming to UK audiences, offering more diversity with eleven channels compared to BSB's five. Eager to keep pace with the United States, Sky Channel was permitted to merge with BSB, forming British Sky Broadcasting (BskyB). To increase subscriptions, BskyB followed the model used by Home Box Office in the United States, which had lured subscribers by offering access to free sporting events. Knowing Britain's national passion for football, the satellite provider purchased the rights to the Premium Football league, and the popularity of the games boosted subscription rates. By the mid 1990s, BskyB was in one out of every five British homes (Broadcasters Audience Research Board Ltd. 1997). By expanding the number of channels offered and reducing the costs of technology, subscriptions rose from 704,000 in 1989 to over six million in 1998 (*Guardian,* February 1, 1999, Sky: the first decade"). But this success came with a price: BskyB was 40 percent owned by Rupert Murdoch's News International, challenging the ideals of the consortium and national control over the system.

Britain's BskyB offers just one illustration of the difficulties that public broadcasters face in fulfilling their mandate in the post-1980s media environment. A new round of criticism from private broadcasters about the unwarranted privileges of public broadcasting was launched. The BBC was considered an elitist bastion that used potential commercial space to promote its own programs, forcing audience allegiance through licensing fees. The public broadcaster countered that it offered quality, commercial-free programming at a cheaper cost than private producers, enjoyed robust viewing figures, and maintained an international reputation for producing some of the most thoughtful news and current affairs programming in the world. Still, the values of quality, cultural sovereignty, and broadcasting as an important public resource were both expensive to realize and difficult to maintain, given the global reach of new technologies and media corporations. The public "wanted their MTV" and were more willing to pay satellite subscriptions than public broadcasting license fees.

In an era of government downsizing, tax cuts, and privatization, politicians focused attention on education, health, and military expenditures. The maintenance of public broadcasting systems moved lower down the priority list of many countries. Public broadcasters were asked to provide more programming for less money, and pressure to include commercial programming grew strong. While most public broadcasters around the world are mandated to give priority to nationally produced programming, the new channels require a steady stream of new programming, or "flow," to maintain audience attention. Because many European broadcasters lacked the funding base to produce this programming, U.S. producers found themselves in an enviable position. U.S. broadcasters were well poised to exploit this situation, for as we saw, they had pioneered the 200-channel universe, and learned from Hollywood how to produce popular entertainment by exploiting celebrities, genres, and promotion with resale in mind. U.S. programming was well packaged, was priced at a mere 1 percent of what domestic production cost, and was ready for exchange through the syndication markets. European broadcasters bought programming and program formats (such as MTV, *Sesame Street*, *Survivor*, and *Who wants to Be a Millionaire*) and licensed characters. Purchases were selective and broadcasters negotiated the right to alter some programming to better suit national tastes. The purchase of programming from the United States certainly did not suppress the production of original European content, nor did public broadcasters buy only from the United States. Still, U.S. programming today remains the cheapest and most readily available means of retaining flow in the expanding Asian and European television universe.

Public broadcasters also had to compete against the tide of satellite and cable programming, which had expanded greatly at this time. The proliferation of television channels available to international viewers today is staggering. According to Tunstall and Machin, the average number of channels available to households in the United States between 1955 and 1975 was two to eight; between 1975 and 1995 the number had risen to between eight and forty; and in the late 1990s, over two hundred channels were available to consumers. In Britain, four channels were the norm until the 1980s, when satellite and cable began to offer a vastly expanded television spectrum. In 2000 digital television came into service, aiming to replace analogue television within six to ten years and to expand the number of channel choices into the thousands.

Digital technology emerged in several forms, bringing several advantages to consumers. One was the ease with which high quality reproductions could be produced; earlier formats had always lost quality when copied. The digital format also integrated with computer and database systems, permitting viewers to use new technology to manipulate and control television programming. Personal television systems such as TiVO, OpenTV, ReplayTV, UltimateTV, and WebTV emerged, allowing viewers to store and access programming that matched their unique tastes. TiVo boxes now enable consumers to digitally store forty, sixty, and eighty hours of programming. Microsoft's UltimateTV has two tuners, allowing subscribers to watch two different programs simultaneously (with picture in picture), record two shows at the same time, or watch one and record one.

Personal television (PTV) and digital video recording (DVR) are like hybrid VCRs which allow audiences to record material, pre-select programming and interact with it. Viewers can choose the camera angles they prefer to watch a football game, ask for additional information about the stars in a show, or link to a Web site to purchase the shirt worn by a celebrity on a talk show. Smart technology systems evolved to monitor programming choices and augment a consumer's stored program choices with new programming similar to that of a consumer's previous choices. This monitoring system has come to provide media buyers with a much clearer picture of audience media preferences than Nielsen ratings ever could.

The spread of these technologies has not come without its challenges. Across the world, new digital media formats raised new privacy and intellectual-property problems, as bootleg DVDs are sold on the Chinese market and young people download MP3 music formats for free, much to the chagrin of major record labels. And the adoption of the new digital technologies has not been as widespread as initially forecasted. By 2000 only one million households in the United States had some type of personal television device and TiVo had reached a total of just 500,000 subscribers (Elkin 2002). Industry experts argued that the expansion of these technologies was dampened by the burst of the dot.com bubble, as the idea of interactivity ceased to signal the magical liberation of full personal program choice, instead coming to mean over-hyped emptiness; Because of this, Interactive TV (iTV) changed its name to "on-demand TV". Another difficulty cited was how consumers remained wedded to old ideas of television. An industry spokesperson noted, "The issue for us and others [in the category] is getting past the inertia of how people watch TV" (Elkin 2002). Perhaps consumers simply do not see how manipulating the same old programs offers them anything new. Nevertheless, personal television remains a hotly debated topic in the media industry. However, the Disney Corporation's 1999 investment in TiVO indicates that the media oligopolies have not yet abandoned the personal television dream. Marketers continue to hope that the new generation of young Internet users will be more embracing of digital technologies.

Audience Fragmentation

During the 1980s and 1990s, advertisers increasingly rewarded those media which could deliver niche audience segments. In 1980 a new network called Fox entered the United States market during a recession, facing stiff competition from the three major networks (ABC, NBC, and CBS). One of the secrets of Fox's success and survival is believed to be its specialty in assembling the highly coveted youth audience segment for advertisers. Advertisers have paid increasingly inflated costs for young audiences under the logic that North American youth had increasing amounts of disposable income and were forming lifelong brand preferences. According to former NBC News president Laurence K. Grossman, "Advertisers pay, on average, $23.54 to reach 1000 viewers in that age bracket [18–34] versus $9.57 per 1000 over 35" (cited in Dee 2002).

Advertisers also rewarded cable companies for their specialty channel approach by doubling their expenditures on cable between 1990 and 1996 (Ross 1997; Freeman 1997). By 2000 cable advertising revenues in the United States were larger then those of the networks, reaching $14 billion. In 1998 British satellite bled 10 percent of total advertising expenditures away from ITV's long-held commercial monopoly. Satellite has become the second largest commercial vehicle in Britain surpassing Channel 4 (British Audience Research Board, 2005). All of these developments were motivated by advertisers' pressing interest in niche audiences and the rising costs of network media buys.

The interest in audience niches accelerated the growth of media monopolies during this period:

> Momentum toward creating targeted spaces for increasingly narrow niches of consumers accelerated despite the consolidation of giant media firms during the 1980s and 1990s. The deals that linked Time to Warner, Viacom to Paramount, and Disney to ABC were not consummated with the aim of turning back the clock on media fractionalization or audience segmentation. If anything, the conglomerates' global reach could speed the segmentation process along, since it gave them the ability to amortize the costs of targeted ventures not just across audience segments in the U.S. but across audience their counterparts around the world. (Turow 1997, 188)

Advertisers continued to want to speak their branded messages to network television audiences, but TV time was a finite resource. Unlike newspapers that could easily expand their space by adding more pages, television has only twenty-four hours a day, and some periods assemble more important audiences than others. Free from regulatory restrictions, the networks took advantage of the demand for their non-programming time, expanding the number of commercial minutes and increasing costs. Therefore, advertisers' move into cable, satellite, and other media was not simply about addressing a cultural change. It was also motivated by an interest in finding cheaper and less cluttered media options than network television.

Clutter

Markets in both Europe and the United States can be distinguished along many lines, but one of the most prominent is the exposure respective citizens have to advertising. According to Asa Berger's (2003, 102) estimates, "Advertisers spend around $800 per person in the United States on advertising, and advertisers spend around $40 per person in all other foreign countries. Indeed, US advertising expenditures are greater ($249.3 billion spent on 250 million people) than all other countries combined ($225.7 billion spend on 4.5 to 5 billion people)."

Britain and many other European countries continue to regulate the number of advertising minutes permitted in each hour of programming. Although commercial minutes on Britain's ITV rose from seven to nine minutes in the 1990s, this is paltry compared to the amount of commercial time on networks in the United States. Between 1980 and 1990 the number of commercial minutes in the coveted prime-time space rose to ten minutes and, by the mid-1990s, to eleven minutes. Competition from cable and satellite providers encouraged networks to include their logos on the bottom of the television screen and promote their upcoming programs during commercial breaks, a practice that added another five minutes to commercial time (Lloyd 1997, 91).

When Disney took over ABC in 1995, there was a great deal of concern that the entertainment giant would bias news content. While interviewing Disney CEO Michael Eisner about the merger, ABC news anchor Peter Jennings addressed this fear by asking whether he was going to have to wear Mickey Mouse ears during newscasts. However, Disney cannot be accused of more editorial bias than any other massive media company. Disney used a more basic means of reshaping ABC news—it offered less of it, giving the network clear instructions to increase commercial minutes. Leaked corporate memos revealed the entertainment giant was openly encouraging the network to favor commercial time over programming time (Freeman et al. 2000).

Today ABC is the most commercial-heavy network of all major networks in the United States. Between 1997 and 1998 ABC increased its prime-time commercial volume by 11.8 percent; in the same time period NBC commercial time was up 6.1 percent and CBS 4.8 percent. Overall the networks aired about six thousand commercials per week, which represented a 5 percent increase since 1983 (Lloyd 1997, 91–92). By 1999 ABC averaged fifteen minutes and twenty-five seconds of commercial time during prime time, and seventeen to twenty minutes per hour throughout its programming (Ross 2000).

Other networks in the United States followed the trend toward decreasing programming and increasing commercials. A 1999 study by the Association of National Advertisers found: "Primetime clutter rose to a high of 16:43 minutes per hour, 59 seconds greater than 1998. Network daytime, always among the noisiest of the day parts, hit a new level of clutter—20.53 minutes per hour, versus 20:01 the year before" (Ross 2000, 68). Network news clutter was 18:53 per hour; late night had jumped to 19:06 commercial minutes per hour (Webster 2000). By 2000 the MindShare's Clutter Watch report noted that NBC had joined the other networks, "airing more than a quarter hour of national commercials and national promotions during every 60 minutes of primetime programming" (Ross 2000, 68). NBC was clocked at having 15.06 minutes of non-programming time, while CBS came in with 14:01 minutes of national non-programming time per hour, and Fox at 14:34 (*Advertising Age*, August 28, 2000).

Ad clutter on cable TV in the United States is worse than on broadcast television. Network TV generally carries twenty-four commercials per hour, whereas cable often carries as many as twenty-eight per hour. By 1997, the sixty-second format made up only 1 percent of network commercials; the decrease of commercial length to thirty and fifteen second format doubled the number of ads (Lloyd 1997, 91). Daytime television had once been important to advertisers who sought to target female consumers, but as women increased their presence in the workforce, this time period became an advertising ghetto. While advertising clutter increased so did the costs of network "upfront spends" for prime time ($3.8 billion in1992, $4.5 billion in 1994, and $8.4 billion in 2000).

Audiences React to Clutter

Throughout the evolution of the fifth phase, advertising studies revealed that audiences were silently expressing a backlash against commercial clutter, voicing their protest by zapping advertisements, time-shifting, and turning to less commercialized media, particularly satellite (Biu Tse and Lee 2001). Zapping has been heavily studied by researchers (Yorke and Kitchen 1985; Greenberg and Heeter 1987; Ainslie 1989; Sylvester 1990; and van Meurs 1998). Kaplan (1985) has examined channel switching and Tauber (1985) has explored fast-forwarding through videotaped commercials. Another form of protesting commercial clutter—physically leaving the room—has been studied by Cronin and Menelly (1992).

Clutter has been found to erode recall and brand recognition, particularly of those ads placed in the middle of the commercial period (known as the pod).

The Cable Television Advertising Bureau undertook a study in the United States which reported: "As pods became longer and more cluttered…audiences increasingly tuned out or undertook avoidant behavior such as zapping, muting, or leaving the room" (Ross and Freeman, 1999). Clutter was found to make some audience members so annoyed that they opted out of the television medium altogether. Clutter variously irritated audiences towards specific ads, all advertising, or commercial programming in general, a disturbing finding for advertisers trying to achieve audience "liking" as a measure of their effectiveness. Audiences in North America made greater efforts to avoid advertising on television than any other media (Speck 1997). Similarly, UK studies identified a cohort of 25 to 30% adults who consistently avoid television advertisements·

In their study of 360 randomly chosen television viewers, Biu Tse and Lee (2001) found that the majority of respondents switch channels during commercial breaks (81 percent). By contrast, non-zappers could recall more brand names and could better remember those ads which appeared at the end of the commercial break. Different lifestyle groups seem to employ different strategies to avoid advertising clutter. Young males often chose video game play over television; women spent time on Internet chat lines, or with magazines that better fit into their hectic lifestyles. Miyagi and Tanaka (1999) found: "Stores, magazines, and occasionally ads in public transportation" were more effective at reaching the young.

Willingness to zap was found to be linked to program type: Audiences are most likely to zap and be annoyed with advertisements that interrupt movies. This is not surprising, as the movie format designed for cinema is fashioned as an extended viewing experience and does not lend itself to direct commercial interruption. By contrast, soap operas, produced specifically as advertising vehicles, were less likely to encourage zapping during commercial breaks (Danaher 1995).

The success of pay per view and satellite television subscription in the UK and in the United States have illustrated that at least some audiences—often those that advertisers want to target the most—were willing to pay for high-quality programming with no or less commercial interference. Advertising revenues on satellite have been used as a secondary income source to providers' primary subscription funding; in 1995 advertising account for less than 12 percent of the total satellite revenue. HBO made its mark, offering commercial-free sporting events, and uncut (commercial-free) versions of movies. The Fox network limited the commercials in the prime time slot around its most popular programs, such as *The X-Files* and *The Simpsons*, and audience ratings rose. A CBS affiliate station, WGNX, "extracted under two minutes of clutter in the autumn of 1999 from its half-hour 6 p.m. newscast and found household ratings climbed 20 percent." It repeated the procedure for the 11 p.m. newscast and saw a similar rise in ratings (Webster 2000).

In 1999 Nielsen reported a 7 percent decline in the television viewing time of the coveted U.S. eighteen to thirty-four-year-old demographic group. Network executives attacked the research company, claiming the decline must have been a data error. While there are many reasons to be critical of the Nielsen rating system, 7 percent is well outside the bounds of sampling error. There is reason to believe that a drop this large is an indication that young viewers have migrated to other media and television options (Ross, 1999). Teens watched less television than other demographic groups, logging in 2.54 hours per day. While this amount of time is still considerable, it is well below that of men, who watched 3.56 hours, women (4.33) and children (3.03) (Berger 2003, 55). In the UK, advertisers' attack on the BBC grew louder, as data revealed that the coveted youth and wealthy audiences chose BBC over ITV.

Throughout this book, we have argued that agencies bridge the relationship between audiences, media and corporations, and have tended to encourage media and advertisers to work together to protect everyone's interests. However, intense conflicts arose between parties during the fifth phase. Advertisers sought quality audiences, in sufficient numbers, at a "fair" cost, delivered with minimum noise from their competitor's messages. Networks raised costs and increased the number of commercial minutes to garner increasing profits. During this time period, a strange situation emerged, whereby some of the most ardent critics of commercial clutter became advertisers themselves (Weber 2000; Freeman et al. 2000, Ross, 1998). Erwin Ephron, a representative of a New York-based media consultancy company, argued that networks grossly over-charged advertisers: "Adding it all up, the early, compressed, clubby, manipulated upfront market is probably costing advertisers an extra 2% to 3%. That's close to $200 million in prime time this year alone, and the networks like that fine" (Ephron 2002).

In 1992, the Association of National Advertisers (ANA) launched a campaign, supported by Proctor and Gamble and the J. Walter Thompson advertising agency. In this effort the ANA sought to break the upfront-buy stranglehold (in which advertisers pay networks a year in advance) in favor of a continual buying structure, in which networks would have to be more sensitive to the market and lower costs. The intervention did not succeed. Jon Mandel, co-managing director of MediaCom New York, argued that the rising clutter threatened to erode the traditional relationship between audiences and commercial television predicated on the audiences' willingness to view advertisements in exchange for programs: "Our concern is that the networks have gone too far and will kill the golden goose. It's gotten to the point that a number of us on the advertiser and agency side feel the networks are threatening the very existence of ad-supported, mass-reach broadcast television by adding too many commercial minutes" (Ross 1998). Instead of adhering to media buyers' complaints about clutter, networks made a business out of it, charging more for ads shown first or last in a pod and adopting a practice known as "topping and tailing" (where a brand is featured for a few minutes right after the end and the beginning of a program, to make the most out of audience attention).

Some argue that networks had succeeded in charging such high prices due to the billions of dollars which Internet companies had invested in television media time: "In the quest for eyeballs, dot.coms came to believe that mass media was their best bet. As a rule of thumb, these companies would dedicate 80 percent of their operating budget to advertising—flooding the airwaves and print media" (Allen 2000). John S. Muszynski, the chief investment officer of Bcom3's Starcom Worldwide Chicago (a media planning and buying company), noted: "Dot.coms came in and spent a lot of money…and it's caused quite a few networks to develop an aggressive mindset in terms of pricing" (*Advertising Age*, January 22, 2001). In 2000 seventeen dot.com companies bought Super Bowl spots. "At least one, Netpliance.com, paid a shocking $3 million-plus for its ad, according to executives—the most ever by a Super Bowl advertiser" (Elkin, 2001). CBS President and Chief Executive Officer Mel Karmazin told analysts recently that while dot-com advertising enriched the bottom line for CBS-TV in 1999, there were no dot.com advertisers in the company's top-twenty list of advertisers, and the company was not banking on a huge dot-com windfall this year (Donaton 2000).

By June of 2001 the dot.com funds had diminished greatly, and for the first time in a decade the cost per thousand for network television audiences fell (Friedman and Goetz 2001). The debate about whether this price drop finally signaled the "end of advertising" emerged again. Given the vast expense of commercial vehicles in this period, this speculation seems nonsensical. In reality what is happening is not the end of advertising, but—as we shall see in more detail later—the rise of new ways of integrating marketplace communication with consumer culture. The network thirty-second ad is no longer the fulcrum of the advertising system. Today media buyers undertake a more mixed-media approach, reaching audiences by distributing their messages across a great variety of media. Since the 1980s shifts to non-television media have facilitated the growth and spread of advertising throughout the media system. Cinema was commercialized in the United States, magazines, press, and radio did well, and there was a significant increase in the sale of out-of-home advertising spaces (billboards, posters, in-store advertising). It is to these other media that we now turn our attention.

Cinema

The Hollywood feature film fell out a favor in the 1970s, and through the 1980s the home video market continued to draw viewers away from theaters.

Never prone to retreating in the face of a challenge, Hollywood movie studios responded by perfecting the timing and packaging of their films. Years of experience had schooled the industry in understanding that genre, star, and publicity were the most important ingredients to market success. Hollywood found that sequels and trilogies could contribute to profit. To address broader audience tastes, Hollywood kept an eye on the independent film scene and the foreign film market, buying the rights to screen select movies for domestic audiences; it was not necessary to control the storyline, simply its distribution. Promotional budgets swelled as up to one-third of the cost of the production of a blockbuster could be devoted to promotion. Trailers became to cinema what music videos were to record companies: The media happily allowed celebrities to plug their movies, as this was cheap programming content. The pinnacles of such promotional efforts are the Academy Awards (the Oscars) and the Cannes Film Festival awards, in which films are aggressively promoted like race horses. The Oscar spectacle, complete with celebrities and designer clothes, ranked with the Super Bowl, World Cup, and the Olympics as one of the major engines of commercial media, particularly for attracting the female audience.

The average cost of producing a film by 2003 had risen to $103 million, and in that same year only twenty-six films had recovered their costs at the box office. However, studios had learned that in the age of synergy, the size of the audience for one particular film had become less important, given that films followed a well trodden path from initial openings, through layers of movie theaters and global distribution, then on to video, HBO, and finally television and reruns. Studios made a great deal of profit, even on very expensive films, due to this long chain of distribution (Tunstall and Machin 1999).

The popularity of the home video market whet audiences' tastes for choice, something old theaters could not satiate by offering only one feature film. Theaters decided that one way to get audiences to come back was to create multiplexes with a number of screens to permit greater choice. However, the construction of multiplexes cut into theaters' profits. Most ticket revenue went back to the studios, leaving theaters to rely on popcorn sales for profit. Selling screen time to advertisers seemed a logical means to fund the construction of multiplex theaters. Through the 1990s the multiplex was replaced by the megaplex, mammoth theaters that emphasized colossal screens. Megaplexes created a total entertainment environment, offering more succulent concession treats and other forms of entertainment, such as video arcades. The theater experience continues to evolve. In the UK, for example, a great revival of film viewing at the cinema has been attributed to the success of some British films, refurbished theaters, and more publicity.

Cinema advertising, common in Europe, had been tightly controlled by Hollywood studios seeking to protect their trailers from dilution by other messages. This protection delayed the commercialization of the movie-going experience in the United States, but studios eventually relented. By 1990 cinema commercials were screened at more than eight thousand of the twenty-three thousand motion picture theaters in the United States. Some audiences initially protested by throwing popcorn at the screen, but their objections were not sufficient to break the lucrative deals between advertisers and cinema. Over time some audiences, like their European counterparts, came to enjoy the high-quality promotional stories presented in the cinema. Cinema advertising is the most expensive to produce, being lavishly crafted, and it is highly esteemed in the industry. By the late 1990s cinema advertising expenditures in the United States had grown to $65 million. Sandler and Secunda (1993) noted that the last three years of the decade saw a growth of these expenditures by 25 percent per year. However, North American cinema advertising did not reach the level of that of the UK, where cinema accounts for 1.4 percent (approximately U.S. $135 million) of total advertising expenditure.

The desire to link brands directly to popular celebrities and programming, combined with the audience's adept use of technology to avoid advertising, has increased interest in product placement and the sponsorship of movies and television programs. The product placement arena has become professionalized, with companies being developed which have the sole objective of negotiating relationships between program producers and advertisers. These relationships can take different forms. First, instead of, or in addition to, having advertisements inserted between programs, in many cases brands are now sponsoring programs—a return to an older practice dating back to the nineteen-fifties and -sixties. Second, there is traditional product placement, in which brands are inserted directly into television or movie storylines (*Friends, Minority Report, Cast Away, The Apprentice*). Third, there is the production of branded entertainment, where the program is developed with the intent of providing a framework to showcase brands. Viewing these changes, Scott Donaton, editor of *Advertising Age*, believes that they signal a "gold rush" mentality to develop product placement links for various types of payoffs. The effectiveness of branded entertainment, product placement, and program sponsorship in stimulating actual consumer purchase decisions is unclear. But to facilitate the relationship between advertisers and program producers, new kinds of audience research measures have been developed and enacted, yet another sign of the growing professionalization of this type of promotion (Nussenbaum 2004).

Magazines

Magazines were niche pioneers, and due to their unique ability to cater to audiences' diverse tastes and interests they have played a key role in the expansion

TABLE 10.2 Percent Change in Ad Share (Main Media, September 2000–September 2001)

Medium	Percent Change in Share
Magazines	1.2
National newspapers	0.2
Radio	0.0
TV	–1.4

Source: AC Nielson MMS, cited in Freeman et al. 2000 ; available online at www.warc.com

of lifestyle and celebrity culture. Many magazine formats also went global during the 1990s. A high proportion of advertising funds were shifted into magazines, which expanded rapidly in the 1990s. By 2002 the Magazine Publishers Association reported a total of 10,625 magazine titles, 933 new publications having entering the market since 1996; over half of these magazines are heavily supported by advertising. According to AC Nielsen MMS, magazines outperformed television in percentage ad share in 2001 (Sumner 2001). The magazine share of advertising expenditures increased by 1.2 percentage points—or 7.7 percent, while television saw an overall decrease in ad spending of 3.3 percent or 6.6 percent (Table 10.2).

Magazines have long helped to feed popular dreams and to offer information and advice to readers, thereby interacting in complex ways with broader cultural changes. Much can be learned about culture and commerce by exploring the successful magazine format. The female magazines market witnessed particular growth during the 1980s and 1990s. With more women in the workplace and busy at home with children, it became increasingly difficult to reach the prized female consumer through daytime soap operas. However, women did thumb through magazines during their commuting time, lunch hours, and at the gym, fuelling an expansion in women's magazines. Working women with high incomes were interested in acquiring resources, information and advice about how to construct new lifestyles and live well. In 2001 the top one-hundred advertisers increased their investment in women's weeklies by more than 25 percent, and in women's monthlies by more than 18 percent (Cardona et al. 2002). Showing their interest in this medium, many of the UK's biggest advertisers, including COI, Procter & Gamble, BT, Renault, and L'Oreal, increased their spend in women's magazines and reduced their TV budgets. The biggest genres remain fashion and advice magazines such as *Cosmopolitan* and *Glamour*.

In terms of the discourse in and through goods, two important tends occurred in women's magazines. One was the expansion of fashion to all other areas of life: Nothing illustrates the spread of style into all areas of life better than the launch of a 1996 publication entitled *Wallpaper*. It emerged at the very moment when a number of designer luxury brands were looking for a place to promote their wares. This magazine taught a new generation of yuppies how to engage in conspicuous consumption without appearing to revel in it. This was achieved by placing great emphasis on modernism, art décor, lifestyle as art, and the home as gallery. Male and female models in designer clothes with vacant looks populated the magazine's pages. *Wallpaper* blurred the line between clothing fashion and the fashioning of space. The *Wallpaper* look drew from Bauhaus, formalism, white on white, and austere minimalist styles, with a dash of the 1960's Op Art and 1970s' shag carpet thrown in for fun. The look became global, copied by wine bars in London, hotels in New York, and restaurants in Paris. The style was recognizable and attractive even to those who did not read the magazine, and it was the publication's ability to be a style leader that attracted massive advertising dollars. *Wallpaper* expanded globally, but never achieved a wider circulation than about 150,000 readers. It was purchased by Time Inc. in 2003 for $1.63 million, illustrating the value that the media places on trend-setting and advertising. By way of contrast, in the 1990s *Ms.* magazine, with three million readers, had to stop publishing because its feminist editorial content did not assemble audiences that advertisers found attractive.

The second key trend in magazine content was the linking of lifestyle to celebrity culture. Learning from Hollywood, fashion magazines in the 1980s fostered celebrity models (such as Naomi, Claudia, and Cindy). By the 1990s celebrities replaced models on the front covers. This merger between celebrity and fashion was part of a more general expansion of entertainment journalism in the 1980s. Carol Wallace, managing editor of Time Inc.'s *People*, noted, "Interest in entertainment now is a global juggernaut," as consumers around the world became fascinated by "the business of the entertainment business, the people of the entertainment business, the products of the entertainment business" (cited in Freeman et al. 2000, 14). Publications such as *Entertainment Weekly* took reporting to a new level, citing expanded information about celebrities, for example the costs of their latest film or record and how it ranked in comparison with other entertainment products. "We sort of caught a wave," said *EW* Managing Editor James Seymore Jr. "There was a hunger out there for this type of information" (cited in Freeman et al. 2000, 14). Audiences wanted to see Hollywood behind-the-scenes.

The magazine *InStyle* was introduced to the North American market in 1994, providing an example of one of the most successful unions between readers and celebrity life. Launched by Time Inc., *Instyle* sought to prevent advertising dollars from flowing to *Hello!*, a European celebrity magazine seeking inroads into the United States' market. *Hello!* cultivated relationships with celebrities who, in turn, permitted photo opportunities in their homes, at their weddings, and with their children. *InStyle* took the *Hello!* format one step further by "filtering" the classic women's magazine format of fashion, beauty, home decorating, food and fitness information through the lives of celebrities. *InStyle* provided readers with information about the brand labels celebrities wore, their favorite restaurants, their diets, and how they negotiated their relationships.

This magazine came to be viewed as a resource for the "choices of people who can choose to have almost anything." The reader of *InStyle* is a "34-year-old employed professional with a median household income of $65,900" (*InStyle* Media Pack 2003). *InStyle*'s managing editor Martha Nelson argued that the celebrities featured in her magazine are considered more real to readers than the model in a typical fashion magazine, because "they have to deal with the same issues everyone does: balancing work and family, what to wear, how to live. It's with a bigger bank account, but it's still a real person" (Kerwin 1999, 6). The survival of magazines depends upon finding the right tone of voice. So for *InStyle* celebrities have to be carefully presented to avoid appearing condescending and insulting the audience by overtly appealing to readers' desire for status. According to its editors, *InStyle* accomplishes this balancing-act by "de-celebrititizing" celebrities—making the famous human.

To fawn excessively over celebrities or to encourage readers to directly mimic a celebrity lifestyle would be considered crass, implying that readers are sheep with no sense of identity. To enable readers to maintain their distinction yet still enjoy association to the famous, celebrities had to be made to appear as authentic working people. *InStyle* surpassed its European counterparts in making it easy for readers to acquire products featured on the magazine's pages by providing phone numbers and reference to Web sites. By 1998, 243 advertisers were purchasing space in *InStyle*, including the all important cosmetic, fashion, automobile, and house furnishings buyers (Kerwin 1998). By the late 1990s the circulation of *InStyle* had jumped to 1.3 million, with plans to expand into German and Australian versions and continuing television specials with ABC and Lifestyle Television (Kerwin 1999). Status competition became rife at the very moment that it also seemed to go underground, so advertisers had to adjust to wealthy audiences' contradictory interest in covert status competition.

Many successful magazines also launched formats tailored to young people, splintering audiences into smaller segments (Locks 2002). Young women have shown a great readiness to buy fashion and celebrity magazines targeted toward their interest in growing up fast and feeding their crushes on male pop idols. A host of women's magazines undertook spin-off publications for teens including *Elle Girl, Teen Vogue*, and *Cosmo Girl*: "In 2001 the teen-girl category will have gone from three major titles to seven in three years" (Fine 2001, 3). For example, *YM*, introduced in 1992, fast became a trusted source of advice. *YM* circulation went from 950,000 in 1992 to 2,150,000 in 1998, a success attributed to extensive consumer research which continually addresses its readers' changing topics of interest. Publishers argued that teens showed an increased interest in celebrity and shopping, and a waning taste for the quiz, puzzle, and general-interest formats of the past, a convenient change of events. The president of *Teen* undertook a redesign of the magazine which she called "Project Ritalin," signifying the hyperactive attitudes of readers who demand continually stimulation and change (Kerwin 1998). Other successful magazines targeted at niche markets during this period included computer magazines, such as *Wired*, launched in 1993; financial magazines *Bloomberg Personal Finance, Family Money, Individual Investor, SmartMoney, Worth,* and *Your Money*; health magazines (forty-eight new health publications since 1995); and men's magazines *GQ, Esquire, FMH,* and *Maxim* all helped to strengthen the men's fashion and lifestyle magazine niche. Many of these magazines went global during the 1990s.

The latest breed of magazines does not blur the line between editorial content and advertising, but rather unabashedly erases it. Titles like *Lucky, Cargo,* and *Shop, Etc.* were inspired by trends in the Japanese media market, which for the last decade have been enchanted by the "magalog," or magazine formats devoting their entire content to product advertising. These shopping channels of print feature regular advertising and product editorials. The images highlight the product, not the model or celebrity, and detailed information is provided on where to find the items. Originally targeted to the female fashion market, new shopping magazine titles have rapidly emerged to compete with those who have already established fairly sizable readerships (i.e., *Lucky* with 950,000). New titles, which focus on targeting the male consumer and those interested in home furnishing, have also emerged.

Newspapers

Newspapers' advertising and classified sections provide a key means for the exchange of local goods. Newspapers maintained a considerable share of advertising expenditures through this period (Graham 1999). In 1997 advertisers in the United States spent $130 billion on press advertising. Large-scale media companies bought up local newspapers in order to reach local communities, although the readers they drew were often of lower income than those who read larger city or national papers. Larger city and national newspapers continued to be utilized by national brand advertisers as well.

The press remained fairly lucrative for its owners, but was nonetheless considered a besieged medium, due to a new generation that preferred to receive news via the Internet, magazines, television, and word of mouth. In reaction, even the most staid broadsheet took on a "youthful persona," which typically included bolder typeface, sectionalized content, and more emphasis on stars and scandal. The trend towards segmentation that began in the late 1960s continued, as images, color, and fonts were sharpened to allow papers to meet the expectations of eyes that had been trained upon glossy magazines. News was supplemented with new sections that addressed many of magazine market's themes, such as lifestyle, travel, finance, health, fitness, and cooking. Emphasis on entertainment and celebrity was highlighted on front-page banners in a bid to secure the attention of those disinterested in "hard news." The sheer amount of information contained in the national papers is staggering. It would take a diligent reader several days to thoroughly read the *New York Times* Sunday edition.

Despite newspapers' efforts to rebrand themselves for the youth market and to produce more refined audiences, the trend over the 1990s showed a decline in newspapers' share of advertising expenditures. In 1988 print advertising accounted for 56.5 percent of global ad expenditures; by 1997 this had fallen to 49 percent. The United States remained the largest single market for press advertising in 1997 (see Table 10.3), taking almost US$53 billion, more than the other nine top-ten print advertising markets combined and four times more than the second-largest market, Japan. European markets took five of the top ten places, led by Germany (US$12.8 billion), UK (US$9.3 billion), and France (US$4.4 billion).

Despite slumps in advertising revenue, newspapers remain the most important information provider, as the press continues to provide the information that other media feed upon. Building upon this strength, newspapers have increasingly packaged information for online and television producers. Further, newspapers remain of interest to advertisers because the people who read them are often opinion makers.

Table 10.3 Top Ten Prin Advertising Markets by Adspend 1997, Current Prices.

Country	US$m
1 U.S.A.	52,843
2 Japan	13,340
3 Germany	12,811
4 UK	9,257
5 France	4,358
6 Australia	2,588
7 Canada	2,586
8 South Korea	2,459
9 Netherlands	2,374
10 Italy	2,144

Source: World Advertising Trends 1999.

Radio

In the 1950s radio broadcasters found themselves unable to compete with network television's large national audiences. They responded by targeting specialized audiences at the local level. Stations fragmented, specializing in singular music formats such as classical, jazz, and popular. Later these formats were expanded to include progressive rock, jazz, soft jazz, country and western. Other stations specialized in talk radio, sports, current affairs, and news. Each format was found to consistently draw unique audience segments. Thus the number of radio stations grew significantly during the 1980s and 1990s. "Shock jocks" replaced "crooners" as radio now sought to "get under the radar" of ad-avoiding listeners. Radio was able to attract a large number of local advertisers who appreciated the niche audiences this medium assembled.

Radio's growing popularity appealed to advertisers. United States residents have an average of five radios in their lives (kitchen, bedroom, office, Walkman, and car) and listen more than three hours per day, mostly during driving time. During the 1980s and 1990s many people began spending an increased amount of time working from home, whereas others experienced growing commuting times; both trends boded well for radio's audience reach. Radio advertising was also cheap and permitted messages to be repeated many times. As radio was often the first place people heard breaking news, it was sold as an intimate and trusted medium that was thought to shape both public opinion and policy makers. It also enjoys a loyal following by the coveted youth market. By 1996 advertisers in the United States were investing $15 billion annually in radio.

Out of Home Advertising

Outdoor advertising is arguably one of the oldest forms of promotion, and in the early nineteenth century there was more such advertising in London than there is today. In the past every square inch of the city was plastered with posters, and streets were clogged with advertising carts—horse drawn carriages which moved around the city bearing large advertising signs. In 1868 city planners became so concerned about the clutter of messages and advertising carts congesting the streets that they made it illegal to post bills, or to assemble more than ten advertising carts in a row. This free-for-all situation was replaced by a system of designated areas where posting was permitted at a price, and public space increasingly became the domain of advertisers. Today, while the City of London regularly rips down postings, it remains a criminal offense for the public to deface an advertisement.

Advertisers have been impressed by the success that brands have achieved with outdoor campaigns. One of the earliest product sectors to understand and exploit the power of outdoor advertising was the tobacco industry. Barred from advertising their products on other media, tobacco companies like Phillip Morris created some of the best-known outdoor campaigns of the later twentieth century: The Marlboro Man became one of the most recognized brands in the United States largely because of billboard campaigns. Increasing numbers of advertisers have come to consider billboards as an effective means of promoting their trademarks; during the 1990s outdoor doubled its share of UK display advertising from 4 to 8 percent, for example (McEvoy 2001).

With outside of the home media, advertising has colonized key spheres of the city. Some environments have a very high prestige and value, for example city centers. Piccadilly Circus in London and Times Square in New York attract millions of people with tourist dollars in their pockets who are keen to see the famous billboard advertising sites. Transportation corridors have become cluttered with advertising. In the United States, highways are sprinkled with some 400,000 billboards. Bus shelters, entire buses, trains, and subway systems have become wrapped in advertisements. Advertising on the back of buses receives increasing exposure due to greater traffic congestion.

New, extreme advertising tactics have emerged to capture the attention of audiences on the move, including sandwich board advertisements placed on herds of cows grazing along train routes to catch rail commuters' attention, and "Arm Guard," a plastic sleeve covered in ads designed for drivers paid to hang their arm out the window during daily traffic jams on Los Angeles freeways (Lloyd 1997). Those who are mobile are often wealthy, explaining why airplane infrastructures have been become cluttered with advertising. Long waits for flights and a prosperous business class have transformed the airport and inside of the plane into coveted locations for advertisers. Seat covers and the entrance and exit of airports are regularly bought and sold to big name brands, whose makers ensure that the products advertised are readily available at duty free shops. And because increased numbers of audiences would not go to the television screen; the screen has been brought to them on buses and transportaion corridors of major cities.

Naomi Klein (2001) has noted how the rollback of public funding for non-profit organizations and public organizations in the 1980s and 1990s led to the use of advertising as an alternative means of funding: Community leisure centers, buildings, and public transit have opened their spaces to advertisers. One of the most controversial issues has been the selling of school children to advertisers. Many schools and universities have accepted money from Coke and Pepsi in exchange for exclusive rights to sell their products to pupils. In 1989 Whittle Communications launched a new television program service called "Channel One," which delivered a daily twelve-minute news program and two minutes of commercials specially targeted to young people via satellite into middle- and high-school classrooms in America (Sandler and Secunda 1993). The controversy over Channel One would later lead several states to ban the service.

Studies have convinced advertisers that billboards offer a cheap way of extending the life of their television campaign. The popularity of outdoor advertising is understood to have increased with the saturation of traditional in-home media (Gleason 2002). Advertisers are encouraged by outdoor sellers to see this medium as a way to "cut through the clutter of electronic and print media," according to Scott Eller of Eller Media Company. Another factor supporting the growth of outdoor media is commuting time: "Today's consumers are spending more time out of home and in their car than they are watching TV. Just ask a soccer mom or a dad who has a 20-minute-plus commute" (Eller 1999).

During this time period, the idea of outdoor media was replaced by the idea of "out-of-home" media, referring to any media opportunity enabling advertisers to connect with consumers once they leave their homes. The widely-held industry belief that two-thirds of all purchase decisions are made at the point of purchase encouraged advertisers to find ways to get their messages closer to consumers (Linnett 2000). This came to be accomplished by a staggering array of media vehicles, including malls, restaurants, and pub toilets. Supermarkets opened their doors to television screens which promoted products, and advertising was included on the computer screen where customers watched the prices of their goods being rung in by the cashier. Promotion was also introduced onto the back of receipts.

The quality of computer-painted vinyl and digital poster production continues to improve. The appearance of billboards has come to be enhanced with dramatic lighting to extend their hours of visibility into the night. Today the use of digital displays is increasing, and demographic mapping and global positioning systems (GPS) technologies promise to enable outdoor campaigns to be designed to target specific audience profiles. Like television and magazines, outdoor companies have begun to offer global audiences to advertisers. The merger of Eller Media Company with More Group created a network of billboard advertisers in twenty-five countries across five continents, enabling campaigns to be run concurrently in New York, Los Angeles, and Chicago, as well as in London, Paris, and Beijing.

Recently a new generation of media planners has emerged who spend their time trying to conceive of new sites to situate advertising to get under the critical radar of advertising-weary audiences. For example, Matt Leible, of New York-based Horizon Media's Out-of-Home unit, speaks with pride of how his firm placed an advertisement on a basketball court in New York City: "It's at the cage, the street basketball court on West 4th Street. That wall is so target-specific to the crowds watching the street ball players. We got [the client's advertising] wall up after a lot of hard work" (*Linnett 2000, 4).* While it once had seemed ambitious to cover a bus with a promotional message, in the fifth phase of media and advertising, cultural intermediaries such as Leible's dream of covering the moon.

Conclusions

The question of how to marshal audience attention loomed particularly large for commercial media and advertisers during this period.

> There are more then 4,000 more consumer magazines than there were five years ago, but the average number of issues read each month is down. There are more newspapers, but weekly readership is down. There are more radio stations, but the average number of hours listening to them is down. There are more television channels but average viewing time has not significantly increased since the 1950s. There is a great amount of selection and a great many more things to do in our lives, but media executives and advertisers have not been able to solve one stubborn problem: there are still only 24 hours in one day. (Forbes 1999)

In the 1980s and 1990s audiences in the United States spent on average thirty hours per week with media. Despite all their new offerings, media firms have had difficulty increasing that figure. Hence, what we find during this period is greater competition between selective media over audience attention. These struggles are often framed as the battle between new technology and old—networks versus cable, television versus other media. But according to Jon Mandel, co-managing director and chief negotiating officer of MediaCom, emphasizing these smaller battles deflects from the larger war which has unfolded in the fifth phase, in which "there is a societal, cultural shift, and it's called lack of time" (Forbes 1999).

By the end of the twentieth century, the old mass media system had not been dismantled so much as augmented by a host of new media. Media formats and genres were refined and offered 24/7. The home video market blossomed and cable, satellite, and digital television increased the number of channels available to audiences into the thousands. Audiences could select from a host of new magazines and radio programs. A more sophisticated network of global cinema, television, magazine, and billboard advertising emerged, cycling formats, celebrities, trends, and buzz between the United States, Europe, and Asia. New technology such as VCRs, channel changers, and personal television allowed audiences to view more of what they wanted when they wanted. At no point in history has there been such a diversity of media options.

Viewing this cultural cornucopia, Jib Fowles announced that the media was no longer controlled by media executives and monopolies but was "completely subject to the fickleness, the choices, and in the final analysis, the control of the audience" (Fowles 1996, 19). We agree that audiences of this period have great choices, but to assert they have complete control is to lean too heavily toward industry rhetoric. Choice is a construction of market relations: Consumers only have the power to select among what is offered. The neo-liberal vision assumes that audiences have pre-formed preferences, but audiences very rarely select programs according to some rational decision model. They graze, making their choices based upon what is made available. They "watch television" as opposed to watching specific programs. The reality of choice on television inspired pop singer Bruce Springsteen to pen his song, "57 channels and nothing on." The new era of media expansion has brought with it reruns, syndications, cheap programming, and more advertising clutter.

The idea that the new media system services a wide diversity of audience segments must also be qualified, as some audience fragments appeared to be more privileged than others—in particular the young, the educated, and the wealthy. Staid newspaper, magazines, and television programs made fools of themselves during this time period by trying to become more hip and trendy to attract the youth market. Those attempts contributed to growing youth cynicism during this period. Celia Lury (2004) has argued that in consumer culture, youth has come to signify more than an age category, more even than a market target. Youth, she maintains, has become a fetish signifying all that is creative, fun, innovative, and exciting.

There is growing evidence that, in the United States, commercial media have been pursuing the chimera of youthfulness, while the reality is changing. During the early baby boom years of the 1960s and 1970s, when youth made up 48 percent of the population, it made sense to orient advertising efforts toward youth. But the demographics have shifted. During the 1980s and 1990s young people no longer had the spending power they once did. Between 1973 and 1990 the real incomes of those under thirty fell 16 percent, and three out of four eighteen to twenty-four-year-olds still lived at home, a figure close to that of the Depression era levels. Youth are not particularly brand loyal, as studies have shown that 67 percent of those aged eighteen to thirty-four would try a new brand even if it went against their customs, compared to 70 percent of those over thirty-five.

At the same time, those over fifty years of age control half of the discretionary spending in the United States, there are more of them than there are of the young, and they are very interested in culture. The numbers of those between the ages of fifty to fifty-nine who go to movies doubled in the last decade, while the figures for teenagers shrank. CD purchases by over-forty-five consumers doubled as well, and yet, less than 10 percent of advertising focuses on those over fifty. Dee asks, "What logic suggests that, because there are proportionally fewer young people than there used to be, because they have less money than they used to, and because it's harder to separate them from that money than ever, advertisers should spend more money trying to court them?" (Dee, 2002, "The Myth of '18-34," *New York Times*, Oct. 13: 58–61). Despite the rhetoric about media diversity, the existence of the eighty-five-year-old living on a state pension and with a penchant for watching variety shows simply does not register on the masters of the new media system, who, at least in the last two decades, have been mesmerized by the image of the eternally young, elite, and cosmopolitan consumer.

CHAPTER 11

Full Service Agencies
Globalization and Unbundling

In the eighteenth century, Samuel Johnson remarked that advertising was so "near to perfection" that no further improvements in it could be imagined. The dramatic innovations in advertising practice since that time have proved him wrong, keeping advertising production in the public eye and prompting never-ending debate and controversy about its evolving social role. From its origins in the nineteenth century, the advertising industry owes its survival to its ability to negotiate relations between media outlets on the one hand and manufacturers needing to advertise on the other. We have referred to this as a bridging function between those domains—and implicitly, between the economy and the culture in which they are embedded.

We have argued that the bridging function between media and manufacturers performed by the advertising industry is not passive. Having achieved its own independence and economic power, the advertising industry does not merely reflect the interests of either of the sectors it joins; it negotiates the compromises between them. The relations between media and advertisers are not just tied together by the advertising industry, but are defined by the conceptions that all hold of the role that agencies play. Ultimately, the bridge once built cannot be forgotten, because the transactions it negotiates become part of the structure and ideology of the marketplace.

We have seen in the previous chapters how shifting assumptions within the advertising industry could change the way person-object relationships are portrayed. Throughout history the agency's developing role both paralleled and adjusted to the changing marketplace situation. Like all institutions, the advertising business is shaped by the broader dynamics of society, its relationships with other institutions, its own internal interests and conflicts, and by the assumptions and ideologies of its members. In this chapter and the next, we will show how, in post-industrial societies where market activity becomes ever more complex, the agency bridge once again had to respond to a global, "mediatized" marketplace and adjust to a constantly transforming cultural context. For this purpose, a purely organizational account of agencies is inadequate. Rather, we must look more closely at the industry's internal mechanisms—and at the techniques, skills, and knowledge that it has accumulated—because these are what actually provide the substance of the agencies' role. The next two chapters seek to map some of the major changes that took place within agency structures in the last decades of the twentieth century.

To sketch the development of the agency industry structure we have interpreted a wide variety of materials, including interviews, the advertising and marketing trade press, marketing studies, and studies of advertising design. The trade press in particular is highly self-promotional and breaks industry dynamics down into sensational struggles between new and old approaches, or between creative personnel and management interests. Yet, as many others have shown, a critical reading of the advertising trade press remains one of the most valuable means of appreciating industry dynamics (Marchand 1986, 1998; Fox 1984, 1997; Mort 1996; Turow 1997).

The Transformation of the Full Service Agency

For fifty years clients had relied on the full service agency to provide account management, creative services, research, and media services that enabled producers to communicate their messages to national and foreign markets. In the 1980s, however, the full service agency began to reorganize, following the recession and deregulation that began in Reagan's United States and spread rapidly to Thatcher's Britain and beyond. In the following pages, we will characterize three trends within the advertising sector that resulted in the unbundling of full service agencies and their repositioning within the global marketing system.

The first trend was new clients' interest in *expanding into global markets*. To undertake global campaigns for their clients, agencies had to be of a particular size and stature and be able to coordinate a full suite of marketing expertise around the world—including research, creative services, and media buys. Moreover, selling into unfamiliar markets demanded staff who better understood the social, political, and cultural contexts of consumption.

The second trend involved clients' willingness to exploit *below the line promotional techniques*—ranging from public relations to telemarketing. Pressured by shareholders to find ways to create greater efficiencies in their advertising expenditures, advertisers turned to alternative marketing activities, which they felt could deliver more refined audience targets at a lower cost than could big media. Outside of traditional agencies, new marketing specialists emerged, specializing in below the line techniques. Some clients no longer looked to the full service agency to help them coordinate their communication, instead hiring a variety of communication specialists.

Third, clients' rethought the role of *media in targeting more refined audience segments* and global markets. Targeting and positioning research became the guardians of efficiency as advertisers took a closer "look at where the brand's best customers are connecting with it" (Adamson and Allan 2001). With the introduction of a host of "new media" channels during the 1980s and 1990s, media planning and buying became more technical and specialized, resulting in a widening chasm between advertising design and media buying practices.

What was the impetus to this realignment of some of the major names in the advertising industry? From the analytical framework we have developed, it is clear that agencies survive and prosper based upon their competence in the close relation between advertisers and the media. While they are themselves freestanding economic actors motivated by financial considerations and providing returns for their investors, agencies also need to be able to fulfill their basic intermediary function. To understand the impetus to the upheavals of the 1980s, we must look at agencies' changing relationships with clients and with media channels.

Pressures Toward Globalization

Advertising executives never tire of pointing out that advertising is a service industry. There is little doubt that the initial impetus for the merger activity in the 1980s was prompted by the changing needs of clients which were growing and expanding their activities to an unprecedented global scale. Companies that were already huge merged in order to reposition themselves in global markets (e.g., RJ Reynolds and Nabisco, and Phillip Morris/Kraft/General Foods). At the same time, Japanese and other Asian conglomerates began to compete vigorously in the United States and Europe.

Very little in advertising is totally new; the mid-1980s were not the first time that agencies had been asked to assist with international campaigns. For instance, the Interpublic Group of Companies (under the direction of Marion Harper) long ago pioneered the idea of international and multiple networks under the aegis of one financial holding company. J. Walter Thompson had opened an office in London as far back as 1899. We can identify three stages in this globalizing process. The first period lasted from the turn of the century to the late 1950s, and is characterized by American agencies opening foreign offices (first in Britain and Europe, and then throughout the rest of the world) to serve specific clients who needed international marketing and advertising services. Before the 1960s, three agencies (J. Walter Thompson, McCann-Erickson, and Young & Rubicam) handled the bulk of international advertising for U.S. firms. As one McCann executive put it, "In general, McCann-Erickson has grown internationally in parallel to key international clients. Some of these (e.g., Esso, General Motors) we have served for over 50 years in various international markets. It has not been our strategy to open an office in a new country and then look for clients. We generally open offices to serve existing clients who have become active in these markets" (Anderson 1984, 90–91).

Starting in the 1950s, this structure proved inadequate to meet the needs of the expanding consumer product manufacturers which began exploring foreign markets that were not restricted to Europe. The advertising options open to these companies were limited. They could hire American affiliates in specific markets and local agencies in markets where there was, as yet, no international advertising presence. However, this led to major problems of coordination and accounting. As Noreen Janus explained:

> In short, the rapidly increasing number of U.S. corporations doing business internationally after the war and even into the 1960s were faced with a very difficult advertising problem: multiple agencies turning out campaigns of variable quality, with little or no control over the company and product image on a world scale, accounting problems associated with multiple agency relationships, and media and advertising statistics that varied across countries. (Janus 1980, 77)

In the second period of global expansion—prompted by client needs, and sensing the opportunities and profits that awaited agencies able to offer international services—more U.S. agencies began to establish overseas offices of one kind or another in the 1960s. The boom was helped by Harvard University marketing theorist Ted Levitt's argument that it was myopic for multinational corporations to ignore the potential of global markets, especially when their products were superior in quality and they were in a position to benefit from the economies of scale afforded by mounting universal advertising campaigns. Levitt believed not only in mass marketing as a leveling force but also in the inevitability of cultural convergence as modernization of third world countries progressed. This mass marketing ideology was given clear expression during the 1960s, when Coca-Cola launched its first global TV ad campaign showing a multinational group of young people teaching the world to sing in perfect harmony in an optimistic celebration of this consumable symbol of American modernity. Coke was able to run this campaign in many countries around the world, achieving economies of scale and uniformity of image in their marketing that made the brand synonymous with global youth.

In the forty-five-year period between 1915 and 1960, American agencies had opened fifty overseas offices; in the decade between 1960 and 1970 they opened 196. American agencies came to dominate the advertising industry in countries all over the world—both developed and developing. As Janus noted, "One striking conclusion may be drawn from these data: U.S. control over the international advertising sector far exceeds its control over transnational industry itself; this is true at both the national and international levels" (1980, 82). Although the number of non-American agencies has grown, even within this scenario, not many agencies could offer services in every market within the world; they were strong in some regions and weak in others. With the emergence of manufacturing companies that sought to exploit to the limit the economies of scale offered by aggregating all possible global markets, a new rationalization was required.

However, a third rationalization emerged, characterized by the combination not simply of individual agencies, but of agency systems. There are a number of strategies available to agencies for establishing the network of offices that the new global emphasis demands. An agency can: (1) take the expensive and time-consuming option of setting up new offices in the markets in which there is a weakness, (2) buy already existing individual national agencies in markets, or (3) buy a network of agencies that complement its existing strengths. This last option was exercised by numerous agencies in the mid-1980s. For example, Doyle Dane Bernbach (which had strengths in New York and Europe) combined with Needham Harper (which had strengths in Chicago and Asia) to form DDB/Needham as a freestanding network under the holding company of Omnicom (which also includes the BBDO International network and a third subsidiary that combined the three firms' regional advertising, direct marketing, and public relations agencies).

Agencies do not simply follow the trends of multinationals. Rather, in their interactions, agencies attempt to encourage companies to elect those marketing options which agencies are best positioned to deliver. The globalization of agencies must be understood as part of the growth aspiration of agencies themselves. The interest in global expansion and mergers coincided with the decline of money that advertisers were putting up for directly advertising-related expenditures in favor of increased promotions, tie-ins, and event marketing in the mid-1980s. This was especially bad news for public companies (those that offered shares to the public on the stock exchange), which were more vulnerable to short-term profit pressures.

The only way agencies could generate more revenue was to attract new clients, and in a sluggish market, the easiest way to achieve this was to merge with another agency and aggregate both companies' accounts. Within this scenario, the British firms, Saatchi & Saatchi and WPP, accelerated the 1980s merger frenzy with their own ravenous appetites for expansion. The Saatchi brothers, Maurice and Charles, along with Martin Sorrel have transformed the global advertising business by treating advertising not simply as a service industry, but as a good investment. The Saatchis started off with a simple ambition: to become the world's largest advertising agency. In 1975 the Saatchis went public, and soon many other agencies joined them on the stock market. To raise money for new acquisitions, these companies simply issued new stock to investors. The subsequent acquisitions are explained in the following way by Preston Rabl, Sorrel's partner at WPP:

> Investors had overcome their suspicions of "people businesses" as they realized that the success of any investment is really determined by management—that is, people. There was then considerable interest in advertising and marketing stocks. In the main, these companies were not large and their management owned sizable proportions of their equity. Hence, there was too little equity to satisfy investor interest and these shares rose to levels where their prices were 20 to 30 times earnings—sometimes much higher. These companies were soon faced with the option of either making acquisitions or

disappointing shareholders, as organic growth could not be sustained at the levels these ratios demanded. (*New York Times Magazine*, July 2, 1989, 26)

As a result of the mergers, advertising is now often regarded as just another business in which the financial managers have wrested control from their creative colleagues.

During WPP's takeover of Ogilvy & Mather, David Ogilvy (a representative of the old-style industry image in which creativity was king) was openly contemptuous of Martin Sorrel, a man who had never written an ad and had no desire to do so (Sorrel started his empire through the sale of shopping carts). While the public image of agencies in the business community changed, it is doubtful that the general public was even aware of shifts taking place in this pivotal industry.

Repositioning in Global Markets

In the early 1980s, as agencies reconstituted themselves for offshore markets, Harvard Business School Professor Theodore Levitt once again emerged with a new prophecy for the marketing community. In a provocative and influential 1983 article, he announced that the age of the multinational corporation had given way to the age of the global corporation. Whereas the multinational corporation adjusts its products and marketing techniques to suit the idiosyncrasies of individual countries (at high relative cost), the global corporation treats the entire world as if it were a single entity and sells the same things in the same way everywhere (at low relative cost). Levitt attributed the move toward global branding to his argument that "the world's needs and desires have irrevocably homogenized" (under the influence of communications and travel). Citing examples from around the world of a curious mixture of traditional belief structures and western consumer goods, Levitt claimed:

> [T]he products and methods of the industrialized world play a single tune for all the world, and all the world eagerly dances to it.... Ancient differences in national tastes and preferences, in modes of doing business and the institutions of commerce, fall before the homogenizing modernity everybody experiences via the new technological facilitators. (1983, 30, 24)

In this latest incarnation, Levitt joined the strategy of market segmentation with the seemingly contradictory one of globalization by claiming that a market segment in one country is seldom unique, and that sufficiently similar groups can be found around the world due to the modernization brought about by technological progress. Aggregating these different market segments into one on a global scale would allow manufacturers to exploit economies of scale that large markets made possible (and, indeed, necessary if manufacturers were to compete successfully in the contemporary global marketplace). According to Levitt, multinational corporations had been too "thoughtlessly accommodating" to local tastes and preferences, falsely presuming that "marketing means giving the customer what he says he wants rather than trying to understand exactly what he'd like." Global corporations, on the other hand, would "never assume that the customer is a king who knows his own wishes," and instead sought to standardize their offerings everywhere. This philosophy favors large-scale monopolies.

With their eyes on the expanding global market, agencies entered a period of merger mania in the later part of the 1980s. While mergers had traditionally been a part of the industry landscape (there were two hundred acquisitions between 1977 and 1985), earlier acquisitions had neither the pace nor the scope of those post-1985. For instance, the largest acquisition of 1982 was the purchase of the William Esty agency by Ted Bates. In 1986, in a celebrated two-week frenzy of merger activity, Saatchi and Saatchi Co. PLC purchased the Bates agency for $450 million. In the ensuing period, numerous other mergers and acquisitions culminated in WPP (a London-based communications company) buying J. Walter Thompson in 1987 and Ogilvy and Mather in 1989. "The ad-agency business is in the middle of the biggest turmoil we've ever seen" (*Newsweek*, August 4, 1986, 41): This statement from advertising president Malcom MacDougall reflected the tremendous changes that shook the advertising industry in the mid-1980s. *Advertising Age* dubbed this period the "Big Bang," occasioned as it was by a wave of business activity that saw some of the biggest giants in advertising merging with, or being taken over by, industry rivals. The formation of global communication companies was underway.

Acquisitions were not simply a business strategy: they were driven by the financial situation within the industry itself. As American advertising growth rates were slowing at this time, they were expanding for the rest of the world. With the growing popularity of global marketing strategies, the creation of new consumer markets, and increasing media deregulation around the world, the United States' share of global advertising expenditures by 2000 had declined to roughly fifty percent. The agencies have to be prepared for foreign markets where there had been growth in the advertising expenditures upon which they depended; in one sense, the mergers and acquisitions were prompted by a simple need to go where the money is.

Although American multinational corporations would continue to control the lion's share of global markets, their long-held dominance within the advertising field would be challenged by agencies abroad. Saatchi and Saatchi aggressively set a new standard in global advertising. As a senior-level Saatchi executive put it: "We missed out on some big opportunities in the early 80s on some big assignments because we were just an English agency. We were determined to play the game in the big leagues and the big accounts now demand, at minimum, European capability" (personal interview, 2003). In 1983 the Saatchis took out a full two-page ad in the *New York Times* and

Today, the most thoughtful companies are adopting a new approach to international marketing.

These companies are moving through the five basic stages in the life of a multinational corporation as seen in the chart below.

And as they pass through stages 4 and 5 the need for pan-regional and world marketing is emerging at the heart of their business strategy.

> *"The globalization of markets is at hand. With that, the multinational commercial world nears its end, and so does the multinational corporation.*
>
> *The global corporation operates as if the entire world (or major regions of it) were a single entity; it sells the same things in the same way everywhere.*
>
> *Corporations geared to this new reality can decimate competitors that still live in the disabling grip of old assumptions about how the world works."*
>
> PROFESSOR THEODORE LEVITT
> HARVARD UNIVERSITY

A New Approach

After the vicissitudes of the 1950s and 1960s, more companies are now reaching the status of having acquired 'critical mass' in various regions of the world. They are now starting to turn from primary concern about 'return on acquisition investment' and 'overhead recovery' towards getting to grips with long-term franchise building across each world region.

At the same time the progressive harmonization of 'headquarters' and 'local' management culture and style, evolving from more frequent two-way movement of personnel, is enhancing the likelihood of successful adoption and execution of pan-regional business strategies.

And meanwhile in Europe, management's strategic thinking is beginning to broaden to match the dimensions of the Common Market as legislative harmonization focuses attention on pan-European issues.

International Growth Priority

Companies have passed through the bygone age when many of them treated 'Overseas Division' as the poor cousin of the organisation, struggling to compete in foreign markets with strongly established indigenous competitors.

The international divisions of many companies are now beginning to 'come of age' and receive their rightful allocation of corporate resource, if only for the practical reason that corporate earnings growth in many multinationals is today often provided by non-domestic markets.

Business System Economics

The strategic value of pan-regional branding lies in the scale economies it affords across the company's business system – to help make the company the low-cost producer.

Where the economies arise will vary by product category, and may include research and development, materials purchasing, manufacturing, distribution and advertising.

The optimum business system for a European beer, for example, is markedly different to that for chewing gum, but the principle is the same. Secure, franchise-protected volumes at the regional scale can allow a company to *build a price/cost/value structure which will eventually put it out of reach of competition.*

Consumer Convergence

In the past, the successes in world branding have been few, and have been achieved by virtue of the sheer will and far-sighted commitment of managements who stayed consistently with a long-term vision for the business. Procter & Gamble is a company in this category that comes to mind.

In the future, the only winners in cross-country branding will be companies who have seen that social developments are making redundant the old idea that differences between nations are decisive in framing marketing strategy.

The most advanced manufacturers are recognising that there are probably more social differences between Midtown Manhattan and the Bronx, two sectors of the same city, than between Midtown Manhattan and the 7th Arrondissement of Paris. This means that when a manufacturer contemplates expansion of his business, consumer similarities in demography and habits rather than geographic proximity will increasingly affect his decisions.

Demographic Convergence

Trends of vast significance to consumer marketing, such as ageing populations, falling birth rates, and increased female employment are common to large segments of the modern industrial world.

Consumer convergence in demography, habits and culture is increasingly leading manufacturers to a consumer-driven rather than a geography-driven view of their marketing territory.

Decline of the Nuclear Family

Some of the most telling developments spring from the same source – the decline of the nuclear family. Observers have attributed this to various causes – the rapid pace of technological development; higher labour productivity which reduces hours of work; and other more metaphysical notions such as the emergence of a 'liberal' philosophy, which increasingly recognizes that a woman's role can exist outside the home.

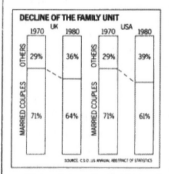

Whatever the causes, the effects in terms of household composition have been dramatic. There are now less children per household, and a declining proportion of households which conform to the two-adult-two-children pattern.

FIGURE 11.1   Saatchi & Saatchi: A Global Agency.

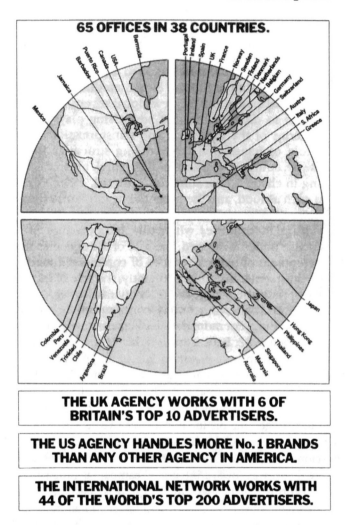

FIGURE 11.1 Continued.

the *Observer*, announcing "the opportunity for world brands" and their own preparedness for the new situation (see Figure 11.1).

Expanding Global Networks

The story of globalization that we have told so far is heavily tied to the spread of American multinationals and the dominance of American and British advertising agencies. It has left untold the fate of smaller agencies in the United

States, Europe, and Asia that were also to play an important part in the emerging global advertising system. Our story also leaves out the role played by the considerable Japanese advertising sector (lead by Dentsu), and interesting lessons being learned by companies like Toyota, Sony, and Nintendo who similarly had to introduce their brands into the American and European markets—often doing so by hiring local agencies. Nor have we discussed the growing U.S. resentment to foreign manufacturers taking over the electronics and car market (a resentment echoing the way other nations sometimes felt toward the encroachment of American designs, values, and brand symbols, not to mention the growing wealth of American elites at the expense of indigenous companies and their labor).

Robertson (1992) suspects that Japanese manufacturers moving into the U.S. market pioneered the post-Fordist business strategy of managing global production networks through flexible local production, distribution, and marketing systems. We also suspect that in working with such clients, agencies learned invaluable marketing lessons about "glocalization" as the alternative to global standardization, lessons that the car industry later used to compete with the Japanese, as evidenced in the launch of the Saturn, where GM explained its rationale for reinventing the car in a series of expensive ads placed in the TV premiere of the popular romantic comedy, *When Harry Met Sally*. Our analysis implies that agencies play an important role in the post-Fordist reorganization of global industrial production generally (Lash and Urry 1993).

Moreover, if the popular image of advertising is that of a characteristically American communication practice, the key roles carved out by WPP and Saatchi & Saatchi tinged the distinctly American voice with a British accent. Indeed, in situations where global brands were developed at the outset (rather than developed for the American market first and then marketed abroad), and where the thrust was toward integrated campaigns rather than "export" campaigns, the British agencies seemed to have a special advantage. With their relatively small home market, and with international trade so critical to their economy, British manufacturers and agencies have had to take the rest of the world more seriously than have their United States counterparts.

With its privileged role within the European market, London was also positioned to exploit the rapidly commercializing European communication channels. Shortly after the Berlin Wall fell, researchers invaded Eastern Europe, plumbing the depths of the aspirations and values of the populations in that zone. Discussions of Euro-branding strategies demanded careful digestion of research which could disaggregate audiences on the national level and reassemble them into coherent Euro-brand segments. With a consumer base of over 400 million, and ten new Eastern European countries added in 2003, the European Union was now carefully watched by marketing researchers and advertisers alike. The center of gravity seems to be shifting away from Madison

Table 11.1 The Big Seven of Media

Company	U.S. Percentage	Worldwide Percentage
Interpublic	6.9	8.5
Publicis	7.5	8.0
WPP	5.4	7.9
Omnicom	5.2	5.1
Havas	1.4	1.9
Grey	1.5	2.5
Aegis	1.6	3.2
The Big 7 (total)	29.5	37.1
All others	70.5	62.9

Source: Analysis of *Advertising Age* and Universal McCann data.

Avenue. Through the 1990s, creative talents in San Francisco, Paris, Denmark, and London provided viable alternatives to those in New York. By the turn of the twentieth century, the advertising sector was dominated by the five large communication giants serving global markets, as shown in Table 11.1.

Each communication conglomerate controlled a combination of worldwide, mid-sized, regional, and independent agencies. For example, Omnicom controlled BBDO, DDB, and TBWA/Chiat Day, all of which had offices throughout the world. Omnicom also controlled U.S. regional agencies, including Arnell Group and Goodley, Silverstein & Partners, among others. WPP profited from the reputation and global reach of J. Walter Thompson, Young and Rubicam, and HHCL/Red Cell. Publicis included Leo Burnett, which controlled 100 agencies on five continents, as well as Fallon Worldwide and Saatchi and Saatchi, with its international network of offices. The global agency Havas subsumed Arnold and Euro RSCG Worldwide. The Japanese company Dentsu was worth $2.06 billion in 2004; ranked the fifth largest communication conglomerate in the world, it was linked with Young and Rubicam's sixty-five worldwide offices in 1982. Dentsu's partnership with the U.S. agency was highly strategic, for it allowed the Japanese car advertisers to benefit from Young and Rubicam's knowledge of the American market.

Targeting the World

The worldwide youth market was quickly seen as the test case for this emerging global marketing juggernaut, because it was the first truly global segment to experience these processes of cultural convergence. Researchers portrayed them as a "global cohort" progressing through the same rebellious stages of the life cycle, pioneering in the new media environments, and confronting both the new pleasures and anxieties associated with the emerging global language of a postmodern visual culture. Most importantly, they were social-ized to become savvy consumers who could read brands as easily as people of yesteryear did books. As Stephen Kline (1995) noted, this global brand strategy was particularly attractive to children's and youth marketers in the 1980s, who found that their marketing opportunities were much augmented by emerging commercial and satellite media channels—especially in Europe and Asia. Peter Sealy, Vice President of Coca-Cola's global marketing, felt these channels favored a global brand strategy: "The time is right. The world has changed. There is a global media now like MTV and a global teenager," he declared. Myra Stark argued that this global teen cohort offered exciting opportunities for marketing: "Trends spread like wild fire through the teen community. You could look at that as a segment, but it's also a community of interest and it erases national boundaries" (Foster 2002)

The possibilities of keeping up with these global teen "communities" was linked to the expansion of youth popular culture—especially music, movies, and television shows which created touchstone references for global teens as well as a host of celebrities—from Madonna to Britney to Beckham—with whom merchants could associate their brands. Building on the global suc-cess of Star Wars and Barbie, many global youth marketers, from Levi's to Disney, saw endless possibilities in marketing to the Nintendo Generation. The strategy they used gave rise the term "McDonaldization" which George Ritzer (1993) used to characterize this mass marketing approach on a global scale. In his book by that name, Ritzer argued that McDonald's global coloni-zation followed from a strategy which privileged efficiency, calculability, pre-dictability, and control. McDonald's ensures that there is a universal quality in the products it develops for the global segments it services. In the process, McDonald's brings suppliers under its control to ensure that there is no dis-ruption in delivery and the uniformity of goods; in Russia, McDonald's helped farmers learn how to grow the type of potatoes the company was interested in buying. According to Ritzer, practices such as these created a growing stan-dardization in global work processes and homogeneity in global culture. In his view, advertising agencies were simply handmaidens to the global ambitions of American multinationals.

But youth was not the only group to attract the attention of the new globalists. The study of global lifestyle segments, particularly as they applied to metropolitan areas, attracted the interest of global marketers who found they could target elite segments within so-called "emerging" markets. Elites such as Yuppies, whether in poor African countries or rapidly industrializing Asia, tended to drive Mercedes cars, dress in Versace clothes, and wear Rolex watches. Manufacturers felt that people who lived in midtown Manhattan had less in common with their neighbors in the Bronx than they did with those who lived in the Seventh Arrondissement of Paris or the hillsides of Kowloon.

Manufacturers therefore planned their expansion in the global scene around global lifestyle niches—a disaggregated network of common lifestyle nodes whose similar demographics and habits could be addressed through global media infrastructures. McCullough (1993), for example, reports that leisure was found in 84 percent of the five hundred international print advertisements he examined, indicating the common obsession of these global elites with travel and recreation.

Although youth and urban elites would be favored targets for national campaigns, other products, from laundry soap to computers, considered reaching broader audiences in the emerging global cultural matrix. Richard Earle, senior vice-president/creative director at Saatchi and Saatchi, saw central control as the key to global colonization: "The winning systems of the 1980's will be characterized by frequent communication among management personnel in different countries, a centralized brand and advertising management system, and centralized advertising production" (*Madison Avenue*, December 1984, 44). Few believed in global control more than McDonald's who, with outposts in 120 of the 190 countries in the world, serves 42 million people a day, half outside the United States. Just as it standardized its burgers, McDonald's looked to standardize its messages. According to Doug Porter, worldwide management director of the McDonald's business at Leo Burnett, McDonald's found success with formats that revolve around "human truths" (i.e., teens will always want to be together, babies are adored in most cultures, etc.) so that "some ads can be quickly globalized.... [Both] Leo Burnett and McDonald's encourage this type of thing because it's very efficient." But he goes on to admit that not all ads run internationally because the "value message" or the "specific product" is inappropriate in some countries (Alison 2002).

Similarly, as global clients and agencies wrestled with the implications of these global brand strategies over the last twenty years, they found there were severe limitations to their assumptions about global media, cultural convergence, and universal market segmentations. Throughout the 1980s, some American brands found themselves in considerable trouble due to their lack of cultural sensitivity. In legendary Japanese examples, agencies were shamed by a series of global campaigns that used an English word for a brand which meant something quite different, often something offensive, when translated into another language. Stories of agency blunders entered popular culture, such as the characters originally chosen to represent Coca-Cola in China translating into "bite the wax tadpole," or Coors' slogan "turn it loose," being rendered in Spanish as "suffer from diarrhea." Agencies learned that although standardization seemed to be a means of saving money, it was a dangerous strategy that could result in considerable local resistance based on traditional cultural patterns, sensibilities, and ideologies—often at considerable financial loss. As Kline has argued:

With a little reflection, it is not that hard to see why Levitt's theory of market-induced convergence fails to provide an adequate account of the dynamic relationships between mass marketing and consumer behaviour. A simplistic economic model of rational consumer choice based on universal use-values proves inadequate to the task of explaining the symbolic phenomena of brand images and loyalties; nor can it predict the effects of changing lifestyles and transplanted ethnic identities within a fluid and constantly changing social environment. (1995, 109)

Globalization and Beyond

Although agencies had long encouraged corporations to see branding as the major tool for advancing into foreign markets, this was no naïve democratic impulse. With satellite TV and the Internet, it was possible to include their brands in global campaign footprints. Yet not all consumer markets would be equally attracted to (or accepting of) global marketers and advertisers. Although Africa and South America had large populations and birthrates that far exceeded those in North America, the piecemeal infrastructures and low GDP of most developing countries did not make them attractive to multinationals. Moreover, constant conflicts in the Middle East and South America dampened enthusiasm for expansion into parts of these regions, despite their relatively high GDP.

The dismantling of the former Soviet regimes and a growing warming toward capitalism throughout the world turned the attention of global marketers and advertisers toward Eastern European and emerging Asian markets. But in many cases, global brands had to fight hard against cheaper local producers who were more adaptive and responsive to local preferences, tastes, and styles, and who held different political views. During the recession of the early 1990s, global brands from the United States sought to cut costs by replacing local advertising management with U.S. management in their subsidiaries, believing that these managers would bring a more aggressive and efficient approach. The result was costly, as some North American managers showed little sensitivity to cultural conditions, permitting local brands to flourish. Business strategists argued that "physical and cultural differences between peoples of the world are far too deeply ingrained to be swept away by the appeal of low-cost products" (Douglas and Wind 1987). Given the choice between paying inflated prices for American brands and cheaper local brands that emanated a sense of cultural awareness, consumers quite reasonably chose the latter. To combat this problem, some giant international brands, like Philip Morris and Coca-Cola, simply bought up the local competition or set up factories for the production of local goods. However, their interest in their global brands began to falter.

Against the Grain

At least partially, we might understand the reorganization of global advertising practices through the 1990s as linked to changes taking place in the geopolitics of our global society. As we have seen, agencies would repeatedly run up against many ideological factors counteracting a global branding strategy. Perhaps the two most important have been environmentalism and anti-Americanism.

Emerging from the environmental crises of the 1970s, global not-for-profit and environmental organizations had joined the fight against globalization, using advertising's creative techniques against the corporations. Greenpeace regarded itself as the advertising agency for the environmental movement, perfecting below the line PR events as a strategy for global protest. *Adbusters*, a Canadian publication, popularized the art of the "subvertorial" and advocated the oppositional use of advertising for environmental and anti-consumption goals. The British publication *Sleaze* provided a similar venue in the UK. Other environmental and animal welfare groups mounted social marketing campaigns (sometimes produced pro bono by sympathetic agency personnel), using the world's screens to fight global brands that were linked with environmental devastation, such as the destruction of the Amazon rainforest. In the early 1990s *The Body Shop* enjoyed a period of great popularity and global expansion, profiting from a self-proclaimed ethical business model which focused on fair trade with developing world suppliers, minimizing and recycling of packaging, and a refusal to stock products tested on animals.

In the face of environmental accusations, multinational brands mounted responsibility ad campaigns declaring their alignment with ecological ideals in order to renegotiate their credibility in global markets. Indeed, from the oil crises of the 1970s onward, oil companies for one had worked hard to establish their environmental credentials. For example, J. Walter Thompson's global campaign for Shell's Pura gasoline is the latest in this company's many attempts to link its global brand with "oceanic themes of purity, timelessness and environmental integrity" (JWT showreel 2003). As JWT explains, it is effective to position brands around this theme because human settlement has long congregated on shorelines, and diverse cultures associate the sea with these values. The Pura gasoline commercials feature tropical fish and birds, and lush underwater environments providing images of human escape, severing the brand's connection to pollution and global warming wrought by fossil fuel use. Yet, *Adbusters* found itself unable to buy time for its "Autosaurus" campaign on an automobile information program co-produced by the Canadian Broadcasting Corporation (CBC) and Volkswagen.

Advertising was now a recognized part of global politics, and American brands such as McDonald's, Nike, and Starbucks were becoming symbols of U.S. economic imperialism. The "McLibel" court proceedings in Britain, and the campaign led by farmer Jose Bove in France, were two high-profile cases in the protests mounted against the so-called McDonaldization of the world (Smart 2003). Naomi Klein contended in her book *No Logo* that behind every glossy global branding campaign lay exploited global workers and mounting environmental devastation. Anti-globalization campaigners struck out against these brand icons and the expansion of global commercialization by rioting at GATT meetings and culture jamming—the practice of defacing or subverting branding messages. Because its brands were most visible, the United States took the brunt of this criticism by the emerging anti-globalization movement.

After the attack on September 11, 2001, commentators noted that American brands wrapped themselves in the flag, but abroad McDonald's and Coke have been running into increasing trouble on purely marketing grounds. The success of the anti-brand Mecca Cola, which claims a large market share in the Middle East and other Arab-speaking markets, serves as a reminder of the latent anti-Americanism that often lurks in global markets. European populations, too, occasionally let their anti-American sentiments flare as the twentieth century waned. One example of this is the Starbucks story: The attempts of a United States-based corporation to bring the tempo and style of Italian coffee culture to England. Although it has done well in England, Starbucks has had a hard time competing in the authentic cafe cultures of Italy and France.

Still, some U.S. brands were unscathed by the growing opposition to global branding. Heritage brands such as Quaker Oats, Dove, and Tide have been in Europe for so long that they continue to benefit from being highly culturally embedded. Other brands advanced through the blatant promotion of American values, particularly Levi's (America, birthplace of the original jeans), Harley-Davidson (American rebels), and Marlboro (the Wild West). Rather than naively embracing American values, these brands encouraged their global customers to say, "I understand it's an American company, but it fits [my] lifestyle" (Alison 2002).

Resolving the Tensions

Working on the front lines, agency personnel were among the first to recognize the various cultural factors that stood in the way of simplistic global branding strategies—from simple linguistic errors to environmental politics. As a key player in globalization and modernity, advertisers found themselves engaged in a struggle to develop language, thinking, practices, values, and images to engage with cultures different from their own. And yet globalization and modernity lay bare complex relationships between traditional cultures and nationalism. Confronted with other traditions, the expansion of advertising and foreign commodities can both threaten and strengthen ethnic nationalism, fuel hunger for authenticity, revive some forms of fundamentalist and anti-modernist religion, and give birth to neo-traditionalist family values in order to prevent old cultural traditions from being swept away in the onrush of progress (Giddens 1995).

To deal with their growing awareness of the complexity of global branding since the early twentieth century, agencies developed three different positioning strategies (with many gradations between them) through which local subsidiaries managed campaigns for the new corporate collective. First, with the universal global brand approach, the central office produces and sends a campaign to be shown in its entirety (usually with just an audio dub into the appropriate language). Second, in the "prototype" or "glocal" approach, the head office forwards a broad brief and a collection of advertising materials (films, videos, print), from which the local team can choose appropriate alternatives for the local campaign, adjusting the basic ingredients for regional tastes but not incurring the expense of multiple production. Third, the "creative work plan," or local approach, involves brand strategies developed by head office that serve only as a framework to guide local researchers and creatives in developing specific advertising executions in major markets. In general, then, there is a continuum from highly centralized to regionally articulated control over both the media buy and the creative. But there is no single hard and fast formula. Rather, a fundamental tension seems to exist in the global market between the modernizing drive to standardize advertising appeals, on one hand, and deeply embedded cultural values and practices (which often resist new consumer lifestyles), on the other. Marketing globally requires a more flexible understanding of the cultural contexts of consumer lifestyle choices.

Global campaign strategies increasingly fell victim to myriad cultural roadblocks, such as time, space, and differences in language and social relationships, as well as how power, risk, masculinity, and femininity are interpreted differently in different national contexts. In a sense all of these factors stand in the way of those seeking global domination (Hofstede 1984; De Mooij 1994). Except for the largest and most adaptive world brands, existing national, cultural, ideological, and ethnic differences often work against universal branding aspirations, except for the largest and most adaptive world brands. By the mid-1980s many advertisers no longer chose common themes and American culture as the backdrop for their appeals, but rather inflected brands with local cultural sensibilities to encourage acceptance. Studies of international advertising revealed that global campaigning was less prevalent and local appeals on the increase (Boddewyn et al. 1986; Hite and Fraser 1988; Whitelock and Chung 1989). Increasingly, a number of advertisers elected to allow more local input into advertising campaigns. In their studies of two European countries, Nelson and Kanso found that "two-thirds of the subsidiaries use the localized approach" (2002, 88). When executives were asked why, they responded that cultural differences prevented them from using a standardized advertising campaign.

Long seen as a bell wether global brand, Coke's rethinking its global positioning in the early 1990s reveals much about the changing circumstances forcing agencies to make "widespread adjustments in the practices and infrastructure of the advertising industry, as newly global agencies reposition[ed] themselves with the 'flexible' unity of global consumer culture" (Kline 1995, 109). As Sealy explained, "it's not 'one sight, one sound, one sell' anymore, which is historically the way we advertised on television. We are going to communicate diversity" (*Advertising Age*, February 22, 1993). It is clearly evident that the globalized marketing sector has begin to rethink, if not the centralization of planning, at least the media plans and execution. As De Mooij concluded in a paper for the *International Journal of Advertising*, "The idea that there are universal values that can be used for global advertising is one of the global marketing myths of past decades. Another myth of global marketing is the assumed existence of global communities such as global teenagers who, across countries, would have more in common with each other than with people of their own country" (2003, 184).

Coda

Between 1980 and 2000 world trade trebled, swelling to over one trillion dollars a day, revealing the scope of the ferment that has engulfed global brand marketing. Although "globalization" has become the preferred title for this rapid expansion in the world trade system, this term understates the continuities in the underlying patterns in global economic exchange. For all the talk of globalization, the vast bulk of trading activity is still concentrated among North America, Europe, and Asia. Of the world's five hundred largest multinationals, those based in the United States, European Union, and Japan "account for more than 80% of the world's stock of foreign direct investment and over half of world trade. These three regions controlled the all important automobile, electronics, chemical, petroleum and pharmaceutical markets" (Rugman 2003, 20, who generated the following list shown in Table 11.2).

Despite the obvious expansion of global (mostly American and Japanese) brands such as Nike, Starbucks, McDonald's, Sony, and Nintendo during this period, some recent writers caution against generalizing about the changes taking place in the advertising of these goods. It all depends on what is meant by a "global" brand. Lannon and Quelch suggest that the best way to measure whether a corporation is global is to consider how much of its revenue it derives outside of its home market. Using this measure, they goes on to note how few American multinationals can be considered global: "Coca–Cola would have perhaps 70% plus of its sales outside the US, Philip Morris's Marlboro brand has about 67%, Nescafé about 50%. Beyond the top ten brands, you start slipping very quickly below 50%—Pepsi, for instance, is only about 40%"

Table 11.2 Multinational Corporations by Country and Region

Country/Region	Multinationals in 2001
United States	197
European Union	143
Japan	88
Canada	16
South Korea	12
China	11
Switzerland	11
Australia	6
Brazil	4
Other	12
Total	500

(Lannon and Quelch 2003 20). Their point is well taken. When we look at the actual role that agencies play in global marketing, we should not over-emphasize their contribution to either global domination or disruption, but rather remember the continued role they play in regional markets too. If we focus on global trade we sometimes forget that agencies from the United States continue to dominate the American scene, while European and American agencies share the European market, and Japanese agencies dominate the Asian market.

By the early twenty-first century, for example, most of the business of Omnicom, Interpublic, Publicis, and WPP is taken up with America and Europe. The European market also makes up a significant portion of these companies' revenues, with WPP deriving the largest share of its business from Europe (39 percent). The Japanese communication giant Dentsu does 97% of its business in Asia. While other agencies clamor to get a foothold within the vastly expanding Chinese market, Dentsu is likely to profit from the inroads it has made in that area. Since the United States remains the most important market for advertising, Omnicom, Interpublic, Publicis, and WPP all have large stakes within that market. While they currently have smaller holdings, Havas and Interpublic could grow, given the inroads they have made within the expanding Latin American market. Similarly, Omnicom's attention to the Indian market is expected to pay off as that market grows. Interesting to note, multinational agencies pay little attention to the African market.

While America continued to dominate the global advertising business between 1988 and 1997 other countries witnessed phenomena growth as the chart below illustrates:

In the decade between 1988 and 1997, real adspend doubled in 24 countries— an indication of the significant advances in both economic development and

Table 11.3 Fastest Growing Advertising Marketings, 1988–1997

Rank	Country	Percentage change
1	China	1,078.0
2	Argentina	715.7
3	Indonesia	703.7
4	Peru	682.4
5	Mexico	423.3
6	Jordan	393.8
7	Saudi Arabia	368.6
8	Cyprus	280.5
9	Brazil	270.5
10	Thailand	269.0

Source: *World Advertising Trends* 1999.

media liberalisation that have occurred in many markets. China tops the list [see Table 11.3] with an increase of over one thousand per cent in this period. Argentina ranks second with an increase of 716 percent. A further three Latin American countries rank inside the top ten. The only decreases in adspend occurred in Switzerland and Finland, both of which have lagged behind in the general trend of media de-regulation. (*International Journal of Advertising*, 1999)

What these figures indicate is the great impact of deregulation and the phenomena growth of global advertising. Given these transitions, it is difficult any longer to confine discussions of advertising to the American context, since advertising now appears a very complex global bridge.

As Rugman (2003, 20) has argued, it is wrong to think that the success of global brands has resulted in some kind of "homogenized" culture.

While the success of multinationals in producing goods and services increases worldwide consumption (or materialism), there is little evidence that the end result of triad–based multinationals is a global culture. Rather, we observe an increase in standards of living, offering consumers greater choice, as multinationals respond to the growth of divergent tastes with niche products and services.

In Rugman's view it is perhaps more appropriate to talk about the role of the agencies in consolidating a triadic structure to the global market system—Europe, the Americas, and Asia functioning as coherent and unique marketing niches. That said, the experience of managing global marketing campaigns remains one of the most interesting developments in the evolving role of the agencies and one of the major reasons that they began to reorganize.

Changing Client Relationships

In the shift toward an ever greater concentration of ownership, advertising agencies were moving to change one of the central assumptions of their industry—that one company could not represent competing brands. Before the 1980s, and unlike other sectors in modern economies, the advertising industry could not rationalize its operations by having its member firms specialize in product types. This was due to a longstanding principle, agreed upon by agencies and their clients alike, that agencies would not handle the accounts of competing brands. Thus agencies could not become experts on how to market one type of product (for example, automobiles), because at any one time they could represent only one manufacturer of that product. This forced advertising agencies to be generalists, with their expertise spread across a range of product types. Some industries—for example, travel, real estate, and theater—used specialist agencies to handle competing accounts, but such agencies provided more of a "listing function," rather than selling services involving creative content or differentiation.

Interesting consequences flowed from the principle of non-specialization: "Unlike so many of the products they represent, advertising agencies cannot segment their market of clients to gain monopoly advantage. If a client is unhappy, it can pick up its business and go to another agency without losing a special expertise that only a few agencies can offer" (Shapiro 1981, 398–9). This is not to say that there was no impetus toward specialization within the advertising industry. Agencies tried, and still do try, to make themselves indispensable to advertisers by devising special services that other agencies cannot offer (for example, unique research techniques); the hefty mark-up on such services accounts for a large percentage of agencies' revenue. Agencies could also specialize by media and, most importantly, by target consumer, offering themselves as experts on advertising to children or to minorities. However, "mergermania" inevitably brought competing brands under the same roof for the first time, prompting many clients to simply transfer their accounts to other agencies. In the aftermath of the 1986 mergers more than $500 million of advertising was reassigned by clients who suddenly found themselves partners (once removed) with their major rivals. For instance, American Honda switched $58 million in business from Needham to Rubin/Poster & Associates to avoid sharing agencies with Volkswagen and other automobile manufacturers.

The lifespan of the client/agency relationship shortened. Randell Rothenberg draws attention to a survey undertaken by the American Association of Advertising Agencies indicating that in 1985 an account remained with an agency for an average of 7.2 years, with larger agencies maintaining client relationships for twice as long. After 1985, clients began to move their accounts at an alarming pace. Rothenberg cites several examples:

When Burger King took its $200 million account from J. Walter Thompson to N. W. Ayer in 1987, in what was then said to be the largest account transfer in history, the new agency celebrated its gain with champagne and Whoppers. The empty Styrofoam cases were still tumbling across landfills when, less than two years later, the fast-food company pulled its business from Ayer and divided it between D'Arcy Masius Benton & Bowles and Saatchi & Saatchi. In 1989, DMB&B won the Maxwell House coffee account from Ogilvy & Mather, only to lose the $80 million account back to Ogilvy in 1990. (1994, 20)

Indeed, the initial client reaction to the new agency mergers was very negative. Most advertisers took a wait-and-see attitude, described by one senior executive as one of "watching like hawks, for that first sign of self- rather than client-orientation by the agency" (personal interview, 1990). Carl Spielvogel, a founder of Backer and Spielvogel (acquired by Saatchi & Saatchi), identifies three types of conflicts and suggests how each will determine the reaction of a client:

There are religious conflicts, like Coke and Pepsi, General Motors and Ford. This is sacred ground, where you don't walk with your shoes on. There are banana conflicts, where you mention a competitor's name and your client goes bananas. Again, tread very carefully. And then there are ultimate-wisdom conflicts; that is, it's a conflict if your client says it's a conflict. Already there's a relaxation of the definitions by advertisers because, it seems, the only agencies that don't have conflicts don't have clients. (*New York,* June 9, 1986, 28)

For their part, the new mega-agencies were very mindful of the need to assure their large clients that their valuable marketing secrets would be safe from competitors. There are two ways in which agencies try to honor this assurance. The first saw agencies more strongly emphasize to employees the need for confidentiality. Most workers are required to sign a confidentiality statement upon joining and leaving an agency. As one creative director humorously put it, "We have an exit speech that says if you say anything there's a dead cat nailed to your door tomorrow" (personal interview, 1990). Second, they create multiple networks under the umbrella of a holding company, so that different accounts can be assigned totally different institutional networks. For example, Omnicom is made up of two freestanding networks (DDE Needham/BBDO), as is WPP (J. Walter Thompson/Ogilvy) and the older Interpublic Group (Lintas/McCann Erickson). In this way, financial coordination exists alongside advertising independence.

In these mergers a new appreciation for the value of brands began to be recognized. For the first time, the accumulated value of brands began to be marked as part of a corporation's assets. Within the crowded marketplace and expensive advertising field, it was a highly valuable asset if a company had a heritage in the marketplace and, better yet, a share of the consumer's mind. The newly constituted advertising corporations sought to leverage the heritage and good will surrounding brands through a practice known as brand extension—attaching the brand to new product lines. Corporate raiders understood brand extension as an important way of creating more profits for a company. By the 1980s some heritage brands (Kellog, Harley Davidson, Heinz) became strong reference points within the mind of consumers. Seeking to take advantage of the value they had accumulated in consumers' minds, the logo of heritage brands began to be extended to other products. Although this practise was not new, it did increase considerably: "In the 1970s, two-thirds of all successful brands introduced were line extensions" (Shergill, 1993). And in the words of another observer, "Since 1987 nearly 70 per cent of *all* new brands introduced have been line extensions or flanker brands" (Morgenson 1991).

The value embedded into heritage brands was recognized as a resource that could be linked to new products without having to invest in costly advertising expenditures, because the brands were held in esteem with consumers already. Disney offers a good example of this interest in brands. In the early 1980s, Disney was losing profits and facing threats by corporate raiders whose principle interest was to break the divisions of the company apart and profit from the heritage of the brand by extending it to many other products (the company was "rescued" in 1984 and kept together).

Corporate mergers also brought many more brands under one company roof. From 1947 to 1984 Procter and Gamble sold a single laundry detergent, Tide. By 1989 the company had four additional varieties. Since 1984 the company has added three additional fabric softeners to its Downy brand. The number of cereal brands rose to 150 in 1989 from 84 a decade earlier. Supermarkets carried 30,000 different packages in 1999, up from 17,500 in 1989, a significant expansion in just one decade (Food Marketing Institute 1999). While there was more and more concentration of ownership at the corporate level, the amount of choice offered to the consumer expanded greatly in these decades. In the post-merger world, corporations that had once dedicated themselves to the production of one type of product found themselves producing a wide variety of products, as running shoe manufacturers began to sell clothes, fashion designers sold bed sheets, and motorcycle makers sold lighters, boots, and luggage.

New Ways of Paying

An interesting consequence of the agency takeovers and mergers was that clients came to look upon the industry in a new way. As the prices that agencies fetched reached astronomical levels, and as some individuals made huge amounts of money (up to $100 million) on the sales, clients began to suspect that perhaps they were paying too much for agencies' services. This suspicion convinced clients to start applying different criteria for working out adequate compensation. Client migration into below the line techniques also contributed to this change, as promotional tactics had never before been sold on commission. It was during this period that the commission system, which has its origins in the space-brokering era of the late nineteenth century, passed.

In the late 1970s almost 70 percent of advertisers based their payments to agencies on a commission of media billings. By 1989, the 15 percent commission no longer dominated financial relations between the agencies and clients. It is generally agreed that only about 30 percent of transactions are now based upon some sort of commission. Most compensation systems are now negotiated on a client-by-client basis, with very few of them yielding as much as 15 percent. The traditional commission system was, in effect, nothing more than a cash flow situation. The agency would pay the media at 85 percent of the amount billed, and would then bill the client at 100 percent. By the end of the twentieth century, this practice was being negotiated—to a reduced commission, a system of guaranteed profits, or a system of cost plus profit. According to a senior worldwide account executive: "You really only have two kinds of systems—one generated on what it costs to make the advertising, the other on volume of placements. Then it's simply a matter of mechanics in terms of how much the client wants to pay for the services delivered" (personal interview, 2003).

Fees for creative work were now paid separately. Typically, before work is undertaken a budget for the project is drafted, rates are then set and paid at the end. Clients find this system agreeable because it provides transparency and control over advertising budgets. These changes had important consequences for the internal relations of the full service agencies themselves. One of the factors which had held creative and media departments together was the 15 percent commission structure. With its demise, each of these departments could bid for individual business; and as we shall see, they did. In London, the Institute of Advertising Practitioners acted as gatekeepers, restricting the entitlement to charge the 15 percent commission to only those agencies of a particular size and standing. This practice helped to keep the number of agencies small and commissions high. The Office of Fair Trading disbanded the screening of agencies by the IPA in the 1970s, arguing that this practice was monopolist. This change resulted in a wave of new agencies rapidly entering the market. The demise of the commission system might thus be seen as increasing competition, driving down rates, and increasing the level of negotiation between clients and agencies.

The climate created by clients' increased scrutiny of their advertising expenditures, and the fact that creative work was now a separate line item, changed the perception of the advertising agency. By the late 1990s other methods of payment arose that tied creative work and media buying to results. Under this model, media specialists or agencies were given a share of the profit resulting from the campaign or media buy. Media specialists were at the forefront, pioneering this payment method. For example, compensation for Bcom3 for the GM account was based upon the fee system which was based on the number of people who worked on and the time spent on the account, as well as unspecified profit margins. Proctor & Gamble also radically changed its payment by switching agency compensation to a straight percentage of sales (*Advertising Age*, September 15, 2000).

Deconstructing the Full Service Agency

We have just provided an account of the formation of larger scale agencies seeking to meet the demands of corporate expansion in a global market, outlining how this resulted in major restructuring of the practices of global advertising. But we need to remember that global accounts are not the only game in town. A second category of agencies, which do not have the capability to operate internationally but deal largely with national accounts, continue to prosper in the spaces left behind. Neil Blackley, a British analyst, neatly summarized the dilemma facing this sector of the market: "Because the ad agency is the meat in the sandwich between giant consumer products companies and giant media companies. You either develop a niche position in the marketplace, as a creative boutique or whatever, or you develop internationally to handle conglomerating clients" (1989, 38).

Blackley's remarks refer to the trend among some agency personnel to work in the cracks of left by the global behemoths during this time period. The new boutiques claimed that large agencies were crippled by risk aversion and conservatism that prevented them from taking the creative leaps necessary to break through the cluttered advertising marketplace. Many discontented (or fired) staff created start-up agencies, pitching themselves to clients as antidotes to the big bureaucratic agencies, with greater creativity and a freedom from kowtowing to shareholders. London had proved to be a particularly fertile ground for start-ups since the 1960s. Some examples of successful London firms included:

> the first wave (of the 1960s and early 1970s), like Collett Dickenson Pearce, Saatchi & Saachi and Boase Massimi Pollitt; the second wave (1980 to 1982), which included Abbott Mead Vickers, Lowe Howard-Spink, Gold Greenlees Trott and Wight Collins Rutherford Scott; and the third wave from around 1988 onwards, featuring Howell Henry Chaldecott Lury, Simons Palmer Denton Clemmow & Johnson and Duckworth Finn Grubb Waters. (*Creativity*, 1 May 2002)

There were several factors contributing to the formation of these new agencies. New technology, such as cell phones, personal computers, and digital transmission to virtual offices, had socialized many agency staff to consider themselves to be part of a moving carnival show. Other factors supporting the formation of creative shops included business-savvy creatives who could both handle accounts and create them, the end of the 15 percent commission, and the separation of media buying, planning, and creativity. According to David Verklin, CEO of Carat North America, New York, the split in agency functions created more space for new niche players, rather than less:

> Media and creative are now so highly evolved outside of each other that these are functions that don't necessarily have to intersect on a minute level. I submit that a greater emphasis is placed on communications between groups, not less, and the continued separation of functions creates opportunities for small, creatively—minded agencies. (Linnett 2000, 4)

Boutique agencies sold themselves not only on their ability to provide cutting edge creative work, but also provide clients with a more personal service. Creative personnel flowed between agencies at increasing rates, as creatives came to consider themselves less like "company men" (they were still predominantly men) and more like fluid, outsourced labor. However, these agency defenders of the "little guy" would often find themselves in a considerable contradiction if they achieved success: Either they would expand globally and become as large as the agencies they once mocked, or they would be bought up by one of the major communication conglomerates.

Two other important factors contributed to the formation of these new agencies. Accounts in London were smaller than those in the United States, where there was a need for agencies of greater scale to handle the size of the accounts. Finally, London creatives were much more likely to reach a wage ceiling faster than their counterparts in America. Ambitious creatives in London had two choices once their careers were established: They could move to the United States or open their own agency. If a start-up was successful, it was fairly certain that it would expand or be bought up by one of the major agency networks, as just mentioned, and this of course placed many start-up agencies in an ironic position. Having secured their clients by arguing that they would edgier, more creative, and more personable than the Goliath agencies, when they were swallowed by the large agencies they had to develop a new storyline to win clients. In fact, little evidence supported the contention that large scale companies were any less creative then niche upstarts; however, creative shops definitely played upon this common assumption to secure their place in the industry.

According to Chris Powell, chairman of BMP DDB, "All you need to start an ad agency is a brass plaque and a phone. Any two fools can do it. And, quite often they do" (*Creativity*, May 1, 2002, 17). The brass plaque he mentioned refers to industry awards. Agency success in the fifth phase, as in the first, continued to require the approval of the cultural establishment. By the early twentieth century, creatives sought to include two types of work in their portfolio, standard advertising campaigns and the awards they had won.

Diversification: Moving Sideways

Earlier we explored how the merger of large agencies in the 1980s could be seen as a strategy to secure profit in a period when manufacturers were shifting their budgets toward global branding. At the same time, smaller innovative specialists were creating a more variegated advertising system. More than a passing fancy, these changes had far reaching impacts on advertising practices, established by the "micro-marketing" paradigm of niche and boutique players creating new services at the fringes of the advertising sector. Sushil Shergill (1993) tracked these changes in the early 1990s, finding that corporations were investing increased sums in below the line promotion (telemarketing, trade promotion, direct-mail, consumer promotions, in store media, sponsorships, public relations)—much of it handled outside the majors. The drift to promotion gained force in the 1980s so that below the line expenditures exceeded media advertising expenditures by 1991 (see Table 11.4).

There were a number of reasons for the popularity of promotion. New computer and scanner technology allowed for better tracking of goods and consumers. Database techniques allowed businesses to more exactly pinpoint or "micro-market," figuring out why given products were not selling and developing more precise tactics for changing the marketing mix to encourage

Table 11.4 Above and Below the Line Promotional Expenditure in the United States, 1991

Above the Line Media Advertising Expenditures $ billion		Below the Line Other Promotional Expenditures[3] $ billion	
Newspapers	30.41	Telemarketing	60.00
Television	27.40	Trade promotions	36.00
Radio	8.48	Direct mail	24.46
Magazines	6.52	Consumer promotions	18.00
Farm/business papers	3.10	POP and in-store media	15.55
Outdoor	1.08	Event sponsorships	2.80
Miscellaneous[2]	24.96	Public relations	N/A
Total	101.95	Total	156.81

Notes. Includes Yellow Pages, weeklies, shoppers, pennysavers, bus, and cinema advertising. Sources include *Advertising Age*, May 4, 1992, 51; reports in *Advertising Age*, *Ad Week*, *Direct Marketing*, and Donnelly Marketing and Nielsen Marketing Research survey data.

purchase. This technology also proved useful in targeting, and finding out more information about particular groups, particularly ethnic groups. The use of electronic coupons gathered key intelligence, helping brands isolate those consumers who could be encouraged by higher value coupons to switch brands. Retailers seeking maximum turn over of goods gave preferential treatment to goods with coupons, leading brand names to increase their promotional budgets. As Shergill (1993) noted, "For every dollar spent on mass media advertising, packaged goods marketers in the US are also spending a dollar on consumer promotions and two dollars on trade promotions. Consumer and trade promotions are now estimated to account for more than seven out of every ten dollars spent by such marketers."

In the 1980s, manufacturers also began to stress near-term business over long-term goals. The new emphasis took place in conjunction with mergers and takeovers of major manufacturers in "leveraged" situations (i.e., takeovers financed by borrowed money that the borrower had to start paying back immediately). In such a climate, immediate sales and profits were much more important than building long-term brand loyalty, and the best way to achieve instant results was through promotions—getting the product on prime supermarket shelves and offering customers incentives (such as coupons, premiums, sweepstakes, games, or bonus packs) to try the product. In store media, consumer promotion and fancier packaging was justified upon the industry belief that up to two-thirds of all purchase decisions were made at the point of purchase.

Below the line marketers argued that, through relationship and micro marketing, they could better target the smaller segments that the mass media could not reach, but which clients considered very important. According to Peter Hurd, the strategic director of GGT group, clients increasingly expected agencies to forget about the older dividing lines between above and below the line, concentrating instead on marketing campaigns that went "through the line" (Rothenberg 2002, 22).

The larger communication businesses we outlined above positioned themselves as one-stop communications companies who acquired increasing amounts of profit from activities outside of traditional advertising. For example, although advertising accounted for only 55 percent of WWP's revenue, other activities, including direct marketing, grew more quickly, making up 23 percent of the company's total revenue. Growth in research and consultancy also grew by 11 percent, accounting for 16 percent of WPP total revenue. Public relations also proved a growing area (8.5 percent total revenue) (*Advertising Age*, 2003). In 2003, Interpublic made 12 percent of its revenue from non-advertising related activity, and Omnicom acquired more than a quarter of its profits from non advertising (*Advertising Age*, 2003). This union of above and below the line technique was a little-noted change within the advertising industry during its fifth phase. Eventually, the distinction between above and below the line was no longer invoked within industry rhetoric; it had ceased to have meaning, as 'integrated communication' became the new buzz word around which debates were rallied.

Media Departments Are Reworked

Of the many changes that occurred within agencies during the fifth phase, the separation of the creative from the media department, the empowerment of media departments was one of the most profound. In this section we look at the transformation of agency media departments and the central role they played in the dynamics of the mediated marketplace.

For fifty years, the straightforward functions of the media department were buying space and time from media, and ensuring that the advertising was shown at the correct time and with the correct frequency. The mass marketing paradigm consisted primarily of the purchase of bulk national audiences, assembled by terrestrial television (ABC, NBC, and CBS in the United States; and ITV in Britain) and the press. Audiences displayed fairly stable viewing and readership patterns, and a system of fixed rate cards measured and costed audiences, making media negotiations infrequent and relatively straight forward. Informal agreements between media and clients limited clutter on television.

Although media buyers were the agency's pioneers, through the twentieth century the creative department became its heart and soul. Little agency revenue was invested in media departments. According to Michael Drexler, CEO of Optimedia: "The big bucks went first to the creative department and then to account management" (Drexler 2002, 22). The awards went to the creative department, not the media. Some of the individuals who worked in these media departments came to feel that their contribution was under-acknowledged:

> As media people we were considered a pretty low life form by the majority of managements; very few media men (and it was primarily men then) aside from the media director ever made it on the agency board of directors; we were underpaid and under-regarded, and no-one outside the department had anything but the sketchiest idea of just what we did. (Jacobs 1995 cited in Banks 1997)

However, these relations began to change in the early 1960s, when a few American media entrepreneurs encouraged manufacturers to provide prizes such as fridges, cars, fur coats to quiz shows in exchange for free publicity. Game show producers traded free air time for the prizes. The entrepreneurs exchanged the free time for something else, or sold it back to advertisers, making tidy profit margins along the way (Ingram 1989). Some of the individuals involved became overzealous in their bartering practices, broke regulatory laws, and ended up in jail.

Full service agencies were pleased by this turn of events, as they did not like anyone breaking the monopoly their media departments enjoyed over space brokering. Frank Muratore, president and CEO of TSB New York, points out that the early media independents were unwelcome: "We were the bad boys of the business. Advertising agencies were screaming that media buying and planning should be under one roof...theirs" (Banks 1997). Account executives in the United States pointed to jailed media independents, and told their clients that such independents could not be trusted, and that clients' accounts were safer in the hands of agencies (Ingram 1989). Although the United States was the site of some of the first and oldest media independents, Time Buying Services (now RDR Associates' TBS Media Management) opened its doors in 1960, the power of the full service agency in the United States ensured that media department remained part of their structure until the 1980s.

The situation was different in Europe. In the late 1960s American corporations sought to consolidate their stake in the European markets, and they needed people familiar with European media channels to plan and purchase air time. This substantial line of media revenue aided the detachment of creative work, a media buyer explains:

> And in this country [Britain] that is how it stayed for 100 years, with media thinking interwoven with the creative process and vice versa. But then some clients started arriving on the scene who did not need creative work, as this was produced elsewhere (often in the US) and wanted someone merely to buy the time or space. (Banks 1997)

In the 1960s Carat formed, a French media independent fed by American funds; it was to become one of the most successful media planning and buying organizations in the world. Through the 1970s several British media independents emerged: For example, Paul Green set up Media Buying Services and sold space for the heavily advertised compilation record label K-Tel. An amalgam of individuals from six media departments left their agencies in 1972 to set up The Media Department. Chris Ingram left media departments at Greys, KMP and Dorlands to launch the first specialist media planning and buying operation, TMD, in 1976 (later Chris Ingram and Associates, CIA). Other media directors left agencies to strike out on their own, including Alan Rich and Don Beckett in 1975, and John Ayling in 1978. By the 1980s, media independents had colonized 10 percent of the total media business (Byles 1992). These European media independents built an important bridge between American advertisers and European markets.

The separation of creative and media departments spread to the United States in the early 1980s. A variety of reasons contributed to the split, one of which was the crisis detected in which clients discovered that agencies were paying too much for inadequate media space or time, and failing to monitor the media adequately to make sure the ads were shown. Herbert Zeltner

(1984) has suggested that agencies, under pressure to find ways to stretch the media dollar, jumped on what appeared to be bargain rates—only to later discover that the time or space they had purchased was inappropriate or ineffective. The deregulation of the communications industry reduced pressures on broadcasters to maintain and provide logs of the ads they broadcast, a problem exacerbated by the agencies' practice of delegating the monitoring function to low-level and low-skilled personnel. As a result, many major advertisers began to supervise their media activities in-house, rather than leaving this entirely to their agency (Zeltner 1984).

Another factor contributing the separation of media departments was bulk media buying. The mega-agencies, by combining their media buying into a consolidated package, gained what is referred to as "media clout." In most countries, purchasing one hour of television time was cheaper than one minute. The pooling of media budgets created large sums of money and offered an effective means of lowering prices from media suppliers, because bulk buys secured funding for media operations, saving administrative fees and the staff costs associated with negotiating many smaller media deals. As one media director put it, "You need to get the critical mass for when you are negotiating with the new media giants. You need a certain amount of volume to get their attention, otherwise you won't get as good a deal" (personal interview, 2003).

Bulk media buying required more sophisticated negotiating skills. Clients expected more, and specialized media companies emerged as the preferred method of media buying time (Green 1992). Agencies began to "unbundle" their media departments as separate specialty businesses. For example, Omnicom and the Ogilvy Group created and shared joint ownership of a third independent group that bought to the specifications of both companies. Saatchi formed Zenith; McCann Erickson, Universal; FBC/Publicis, Optimedia; and Lintas, Imitative. And the media specialist function drew the spotlight in 1995, when Bates and Saatchi & Saatchi unbundled their media buying and planning to create what is now Saatchi's Zenith Media Worldwide, New York.

Cost sensitive companies seeking to minimize waste in their media planning and buying saw the big holding companies (such as Interpublic Group, WPP Group or Omnicom) as better able to create the economies of scale and smart buys. Major corporations in the United States began to seed their funds into specialized media planning and buying companies. In 1997, Procter & Gamble made history in awarding New York-based Televest $1.2 billion to oversee the planning and buying of television for all of its brands. Proctor & Gamble also centralized about $180 million in print media planning and buying with Bcom3. This was a very radical change: "Prior to this, P&G had nine brand agencies managing media planning for each brand, using an agency of record for print buying only" (Lloyd 1995, 95). By 2000, media specialists had become the norm for many of the top 100 advertisers. In 2001 General Motors awarded its $2.9 billion media planning account to media specialist Bcom3, of the Starcom MediaVest Group; Unilever, overseeing global brands including Dove, Lipton, Pond's and Wisk, awarded its $700 million U.S. media planning and broadcast TV buying account to WPP Group's MindShare; and Kraft Foods consolidated its $800 million North American media planning and buying account at Starcom MediaVest Group (Freeman 2001). Novartis (the marketer of the Gerber baby line), the pharmaceutical giant Pfizer, and Hewlett Packard also joined the growing list of companies investing in media specialists (Goetzl 2002; Goetzl and Linnett 2001; Elkin et al. 2002). Some saw this as a shift to a new style in agency hiring away from individual agencies toward large media conglomerates and holding companies (*Advertising Age*, January 22. 2001).

According to *Advertising Age*, by 1994 the top twenty agencies were linked to or owned a media specialist in one part of the world, often in Europe (see Exhibit 1). The ten largest have unbundled media departments (such as WPP Group's J. Walter Thompson, Ogilvy & Mather and Young & Rubicam; Bcom3 Group's Leo Burnett; the Interpublic Group of companies; McCann-Erickson; and Omnicom Group's BBDO). By the early twenty-first century, technically, the full service agency no longer existed.

Because media is more lucrative than advertising, the billing of the top media independents exceeds those of the top agencies: "Zenith Media....an offshoot of Saatchi & Saatchi...had billings in 2000 of £660 million. The top advertising agency in 2000, Abbott Mead Vickers BBDO, could only manage billings of £410 million" (Jacob 1995). In just 30 years, a "Big 7" of media–buying conglomerates has emerged (see Table 11.2): Interpublic, Publicis, WPP, Omnicom, Havas, Grey Global, and Aegis Group's Carat. These media companies have increased their presence in the U.S. media market, undertaking 29.5 percent of the media purchases; worldwide, these media specialists had increased their control of media purchase from roughly 34 percent in 1990 to 37 percent in 2000 (Mandese 2002).

While the chart above illustrates that the Big 7 control a significant component of the worldwide media purchase, media buying also remained in the local hands of mid–size agencies, or advertisers themselves. Another noteworthy point is how Europe had come to dominate the field of media specialists. Carat, in particular, exerts considerable influence over U.S. media planner and buyer practices (Linnett 2000; Tunstall and Machin 1999). These changes in the full service agency structure speak to the growing expansion of the commercial media bridge that permitted greater flow of goods, media, and advertising between Europe, America, and Asia. The formation of the media buying operations were twinned with the expansion of global media was saw in the last chapter. The separation of media buying from agencies contributed to "big deal making, involving multimillion dollar investment" in which "clients purchase media space across the entire inventory of a media company and are assured a special cost-per-thousand" (Linnett 2000). Sean Cunningham, executive vice president and media director for Universal McCann, New York, celebrated the changes in agency structure, seeing them as a growing recognition of the importance of media within marketing cycles: "I think the word 'unbundling' does little justice to the changes in the media landscape. This is all about recognizing media as being a fundamental component in the sales and marketing process" (Drexler 2002, 22). The globalized and mediated marketplace had arrived.

New Interest in Mixed Media

Top 100 advertisers began to endorse advertising outside of the thirty-second television spot. Industry heavyweights such as Bob Wehling of Proctor & Gamble told colleagues at the American Association of Advertising to focus not simply on "effect" but on "surrounding the consumer by blending the various media into a harmonious mix" (Lloyd 1997, 93). The ever-controversial Martin Sorrell, chief executive of WPP, argued that for forty years in the UK and in the United States agency profits and reputations had centered on "30 second spots for network TV." He warned that advertisers must change or be made redundant by the "irreversible changes taking place in the world of communications, none of which favored network TV." Sorrel noted that the future lay in "a much wider understanding of the meaning and nature of creativity than we commonly hold today" (Lloyd 1997, 94).

According to Steve Sternberg, senior partner at BJK&E Media, New York, one of the reasons for this changed approach to media was simply the "tremendous number of choices that exist [today] compared to 10 to 15 years ago" (Ross 1997, 1). Advertisers were also convinced that some of the audience segments they wanted to reach the most (the young and the rich) were becoming more difficult to get at through television. They were also impressed by studies suggesting that people moved cross media and that by coupling two different types of media, greater exposure at lower cost could be achieved. Others argued that the fragmentation of the media environment had encouraged new thinking about how to best to reach audiences. Bob Giacomino, senior vp-media manager for Grey Advertising, New York noted that clients thought about media in a new way:

> Clients are regarding media in a different way-that it's not just plugging [gross rating points] into a computer or finding the lowest [cost-per-thousand viewers or readers]. There is a lot more emphasis placed now on how to use media in different and smarter ways that media contribute greatly to the success of a campaign, that it's not just creative that sells products. (Freeman 1997, 18)

Even in Japan, the tide had shifted away from mass media, as A. Benington of Deutsch's media department noted, "It's not about tonnage anymore; it's about what is effective"(Linnett 2000, 3). The decision to use mixed media was also made easier due to media consolidation. Traditional concerns were that spreading media budgets too thinly across media diminished buying clout. This was no longer a worry for media conglomerates that now happily customized media packages across their many holdings, often willing to add value with favorable editorial mentions as well (Rothenberg 1991; Sandler and Secunda 1993).

Advertisers began to shift their budgets beyond the 30 second spot. Mark Kerray, vp of the electronic giant Philips, noted that one of the key reasons for awarding Carat its $600 million media buying and planning account in June of 2001 was an interest in communicating outside of the thirty-second TV spot: "We want to turn the process on its head....We are looking for a more fully integrated communications plan that leads to sales" (Elkin and Linnett 2001, 4). The auto parts giant Unilever also rethought its use of the 30 second television commercial and began to "look at the entire media marketing investment earlier in the process" (Neff 2000, 2). Other blue chip companies such as Kraft and Chrysler followed the trend, moving away from television advertising (Linnett and Thompson 1999; Friedman et al. 2001). In 2000 Wehling noted that there had been a considerable shift from planning centered around television with left over budget used on other media, toward starting "with consideration of a full range of media and communication approaches, from direct mail and event sponsorship to conventional TV advertising" (Neff 2000, 3). By the end of the twentieth century, an *Advertising Age* survey (Fine 2000) showed that 55.5 percent of ad buyers and 70.7 percent of sellers said that they bought or sold cross-media ad packages; another 50.3 percent of remaining buyers and 47.5 percent of remaining sellers said that they would do so within the next year.

Media planners and buyers would orchestrate these more complex media strategies. A spokesperson from BBDO summarized the wide range of decisions for which contemporary media planners were now responsible:

> Broadly speaking....strategic media planning covers decisions such as which media to use, what creative format to employ (e.g. space size or time length), how the campaign should be distributed (e.g. in a concentrated burst or a more even 'drip' over a longer period of time), and a number of other decisions such as positioning requirements, seasonality and editorial considerations. Other considerations within the strategic plan include target audience definition; competitive strategies; the likely effect on advertising recall (and ultimately sales) of different media mix strategies; the relationship of the media plan to both distribution and sales patterns; and an understanding of the media consumption habits of the chosen target audience. (Linnett 2000, 4)

To undertake media mix programs, planners had to understand the differences the various media offered in terms of creative scope, audience reaction, cost, and the unique seasonal strengths of each media. Planners were encouraged to exploit the "intrinsic value of an additional medium...to extend the creative effectiveness of a campaign; and to produce synergies" (Belch and Belch 1998, 163). Canadian creative executive Marty Myers explained how the industry had come to understand the different powers of each medium:

> Different media work differently. Print is linear and it's a left-brain medium—it's linear, logical, rational, it goes a-b-c-d. Everything follows in sequence. If you have a long story to tell, if you have a success story, if you have facts, if you have news, the place to go, at least initially, if you need space to work in, is print. If you have a story that isn't a story, if you have to deal in clouds like perfumes and stuff (though that will work in magazines too with visuals only), if you have an emotional story to tell, your best bet is probably the right-brain medium which is clearly television. It works a different way entirely. You don't have time to make a rational argument—you use a metaphor, something out of the other art forms. You do something out of music, out of film, out of drama—the really good creative people know a little bit about marketing and a lot about the arts. (personal interview, 2003)

Beyond the Thirty-Second Television Format

As our bridge model reminds us, however, media planners and buyers did not simply navigate the commercial media; they actively knitted a new media landscape and set of relations. Planners moved beyond the thirty-second commercials in several different ways. The lifting of the FCC ban on infomercials that occurred in 1984 in the United States led planners to rush into this format. By the 1990s, 85 percent of local American television stations accepted infomercials, generating $250 million in revenue (Jaffe 1990). Promotional links were made through the many new shopping channels that emerged on cable television. Planners also increasingly sought to link one medium to another, particularly the Internet or 888 phone lines that lead consumers to brochures, additional information, or actual product purchases.

Product placement expanded exponentially through the 1990s. Tim Hanlon, director of emerging contacts for Stardom IP Worldwide, noted that resistant audiences made product placement and sponsorship more important than conventional advertising:

> The issue of commercial zapping also needs to be figured out. We need to reintegrate the message, and I think you'll see more in-programming experiences. It's almost the '50s all over again with sponsored shows, star performer/spokespersons [like Arthur Godfrey], product placement and more signage scenarios. (Tiegel 2000, 6)

The trend toward product placement was confirmed in a study of 24 hours of major network television which counted 818 free mentions of advertised products (Hume 1990). Popular music also became an important vehicle for promotional content. Music acts were courted by public relations people, and given gifts to wear or use in the hope that the brand might get "name-dropped" in their songs, seen on stage, or in the media coverage of these stars. Newspapers and magazines, which endured a significant loss in their revenues after the early 1990s recession, had reduced staff. To fill pages, harried staff began to accept the Internet search engine Google as a valid news source and public relations department releases as first drafts. This was particularly true for the new sectionalized segments of the paper (travel, money and jobs, and lifestyle). By the end of the twentieth century, it was estimated that up to 70 percent of news stories were generated by corporate public relations. "Advertorials" and advertising supplements also became common features (*Observer*, 2003).

The desire to link brands directly to popular celebrities and programming, combined with the audience's adept use of technology to avoid advertising, has increased interest in product placement and the sponsorship of movies and television programs. The product placement arena has become professionalized, with companies being developed which have the sole objective of negotiating relationships between program producers and advertisers. These relationships can take different forms. First, instead of or in addition to, having advertisements inserted between programs, in many cases brands are now sponsoring programs—a return to an older practice dating back to the 1950s and 1960s. Second, there is traditional product placement, in which brands are inserted directly into television or movie storylines (*Friends, Minority Report, Cast Away, The Apprentice*). Third, there is the production of branded entertainment, where the program is developed with the intent of providing a framework to showcase brands. To facilitate the relationship between advertisers and program producers, new kinds of audience research measures have been developed and enacted, yet another sign of the growing professionalization of this type of promotion (Nussenbaum 2004).

Media planner Jarrod Moses, president and CEO of New York-based Alliance and partner to Grey Global Group, has argued that advertising's future lies in Hollywood. Alliance specializes in product placement and promotion deals with film studios and talent agencies. "We work directly with studios developing scripts and other properties, looking for cross-marketing opportunities. Sometimes I even write scripts myself in order to work with a brand equity" (Linnett 2000, 4). Other nascent branding techniques came to include long-form video, episodic vignettes and video-on-demand. Some examples included "advertainment" showcases; for example, BMW Films commissioned well-known film directors (such as Ang Lee, Tony Scott, Guy

Richie, and Alejandro Gonxalez Inarritu) to create short films starring a BMW car (Elkin 2002). These shorts were downloadable on the Internet. The ten-minute format allowed a level of drama and intrigue difficult to replicate in a thirty-second ad. It also enabled the car to be shown travelling and handling at high speeds not permitted by advertising regulation.

Cross Media

Media planners also worked below and through the line to develop new promotional means for advertisers, negotiating event marketing or tie-ins, in which a brand name was linked to a high-profile event (for example, in sports or film) or to another significant brand name (such as a Coke promotion at Little Caesar's restaurants). To maximize promotional benefits and minimize media costs, corporations decided it was better to unite than compete. For example, in 1997 McDonald's and Disney signed a 10-year cross promotion plan to maximize their global synergy by sharing advertising and employee training techniques. The sale of McDonald's French fries rose a significant 7.5 percent when "they were cross-promoted in movie theatres and restaurants with Disney's holiday film *Flubber*, the company said" (Kramer 1998, 24).

The problem of "getting under the radar" of young audiences who seek to avoid advertising messages simulated several new creative techniques. Buzz marketing began in the early 1990s as a technique to reach the elusive youth audience. Unconventional creative executions were placed in non-prime advertising media ("wild" posters, mysterious billboards, and late-night television ads), in a move illustrating planners' skills at finding the "underground" media. With their new research in culture, promoters also realized that young people congregated around political causes, leading to the practice of linking promotion to anti-promotion campaigns. In protest against the co-opting of public space by advertisers, "culture-jammers" defaced advertisements with stickers offering alternate messages. Advertisers followed suit with "wildcat advertising," in which one brand subsidized another's billboard costs by paying for the right to place a sticker of its brand over the original billboard ad toward the end of its display period. This (possibly naïve) technique was thought to give advertisers street credibility because it appeared to be the work of respected culture-jammers.

More elaborate happenings, created events, and hoaxes continued through the 1990s to create a buzz or word of mouth reaction—a virus incident that would be spread among youth culture circles. For example, guerrilla marketers entered Internet gaming sites and chat rooms covertly to shock users. Starcom launched Nintendo's *Perfect Dark* by creating a hoax recruitment advertisement on a job Web site frequented by the male target audience, asking for "aggressive, intelligent young workers" to join Datadyne, a fictional company featured in *Perfect Dark*. The authenticity of the advertisement caused a stir in chat rooms. Amy Sabo, Starcom assistant media director, noted, "We planted the idea that this might be a real corporation, and then watched it unfold. That's getting more involvement than a 30-second spot. It's not on the street, but it was in the place where these guys hang out: online" (*Agency Magazine*, 2001).

Fallon McElligott created an online game staring Buddy Lee, a Kewpie doll, publicized through an online low-tech looking video clip which looked like gamers themselves had created it. Players advanced in the game by retrieving special codes found on the tags of the jeans in stores, using play to link consumer and commodity. Ron White, president of Fallon Minneapolis, noted that in order for a brand to find success with young audiences, "they have to discover it.... The element of discovery is crucial.... Push marketing is less complicated, but isn't as effective with this group" (*Agency Magazine*, 2001).

These unconventional techniques had an added bonus—they were cheaper than conventional media spends. According to Alex Bogusky, creative director and partner at Crispin Porter & Bogusky Advertising:

> If you have $120 million, you can use traditional media and it's really effective. But if you have $2 million, or even $6 million, you can disappear. The popularity of guerrilla is in part coming out of the fact that traditional media is becoming more and more difficult, especially if you are on a limited budget. A good guerrilla marketing campaign has the ability to become viral and spin out of control in a good way.... you get many more impressions than you paid for. (*Agency Magazine*, 2001)

Media planners sought to turn new media, including wireless phones, video and computer game environments, and both personal and interactive television, into promotional vehicles. The online version of Electronic Arts, The Sims, not only allowed players to simulate a society and characters, but permitted Intel Corp. and McDonald's to place products in the gaming environment. Players' advancement in the game was aided by interacting with the brands. Wild Tangent, a software design company in Seattle, is one of the leaders in the commercialization of gaming space, working with Sony Electronics, Nike, AOL-Time Warner's WB network, Toyota Motor Corp., and Verizon Online (Elkin 2002). Personal television provided audiences with the ultimate tool for avoiding advertisements, but through the eye of media planners it was turned into a wondrous new promotional tool. David Verklin, CEO of New York-based Carat North America, argued that shift TV programming (e.g., OpenTV, ReplayTV, TiVo, UltimateTV, and WebTV) would enable viewers to spend more time with advertising, not less, for clients would seek out advertising of interest and follow hyperlinks to find out more (Ellis 1999). New technology by Wink Communications, in five million U.S. homes, allowed audiences to watch television and click their way to product information and purchases

(Elkin 2002). AT&T Broadband software was developed to allow personalized messages to be directed to cable users based upon a database of their programming interests. Projecting these links between technology and promotion into the future, new media guru Nicholas Negroponte announced the end of the traditional advertising paradigm in which messages were "pushed" at audiences, and the beginning of a new paradigm of "permission" marketing in which audiences own interests "pulled" them toward marketing messages.

Media Research

Traditional audience ratings that were developed in the mass media age, like Neilson (in the United States) and BARB (in the United Kingdom), gradually came to appear ineffective and out of date for providing planners and buyers information about the fragmented mediascape. The validity of Neilson and BARB audience data techniques had been increasingly questioned, so these businesses responded by including new technology to track audiences' use of VCRs or personal television. BARB constructed a new sample, admitting that the old sample frame had been weakened due to the revolution in audience viewing patterns and changing technology. These ratings changes occurred within the context where media executives sought more and more detailed audience data, "such as additional demographic details, minute-by-minute ratings, ratings for ads as well as editorial content, a broader picture of the media each audience member consumes, and a measure of an ad's impact" (Hughes 2001, 2). Media planners secured their success by providing added value media research services, such as special analysis of audience data, and planners invested in "analytical tools and systems, to support more in-depth strategic planning" (Drexler 2002, 22). Optimizer tools computerized media buying, allowing agencies to sift through data and determine the best media buy for reaching a client's target audience. (Hughes 2001; Elkin 2001). Planners also won kudos from advertisers by offering specialized services for reaching particular niche audiences. For example, Havas opened a new division dedicated to reaching the Hispanic community, which then comprised 13 percent of the population of the United States, while others promised to sort out and assemble Eastern European audiences for advertisers (Linnett 2001).

But nothing brought more of a glint into advertisers' eyes than some of the new visions for linking media and market research. The emergence of UPC scanners, television meters, desktop marketing systems, and telecommunications technologies could track consumer behavior and deliver messages with a precision that was unprecedented in marketing history (Shergill 1988, 1990). Single source data (the simultaneous electronic tracking of television viewing and product purchasing behavior) promised to eliminate the wastes found in the media buying system (Shergill 1989; Assael and Poltrack 1991). Full integration of online and offline media buying was been explored by a number of companies. One example was Arbitron's Portable People Meters, pager-sized scanners which panel respondents wore all day and which recorded consumers' media diets by detecting embedded audio codes.

AdForce was one of the companies developing integrated market and media research. An AdForce spokesman explained that the "marrying [of] demographic and psychographic information from direct marketing databases with Internet behavior profiling and location-based targeting" in their system would enable consumers to be targeted wherever they are—in their car or in front of their TV set. Global positioning systems and deals between carriers and radio stations would enable media planners to use integrated research to enable consumers' radios to function like cell phones, receiving targeted, personalized promotion. People listening to the same music station would receive different, targeted advertising messages. Cravens was careful to note that consumers would have to agree to such forms of promotion (Gilbert 2000). His caution may well be warranted. One of AdForce's competitors, Doubleclick, had tested similar promotional vehicles among consumers. Controversy from special interest groups about invasion of privacy caused the company to stop such initiatives, adding a different perspective on the idea of "permission marketing."

Conclusion

By the twenty-first century, the full service agency technically no longer existed, as research and media departments were unbundled. Agency structures were reassembled deep within the organizational structures of the massive transnational communication conglomerates. The power of the agency continued to flourish, however, as these communication behemoths' preference for contracting out services, their massive financial clout, and their inherent conservatism fueled the expansion of niche communication businesses that specialized in everything from public relations to branding strategy. Advertisers could select from a dizzying assortment of specialized communication services, many owned by the very same major communication giants.

This period was also accompanied by a renewal of the old debate about "the end of advertising" (Zyman and Brott 2002). The use of both below and above the line techniques and the expansion of new media and promotional formats actually resulted in total spending on advertising being reduced during this period. The growing empowerment of audiences to interact directly with businesses through the Internet, as well as their high levels of resistance and growing promotional literacy, made it appear that the magic of advertising was diminishing. And yet, this renewed debate about the end of advertising was taking place during a period in which advertising was busily migrating to all spheres of society (Wernick 1991), was becoming more fully meshed with popular culture, and was increasingly seen as responsible for many forms of "deviant" consumption, in which many individuals were left with obesity, alcoholism, smoking, and debt. But we cannot support the view that all of this somehow is likely to herald "the end of advertising." What is happening in the most recent period is, in our opinion, better understood as a new era of marketplace communication, where the horizon of promotion is more difficult to ascertain due to its intensive embedding within cultural dynamics.

CHAPTER 12

Structure and Agency
Tensions at Play in Advertising Design

In the last chapter, we explored how globalization, an empowered media planning and buying sector, technology, and clients' growing interest in promotional activities led to an unbundling of the activities in the full-service agency.
In this chapter, we focus on how creative departments reacted to these many
changes and we explore some studies about advertising design, in order to begin to sketch how advertisers sought to negotiate with audiences in the mediated marketplace.

The discourse surrounding creative practice in the post-1980s was riddled
with contradiction. Some pronounced advertising dead, while others maintained that it was in the throws of a creative renaissance. In the 1990s Thomas
Frank said that advertising was undergoing a creative revolution as great as
that of the 1960s; Frank Mort announced a "third wave" of creativity; and
Sean Nixon saw a turn toward a more richly aesthetic and emotional mode of
address. Mica Nava (1997, 46) argued that the challenge of speaking to promotionally disinterested audiences lead creatives to produce more highly entertaining and aesthetically appealing designs during this period:

> Cynicism and boredom about ads are widespread and part of a more general
> neurasthenia of postmodern culture. In fact the battle of the advertisers to
> overcome this boredom is what has led to the creation of so many witty, so-
> phisticated, intertextually referenced and visually appealing ads. This in turn
> has produced more discriminating and skilful consumers.

Liz McFall (2004) offered evidence from the 1920s that illustrated the existence even then of highly emotional and aesthetic appeals in ads. Early advertisers undertook targeted campaigns, were concerned about clutter, and
believed their audiences were savvy. Thus, McFall questioned the assertion that
any of these items represented a "new" era for advertising.

The so-called advertising renaissance did not stop the industry trade press
from declaring the "end of advertising," however. Media planners—advancing
their own position—argued that creatives had lost their influence in the marketplace, were not keeping up with technological changes and were becoming
a conservative force that held back innovation, referring to them as "Luddites
wed to the dying 30-second TV commercial model" (Hatfield 2002). Others
pointed out that creatives could no longer "bully" media departments into purchasing the media space they most preferred, typically television and cinema,

arguing that "clients ask first for media thinking, not creative cleverness" (Drexler 2002). A planner from Carat portrayed creative work as mere "headline writing" and asked why creative work was not outsourced, as it was in the Hollywood model(Crain 2001). The industry buzzed with news that clients were looking outside of agency creative departments for original ideas.

> Creative ideas, once the preserve of copywriters and art directors, now can come from anywhere: from planner or account exec to record company big cheese, trend-spotting futurist to celebrity agent, and even from the new breed of "membrane" who links Madison Avenue with Hollywood. Creative departments need to regain stature, confidence. (Hatfield 2002)

These conflicting stories are troubling only if one expects advertising history to follow a singular linear thread of progress. It simply does not. Advertising is a highly conflicted and vastly diverse practice and change is cyclical, meaning that the conclusions we reach depend on interest and perspective. Conflicting viewpoints are the norm, not the exception. As a matter of fact, advertising did die during this period—and at the same time it went through a creative rebirth.

Reasserting the Creative Spirit

Few creatives were pleased with the accusations made about them during this period, and few accepted the characterization that saw them as malleable, conservative and dispensable figures of the advertising enterprise. Some of them retaliated with arguments designed to rescue recognition of their importance in the industry. Ogilvy and Mather's Chris Wall worked out his frustration over the industry's treatment of creatives in a response to the question: What will the industry be like in the future?

> For a period of seven years commencing in 2021, the virtual elimination of creative talent costs will lead to outrageous profitability for communication holding companies—who, absent talent costs—will continue to charge top dollar for low or no cost labor. In 2028, however, a new piece of procurement software will make it possible for clients to identify consumers who are capable of actually "selling themselves." Customers will write e-mails to themselves explaining why they love the products they buy and urging themselves to buy more which will be sent back to them by gigantic servers...."Word of mouth" advertising will be replaced by a new and more effective hybrid: "word of self." The final creative person in all of advertising will be laid off in September of 2029....Ironically, agencies will continue to exist—however, there will be only two jobs remaining in the agency itself that clients are willing to pay for: PowerPoint operator and focus-group attendee. (*Creativity*, May 12, 2004)

Creatives reminded all those who would listen that the entire advertising enterprise hinged on their unique talents. Defenders like Chuck McBride of TBWA/Chiat/Day rallied the troops, reminding colleagues that "the only thing we have as an industry, is our ideas. Without them, we're just professional opinion-givers" (Donaton 2000, 26). Creativity is advertising's unique selling proposition, according to Peter Mead, co-founder of Abbott Mead and Vickers: "Our aim is to destroy the view that advertising is a commodity. It is the creation of an elusive spark of originality which can fundamentally enhance a client's business" (Muirden 2003).

This separation between creativity and business was a familiar refrain of creatives who had long harnessed the authority of the arts to justify their practices—and for good reason. Creativity is a deeply valued concept with long lines of resonance in the cultural sectors. Colin Campbell noted how, during the eighteenth century, creative artists came to embody a set of moral and spiritual aspirations in Western societies as they became more secular. The very act of naming themselves "creatives" shows how advertisers sought to secure cultural privilege. Advertising has long been considered a "profane" art, as much by those inside the agency as without. Creatives admit they do commercial work for the money, while their passions lie in traditional artistic pursuits such as novel writing, film directing, playwriting, or painting (Shapiro 1981). Film director Tony Scott summed up this sentiment when he noted, "I do thirty seconds for the money and ninety minutes for the ego". Still, to shore up their respectability, commercial artists, while deriding their craft, have also attempted to turn their commercial canvas into something more than the crass selling of messages, in order to impress one another and the artistic elite. In interviews, art directors commonly rank advertising low on the cultural hierarchy list, yet proudly brandish their CLIO and EFFIE awards as the badges of their supreme achievement.

The theory of the cultural intermediary thus provides an explanation for the creatives' drive to impress, as well as for their sense of inferiority and the drive to overcome it. Pierre Bourdieu located a middle-class grouping in his analysis of French statistical data who to "escape from being demoted to a lower class... produce new professions or readapt the professions their qualification give them access to, so that they are more in line with their pretensions" (1979, 167–68). Unable or unwilling to secure traditional professional jobs or those to which they aspired (poets, novelists), educated individuals colonized the cultural industries to become advertisers, fashion designers, media workers, therapists, and gallery owners. Together, they form a broader cultural formation of workers concerned with aesthetics, design, fashion, and art. They see the cultural industries as the key to their social advancement, thus are highly attentive to cultural capital. Their concerns about achieving social advancement and preventing social disgrace explain why cultural intermediaries are particularly anxious about their health and appearance. Fixated on the bourgeoisie lifestyle, cultural intermediaries both popularized it and took up unconventional, counter culture tastes to exert social distinction against it.

Due to their strategic location in the art culture system and access to media, advertisers popularized their particular lifestyles, which suggest why health, appearance, aesthetics, and cosmopolitan up-market style have come to permeate the mediated marketplace. From this perspective, the Rosetta Stone necessary for unlocking agency practice lies in reading the actions of advertisers as part of the symbolic struggles of workers engaged in a bid for class distinction. The story of the agency is first and foremost the social plight of the cultural intermediary; the influence of new technology, research, or the changing interests and needs of the consumer are secondary influences.

In his detailed history of masculinities in the 1980s, Frank Mort illustrates how advertisers worked in consort with designers, photographers, and independent journalists who "exerted a strong sense of authority in the search for new markets," and together constructed a new commercial discourse of masculinity. "Taste leadership" was recognized as a key feature in the dissemination of goods, and the "habitus of these cultural professionals was overwhelmingly metropolitan" (Mort 1996, 8). Advertisers have long provided consumers with advice about how to live and models for different styles of life, but Mort (1996) and Nixon (1996) illustrate how during the 1980s a third wave of creativity crashed upon the shore of consumer culture, washing up a new range of aesthetic and lifestyle options. The inspiration for these lifestyle motifs were derived from the lifestyles of advertisers' and other cultural intermediaries, not from research or marketing strategy.

As cultural intermediaries, advertisers were deeply sensitive to consumer culture innovation–watching the latest movies and keeping aware of the latest fashion, novels, club activity, and Web site happenings, along with general news events. Creatives' place in the agency and in their peer communities depended on their knowledge of the cultural field. The drive to produce award-winning work, and the industry's reverence toward it, illustrates how social status overrides the focus on business matters and audience preferences. Indeed, Polonsky et al. (1995) found no correlation between the income and billings of the top fifty agencies and the number of awards they won. And creatives were found to enjoy award winning ads much more than audiences did (Kover, James, and Sonner 1997).

The theory of the cultural intermediary thus provides a powerful explanation of advertising practices, but like all good explanations, it is a partial one. Advertising is not simply a closed system of cultural intermediaries watching one another, nor have creatives ever had the complete luxury to produce "art for art's sake." At the heart of the creative process is not just creative talent but an ability to reach people and, ultimately, to understand people and their worlds. Advertising is an art with a purpose, namely, to make what happens in the marketplace interesting to consumers on a permanent basis. Advertising is neither exclusively selling nor exclusively communication—it is "marketing communication." In the next section, we highlight important trends in the research and audience circuitry that impacted negotiations between creatives and account managers concerned with brand positioning in the mediated market.

The metropolitan look of the *cognoscenti* (those in the know) and the cultured lifestyles of advertisers during this period competed with other forms of address, such as the mass family targeting that continued to be produced for Wal-Mart and Proctor and Gamble, who demanded returns on their advertising investment and stringently evaluated the effectiveness of their campaigns. In the highly competitive mediated marketplace, businesses scrutinized advertising costs with new rigor. New corporate culture priorities revealed a certain loss of confidence and a tendency to play it safe and not take creative risks. Debt-ridden mega-companies were under pressure to find efficiencies and savings, and when running down the balance sheet, advertising jumped out as the most fanciful and dispensable investment. Many corporations loathe the alleged "navel-gazing" of creative departments—particularly P&G, which controls such a massive advertising budget that changes in their advertising spends influence others. This was a period of not only creative flowering, but in the words of one media director, cost cutting: "Pressures have got down to the creative level because clients are not about to invest in a super production. They are looking to cut corners" (personal interview, 2003). Advertising dollars were redirected to promotions and event sponsorship, where returns were more measurable and immediate.

Variation on the Idea of Creative Struggle

Fox (1980) held that at different moments in history, advertising agency battles erupted between creative and research departments in their attempts to shape the practices of the advertising industry as a whole. Agency work was characterized as a tension between creativity and marketing research in the twentieth century. The oscillation between them was not just a sliding back and forth, but part of the ongoing evolution of the modern agency system and its research and communication design practices. Our studies of industry dynamics indicate that the discursive separation of the artistic and rationalizing elements of the agency is more difficult to find in practice; as these elements blend and blur, leading to considerable dynamism and innovation. We find evidence that increased pressures were placed on creatives to justify their budgets, and their work was subject to more efficiency measures; at the same time, there appeared to be a growing embrace of creative work by audiences, clients, and researchers.

Because advertising is such a broad and diverse form of social communication it is not surprising that it excites contradictory opinions. Advertising at various times is simultaneously liked and disliked, threatened, and secured. During the 1980s and 1990s clients demanded greater efficiencies, media planners vied to take over the industry, and audiences used technological tools to zip, zap, and avoid advertising; all of which posed very real threats to those working in creative department. At the same moment, however, they achieved new heights of popularity. The reasons for this are many. First, contemporary creatives inherited the esteem won by their predecessors in the 1960s and the "creative revolution" they had carried out then. By the 1980s advertising was no longer as heavily tainted by the Aspidistra (Orwell, 1936). English graduates from Cambridge eagerly entered agencies, as jobs in the cultural industries such as advertising were held in high esteem. Even though audiences continued to dislike advertising, they were deeply intrigued by creatives. Popular culture producers sought to profit on this fascination, thus many versions of the advertising creative circulated in popular film, television and art (for example, *How to Get Ahead in Advertising, Thirty Something,* and *Leitchenstein*)

Second, the audience addressed by creatives had changed. Ad designers in the 1920s were separated from most of their audiences by a great educational, regional, and gender divide. Trained in art departments where the line between high and low art was seriously maintained, early creatives developed a particular type of snob appeal (Marchand 1986). By the 1980s, however, their successors were speaking to an urban population who had enjoyed the expansion of higher education. The distance between advertisers and their audience closed slightly (although not along the lines of gender and race). While creatives continued to seek awards and to please their peers; the legitimacy of the high culture arbiters, as we learned, weakened. Scholars now celebrated the artistic achievements of advertising (Nava, 1997; Titchell, 1996; Richard et al. 2000) . Changes in advertising design contributed to greater audience involvement. For the new generation of creatives, fame, celebrity, and respect in popular culture were new benchmarks, particularly for those working in dramatic and humor genres. They were less "artists" (self-possessed, introspective, unmoved by popular opinion) than "artistes"—popular entertainers. A representative sample of the British population felt that the "majority of the population are quite positive toward advertising, but some feel that sometimes ads just go too far." However, a similar proportion felt that some people "are just too sensitive about the things they see in advertising" (ASA 2000; ASA 2001; ADA 2001a).

Advertising is a very public job. Because the finished product is on public display, a good deal of concern is lavished on the quality of the advertisements that are finally produced. As one art director remarked, "What we do is a public thing. Everyone sees it on television. You know that everyone is seeing something that you did. A banker, no matter how successful, is never a star. His work doesn't get seen" (personal interview, 2003). Creatives engage a considerable amount of ego in their craft. Thus, the price for failing at this craft is not simply economic income loss (for self and agency), but loss of face. This ego investment in their work links them emotionally to their audiences, not just their peers. A creative director said,

> I like the idea of pleasing people. In the midst of all the junk on TV, the advertising is better than the shows. It's a matter of pride with me. Advertising is filled with people who want to do good work. This may be because it's a public business. If we do something terrible, we're going to be embarrassed. (Schudson 1984, 77)

Creatives are painfully aware that popular cultural programming is enjoyed more than their creative messages. It is not just the brief that drives them to make appealing entertaining, emotionally laden messages—many of which downplayed product and sells mission—but also an attempt to avoid the sting of public rejection. To win over the audience, some creatives look to their personal experience. According to advertising creative Amil Gargano, "I said that you take personal experiences and you see whether or not they have any relation to the problem at hand. And being a human being you're part of the human species—chances are your problem probably has a correlation to somebody else's" (Ellsworth 2002). They talk about their craft as a powerful force beyond their control, as something difficult to put into words. When asked where the inspiration for advertising comes from, one practitioner replied, "Human nature. Human creativity drives it. It is still that visceral, gut instinct that put into the right or wrong hands of someone will sell you a bag of goods" (O'Barr 2001).

In his in-depth interviews with account executive, planners, and creatives working in leading London and New York agencies, Hackley (2003) found different ways of conceiving the consumer. Account planners and managers felt that the key to engaging consumers was to decode them through formal research, and to then develop communication tailored to the findings. However, creatives felt no need to "discover" the consumer, rather they already felt that knew who they were, and they pictured the consumer as bored and inattentive, living drudging lives. They felt that their role was to satisfy the audiences' need for stimulating beauty, humor, and drama. Empathy, not research, was the key to reach audiences. Creatives felt that good work sprang from those who developed the spectacles and fantasies that tapped into the child inside them—inside all of us. They reported that regression was an important aspect of their craft.

Third, creatives were supported in their craft, not always opposing researchers, account managers, and clients as earlier reports have suggested. Creative departments continued to be distinctive workshops. In their studies of London and Japanese agencies, both Nixon (2003) and Moreau (1996) found that creatives undertook strategies to distinguish themselves from others, wearing more informal clothing, and arriving late for meetings. Creative departments were populated with highly self-promotional and expressive individuals; some of creative's art school graduates moved into the forefront of business, advancing over Harvard MBAs. By in large, account executives, who continued to mediate the relationship between client and creative, were slightly more conservative in their dress and behavior—although all workers during this period conformed to more casual business attire that accompanied the loosening of cultural boundaries discussed in Chapter 9. Nixon found that those working in account management and research were more likely to hail from middle- and upper middle-class backgrounds, and from more elite educational institutions.

On the other hand, no formal qualifications are necessary for entry into creative work; one does not even need technical skills such as drawing ability, so long as one is imaginative. Nixon found that the 102 creative departments he studied were mostly populated by those from lower middle-class or working-class backgrounds, with technical or art school training. Competition for entry into this hallowed domain was very intense, often requiring hours of volunteer work, a self-funded portfolio of good work, superior networking, and self promotional skills. A BBC documentary (2002) which followed the plight of three young potential creatives chasing after a single job in Grey Advertising revealed thick entry barriers, as candidates were pitted against one another, against a superior agency team, and subjected to intense criticism. Self-presentation and social skills were evaluated as closely as the ideas produced, if not more.

Money alone cannot explain the attraction to this profession. The creative department resonates with the dream of making it on pure talent and imaginative prowess. In her study of how young audiences conceived those who work in the advertising industry, Stephanie O'Donohoe (1996, 23) found that their understanding of the industry was "largely derived from films and television programmes featuring characters who worked in agencies, from television documentaries about aspects of marketing, and from features in magazines and newspaper stories." They saw those who worked in advertising as having quite exotic jobs and described advertisers as "hip," "on the scene," "tuned in," and believed they must derive great pleasure and satisfaction from "creating things."

Those who hold creative jobs might well beg to differ, but one truth of the industry is that gender and ethnicity remained formative barriers for those wishing to obtain a dream job in advertising. Creative departments are overwhelmingly populated by white males. The last time a woman was inducted into the Advertising Hall of Fame in New York was 1974 (Advertising Women of New York, Good Bad and Ugly Award, 2004). Nixon's unique analysis of creative department dynamics highlights how privilege is maintained by exclusionary gender practices enacted in language and behavior. The distinctions between those who work in creative departments and the rest of the agency have been neglected in discussions focused on the broader category of cultural intermediaries.

Agencies gave thought to finding management structures to foster creativity. Generally creatives are permitted a good deal of freedom to break norms, to behave in unorthodox ways (at least more than the agency secretary), and to be temperamental. In particular, star creatives are pampered, possibly out of a fear that they would join other agencies or start their own creative shops. Given the pressures they face, a certain amount of loose rein is required to enable them to take full responsibility for their craft. One pressure is the challenge of making compelling advertisements. It is possible to argue that producing advertising is harder than producing popular cultural programming because creative messages have to move us in some way, to make us think or react, to pull at our emotions, desires, and dreams, and ultimately to affect our behavior after the time of viewing. Designs that do this are more difficult to conceive than those that simply attract attention on permanent loan, so to speak, like popular cultural programmers. Few creatives were so deluded as to believe that all audiences embraced their work. They knew quite clearly that advertising was interpreted differently from other popular cultural messages. According to Paul Cappelli of The Ad Store:

> In a movie, you're more willing to suspend your disbelief. In a commercial…you're starting from the idea that "It's a commercial: I hate you. You're going to try to sell me something: I hate you." So how do you, in 30 seconds take them from "It's a commercial. I know you're going to try to sell me something, so I'm going to lock down right now." Here I go, to, "Holy shit! He got me; he absolutely got me." (O'Barr 2001)

Another pressure is the severe time limit (usually thirty seconds) on the communicative act. Ads must do their work quickly. Advertisers want to utilize every split second of their costly time. Unlike film directors who have two hours to build a storyline, the advertising creative has to make an impression instantly. A third pressure is media clutter, which means that creatives have to conceive of techniques for making their ads stand out in the crowd. Moreover, media-literate audiences have grown cynical toward advertising: With their fingers on VCRs, channel changers, and other ad-avoidant technologies, it is all too easy to press the button when confronted with irritating messages. Audiences mount strikes, withdrawing their interpretive labor, and find new pleasure in cynically decoding and poking fun at "cheesie" advertising messages: "They're bombarded with messages, and they're very savvy about how those messages are interpreted. They don't want to be told things. They want to be engaged, and it's very different how you market to them" (Alison 2001).

Young audiences, raised in a media- and marketing-rich culture, are particularly cynical toward messages, and along with the educated elite are leading a rebellion calling for more diverse and authentic modes of address. Fourth, due to the timelines of campaigns, ideas must be developed quickly, even though truly innovative ideas are known to take considerable time and thought to produce. Fifth, agencies have less control over the look of the final product. When advertising was produced simply by a copywriter and artist, the product could be fairly well controlled. Today's television and cinema ads bring together large teams, including production houses, stylists, and caterers. Thus, the final broadcasted ad can end up looking very different from the storyboard. Increasingly, advertising is as much about managing social relations and orchestrating innovation as it is about image creation.

Sixth, despite dwindling advertising budgets a great deal of money continues to be invested into advertising production. By the late 1990s it cost about $350,000 to buy a thirty-second television spot and $500,000 to make the commercial. As Asa Berger (2004, 57) pointed out, "A thirty-minute program, if it cost as much per second as a television commercial, would cost $15 million—that is the price of making a low budget movie." Million-dollar commercials are no longer a rarity, and no expense is spared. The increased use of celebrities and location shots contributed to rising advertising spends. What we see on the screen is the best possible performance and execution of the communications strategy. North American broadcasting today is an ironic scene: The things people presumably want most—the shows—are produced as cheaply as possible, just so that the screen will be filled and hold our passive attention with its flickering images, while the things that people often say they do not want—commercials—are produced with lavish care at great expense.

Agencies utilized several techniques to harness the creative spirit of their workers, and we will explore a few of them here. During the most recent period, agencies have been typecast not simply by their designs, but for how their creative departments are organized. Creative quarters were unveiled for promotional ends. The esteemed independent London/New York agency BBH, which has held the lucrative Levi's account since the 1980s and has captured numerous creative awards, takes a classical approach to creative management in which earlier masters such as David Ogilvy would not feel uncomfortable. The BBH promotional video showcases elder founding father creatives seated in leather chairs, dressed in casual but smart black attire, frankly discussing the creative impulse and philosophy behind their award-winning designs. Emphasis is placed on the creative work produced and the strategy behind it. Creatives in this organizational arrangement are sages who marry art and business in an intelligent, imaginative, and witty fashion. They speak to a viewer whom they believe is intelligent; their tenor is mature, serious, akin to an art or cultural historian. Creativity here is linked to discipline, strategy, and puzzling to find the unique angle, summed up in the agency tag line: "When the world zigs, zag." One of the principals of the agency, John Hegarty, argues that good advertising takes everyday ideas and twists them.

The BBH's creativity philosophy is distinguished from another school of thought that romantically links creativity to imaginative childlike behavior. The infantile moment, unconstrained by rules, discipline, and adult responsibilities, has a long been linked to creativity. The logic of this philosophy would have it that working conditions should encourage childishness; and it would appear that this happens, as one creative director noted, "I encourage immaturity in the creative department" (Akert 2001). The promotional video, *The Package*, by the American advertising agency Crispin Porter and Bogusky, offers another example of this creative philosophy. The clip follows the office pranks of the creative teams. It begins with a pan shot of masked creatives and the voice-over, "We have too much time. We have too much money," which provides the pretext for the midnight stealth mission carried out by the group in which they rent a moving truck and acquire several massive bags of Styrofoam packing pellets used to fill the office of their colleagues. After filling the room, they play in the space, which is not dissimilar to the "ball" rooms provided for children in McDonald's.

The young men paddle and jump about in the pellets which permits their body to free float and thrash about unharmed, buffered from harsh material reality. Those who pulled the prank enjoy a sense of mischievous glee, denied to their colleagues who occupy the office, who, in the morning, open the door to experience a mess, not a play space. The perpetrators abandon the scene, and like children, take no responsibility for cleaning up their mess. The defacing of another's office is an assault on their workmates' territory and integrity. After coughing up a Styrofoam pellets the victims of the prank seek revenge. Gathering the pens, water bottles, and phones of their colleges, they exercise to sweat themselves up and place the objects under their arm pits, in toilet water, and rub them on their genitals and rear ends. Their colleagues are filmed placing these "dirty" objects in their mouths. The clip ends with the philosophy: "Don't seek revenge; seek advancement" (Crispin, Porter, Bogusky, *The Package*, available online at www.cpbmiami.com, accessed July 22, 2004).

Agency creatives here are playful children engaged in vengeful struggle—little emperors undertaking creative destruction. The creative department is presented as a romper room where fertile imaginations endlessly dream up new stunts. While most of us have to simply adjust to the stress and monotony of office life, the creative ethos must resist this in order to maintain its integrity. The type of play presented is highly gendered in its competitiveness: the bathroom humor, revenge motif, and appeals to military strategy. It has become increasingly common in large agencies for staff to be pitted against one another to encourage creativity. Thus the clip both releases some of the competitive pressures that creatives face, as at the same time it mimes them in play. The promotional video informs potential clients that the creativity embodied in the agency is predicated on freedom and indulgence, and suggest that clients must support this ethos.

Another myth about creativity that circulates in the industry is that hierarchy and bureaucracy are its antimatter. The London agency, St. Luke's, sought to strategically erase the line between work and play, and obliterate departmental boundaries to encourage not just creatives, but everyone in the agency to get in touch with their creativity. An agency documentary revealed how the office was organized in an open seating plan with campaign rooms instead of departmental divisions. All agency staff was encouraged to roam. The tools of leisure were on continual offer—free food, drink, popular culture, and couches to relax or nap—in an effort to erase the line between work and play. Staff events had a carnival-like theme where senior management drank and played silly games with the staff, to erase power divisions. All employees had shares in the company and some voting rights in relation to agency decisions (although one's position and the different number of shares held continued to exert power). The offer of shares to all employees was fairly distinctive—perhaps inspired by Prime Minister Thatcher and her emphasis on everyone being a shareholder in Britain—but the open layout and casual relations between agency departments were imported from the well known Los Angeles agency Chiat/Day which, since its inception in 1968, had experimented with a "laid back California style" for creative work. One of the founders of St. Luke's had worked in Chiat/Day's London office until it was acquired in 1995 by TWBA, illustrating the fact that not only creative approaches, but management structures as well, continue to cross the Atlantic in the mediated marketplace.

We have drawn attention to one final (and by far the most radical) change in organizational structure that, we believe, signals a new mood in client creative relationships. Most U.S. agencies, and the majority of those in Britain, maintain that advertising works best if creatives are sheltered from clients and their demands (and conversely, if clients are separated from the antics of creatives). Hence, agencies have typically used the account executive as a mediator between these parties. By contrast, Mother Ltd., London (and its New York branch opened in 2004) took the novel step of allowing creatives to negotiate directly with multinational executives on accounts as large as Coca-Cola. A "kitchen table" approach was adopted by this agency, which dispensed with the account executive—the key middle-management position. To further eliminate bureaucracy and any taint of a paint-by-numbers strategy, creatives worked without a formal brief. Instead they, producers, and clients sat down together and "jammed." Innovations like these in agency relationships are made possible because over time some clients have become more creative-friendly. As the following quote suggests, clients better understood the nature of creative work today: "Clients are much smarter now.... They've taken all the courses on how to get the most out of the creative mind. They're much, much better than they were in the 1970s and 1980s when I was growing up in the business"(Akert 2002).

Mother Ltd. also suggests that creatives, in turn, have become more business-friendly. This management structure had a fortunate spin-off, in that it allowed Mother Ltd. to attract some of the best producers in advertising, and may well have helped it become one of the most successful new independent agencies of the late 1990s. This approach also suggests a new level of unbundling of creative service from the traditional full service agency model, leading to a situation in which creative work is outsourced as it is in the Hollywood business model.

Research

The final piece of evidence that we offer to illustrate change in creatives' role is their relationship to research. Again, the picture is contradictory. Creative work continued to be threatened by clients' demands for research to prove advertising efficient. At the same time, new forms of creative-friendly research emerged. Research was part of the professionalization of the modern agency and long has remained a prominent feature of agency practices. Well before post-Fordist thinking made it fashionable, agencies were contracting various kinds of research for different stages of their evaluation process. The traditional stages of research are as follows: The first stage involves discussions among the creative department, the client, and the account team about the aims and direction of the campaign. Information about problems with past campaigns and past ads, about the market segment being targeted, about the views the target market holds about the product and simple facts about the product itself are all vital at this point. Also important are general market information and knowledge about what rivals are trying to do; much of this information can be provided by the client or the agency itself.

Costs prohibit a full-range of research procedures, except for large national/global accounts, including most television campaigns that are so important and have so much money behind them that they are carefully researched. Once the brief has established the marketing problems and the creative team has devised various solutions, storyboards (a series of photographs or animated drawings) and an accompanying soundtrack are produced. Several storyboards will be presented to the client, who normally decides to test one or more of them. Focus groups may be used to review the storyboards, and audience opinions become the basis for future decisions. Tests may also be conducted with larger groups of consumers in shopping malls or in special studio settings, to get measures of "communication and recall," indicating how likely consumers are to purchase the product advertised, or "intrusiveness and recall," indicating how well an ad is remembered the next day. The results may lead the client to ask for modifications and fresh tests, or to authorize the production of one of the storyboards into a finished commercial.

Once again, when the full commercial has been produced, a battery of research instruments may be employed, including reruns of the communication/recall and intrusiveness/recall tests of brand or brand values. Other tests may also be run, such as "message take out," exploring whether consumers took away the "reasons" for purchase communicated in the message. Measures of physical reactions imperceptible to subjects were developed, such as Wesley procedures which use galvanic skin devices to measure perspiration (on the assumption that emotional responses that cause perspiration are related to what is happening in the commercial message). Other techniques track brainwaves or eye movement or analyze subjects' voices.

In addition to these somewhat "artificial context" tests, finished commercials may also be tried in a test market. Results can then be evaluated by monitoring sales figures in those areas. Thus, measures other than sales are used as indications of effectiveness. A preferred approach is day-after recall, where telephone calls are made at random the day after the commercial is shown until two hundred people who saw the programs containing the commercial have been reached. These respondents are then asked which ads, and what specifically about them, they can remember. If the test results are satisfactory, then the client will approve wider distribution of the commercial, but it is not unusual for a particular advertising strategy to be cancelled even at this late stage if the tests do not provide sufficiently strong support.

While clients and account executive are quite fond of the tangible reassurance that research provides, creatives are less favorable, and have become some of the most ardent critics of evaluation research. They protest that research tests are rarely representative of the target audience, and that the minimal funds invested in research, and the short time in which it is produced, leads to questionable validity claims. Research done over the phone or in focus groups is nonecological, for it asks people to discuss in detail advertisements that they might otherwise ignore; home viewing is known to be distracted, and disrupted. The testing of memory via "recall" was not shown to be linked either to sales or advertising impact. Ostensibly, the purpose of research is to evaluate the effectiveness of the advertising messages produced, but many people in the agencies say that its real purpose is to provide a rationale for decisions taken by representatives of the client company (they sometimes refer to it as "smoke-screen" research).

> The truth is, much of that research is hocus-pocus. The reason most clients research advertising is not to find out if it's effective, but to conform to the system in their company, so if advertising doesn't work, they're off the hook. So they let the research make the decision and evade the responsibility. (personal interview, 2003)

Others argue that agencies are less in the business of designing communication than in providing justifications for their practices, and that research plays a key role in this mission. Asked whether advertising strategy is linked to research, Cappelli responded that it was the other way around:

> If you get people in advertising to sit down with you and talk honestly, they will admit to you that a lot of the strategy for campaigns is done after they've seen the work, after they've seen the creative. They will retro-fit the strategy to fit the creative. We are a rational industry. We will rationalize anything to make it work. (O'Barr, 2001)

What creatives resent most is research that impinges on their designs: A 1998 Boss Man advertisement provides an example of why. Focus groups revealed that the Boss Man, promoted primarily in magazines, was too "modelly" and "stiff"—nothing but a "clothes horse." Hence, a television commercial was commissioned to give the Boss Man a personality by showing show him holding his composure under pressure—a not-so-subtle way to associate the brand with coolness.

Under the Hollywood logic that maximum drama creates maximum coolness, the Boss Man was placed in the stressful situation of having his luggage searched at an airport. The original storyboard showed a sniffer dog snarling in the background, and the Boss Man and security guard staring one another down. Although in keeping with the brief, the storyboard was rejected. Research intelligence suggested that consumers reacted negatively to the thought of dog saliva and fashion being put together. The extended looks between the security guard were taken as a signal of homosexuality, which the client feared might alienate the wider heterosexual market. Thus for the final take the ad was changed: The dog was bathed to give him a shiny coat, muzzled to mask drool, and a female security guard was added to blur sexual connotations (Nava 1998).

The encroachment of research in creative design processes had been building since the early 1980s recession, when advertisers pressured agencies to prove that creative work was cost effective. Clients who dabbled in below the line techniques had learned they were cheaper and more accountable. Clients wondered why advertisers could not deliver the same. Agencies had to report the results of their budgets (Salmon 2000), and studies revealed that through the 1980s creative work was increasingly subject to research evaluation and that creatives responded negatively to this intervention (Morgan 1984, 1985; Vaughn 1982, 1983; Wells 1983). Some spoke out, arguing that micro-management via research killed their originality and hampered their agencies' advancement in the mediated marketplace.

> I've seen research reach a zenith five years ago and it became impossible because it began to kill creative activity. Not focus groups but doing in-depth studies one-on-one with trained psychologists and eye camera where the eye is dilated—it was big money. And what happened was that time and again

brave agencies and clients were not subjecting their ads to that and were beating the pants off the others. (personal interview, 2003)

The puzzle of how to accurately measure advertising effects was certainly not solved in this period, so measuring the worth of creatives remained elusive and pointed the finger back at producers. Creatives fought back against promotion, reminding clients of the importance of brand loyalty. Some further noted that "promotions destroy brand loyalty. Consumers have deal loyalty, not brand loyalty" (personal interview, 2003). Giving a deal was seen as a slippery slope to lower profits and taught the consumer bad habits (i.e., to look for a deal); whereas investment in brand image created both distinction and premium price. Creative defenders argued that promotions were ultimately strategies of price competition, strategies that, if followed, would lead to losses for every one (except the consumer). The point was to invest in provocative creative work to built loyalty (Love 2002). Those few corporations that invested heavily in creative work (such as FedEx, Nike, and Visa) stood out against the trend to cut corners on creative budgets.

Creatives also struck it lucky with the emergence of a new vein of research. Traditional measures of effectiveness had difficulty explaining how highly emotional and dramatic ads made their impact. Focus groups participants spent more time discussing whether they liked the ad, the marketing motivations behind it, and their emotional engagement than answering standard effectiveness questions (such as recall, message take out, or willingness to purchase). Researchers, in a novel move, took the step of testing whether "liking" and "emotion" was actually related to market response, and confirmed that liking the ad positively transferred values and emotions from message to brand and increased willingness to purchase (Edell and Burke 1987). Research also began to explore the power of feelings in understanding advertising effects (Mitchell, 1986), the effect of verbal and visual components on brand attitudes and attitudes towards the advertisement (Petty and Cacioppo 1986), the elaboration likelihood model of persuasion (Leather, McKechnie, and Amirkhanian 1994), and the importance of likeability as a measure of television advertising effectiveness. By 1993 over thirty-seven studies had confirmed the link between liking the advertisements and feeling positive toward the brand (Decock and De Pelsmacker 2000). This scientific "eureka" is, of course, a matter of common sense to most people; nevertheless this line of research legitimated liking as a measure of effectiveness, and in so doing brought the interest of creatives and researchers together. The galactic battle painted by advertising historians between creatives and researchers (Fox 1980; Frank 1997) is not so black and white, nor as adversarial, as it has often been portrayed.

The introduction of the account planner also drastically changed the role of research in agencies. Developed by Stanley Pollitt of the UK agency Boase Massimi Pollitt in the 1960s, and transported to the United States in 1970, the account planner was charged with uniting consumer, audience, and research (Barry, Paterson, and Todd 1987). The account planner joined the table with the account management and creatives to keep parties focused on the development of culturally relevant brands. The account planner was the consumer's representative, the brand's champion, and the communication plan's architect, with knowledge of consumer behavior, gleaned through research, brand marketing, and communications. Planners used their skills to "lead, shape and finesse development of brand strategy to the point where writers, art directors and media planners can take over and create the campaign" (Ephron 2002, 36), playing a central role in the construction of the creative brief. Once institutionalized, the account planner helped to ease the tensions between research and creative, and began to erode the distinction between advertising and marketing research, consumers and audiences.

Creatives appreciated research input at the beginning of the campaign. Focus groups, in which a group leader guided representative consumers in talking about themselves and their relationships to brands and products, were the least precise and predictive of all methods, but the most appreciated. The videotapes, or observed results of focus groups, did not show up in hard (factual) data, but provided hints and hypotheses from which the creative team could set to work. Marty Myers commented: "We use it for input before we tackle the creative problem. Before we do, I like to go out and probe and do focus groups and interviews to find out what it is that the public appears to want, to feel what their state of mind is, how they're shopping, what they're doing" (personal interview, 2003). The large-scale quantitative psychographic studies undertaken in 1980s were supplemented through the 1990s by qualitative research, primarily because it was cheap, flexible, and produced findings quickly, thus feeding the growing interest in tracking the fast changing market. More continuous research was necessary, as advertisers no longer spoke to a generalized mass consumer, but to distinctive market segments, each with unique lifestyle and lifecycle issues. Although many advertising jobs were lost in the 1990s recession, some jobs returned; but most of the positions were for researchers. While researchers are "hired guns," should unique ideas emerge from their findings, creatives have no qualms about using them in campaigns and taking the kudos. Some campaign ideas did emerge directly from research participants' mouths, as the creative above had foreseen.

Researching Culture

As agencies expanded into global markets through this period, they grew to appreciate that consumers existed in cultural contexts. They sometimes learned this lesson the hard way, thus it stuck with them. Researchers therefore embraced a cultural perspective, and anthropological research became a trend in Britain and the United States through the 1980s, as researchers focused on subcultures, tribes, the belief systems consumers held, how people mapped goods in their minds, and communicated in and through them. Researchers undertook ethnographic work by hanging out with teens, and looking in their closets, lockers, and cupboards for clues to the values that would be most culturally relevant with consumers.

Professional researchers went "cool hunting" and provided market intelligence to advertisers. This approach was not interested in representative samples but rather in finding style innovators, or cool teens, who, according to Malcolm Gladwell, had "personal influence, within specific social networks." Contemporary trends in fashion were not so much tipped off by social envy, noted Gladwell (1997), as by "the respect and admiration and truth of their friends" that the cool teens enjoyed. Market intelligence had moved beyond static models towards more fluid and predictive approaches. Trending became a growth industry, as the point was not to study consumers after the fact nor gather their opinions, but to stay one jump ahead of them. Researchers provided resources for creatives by updating them on the changing patterning of the culture. The senior vice president of Saatchi and Saatchi Advertising in New York, who oversees large-scale studies of consumer issues, identified trends to help marketing strategies and brand building: "My function in the agency is to bring the knowledge in the world into the agency, that is, to bring the knowledge out in the world into the agency and see that it gets circulated through the agency" (Foster 2002).

Within the mediated market, style trends were thought to "buzz," or circulate through word of mouth and media channels. Young people discussed advertising as they might a television program or a film. O'Donohoe recognized that, particularly for young people, the boundary between advertising and mass media was "fluid," and that "they brought their understanding of music, film and television programmes to bear on their interpretation of ads" (1997, 23). Promotion was "social glue"; tag lines were everyday colloquialisms. A study by the ASA (2001) revealed that advertising provided "a universal subject" that give people a shared topic to talk and laugh about. Instead of measuring recall, advertisers were interested in campaigns that buzzed: "One of the things we like to find out is whether these commercials are getting talked about, maybe on the radio, maybe at school" (Alison 2001). Those advertisements and branded entertainment features that caused a buzz in their target markets became a new measure of promotional success, even though it was very difficult to describe with any accuracy the relationship between the buzz and actual sales or brand awarness.

Cultural research helped agencies gain a new appreciation for how the brand fit into consumers' lives and their contribution to this process. Creatives clearly understood that they did not control brand meaning completely; rather they negotiated it with consumers. They worked hard to get a share of the consumers' mind, which they often believed was distracted by other brand symbolics and competing information and concerns (such as love interests, spats at work, the Atkins diet, and new movies):

> It's [the brand] a language; it's like your choice in clothing. There are things I would never wear because that's not the way I see myself. In the same way there are brands that I use. One of the ways, but no means the only way, because one of the ways consumers create meaning for themselves—who I am, where I'm situated in this universe, how I want to live. And since we live in a consumer society and buying things is necessarily a major act, the brand we surround ourselves with help us answer those questions. (Foster 2002)

Agencies appreciated that the brand was one means by which consumers construct meaning, but not the only one. In the fast changing mediated market, brands had to do more than project a personality; they also had to maintain a dynamic relationship with the consumer. According to Robert Foster, the "ultimate goal was to turn a brand into a 'love mark' so that it has mystery and passion and intimacy and al those other things that go into our most important and meaningful relationships".

The power of the brand was rearticulated; and although the story had been told before, it was given different inflections now, and was dramatized in the telling. The argument for creative branding went as follows: In a mature marketplace, where people's lives are saturated with goods and copying products is made easy by new regimes of customization and technology, the rational appeal emphasis that sold products by providing consumers a "reason why" to buy is no longer tenable. There were no longer any really new or improved product features; rather, all products had entered into the realm of the Coke and Pepsi symbolic wars, where the quality of the brand, not the quality of the product, was at stake. The only way to distinguish goods nowadays is symbolically through image, word, and the building of brand values. Creatives reminded both colleagues and clients that brands had new psychological significance for consumers.

> In a marketplace in which products can be knocked off so quickly, the type of advertising used has to change. It isn't enough just to suggest rational reasons why people want to buy your brands. You also have to connect them emotionally with the consumer; and consequently, what we do when we are working with psychologists and anthropologists is try to open this whole level of emotional connection. (personal interview, 2003)

Harvard marketing professor Douglas Holt (2003) has argued to the business community that they needed to stop trying to win a share of the consumer's "mind," for this paradigm is irrelevant in the mediated marketplace. He maintains that consumers now use brands "like film, books, television, sports and other popular cultural products, to construct our lifestyle narratives about who we are and whom we want to be." In his study the top twenty brands, Holt found that those who successfully negotiate with consumers "provide the myths and stories that consumers use to organize and understand their world, filling in the role that religion once played." Top brands are not conservative; rather, they enter into the heat of a "cultural contradiction," becoming involved in an event as a "cultural activist," contributing original expression to the culture as an artist, and developing an "authentic populist voice (which was not necessary "true," but which was so "compelling that believers feel it must be true." For Holt the age of the "iconic" brand has arrived, and success is no longer linked to understanding consumers through their mind, but rather through the culture in which they live. In the 1960s, Thomas Frank raised concerns about how advertisers put rebellion and counter-culture values in the service of consumption. By the twenty-first century, if we accept Holt's reading, brands had become our "comrades in arms," animating our cultural struggles.

Audience Negotiations and Emergent Advertising Designs

In the previous sections we have sought to characterize the changing role of the creative in the post-1980 period. In this next section we explore some of the advertising design formats that added to the already complex repertories established by the 1980s. These new formats reflected a different quality in the relationship between creatives and their audiences. Advertisers have stated over and over that audiences were more "savvy" than ever before. It was plain to researchers and to some academics that audiences did not necessarily accept any of the intended conclusions drawn in advertisements. Goldman, Parson, and Kersey describe the tug of war between creative and audience as follows: "Jaded viewers frequently become resistant to deciphering ads because they variously perceive that ads are stupid, manipulative, consumerist, fill in your blank. The continuous tug of war between advertisers and audiences plays itself out this way, back and forth between them" (available at http://www.lclark. edu/~goldman/global/pagesintro).

When questioned by researchers, audiences revealed a great deal of interest in advertising practices. They know very well that they are "targeted" and they often use marketing language to decode advertisements (O'Donohoe 1997). A representative sample of the British population found the public "more critical of advertising than it has ever been" (Tylee 1998). As we have seen, advertisers construct a vision of the consumer which informs their designs. Likewise, an awareness of the "savvy audience" has led to the conclusion that consumers, too, construct notions of the advertiser. Friestad and Wright developed a model asserting that consumers "interpret and cope with marketers' sales presentations and advertising" with knowledge they develop over time "about the tactics used in their persuasion attempts. This knowledge helps them identify how, when and why marketers try to influence them. It also helps them adaptively respond to their persuasion attempts so as to achieve their own goals" (1994). Knowledge of persuasion techniques is gleamed from common sense skepticism, word of mouth, exposure to the media, formal education (which often includes media literacy material), and mainstream media reports about the practices of advertisers.

Consumers are not necessarily always "goal seeking," for indeed many actions in the marketplace are habitual or arrived at during the point of purchase, and power circulates in the relationships between advertisers and audiences. Still, the general idea that advertisers and consumers interact through the folklore each holds about the other is a useful way of thinking about the creation and reception of messages. What is described by Friestad and Wright might be part of the more general process of "reflexivity" recognized by social theorists, which implies an active processing of signs, not simply to achieve goals, but as part of the creation of social relationships and self identity, and allows potential for critical awareness (Lash and Urry 1994).

We find that advertisers have been preoccupied with three concerns since the 1980s: first, how to reach audiences in a cluttered mediated marketplace; second, how to develop a means of speaking to international audiences; and third, finding a way to create acceptable messages for a culture in which attitudes toward women and ethnic minorities were points of conflict.

Designing for Impact: May I Have Your Attention Please?

Throughout their history, agencies have been striving to secure audience attention. But in the mediated market there is a new urgency to avoid being "zapped" or "zipped" by critical and bored audiences. For this reason, creative teams concentrate on generating more impact, more drama, more emotion, and more radical messages. To build intrigue and attract attention, advertisers draw on techniques they have accumulated over the years—music, noise, celebrities, humor, intensive visual imagery, and drama (Admap 2003). Children, animals, and humor (known crowd pleasers) are used endlessly, particularly on television (Decock and Pelsmacker 2000). Competing not only with other advertising messages, but all popular cultural products—film, video games and television—creatives secure audience attention with messages that have a rich filmic look and feel. Ads masquerade as movie trailers, sporting events, music videos, videogames, vignettes, reality TV programs, soap operas, and celebrity talk shows. Unwin's study of audiences suggests that advertisements that are "written in the language of a movie, a celebrity, a profession, or any familiar style...can be created more easily and can communicate more effectively than advertising written in usual advertising style" (Unwin 1982). In the thirty-second format, state of the art cinematography is the key to delivering maximum impact in minimum time.

> Nowadays, the basic new technique is your vignette commercial. In my opinion, it's a classic film approach—meaning that there's often no dialogue and the style emphasis is on the visual. The key thing to remember about the vignette commercials is that you can get so much more information into them. In fact, the vignettes more or less originated in response to the switch from 60 second to 30 second spots. They're a wonderful way to pack in information: all those scenes and emotions—cut, cut, cut. (Aden 1981, 180-2)

MacLachlan and Logan (1993) found that the average film shot length declined as the number of shots per commercial grew. In 1978 the average shot length was 3.8 seconds, but by the 1990s, 2.3 seconds. In 1978, there were on average 7.9 camera shots in a thirty-second advertisement; by the 1990s, the average had grown to 13.2 shots—a 33 percent increase. The only programming with shorter shot lengths than advertisements is MTV music videos (which are commercials themselves, of course). Having grown up in a media-saturated world, young viewers are thought to process information more quickly and to be more capable of multi-tasking than were prior generations. Doug Potter, vp marketing at McDonald's, observed that his firm's target audiences easily absorb the rapid-cutting messages:

> So that's the kids today and they are pretty able to soak it all in because they're growing up with MTV and VH1....If you look at kids today...one of the things that we see is the multitasking. They're on the phone, playing on the computer, with the radio and TV and it doesn't faze them. (Alison 2001)

Some clients still insist on information-packed executions with extended shots of the commodity. Yet, given the success of Nike and Levi's, it is easy to believe that this generation prefers fast-paced ads:

> Clients haven't changed that quickly, unfortunately. A lot of clients still think "slow it down, take it easy." But a lot of clients like Nike, Levi's, especially with the younger audiences, you can communicate a lot of information much quicker with much fewer words. So I think that's the big change. (personal interview, 2003)

Effectiveness is not just a matter of great creative work, but also of timing—raising in research communities questions about the weight or number of times that television messages needed to be repeated. Research revealed that high-impact messages were comprehended after one viewing—not the traditional three. Agencies alerted clients to the looming problem of wear out—the rapid rate at which audiences could became bored with the messages. In the past it was believed that some messages required time to "wear in," to allow audiences to become familiar with the characters or puzzle over an advertisement's meaning. Increasingly, ads that overstayed their welcome stimulated a negative affect toward the brand, or were zapped. Since timing is everything, more attention was devoted to cultural dynamics. Media planners carefully calibrated the comings and goings of commercials, but it was up to creative departments to come up with novel designs for the fast paced cycle of promotion. The young consumer was understood as a moving target, and creatives believed that they had to keep pace, or be one step ahead of them. Levi's, for example, was dedicated to keeping symbols "fresh" and continually renewing campaigns. Although its core brand values (freedom, original, and authentic) were rarely altered, what was meant by cool in the 1960s differs from cool in the 1990s; and creatives had to find the symbols that new generations could relate to. One creative commented:

> In a sense now, the message is evolving, it's staying ahead of me. Or staying with me. And that's what brilliant advertising does, it tracks the consumer. If you keep on saying the same thing to the consumer, he's going to move out of your window. So your window always has to move with him and try to anticipate where he moves next. (personal interview, 2003)

Nike would go one step further. The brand had originally evolved around the core value of athletic prowess and health, but by the late 1990s the "swoosh" was associated with a variety of themes, as the brand switched its core brand value to be simply the zeitgeist of cool (Holt 1999).

To fashion emotional scripts, agencies employed the best talent they could afford: Hollywood filmmakers, rather than TV producers. The commercial had become an art form wherein communication triumphed over crass selling. From the 1980s onward this meant that filmmakers had come to believe that doing ads would not hurt their Hollywood careers:

> The medium is taken seriously enough to have attracted the interest of no less a talent than Richard Avedon, whose Brooke Shields ads for Calvin Klein drew a great deal of attention a couple of years ago.... What's interesting about these ads is that they aspire to something like high art. (Hirschberg 1983, 55)

A host of other directors—Michael Cimino (*The Deer Hunter*), Alan Parker (*Fame, Midnight Express, Angel Heart*), Howard Zieff (*Private Benjamin*), and Adrian Lyne (*Flashdance, Fatal Attraction*) flit between movies and ads. Tony Scott, who has made modernist Diet Pepsi ads, also directed *The Hunger* and *Top Gun*). His brother, Ridley Scott (*Blade Runner, Alien, Gladiator, Black Hawk Down*), directed the innovative Chanel "Share the Fantasy" ads. Even nonmainstream directors like Mike Leigh, Spike Lee, and David Cronenberg sold their talents to Kleenz and Nike. Others established themselves as experts in various commercial genres. Steve Horn, for example, is a director specializing in emotion and feeling. Joe Sedelmaier is a master of offbeat comedy commercials. Music video directors also moved between promotion and cinema—Spike Jones moved from *Beasty Boys* promos to directing *Being John Malkovich* and *Adaptation*.

During this time, agencies also cemented their historical links to celebrity culture (Kaikati 1987). Following the directors, Hollywood PR people pushed their stables of stars to reach disaffected audiences. Celebrities enhance brand values. They are immediately recognizable, thereby effective in cutting through the clutter. A 1995 study in the UK revealed that celebrity campaigns were more likely to gain national headlines (Erdogan and Baker 2000). By the end of the twentieth century, it was estimated that approximately one-quarter of all commercials in the United Stated contained celebrity endorsement (Shimp 2000); in the UK the figure was one in five (Erdogan et al. 2001). Yet, while some advertisers experienced increased sales after signing a celebrity, the exact correlation between star endorsement and sales has been hard to establish, especially given their Hollywood price tags. According to Kaikati (1987), a celebrity-weary population could bring a brand down. Fame is a fickle beast that advertisers have difficulty controlling: The stars' flames can burn out before the contract was up, tarnishing the brand's appeal; negative information about a celebrity could infect a brand. Still, advertisers' interest in harnessing celebrity culture substantially increased.

Those who work in film knew that the perfect dramatic shot is nothing without accompanying sound. So too, sound design went beyond the catchy jingle. With an ear to the underground, music houses produced more bizarre and novel sound tracks for ads (Block 2003, 6). Agencies had long fed on popular music, but the relationship was reversed as artists began to gain record company contracts after popularizing their music in advertising. Cultural resistance toward "selling out" wore down as advertising was legitimated as a form of entertainment. To secure and maintain musical success in the mediated marketplace demands considerable self-promotion; musicians recognized that advertising is just another promotional tool—and that it seemed foolish not to adopt the practice of making a well-paid music video. Highly respected musicians signed on to the growing roster of licensing deals. Bob Dylan sold rights to his song "The times they are a-changin'" to promote Internet banking; Madonna and the Rolling Stones have taken money from Microsoft. In 2000 Sting sold Jaguar automobiles the rights for a song on his poor-selling album. Licensing is expensive: Original music from music houses can cost $10,000 to $50,000, licensing between $250,000 and up to $14 million—the sum paid to Celine Dion by Chrysler).

Humor also continues to be liberally used, since it is known to cut through the thickest audience resistance, and is believed to secure attention, engagement, liking, and positive affect towards the brand (White 2003). Audiences willingly will sit through a sales message for a laugh. As one creative noted:

> People respond to humor more than anything.... [The] younger target, especially a young, male target, if you don't entertain them in some way—it doesn't have to be humorous but you have to entertain them—they will not take your commercial seriously.... If it is boring or phoney or hyped in any way they have contempt. It's a very tough market. (Akert 2001)

But humor is also troublesome. It works best for the young, but it is highly subjective and culturally specific; thus it is rarely used in international campaigns. Humor is more useful for promoting some products than others: Almost all beverage or snack food ads try to get a laugh, but because humor is thought to reduce credibility, it is rarely used for status and identity goods such as jewelry, fashion apparel, or cosmetics (White 2003). In 1973 only 15 percent of U.S. advertisements contained humor; by 1989 24 percent did, and by 2001, 33 percent did (Toncar 2001). In the past, UK and Japanese creatives have been more likely than Americans to use humor; yet by 2001 American creatives were as likely as those in the UK to employ it. However the types of humor used remain culturally distinct: "Understatement was used in 16% of all humorous UK ads, but in just over 1% of all humorous U.S. ads, while jokes were used significantly more often in U.S. ads (37% vs. 19%). In addition, UK ads used more satire, and this difference approaches significance (18% vs. 10%)" (Toncar 2001).

Stimulating Curiosity: The Shocking and the Bizarre

Some creatives made their mark by disrupting and disturbing audience expectations, using their thirty seconds to create bizarre, shocking, and alienating messages. Believing that curiosity stimulates attention, creatives gave audiences images to puzzle over. An example is found in the work of the London agency HHCL, who opened shop in 1987 with the promise of providing "radical professionalism" that would storm the Bastille of traditional ad design. In the early 1990s, HHCL won the account of the British telephone bank, First Direct. To promote the service, creatives employed stark images of buckets and other household items. One television ad depicted a clothes line moving gently in the breeze with colored pegs clipped to it, set to the sound of Inuit chanting songs. The spot ended with a quick flash of the brand. Viewed from the context of other ads, the message was alien. First, it was a thirty-second long single shot, strange to eyes accustomed to rapid firing MTV editing; second, it had no throbbing music, no high action antics, no celebrities, no "in your face" humor; third, it was a shot of everyday domesticity. Not only did the spot not feel like an advertisement, it was highly postmodern, in the sense that it was impossible to stitch together the signifier (clothes line and chant), to the signified (the bank). The point of the ad was to break clutter, to encourage people to scratch their heads—the brand value which was communicated was, "we are different." HHCL became highly successful for its bizarre shtick through the early 1990s, expanding globally and inspiring other new agencies (such as Mother). But by the end of the twentieth century, such radical tactics had become exhausted, as audiences quickly learned the game. HHCL designs were a bit like Marcel Duchamp's famous toilet—out of place at first, thus shocking, but commonplace afterward. The foundering agency was recently brought under the wing of WPP and renamed HHCL Red Cell.

Creatives used shock tactics to get audience attention. Ads showed rabid wolves attacking marching bands; characters had their limbs bitten off by sea mammals, chopped off by axes, and ground in wood chippers. Creatives with a brief to promote a mobile phone text-messaging feature scripted a young man in a contest of wills with his ferret. While the ferret growled, the young man stuck his tongue out at it. The ferret catapulted to his face and sunk its fangs into the man's tongue. The man leapt up, attempting to pull the ferret from his face, only to inflict more pain. "Folie" artists simulated horror film quality sound, with the screeching ferret and wailing victim. The phone saved the day, as the man punched an SOS call into his phone. The tag line noted: "For those times when you can't talk." Creatives tapped into the naughty pleasure of seeing physical harm inflicted on others.

New digital technologies and advances in special effects greatly enhanced creatives' ability to produce fantastical ads cheaply. Shock was considered an economical means to get a brand noticed. A senior creative at Freeman and Partners, an agency typecast as the "kings of shock," claimed that the firm was driven into the genre due to its clients' low budgets: "We don't have the No. 1 brand in the categories.... The budget is always 10 percent of the main competitor's so what are you going to do with that 10 percent? Something to get talked about." The agency's creative director, Eric Silver, noted, "Our goal is to get viewers' attention by any means" (Walker 2002). Creatives argued that shock techniques were appealing to youth raised on a diet of cartoon violence and sick *Saturday Night Live* humor. Heavy-hitting humor—such as *Beavis and Butt Head*, and *America's Funniest Home Videos*—grew more frequent in the United States. Cutting through the clutter seemed to leave little room for delicacy: "Subtle humour may not be viewed as an effective way to break through the clutter of the U.S network television environment" (Walker 2002) But these ads often troubled animal rights groups and parents.

For example, one British spot depicted a young man vomiting up a dog, who shook stomach contents off himself as he growled at the young man, only to disappear when the young man took a breath mint to cure his "dog breath": Halitosis had come a long way. This advertisement inspired 580 calls to the regulator from angered animal rights activists and parents. Animal rights activists despised the disregard for animal care (although both the ferret and dog were hyper-real, digitally rendered animals). The ad was pulled, but the press coverage of the controversy provided free media time for the advertiser. The ferret spot caused a similar stir in the U.S., but the young female creatives who produced the spot defended their work: "We weren't too worried, because the people who would think it was gross weren't exactly in our target market" (Walker 2002). Indeed, the displeasure of older consumers became welcome, as it was thought to fuel youth's embrace of certain brands for the rebellion value they offered. Young males caught in oedipal struggles to distinguish themselves from the command of their fathers' particularly admired inappropriate ads. MIT professor Henry Jenkins argued that, in the North American context, shock ads felt freeing and liberating to a generation raised on political correctness (Walker 2002).

Rebellion continued to litter the design landscape; but the more rebellion was commodified, the harder advertisers had to labor in order to produce the same result in the 1990s. Consumer generations had moved on. For the post-baby boomers, raised under more liberal child rearing techniques and situated in a culture where manners, clothing, and institutional relations had relaxed considerably, rebellion took on new meaning. On one level, cultural revolt had to become more biting; on another, rebellion was not called for, as studies indicated that many contemporary youth had very close relationships with their parents and, in fact, rebelled by being conservative, seeking safety and reassurance as much as independence.

As advertisers' messages grew harder, the sales pitch grew softer, particularly in the United States. Since the 1960s creatives had tried to dampen the hard sell, which they deemed inappropriate for addressing audiences who loathed being told what to do and buy. Advertisers in this country looked to British and Japanese creative work for clues on how to address audiences disrespectful of their commercial designs, for European and Japanese advertising had developed a more soft sell emphasis. A comparison of Japanese and American advertisements revealed that Japanese ads used more humor, celebrities, and female voices. Ads were less likely to mention product price, warranty/guarantees, safety, overly boast about the product, or bribe the consumer into submission. Hard sales were considered rude and contemptuous of consumer's intellect and the company's integrity (Lin 1993).

UK creatives had developed an international reputation for their subtle, indirect style of humor, and those in the United States had begun to believe that their savvy and reflexive audiences might be appeased with softer sales. An art director explained:

> We took some lessons from them [European creatives]. We in North America used to be conceited and think we knew it all, but we learned from them. TV was the reason, because they had been doing the magazine format with all the ads together and this was a later development here. They had 20 commercials altogether, so the question was how do you get them to remember

you if you are #4? How to stand out and be memorable? If you adopt the hard sell approach the consumer might say, "Oh, who needs this, I'll go get a beer." In England and in Japan they learned to be subtle, entertaining, amusing. So more emotion came to this country. We learned from that. So you get attention and interest and people remember the product. There's a great creative drive. (personal interview, 2003)

In a classic illustration of a soft sell, creative director Paul Cappelli explained why he ignored the advice of others who suggested to pour Coke on the pinecone as the magic fertilizer that made the gigantic Christmas tree in New York's Time Square grow in his award winning commercial (grandma's fruitcake was used instead): "I said, 'Eh, it's just a little too much. It's better as the toast. It's better as the cigarette. It's the afterglow. It's a job well done. Here's the reward.'" Paul Cappelli also noted that emotional advertisements were "very difficult to pull off so they don't come across as sappy and schmaltzy, but come across as genuinely heart-tugging, emotional commercials" (O'Barr 2001). Advertising creative Max Sutherland argued that the "reason why" hard sell format had offered consumers a tangible selling point, thus was not subject to the same scrutiny as ads that sought to entertain or emotionally move consumers. Audiences must allow their heart string to be tugged, but they would not be jerked about by messages they found inauthentic or uninteresting.

Audiences had little real political power to shape the mediated marketplace. Nor did they have the symbolic privileges of advertisers. However, they did have a modicum of control over where they spent their attention; so to secure consumers' interpretive labor, advertisers had to listen, at least partially. The softer sales pitch illustrated the outcome of an advertiser/audience negotiation. Advertising increasingly looked like popular culture. Some argued that the sale in advertising of this period became so soft that messages were transformed into a "new kind of ambient short-form entertainment" (Gimein 2002). Audiences greatly appreciated the changes in design. Over two-thirds of the adult population in Britain reported that they "enjoyed seeing advertising" (ASA 2000). Another study found that audiences felt advertising had become more clever and invited more involvement: "Advertising is cleverer now, very much so...because you have got to watch the advert, pay attention, to get what they mean" (Ford, Hutchinson, and Rothwell 2002, 15). Audiences highly valued this change.

Speaking to the Other: The Values of Advertising

Advertisers negotiated means with foreign audiences in their global advertising designs. Much of the research relating to global advertising has focused on the question of cultural convergence as measured by social values and lifestyles represented in advertising. Values can be thought of as a specific culture's preferred ways of conduct, end states, or beliefs (Rokeach in Caillat and Mueller, 1996). Pollay and Gallagher (1990) found that North American advertising focused on "certain attitudes, behaviours and values, lifestyles and philosophies," and they believed that over time, advertising normalized "materialism, submission and seduction, selfishness and greed," leading to a dissatisfaction with life, "disrespect of family elders, tradition and authority," and a potential rise in crime rates.

Anthropologists have long believed that cultural values differ widely, particularly around such socially embedded issues as status, gender, family, ethics, and mores. Even countries that speak a common language may require multiple kinds of advertising address. De Caillat and Meuller's study of beer advertisements in the United States and the United Kingdom found considerable differences in how brands were presented. The ads for American beer emphasized individuality, modernity, and achievement and used direct speech; whereas British beer ads were more likely to emphasis history, tradition, and eccentricity and use an indirect form of address. Emotional and sexual appeals were also used much more frequent in American ads, while British ads presented humor in over 90 percent of the sample. The longer history of pub culture in Britain and the legacy of Christian principles and prohibition in the United States were used to explain why British beer ads showed beer drinking as an everyday event, and lone drinkers. The U.S. commercials situated beer drinking in celebratory settings and never depicted a lone drinker (considered a sign and promotion of alcoholism in that culture). De Caillat and Meuller (1996) noted that differences like these draw into question the viability of standardized campaigns:

> The nature of this study makes the argument for specialization particularly strong: In two countries where most marketing factors are strikingly similar—physical environment, economic development, industry conditions, marketing institutions, language and legal restrictions—the differences in culture alone are significant enough to warrant a specialized advertising approach. (Caillat and Mueller 1996)

In another sample of British and American television advertisements, Katz and Lee found that lifestyle and personalization occurred more frequently in American commercials than in British ones. They argued that television advertisements in the United States were more people-oriented or subjective, showing how the product fit into the viewer's way of life, and/or how it was right for the average viewer. In the United Kingdom, advertisers paid more attention to what the good or service was or did. This finding was consistent with others revealing that British ads tended to be more informative and rational (Weinberger and Spotts 1989;Frith and Sengupta 1991). However, these studies also found that the depiction of cultural values varied considerably by product category (Katz and Lee 1992).

Yet, as Harvard business professor John Quelch argued, there was also "ample evidence that consumers around the world are very similar in their aspirations, emotions and ways of thinking" (Lannon and Quelch 2003). Indeed, he noted that locally-embedded advertising managers sometimes accentuated cultural differences, because their job depended on being aware of them. To resolve the tension between the cultural embeddedness of consumption and the efficiencies of globalization, advertising creatives turned to what became know as the "international style," based on universal themes of fun, progress, and family. Escaping the language barrier, international ads tend to be highly visual, and to use animals, cartoons, or celebrities as a means of creating character identification without making reference to a particular ethnic group. Others have argued that international campaigns should tap into archetype images, stories, fairy tales, and ancient heroes, as tales that offer universal insights into the broader human condition would be accepted in all cultures (Heaven 1999, Howard-Spink 2002).

Aware of the cultural embeddedness of values, corporations from the United States now go softly into many foreign markets. In 2004, Coca-Cola employed the theme of social harmony in a multicultural world in an advertisement produced by Mother Ltd. UK. Produced for the British market, the ad depicts a young black woman walking down the street handing out bottles of Coke to pleased onlookers, singing a song about how she wished she could "give all the love that she had" (namely, a bottle of Coke). This touching rendition of racial harmony so impressed corporate headquarters that Coke decided to run the campaign in the United States. In fact, Coke's current "think local, act local" strategy attempts to downplay the drink's "image as an emblem of American culture" (MacArthur 2004), which doesn't play well against brand rivals like Mecca Cola (which has boomed in politically sensitive areas like the Middle East) or fruit drinks in India. With $20 billion in global sales, Coke's global branding efforts in 2004 would be almost exclusively focused on global sports events like Euro 2002 football and the Olympics (which it has sponsored since 1924) in Athens, providing its preferred channels to a global audience in an international marketplace characterized by fragmentation and niche messages as much as universal appeals (Walsh 2004).

In the wake of these changes, advertising's visions of a cosmopolitan, affluent, worldwide lifestyle of consumerism were tempered by a revolt arguing for the indigenous, the authentic, the sustainable, and the diverse. Never before had there been such a vogue for the ethnic, the organic, and the exotic. World music, ethnic art, global cinema and theater, multicultural advertising, tribal fashion, fusion cuisine, Eurasian architecture, oriental design, Eastern religion, alternative medicine, new–world literature—the Western consumer was attracted more than ever by the cultures and products of distant lands. The exotic global otherness of the world was, after all, the reason why people traveled and ate out. In the United Kingdom, curry became the unofficial national dish. The diversity of values in contemporary advertising was itself one of the strongest indications of globalization.

East of Eden

While the United States had the capital, the corporate culture, and the military dominance to straddle the globe, it lacked one of the most important factors for continued economic expansion: populations whose circumstances were changing. By contrast, much has been written about the opportunities provided by the emerging Asian nations. By the year 2010, Asia will account for 59 percent of the world's population; growth rates in Asia will be more than four times those in Europe (Chiarelli 2003). Over time, the productivity and birth rates of Asia made this region too important to ignore any longer. The interest of global advertisers was strong, given Asian countries' potential billion consumers, particularly an increasingly affluent middle class. But until 1996 the lack of media had stood in their way. This changed under the forces of media expansion we outlined in the previous chapter.

In China, until 1996 Coke was chastised as "spiritual pollution" and McDonald's was experiencing problems in its Beijing outlets; thereafter the Chinese government's easier acceptance of foreign investment and the opening up to commercial speech precipitated major changes. The global media erected to unify the country was now accessible to corporate interests. Changing conditions in China proved increasingly tempting to global brands both from Japan and the United States. Laying communication cables is one thing, speaking to consumers is quite another, however: The West still faced the enormous challenge of learning to speak to these ancient but rapidly changing Eastern cultures. But by 1997 all the major agencies (Saatchi and Saatchi, JWT, Leo Burnett) had offices in China working on this problem (Wang 1997).

North American advertisers often sought to parlay the global popularity of Hollywood celebrities and pop music to transcend local cultures (Erdogan and Baker 2000). This strategy, long an accepted part of the Japanese advertising scene, was tried throughout the burgeoning Asian world, where American film stars sung the praises of products they would never be associated with in their home markets. But in Japan there was evidence of a retreat from using washed-up Hollywood celebrities whose brand value was increasingly lost in translation in global markets. The power of the Western celebrity in Asian regions faded gradually, often replaced by the more familiar voices of the booming Canto media. Short of a few celebrities of Beckham-esque stature, the use of white faces to advertise luxury brands, common in the 1970s and 1980s, more or less died out in some Asian markets. As one marketer put it, few see "any cache in white people using things anymore". Advertisers in Asia gave up mixed-race and Eurasian in favor of local talent (Lord 2004).

Researchers also sought to confirm whether Asian cultures shared the same basic emotions, arguing that Chinese campaigns could be built around these universals, if they existed. For example, Huang (1998) found in a sample of 247 students from the United Kingdom, Taiwan and mainland China, that although participants responded differently to social emotions such as humor, warmth, and surprise, they responded identically to basic emotions such as happiness, love, and sadness. Mooiji (1998) similarly illustrated the challenges of humor in international advertising, because it so often hinged on cultural context and understanding that does not travel well; other studies showed that another marked feature of the international style was that it was less funny than local addresses (Appelbaum and Halliburton 1993). High levels of practicality in North American advertising were also noted by Pollay (1983) in a major historical study of advertising values: among all the universal themes of friendship, romance, and fun, practicality persistently ranks the highest. Richards et al. (2000) also confirmed this finding in British financial, credit card, and car ads over the post-1950 period, revealing an increase in practical information over the time period. The evidence was stacked against the thesis that there had been a great shift to highly emotive, symbolic values within so-called postmodern cultural formations.

In a sample of 800 television ads from the United States between 1996 and 2002, Goldman and Papson found evidence of the revival of modernist values so typical of the booming hi-tech world, which tied "individual well-being with the 'twin gods' of social progress and scientific achievement" (Goldman et al. 1998–2003). Others noted that modernity and the powers of new technologies were the oft-repeated dominant values found in China and Hong Kong print and television advertisements, particularly international or joint product advertisements for high tech products (Cheng 1994; Cheng and Schweitzer 1996; Chan 1999). In the information age, there seemed to be a growing cultural convergence around a progressive modernist ideology.

But modernism is not identical with pragmatism. Several studies exploring whether Asian advertisements were moving from a utility frame to a symbolic frame (as Western cultures were assumed to have done) have been more equivocal. In a study of 572 Chinese magazine articles, Cheng (1994) found a shift from utilitarian to more emotional and symbolic values; Cheng and Schweitzer (1996) reached a similar conclusion after exploring 500 Chinese television commercials. However, other studies made the picture more complex. The very premise that ads from the United States and the United Kingdom had moved to a postmodern condition rooted in spectacle and unconscious differences, beyond reason, utility and practicality was disconfirmed. For example, Keown (1992) found that television and radio ads from the United States contained higher numbers of information cues than those aired in China and South Korea where advertising was highly regulated. While commercials from the United States blended symbolic and utilitarian values, Chinese ads relied heavily on symbolic values alone.

Looking for a More Sensitive Voice

The deregulation of the marketplace and the expansion of the mass media coincided with a heightened concern for advertising representations. Commercial media were recognized as key socializing institutions, fully integrated into cultural dynamics. As a cultural resource incorporated in identity projects, advertising was heavily scrutinized and subject to new expectations. Corporations won the rights to self regulate and extend their positions, under the expectation that they would behave responsibly. Audiences were aware that these institutions produced both good and bad, and, quite rightly, expected corporations to behave in socially appropriate ways (even if consumer folklore suggested they probably would not). Advertising became a window through which the public judged the morality of the corporate world.

On university campuses in the 1980s, particularly in North America, language and images became subject to radical critique (supported by cultural studies, postmodernism and post-structural academic movements). Discursive categories (such as Oriental, mankind, and cripple) were challenged, and expectations grew for more inclusive and equal representations. There grew up an expectation that the representations in advertising should be progressive. While older people continued to be offended by advertisers' use of sexual images, violence, and bad language, young people were much more concerned about how people (particularly vulnerable groups) were portrayed (ASA 2000). Yet, young consumers also felt that people should not be 'over sensitive' about advertising images. Many agendas flowed through the politics of representation. Some were more progressive than others, but this does not detract from the point that a struggle over symbols was inflamed during this time.

Indeed, advertising had long been a contested terrain (Nava, 1997), but concerns now expanded. Advertising did not simply denigrate culture or serving as a handmaiden to capitalism; now it was also held accountable for how it depicted audiences, particularly women and ethnic minorities. In this section, we explore these issues. We cannot provide a comprehensive review of the complex and contested terrain of representational politics. Our aim is to touch upon these issues in brief, to illustrate how advertisers sought to negotiate with audiences' changing concerns about stereotypes.

Housewife, Superwoman, Partner: Advertising's Representations of Women

Since the 1970s opposition had grown toward the way advertisers represented women (White 2002). Whereas gender politics had traditionally been carried out on the street, in parliament, and within domestic spaces, Janice Winship noted that advertising became the key site of gender struggle: " Negotiations of gendered relations are not only increasingly played out in media text, but that audiences also articulate their own views by reference to them" (2000, 48).

Women were increasingly politicized about their representations in the media. Young women on university campuses were schooled with powerful educational videos, such as Jean Kilborn's "Killing Us Softly" series (Kilborn 2000), which showed the many representational crimes that advertisers inflict-ed upon women, and Sut Jhally's "Dream Worlds," which revealed the unwhole-some depictions of women in music videos (Jhally 1995). Women's political organizations added representations to their list of concerns. Ford and LaTour (1993) studied the attitudes of 130 members of the National Organization for Women (NOW) and 94 women from the League of Women Voters (LOWV), and found that members of NOW were highly critical of images that objecti-fied women, limited their role to the home, or offered unrealistic standards of slenderness or beauty. The opinions of these politicized women argued that advertisers were particularly influential in the culture as a whole; and they advised that creatives "should be particularly wary of stressing the wrong ele-ments" in their advertising (Ford and Latour 1993).

Advertisers did not seem to be keeping pace with the changing roles of women in society. Women make up 52 percent of the population of the United States, yet are under- represented in advertisements. Dual incomes are the norm, and 60 percent of women now work outside the home, as op-posed 25 percent in 1950 (Engel, Blackwell, and Miniard 1993). Women are replacing men as the principle breadwinner (Googins 1991) and have adopted new attitudes to marriage and children, yet they continued to be presented in two predominant roles: carer or sex object. Women were more likely to be shown in the home engaged in housework, while men were more likely to be shown in empowered professional roles or at leisure (Jaffe and Berger 1994). Debate centered around the impact of advertisers' unachievable body images on women, particularly on young audiences. Women in ads continued to look younger than men, implying that older women were unimportant or non existent. Women were interpreted by audiences as looking more pleasant and decorative than men, who appear "serious" and confident (Waters, & Ellis 1996, 101). As Kilborn graphically displayed in *Killing us Softly III*, men have gotten bigger and women smaller.

There is nothing inherently "natural" about the use of these particular gender images, and not all countries display women in the American way. A major comparison of the portrayal of men and women in magazines found that Swedish magazines were more likely to present women in recreational roles, whereas ads from the United States were more likely to show men and women in decorative roles. Within the women's magazine category, Swedish magazine advertisers portrayed women in working or recreational roles, and less in decorative roles in comparison to magazine advertisers from the United States (Tjernlund and Wiles 1991).

Aware of the contention that surrounded their representations, advertisers from the United States attempted to negotiate a new mode of address. Two new female stereotypes were offered. In the 1980s the "superwoman" appeared, a yuppie female who did it all—achiever at her job and a six-figure income, maintainer of an immaculate home, with beautiful and well-adjusted children, and a sexy figure. Women were shown buying for themselves, not simply for their family. The superwoman image did not survive into the 1990s, however. As one critic put it, replacing the harried housewife with the superwoman was hardly progressive. Advertisers tried again, presenting women working with males in the domestic and work arena. These "egalitarian depictions reworked both male and female representations" (Jaffe and Berger 1994). Klassen et al. (1993) used Goffman's frame analysis, "which concentrates on postures, facial expressions, relative sizes, positioning and placing, etc." and confirmed earlier studies that found that "a disproportionately high number of advertisements…portrayed women in 'traditional' poses," but that 'equality portrayals' were rising." More recently, there appears to have been a trend towards role reversal in the representation of women. A British ad for the Alcopop Archers showed a barman contorting into a variety of stereotypical female fantasy poses—a fireman, a French lover, a stripper, a caveman—with the tagline "one for the ladies." However, since they are straightforward binary opposites, these role reversals did little to alter traditional gender stereotypes.

Jaffe and Berger (1994) interviewed married adult women to explore their attitudes towards three dominant advertising representations of women: traditional, superwoman, and egalitarian displays. They found that the egalitarian motifs were preferred, even by women who self reported to be more traditionalist and conservative (see Table 12.1).

A host of studies have confirmed that portrayals of women have a considerable impact on the marketing of a product, and that women preferred modern role models (Jaffe 1991; Jaffe and Berger 1988; Leigh, Rethans, and Whitney 1987). Critics such as Rena Bartos (1995) used evidence like this to remind advertisers that it was bad business not to acknowledge women's resentment

TABLE 12.1 Mean Advertising Effectiveness by Positioning

Mean Ad Effectiveness	Traditional	Superwoman	Egalitarian	Significance Level
Purchase interest	2.76	3.72	4.50	$p < 0.001$
Affect	2.68	3.70	5.00	$p < 0.001$

Source: Jaffe and Berger 1994, available online at www.warc.com.

toward their designs. She argued that advertisers should seek to please women the most, given that they account for 80 percent of all purchase decisions. Bartos encouraged advertisers to undertake more research and listen to women's concerns. Women have complex lifestyles and lifecycles, and their needs vary according to whether they were "married with children, married without children, not married and with no children, or not married but with children." Women also make different investments in their careers, some seeing work as just a job, while others experience their careers as a significant part of their lifestyle and identity. There is no easy formula for speaking to women, Bartos concluded, advocating a "dialogue with the consumer" at the start of each creative project to ensure that the representations they produced were "personally involving and relevant to those consumers" (1995).

But Worlin's (2003) exhaustive meta-study revealed that for every study undertaken between 1970 and 2002 to depict women that illustrated an improvement in gender representation, there was another showing that representations of women had become worse. Depressingly, the most progressive representations of women occurred at the height of feminist agitation, in the 1970s. Advances in female representations in ads have been cyclical since, subject to backlashes and backslides. Why have advertisers' depictions of women not been more progressive? One explanation pointed to a 1990s feminist backlash in which young women grew resistant to what they took to be the overt political correctness of some feminist positions (Feludi 1992). These women sought to distance themselves from what they perceived as middle-class versions of womanhood, understood as a form of male bashing, a denial of women's sexualized enjoyment, and the pleasures they derived through looking at fashion magazines.

Quinlan (2000) argued that advertisers' failure to communicate thoughtfully with the female sector happened because males dominate agency creative departments. As Nixon illustrated, creative department attract particularly brazen males with interests that are far distant from how women "think, talk, and interact" (Nixon 2003). Critics have argued that "it matters who makes it," but to date there has been little success in breaking down the gender divide in creative departments. Sex is an easy, tried and true cultural trope, and of all the tools in the advertisers' handbook, it remains a best seller. According to Jack Solomon, "The sexual explicitness of contemporary advertising is a sign not so much of American sexual fantasies as of the lengths to which advertisers will go to get attention. Sex never fails as an attention-getter, and in a particularly competitive and expansive era for American marketing, advertisers like to bet on a sure thing" (quoted in Berger 2004, 83).

A content analysis of 2,209 network TV commercials selected from different time slots found women in daytime programs tended to appear as American housewives and in subservient roles. During male-dominated sportscasts, women morphed into sex objects. In the prime-time evening slots, when professional women were in the audience, "women are portrayed in more egalitarian and sophisticated fashion" (Craig 1992, 100). What this study reveals was that the fragmentation of the media provides advertisers with increased leeway to address various audience segments with different stereotypes. This again should caution researchers against discussing advertising representations as a whole, for they change significantly depending upon media and time of showing.

Many women dislike how advertisers represented them, but their political discontent tends to manifest in ways that do not threaten advertisers. Pollay and Lysonki (1990) found that although both men and women in the United States, Denmark, Greece, and New Zealand had all grown more resentful toward sexist depictions of women in the 1980s, none were willing to undertake product boycotts. As the authors noted, "Few are motivated to put their money where their mouth is, even after consciousness-raising." Judith Williamson (1978, 167), arguing from a broader perspective some time ago, saw the lack of any real attention to the criticisms of the female audience as simply another illustration of advertising able to absorb criticism: "Advertisements can incorporate anything, even re-absorb criticisms of themselves, because they refer to it, devoid of content. The whole system of advertising is a great recuperate: it will work on any material at all, it will bounce back uninjured from both advertising restriction laws and criticisms of its basic functions."

In a review of British television advertising Renee Dickason (2000) noted that advertisers' representations of gender had attracted the attention of the wider media, and found evidence that advertisers had changed their mode of address to women: "The 1990s undoubtedly witnessed a change in attitudes and greater balance between the sexes." But advertisers remain very conservative in their representations of the sexes, and she concluded that "the question of the relations between men and women in the 1990s had become more complicated, although how far advertisements need to respect propriety, and the extent to which they represent a true or aspiration vision of contemporary culture, remain unanswered questions."

We find many limitations to the power of audiences. In the niched marketplace advertisers tailor their stereotypes of women to suit different audiences. They continue to rely on women's tolerance to buy brands and watch television programming designed for men, and they are not inspired to radically change their mode of address toward women, for opposition from some quarters rarely translates into harsh consequences for them. Still, the attitudes of audiences have entered into advertisers' folklore about consumers, and so when sexist tropes are used today, they are cleverly disguised beneath a veil of tongue-in-cheek humor.

The Darker Shade of Pale: Negotiating Ethnicity

In the global marketplace good ideas and capital flow everywhere easily, but so do people. Urban centers all over the world have become rich mixes of different immigrant groups. Former empires like Britain and France, along with their former colonies, wrestle with the process of decolonization. New global conflicts create refugees, camps, and asylum-seekers needing safe havens. Awareness of racism has grown, and at least on paper is no longer tolerated in cultures which think of themselves as democratic and that had witnessed the Holocaust, the civil rights movements of the 1960s, and the struggles in South Africa in the 1980s. Advertising has been caught up in these larger social and cultural processes and has been subjected to criticism for its representations of "the other" (O'Barr 1994).

This period saw a rise in the number of ethnic representations in advertising, a change motivated by several interests. First, to avoid criticism advertisers must find ways of keeping pace with contemporary cultural values, and at least in urban centers there is a growing valuing of diversity and concern about open racism. Second, as we saw earlier, "the other" is a useful trope for associating goods with a sense of novelty and exoticism: The educated middle classes in particular have a taste for the "cosmopolitan" and diversity (Holt 2000). We also observed how blacks have been popularized, particular in contemporary music cultures.

The interest in reaching out to ethnic communities was also based on the interest in building new markets. As politicians increasingly awoke to the importance of the ethnic vote, advertisers and marketers became conscious of the growing economic strength of ethnic markets. In 2003, the Hispanic market made up 13 percent of the U.S. population and comprised over 40 percent of the population of the city of Los Angeles in 2003—a number that is still expanding. This market was estimated to control $630 billion in spending power (Torres and Gelb 2002). African Americans are also a powerful force, many having moved into the middle classes, accounting for 10 percent of the population. Asians have been the fastest growing population segment in the United States. Overall, ethnic minorities are thought to account for 30 percent of all consumer purchases in the United States. Ethnic minorities account for approximately 8 percent of Britain's population, and 30 percent of London's population. In 2003 British advertisers were encouraged by the Institute of Practitioners in Advertising to make a more concerted effort to chase the estimated 32 million pound nonwhite market. Industry officials encouraged advertisers to address their attention to what they called this "brown pound" demographic. In short, market expansion and cultural change were inseparable components in the politics of minority representations.

By 2000 nearly 50 percent of the top 1,000 international companies were engaged in ethnic marketing. Many ethnic groups with different languages have their own media, which is influential in purchase decisions. For example, Rosslow and Nicholls (1996) found that Hispanics were more likely to purchase goods with messages that were in Spanish and shown on Spanish rather than English television; this was true for both Spanish-speaking and bilingual viewers. Interest in the ethnic market fueled the drive toward niche marketing in cable television, Internet, and below the line strategies. In the United States, marketers learned that middle-class blacks watched very similar programs to middle-class white consumers, and shared similar values and tastes; thus, they were targeted with similar advertising appeals (Turow 1998). But more disadvantaged blacks showed differences in their preferences, particularly in relation to the situation comedy genre. As we learned above, humor is greatly influenced by cultural context.

As with women, ethnic minorities do not get jobs in significant numbers in the advertising industry in the United States. African Americans account for 10 percent of the total workforce, but only 5 percent in the advertising industry, and are rarely in creative positions. Although the advertising industry, both in Britain and the United States, continues to announce its interest in hiring more blacks, this goal seems difficult for the agencies to achieve. But the number of ethnic minorities represented in advertising did increase. According to research by the Institute of Practitioners in Advertising and Extreme Media, in one year (2003/2004) the number of ethnic minorities in British advertising rose from 2 percent to 7 percent due to awareness initiatives and the drive for the "brown pound."

But how people were represented remained a concern. Taylor and Lee (1994) found that the ethnic groups represented in ads varied, depending upon the target audience for a given magazine. In a random selection of top ten U.S. publications in business, women's, general interest, and popular science/ mechanics magazines, researchers found that Asian Americans dominated technology and business publications (75 percent), whereas black models occurred in only 35 percent of the tech advertisements. Asians also dominated business publications (72.3 percent). Yet Asians were less likely to appear in female or general interest magazines, appearing only once in two hundred *Vogue* fashion ads and twice in *Time* magazine advertisements. Over 50 percent of the black and Hispanic portrayals were in the women's and general interest categories. Asians appeared in business settings in 60 percent of ads, whereas black and Hispanic models were more likely to appear in outdoor, home, and social settings. Asians were more likely to be portrayed as coworkers (60 percent) than blacks (40 percent) or Hispanics (48 percent). The authors argued that depictions of ethnic minorities reinforced common stereotypes: Blacks and Hispanics are shown as being more social and physically competent, whereas Asian Americans are depicted as "intelligent, hardworking, technically skilled, serious, [but] not socially adept or fun loving" (Taylor and Lee 1994).

Fletcher's (2003) study for The Broadcasting Standards Commission in Britain explored 273 hours of prime time television (i.e., from 17:30 hours to midnight) in the United Kingdom's three terrestrial commercial channels for a two-week period in the autumn/winter 2001 and spring/summer 2002, capturing a total of 5,591 ads. One in seven commercials represented an ethnic minority. Overall, blacks appeared more than other minorities, with Asian people represented the least. It was consistently found that advertisements with ethnic minorities had more participants. Thus, it appeared that the compromise advertisers seemed to make toward the demand for ethnic representations was the "diversity" shot, which showed white people alongside people of other ethnic backgrounds. White characters continued to assume the most prominent and major roles. Thus, ethnic minorities were notably less likely to become major participants than their white colleagues, even when they appeared in the same ads (11 percent vs. 17 percent). Furthermore, their white counterparts in the base comparison sample were twice as likely (30 percent) to enjoy a major role (Fletcher 2003). Similarly, a study of a three-hour sample of prime time network television commercials from the United States found that 26 percent of the messages contained black characters, and only 6 percent Hispanic (Wilkes & Valencia 1989). As with the Fletcher study, nonwhite characters were most likely to be found with large numbers of other characters, and were rarely depicted as a central character.

The use of the "black body" stirred particular concerns. Blacks were most likely to appear in ads as athletes or music stars. Celia Lury (1996) argued that ethnicity has long been known as an important tool for making goods appear novel. She noted how black characters were fetishized in advertising; for example, black female fashion models were more likely to appear as exotics in leopard and jungle prints. Bristor et al. (1995) completed a nonrandom study of television broadcast ads in North Carolina. They also found that the advertisements drew upon cues reflecting white cultural values and ideals of physical beauty.

Some evidence suggested that both blacks and whites reacted positively to depictions of black characters. Appiah (2001) showed 173 black and white youth advertisements in which the race of the main characters had been digitally enhanced and race-specific cultural cues were included, while all other features of the ads were maintained. Black adolescents with strong ethnic identity most staunchly identified with the black characters in the ads; but so did those polled who had weak black ethnic identities. Similarly, white adolescents found "black character advertisements with varying degrees of black cultural cues as appealing as similar white character advertisements" (Appiah 2001b, 29). Indeed, a study found that both women and nonwhites were more sensitive to stereotypes and thus had a greater appreciation of progressive depictions.

As with the representations of women, the industry appears to have made some changes in their representations of black people. But these changes remain limited and controversial. A recent ice cream advertisement which used the rhyme "eeny, meeny, miney, mo" was chastised by a coalition of black groups who found the ad racist (the rhyme typically ends with the line, "catch a nigger by the toe"), which threatened to launch a consumer boycott. Simon Woolley, a spokesperson for the group, said, "The amazing thing is what this says about the advertising industry. It shows how few minorities there are in senior roles in these companies" (Muir 2004). These continued accusations, particularly when aired in the newspapers, threaten the industry's drive to show that it is more open to diversity.

Conclusions

There were several ways audiences registered their interests and helped to change advertising design during this period. Some formally complained to regulators. Others, when given the chance to talk to advertisers in focus groups, told them what they disliked and this information cycled through agency gossip and chains of beliefs about consumers. Some boycotted. Some spoke directly to producers. And, as we saw in Chapter 10, many used their zappers, or turned away from commercial media entirely. All of these actions changed advertisers' perception of consumers, who were increasingly seen as willing to use their media literary and withdraw their personal "engagement" with advertising. Brands need the goodwill of consumers' meaning-making capacity to survive, however. In response to these negative reactions, advertisers produced more attention-getting, stimulating, and "clever" products. They made concessions to local interests within their globalization strategies and offered more inclusive (albeit still limited) representations of women and ethnic groups.

In return, audiences warmed to advertisers who matched contemporary values in relation to women and ethnicity; many in those audiences appreciated the softer sales pitches and took pleasure from the dramatic, artful, emotionally packed, and stimulating messages. Creatives enjoyed the growing public appreciation of their work for it unshackled them from the sense of inferiority they often feel toward their commercial craft. Stephanie O'Donohoe found a collusion of values between audiences and creatives during this period of advertising, but she identified a "collision" of values as well, since "practitioners also seemed quite threatened by the 'punters' advertising literacy, as it could provide them with the means of distancing themselves from advertising's effects and mystique" (1996, 24).

CHAPTER 13

The Mobilization of the Yuppies and Generation X

Introduction

In the 1980s advertisers developed new research and communication for diagnosing culture and mobilizing consumers. Advertisers were one among other cultural intermediaries, marketers, retailers, designers, and media, all of whom were negotiating lifestyle niches in the mediated marketplace. In the sections that follow we trace the development and communication directed to three target markets that received an inordinate amount of advertiser's attention, despite their making up a very small part of the total market.

We begin with the yuppie, one of the earliest lifestyle target groups but one which received the greatest attention. Indeed the yuppie captured the imagination not only of marketers and advertisers but also of the general public. Popularized through the media, the yuppie became a cultural resource used by people to map both their own identity and that of others. The yuppie profile was born in the early 1980s, but by the end of the decade it was drawing sharp critiques from film and literary producers who cast the yuppie as the villain within their morality tales of ruthless greed and corruption. But in the end the strongest venom directed toward the yuppie came from the young middle-class cohort just behind the yuppie's baby-boom generation: Generation X. As this new cohort came of age they presented marketers who were still blinded by the yuppie phenomenon with a considerable challenge, for they had to learn quickly how to appease a group who proved to be angry toward any forms of blatant promotional appeal. The formats that had worked for the yuppie did not pass muster with this promotionally-savvy and media-literate generation. Through their experience of the clash of taste cultures that unfolded between the yuppie and Generation X lifestyles, marketers learned about the importance of lifecycle and generational targeting.

Therefore, in the next chapter, we look at the advertising directed at Generation X to understand the strategies used to speak to this audience. Then, in chapter 15, we turn our attention to the construction of the culturally-oriented consumer whom we refer to as the *culturati*. Through a case study of a sample drawn from four thousand *Vanity Fair* advertisements appearing throughout the 1990s, we recount how the late-modern culturati were assembled by magazine publishers and explore the unique style of address used to speak to this audience and its contradictory tastes.

Institutionalized Lifestyle: Yuppie

The yuppie—the famous acronym used for young urban professionals—embodied a renewed work ethic and economic mentality that made them the good children of the Reagan years. The yuppie might be thought of as the new "dandy" of this period, for they signaled the return to a uniquely stylized form of consumption. In this chapter we present a short history of the yuppie, for within the rise and reworking of this consumer type important tales about the changing politics of the mediated marketplace are revealed. We focus on aspects of the yuppie's construction and circulation to explore the exchanges between marketers, advertisers, and the public.

In 1981 the yuppie emerged from the womb of new psychographics and lifestyle profiling tools and was rapidly embraced by advertisers and marketers. Yuppies, roughly thirty years old by 1985, were squarely situated in the baby boom generation. They resided in cities and highly populated inner suburbs. They had used a widening access to higher education in the 1960s to become professionals, lawyers, accountants, executives, and business consultants. Deregulation increased the demand for professionals to oversee the changing economy and numerous corporate mergers. The yuppie populated Wall Street's stock market and orchestrated entertainment contract law in Los Angeles and corporate mergers in Chicago. While they were not the architects of the new political economy, they were its loyal foot soldiers.

According to Cornell West (1994, 346), "the triumphant conservatism of the 1980s squeezed out the 'fat' and made American business more competitive in the global economy. This new environment required a totally dedicated worker willing to become a 'corporate man' and act in the interests of profit without management coaxing." The yuppie rose to the task with a steely work ethic and an entrepreneurial streak, both traits distinguishing them sharply from their hippie counterparts. The yuppie was celebrated as the key ingredient necessary to push America forward into a much more competitive global marketplace and to deliver everyone from the evils of the high inflation, the bloated social programs, the economic inefficiencies, and the liberalism of the 1970s.

The first generation to embrace the "air economy" (Leadbeater 1999), they worked on contract and without union supervision. They faced off against the new pace and risk of the workplace. Freed from the coffee breaks of the union era, yuppies hardened themselves to the long hours and total commitment the new workplace demanded (West, 1994), and the media published their bonuses taken as a sign of a renewed economic boom. The old taint of "working for the man" did not seem to apply to them, because many of these professionals worked for themselves. The yuppies' rugged capitalistic individualism was endorsed and promoted by the U.S. and British governments, which were turning them into national heroes. Yuppies appeared on the cover of *Newsweek*, in an article that failed to point out that they were working three times as hard as their parents' generation. But unlike their forbears, few yuppies believed their hard work would secure them a place in heaven. Cornell West suggested that the yuppies' work ethic was not motivated by spiritual issues rather the pursuit of "power, property, and pleasure." In a similar vein Piesman and Hartley (1984) sensed that the yuppie worked to fulfill the aspiration for "glory, prestige, recognition, fame, social status, power, money."

Wentz (1985) argued that yuppies represented an archetypical American lifestyle—specifically, the business rogue who made it by his cunning on the stock market floor and was handsomely rewarded for his efforts. This path to social mobility was thought to be more difficult to achieve in Europe given the legacy of class, and the ceilings placed on executive salaries. Yet the yuppie profile seemed to travel well and was used to describe consumers in Germany, Holland, Spain, and Italy. Frank Mort documents the cycling of the yuppie in advertising, marketing, and media discourses during the 1980s: The yuppie template seemed well suited to explain the new generation of young men and women who worked in the expanding financial and service sectors in the Thatcherite deregulation years. Mort argues that the yuppie was an American import that was reworked and applied in the London marketplace:

> The icon of the young urban professional was originally an import from New York's Manhattan. His translation to a London setting produced a particular reading of the persona. Pre-eminently the yuppie was the personification of Britain's unstable economy and commercial culture during the 1980s. Part hero, part victim, he was a creation of the short-lived boom. (Mort 1980, 171)

As in America, the British yuppie embodied a work-hard, party-hard reputation and embraced long hours and the stress of the workplace for the bonuses. One financial firm famously provided its workers with red Ferraris as a perk of their job. Mort traces the history of how Next, a retail business, targeted the yuppie, believing that "the fun clothes of the 1970s were totally inappropriate for a new generation of the would-be affluent' who were understood to require 'respectable workwear,' with a touch of fashion in the styling." The yuppie was also shaped within the reordering of the ethos of consumption. As American researchers probed ever deeper into the yuppie profile, they found that this cohort held a unique amalgam of values which made them more than gross materialists.

In addition, political parties wanted to know what the political persuasion of the yuppie was so they could harness these national heroes to their cause;

thus research was commissioned to explore the values of the yuppie. The yuppie did not map easily onto traditional politics, and some wondered if they represented a new class. Distinct from the rest of the population, yuppies endorsed values that became associated with "style" politics. This political position was identified by Miller and Levitin in 1976, who argued that one of the youth culture movements of the 1960s and 1970s had instilled a "new politics" concerned with civil rights, women's right to control their own reproductive capacity, sexual freedoms, and animal and environmental rights. Yuppies, more so than the rest of the population, endorsed these political positions (Berelson et al. 1954, 184–5). Yuppies were more likely than the rest of the population to vote against capital punishment, to endorse liberal foreign policy, to be pro-choice for women, and to favor equal opportunities for minorities (Carpini and Sigelman 1986). In terms of their values they celebrated "new anti-authoritarian norms and celebrated the politics of the left." Ingleheart (1977) argued that these seemingly new values were part of a shift toward a post-materialist value system more suited to the postindustrial society, where the production of material things was less important.

However, the yuppie also did not embrace traditional leftist ideals of economic equality; rather, they were highly financially conservative and on matters of money their views matched those of the most ardent Republican. They loathed state intervention in the marketplace and consistently advocated the lowering of taxes. In this attitude, they were not alone, studies during this period revealed few—except the very poor and less educated—supported economic radicalism. Those with higher income and education did not believe in sharing privilege. The yuppie politic was thus contradictory.

> The fact that yuppies are indistinguishable from other Americans in their opposition to programs designed to equalize wealth is more interesting, for it serves to emphasize that even though yuppies are apparently more liberal than other Americans, their leftist leanings stop well short of opposition to the basic tenets of individual enterprise. (Carpini and Sigelman 1986, 506)

Nevertheless, yuppies supported more democratic participation in politics and a widening of the opportunities for women and minority groups, and although economically conservative they rejected wealth as the standard of social status. Thus while the national spotlight was shone on the yuppies' financial success, they seemed to gain their esteem from conspicuous consumption habits: "The ambition and conspicuous consumption of the yuppie made them darlings of media and advertising circles 'quotes'" (Strazewski 1984). They conveniently filled the gap of the traditional rich (WASPs, the Hollywood elites) who no longer clustered together in easily identifiable ways.

The yuppie displayed a significant sense of entitlement over the objects of the good life, rather blatantly abandoning the older values of thrift and monetary accumulation. Part of the ideology of this historic period in both

American and Britain was that one should not feel ashamed about one's success, but rather enjoy it in the field of consumption. William Palmer suggested that the yuppie coupled their "work hard" mentality with an equally competitive "party hard" ethos which required a great deal of spending to maintain: He described the yuppie as:

> driven to make large amounts of money quickly, to succeed in a ruthless competitive world, to acquire the most expensive material goods, to spend rather than save, to party extremely hard as a reward for working extremely hard, to sacrifice human relationships for one's job. (Palmer 1993, 20)

The taste of the yuppie was guided by a distinctive style sensibility. Belk (1986) argued that yuppies were the architects of a new style of nonmaterial consumption. They gravitated toward sparse minimalist industrial designs, designer goods, remodeled hotels and restaurants. Functionalist styling held a particular appeal for the American yuppie who took up the modernist tastes of the educated European classes: Indeed, the American yuppie had a very sweet tooth for European design. Swiss-designed Rolex watches, Italian-designed Valentino suits, and German-engineered BMW cars became yuppie emblems.

Yuppie taste was also complicit in forging new relationships with domestic space and with transforming the "industrial" into the everyday. In *Loft Living* Sharon Zukin documented the flight of industry from factories and docks areas of the city as manufacturing declined. These abandon buildings attracted artists who simply squatted or acquired the cheap property. That these areas soon became some of the more trendy parts of the city, with soaring property prices, was not a particular surprise to Zukin, for in modern society sectors of the middle classes had long mimicked the lifestyle of the artists. In Paris, for example, bourgeois students long ago took up residence in the former garrets of the artists. So too would the young urban professional follow the artists into the industrial loft areas of the post-industry cities. Artists, notes Zukin, also whetted the appetite for industrial design, having made in the 1970s a conscious aesthetic choice to strip away "the artifice of décor" in order to find "beauty in unadorned functionality" (Zukin 1982). As fabricated as it was, industrial design, with its lack of artifice, seemed "real" and "raw."

City lofts were a far cry from the white picket fences and backyards of the suburbs, and not particularly child friendly, but they suited yuppies who were likely to forgo marriage and children. This change did not represent a complete rejection of marriage and family institutions, for many yuppies did eventually marry; rather, the new demands of career simply did not seem to allow them to go through the same lifecycle patterns as their parents. They delayed marriage and children (having fewer offspring as well). These marriages were more likely to end in divorce, but yuppies were serial bonders, and many married more than once. The yuppie cohort found the yoke of traditional norms, role maintenance, and institutional requirements stressful, and they turned to self-help and psychotherapy to see them through, fuelling a boom in these practices (Ballah et al. 1985; Turner 1976; Veroff et al. 1981; Yankelovich 1981).

Zukin notes lofts were most popular with newly liberated female professionals, single males, and gay couples. New scripts of domesticity were mapped in the former industrialized spaces: "Loft living has played an important role in 'domesticating' the industrial aesthetic. The factory origins and the present mixed use of many lofts suggest, in the interest of authenticity, the adoption of the industrial style." Whereas the suburban home was thought a refuge from work, the loft space, blended work and life in a new intimacy. The people who took up loft living mapped their vision of domesticity on an industrial scale. Some sought to replicate the restaurant experience in the home: "The exaggerated scale of a loft provides a natural setting for the new cult of domesticity that worships restaurant and supermarket equipment, industrial carpeting, and Pirelli rubber tiles" (Zukin, 1982 71). They brought the restaurant into the loft, inserting industrial steel refrigerators and chef's stoves. The concept of the formal dinning room was erased as the kitchen became the focal point of social exchange, and the cooking space was exposed and looked out to the a dining table. Entertaining friends (less so family) became a highly coveted ritual. Industrial areas were also often designed for ease of cleaning with few objects in a space. This sparseness also invited aesthetic appreciation of the few objects in the room, laid out with art gallery precision: Clutter distracts the eye. The emphasis on industrial design led to a popularization of metal and glass within the interior of the homes. Yuppies popularized factory dome lights, warehouse shelving, and steel mesh.

The yuppie's interest in paring down and revealing the authentic underneath the edifice also fueled a restoration movement. Yuppies with children often found lofts unsuitable and bought houses and restored houses. When their parents had moved into rundown older homes after the war, the impulse was to make the home comfortable by covering the old fashioned hardwood floors with wall-to-wall carpeting, replacing traditional windows with aluminum ones, and painting the home in the latest colors. A generation later baby boomers ripped up the carpeting to reach the authentic hardwood floors beneath. This was the generation who returned to the junkyard to retrieve the wooden toilet seats their parents had thrown away. A booming business in authentic doorknobs and leaded glass windows emerged. Carpenters became wealthy reinstating pantries and the open cupboards of yesteryear. Stephen Gordon, founder of Restoration Hardware, became wealthy selling new old goods that he brought to life with accompanying nostalgic essays, for example, salt shakers are associated with "childhood memories of family dinners" (Neuborne et al. 1998). In 1987 an American television series called *Thirtysomething* followed the yuppie into their child raising years in their "authentic" homes. The show reveled in the intimate talk of yuppies' concerns and dealt with issues of their sexuality and identity crises. The two lead male characters worked in advertising.

Zukin suggested that the interest in objects of the past was a nostalgic act to bring some stability to a fast-moving present. As each generation of machines becomes more complicated, she says, we withdraw "into dreams of obsolete machines and see ourselves among windmills, clipper ships, even trolley cars" (Zukin 1982, 73, 74). In essayist Robert Harbison's view, "there is no nostalgia like the nostalgia for simpler machines, which are now imbued with the warm glow of a smaller past. As we moved into the transistor age the appeal for bigger more solid objects became more sentimental" (quoted in Zukin 1982, 73). To some extent the taste for industrial trash baskets, reinforced steel shelving, and hospital faucets is also a flight from the throwaway mentality of our plastic culture: "People find art in industrial forms when their industrial use appears to become obsolete. Like Gothic ruins in the nineteenth century, artifacts of the Industrial Age now inspire nostalgia for the past. This sentiment grew as the pace of change speeds up" (Zukin, 1982, 73). The restoration impulses of the yuppie had a considerable impact on the economy, creating new businesses and seriously inflating property prices. After yuppies got through with restoring the former homes of the working classes, no one but professionals could live in the area.

Yuppies were also linked to the boom in health-related media, products, and services. Increasing amounts of disposable income were devoted to fitness related apparel through the 1980s. The yuppie seemed to find spiritualism in the healthy body, materialism, and the aesthetics of commodities.

The media and advertisers circulated the yuppie lifestyle throughout the mediated marketplace. Yuppies were partial to magazines, for their demanding careers left them little time for television. Magazines also permitted the careful study of lifestyle objects and the acquisition of cultural capital. The yuppie template was a driving force behind the mass of new publications that emerged in the early 1980s that offered lifestyle advice, particularly the artist's lifestyle. *Metropolitan Home*, launched in 1981, fed the yuppie phenomena by providing creative design inspiration for those wishing to live a "simple but stylish life." The publication's mission statement emphasized a dedication to craftsmanship (from around the world), enduring style, self-expression, and accessibility. In short, it invoked the liberty of fashion which so moved yuppies. Like shoppers before them the yuppie enjoyed catalogues, but the new yuppie equivalent of the venerable Sears and Roebuck volume was Richard Thalheirmer's *The Sharper Image*. Despite their love of nostalgic items yuppies also embraced the latest technology, and this publication was a virtual candy story of technological toys which earned close to $80 million in 1983. Yuppies also increased the fortunes of older publications, in particular the *New Yorker*, which had supplied lifestyle advice to the urban, creative elite since the early twentieth century.

Designers retooled to address the yuppie market. In a trade press during this period it is possible to find many articles coaching designers in the tastes of the yuppie. For example, gold merchants were informed that with no families to support yuppies had more disposable income to spend and that they were more willing to take on debt. The merchants were encouraged to play upon the yuppie's weakness for fashion and trends and be aware that they were adventurous and impulsive shoppers. Designers learned that "avant-garde designs and unique character pieces" were more likely to hook the yuppie than were traditionalist designs. The yuppie was said to loathe "gaudy designs" and to prefer the "uncommon, gracefully functional stuff" (*Wall Street Journal* 1984). Advertising agencies did very well by promoting designer brands to yuppies. Some of the most successful included Ralph Lauren (sales reached $1.3 billion in 1986, representing a 400 percent increase since 1980) and Calvin Klein. The yuppie's liberal attitudes toward sex paved the way for the inclusion of the male body and gay male target. If cultural consumption was the main area of competition, than males had to become more involved. The changing nature of work also contributed to this, since few any longer got their hands dirty at work; rather, they were more involved in the social interactions of white-collar work, which put more emphasis on "looking good."

Financing the yuppie lifestyle was difficult in a period when real incomes were declining. Yuppies possessed more disposable income, making on average $30,700 compared to the $26,900 of other consumers (*Marketing News*, 1985), but they were also more likely to embrace debt, showing little concern about financing their visits to fine restaurants via credit cards. A 1985 study of 1,300 consumers undertaken by Marketing Facts Inc. revealed the yuppie was more likely to spend on consumer products than other consumers and was more willing to use credit cards, bank machines, financial products, personal computers and merchandising catalogues. They paved the way for the acceptance of higher levels of consumer debt. Combined home mortgage and consumer debt in the United States rose from $1.3 trillion in the late 1980s to $3.4 trillion in 1990, about 50 percent faster than consumer income. In Britain by 2002 the average consumer "owed £3,383 on credit cards, loans and overdraft, a 52 percent increase on the previous five years (*Guardian*, December 13, 2002). Fisher (1985) found the percentage of the GDP made up of domestic consumption remained at 60–65% during the yuppie high-water point, exactly the same as in the 1950–1960s. Still, the popularization of the yuppie lifestyle influenced the type of goods available in the market and a greater willingness to take on debt.

For advertisers yuppies were their Great Gatsby, thought to fuel the engines of the consumer culture with their luxury consumption patterns. Advertisers and marketers embraced the yuppie for their conspicuous lifestyles. Their taste for functional and minimalist aesthetics and renovation motifs continued to animate contemporary consumption practices, along with health consciousness and an interest in fashionably casual clothing. They were arguably at the forefront of the "foodie" and restaurant culture which boomed through the 1990s. Despite the growing economic gap between the rich and the poor and the decline in real incomes, advertisers reminded the hardworking yuppies that indulgence in the consumer culture was their due, and that they were fully entitled to the toys of the marketplace. Advertisers publicized conspicuous lifestyles.

The Decline of the Yuppie

It was representations like the BMW ad that would make yuppies a victim of their own hubris. The golden age of the yuppie was short lived, as the contradictions of the "economic miracle" of the 1980s boom began to unravel. Several different forces attacked the yuppie vision of the world. Researcher noted the numbers of yuppies simply did not add up and began to ask why this particular lifestyle group had so dominated media and advertising. The yuppie also became a whipping post for cultural producers, who raged against what they took to be a symbol of all that was vulgar, materialist, and uncaring about this decade. Finally, the yuppie was caught up within a generational conflict, as a new generation sought to distinguish itself by rejecting the yuppies, their opulence, and the media and advertising institutions that had created this Frankenstein monster.

In 1985 the yuppie phenomenon was picked apart, starting with the observation that their numbers had been exaggerated. At times it had seemed the entire baby boom cohort were yuppies. The General Social Survey data from 1972–1985 revealed that yuppies, defined as professionals between eighteen and thirty-nine years of age and living in areas of at least 100,000 residents, were "an extremely small proportion of both the population as a whole and of the relevant sub population." Those who displayed all three of the key yuppie profile traits made up only 2.4 percent of the population, or 4.2 million persons of the baby boom generation, a sizable number to be sure, but not large enough to justify the inordinate influence of the yuppie on the marketplace (American Demographics 1985). Empirical studies of seven countries revealed "no evidence that yuppies form part of a broader category of young left-wing professionals constituting the 'new class' of the 1990s." In the final analysis "the idea of a syndrome of distinctive yuppie attitudes [was] rejected for the seven countries" (Ester and Vinken 1993, 672).

American Demographics in 1985 found no evidence of a coherent yuppie cluster, but instead a "hodgepodge of disparate elements, each with its own peculiar effects" rather than a "gestalt":

> We have uncovered virtually no evidence that would support the yuppie class thesis, the notion that a synergism among the component elements of yuppiedom makes yuppies somehow *sui generis* politically. More than 85% of the impact of being a yuppie is the result of being young and of being professional. The generally liberal stands of yuppies are explainable without reference to any yuppie class or new class notion and a very traditional group politics thesis performs quite nicely indeed. (American Demographics 1985, 23)

Marketers, media, advertisers, designers. and other cultural intermediaries cannot simply conjure a market segment out of thin air. Like all good spin, the yuppie story was based in some element of fact. But how those facts were turned into a coherent market segment of such great influence is part of the magic of the marketplace. The yuppie was a convenient category for understanding and stabilizing a chaotic marketplace at a moment of great political change. Politicians adored their rugged work ethic. The media could not get enough of the yuppie: According to Shapiro (1991) between 1983 and 1991 the term "yuppie" was featured in more than 22,000 magazine and newspaper articles. Specialty media formed to address them, and marketers and advertisers encouraged businesses to believe that there was profit to be hand in finding ways to fulfill the lifestyle interest of the young, urban professional. The yuppie soap operas dominated media space despite very low audience figures.

The promise of the mediated marketplace during this period was that it would deliver more customized and diverse goods to better meet the interests of consumers' unique tastes. But the inordinate influence of the yuppie illustrates that the mediated marketplace remained deeply biased. The yuppie profile thus became a site of struggle as others rejected the privilege of yuppie values and taste in the marketplace. Others became resentful towards the yuppie construction mobilized by advertisers: Romantic revolts by artists gave collective words and images to rally opposition to the yuppie. The attacks within popular culture reached a boiling point in 1987 as the economic miracle of Reganomics began to unravel. The highly publicized trial and jailing of yuppie junk bond trader Michael Milken was a media morality play which came to symbolize the greed and corruption of the period. The problem with these revolts is that they personalized the larger processes of inequality and change.

Creative members of the baby-boom generation attacked the yuppie. Thomas Wolfe chose a yuppie for the central character in his first novel, *Bonfire of the Vanities*. The story focuses on Sherman McCoy, who had a six-figure Wall Street job and a life of privilege and taste. McCoy is caught in a twist of fate in the South Bronx when his girlfriend runs over a black teenager. McCoy tries to run away from the tragedy but the act leads to the dethroning of his privileges and a jail sentence. *Bonfire of the Vanities* went to the heart of the yuppies' contradictory morality, suggesting how money, success, and opulent consumption draw one away from liberal politics. Wolfe revealed his contempt for the yuppie, who in his mind was not even a decent plutocrat, rather simply a money loving *poseur*:

> A plutocrat is one who rules through money. A plutographer is one who merely wants to live a life that looks like, that graphically depicts, the life of the plutocrat, without any of the plutocrat's responsibilities. Hence the most famous of the *yuppie* passions, the passion to be seen at this week's restaurant of the century. The *yuppies'* problem is that they have no Aldous Huxleys, Reichs, or Marcuses to adorn them with wreaths of moral and intellectual respectability. (Wolfe 1990, 37)

Oliver Stone's *Wall Street* was also released in 1987, and although it was panned by the critics it vividly put flesh on the unattractive yuppie archetype. A classic morality play, *Wall Street* tells the story of a young man's quest to emulate an elder; however, the lessons passed down are disturbing. The action takes place on the trading room floor, where history is now made. Gordon Gekko, the central character, reflects the ambitious side of the yuppie, enjoying the endorphin rush of working in the high-stakes world of finance. He displayed immaculate grooming and fine taste. Gekko celebrates the rampant capitalism devastating the manufacturing sector in America as owning became more important than making: At one point Gekko says, "I don't create anything. I own." He celebrates the pursuit of individual interests as the best means to secure the public good. In a speech to the shareholders of Teldar Paper, a fictitious company, Gordon Gekko makes his plea for greed:

> The point is ladies and gentlemen that greed, for lack of a better word, is good. Greed is right. Greed works. Greed clarifies, cuts through and captures the essence of the evolutionary spirit. Greed, in all of its forms—greed for life, for money, knowledge—has marked the upward surge of mankind and greed—you mark my words—will not only save Teldar Paper but that other malfunctioning corporation called the U.S.A. Thank you. (*Wall Street* 1987)

Projecting onto Gekko an unselfconscious embrace of material wealth over social relationships, Stone, like Wolfe, attacked members of his own generation. Wolfe loathed the yuppies' uncultured posing, Stone their selling out to capitalism. But the most chilling yuppie character assassination emerged from the pen of the young novelist Bret Easton Ellis, who belonged to post-baby boomer generation. This generation, as we shall see, was particularly resentful of the yuppie. In Ellis' satirical novel *American Psycho*, the yuppie character, Bateman, is engaged in constructing a highly stylized, designer brand, immaculate lifestyle, including all the yuppie accompaniments—minimalist furniture and European styling, with the same loving attention he devotes to graphically murdering women (*American Psycho* 2000).

Ellis was part of a new generation which played a considerable role in a values shift that occurred in the late 1980s. The key proponents of this new value system were young people, the so-called Generation X. Researchers began to recognize this value shift, and market spokespersons promoted the need for a new way of relating to the consumer that was less brashly materialist and competitive, or kindler and gentler (Akert, 2002). The power of the yuppie was drawn into question. ABC and advertisers withdrew their support for the yuppie cohort and the yuppie soap opera *Thirtysomething* was cancelled in 1991 due to low audience figures.

Lifestyle Marketing and Generation X

Baby Boomers and Youth Markets:
The Establishment of Generational Marketing

In pursuit of newer markets, marketers and trend forecasters such as Yankelovich and Partners had identified the consumer potential of the soon-to-be-called Generation X phenomenon by the late 1980s, as their interpretation of demographic and social survey data began to show definitive trends occurring amongst teens and twentysomethings. The group of roughly 52 million North American youth that came of age during the fall of communism and the establishment of the PC as a household appliance, were, to the surprise of some observers, behaving differently than their idealistic parents had during their own youthful hippie hey day in the late 1960s. The new youth, marketers found, seemed to not only be anti-consumerist and thrifty—a stark contrast to the conspicuously decadent lifestyle aspirations of their predecessors—but pessimistic about everything. Marketers were now faced with a youth market that appeared to be shunning the consumerist opulence of the 1980s, who were apathetic about things political and "big business," and who cared about the environment (and blamed the boomers for its demise). By 1989 headlines trumpeting warnings about the "graying market" and "dwindling bottom lines" began to appear. The apprehension that marketers began to experience in the late 1980s and early 1990s seemed to be confirmed when the economic bubble of 1980s burst and the recession of the early 1990s began. Market strategists soon began the full frontal assault they felt they needed to win over their dwindling market shares; conquering the youth markets—the future consumer of economy-sustaining big-ticket items such as houses and cars—was top priority.

Some sectors of the media accentuated the cultural revolt against the yuppie. Taking the opportunity to turn the changing of a decade into a newsworthy event, some announced a move toward more social values and a turn away from the driven ambitions and materialism of the 1980s. The yuppies, actually no more or less materialistic than their parents' generation, did appear to be much more comfortable with an open display of status, and they wore their ambition on their sleeves. This consumption bravado was driven underground within popular culture and advertising representations through the 1990s.

There was a growing realization among marketers and advertisers that the consumer profile of the yuppie and the baby boomer, which had been so useful to the positioning of goods in the marketplace, had began to lose sway. The yuppie had provided a plausible, if not always entirely accurate explanation for a lot of casual observations, was such a helpful trope within "journalistic routines" (Gitlin 1980, 99–100). Advertisers in particular liked the yuppie for, although they were selective, they seemed to enjoy consumption and advertising, and creatives, despite their considerable bravado, like to be liked by the audiences they address. But advertisers began to detect a resistance towards the yuppie-oriented forms of communication. The tried and true formats were resisted by the new generation of consumers.

In focusing on the baby boomer and the yuppie they forgot that boomers were made up of many sub-segments of a greater market. And, while marketers throughout the 1980s continued to be obsessed with the yuppie horde, market sales figures slowly began to detach themselves from initial upwardly flowing sales forecasts. BMW watched its sales decline steadily after 1985 but did not de-link its products from the yuppie until 1994 (*Advertising Age*, October 3, 1994). The reality of a sputtering and aging boomer-segment awoke marketers to the need for new marketing strategies that would help them deal with a tired and recession-impacted retail market. In response, marketers found a need to step out of their boomer tunnel vision and in doing so they would look to the sector of the market that they had learned was an eternal wellspring for them: youth. The task facing them was to enchant newer and younger consumers, which had been forgotten in the wake of yuppiemania, to the pleasures of conspicuous consumption.

The generation growing up in the wake of the baby boomers was a good market segment to be selected for many reasons: Late adolescence and early adulthood have long been an important period in the consumer lifecycle, because it is a time when disposable income is increasing, brand preferences are stabilizing, and taste cultures and consumption styles are forming. By the late 1980s marketers began to take seriously the new generation of youth born post-1964 that had, until then, been mainly ignored except by staple youth products like snack food, pop music, and Coke. The origins of this generation were disputed: Some argued that they began in 1961 and ended in 1978, others felt that the correct dating was 1965 to 1981. Although most agreed that the Generation X was smaller than the baby-boomer cohort, they were of interest due to the estimated $125 billion in discretionary spending they were thought to control (Benezra 1995).

But during the late 1980s this media saturated cohort of latch-key kids appeared to be turning into a diffident and complex target market that was refusing to follow the frenzied path to success carved out by the yuppie cohort. Researchers were beginning to reveal that the experience of viewing the turmoil of the 1980s through the TV screen had produced a segment that was more media savvy, environmentally aware, and critical of the rampant consumerism of their parents. Early discourses about the change in youth trends were, in actuality, a mix of popular culture anecdotes; the promotional industry's efforts at deciphering early demographic observations; actual sub-culture trends; and early market research data mixed in with over-hyped news accounts of a hapless "lost generation"—but this was not the name that would stick. The name that did rally interest and lingering resonance did not emerge from the workbench of the market researcher, but in a 1991 novel by Canadian writer Douglas Coupland, *Generation X: Tales for an Accelerated Culture.*

The now legendary novel told the story of three late-twentysomething, angst-ridden friends who had decided to opt out of the rat race. Since then, it seems, we have all come to know, rather uneasily, the term "Generation X" and the group of supposed "directionless" and "apathetic" young adults that, according to popular media accounts, make up its numbers. Generation X seemed to take their riffs more from Sid Vicious and the punks than Lennon and the Beatles; while the former tried to build an alternative reality, the latter was satisfied with deconstructing that that existed, reveling in the label of the outsider and misfit, and rejecting everything, particularly liberal demo-cratic values, in favor of nihilism. Punks elevated mock and shock to a high art form which seemed to define their taste for Generation X. Fulfilling their time-honored role as town criers, the marketing and advertising trade press began to spread the Generation X name throughout the mediated marketplace (Zinn 1992; Donaton and Levin 1993).

The term "Generation X" added more fuel to a socio-cultural fire that was already ablaze with tales of "generational wars." Coupland's novel struck an immediate chord with marketers. *Generation X* seemed to be the articulation they needed, an articulation of the cultural phenomenon they had been ob-serving for a few years already. The discovery of Generation X emerged at the same time as a new West Coast music scene, bands such as Nirvana, Sound Garden, and Pearl Jam. The baggy pants, chained wallet, and flannel shirts worn by members of these brands sought to distinguish the musicians from the glam heavy metal bands, with their tailored and well-groomed look of the yuppies. This romantic, anti-fashion fashion revolt aligned with lumberjacks and street cultures.

The bands became highly successful commercially by maintaining an anti-commercial stance, refusing media appearances and instead pressing the flesh to sell their music. The angst-ridden music emerged from middle class white boys who had experienced the emotional torment of begin brought up as spoiled children. Members of the generational cohort were variously labeled "slackers, cynics, whiners, drifters, malcontents." A *Washington Post* headline captured the patronizing attitude that baby boomers apparently held toward their successors: "The boring twenties: Grow up, crybabies." And yet this sounded like nothing so much as the impotent resentment of an earlier ruling, cultural elite whose time had passed.

Although the designation "Generation X" is familiar to most people, the exact make up of those who supposedly are a part of this fluid young generation has proven to be elusive to marketers, media executives, commentators, and academics alike. Coupland described them as a generation at odds with the mainstream of consumerism, resisting the attempts of marketers to pigeon-hole and package them as an audience for advertisers. He had sympathy for this generation and received thousands of dollars from the industry to lecture to them about his deep insights on Generation X. Greater Talent Network booked filmmakers associated with Generation X to lecture to marketing executive about their generation, and young marketers quit their jobs, made videotapes of Generation X types in their habitats, and then sold the tapes to clients like Liz Claiborne and Mattel Inc. for thousands of dollars (Heath 1996). Generation X thus contributed to the new trends within market research of ethnographic research and cool hunting.

Coupland's account of "the lost generation," however, soon began to show flaws. Marketing campaigns geared to Xers, depicting scenes of slackers—angry and cynical toward everything and everyone—soon began to falter (see Figure 13.1). Researchers were implored by the industry to find ways of producing better data about generational cohorts who were in constant evolution. Generation X did not seem to cohere in the way that the baby boomers had. There were few definitive heroes in the new generation (the reasons for which ought to have been obvious, since they were anti-hero oriented). They were shaped by a marketplace of relatively peaceful times (except for the Gulf War), experiencing no grand historic events such as those which had united earlier generations, such as the war in Vietnam (Schoemer 1995; Morrison 1994).

Generation X as a Cultural Phenomenon

While exaggerated and somewhat cartoonish descriptions of late-1980s and early-1990s youth plagued marketers early on, they were not mistaken in identifying differences between Generation Xers and their parents' generation. Demographically, the baby boom had ended in 1964, when the newly introduced birth-control pill and changing socio-cultural attitudes and mores led by the youth movement of the 1960s began to come to the cultural fore. Births per thousand dropped drastically in 1964 and remained at much lower levels than during the lowest baby boom years. This simple fact alone ensured that, when this relatively sparsely populated generation came of age, the economy would be impacted. But the extent of the impact on the retail sector and job markets at the time could not have been predicted. Thus, it is

Condoms, it's repression man, it's just another tool of the establish-ment....to bring us down!

They *say* we gotta use them, but who are they!! They wanna control us with their condoms, but not me man.

Cause I ain't wearing one!

Woman: Sheik. Use one or get none.

Young man: While these are cool. Well I would use them. Yea, I'd use them, and I'd like them, and I'd use them all the time.

Announcer: Sheik, get some.
Young man: Thank you, thank you Mr. Sheik.

Figure 13.1 Sheik Condoms, "Repressed Teen."

inevitable that those born between the end of the baby boom in 1965 and the beginning of the conservative Reagan years in 1980 (when birth rates again began to pick up) would, in some way, possess some unique characteristics differentiating it from previous generations. Socio-culturally, the differences also proved profound. Authors and academics such as Boutilier (1993), Holtz (1995), Strauss and Howe (1991, 1993), Bennett and Rademacher (1997), and Paulin and Riordin (1998), paint a bleak picture of the formative years of many Gen Xers: single-parent families; fractured home-lives; inner-city crime, and rising racial tension in the United States; the potential break-up of Canada; and memories of failed institutions—Watergate, the Iran hostage crisis, Iran-Contra, the pork-barrel reputation of the Conservatives, and crippling recession and inflation—that dethroned the once-mighty establishment.

In addition, the pressures of a rapidly changing marketplace, diminishing job prospects, and the unrelenting demands of a technologically defined and fluid postmodern world forced youth in the early 1990s not only to stay in school longer, but to depend more and more on their parents in later and later years of their lives (Statscan 1996; Boutilier 1993). Indeed most of the changes that differentiated Gen X culture from youth of other generations seemed to be associated with life-cycle changes linked to the economic realities in which Gen Xers came of age (Nevitte 1996; MacManus 1995). Most important for marketers, these realities inevitably meant that Xers were also marrying later and prolonging starting a family to later years thus, subsequently, prolonging purchasing life-cycle products such as homes, cars, and RRSPs.

Although many post-boomers were brought up as latch-key kids and were raised in single-parent homes in tough economic times, the angst of the early 1990s—which undeniably was and, in some cases, is still there among certain sub-cultures and members of this age group—began to turn into dogged determination to get ahead in the mid- to late-1990s (Nevitte 1996). As Holtz (1995, 208) tells us in his conclusion to his Gen X book *Welcome to the Jungle*: "While this generation has sometimes seemed paralyzed with indifference or apathy, recent years have seen and increasing willingness to speak out and…our influence in society has begun to accelerate." Undeniably, then, Generation X was, and remains, a distinctive cultural phenomenon.

Advertisers' Renewed Response to Generation X

In focus group settings teens and young adults told ad creators and marketers that advertisers' depictions of them were all wrong. As one marketer stated, "Xers feel that they are anything but the way they've been depicted in most advertising aimed at them" (Freeman 1994). As newer, more thoughtful marketing data began to emerge, marketers began to discover that Gen X wasn't the absolutely ambitionless, hopeless, and angry-at-everything generation they had pictured. Yes, many in the generation did have fears about the future, but many were also ready to take on the challenge of a "new economy" —a knowledge-based, technology-driven one. Marketers began to also discover what many social scientists such as Buckingham (1994) and Freeman (1995) already knew: that Gen Xers were more educated than any other generation before them; that they were "weaned" on television and pop culture; and that they were very comfortable with the emerging technologies of computers and the Internet.

Marketers found out, through costly trial and error, that in their early angst-encoded marketing messages they were addressing Xers all wrong. Gen Xers were much more than the derisive marketing label with which had been tagged; in fact, they were a diverse, multi-ethnic, and complex generation of cautiously optimistic, media- and technology-savvy future leaders. Rushkoff (1994, 4) sums it up best in his introduction to his book, *The Gen X Reader*: "For Gen X is the nightmare of a postindustrial, postmodern age. We are a marketing experiment gone out of control." Marketers retreated and re-grouped. They had to change their methods of "hailing" the new, savvy generation. And, as our analysis of 1990s advertising shows, they did.

Marketers and advertising designers learned the hard way that cute, over-generalized labels and simplified preconceptions did not accurately describe this diverse, multi-ethnic, and eclectic group. Nor, surprisingly, did the hyped-up, caricature-like MTV styles of address seem to suit most in this young-adult group that we casually refer to as Generation X. But in order to understand a more nuanced profile of this generation—and ultimately understand how advertising came to address them with emotion—we must first look back to its predecessor, the baby-boom generation, and to the beginnings of attitudinal and lifestyle marketing segmentation.

How Marketing Learned to Address the Complex Gen X Culture

In the state of socio-economic flux that has defined the Generation X cultural phenomenon, it is no wonder that addressing this cohort proved to be a tightrope walk for marketers, especially because they still freely admit that they do not thoroughly understand who they are (Redhead 1997; Guccione 1995; Anonymous 1997). Nor can they do so completely within the paradigm of marketing. The act of target marketing seeks to simplify and crystallize an entire sub-set of the population as a "group of individuals who share a central ethos, or a set of values and common understandings about how these shared values will be enacted in attitudes and behaviors" towards a product, a brand, or an advertising message (Prensky and Wright-Isak 1997, 70). This effort grew in complexity because, as Kline (1993, 284) argues, "target-marketing depends on the degree to which these clusters can be addressed as audiences through the available communication channels." Herein lies the problem. More than any other generation, Gen X did not act in homogenized ways (Holtz 1995). Traditionally, the "communication channel" of advertising, through its narrative and person-codes, represents a target market as a prototypical ideal. As Englis and Solomon (1997, 27) suggest, "By depicting only selected or stereotypical perspectives on what a prototypic member of a particular lifestyle category ought to look (and behave) like," marketers hope that the personalities will empathically resonate with the intended target segment. Marketers have learned (through expensive trial-and-error), however, that this does not work in the same manner with Gen X audiences. The reasons for this are two-fold.

First, Gen Xers are "savvy media consumers" (Zukin, 1997, 11) and as such know what makes advertising tick. As Zukin explains, "They have been consuming media since they were born, and they are experts at it. It is almost impossible to fool them and they do not like to hype or succumb to it." Marketers seemed to have finally accepted this. As Toronto-based advertising executive Edward Caffyn confesses, "[T]hese guys are supersmart. They've seen through our little strategies and they know who pays our bills. They relish the fact that unlike previous generations, they recognize advertising for what it is—a grubby sales pitch" (1997, 13). Author Karen Ritchie argues that Generation X was particularly critical toward selling messages: "The first time you realize the super toy you wanted is really only four inches tall you learn a hard lesson," says Ritchie. "We created a whole *generation* that believes advertising is lies and hype."

Previous generations had grown up with different conceptions of media and advertising. Boomers had been living life vicariously through advertising and mass-media depictions of themselves throughout the 1970s and 1980s. Personalized-format ads and lifestyle ads in *Playboy* and *GQ*, and commercials sponsoring programs such as *Lifestyles of the Rich and Famous* and *Dynasty*, educated boomers in the finer art of Me Generation "conspicuous consumption." As the novelty of the TV began to wear, media and marketing's position of privilege began to wane. Thus, while the pre-boomer generations in the 1950s had been awed by the new possibilities of TV broadcasting and were looking for subliminal messages in advertising, Xers were being weaned on the intricate forms of media culture through the ads and commercial paradigms that sustained the explosion of programming and new channels throughout 1980s and into the 1990s. Slightly overstating the point, but nevertheless getting the message across, Owen (1997) says, "Gen X was baby-sat by TV." It is not an exaggeration, however, to claim that Xer's socialization was deeply embedded within media culture. Watching Saturday morning cartoons, *ABC Afterschool Specials*, *Sesame Street*, and MTV, they quickly adapted to new, intricate production techniques that carried more information in less time. They also grew up intuitively knowing that all ads were a selling tool, a way to make them spend. To prepubescent and teen Xers, this was a way of life, the order of things "out there in the real world."

Second, as the benefactors of a prolonged and open immigration policy in both Canada and the United States, North American Gen Xers were the most ethnically and culturally diverse cohort in history. For example, as of 1992 U.S. Xers were 14 percent black, 12.3 percent Hispanic, and 3.9 percent Asian, while the majority, almost 70 percent, was Caucasian, ethnic backgrounds were as diverse. In comparison, the U.S. population as a whole was 74.8 percent European ancestry, 12.4 percent black, 9.5 percent Latino, and 3.3 percent Asian (Zinn et al. 1992, 77) In addition, the generation is defined by the many subcultures and taste cultures that flavored it: skaters and club-hoppers, tattoo-wearers and body-piercers, snowboarders and surfers, ravers and rockers, Christian youth and charity volunteers, Bay Street and Wall Street wannabees, net-heads and hackers, Bangra rockers and rappers, techno-geeks and radicals and conservatives, and everything in between. While this ethnic diversity and endless sub-cultural fragmentation gave Gen Xers a tolerant and rich cultural experience, it is precisely this dense multicultural make-up and experiential adaptability that made the Gen X market so difficult to "market" to.

To their peril, what marketers had neglected to understand about Generation X was that it was highly racially diverse. For example, the black and Hispanic members of this cohort were shaped by their own subcultures in ways that caused them to differ sharply from the white majority. As Hispanic author Lalo Lopez wrote in *Next: Young American Writers on the New Generation* (1997, 4), "I'd like to be a slacker, but my family would kick my ass." The dominant Generation X sensibility did not map upon those of poorer ethnic communities, an issue that Lopez drew to the surface when he noted: "A poor Mexican worrying about esoteric emotions like angst? Get a job."

According to David Watkins, then a 26-year-old vice president of the marketing company Dstreetz, "If anything I think we should be called the hip-hop generation." The impact of rap and hip-hop artists on record sales and fashion has far outstripped that of Nirvana, Grunch and Flannels ($800 million worth of records last year, roughly half bought by whites). Fashion associated with hip-hop proved an even more lucrative business than record sales. For example, when rapper Snoop Doggy Dogg wore a Tommy Hilfiger rugby shirt on a 1994 *Saturday Night Live* show, he started a fashion trend among young white suburban males who developed a taste for Hilfiger baggy jeans and oversized jackets. Company sales rose from $53 million in 1991 to $847 million in 1998.

Advertisers have found that among the most successful Xer ads are those that overcome Xers' cynicism towards media hype by ad designers self-reflexively parodying themselves. The ad exposes advertising's "lie," "sleaziness," and "hucksterism," again addressing Xers' cynicism toward media hype (Shenk

1997). It becomes clear, however, through reading the recent marketing industry literature, that marketers and ad designers are starting to acknowledge and address this diversity. Commenting on their diversity, Caffyn (1997, 13) provides further insight into the industry's confusion around addressing Gen X: "Over the past years, in our eagerness to relate to young adults, we've attempted to portray a vision of 'young adult cool' [see Figure 13.2] hoping that they'll like us because we're cool too. But the take-away by young adults is that the advertising is an attempt to fabricate a culture for them. The whole issue is compounded by the fact that these young adults... reject commonality. They focus on and celebrate the differences among themselves. In reality their only commonality is their diversity."

Marketing's Changing Perception of Gen X:
From a Cynical Anti-Consumer to an Avid but Picky Consumer

The great minds of the twentieth century have generally rejected sentimentalism, even defining its essence as false, exaggerated emotion; and we tend to find mawkish or even comical much that the Romantic age prized as moving and beautiful. Yet there was more than cheap self-indulgence and escapism in this fevered emotionalism. Its proponents argued that one could be morally and spiritually uplifted by cultivating a greater sensitivity to one's feelings. The cultivation of empathy for the sufferings of others could even be a vehicle for social change, as in the works of Charles Dickens. That this emotionalism was sometimes exaggerated or artificial should not obscure the fact that it also contained much that was genuine and inspiring. It is not clear that we have gained so much by prizing in our modern literature attitudes of cynicism, detachment, and ruthlessness.

As Ritchie claimed in her book, *Marketing to Generation X*, (1995, 3) earlier marketing discourses on Gen X strongly implied that "the youngest and least educated segment of Generation X actively rejects status through material possessions ... and the best-educated and most affluent choose to fit in and play it safe." This, as marketers soon learned, couldn't have been more wrong. Early Gen X ads depicting cynical, angst-ridden, anti-establishment, anti-consumers, modeled on Coupland's characters, began to show their flaws by the mid-1990s (Freeman 1995). Indeed, for the reasons mentioned earlier, marketing's traditionally accurate picture of target markets gleaned through demographic and psychographic data (traditionally perfected through attitudinal segmentation) was intensely challenged with the appearance of the Gen X market.

On the contrary, advertising's highly concentrated image-laden messages played a central role in this socialization of these future consumers. Indeed, in the lifetime of Xers, from the mid-sixties to the present, the most prevalent form of socializing force has been the TV commercial (Fowles 1996). As Kline

The only thing as good as your
Crispy Crunch is someone else's.

Figure 13.2   Crispy Crunch "Bathtub" campaign.

(1993, 13) points out, "the market is a growing force within the matrix of socialization" of youth. Statistical evidence underscores this influence: By graduation the average child has spent 20,000 hours watching TV and has been exposed to 18–21,000 advertising messages per year. In contrast, that same child has spent 11,000 hours in the classroom (Kline 1993, 17).

If this generation was apprehensive toward the workplace it was not purely a matter of choice, but much more likely a rationalization for getting to grips with an economic period in which the hopes of youth were stunted. Carrying a national debt in the United States of $4 trillion, and leaving college in 1991 owing an average $7,000 in loans due, almost double what boomer graduates in 1977 owed, Generation X entered "arguably the worst job market since World War II." Few made enough money to live on their own, and hence 46 percent lived with their parents. Studies of college-course enrollment showed a steady gain for the business major, which doubled from 12 percent of all degrees granted in 1970 to 25 percent in 1985. UCLA's Higher Education Research Institute, which polls the attitudes of the nation's incoming freshmen, reported a similar change in attitudes. This generation had become more career-conscious and money-oriented with each passing year. According to Ratan (1993), "The Bureau of Labor Statistics forecasts that nearly one-third of college graduates from the classes of 1990 through 2005 will take jobs whose content doesn't really require a degree, up sharply from 19% in 1980."

In 1966, 84 percent of all incoming freshmen had reported that "developing a meaningful philosophy of life" was their most important goal; only 44 percent felt that "being very well-off financially" was most important. By 1990 the trend had reversed. Only 37 percent now felt that a "meaningful philosophy" was the most important life goal; 76 percent now answered that "financial success" was their primary aim. As Stuart Himmelfarb, then president of the polling firm CollegeTrack, explained in 1989, "These young people have bought into the process" of defining success with money. Despite this clear evidence of a fundamental shift in basic values, the media began to frame Generation X as a cohort of slackers. In a cover story entitled "Proceeding With Caution," *Time* pointed out that headhunters found that young women did not want careers, but were more interested in escaping the 9-to-5 grind.

Stories followed in the *Wall Street Journal*, the *New York Times*, and the *Chicago Tribune*, to the effect that the new generation lacked career ambitions. This statement was typical: "The young work force is considered overly sensitive at best and lazy at worst" (Lipsky and Abrams 1994). The recession of the early 1990s was devastating, and the Generation X slacker became the scapegoat, allowing the problems of the nation to be "given a face." The idea that young people did not care about jobs may have helped preserve jobs for those over thirty: Over 55 percent of the new jobs created in 1990 went to workers over thirty, a considerable departure from all previous recessions, when college graduates, cheaper to hire and easier to train, were given the jobs. The slacker image also gave the impression that this group's lack of interest in material success was to protect them from the disappointment of not finding a job in a period when no jobs were available (Lipsky and Abrams 1994).

However, newer data suggests that by the early 1990s Xers had not, by any stretch of the imagination, rejected the notion of consumerism. Throughout that decade, for instance, Xers dominated the market for designer jeans and athletic shoes (Hornblower 1997); however, it is also telling that these two items are important sub-cultural totemic items that were integral in identifying an individual within certain sub-groups and taste-cultures. Their normalization to the culture of promotion as the status quo—the way the world is—that began early in life for Xers indeed carried forward to their early adult years. To marketers' relief, these early accounts of Gen X anti-consumerism were mostly due to costly misreadings of the market by consumer researchers clinging to non-representative niche sub-culture and taste-culture data, as being indicative of an entire subset of the North American population.

Thanks mostly to the hype around Coupland's "McJobbers," early and erroneous attitudinal segmentation studies positioned almost all Gen Xers as "postponers." According to Zukin, "those with [this] orientation, about four in ten, are the culprits who have defined Gen X in popular culture, and this segment is perhaps the generation's worst representatives." Zukin explains who falls into this category: "Postponers...are rooted in the present.... Postponers watch. They are trying to discover what to do with their lives and are unsure of the future.... Seeing their jobs as just a way to get money, they live paycheck to paycheck, spending impulsively and fitting the 'slacker' stereotype" (1997, 13).

Suddenly, the view changed: "Then books and articles began to recast young Americans as ambitious, savvy, independent, pragmatic, and self-sufficient. For instance, Time magazine described its 1997 article entitled "Great Xpectations" this way: "Slackers? Hardly. The so-called Generation X turns out to be full of go-getters who are just doing it—but their way." A telephone poll of seven hundred adult Americans (three hundred boomers, two hundred matures, and two hundred Gen Xers), taken for TBWA Chiat/Day and Yankelovich Partners Inc. in May of 1996, yielded this picture: Compared to boomers, matures, or the generation before them, the Gen X cohort was more likely to be optimistic about getting where they wanted to go in life; preferred to work on their own; felt that the only meaningful measure of success was money; were less likely to want to do things differently in their lives; and were faithful to the American dream that if they worked hard they could achieve what they wanted (Time Magazine 1997).

Other research suggested that twentysomethings were as likely as the boomers to be unhappy with their life (of those polled 25 percent Generation X agreed; 26 percent baby boomers agreed). Boomers were 8 percent more likely to report that they felt dissatisfied with "the way things are going in the United States," a finding that challenged the accusation that Generation Xers were whiners (Giles and Miller 1994). Some of the trends which began with the yuppies were carried on by Generation X, however. They continued to reject the institution of marriage, with only 40 percent of young people being married in 1992, compared to the 67 percent who walked down the aisle in 1970. And although Calvin Klein would boost the sale of his products by promoting a "heroin lifestyle," and the suicide of Kurt Cobain would be elevated to cult status, heroin was not a chosen drug by this generation, nor did the suicide rate change because of them. TBWA Chiat/Day's Adam Morgan sums up the cost and impact of marketing's initial views of Gen X:

> Today forecasters...are acknowledging that their first X rays of the new generation were distorted. The baby boomers of the media and marketing world were desperate to explain a generation they didn't understand. It may be the most expensive marketing mistake in history. (Hornblower 1997, 60)

Generation X was Materialist

As the 1990s wore on Gen X hungered for a new cultural idiom of its own, a new voice, a new form of cultural expression which reflected its experience of being children of preoccupied parents, forced into facing the grittier realities of recession and AIDS. They distinguished themselves as being less hypocritical than their flower-power-turned-yuppie parents and were more than just rhetorically sensitive about gender equality, the environment and world issues, and striving for a more fluid and open lifestyle. Eventually, as early Gen X ads failed, marketers learned (around the mid 1990s) that Gen Xers were mainly positive and future oriented. As Yankelovich and Partners report in Smith and Clurman's *Rocking the Ages* (1997, 190), Xers show no statistically significant difference in the numbers of them who desire a financially comfortable retirement [78 percent to boomer's 78 percent and 81 percent to matures] and, surprisingly, slightly led the other two older generations when asked if they aspire to own their own home one day [1 percent to boomer's 79 percent and mature's 74 percent].

And although they were more cynical than older cohorts toward things traditional and institutionally based (including the institution of advertising), they certainly did not reject consumerism, including the postponers among them (Zukin 1997; Nevitte 1996; *Toronto Star* June 12, 1997). Instead of being against the consumer lifestyle, they were merely more selective about what they consumed. Xers were, in general, less loyal to brands than were boomers, but still "the data indicate that some segments of the generation are indeed loyal, at least sometimes...and the experience of certain marketers (i.e.,

Nike, Doc Martins, The Gap, Saturn) bears this out" (Ritchie 1995, 135; see also Goldman and Papson 1996). Rather than being *rejecters* of consumerism, Xers were purchasing and spending on things that increase their sense of esteem and belongingness. Socialized by the marketplace and the mass media, Gen Xers were also sophisticated citizens of consumer culture, not keen on being given the sales pitch and needing a good reason to spend time within the marketplace. Thus, their shopping behavior usually involved socializing with friends in stimulating and multi-faceted environments (e.g., malls, ethnic restaurants, and coffee shops; specialty "customer first" and "shopping experience" stores; the new superplex entertainment centers; and so on). Their mass media choices had to be engaging, varied, full of choices, and interactive.

Most importantly, Gen Xers desired intensely entertaining marketplace and mass media experiences, and advertising also fell under these same criteria. To Generation X, the marketplace, advertising, and mass media continue to be a seamless fabric of popular culture, one not more important than the other, and all interacting in a complex web of intertextual references and commonly shared experiences. As well entrenched postmaterialists, however, they reject overt marketing and "being sold to"—but not consumerism per se. As such, the savvy Gen X consumer marketers argue, can be reached by advertising "if it's more informative than persuasive. They particularly like Web sites that enable them to get product information that they want and need. Still, the best communication for them is person-to-person and word-of-mouth. (Morton, 2003, 42)

> And, as reported by commentators advertising itself is now one of these reference points, with an active mythology of its own (see Fowles 1996 and Goldman and Papson 1996). According to Smith and Clurman, "64% of Xers...say that 'Material things, like what I drive and the house I live in, are really important to me'"; surprisingly enough, less than 50% of boomers (products of the "Me Generation") believed this. (quoted in Hornblower 1997, 66)

By the mid 1990s the Generation X market had proved to be an annual $125 billion dollar powerhouse (Ritchie, 1995). But tapping into this rich market required the nimble tightrope walk that is Gen X advertising. The cynicism and resistive stance that marketers experienced among this generation was really a media/marketing savvy reading of advertising's traditional ways of communicating (its "idealized depictions" and "most" and "best" traditional advertising rhetoric). In response, new media channels were supported by advertising which contorted its standard format and style in order to appeal directly to Gen X's media savviness. Subsequently, by the mid 1990s progressive advertisers began creating the "ad-savvy" ads that reflexively decontextualize advertising codes and techniques (see the further discussion of this point later in Part 4). Thus, the "cynical voice" ad, such as the Sheik Condoms' "Repressed

Teen" campaign (see Figure 13.1), gave way to the "ad-savvy" ad represented by Labatt Genuine Draft's "Hi I'm Joel, and this is my beer commercial" campaign (see chapter 14; Figure 14.3).

Generation X: Marketing's Waterloo

Marketing to Gen X, therefore, posed a new problem. Because of this cohort's media-message savviness, honing in on its consumption communities and target markets through attitude segmentation became exponentially more problematic for marketers. As more and more focus groups revealed increasingly resistive and disbelieving audiences, advertising designers responded with marketing communication techniques based on surrealistic design concepts, absurd cartoonish fantasy worlds, postmodern stylizations, and self-reflexive and irreverent themes. Some ads worked and some did not; most advertising—and especially television commercials—had a distinctive edge to them that differentiated the new youth ad from traditional advertising design and positioning.

A sense of "rupture" in advertising messages took place in the Gen X ads, not only through the disjointed visuals and highly evocative and emotive MTV-ish narratives, but also within the ideological space of the ad, where advertising's old meanings—its perpetually happy, idealistic, congenial worlds, made better by the product—became farcical to an audience leery of promotional culture's hype and unbelievable claims. Identifying "the ideological fractures and divisions in television advertising" (Goldman and Papson 1996, 256), corresponding to the modes of address that arise when consumers are pigeon-holed into target audiences based on lifestyles and psychocultural categories, marketers attempted to gain back credibility with the postmodern Xer viewer through a complex redefinition of advertising. Central to this is the struggle by marketers to regain advertising's sense of authenticity with the new consumer.

CHAPTER 14

Negotiated Messaging for Generation X

The youth rebellion of the 1960's prepared marketers to undertake stylistically altered new marketing practices and advertising modes of address, in order to reach and reinvigorate a seemingly disaffected portion of the new consumer youth market that was detected in the late 1980s. Advertisers approach this market in a new way; not simply as an age cluster that had particularly oedipal struggles, but as a cohort that shared particular historical events. Generation X, as we saw in the previous chapter, was imagined as a uniform whole, but cracks within this idealized grouping became increasingly apparent as marketers attempted to address them. It turned out that the readings of even a small group of this cohort were shot through with different inflections relating to nationality, gender, ethnicity, class, and perhaps most importantly, knowledge of media history. They all came to advertising with particular expectations and looked for their values to be reflected. We find audiences and advertisers engaged in a serious and complex struggle over meaning.

Being media savvy, this cohort rejected conventional media forms, and its members were more likely to zap and tune out a media presentation (promotional or otherwise) than older generations. Marketers dealt with this problem through opening up new channels (MTV, targeted magazines, fashion outlets) and developing alternative production values and presentation styles (shaking camera, rapid cutting, jump shots, streeters as authorities) to provide entree for emerging cultural forms (grunge, alternative music). Thus, highly entertaining and emotion-laden narratives led the efforts to develop affinity with the young new consumer.

As cultural critics such as Williams (1982), Fiske (1987), Barthes (1993), Lewis (1997), and Buckingham (1999) have shown, we can move beyond merely reading media products textually (i.e., as only a vehicle to promote a product, as an individual thirty-second narrative, etc.) and also use media texts as "interpretive keys" in order to reveal the multi-dimensional complexities and the importance of symbolic communication in contemporary life. According to author and cultural critic Douglas Kellner, "media culture provides the social allegories which articulate class and social group fears, yearnings, and hopes... [providing] a diagnostic critique with insight into the situation of individuals within various social classes and groups, like youth" (1995, 125). Thus, through our analysis of marketing communication messages aimed at Gen X, we can use advertising as that interpretive key that helps us explore the complexities of both youthful culture and contemporary marketing's efforts in responding to its complexities.

Advertising contributes to the *creation* of new symbols, and indeed, new "taste cultures" (Bourdieu, quoted in Lury 1996). As Jib Fowles contends, "Advertising draws on popular culture's repository of symbolic material (images or text or music) in an attempt to fabricate new symbols with enlivened meanings." (1996, 9) To Fowles, echoing Kellner, advertising appropriates cultural symbols and then repossesses and disseminates those symbols back to society in new ways, usually in very creative but often quickly forgotten message packages. Wolf (2003) bridges this critical perspective with the pragmatics of the advertising industry; he contends that successful contemporary advertising must become an entertainment outlet. In other words, to postmodern marketers, ads in and of themselves must be integral in the meaning generating system of popular culture. Advertisers must recognize that, to Gen X markets, advertising is judged upon the entertainment it frames itself around; it is part and parcel of that entertainment. To Wolf, advertisers ignore this truth at their own peril.

Entertaining presentations, then, produced on the Xers own terms, proved to be the olive branch marketers needed to gain legitimacy with the new consumer. According to one youth marketer, "[Xers] are willing to strike a pact with us, and that pact is, if creatives humor and entertain the Gen X viewer, then they will stay, watch, and even actively engage with the ad" (Calfee 1994, 13). This neatly sums up the complex counter-transference that occurred between marketers and their niche targets. Kratzer and Hodgins (1997, 16) uses market research data to confirm this: "Both qualitative and quantitative results revealed that entertainment is the most important element in [Gen X's] favorite ads." This cohort has a complex relationship to popular culture, showing both considerable disdain toward it but also relying on it as the key arena for forging its shared cultural experiences.

Case Study: Constructing a Generational Consumer

In this section we explore some of marketing's new tools of persuasion in its thrust to regain legitimacy in the mind of the new consumer. We do so by reporting on our content analysis of two hundred television commercials randomly selected from a database of almost fourteen hundred Canadian and U.S. prime-time TV commercials recorded in the Vancouver, BC market between 1994 and 1996.[1] Of the two hundred diverse ads from an assortment of product categories, fifty proved to be ads geared to young adults (eighteen to thirty-four). To distill the findings of this study we present five campaigns

---

[1] The database we used for this study, the Simon Fraser University Media Lab's "Emotadlib" database of primetime TV commercials, is itself a subset of almost 4,000 TV commercials recorded throughout the 1980s and 1990s. The database is archived at the School of Communication, Vancouver, Canada.

best exemplified prominent Gen X design trend, comparing them to commercials geared at other generational target markets. Our typology of Gen X ads documents how advertisers struggled to reach out to an amorphous and fluid demographic.

Our study explores how advertising to Gen X came to typify a particular historical negotiation between advertisers and resistive consumers, resulting in new, emotion-based marketing efforts endeavored to position commodities in the minds and culture of the Gen X consumer. We also analyze interview data gathered from young adults' discussions of advertising geared at them. This research indicates that to the media savvy generation criticisms focused on message style and product "pitch" rather than fundamental critiques of consumerism or promotional culture.

The Gen X audience, more than any other audience in history, is defined by a savvy cynicism and apprehension toward the hype-ridden market that colors and complicates the act of "defining self in terms of consumption." Goldman and Papson (1994, 1996) have given a good account of the new voice of marketing that emerged to re-integrate what they call the "alienated spectator." The essence of their analysis is that to engage a resistive audience advertising designers explored an angry and anti-conventional, frame-breaking and self-referential, yet at the same time intense and vivid, montage or storytelling stylistic format, borrowed in part from cinema and rock video format. Summing up their mainly interpretive analysis of early to mid-1990s young adult advertising, Goldman and Papson (1994, 23–53) found that ads geared to North America's new, savvy consumer contained the following elements:

Sanctioned negativity: The exposure of negative social worlds and acceptance of stresses of urban life.

Sub-cultural fit: Presentation of style as a mode of allegiance and belonging; subversion as the language and fashion of the street dominate; direct integration of target groups' symbolic markets.

Intense emotional appeals: A heightened sense sensuality, excitement, and risk through taking the camera where it has not been before; carefully crafted narrations; and gritty, real gesturing through carefully crafted narratives or rapid-fire barrage of images, stylized form of cultural noise and abstracted editing.

Sexual identity: Hints of gender blending such as males as sexual objects; reshifting of female depictions (the woman who once draped over the car transformed into a perky advocate for the auto company; a slightly different voice which is both more ironic and more appealing to the young (and now increasingly female) audience.

Humor and irony as the way through cynicism: Drawing upon audiences' stocked knowledge of popular cultural codes to present visual puns; stereotypes, self mocking forms of humor.

Realism and reflexivity: Advertising attempts to "give you back as you are," as opposed to presenting an idealized you; ads reveal themselves, the camera is shown, or shakes, or presents grainy images; back to black and white.

Intertextuality: Advertisers call on viewers' memories and their hostility toward formulaic and invasive advertising strategies of the past; celebrity as spokesperson, as character; photographic style or scene from a film or TV program; references to other advertising/product genres.

Our own analysis confirmed Goldman and Papson's notion of a new voice and approach in youth marketing that, we observed earlier, not only conveys a revised view of the world, but a new structure of feeling as well: Marketers were using both popular culture and media analyses of youth trends to inform a rethinking of ad design and to construct a new mode of address. Paralleling some of Goldman and and Papson's findings, our content analysis revealed four important themes and two sub-themes that consistently show up in marketers' attempts at earning the coveted voice of authenticity in their ad messages geared at media savvy, young-adult consumers: (1) images of shared values and ideology; (2) images of belongingness through, for example, depictions of stylized group activities and intra-generational diversity; (3) the theme of countering cynical, resistive readings though irony, humor, and reflexivity; and (4), myriad design techniques using postmodern design strategies such as hyperreality and hypersignification and intertextual references to popular and media culture.

Images of Shared Values and Ideology

Although all ads, to a certain extent, have image-building qualities, Stewart & Furse (1987) define the specific image-building ad as one that primarily attempts to "create desire for the product without offering necessarily a specific product claim" (1987, 140). This element of commercial culture is key in Gen X advertising: The product consistently gives way to the image of the characters, the situations portrayed, and the denotative meanings, allegories, and symbolisms suggested. Heavily image-based advertising was used to speak to Gen X. Indeed, 84 percent of our Gen X ads were encoded as mostly "image building" ads as opposed to 54 percent for all other ad types.

Through ideological values-matching, the Gen X ad is often accompanied by the creation of manifest emotive moods of "freedom from the mundane and the everyday" (36 percent of Gen X ads vs. 6 percent of all other ads), usually denotated by exuberant group activity and through technology or highly evocative artistic and optimistic music video-like presentations. While most advertising traditionally encodes the theme of freedom through the freedom of choice offered by the marketplace, Gen X ads specifically use freedom as a theme in their depictions of diverse people, as well as in their depictions of technology as an instrument of liberation from oppression and/or the mundane quality of postmodern living. These ads also celebrate hedonism as freedom (16 percent Gen X ads vs. 2 percent in all others). Sexual freedom also tends to be a common theme in the freedom-as-ideology, image-building ad: "sensuality" was coded in 62 percent of Gen X ads versus 50 percent of all other ads.

While themes of freedom are present in many Xer ads, by far one of the most powerful strategies to authenticate Gen X ad presentations is to use narratives that underscore individual emancipation and empowerment. One ad campaign that does this is the humorous but poignant Saturn "Vanity Mirror" campaign (see Figure 14.1). The Saturn piece is a perfectly executed example of an ad using ideological agreement. Through the characters' well-understood statements, attitudes, and realism, the ad creates acceptance of the key message of the piece, namely, that Saturn is indeed "A different kind of company" and "A different kind of car." The ad in its entirety fits precisely the image of the 1990s' upwardly mobile, cautiously optimistic, and empowered Gen X viewer. The piece is, in essence, a slice-of-life, a counter-argument ad that directly addresses the "big sell" hucksterism experience of most car purchasers, and humorously turns it on its head by mocking the typical image of a car salesman. This ideological positioning is intimately understood by most young, especially female, viewers and, in a typical Gen X mode of address, uses an ideological appeal instead of a product-centered strategy to differentiate the ad message.

The ad specifically addresses female car buyers by empathizing with the patronizing and condescending attitudes they often experience from male-dominated industry "experts." Throughout, we see her being given the runaround by male car salesmen at various unidentified dealerships, being treated as an inferior person because of her gender. We are taken into the subjective position of the woman with a female narrator's voice: "I thought the days when women were treated differently then men were long gone! Then I tried to by a car..." she explains with a disheartened tone at the start of the piece. The second half of the piece sees her at a Saturn dealership where, she states in an upbeat mood, "Dave Peters took the time to answer all my questions." She then not only ends up buying a Saturn car, but, because she loved the experience of buying the car so much, we see her in the last scene of the narrative actually working for the company selling Saturns.

The ad empathically invites the target viewer (females in their late twenties to early thirties) to share in the frustration and humiliation faced by the narrator protagonist. Her constant failure to get the various male salesmen to take her seriously exasperates her, and the viewer feels her mounting frustration. The caricatures of the salesmen are well understood by the target market and portrayed well in the ad's various vignettes. "What a great day to buy a

Car Salesman 1: What a day to buy a car!

Women: I thought the days of women being treated differently from men were long gone.

Car Salesman 2: This is the vanity mirror, so you can check your makeup.
Woman: Then I tried to buy a car: something reliable, sporty.

Car Salesman 3: How much were you looking at spending?
Woman: I was looking at spending $12,000.
Car Salesman3: Rich can look after you. I will be back to you real soon
. . .

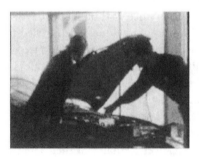

Woman: When I got to Saturn, Dave Pierce took the time to answer all of my questions.

Woman: Not only did I buy a Saturn, I thought it might be fun to sell them. You know what I like best about working here? Showing guys the vanity mirror!

Figure 14.1 Saturn "Vanity Mirror" campaign.

car!" exclaims one of the cheesy male salesmen as the protagonist chokes while politely smiling and obviously feeling jilted and talked down to. "This is the vanity mirror so you can check your make-up" says another salesmen as we see her sitting in the passenger seat of a car, in a competitor's showroom, with the salesman's face appearing in the vanity mirror. Again the viewer feels her quiet pain while the ridiculousness of the situation grows exponentially into funny but bitingly poignant statements of the lack of female empowerment in certain sectors of the marketplace.

The second half of the ad sees the protagonist finally going to a Saturn dealership where, she thankfully tells the viewer, "Dave Peters took the time to answer all of my questions." Here the protagonist finally feels like she is being understood and treated as an equal. This, in turn, has an empowering quality about it and, most importantly for the ad's designers, the ideologically congruent and positive mood is transferred onto the Saturn brand.

In sum, the ad is an attempt to establish a positive image of the Saturn experience and product in the mind of its twentysomething, upwardly-mobile and single female target. Through the protagonist's testimonial we see a before and after presentation of what purchasing a car is usually like and what purchasing a Saturn is like by way of comparison: positive and empowering, pleasurable, and worth repeating. The reflexive tone (casting car salesmen in a negative light, seeing the customer getting jilted) is underlined by the irony at the end, when we observe the jilted protagonist actually liking the Saturn experience so much that she ends up working at the company: "Not only did I buy a Saturn.... I thought it might be fun to sell them." The ironic empowerment is witnessed in her comment toward the end: "You know what I like best about working here? Showing guys the vanity mirror." This narrative technique is tailor-made for the savvy viewer; the ad doesn't have to blatantly state that buying a Saturn is a better experience, it humorously and engagingly implies it in the quick-cutting narrative. Attracted to the ideological fit of the ad, the viewer then willingly fills in the obvious blanks.

What the Saturn ad does especially well is to subvert standard stereotypes. Indeed, stereotyping the crafty and distrustful car salesmen helps to deflect empathy from them and, consequently, increase the empathy the viewer has toward the protagonist. Stereotypes quickly loose credibility with the new consumer. As Hornblower (1997, 68) reminds marketers, advertisers must strive to "communicate messages in a simple, straightforward fashion...[because]...if you can't find that authentic voice, they will discount you." By doing their homework the Saturn ad designers reach into the psyche of the female Xer and articulate her apprehension toward the ritual of buying a new car, then reversing the feeling by casting the event in an emancipating way. Commenting on the same ad, Marchetti (1995, 65) confirms the success of the Saturn approach:

> Commercials that stereotype us continue to flood our TV set.... On the other hand, some commercials are wising up to our generation. Like the new commercial for Saturn cars. The commercial works—it reminds me of the day I picked up my first set of wheels. Companies like Saturn are finding an *authentic voice.*

Rather than MTV-like, grunge-encoded, angst-laden scenes, ads like this communicate the most important values of the Gen X new consumer: "genuineness, honesty, and pride." David Taylor, corporate communications director at Coors, notes, "Research reveals that Generation X as an audience is one that likes to hear honest, direct messages about the product." Renee Frengutt, president of New York-based Market Insights, concurs, "You have to find something that will resonate with them without making it obvious that you are trying to target them" (quotations from Marchetti 1995, 65–68).

Images of Belongingness Through Depictions of Intra-Generational Diversity

Closely related to the ideological values-matching ad, depictions of diversity in the person-codes is another strategy used often by advertisers to find authenticity. One of the methods of encoding images of diversity into ads is through scenes of intra-cohort group activities and belongingness. Many boomer ads depicting belongingness concentrated mostly on family values; 21 percent of all other ads were coded with family values. But Gen Xer ads encode depictions of belongingness and social groupings by centering them around peer group activities (34 percent of Xer ads vs. 15 percent for all other ads). Despite their worship of rebellion and romantic individualism, this generation—like those that proceeded it—is in desperate need of social contact and approval, and must rely more on peer groups for that expression, given the family and generational divides that now exist. These groups are engaged in fun times or social situations such as rituals and rites of passage (34 percent Gen-Xer ads vs. 10 percent all others). The ads also include many non-Caucasian characters to appeal to this cohort's valuing of diversity.

Some advertisements developed quirky storylines or cultural vignettes to which the logo of the brand, which is then briefly attached at the end to signify authorship. Levi's has had great success presenting youth with branded entertainment. These types of ads, according to David Spangler, a director of marketing, work because they bury the sales message and speak to the audience as intelligent viewers: "The ads are low key and that's just the point....Kids say, 'You're talking to me in a way that's respectful. This is not about you selling me jeans. It's about you and me being friends' " (in Shenk 1997, 80). We find in this quotation the interest of creatives in being perceived as "friends" with their audiences, in being "liked." One way in which this is accomplished is by providing the young adult audience with entertainment instead of direct sales pitches. Working through the marketing problem posed by Generation X helped designers to develop templates that were more sensitive to the tone of voice their audiences preferred.

A good example of presenting the brand encoded with scenes of diversity and social groupings is Molson Canadian's "Road Movie" campaign. The brand takes on a secondary role to the images of youthful freedom, irreverence, partying, the carefree life, and exuberance. The brand itself does, however, play a key role as the central prop that celebrates and unifies the diversity of Gen X youthfulness, bringing together the desirable group affiliations and rites of passage. This "decentering of the product" is perhaps the most common way of presenting the brand in the Gen X ad, for its is non-obtrusive and complimentary to its audience, addressing the new consumer's desire for less hucksterism and a more useful, tasteful, and targeted promotional strategy. Commenting on this aspect of the Molson Canadian piece, one prominent Canadian marketer states, "The Molson Canadian 'I am' campaign is about presenting the identity of the brand and its take on life. Ad by ad, the campaign lays out the essence of the identity and asks the viewer to decide whether to accept it or not" (Caffyn 1997, 14).

The ads—emulating a David Lynch road movie—speak to the new consumer at several levels, appealing to their sense of ethnic tolerance, social liberalism, and independence. The brand is linked to escapist rites of passage, associated with the "weekend at the cottage" part of Canadian mythology. The ad is a multilayered visual montage of vignettes presented in extremely quick scene cuts, making the piece feel at once hectic and chaotic, but also unified in its central theme of freedom in youth. The montage style is readily understood by a Gen X target market weaned on MTV and MuchMusic. A male Gen X narrator speaks in a poetic but mundane voice that subtly complements the visual imagery by juxtaposing the machine-gun editing and shaky camera movements with a monotonous tone of voice. This contrast gives the scenes of youth—leaving the city, driving, hitchhiking, and doing wild things to escape with friends to the country on weekend outings of hedonistic reverie—a sense of planned chaos.

While the characters are wild and out of control, this scene occurs only for a contained period of time—after work and school on weekends. For unlike their unfocussed boomer parents in the drug-induced haze of the 1960s, those portrayed here know exactly what they are doing and that there are high-paying, high-tech jobs awaiting them back in the city. It speaks to the work and consumption divide, modeling the "controlled de-control" Featherstone sees as typical of the new middle classes. The way to unwind from the frustrations of the cubicle-and-fluorescent offices, the ad states, is to let loose on weekends and party as hard as they work.

Unchained, linked to a native in-
stinctive appetite to break free

. . . wheeling.

Leaving the cities limits behind,

(The sight disappearing in the rear-
view mirror.)

Why...because I AM CANADIAN
(music).

Figure 14.2　Molson Canadian "Road Movie" Campaign.

The ad type is a youth-manifesto ad (ideological appeal); the complementary scenes of young people all over Canada getting into their cars and heading for the open road, presented in its fast-paced montage setting, speaks directly to the generation's disdain for being tied down (this is after a cohort subject to a fluid job market and delayed passage through the lifecycle). The ad implies you can have it all. An oppressive life of socio-cultural expectations and mores need not lead to the sacrifice of individual self-fulfillment (which is their own cynical view of the boomer generation); rather, the ad shows what young Canadians are doing about it: bucking trends, becoming millionaires at twenty-seven, staying in school longer, enjoying mom and dad's cottage). In essence the ad speaks of a massive and unified thumbing-of-the-nose at society by a corporate multitude of once disenfranchised young adults who are saying, "To hell with the status quo and working 9-to-5 and all of the trappings of the boomers, we're doing things our way"—reclaiming leisure from yuppie driven work-a-holism (of course the 9-to-5 had to be dismantled for the new workplace that for many now demands well in excess of eight-hour days).

Anticipatory codes of foreshadowing and interpretive cues are designed throughout the ad. Music is one of the main ways of cuing desired meaning and viewing stance. For instance, scenes of "…leaving the city behind…" at the beginning of the piece are underlined by a driving, pulsating drum score. The driving drums, in their incomplete staccato, speak of a yearning feeling in the characters to let loose and break free. The viewer, already familiar with the technique in pop music, is expecting more instruments; and when those instruments arrive, the viewer has already been cued to a forthcoming change. With the full instrumental music coming in when we see the confines of the city being left behind, the viewer is further signaled to react negatively to the unsympathetically cold city and positively to the freedom promised in the open road. Connotatively, the cold drums represent the staccato of repetitive city life; the music, the free-flowing improvisation of a wonderful weekend with friends in the vast and inviting outdoors.

Another design technique that colors the piece with rebellious resonance is the use of shock and irreverence in the characterizations. For example, the ad is peppered with scenes of the young men doing wild things, such as urinating in unison at the side of the road. This shock-value scene differentiates the cohort from older viewers and the brand from its more stodgy competitors. The comic relief of this scene also complements the ad's rebellious tone and alleviates some of the pounding, unrelenting montage, encouraging the viewer to continue to engage the ad. The point is no longer to imply the consumer's magical transformation; rather, it is to de-center the product within an engaging narrative and hope that the consumer will be engaged. Account executive Brent Hodgins of Leo Burnett in Toronto puts it best:

> Teens get it—base your creative on reality. Many ads fail by virtue of claiming that teens will be cool by using your product. You must instead demonstrate its relevance to their culture and let them draw their own conclusion. (Lahey et al. 1997, 16)

The Molson Canadian "Road Movie" piece demonstrates effectively and powerfully what beer in general, and the Molson Canadian brand in particular, means to Canadian Xers: a cultural icon of social bonding with friends. When communicating to Xers, one of the most effective strategies marketers employ is to tell viewers about the product and the brand by somehow creatively weaving the product in celebratory, unifying, belongingness scenes. The highly rationalistic and materialistic product/brand benefits of the "Product Information Format," and the idealistic images of the consumer in the Product Image, Personalized, and Lifestyle Formats, give way to the product or brand positioned not as the savior of the consumer, but as a constitutive element within the symbolic world of the user and his or her sub-group. Whereas the Lifestyle Format had to match the look of the target audience, these appeals must map the production values and ideology of the group, as well as their taste and humor, without appearing to be too earnest or eager to please.

Addressing Audience Cynicism
Through Reflexivity, Humor, and Irony

The original response to Gen Xer cynicism was to show a cynical slacker-type, disgruntled and disenchanted with the world. While these early Gen X ads failed miserably, they were upgraded to fit Gen X's focused cynicism. The object of Xer cynicism in the new ads becomes, self-reflexively, the very media that produce the ads. This paradoxical message positioning agrees with the cynical value judgment of the Xer audience toward media hype and rewards the Xer viewer's media savviness.

A way of executing this strategy, Lahey et al. (1997) suggests, is to design ads that are quirky, at times bizarre, and always irreverent when addressing the Gen X viewer. And, most importantly, it means breaking down the once sacred industrial age advertising strategies and revealing the jaded edges and persuasive strategies of Madison Avenue itself in self-mocking narratives. This means both not being afraid to be an ad and to give Gen X audiences the straight pitch, but with an ironic or satirical twist and parodying the tools of the trade, which Xers intimately understand.

The Generation X consumer, according to Goldman and Papson (1996, 256), was "hailed way too often" with tired messages of "most" and "best" claims. To directly address "the pressure ... to find fresher, more desirable, and more spectacular images to enhance the value of products," advertisers throughout the 1990s positioned their products, messages, and concepts within new forms of thematic delivery that capitalized on the knowledge of a more media-savvy audience became more open to traditionally taboo advertising topics and techniques. Generation X having been targeted, ads found their meaning in challenging traditional advertising narratives. The use of more negative emotional themes captivated audiences. Guilt, fear, and anxiety were scripted into messages in graphic ways (Burnett and Lunsford 1994). Of the two hundred prime- time commercials we analyzed, "guilt" was encoded in 10 percent of Generation X ads and 13 percent of all other ads, but "anxiety" was found in 28 percent of Xer ads and 13 percent of other ads. Advertisers tapped into the general malaise and angst of suburban youth. Negative theme ads are more prevalent than twenty or even ten years ago.

Early understandings of this market segment painted them as being overwhelmingly negative, politically disengaged, socially and politically distanced, full of cultural ennui, cynical, and flippant. They seemed to refuse to engage in stable brand relationships and placed more credence in what their friends had to say about products than what marketers said. Marketers began to muse that to reach this generation required one to establish street credibility, undertaking what is called "bottom-up branding." One way this was accomplished was by creating advertisements that poked fun at the very practice of advertising and marketing. Barq root beer, holding second place in the American root beer market, engaged Generation X by making fun of its own marketing. The band used an "edgey" personality and a string of wacky, almost sophomoric promotions. Barq's marketing director noted, "We use a lot of self-deprecating humor and have a lot of fun at our own expense....the intent is to form a relationship in a non-pretentious, non-patronizing way" (Shenk 1997, 80).

The new generation of consumers appreciated the willingness of brands to deflate their marketing seriousness. Ads like this illustrate how humor was used to target Gen X. Of the fifty Xer ads we analyzed, 60 percent continued humorous narrative themes compared to 37 percent of all other ad types. The design techniques of "Irony" (28 percent of Gen X ads vs. 13 percent of all other ad types) and "Parody and Satire" (42 percent, of Gen X ads vs. 26 percent all other ads) became standbys in the advertiser's Gen X toolbox. For example, Coca-Cola promoted Sprite with its "Image is nothing. Thirst is everything. Obey your thirst" campaign. One spot mocks the constant association of soft drinks with partying by showing some characters who find a can of "Junky" soda on the beach, open it, and find a "party in a can." There is a cut to two young people watching the ad on television; one opens his Junky soda and no party emerges. The tag line warns in the voice-over, "Trust your taste buds, not commercials." The ad seems to unpack the magic of advertising conventions. In these ads image is mocked as shallow and inauthentic. But as Mark Crispin Miller, professor of media studies at Johns Hopkins University, notes, "If they really believed that 'image is nothing' then they wouldn't bother to mention it.

Repudiation of image is itself a most seductive image" (interview in *Merchants of Cool*, PBS Documentary 2001).

"Reflexive" ads, a predominant Gen X promotional strategy (34 percent of Gen X ads vs. 7 percent of all other ads), are used in "turning criticism into positioning concepts ... [by rerouting] viewer criticism." By exposing "the metalanguage that composes the underlying code of advertising," these ads give credence to the viewers, treating them as peers who are not being talked down to (Goldman and Papson 1994, 42). In these ads topics once considered taboo by the ad world are now fair game. As Hornblower eloquently states, "...they are as skeptical of the media as they are of politics. The hippest ads tap into their hostility towards hype.... Sprite rocketed from seventh to fourth best-selling soft drink after scrapping its schmaltzy jingle, 'I like the Sprite in you,' in 1994 in favor of the slogan, 'Image is nothing. Thirst is everything. Obey your thirst'" (Hornblower 1997, 66).

To counter disgruntled consumers who have been "hailed too often," ad creators have learned to turn to self-reflexivity, as ad creators Caffyn and Hodgin (1997) confirm. Gen Xers care less about what angle or bias ad opinions and media messages have, as long as they are up-front about the opinion (part of their diversity). An example of an ad that exposes advertising's "grubby sales pitch" is the KISW Rock 99.9 FM "Gratuitous Sex" campaign. The ad admits to marketing's "greasy paws of advertising" (Lahey 1997, 13) right in the ad, self-reflexively. The ad exposes advertising's "lie," "sleaziness," and "huckster-ism," addressing Xers' cynicism toward media hype. We hear the narrator in the plane of discourse together with text underlining his commentary and strummed rock guitar music throughout. We are informed that the station "won't show any sexy videos. No provocative positions. No sexy videos." It then pokes fun at the advertising genre by bringing the banality and formulaic arguments lobbed against advertising by its critics to the forefront: "We know you're too smart for that." The ad then shows a 10-second montage of sexy videos, women in provocative positions and animated, driving rock music, and the narrator states, "We lied."

Another poignant example of the reflexive ad is Labatt's "Joel" campaign. Labatt has turned the self-reflexive ad into an art with its "I'm (*fill in the blank*) and this is my beer commercial" campaign. The elements of advertising are exposed by Joel, who seemingly constructs the ad, with all its inherent jingoistic and formulaic elements, in the course of its being shown. Joel is in control, explaining how a beer ad is put together ("...and we can add music, and color, and poking fun at the government regulations, noting 'Now, we can't actually drink beer on TV, but, we can hold it!'"). He proceeds to magically construct the ad (and in doing so, of course, to deconstruct it) by adding the music, the people, and the colors, then keying in the announcer, while at the same time being a part of the action. Joel simultaneously straddles the line between the plane of events and the plane of discourse.

Hi, I'm Joel and this is my beer commercial.

Now we can't actually drink draft on TV, but we can hold it.

And we can add music, color, and some people having a great time.

Queue the announcer.

Announcer: OK Joel. Labbatts Genuine Draft goes down real easy because its real draft.

OK, tape, that's it. Can I open this draft now?

Figure 14.3 Labatt's "Joel" Campaign.

The absurdity of beer ads is exposed in the obnoxious voice of the male announcer after Joel cues him: "OK Joel. Labatt's Genuine Draft goes down easy cause it's real draft!" But before he cues the announcer there is an abrupt transition when a scratchy-needle-on-a-record sound abruptly cuts the music and the color, converting the ad to black and white. People in background stop partying and the announcer reads his lines in an over-stimulated manner. People partying in background are then seen as actors in a commercial, being made up and working on the set of the ad. Here, the piece exposes the dominant theme of traditional advertising, reflexively turns the "happy worlds" theme on its head and using it as a deconstructive technique—in a direct appeal to the media-savviness and jaded character of the Gen X viewer. Joel proclaims that the ad is over ("OK. That's it. Music, please.") as he motions to someone off-screen to start the music, and color seeps in as a wipe, colorizing the entire image on screen, when Joel commands it: the return of the happy advertising world used to reflexively expose the meta-narratives and techniques of advertising formats. The ad becomes its own hyper-reality—the object of scorn whose fantasy cannot be resisted. Thus the narrative is resolved by leaving the viewer within the party world of alcohol advertising.

This ad can be called prototypical Gen X because of its reflexivity—the nonchalant, yet in-control attitude of Joel, a typical Gen X type, outfitted in signifying dress, inwardly optimistic toward his own life (he is happy and confident in the ad), yet outwardly indifferent in appearance. The ad directly addresses Gen X in the familiarity its message has with the media, as Joel deconstructs the overused 1980s beer commercial party atmosphere ad, at the same time as the ad affirms it. The fluidity of the deconstruction, and the ease of Joel's control, indirectly places the dominant position of the discourse into the hands of the viewer, in an attempt by Labatts to be a transparent company, thus adding credibility and authenticity to its product. The ad takes on the critical point of view of the viewer toward beer ads, exposing the "beer ad hype" of competing Bud and Coors campaigns.

Strategies of Youthful Style, I: Hyper-Reality, Hyper-Signification, and Postmodern Design Strategies

"Hyper-reality" and "Hyper-signification" (58 percent of Gen X ads vs. 16 percent of all other ads) are an exaggerated, TV-mediated reality. Commercials become hyper-real by "technically modifying the encodings of realism and drawing attention to the codes of media realism," and by using "video techniques that encode a heightened awareness of reality" where "technique overwhelms substance as a semiotic system" (Goldman and Papson 1994, 25, 31). Goldman and Papson give us some examples of how ad design forms hyper-real depictions: shaky camera work, the "searching camera," "photographic techniques that de-center products" and central objects, unfocused subjects, and a jarring, fractured narrative that leaves the viewer to piece together meanings. In general, hyper-signifiers in ads "emphasize the detailed contours of material objects and human gestures" (Goldman and Papson 1994, 35) in unconventional ways—ways that "hyper-realize" an ad to portray extreme or outlandish situations.

Through the 1990s it was common for producers to layer images with text, to use the roving camera and montage-like editing techniques and contrapuntal music effects, à la Marshall's "typography of text and visuals" (1997) found in Channel Zero productions but pioneered by Moses Znaimer at Toronto's CityTV (Wiseman 1996). This technique has been called postmodern because it "...maps the interplay of surface phenomenon, as a system of collage and citation that 'floats above' any determinate or determining ground" (Delany 1994), breaking with the traditional rules of simple linear imagery and storytelling. In postmodern productions, such as Channel Zero's *Planet Street*, text, imagery, and music merge in a "highly stylized" form of narrative (Orr, 1997) that necessitates the viewing of the text several times to fully understand the messages portrayed (Marshall, 1997). McAllister noted that the increased use of text in advertising could also be seen as a strategy for overcoming the audience's zapping and muting tendencies. Written words are useful because they can convey meaning even when viewers turn the volume down, and also they make ads stand out in the sea of images.

> It has become impossible to differentiate one image from another. For a form of communication that has as its first goal to attract attention, this sea of images is an oppressively swallowing sea. Thus, in part to escape a trap that they themselves have created, advertisers must turn to the written word...to stand out. (McAllister 1997, 98)

An example of a hyper-real and hyper-signified ad is a message from Money Mart headed "Not a Number." The advertisement is a montage of various Xers proclaiming they will not be prisoners to the hard sell, or technology, or lack of personal service, and especially they will not be considered merely a number. This anti-establishment protest ad, is pure counter-argument, appealing directly to the known resistive readings of the Gen X cohort. The ad honors individual identity and self-expression and a marketplace where the consumer is king. The ad was designed against the cultural backdrop of spreading call centers, Internet banking, and other "self-serve" technological strategies implemented by the financial sector.

The ad is hyper-real in its layering, making use of roving camera shots, fast edits, quick zooms, and pieced-together dialogue and narrative to form one unified but fast paced message. The ad takes Jean Rouch's *cinema verité* to the stratosphere of postmodern design. Mimicking the fast-paced, visual montage techniques of the music video genre, the narrator's voice is gritty and direct, exclaiming exactly what it is that ticks off this generation about the lack of customer service. Along with a tapping into Xers' knowledge of music video and television techniques—speeded-up video of the cityscapes, the double-take edits—it also references the computer savviness of the cohort with fast flowing images, numbers and bar codes. Generational conflict is played upon as the boomer appears: an overweight, mean-looking, hectoring, middle-aged man in a cheap suite in a room with taxidermy on the wall behind him (a very politically incorrect scene). This is juxtaposed with the long-haired free-spirit man exclaiming, "Enough people tell me what to do already!"

The ad rejects the condescending treatment of the consumer, demanding: "I want to talk to a real person.... No attitude, thanks." Citizen empowerment is the answer. "I am not a number.... I want to talk to a real person ... faster.... I hate line-ups...." The ad also communicates product attributes as the character explains why he likes Money Mart : "I want to cash a cheque ... pay some bills ... no attitude at all...." The appeal for individual expression and more authentic interactions is also stressed in comments such as, "I am not a number," "Machines? No machines!" The ad speaks to Gen X's resistance to technological determinism, which distinguishes them from the baby boomer's insistence that technology is the end-all-and-be-all of modern life.

Strategies of Youthful Style, II:
Intertextual References to Media Culture

The use of media culture and pop culture references in ads to reflect and suggest new meanings is known as *intertextuality* (Fowles 1996). Gen X targeted ads in our sample were more likely to accentuate the intertextual (42 percent of Gen X vs. 27 percent for all other ads). The ads "comment" on familiar popular culture themes and topics and popular cultural icons, and contain references to other goods or previous ad campaigns, ideologically or socially familiar themes, and indirect references to other media.

In a hair color ad we find TV culture itself used as a main theme. A young, vivacious, bubbly and "flirty" woman sits in front of the television set flipping channels while trying to persuade the audience to try Flirt hair color. She flicks through the channels with her changer, making commentary on different characters' hairstyles, all of which she believes could benefit from treatment with Flirt: "Wow! Looks like some of you still haven't tried Flirt, the conditioning color enhancer. Look, it just gives your color a kick," she says. In its intertextual mode of appeal the ad denotatively uses snippets of nostalgic 1970s TV programs to underline the easy-to-use image of the product.

Much of the framing of this commercial positions the viewer within the television set, and thus metaphorically the audience is also without the enhancing powers of the product. She is pictured in deep interaction with her television set, as her conversation is influenced by what she sees on the TV material she is watching. The logical form of the discourse of the entire piece is an analogy: coloring your hair with Flirt is as easy as flipping channels. It is also as noncommittal as watching TV: You can just zap your way to a new color and zap it away should it not be to your taste. The TV clicker appears as a magic wand of transformation. The ad also directly addresses the zapping tendencies of most viewers by portraying the protagonist using a TV clicker to *flip past the commercials!* This connotatively encodes reflexivity and tells the viewer that the advertisers understand the hyper-real, fragmented media-scape. In a sense, the ad is reassuring the viewer's guilty-pleasures side, implying that it is OK to "veg out" in front of the "boob-tube" and let the clicker "do the walking."

As one marketer stated recently in *Marketing Magazine*, "Clearly, teens now have a wider cultural array from which to choose.... They use this breadth of choice as a cultural smorgasbord—a little hip-hop plus a little '70s retro with a dash of ethnic 'finds'—in order to build an image" (Kratzer & Hodgins 1997, 16). Most of this "cultural array," however, is firmly ensconced within mass media images, clearly and overtly capitalizing on this wider cultural array through their multi-ethnic person-codes, intertextual references to pop culture, and eclectic depictions of group activities, fashions, and music tastes.

Nostalgia is mostly a boomer ad technique (31 percent of all other ad types compared to 14 percent of Gen X ads), but when it is used in Gen X ads references are typically to media memories. Gen X's nostalgia lies in using the hyper-signification of shared media experiences: "This has been accompanied by an increasingly pervasive practice of rummaging through the old bins of television images in search of image fragments that can be recycled and re-framed," what Olalquaiaga, according to Goldamn and Papson, calls a "self referential kitsch-kitsch." They add: "The ability to appreciate old kitsch represents a higher order of consumer authenticity" (Goldman and Papson 1996, 257–8).

In the clutter of the contemporary, "hypermedia" landscape, getting the viewer—and especially the media saturated and younger Generation X viewer—to watch and engage with the ad message has been a major challenge. Ad creatives have addressed this problem with the "emotive ad": ads designed with intensely multitextual and rich empathic situations, dramatic presentations, shared cultural symbolism, and ideologically congruent images interlaced with engrossing and entertaining emotion-laden narratives. The emotive ad has been around for several decades, but its prevalence has significantly increased. Consumer behaviorists such as Moore and Harris recognized advertising's more frequent use of dramatic emotional narratives to break through the clutter of a multi-channel universe and make the advertising's appeal "more distinctive and, hence, perhaps more persuasive" (1996, 37).

Holbrook and Batra (1987) place such high importance on emotions being embedded within advertising that they have conceptualized an ad's emotional content as the "personalities" or "emotional profiles" of advertising. Emotion has been institutionalized in commercial practice. Pragmatic academic researchers explored the importance of emotions embedded within ad messages as not only differentiating elements within the advertising's narrative, but as *mediators* between an ad's content and viewer attitudes toward the ad and the brand (Holbrook and Batra 1987; Moore and Harris 1996; Thorson and Page 1988). The ability of an ad to invoke positive affect was increasingly understood as a key component of advertising effectiveness.

Our review of Gen X advertising revealed that advertisers employed several strategies to legitimate their practices before the eyes of a cynical youth audience; at the same time these strategies came to symbolize and constellate a niche market. In order to increase the retentiveness in memory and felt impact of the message, and to negotiate a sense of authenticity with their audiences, marketing communicators have been entrenching the shift to a communication conception of persuasion. This is centered around designing with affect and cultural symbols, as a critical element for survival at a time when the audience was imagined as being particularly resistant to messages. And, as our content analysis makes clear, these new strategies are on the whole entrenched in intertextual cultural references and ideologically shared experiences. This motivating symbolism is freely drawn from images found within popular culture, and the consumers' capacity for visual literacy can draw out minute references which become the resources of a shared culture.

The advertiser's romance with the young adult audience began in earnest in the 1960s, but it was the experience of enchanting Generation X that solidified youth as a key market segment whose tastes were inflected through culture. For example, MTV style editing has become *de rigeur* in television advertisements regardless of target, and as copywriter Ernest Lupinacci notes, the theme of rebellion has become an industry standard for distinguishing brands that cannot be distinguished by quality:

Without doing much research, you could conclude that in the last half of the twentieth century one of the most popular ways to market a brand was to position it as the alternative to the current, and in the vernacular of the times, seemingly "uptight" category leader. So wild, visionary Pepsi-Cola was, as opposed to Coca-Cola, "The choice of a new generation," daring Burger King let you "Have it your way" instead of McDonald's way (Vagnoni 2002).

Those brands that flourished with the target market developed an affinity with them and provided symbols that they found useful in their identity struggles. According to marketer Ian Forth of Britain's BMP DDM Needham agency, in a postmodern culture where social relationships are continually torn asunder and remade, brands become a source of consistency which can be referenced within life narratives and as shared cultural experiences with others: "As contemporary life and contemporary media fragment, strong brands will become more relevant, providing a beacon of consistency and reliability amid the clutter and chaos. Hence...advertising can play an important contributory role in investing products with emotionally motivating symbolism" (1996, 23).

Those design elements that fully exploit the entire spectrum of emotional appeals proved to be a pivotal tool for advertising designers. Exemplified in 1990s young adult-market advertising, many campaigns now include design strategies that exploit emotional encodings, including, in addition to the "hyper-real" and "hyper-signified" narratives already discussed, intertextual and "nostalgic recollections of media memories," the use of irony and satire, and heavy uses of Brechtian-like postmodern stylizations (Fowles 1996, Goldman and Papson 1996). Whereas earlier postmodern critics such as Jameson (1991), borrowing from the Frankfurt School, would derisively label these techniques the culture industry's "aesthetics of pastiche," our study shows that the marketing world uses these pastiche aesthetics, self-referential humor, and themes saturated with kitsch and nostalgic intertextuality as blatant and increasingly successful advertising design strategies. They are successful because, as we discovered though our focus group interviews, they appeal to the new consumer's media-acculturated, reflexive, and media-weary palette.

The Case of Advertising Reception and Generation X: Layers of Resistance to Advertising Messages

Having explored how the industry constructed its understanding of the Gen X cohort and the types of messages encoded to rally this disaffected segment, we now turn to exploring how individuals from this cohort interpreted the promotional messages directed to them. To focus our study we sought to delineate more clearly the "resistance" of this cohort, which is considered to be a defining feature of their generational character. A review of the reception research literature reveals three different usages of the term resistance by cultural critics. These three definitions are explored in light of interview data gathered from discussions of advertising by young adults. Findings are then placed back within the historic context discussed thus far in order to explore more fully the impact of generational resistance to various aspects of consumer culture.

Resistance in Reception Theory

Resistance in reception research was originally concerned with persuasion. McGuire (1968), a founder of this approach, defined resistance as taking place within a process of counter-argument in which the subject understands the message but develops a cognitive response which denies or rejects the content.

The ability to develop oppositional arguments was assisted by the stock of counter arguments individuals possessed prior to the reading. McGuire's communication model universalized and naturalized notions of resistance through being situated outside the complexity of structural relations. Hall's encoding/decoding model (1988) provides a corrective. For Hall encoding (message construction) and decoding (readings) took place within the framework of class ideology, where individuals could be seen as taking up three distinctive reading positions (136–8):

1. Dominant-hegemonic: "operating inside the dominant code";
2. Negotiated: creating exceptions to the dominant code while still accepting its legitimacy;
3. Oppositional: "de-totalizes the message," reconstructing it "within some alternative framework of reference."

Hall subsequently conceded that his model treated "the institutionalization of communication as too one-dimensional, too directly articulated to a dominant ideology." The model's generalizability was hampered by never being fully empirically tested and based upon the narrow subject areas of news and union disputes. Still, Hall refused to relinquish the position that structural power works through language: "Power needs something out of language. It needs something out of the shaping maps of meaning which the population is going to use to understand events...." Ideology, he continues, "cuts into the infinite semiosis of language" and "wants to make a particular meaning" (Hall 1997, 263).

Kristeva's (1984) notion of intertextuality challenged the notion that texts were the isolated products of authors, noting that meaning always draws upon language which is already present. Each utterance is supported not only by a quotation of another text but can only make sense in relation to the texts around it. New combinations of signs "place and displace" old and new meanings while they build upon that which has gone before. Writing is always "rewriting" and authors cannot take credit for meaning, for its origins are derived outside of what is "texted" in language, namely, the cultural context and the unconscious mind of the reader.

At its most extreme, this view implied the "death of the author," since it represents each act of interpretation as utterly unique and productive, derived from the act of interpretation for which the symbols of the text play a supporting role in a larger concert of meaning. From this perspective idiosyncratic readings are not deviant; rather, they are to be expected. Indeed, given that each reader comes to a text with a unique history, an infinite set of interpretations would be expected to cut across the intended meaning of the text. Hall, however, questions the limits of the "infinite playfulness" of signification and the way this perspective is considered to be emancipatory, or at least potentially emancipatory, for the individual (Fiske 1987; Barthes 1993; Buckingham 1997).

Morley, one of the few researchers to have produced empirical research on the processes of decoding, argues that "the imperative is to find a way of steering between the dangers of an improper romanticism of 'consumer freedoms,' on the one hand, and a paranoiac fantasy of 'global control,' on the other" (1993, 227). Hall urges the need to be "sensitive to both the 'vertical' dimension of power and ideology and the 'horizontal' dimension of television's insertions in, and articulation with, the context and practices of everyday life" (1993, 276). The emphasis on studying readings from an idiosyncratic and psychological basis is also endorsed by Livingston (1990, 167), who in her study of soap operas sees the need to go beyond social indicators: "The determinants of this range [of responses] were found to be not simply sociological (age, sex, class), but also psychological (identification, evaluation, recognition, sympathy)." In particular she points out the importance of narrative, character, motivation in the formation of unique readings: "The difference is in how they interpret characters, are what allow viewers to become involved emotionally with them and to take sides as the narrative unfolds".

Semioticians such as Eco (1981) and Barthes (1993) note that some texts are more open to interpretation than others, and they have attempted to contribute to the understanding of message reception within the 'horizontal' domain of everyday life, through pointing out that individuals derive real pleasure from texts. McQuarrie and Mick (1992) empirically test the notion of "pleasure" in their study of advertising interpretation. Their work confirmed the polysemic nature of the text, illustrating that the array of interpretations individuals created was much greater than those produced through semiological examination alone. Advertising contains various levels of ambiguity or multiple meanings, which are clued through resonance with meanings stored up in the individual's memory. They argue that pleasure is derived from the reader's ability to decode the multiple meanings of the ad. Yet, not all individuals derive the same degree of pleasure from this quality of resonance in ads, since "some people cope well with ambiguous stimuli and situations, while others dislike and avoid them" (McQuarrie and Mick 1992, 11).

From this perspective advertising is considered to be an aesthetic rather than a rhetorical product, canceling out the viewers' ability to present counter-argument because the bulk of their attention and energy is funneled into the decoding of the text. Audiences appear to take pleasure in their judgments of advertising aesthetics and to enjoy playing the role of the cultural critic. O'Donoughue, for example, found that young adults could interpret ads in a cynical and ironic way and derive great pleasure from doing so. As McQuarrie (1992) notes, a "self generated resolution to the ambiguity and incongruity" of the message may enhance favorable brand attitudes, because in solving the symbolic puzzle the subject is able to "congratulate himself on his astuteness."

We have seen how advertisers during the last two decades of the twentieth century increasingly moved toward a more dramatized and emotional style of ad design. Studies undertaken at the time of this transformation revealed that audiences react to these types of advertisements in unique ways, differently from their reactions to ads which attempt to rationalize or to present an argument or reasons for product purchase. The positive regard toward dramatically-scripted advertisements discovered by Deighton, Romer, and McQeen (1989) could be related to the level of sensationalism surrounding characters and narratives. Deighton et al. found supporting evidence for the thesis laid out by of Wells (1988) and Englis (1995), namely, that television ads can be defined as "...either arguments or dramas or hybrids of these forms." They have proposed a *Dramatization Scale*, with argument and drama at the extreme points on a "...continuous scale with plot, character, and narration as attributes that mark transitions along the scale" (Deighton et al. 1989, 335). They go on to claim that, where argument appeals to reason, the scale moves down to a more empathically persuasive based rhetorical form as in drama centered commercials.

In short, these authors conclude that the use of drama increases the emotive force of the ad and opens up the persuasive mechanisms of commercials to entertainment-centered accounts that are not subject to refutation. In these ads the viewer is asked to "step into the fantasy world of the ad..., to step into the role of the character in the same way as we would in a movie." Ultimately, Sutherland concludes, "These ads appeal to us emotionally" (1989, 68, 81). Our study of ad content also shows that, due to the importance of authenticity to savvier Gen X markets, ad designers are to a large extent appealing to the realm of the emotional and the dramatic, and not as much on rational/functional/utility arguments to reign in the new consumer. Indeed, "materiality," "rationality," "functionality," or "utility" codes were present in only 32 percent of Xer ads, but were present in 74 percent of all other ad types (i.e., boomer ads) using these rhetorical strategies. In turn, more Xer ads were coded with the highly emotive elements of "sensuality," "sexuality," "anxiety," "imaginative appeal," "fantasy themes," "belongingness," "irony and satire," and "comedy and humor."

On the other hand, argument-based ads that rely less on emotive rhetorical force are at least open to refutations, rebuttals, and even being proven false in their claims. Sutherland (1993), borrowing from the techniques of the cinema, hammers home the importance of drama in subverting viewer resistance by exploring the notion of "vicarious participation"—engaging the viewer through immersion or inclusion into ad's narrative that is solely based on the dramatic eloquence of the ad. According to Fiske (1987, 21), dramatic presentations work because drama cannot be shown to be false due to the fact that they are not open to argument, relying instead on what Fiske calls a "dominant sense of reality." A successful ad that uses dramatic engagement is not based on the success of relaying the product's beneficial attributes, but rather relies on how entertained (or engaged) the viewer is when viewing the commercial. This does not mean that these advertisements are not subject to criticism, for they are; but any such criticism will be framed by the criteria of engagement, not argument—the simple exercising of individual taste in deeming something either good or bad.

The emphasis on dramatization, sensationalism, and emotional appeals has become fundamental to adverting design, as marketers are being advised to construct messages which account for the "emotional" dimension of cognitive processing (Zajoc 1980). Burke and Edell reiterate the argument made earlier by Holbrook and Hirschman (1982) about the need to understand consumers' "feelings, fantasies, and fun," as part of the overall consumption experience, in light of the later empirical research which shows a significant correlation between affective reactions and message processing (MacKenzie et al. 1986; Parker and Young 1986). They point out the need to make a distinction between judgments and affective response for "even though an individual may describe an ad as "amusing" (i.e., determine that the ad has the characteristics of an amusing ad), that individual may not be amused by the ad" (Burke and Edell 1989, 70). Their study illustrates that feelings influence not only readings of an advertisement, but also brand attitude and evaluation, whereas from this perspective resistance would involve negative feelings or dislike which would lead to message rejection.

Another form of resistance is exemplified in the work of researchers who attend to sociality and signifying processes. Hebdige (1988) revealed the way sub-cultural groups array symbolic markers and signifying practices to differentiate themselves. De Certeau (2002) questions the nostalgia for a past uncorrupted by popular culture and advertising references, arguing that people "make do" with the texts provided to them and use these to construct meanings in creative ways. Audiences bring distinctive ways of reading and of subverting the dominant readings which advertisers seek to convey. In their study of popular television programs, Ang (1991) and Radway (1988) have noted the way in which individuals can be seen as forming "interpretive communities" whereby one's perception and interpretation of a message is shaped by historic, regional, and social positioning. Jhally and Lewis (1992), in their study of *The Cosby Show*, confirm this finding in revealing a complex interaction between the social cultural categorizes of race and class in different interpretations and enjoyment of the show.

Goldman and Papson (1996) have called this heightened cultural appropriation "Sign Wars": the use of intense image creation in order to differentiate niche markets and target markets through the marketplace culture's appropriations of cultural symbols imbued with culturally understood meanings. It is an equation that equals a "commodity sign." Commodity signs, therefore, psychogenically and psychographically select and differentiate markets. Throughout the 1990s marketers targeting Generation X, for instance, attempted to appropriate and use symbols common to certain sub-groups, sub-cultures, taste-cultures, or symbols residing in youth culture (read "pop culture) in general. For example, Nike versus Reebok meant Air Jordan fame versus Gangsta rap from the hood hip.

Resistance styles in Generation X viewer readings

The preceding discussion suggests that three overarching forms of resistance run through the reception research literature, which we have designated as follows:

1. Ideological resistance: based upon the deconstruction of the text and its reconstruction based upon an alternative framework, such as socialism, feminism, anti-racism, anti-heterosexism etc (Hall 1997);
2. Modes of address resistance: challenges based upon idiosyncratic interpretations strongly informed by affective and aesthetic elements (McQuarrie and Mick 1992, Burke and Edell 1989);
3. Lifestyle resistance: discord between the message and the symbolic markers and values used to designate the reader within affiliation to others (Hebdige 1988; Fiske 1987).

To further explore these ideas of resistance, so closely associated with the Generation X cohort, we conducted an experiment in which six prototypical young-adult targeted advertisements, drawn from prime-time television over the period 1994–1996, were shown to ten young adults. Respondents in this group are referred to here by number (i.e., 003, 006, etc.). Semi-structured interviews, approximately two hours in duration, were conducted to produce the data used here as a preliminary exploration of resistance in readings of promotional messages. The advertisements selected promoted specific products and contained style elements thought to be attractive to the subjects' age cohort (nineteen to twenty-five); most were similar to those analyzed above, and three were actually analyzed in our content analysis. One outlier ad targeted at baby boomers, a Ford ad, was included for a point of comparison. The ads used in the study are listed below along with a short denotative description.

1. Crispy Crunch "Car Logic"
   The scene opens picturing a young couple in a car. The young woman distracts the man in order to steal his candy bar.

2. Saturn "Vanity Mirror" (Figure 14.1)
   As previously described, this ad depicts a young woman shopping for a car, confronting a variety of salesmen. Most impressed by her treatment at the branded car's showroom she becomes a company employee.
3. Ford
   Lindsay Wagner, a television star from a 1970s drama, explains the value and financing of a family style car. This ad is targeted at a baby boomer audience.
4. Sheik Condoms "Repressed Teen" (Figure 13.3)
   Commented on earlier, this ad depicts a young man dressed in baggy clothing with a flannel shirt tied around his waist. He stands in front of a building with columns, ranting that he is not going to take it anymore and that he refuses to be oppressed. A young woman walks by, gives him a condom and tells him to "just use it."
5. Rold Gold Pretzels
   A character from a popular television comedy appears in a high school prom dream sequence in which—given his small and out of shape body build—he carries out hyper-real acts of strength and agility, beats up the bully, and wins the girl.
6. Pringles Potato Chips
   A series of shots focused on young people dancing to music and eating potato chips.
7. Joel Genuine Draft (Figure 14.3)
   As previously described, a young man walks the audience through the making of his own beer commercial.

Our interviews confirmed the view outlined in academic theory and empirical studies and held intuitively by marketers: Young adults do not always agree with the dominant messages conveyed in advertising. Those interviewed generally expected ads to entertain, to convey a sense of authenticity they found acceptable, and to acknowledge their media-rich life-world. They derived forms of pleasure from the text even while criticizing it. The most typical type of resistance is best understood as lifestyle or modes of address, rather than ideological resistance. Few completely rejected the premise of the advertisement and offered an alternative, and the few examples of ideological resistance we encountered were neither forcefully nor consistently sustained. This tells us that the central concern of readers is not to reject consumerism, but to challenge the styling of goods and media tastes that neither conform to nor complement their own. Still, these readings reveal that advertising is a site of contemporary struggle over meaning. Viewers expect creatives to match their values, particularly in relation to the representations of women and race, and viewers also expressed a sense of entitlement for high quality novel advertisements.

While storylines and styling were discussed, our subjects devoted most of their attention to decoding the characters within the advertisements. The transcripts of interviews reveal a great deal of sensitivity to the hair and clothing styles of advertising characters, perhaps confirming Goffman's (1979) perception that hair is an early warning system informing the viewer of the type of social interaction that is likely to unfold. Viewers more readily commented upon the styles they did not like than those they did:

> Respondent 003: I don't like the long hair....I like guys with really short hair.

> Respondent 006: She's got a really bad perm.

> Respondent 009: A taupe, really cheesie jacket, blazer or something and her hair! There is nothing you can really relate to when you look at it except her haircut, which is like—really bad.

> Respondent 003: This is not a look I like, I don't like Joel's look.

Identification with characters might be understood to run along four different, but not mutually exclusive lines: personal, social, lifestyle, and intertextual. With personal identification, the reader projects himself or herself directly into the storyline or character offered in the ad. For example, one participant noted that the chocolate bar ad in which a young woman steals her mates chocolate bar, was "funny for me," for she identified with the character's transgressive behavior: "I am always sneaking chocolate or eating off of other peoples food, when I'm not supposed to" (respondent 003). Another respondent, after viewing the couple in the chocolate bar ad, noted, "I could see me acting like that in a relationship" (respondent 011); and another, "I have a boyfriend and I can see how it would be funny to go into the washroom and steal a chocolate bar from him." Still another respondent said, "I like it because I can relate to it, 'cause I went through it. So, in that way, I just think it is a cute commercial" (respondent 006). Personal identification produces a powerful form of positive affect. When readers are able to find themselves in commercial representations a powerful affirmation and values match is created.

Viewers also made sense of the ads by reading them through their immediate social relationships, mapping peers and family members onto the characters. Through this process the characters were made intimate, familiar, and credible to viewers. Examples of these types of responses include statements such as: "He reminds me of a lot of my friends" (respondent 011); "I have to identify this with my bother" (respondent 005); "It reminds me of my friend's place, cause she has a similar place" (respondent 001); "I could totally understand what she was saying. I liked her character too, 'cause she seemed like a friend type person" (respondent 007). We find here a bleeding of the commercial domain into life-worlds through the act of interpretation.

But viewers also moved outside personal reference points, bringing their storehouse of lifestyle and social segmentation knowledge to bear in their readings. For example, "class" was used as a convenient way of describing the differences among characters. While these readings of class and economic positioning rarely ruptured the seam of the intended message, definitions did vary. For example, one viewer felt that the grunge look of the condom ad character signified middle-class bohemian and a sense of overindulgence. This reader disapproved of the character's ranting about the plight of the world, believing this rebellion, coming from a spoilt middle class, to be simply a form of attention-getting. Showing an ability to align with the practice of advertisers, the reader recast the ad: "It should be a black African American cause, or something, the conspiracy thing.... It's a white kid out there, skater, probably has everything he wants, he doesn't have the right to be so irate and so, because there are so many other things going on. You know, the States" (respondent 003). Another respondent noted, "He thinks he is oppressed but he is not" (respondent 004).

We make two observations about these readings. First, the resentment viewers displayed toward the main male character within the condom ad would be applauded by advertisers, who had encoded a persona they hoped young people would react negatively toward. Disdain toward the male character heightens the affirmative action of the young woman who tells him to stop ranting, take action, and wear the product. In short, the audience aligned with the female character, as readers sought to distance themselves from the ranting, opinionated behavior of the male character. Respondents honored gratefulness, pragmatism, optimism, and concern for the less advantaged. Second, we suggest that these interpretations are inflected with nationality, as these Canadian readers drew upon their stock knowledge of American values to critique the ad. We would assume that part of the pleasure derived from these readings related to how they simulated feelings of national identity and superior moral standing.

But while some readers interpreted this character as being affluent and middle class, others felt he signified working-class sensibilities, and while those quoted previously read the character's look as grungy and edgy, to others he was scruffy and dirty: "He looks scruffy! Yeah, he is not, like, clean. But I guess, to me, he looks more like working class type...everyday Joe kind of guy" (respondent 007). Another did not find the character in the beer ad unattractive, instead saying he looked slovenly, as if he had been in prison (respondent 011). For several respondents the grunge styling presented in the Gen X advertisements was associated with dirt and dishevelment, causing anxiety. Based on our sample, at least, advertiser's taste for the "bohemian" look does not seem to register with all young readers.

Our viewers distinguish characters through lifestyle categories more so than class. Thus another way the working class was referred was as "trailer trash." One viewer noted: "Like they were wearing really cheap clothes, it looked like. It just seemed really kind of like boppy American, kind of like trailer trash-ish" (respondent 003). Although he had no props, the character in the condom ad was continually described as a "skater," a "skate-boarder," but also a "gangster," "generation x sort of guy," and "typical left-wing radical" (respondents 003, 004, 005, respectively). The character in the Ford ad was read as "mother-ish," "probably with children" (respondent 003, 011). Readers filled lifestyle narratives into the characters, and these interpretive acts made the characters more rounded, vivid, alive. This categorization also eludes to the processes by which viewers map characters onto culture to make sense of them.

Finally, participants also engaged in intertexual identification, drawing upon their knowledge of the media world to make sense of the messages. Hence the condom ad character was "sort of like that Bill & Ted's excellent adventure or Pauly Shore—you know, one of those really young comics, maybe kind of like Jim Carrey, you know kind of spacey" (respondent 011). As for the girl in the Saturn ad: "Um, she looks like Dana Scully on X-Files" (respondent 005); Joel in the beer ad was "like his hair and his clothes of Bud Bundy—one of the Bundy kids" (respondent 011). Those that recognized the celebrity used within a commercial brought this to the interviewer's attention, with some pride: "I think George draws your attention to it, well he *is* George on *Seinfeld*" (respondent 001). Some used the actors' real name, others their media name: "I always think *Bionic Woman*" (respondent 003). The sexuality of one female character is referred to with reference to media stars, past and present: "You know, she looks like Anna Nicole Smith kind of meets Marilyn Monroe or whatever" (respondent 003). Knowledge of brand styles was also used to read the messages; thus one of the advertisements was "totally Eddie Bauer" (respondent 003); another "like that Gap look" (respondent 006) and still another, "You know, like Liz Claiborne" (respondent 009). This type of discourse, which maps the world via popular culture and brand knowledge, is very similar to how advertisers pitch their ideas to one another. When advertising creatives speak of their craft they frequently do so in a short-hand of popular cultural style references which become their common language.

Audiences took issue with how advertisers represent women and race. Earlier we learned that the inclusion of minorities within advertising was increasing; however, non-Caucasians continue to be overrepresented within group depictions. The people we spoke to showed that they were aware of a "diversity shot" pattern in advertising, and they did not necessarily react positively toward it. One respondent noted, "This one is like a bunch of Caucasians but with one black woman, so I just thought, 'Ooh! That's kind of racist" (respondent 009). Several respondents in their recounting of the ads remembered a clip from the

Pringles advertisement that depicted an African American woman with chips in her mouth, mimicking a duck's bill. Most interpreted this image as "weird" or "stupid," but some took issue with the offense it might cause to black people, as the following comment indicates:

> It is like the chips, when put in this way, emphasizing on her mouth, and they are using a black people. I think like "why don't you use the white people to do this? Black people in general, I'm not saying all of them have big mouths, and they are emphasizing on it...not very good. Not good. I think they would find it offensive. (respondent 010)

These comments and others found in the transcript illustrate that audiences read race and empathize not only with advertising characters but with their intended readers. Advertising in instances such as these becomes a moral tableaux in and through which readers seek to protect others from perceived harm. Readers were also attentive to how women were represented. While female respondents were more likely to comment on the representations of women, some male viewers found the old troupes of sexism tired and boring. Several viewers expressed their dislike toward ads that they believed objectified women, or presented them as submissive and not clever. It was not just the images of women, nor the plot lines that participants took issue with, but also the tone of their voices. One respondent disliked the squeaky voice of a female character: "It just bothers me because, you know, women probably don't talk in those tones or talk in high-pitched or talk in certain ways, but are taught most of it to talk like that. And it just seems really, I don't know, un-progressive" (respondent 003). Female characters were expected to have their own minds, as one participant noted, "She is nothing, she has no mind of her own in this commercial....It just makes girls look so silly and stupid" (respondent 001). Readers also highlighted the differences they saw between the representations of men and women. One viewer noted that in the reflexive beer commercial while males were presented as "authentic," whereas girls were relegated to mere props: "I don't like how they are dressed...it is kind of offensive. They are not even looking at them as people, they are just meat, I mean they don't do that to genuine Joel, but they'll do that to all the women." (respondent 007)

The differences between the sexes were also highlighted in readings of the pretzel ad, which depicted a male fantasy (fight and sexual conquest) that female readers found difficult to relate to. One reader, speaking of the woman in the ad whom the males fight over, noted: "She finally is won by and owned by a male. She is like a prize—a trophy....It is stupid" (respondent 010). Still other readers found the stereotyping in this ad to be acceptable because it was read as "obviously" or "reflexively" mythical: The characters were read as allegories, which permitted readers to find humor and cleverness, rather than demeaning depictions of women, in the ad. Reflexivity, irony, and playfulness appear to be able to deflect criticism from the text. For one reader, the match between the geeky male and over the top beautiful woman seemed to be the stuff of fantasy where stereotypes take on different hue:

> They have done her up to be even more, of this kind of, goddess looking thing. And in the gym too. So in a way it is not as offensive because at least they are obviously doing it to be funny. And George is not trying to come across like he is any [big deal]. Putting those two people together is not that offensive. If they had a big stud guy coming in and she was really believably a model or something, then it would be obnoxious. (respondent 003)

There were many other examples in the transcripts where the approval of readers was won with clever storytelling, humor, "meta"-stereotypes, and reflexivity, such as these:

> It is sort of like, the mini storyline that everyone knows like the high school reunion, and the bully and the pretty girl and the geek. You know, how they play on that story-line and the characters are still, like, stereotypes in this commercial, but it is different. It is drawing upon a story. I have to say that I like it cause they are not hiding anything, they are not trying to put one over you or anything. They are totally exaggerating it. (respondent 005)

> It is unrealistic but it is effective because it is funny. It is a commercial about the commercial about a commercial. So, it is different from regular commercials. Like it is completely different from that Pringles commercial—which is the typical commercial. (respondent 011)

> It is fun. It just seem like it is fun. It is a joke. It's funny; it reminds me of something like a *Married with Children* episode or something like that. (respondent 001)

Thus, it is clear that ads could deflect media criticism if they acknowledged the media savviness of their audience and presented signs of "pure entertainment." As the response below indicates, some of the young adults are less critical of entertaining messages that sought to offer obvious points of identity:

> In the Pringles ad they think I am supposed to be relating to them [characters]—I am supposed to be like them. But the Pretzels ad, I don't feel like I am supposed to be them. It is purely entertainment. (respondent 011)

However, advertisers were also praised for what were understood to be progressive depictions of women. Viewers were particularly appreciative of the car ads, which presented women in a sales position, or a role that defied stereotypical femininity. The Ford car ad received praise because the character bore all the marks of a "mother," "wife," or "homemaker," but "she is selling trucks," which made the ad "cool." The Saturn car ad allowed one female viewer to affirm her belief that men are concerned about their appearance, and this validation of belief created a very powerful affective relationship toward the ad: "Like when she says at the end 'you know I like showing the guys the vanity mirror,' I go 'right on'—'cause you know guys use it" (respondent 011). One respondent was happy to see a woman selling the car with brains instead of brawn: "I like it...it is different.... like, she knows what she is talking about, not like one of those 'bimbos' who is always selling the cars" (respondent 007). That the producers of the Saturn ad are praised for showing women as empowered and employed, when they have been so in fact for some time already, illustrates the inherent conservatism of advertiser's depictions of gender.

Despite its pro-female storyline, however, some read the Saturn ad as a threat to their identity. Two respondents found the "corporate culture" overtone of the ad uncomfortable. One viewer found the brand "cultish," noting: "I don't like the way they are drawing people in, I think it is eerie...like the way they talk, like it just seems like a religion thing or like Amway" (003). For another the ad invoked a club he or she did not want to be part of: "Um, it seems like you have to buy a car to be in this club. But do you really want to be with these people?" Here we find the complexity involved in communicating corporation belongingness. Some viewers conveyed a keen awareness of corporate targeting, and for them the ad invoked paranoia, posing a threat to their independence. Individuality is held sacred in a consumer culture, and this message, which invites the reader to become part of the group, violated this value for them. Demassification is clearly at work in readings such as these. The worshiping of individuality was also reflected in viewers' expectations that advertisers should provide strong and believable personalities in their messages. Weak characters were generally disliked.

> Like, she doesn't come across as an exciting or fun person, or intelligent or.... It seems as though she is just a spokesperson in the commercial. Just talking, like she got hired by the company to talk about these cars. (respondent 006)

> Like, he doesn't seem to me like he necessarily had a personality or like a...he was just kind of... you know, promoting this product. He didn't seem like an actual person. (respondent 007)

Participants also reflected an awareness and active participation in the process of targeting. Age appropriateness was particularly important for these viewers, who resented having to watch ads which they deemed to be oriented toward "old" people. Recall that the spark that ignited the Generation X debate was a recognition of disgruntled young viewers who felt that the media overly favored the tastes of the baby boomers—which, by in large, it did. Readers staunchly upheld a divide within the marketplace between young and old and refused to be associated with the latter. These young readers were particularly ageist, drawing strict generational divides: "I didn't like it. It made me feel old" (respondent 004); "I don't know...just that she is totally, old, and I don't really care what she says…" (respondent 006); "I think if like the people were younger I would be more likely to stay with the ad" (respondent 010).

One respondent who loathes the depiction of young people offered in the Pringles ads, imagined that it must have been produced by an out of touch "old" person: "I can just imagine who wrote this commercial and who directed it—a bunch of old guys! Who think that young people are like that they are totally not!" (respondent 011). Scorn was heaped upon the boomer character played by Lindsay Wagner because, although she was "mommsy" and empowered, she was also "old." One viewer put her in her place by displaying cultural snobbery, drawing a clear demarcation between the world of popular culture and advertising, and invoking the residue belief that good actors would not stoop so low as to appear in commercials: "Poor thing, I guess she needs the money, she has got bills to pay. You kind of go, oh! The graveyard of lost stars…and stuff" (respondent 003).

Nor, however, did viewers appreciate ads, which they felt contained messages that were too young, for example: "It just reminded me, it's like an irritating ad that would be on Saturday morning kids' cartoons" (respondent 003). Readers not only participated within the processes of targeting by articulating their specific tastes against others: some also showed their understanding of the position of the advertiser, displaying an awareness that their criticisms toward messages not directed to them was of little threat in the age of market segmentation. As respondent 009 stated, "They are not targeting me anyway, so they wouldn't care, right?"

Entitlement

Viewers expressed a strong sense of entitlement for quality ads, which illustrates both the nonacquiescing character of some youth as well as a culture where their demands were encouraged and, occasionally, met. Participants expected the ads to be clever, well produced, expensive, well acted, creative, and well targeted. They dismissed ads that were not creative, and referred to them as just "typical commercials," which meant the ad lacked a storyline, or that it failed to get them to suspend their disbelief. There was some indication that quality for these viewers meant a "cinematic" look, because poor quality ads were described as "very TV-ish." Indeed, as we have seen, the amount spent on commercials far outstrips the amount spent on television programming, and audiences expect to get their money's worth.

Those ads that were not well produced seemed to surprise viewers who felt that advertisers should, as a matter of course, understand that they had to produce quality images to secure audience attention. Indeed, participants spoke as if quality ads were their due—they felt entitled to be entertained. Criticism was directed toward the "director" and "producer" as respondents wondered how they could make such poor judgments about how to engage their young audiences. Viewers took the opportunity to insult producers on their lack of creativity. As respondent 007 put it, "I just think it really, I wonder who produced it. I found it really boring and stuff. And just not creative at all!" Expecting brilliant location shots or fantastically digitally-rendered, hyper-real environments, respondent 001 was disappointed by the Pringles ad: "It seemed like a cheap commercial... probably like some studio with some colored background kind of thing." We also found evidence that audiences expect a particular type of authenticity from the messages as well as good acting: "I don't think it is natural behavior. It seems staged (respondent 001); "I can tell he is just acting...I just think he is really fake. Like I can see right through it. Yeah, I just don't buy it" (respondent 006).

Great scorn was heaped on the Pringles advertisement, which depicted characters treating the product with adulation. This type of promotion did not give the viewers anything in return for their attention and the mood of reverie toward the product was considered "tacky" and distasteful. Respondent 005 stated, "Like the whole group is so... so involved with these chips and it is like too much." Respondent 005 said, "They are tacky....Oh, I hate it. I just hate it. It is irritating!" Respondent 011 commented, "Just reminds me of another, kind of, American nightmare." Resondent 003 succinctly said, "Irritating."

Readers, as inhabitants of the mature marketplace, were intolerant of "product worship." They expected advertisers to forget about the product and provide them with intriguing characters and storylines. As we learned earlier, some brands invested a great deal in advertising, producing very engaging messages of high quality. There is some evidence that readers expected all advertising to meet this mark and that they were disappointed when it did not: "It doesn't look very sophisticated, in a way. Like, what ads today are like, you know they are very, kind of, you know really trying to get your attention" (respondent 009). These audiences are ad critics—commercial snobs.

Ads that were richly textured with irony and double meanings were labeled as "sophisticated," "clever," "funny," and were generally well liked. While texts with double meanings and symbolic puzzles held the potential to alienate the reader, their ability to capture attention and invoke powerful epiphanies created powerful positive affect: "Oh, I get it, neat!" (respondent 003); "I see what they are trying to say" (respondent 001); "I didn't get it the first time, but now that I see what they are saying, cool" [laughter] (respondent 006).

There was also evident that readers could acquire pleasure even while contesting the meaning offered in the advertising text: "I felt a sort of satisfaction, looking at them and being able to say, Oh they are goofs!" (respondent 005); "It is interesting in its own stupidness" (respondent 011); "Yeah, he is really annoying actually. But I enjoy watching the ad, I don't know why, but you know, he is a stupid character. It catches like, my attention, like 'Oh! There is that stupid guy!'" (respondent 009); "It is kind of irritating because the guy is so hyper and he is screaming. But it works" (respondent 011).

It was not just the age of the characters that was clocked by readers but the styles advertisers offered. During this period, advertising designers were at pains to refresh the symbols in ads to keep audiences constantly engaged. We found participants responding to these changes judging ads as "in" or "out of style." Participants generally appreciated messages they interpreted as "on the pulse"—they liked novelty. Nineteen-eighties yuppie styling was subject to romantic revolt, being seen as "crass commercialism," "American values," and generally unrefined, lacking in entertainment value, and exhibiting a deficit of reflexivity.

> I think it is really tacky and they are stuck in the '80s—like nobody wears those colors any more. It is very, very eighties, very American actually. There is no theme, there is nothing there, it is just like you see these people having a good time eating chips there is nothing to it! (respondent 007)

> Just there was a woman in the ad, she has shirt, curly sort of hair and she was wearing this orange headband, which I thought looked really bad. Totally '80s! (respondent 006)

> It is irritating. Yeah. Looking at it now, it kind of looks like an '80s commercial. (respondent 001)

> It just seems really out-dated, sooo '80s. (respondent 003)

Audiences read the ads through the frame of a dominant style template, as particular colors and fashions came to signify an entire complex and chaotic decade. Advertisers, who helped to construct these fantasies of unity, have come to engage this style-knowledge of audiences in their designs to communicate to young people. References to "out of date" symbols were not necessarily a negative experience for readers. While the 1980s were unanimously subject to ridicule, the retro-'70s style held great appeal.

> They hit it well with the '70s music. I mean it is really fun—the '70s are cool. I think too, when you hear music like that, like now they have it in lots of clubs and they have, like, retro-nights and things. So it is instantly, kind of, right-on there! Like right on the pulse, kind of thing. It drives you because it is fun. Something you are experiencing in a certain age group, I guess. 'Cause, I don't know . . . my parents would think differently. 'Cause it would be old to them. (respondent 003)

The appeal to retro styling, recognized as part of the processes of postmodernity, may also be informed by generation dynamics. The 1970s perhaps appeal to Gen X because this period was often the scorn of many die-hard 1960s counter-culture members, and thus it could be re-appropriated by the market and provide symbols that appear new, fresh, fun, but also useful for "clique maintenance." Media and marketing industries play a considerable role in popularizing and working within the cracks of generational divides.

Summarizing the New Consumer's Resistive Readings

Our semi-structured interviews seem to support well the academic theory, our content analysis categorizations, and marketing communication wisdom: Contemporary young adults are sophisticated judges of promotional messages. They are able to comprehend and find pleasure in texts complicated by ironic, cynical, double meanings and intertextuality, and they expect advertising to be more than just "typical ads." Identification is closely related to resistance, and the characters in ads which were unable to resonate authenticity, credibility, and entertainment, and to ally with age demographics and personal sub-cultural tastes, were at best ignored, at worst heaped with scorn. The sample ads presented to subjects invoked heated emotional statements, and subjects quite freely expressed their opinions on matters of aesthetic judgment and character interpretation.

Readers felt entitled to receive entertaining ads from the marketplace. According to Fowles (1996, 106), the light entertainment of the commercial media system serves as an "elixir" for the emotional management needed to deflate the pressures of everyday postmodern life. This is accomplished through the "vicarious discharge of the somatic components of emotions...and the space of emotional reparations" that pop culture and its discourses offers. When ads become intertextually linked to pop culture, they also become a "psychological tonic," much like movies and commercial TV programs are. Emotionality is now the technique of choice in subtly hailing the mature, cynical Gen X viewer. The consumer, thus, stakes his or her claim not on the ad's product but on its entire narrative universe: its manifest message, its multilayered meanings, and its latent subtleties, analogies, and parodies.

But entertainment is not simply a psychological factor, but part of a social struggle between audiences and advertisers. These types of messages not only provide gratifications but also points of discussion in social groups and a common language between audiences and advertisers. Young audiences are not only looking for pleasure, but representations that match their values. The transcripts revealed audiences engaged in a negotiation or pact with advertisers in which respondents indicated, in effect: "If you please me, I will give you my attention." This sense of audience entitlement does not spring fully formed as the authentic statement of audiences; rather, it must be understood as being shaped within the nebulous subject position constructed for audiences within the marketplace. For years the marketing ethos had claimed that the consumer was king (or queen). We find that within their interpretations, young people are claiming what they can of their entitlement to this ideology.

While much has been made of the blurring of boundaries that occurred during this period of so-called postmodernity, we find audiences and advertisers engaged in the construction of new dividing lines. A considerable amount of interpretive labor is devoted by young people to distinguishing themselves and their symbolic worlds from those of the boomers. This generational struggle appears to be one of the few factors that unites these readers. Like the yuppie template, Generation X created a conceptual unity over a diverse and chaotic public, perhaps best described as young, white, middle-class males from North America's West Coast. There was more diversity in readings than unities.

In this period of growing acceptance toward the role of advertising within society, we still find a form of resistance which does indeed conform to the rigors of rational ideological critique. Hall's emphasis on the need for critique to be rooted within a broad rational framework, which looks beyond issues of personal taste to systemic inequality, is still the most sound prerequisite for the mobilization of dissent. However, there remains a need to listen closely to the lived expressions of audiences and factor them into the framing of research questions, such as: How did "emotionally" and "aesthetically" based dissent come to dominate? In what way can texts be seen as closing ideological critique through the presentation of symbolic puzzles or drama? Why are critiques of lifestyles and modes of address so easily formulated, as opposed to more broadly-based criticisms? How do style critiques deal with broader issues of social inequalities, e.g., the scorn for the symbols of the 1980s? Can aesthetic critiques be mobilized?

One way these audience readings might be more fully appreciated are to view them as cultural critiques, to think of advertising as part of the process by which audiences seek to secure distinctiveness. As we have seen, few of the respondents argued that advertisers' depictions were "wrong." These messages simply do not lend themselves to "truth" claims. Rather, respondents challenged the intelligence and taste of the advertiser—using words like "stupid" and "silly" in their attacks, which reveal an assertion of the ownership of cultural capital. Audiences constructed models of commercial producers' motives and persuasive techniques and utilized these to decode and defend themselves against intended messages. Viewers most vividly expressed their tastes through their distaste, indicating that research might focus more upon "displeasure" than "pleasure" in the text.

CHAPTER 15

Mobilizing the Culturati

Pierre Bourdieu theorized a cultural field in which taste distinguished individuals, and people struggled to advance or secure privilege. Taste cultures were linked to particular types of resources or cultural capital and class, which he argued could explain people's differing relationships to goods. He identified a group, namely, cultural intermediaries, who were particularly fixated on advancing its social place within the cultural field and was "interested in how they used the quirkiness of their tastes to set new fashions, offsetting the power of the upper class and traditional elites. These issues became important to both consumer culture and the economy as the upper middle class and their pundits grew more affluent, and also more influential, during the eighties, in Europe as well as in the United States" (Holt 1998, 39).

Academics and popular writers through the 1990s showed great interest in this group, using various names and attributes to describe them. Featherstone (1991) spoke of a new middle class, Campbell, a romantic consumer, Belk, anti-materialist consumers; popular writer David Brooks, BoBos; and Boyle, the new realists. All these authors recognized this group as having unique taste and using the aesthetic aspects of goods in distinctive ways. However, there was debate concerning the exact size and characteristics of this group. Belk estimated they made up about one-third of the American market, whereas Boyle put them at two-thirds of the British. Featherstone was criticized for implying that everyone had become the "new middle class" (Lury 1996; Warde 2002; Wynne 1998). Jansson (2001) argued that it was more important to think of modes of consumption, contending that the aesthetic or romantic ethos was just one orientation to goods amongst many others, and that it was possible for one individual to align with different modes of consumption depending upon context. These debates signal a serious rethinking of how the relationship to goods held by particular groups, but it was not only academics that took note of this culturati group. In the 1990s marketers and advertisers also took a keen interest in this group, and in this chapter we seek to illustrate how the culturati were mobilized by the commercial media.

To begin, it is useful to put some flesh on the culturati and their particular consumption patterns. To do so we turn to an empirical study undertaken by Holt (1998), for it provides a detailed image of how consumers relate to goods differently. Holt used Bourdieu's schemata to explore whether American consumers distinguished themselves by taste. He believed those with higher levels of education, access to cultural institutions (i.e., a working-class girl who becomes a ballerina), professional parents, and higher income (although not as determining as the other criteria), would have distinctive consumption patterns. Holt felt it should be possible to detect a migration of some groups from the economic field to the symbolic and cultural field, where their taste was guided more by "aesthetic and international styles that fit with cultural elite sensibilities and that are socially scarce" than by economic considerations (1998, 218).

Holt undertook interviews with consumers about their consumption habits, isolated key themes, and classified participants based upon their education level, family background and occupation. He confirmed Bourdieu's thesis, finding participants with high cultural capital displayed a significantly different relationship to goods than those without, confirming that the consumption of those with high cultural capital was more influenced by abstract aesthetic considerations. Table 15.1 summarizes his findings.

Holt found for those with high cultural capital, the cultural aspects of goods overrides their exchange value. The tastes of the nouveau riche continue to be shaped by education and family background, despite the influx of money; the newly-monied elect economic status displays—expensive restaurants, luxury cars, fur coats, and other obvious displays. Those with high cultural capital reject this pattern of consumption. They rarely go to expensive restaurants, even though they can afford to, because they have found these eateries to be impersonal and gauche. Understatement and knowledge about goods and services were valued.

Those with high cultural capital enjoy talking about goods and displaying their connoisseurship, and feel confident about providing an opinion on the quality of goods. Goods offer opportunities for self-expression. The symbolic aspects of goods support lifestyle construction and the articulation of taste. They fuss over the detailing of goods, taking every opportunity possible to talk about and form judgments toward goods. Selecting the most expensive good is a cheap way to express taste; thus, these consumers prize their ability to use their connoisseurship to find high quality at a cheaper price. Those with high cultural capital have satiated palates and hold "world-weary" and "bored" attitudes toward goods, which perhaps explains why they enjoy entering the world of the "other" through motifs of exoticism.

Cultural elites undertook a complex mixing and matching of goods to forge distinction and sought unique consumption experiences. They looked beyond their local groups to international elites for their consumption cues. The comfort and sentimentality of Victorian aesthetics were rejected for the abstract, cold, hard and elitist styles of functionalism and modernism. They also nostalgically appreciated the paucity of the peasant and artisan lifestyle. Goods that they considered to be mass-produced were vehemently rejected in favor

Table 15.1 Qualitative Differences in Consumption Patterns and Levels of Cultural Capital (Education, Family's Professional Background)

High Cultural Capital	Low Cultural Capital
Goods as form of self-expression	Practical problem solving, status, and celebration
Distant formal gaze toward goods; playful use of goods in which materiality taken for granted, creative contemplation	Appreciation of goods that realistically capture personal and bodily pleasures
Pleasures of the mind interest in cosmopolitan, and exotic, seeks to enter the world of "other"	Local, autotilic, collective, wary of entering the world of "other," preference for popular destinations
Appreciation for functionalist modern aesthetic	Country and Victorian aesthetics
Anti-fashion, prizes unique and originals style, one of a kind; dehomogenize, demassify, and decommodify goods by stressing their authentic engagement and knowingness of good	Developing skills with like minded, subjectivity not constructed through individuated consumption
Material paucity, peasant eclectic, artisan, casual	Abundance and luxury
Identity in communication of lifestyle	Identity in social affiliation, passion pursuits
Connoisseurship, fine grained vocabularies teased out of goods comparing good to other good, discussion of quality, opinionated, but if good unknown, will defer to expert, great enthusiasm for minutia	No passion about talking about goods, rather goods used to tell stories and convey information about local meanings—model and style of less interest
Eclecticism allows for construction of distinctive tastes in categories combination for exclusion and identity, weary of following style, prefers creative mix and match (*bricolage*)	Specializes, developing skill and social capital in one category that becomes key resource for constructing self and others
Consumers across genres	Consumes within genres

Source: A summary of point from D. Holt, (2000) "Does Cultural Capital Structure American consumption," in J. Schor, and D. Holt (eds.) *The Consumer Society Reader* (New York: New Press, 2000).

of "original, one of a kind" objects. However, some goods deemed obviously mass-produced could be incorporated into their lifestyles, if they were carefully packaged in irony and could be enjoyed as "kitsch."

Those with less cultural capital tended to consume within, not across, genres and had less jaded palates. They enjoyed the usefulness and bodily pleasures that goods offered and embraced abundance and luxury. They marked their status and identity on social relationships and skill, not on their knowledge of goods. They appreciated local and collective meanings of goods, preferring the popular to the abstract and bizarre. Since their identity was rooted in local pursuits and the development of skill and social capital, the "world of the other" held less appeal. They did not consider it shameful to use shared meanings of goods and expressed passion or dislike toward goods instead of disinterest. Goods allowed stories about local events and personal skills to be told. These participants had less interest in discussing the style, make or model of goods. Indeed, Holt had difficulty getting these consumers to talk—where as those with high cultural capital could not contain their discussion about goods. Sharon Zukin (2004) also found that some of the shoppers she spoke to enjoyed discussing the aesthetic merits of goods, while others concentrated on getting a good deal and finding useful goods.

These studies illuminate some of the complex relationships to goods, but they cannot be disentangled from the new media and advertising practices that emerged in the political economy of the 1980s and 1990s. During this time advertisers and marketers reached out to consumers with higher levels of cultural capital. The globalized media offered "international" styles that catered to the culturati's interest in cosmopolitanism. One publication that played a significant role in assembling this niche was *Vanity Fair*. In what follows we explore the type of audiences *Vanity Fair* assembles and how its advertisers seek to negotiate with the culturati in their designs, by way of a case study of 4000 *Vanity Fair* advertisements drawn from the period between 1990 and 2002.

Vanity Fair: Assembling the Modern Cultural Niche

Advertisers do not create niches alone, but in concert with media and designers. The intimate tone of magazines makes them one of the best niche market tools of all the media. In the early 1980s the consumer magazine sector expanded to meet advertisers' interest in more refined market segments. Despite ample funding and good editorial stewardship a great number of these new publications failed. Those that succeeded in negotiating the changing tastes of consumers and advertisers alike tell a unique story about culture, media, advertising, and research. *Vanity Fair* was one such publication. After its relaunching in 1983,

Figure 15.1 Advertisers offer gold, platinum, and other metals as something that will endure, mark time, and contribute to the ceremonial world.

subscription and advertising revenue climbed and the publication proved to be virtually recession-proof. The magazine assembled its niche audience with a unique mix of cultural content and positioned itself as a cultural guide, hosting a prestigious Oscars gala party, breaking exclusive celebrity interviews, and taking positions (mostly safe) on international and domestic politics. Editorial attention is paid to the business elite and a small degree of homage is paid to politics, but the majority of the articles focus on culture, fashion, and celebrity (cultural events calendars, articles on architecture, art world battles, stories of socialite murders, and interviews with designers).

This blend of content attracts a core readership with high levels of interest in cultural capital, who are affluent, educated and diverse (mean age, 40; mean income, US$80,000). *Vanity Fair* has carved a formative global marketplace niche, one of the few magazines able to use the same cover for international distribution. The editor, Gaydon Cater, describes his readership: "I have a fashion readership. I have a political readership. I have a literary readership. I have New York's social scene, Hollywood. I have America. I have Europe. And then you have men and women. It's a very complex magazine."

The publication has capitalized on its enviable brand heritage. The term *Vanity Fair* has strong links to literary tradition. The bohemian novelist William Makepeace Thackeray entitled his detailed study of London society *Vanity Fair*; in his 1848 novel the title phrase refers to "a place where all is frivolity and empty show; the world or a section of it as a scene of idle amusement and unsubstantial display" (*Oxford English Dictionary*), a place where individuals sought status, success, and wealth. In 1868 Thomas Gibson Bowles began a magazine called *Vanity Fair: A weekly show of political, social and literary wares*, which critiqued bourgeois lifestyles and valued culture over wealth. Concentrating on reporting social and cultural events, the publication achieved popularity, not necessarily due to its literary analysis but to how its skilled artists used caricatures to poke fun at public figures. The publication was disbanded by the turn of the century.

In the United States in the early twentieth century a young advertising executive named Condé Nast left his position at *Colliers*, a highly successful weekly magazine with a huge circulation. Nast believed the future of the marketplace lay in targeted, or what he called "class," magazines that catered to the taste of readers with similar incomes or interests. In 1909 he purchased *Vogue*, followed by *Home and Garden* in 1911. Each publication secured a viable "class" audience and attracted aspirants interested in the lifestyles of the fashionable set. In 1914 Nast launched his first self-created magazine called *Dress &Vanity Fair*, initially targeting the urban male dandy. After a few years, *Dress* was dropped from the title. The editors of *Vanity Fair* aspired to create the American version of the British publication *Tatler*, a highly successful journal of cultural commentary that according to its original publisher, Richard

Figure 15.2 The commodity and nature blur as advertisers repeatedly use images of unspoiled nature to promote products.

Steel, provided "accounts of gallantry, pleasure and entertainment." Yet, *Vanity Fair* had difficulty establishing itself. Its editors" inferiority complexes toward European culture lead them to obsess over high cultural excellence, making the magazine a terrible bore. The editors also paid scant attention to their audiences' interests, showing little regard for circulation figures or financial success—indeed from a cultural perspective, at this time, advertising and subscription income increased economic value, but was thought to cheapen the cultural value of the publication.

> As nearly as any evidence can suggest, the editors and writers of *Vanity Fair* were genuinely uninterested in the commercial part of producing a magazine. There was little or no communication between the business and editorial offices and the business executives" names did not even appear in the magazine for most of the years they made possible its publication. (Hoffman 1980, 50–51)

The editorial focus on high culture did not suit the more modernist and populist tastes of the expanding 1920s consumer culture. Over time *Vanity Fair* editors learned to be less strict in its definition of culture and began to include stories about Hollywood, sport, celebrity, and caricatures along with high culture content. This blending of high and low culture gave the publication a "modern" feel and the magazine became branded by its bold and distinctive covers. The publication became the place to find the latest and most respected cultural news. Sales boomed. By 1929 New Yorkers, Londoners, and Parisians recognized *Vanity Fair* as the leading magazine of its type. Despite this global brand recognition, however, *Vanity Fair* was unable to weather the storm of the interwar period and folded in 1936. For forty years the title lay dormant.

At the height of yuppie mania in 1983, Condé Nast (the company named for its founder) relaunched *Vanity Fair*. The publication was positioned as a highbrow literary magazine with the challenging mission to create "a record of current achievements in all the arts and a mirror of the progress and promise of American life." The new magazine offered in-depth biographies of political figures, current events, and topics thought to be of interest to educated audiences. But the high and low culture balance failed to impress audiences or advertisers. *Vanity Fair* floundered on the seas of the highly competitive 1980s magazine market cluttered with new lifestyle and entertainment magazines.

Showing its serious commitment toward making the publication the American *Tatler*, the publisher attracted a former *Tatler* editor, Tina Brown, as the editor of *Vanity Fair* in 1984. Brown popularized the magazine, modernizing its highbrow sensibility by increasing celebrity content. Her famed editorial formula was "60% Hollywood, 10% Ethiopia" (we might assume the other 30% was advertising). Brown increased the use of artful photography to

Figure 15.3 Those with high cultural capital have satiated palates and hold "world-weary" and "bored" and indifferent attitudes to luxury goods.

make the publication distinctive, and paid six-figure incomes to secure talented writers. She set about making celebrities of these writers by including beautiful author bio-pics at the beginning of each issue. This vanity style of publishing allowed the culturati to acquire knowledge of the names and lifestyles of cultural producers. The writers also brought a distinctive tone to the publication, which plays a key role in reaching niche audiences. One of *Vanity Fair*'s celebrity writers, Christopher Hitchens, a popular political journalist and regular contributor, explained how the *Vanity Fair* audience appreciated an intelligent and witty tone:

> With *Vanity Fair* the readership is so enormous, so it's very important that I don't try to think who the audience is. But, again, I try and write for everyone to read, as if I was addressing an intelligent and humorous friend....The great discovery you make is that that's how people quite like to be talked to. If they suspect for a moment that you're thinking, "Well, wait a minute, there are lots of trailer park readers of *Vanity Fair*, I better put in something for them," they will sniff you out in a second, as they should. They will know right away if you are being in the least bit condescending. And so that's how I write. (Institute of International Studies 2002)

Hitchens said the *Vanity Fair* audience did not expect an obvious political orientation, like other magazines; still, a general liberal slant was appreciated. This intelligent tone, neither too condescending nor too challenging, which did not obviously take itself too seriously, perfectly matches the values of contemporary culturati.

Brown left the publication in 1992, but *Vanity Fair* continued to grow out of its contradictory editorial formula. The new editor expanded the celebrity emphasis, putting one on every cover. Along with showcasing entertainment and media business, he added Hollywood and music issues. *Vanity Fair*'s Oscars party associated the publication with the "in crowd" and allowed the editor to snare exclusive interviews with hard-to-reach stars. But he and his band of high-paid writers also took stands on international politics, particularly war, revealing their liberal orientations in the jabs they took at Republican politicians. Some of these statements received coverage in the media—creating the coveted buzz. Thus these carefully orchestrated statements of rebellion enabled the publication to establish itself as "free thinking." *Vanity Fair* carefully built upon the heritage of the brand positioning itself as the place to hear the latest cultural news.

The audience assembled by *Vanity Fair* was highly attractive to advertisers, due to its high income and education levels. The readers were considered "style leaders" and, due to their perceived marketplace force, a premium price was charged to those seeking access to this audience. A typical full-page color advertisement cost up to $100,000, more than similar space in any other Condé Nast publication, including the venerable *Vogue*, *The New Yorker*, and *GQ*. A

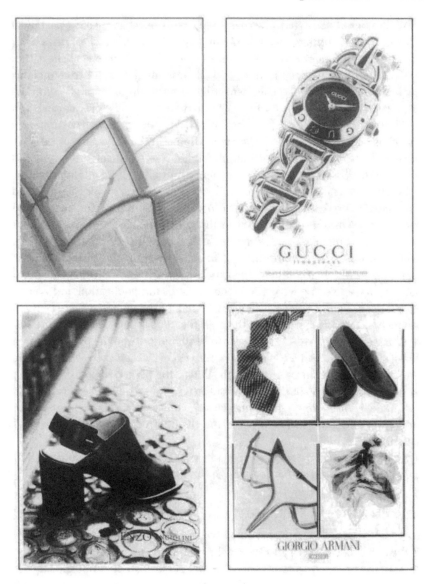

Figure 15.4 Fables of austerity replaced fables of abundance as the advertisements presented single goods for careful reflective study.

small number of dedicated advertisers repeatedly purchased space, particularly for fashions (clothing, shoes, and handbags), jewelry (watches, rings, necklaces etc), automobiles, cosmetics, home fashion lines. Marketers believe these types of goods excite deep feelings and desires, but also instill contemplation due to their cost: Marketers call them "high emotion/high rational" commodities. Advertisers rarely use humor to promote these goods for it dampens the credibility thought necessary for their sale. Laying out thousands of dollars for a watch is no laughing matter. The publication also caters, to a lesser extent, to tourism, finance, and communication. Condé Nast's dedicated food publications tend to absorb food advertising, hence only a few food ads appear.

Vanity Fair contains full page, and often double or quadruple page, advertising rendered with the best photographic techniques and increasingly printed on premium quality paper. Although financial, communication, and sometimes cosmetic advertisements can be copy-heavy, image dominates most messages. The ads are difficult to separate from the aesthetically rich photographs which accompany the articles. Some brands appear so regularly that they have become woven into the fabric of the publication and readers' expectations. *Vanity Fair* launched the careers of the yuppie designer brands, Calvin Klein and Ralph Lauren, through the 1990s. Between 1992 and 2002 advertising revenue "rose 121 percent to $140 million, and the publication was selling close to 2000 advertising pages per year" (Deeken 2003, 46). Creatives had slightly freer reign in their designs due to the perceived sophistication of the readership. In one of his editorials, Carter praised advertisers as the force that made *Vanity Fair* "a great magazine." *Vanity Fair* today epitomizes the integration of culture and commerce and the union of advertising and media content.

We now turn our attention to how advertisers negotiated meaning with the *Vanity Fair*'s culturati audience through the 1990s.

Luxury Is a Bore

To appeal to the culturati, *Vanity Fair* advertisers would be expected to accentuate the cultural aspects of goods over the economic; social scarcity over financial scarcity; uniqueness over rarity. On first glance this does not appear to be the case. The advertisements overflow with references to expensive luxury objects. The many jewelry ads feature an unremitting display of gold, pearls, and to a lesser extent, diamonds. These many images of sparkling metal and jewels meant thumbing through this publication was a treasure trove of wealth-based aesthetics. All of these objects bear a historic relationship to the economy and traditional elite. Gold has captivated the human mind for centuries, served as the basis of Western monetary systems, and has been a favorite of elites since 2500 BC. Most modern economies have ceased to tie their currency to gold,

Figure 15.5 In the mid-1990s androgyny, lesbianism, and fetish sexuality sporadically appear within the dominant images of heterosexual romance. Advertisers acknowledged an easing of sexual norms and mimicked the sadomasochistic style fashion designs of the period.

thus opening the metal up to a new range of meaning outside of economic circles. Gold is now simply a color spread through the publication, a common backdrop to invoke not wealth but a sensual, shimmering, unique feeling. So plentiful is gold that a model is sunk into a pool of it; gold buttons and chains endlessly encrust fashions. Gold is less likely to be promoted as an expensive bauble than as a marker of "stability" and tradition. Advertisers offer this and other metals as something that will endure, mark time, and contribute to the ceremonial world. For example, an advertisement for platinum invites readers to imprint their emotions upon the metal: A couple about to kiss "etch a moment in platinum" that will "live forever." The metal shows you "how you make happiness immortal and how you make a moment a milestone." These appeals might be considered nostalgic; at a moment when the endurance of relationships is sporadic and fluid, metal speaks of staying power (see Figure 15.1).

While the lack of natural pearls could offer a tangible selling point, and their rarity used to heighten interest, today farmed cultured pearls are in great abundance. Yet advertisers have found other ways to link them to value. Images of unspoiled nature are repeatedly used to promote pearls, perhaps to provide mass produced pearls with the aura of the original. Pearl necklaces are wrapped around bunches of flowers or vegetables. Pearl jewelry shaped like flowers float through the air mixed with actual blossoms. The commodity and nature blur. Jewelry designers have long referenced nature, but in some of the ads it appears that nature now reflects the commodity world (see Figure 15.2). The commodity is presented as preferable to nature—shoes offer more comfort than bare feet; bees flock to the commodity instead of flowers. Several of the ads made reference to the DNA structure of the commodity.

Traditional luxury goods (cars, furs, caviar, and champagne) no longer invoke automatic reverence: The ads present luxury goods as a bore, acknowledging the jaded palates of their audiences. Traditional luxury goods are tainted with a sense of duty, lack of emotionality, and stuffiness—the dust of yesterday—sentiments no longer acceptable to audiences seeking novelty, freedom and distinction. Symbolics during the 1990s became intolerant of displays of economic status. Thus, advertisers re-wrote the narrative of luxury, poking fun at it or adding quirkiness to the objects of affluence. One ad depicts a young woman in a convertible sports car, hair pulled back in a classic European ponytail. She wears a Chanel-type suit and has designer sunglasses pushed up on her head. She bears all the marks of a cultured consumer, but the outlandish fur casing that covers her steering wheel pulls the stuffiness out of her. Her personal customization asserts her identity, adding fun and character and aligning affluence with the working classes who have long altered mass produced goods to make them more of their own (e.g., mods' scooters). Another advertisement depicts a young woman seated in a first-class seat of

Figure 15.6 Advertisers recognize and exploit the fact that the game of cultural capital is often experienced as a solitary sport, even though it is complexly bound to the social processes of class distinction.

what might be a private jet. Her obvious wealth (fur, leather, private transport) is dampened by her unusual looks (young and funky) (see Figure 15.3).

Mocking traditional symbols of luxury serves to scrub them of their seriousness and preciousness. It is possible to surround oneself with ostentation, but it must be done knowingly, tongue firmly planted in cheek. A campaign for Stella Artois beer depicts a cat about to feed from a can of premium caviar with the tag line "reassuringly expensive." Another advertisement displays pearls wrapped around tins of black caviar announcing the "new black"—the new commodity symbolically usurps and surpasses the power of the old sources of luxury. The ads also tell cautionary tales about conspicuous consumption. To build esteem without emotional dryness, another ad notes that the commodity is "more upper" than "crusty." Advertisers do not define luxury for consumers. For example, a car manufacturer invites readers to define their own luxury. The object is no longer the source of esteem, rather the consumers" cultural taste is celebrated—their ability to distinguish objects reflects their superiority. Thus, champagne is "for people who know," and jewelry is recognized by those with "instinct." Another car advertisement, for the Acura RL model, praises the viewer for using knowledge, not a price tag, to judge value with the line, "knowing you could buy a Porsche and not needing to."

Nineteenth-century culture obsessed about classifying and stockpiling objects. Early shopkeepers and advertisers, as Jackson Lears has brilliantly illustrated (1995), stressed the abundance of goods on offer. Traditionally wealth was linked to accumulation and a bountiful larder. Yet throughout the affluent twentieth century tales of abundance began to compete with stories of austerity. Austerity might be considered particularly attractive to who seek some distance from the abundance of mass produced goods. Piles of goods too easily invoke factory processes and homogenization. Displays of abundance threaten the advertisers' appeal to "uniqueness," which is the key to making objects amenable to cultural capital dynamics. Abundance for middle-class consumers too easily appears gaudy, common, trashy, bargain bin. These factors might suggest why the sample of ads contained repeated displays of lone commodities, or at most, clusters of two or three objects.

These singular objects were offered upon a stark canvas, as the sophisticated *Vanity Fair* consumer no longer seems to need products to be boasted by the person or setting codes. These motifs challenge the argument that the product has disappeared in contemporary advertising. In their study Richards et al. (2000) recognized a trend toward neo-materialism in the post-1980s period. Indeed, this study too found many attempts on the part of advertisers to make goods "weighty." This materialism appeals to the capacity to daydream. As the early architects of the department store learned long ago, singling out objects prevents distraction and encourages maximum aesthetic appreciation. These lone objects need only their brand name to promote them. Objects have become art within the game of cultural capital, thus do not need to be associated with high culture to the same extent. *Vanity Fair*, in this sense, acts like a catalogue, which one flips through to acquire cultural capital by studying the latest objects on offer.

Advertisers present some goods in playful and witty ways, but overall these objects of desire—fine watches, fashion, and leather goods—are displayed for serious contemplation that would be disrupted by humorous assaults. These objects of identity and status invoke deeper contemplation than coffee filters, paper towels, and laundry detergent, and advertisers acknowledge this. The result is an overall advertising tone that is knowing and self-possessed. In the way they present these commodities to us, advertisers have privileged cultural over economic capital.

Social Relations

Advertisers highlight aesthetic values over social ones as objects, looks, and creativity are celebrated. There remain some social appeals, to be sure; for example, Timberland shoes reminds the reader to "open your eyes what's important is right in front of you" (accompanying your family). In the old days perfume and diamond ring advertisements commonly referred to romance. Advertisers have made modest concessions to changes in gender relations. The "sensitive" male appears from time to time, packing the children into the car, lounging with his family on the family bed or in a hammock. Mothers and children appear, but at times it is difficult to ascertain whether the baby is actually related to the adult or is just serving as one more interesting prop. In the mid-1990s androgyny, lesbianism, and fetish sexuality sporadically appear within the dominant images of heterosexual romance, as advertisers acknowledged an easing of sexual norms and mimicked the sadomasochistic style fashion designs of the period. Models in highly contorted poses draw the eye to voyeuristically inspect what appear to be mangled body parts. Fashion photographers have little scope to render shock and surprise, thus in rather tiresome fashion continually turn to limp and dead-looking figures, or to poses of potential violence. While women are most often displayed as the living dead, men also appear from time to time in masochistic poses for women (see Figure 15.5).

By in large, characters turned their attention to the camera or to the commodity, rather than one another. The vast majority of the ads contain a single individual, a product, or parts of the body. The human body remained an important prop, and was used at times as a medium upon which the logo was written. The valuing of aesthetic appreciation is neatly revealed in an advertisement for cut crystal. A woman sits at a table in a well-appointed room, which we presume is her home. She reads a novel. On the table sits a crystal bowl. The caption reads: "You are never alone when you are in the presence of beauty" (see Figure 15.6). Another advertisement displays a young woman shopping on line during a party, with the line, "it's her party and she'll shop if she wants to, blue fly." Aesthetic pleasures are highly personal, disrupted by others. Advertisers recognize and exploit the fact that the game of cultural capital is often experienced as a solitary sport, even though it is complexly bound to the social processes of class distinction.

On one level it could be said that these relations are troubled. These ads are disturbing due to the blatant disregard for elementary sociality, and the unease stimulated by the thought of depending upon things rather than one another. They signal alienation. Another reading might conclude that the ads show new motifs that de-link individuals from traditional social obligations and sexual norms. For those so released these images are not necessarily alienating, but something to be celebrated. Pollay and Gallagher (1990), however, observe that advertisers' disregard for social relationships does little to promote a healthy society. In their study, they that found North American advertising focused on largely on anti-social behaviors, "values, lifestyles and philosophies," and they suggest that over time advertising has normalized "materialism, submission and seduction, selfishness and greed," leading to a dissatisfaction with life, "disrespect of family elders, tradition and authority" and a potential rise in crime rates.

Following the cultural trends toward more relaxed behaviors in public space, the ads reference comfort. The expansion of fashion would not be possible without the dismantling of the dress codes of the past. Traditional attire might not have been all that comfortable, but it did provide clear guidelines about socially acceptable dress. The relaxing of fashion codes confuses the domain of leisure and work. This blurring of boundaries offers a perfect space for debates about cultural capital to be asserted. Advertisers schooled consumers in the new "casual" look. One ad tells the readers to understand their product line as "clothes you live to work in," another informs the reader not to be anxious about wrinkles, because "wrinkles are not an issue"—this is casual chic that goes from behind the desk to relaxed living and everywhere in between.

A several-page fashion spread entitled *Work* presented office workers in playful poses (on top of the photocopier, in the office waiting room; clothes appear in in-boxes) to align the brand with informal but neat office attire. Another message proclaims: "You don't just want clothes. You want clothes that make you feel completely at ease with yourself. Like when you were six" (Lands End). The easing of formal dress codes liberates consumers from the straightjacket of the three-piece suit and high heels and allows them to be "more themselves." However, individuals are subject to new codes, which require a sophisticated knowledge of what dressing up and down demands, a more diverse wardrobe, and constant vigilance to how to appear appropriate in context.

Advertisers reminded readers of their power to continually transform. The ads variously urge the reader to "live in the moment"; "let the moment be your invention"; "you make it happen"; "reinvent yourself"; "create your own spotlight"; "create your own dream"; "every day is another chance to feel healthy." Risks are presented as necessary to add novelty and excitement to life, and the only hazard the reflexive individual faces, according to Johnnie Walker scotch, is "not taking a shot." The subject is presented as "self-propelled," with no obligation to negotiate with others. Advertisers acknowledge their readers, struggles to maintain and build identity.

But in this "to be looked at world" the camera is always running and women in particular are instructed that their cultural capital resides not simply in what they know but in how they look. The rhetoric of freedom and transformation runs up against a profound contradiction in cosmetic and plastic surgery advertisements, which remind women of the eyes and the critical judgments that are constantly upon them, a message which rings true to the self-aware who watch and judge others. The body is presented as a form of social and cultural capital that depreciates with age or weight gain. Commodities offer relief from self and social scrutiny and time. Thus, a new bathing suit means "you don't

Figure 15.7 Advertisers recognize their reader's interest in believing that the rare oils of an exotic plant hold superior medicinal properties to chemicals cooked up in a laboratory. Thus, there are no advertising restrictions on the words "pure" or "natural"; they are empty adjectives, signifiers emitting a myth of wholesomeness.

ever have to feel self-conscious on the beach again" (Lands End). Cosmetics enable women to stop lying about their age and begin "defying it" (Revlon). Others permit the erasure of time ("erase time; alter perception; create a new reality prescriptions; power over time": Lancôme).

Cosmetic and plastic surgery advertisers are careful not to dismantle the ego of their potential clients. Hence, the procedures are said to not so much transform people but to allow their unique character to shine, or serve as positive additions to the great person one already is.

> Dr. Murad believes you should be defined by your character, no your character lines. Murad, I am confident. I am beautiful. Have you ever imagined yourself with more shapely breasts? Confident, sensual and beautiful—simply more of what you already are. When you choose McGhan Medical, you choose with confidence (McGhan Medical).

Face painting and cosmetics, once part of the world of artifice, stage, and theater, have become the means to find and maintain self-integrity. Beauty potions are decidedly anti-modern: The active ingredients are rarely associated with the wonders of science but are presented as "natural" and "pure" elixirs. Advertisers recognize their reader's interest in believing that the rare oils of an exotic plant hold superior medicinal properties to chemicals cooked up in a laboratory. The appeal is to feel more authentic by incorporating nature, instead of science, into one's life. There are no advertising restrictions on the words "pure" or "natural," thus they are empty adjectives, signifiers emitting a mythical wholesomeness (see Figure 15.7).

Individuating

The impulse toward "demassifying," or disentangling oneself from the project of modern progress toward a more distinguished and authentic existence, is recognized and reflected back to consumers by advertisers. In conditions of modernity, where maintaining identity and individuality is an ongoing struggle, commodities are more often offered as a means of standing out from the crowd than standing in it. But as we have seen earlier, there is a contradiction here, in that to feel unique consumers have to believe that they have discovered their own style, not simply followed what is offered by advertisers. Hence, advertisers leave blanks in their messages for consumers to fill themselves in; for example, wearing Paco brand men's wear "will get you remembered," but "what people remember is up to you." A premium cosmetic company does not presume to tell consumers what is "important," rather it reminds them they already "know what is really important." Gap offers its jeans as a conduit to a distinctive life: "The most important act is always to desire to stay unique; the most defiant act is the ability to do so; the most conclusive act is that you make it right." The ad concludes on the contradiction, "Put your jeans on."

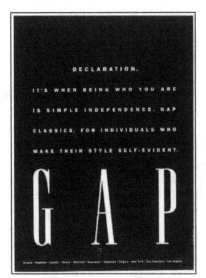

Figure 15.8 In conditions of modernity, where maintaining identity and individuality is an ongoing struggle, commodities are more often offered as a means of standing out from the crowd than standing in it.

Another key aspect of the rhetoric of individuality is that a strong personality can transform mass commodities into unique objects. The ads celebrate the individual's unique assembly of goods in her or his life. Hence, regardless of how many other people have the same jewelry, "every woman has a signature. Every woman has a favorite pair of earrings, a cherished ring, a bracelet that seldom leaves her wrist. These are invariably the things which define a woman's style." A Delaneau ad acknowledges the priority of social over economic scarcity with the tagline, "the object is not rare you are." A Virginia Slims advertisement shows a woman with the caption, "I deserve more than one size fits all." Customized scents provide the opportunity to feel that people are contributing to the manufacturing of the product, making it seem "their own": "You. Bottled. What would you be if you came back as a perfume? Find out with plant & flower perfume Aveda personal blends. A line of body care made just for you."

These appeals reflect the new customized processes of product that permit more diversity of goods. The appeal is to a world that conforms to the unique needs and idiosyncratic lifestyle taste of each individual. It is no longer simply the product that transforms the consumer, but the powers of the consumer's cultural capital to make mass-produced goods into unique objects.

Romantic Landscapes of Escape

We carefully studied the settings advertisers chose to place their wares for clues about cultural consumption. The studio drape or plain wall of color was the most dominant frame for commodities. This type of setting allows objects to be viewed in isolation, privileging the aesthetic dreams of the audience, not the backdrop tastes of the stylist. Still, some repeated landscapes took on iconic status. Couples almost without exception are shown against two backdrops, a ceremonial space such as a formal party, or wedding, or a landscape of escape such as the beach or countryside. If there is a dominant message in the sample it is water, appearing in beach motifs, when characters are boating on the open sea, and in streams. Water appears on bodies to signify rain, dew, excursion, and sexual readiness. Water speaks of freshness and purity in cosmetic ads.

In the context of all this wetness the periodic use of the desert presented a notable contrast. The desert symbolizes the Western imagination, an open field of challenge to test one's rugged individualism, where one lives according to self made laws. And in unsubtle contrast other brands distinguished themselves by using backdrops of the Far East. Lears noted how through the romantic movements of the mid-nineteenth century Oriental villas and Eastern ornaments "signified imaginative participation in a world of exotic, sensuous experience and titillating theatricality, perhaps even a faint and fitful dream of personal transformation. Orientalism was commonplace in ladies magazines as early as 1840" (1995, 63). In the sample landscapes where the "East" is invoked models hold camels, a couple is pictured at archeological digging sites or near ancient ruins. The East is a convenient symbol of difference for the Western mind, thus provides an opportunity to examine or reaffirm one's "self." It is interesting that advertisers continue to draw upon such stark binaries as East and West when the processes of globalization have so severely challenged them. How these references to the East are interpreted by the many Asian immigrants living in North America is an important question (see Figure 15.9).

Advertisers play upon the romantic ideal of going to a different place to find out who one is, and test wits against the unknown. For example, in one Audi ad a car becomes a tool of self-transformation. The car is pictured on top of crumbling bricks, the caption reads where the "pavement ends, life begins." The sun-drenched landscape of the ancient world is reflected on in a confessional journal depicted in script writing: "The eastern desert June 1: The first time I made my own road, spoke a language I didn't know, got lost on purpose, measured time in cups of mint tea." We are invited to leave the civilized world behind and explore realities beyond the everyday. The unknown replaces the anxieties of the urban environment. These landscapes ask the reader to enter another world, another place of pleasure, and the world of "another." The pilgrimage may be the last initiation rights in a culture of largely individualized rituals. The search for the other and distinction has become more frantic.

The sample also contained many references to characters surrounded by the tools of mobility. While early advertisers used the automobile to communicate social prestige, as a commonplace object the car has become simply a tool of movement. Importance is placed not the object of mobility, but the act of mobility. Models are chauffeured about in the back seats of cars. Social status is now found in the display of the couple or individual running from their private car to a private plane in a potent visualization of mobility and escape. Models increasingly appear in airplanes. Bauman (1998) reminds us that in the global society the new elites are highly mobile.

Mobility and travel, however, contribute to the jading of palates and promote a "been-there-done-that-seen-it-all" sensibility. Thus the East and the country field are often no longer far away, or exotic enough to stimulate dreams. For this target market the world is simply not enough. Therefore, advertisers are pressed to construct worlds beyond. Hence we find in the sample landscapes of surreal dimension. Examples include a swimmer who lands his propeller plane on the polar ice cap to take a quick dive into the crystal clear waters; a woman riding a large hairy animal tows a motorcycle behind over a surreal agricultural field. These settings are made possible with advances in photographic and computer-animation techniques and audiences who not only tolerate, but also take pleasure from, the sense of the strange.

Figure 15.9 To the Western imagination, the desert symbolizes an open field of challenge to test one's rugged individualism, a place where one lives according to self-made laws.

Showing In

The ads also take us inside private spaces. The aestheticization of everyday life requires careful attention to all objects in one's environment, particularly the home. The home is an extension of personality, an articulation of cultural capital. Living spaces and the project of self are integrated. The home is not a reflection of ethnic or family background, but rather of who one is. However, this target audience has a need to avoid ostentatious displays that make them seem common. Thus, "showing off" is replaced by the more romantic gesture of "showing in." Viewers are invited to take pleasure in the beauty of interiors. Space here is meant to reflect individual style, not individual wealth. The home interior becomes a work of art, shown to others for their aesthetic enjoyment.

Showing off means designing the home to ensure that maximum status value is achieved. Showing in veils status competition by focusing on taste and beauty. Beauty supersedes tidiness as the key criterion upon which to judge a home. Many "designer" brands expanded from clothing to furnishing, bed sheets, curtains, and other coverings during this time. The home became subject to fashion cycles, as the body had with clothing. Thus the interior of the home showcased new decorative goods, or became a lifestyle backdrop for the commodity. Designers and artists lead the way in displaying their interior lives for emulation. The Coco Chanel brand is promoted with reference to a room labeled "Chanel's famous Paris salon." We see Ralph Lauren in his modernist apartment. Prada shows her models in sparse European style homes, while Versace displays theirs in opulent rococo interiors.

Globalization and Time Place Compression/Universals

Modernity is promoted in a few advertisements for telecommunications and cars, where advertisers seek to close the gap between people in the global market by way of universal concepts. One advertisement for AT&T notes, "There's only one human race. Yet isn't it remarkable how so many things can actually separate us? Things like time. And distance. And language. Well, imagine it you will a world without limits where close and familiar replace foreign and distance. If you're an AT&T customer, the world is now within your reach." An insurance company promises to "be everywhere," and a car company reassures its American consumers that they will receive the same personal courteous service as their Japanese customers do.

But the discourse of distinction drowns out the themes of universalism. Universals too easily disturb the culturati's taste for novelty, uniqueness, and peasant culture. The globalizing marketplace and sameness of goods sharpened advertisers efforts to make goods appear authentic. In most ads globalization is signified with reference to a key destination—a global division of labor.

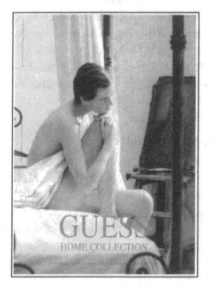

Figure 15.10 The home became subject to fashion cycles, as the body had with clothing. Thus, the interior of the home showcased new decorative goods and became a lifestyle backdrop for the commodity.

Paris serves as the setting for French perfume and fashion ads. The streets of London promote Burberry and London Fog trench coats. Tommy Hilfiger signifies America with repeated red, white, and blue coloring. Vodka is associated with Russian socialist realist art. The craftsmanship of Swiss watchmaking is rehearsed endlessly in our sample. One ad tells the reader that Mexican culture is found in tequila: "A fine tequila is a window into a nation's soul." "Cuervo 1800 is a distinctive expression of the culture and history of Mexico."

Symbolically Demassifying and De-commodifying Goods

Advertisers have utilized several techniques to scrub commodities free of the taint of mass production, which is so unpalatable to the taste of the culturati. Goods are promoted as craft objects produced by hands and talented minds, not global assembly lines. Appeals to functionalism and classicism are used to disassociate goods from the cycles of fashion and trends and trashy over stylized goods.

Nostalgia

The mediated marketplace rapidly cycles objects. Invoking traditional craft labor to promote goods provides the means to slow down these processes and symbolically remove goods from the cycles of exchange. Watches and some types of handbag brands favor traditionalist appeals: The ads emphasize the "craftsmanship" and the "hand made" quality of the goods. Craftsmanship instills a sense of durability and anti-fashion. Promotion focuses on brand heritage and the legacy of skills accumulated in the making of the product over the years. The Swiss watchmaker, for example, is endlessly celebrated as the master craftsperson. Fine leather goods are sold in a similar way. For example: "Every Coach bag is inspired by a tradition of American craftsmanship."

For Grant McCracken traditional cultures sought out durable goods that could endure the process of handing objects down through the family. In the contemporary market, relations to goods are transformed as fashion and individual taste become more important in consumption patterns. Families tend to pass down property and money. The inheriting generation now often rejects the style objects of their elders, either burning them or having a garage sale to unload them. The new relations to goods do not require objects to last. The practice of object "inheritance" and durable goods thus takes on a nostalgic tone and reenters the promotional frame in a symbolic effort to make good unique against the backdrop of a throwaway object world.

> A gift that will last forever.... Since 1832 Bailey Banks & Biddle has been providing the finest jewelry, watches and giftware to a clientele accustomed to such things,... pieces that will look as exquisite on future generations as they

Figure 15.11   In most ads globalization is signified with reference to a key destination. Paris serves as the setting for French perfume and fashion ads. The streets of London promote Burberry and London Fog trench coats. Tommy Hilfiger signifies America with repeated red, white, and blue coloring. Vodka as associated with Russian socialist realist art.

do on their original owners. Anything less, we feel, would be letting down our founders. And your heirs.

Nostalgia is also found in the many references to script writing. Handwriting is a popular typeface, appears in many ads, and is imprinted on objects. The expansion of computers and the dot.com frenzy of the 1990s is largely veiled in the ads, perhaps because the computer revolution too easily invokes a sense of mass production and impersonal relations: As keyboards replace the pen, writing nostalgically links the viewer to a world when people had the time to write love letters and poets and writers left traces of their thoughts in their own hand. An advertisement for an expansive Mont Blanc pen reads, "In times that are changing ever faster, we need things which preserve the moment." Script writing invokes a sense of authorship. It is a craft skill that one learns as an art form. Handwriting is unique.

Working Class

The counter-culture movements of the 1960s legitimated the working classes and street as sites of authenticity, and *Vanity Fair* advertisers reached into these sites to bring distinction to their brands. Referencing the poor in relation to expensive high fashion goods also takes the edge off signifying status seeking. A Calvin Klein ad uses a burnt-out flat black Ford, not as symbol of downward mobility, but as a romantic embrace of cool rugged individuality. This is the getaway car of the Hollywood outlaw—the California cruiser. An expensive bottle of water is associated with a battered pickup truck and dirt road. The advertising references trailers and broken down old cars. Dior covers his models in dirt to symbolize a gritty, edgy, authenticity, a look which is symbolically novel because it contrasts the orthodox fashion rules of good grooming and cleanliness.

Where young people in the 1960s wore jeans in solidarity with the working classes, jeans today are designed with rips, and dirtied, for authentic effect. A jeans advertisement presents its beautiful models on a ripped-up couch. As factory farm processes reduce farming jobs, the symbols of the agricultural field romantically remerges in advertising to animate consumption. Guess Jeans models work rice paddies, another model poses on a tractor in a field. These messages suggest a rejection of the glossy world of high fashion, an anti-statement. The use of these types of symbolics might be partially explained by an interest in building authenticity and distinctiveness. They also indicate the profound discomfort that the culturati feel toward both their class placement and the privileged world of style that their identities are so closely bound up with (see Figure 15.12).

Classics and Anti-Fashion

Advertisers refer to the "classics" to disassociate goods from commodity cycles. Classicism covets the creative output of the ancients. In the late eighteenth century neoclassicism worshiped classic objects for their restrained, harmonious, ordered, calm, and balanced designs. Some assumed that the literature, art, and architecture of the classical period epitomized the most beautiful forms imaginable, monuments of grandeur thought to defy replication—as Platonic archetypes, timeless objects. Classic objects are removed from history, possessing a depth that is beyond mere decoration. When judged against these templates, most contemporary designs are found lacking; thus the classic forges symbolic distance from the herd. The classic is of higher rank, removed it from the cycles of fashion and mass production into the ether of essential forms.

Roman columns and ancient architectural lines formed backdrops for commodities more often than did fine art. Those who use classic products assert a "taste" that is not moved by the whims of fashion. Tiffany's speaks of its style as "classic conception and craftsmanship." Ralph Lauren presents is knit polo shirt as a fine bottle of wine getting "better with age," and achieves a status beyond fashion "spanning generations, to be worn by fathers and their sons, and mothers and daughters," becoming not a mass produced and distributed item, but the high water mark upon which all other clothing is judged. In making reference to "classics," classic cuts, or the classic Chanel suit, these ads remove the anxiety of market choice—the classic cannot be wrong, for it is an eternal and timeless object.

Goods are disassociated from fashion cycles. For example, we are told that the model in an ad has "never been fond of throwaway chic. She looks for the kind of styling that makes a jacket current today and classic a decade from now." Talbots offers "fashion without an expiration date," and stresses that it is not designing for the catwalk, but the everyday, presenting the tongue in cheek caption: "Clothes designed for models: role models." Rolex is "fashion proof" and "virtually impervious to dust, dirt and water, not to mention the shifting winds of fashion." Karastan rugs are not "in for spring" but for the next sixty years," and Cyma Signature is the watch for "discriminating Americans who would prefer not to wear the watch everyone else is wearing." A Timberland shoe ad acknowledges that "seasons of fashion come and go, but Timberland quality outlasts them all." All of these appeals reflect the middle class contempt toward following trends, and the process of demassification.

Some advertisements turn the viewer's attention from the surface image to the "depth" of the commodity. For example, the Virginia Slims model warns that if we judge her by her looks "you're just scratching the surface." The watchmaker Piaget uses the slogan, "beyond the style, the emotion," and

Figure 15.12 The counter-culture movements of the 1960s legitimated the working classes and the street as sites of authenticity, and *Vanity Fair* advertisers reached into these sites to bring distinction to their brands.

Wenger watches ask us to look beyond the "pretty face" of the watch to "its heart and soul." Neiman Marcus distances itself from an association to surface styling with its caption "art proves more than mere decoration." The object is distanced from the realm of "mere image" and made weighty, meaningful, and emotional. The liberal politics of the readers is engaged in advertising space devoted to social marketing messages from the World Wildlife Fund and Amnesty International, which lend an air of gravity to the occasion, suggesting that some things are more important than fashion.

Functionalism

The yuppie interest in industrial design, modernism, and functionalism is found in the ads and might be considered a third way in which goods are "de-commodified." The functionalism expressed by European architects prized form over style. Modernist designers made arguments about the importance of balanced and refined forms. Functionalist designs and shapes were the classics of the modern period. Hebdige (1988) argued that in the 1920s European functionalist designers rejected American design trends, which some of them felt catered to the public with ornate "surface" styling. American design idioms such as "streamlining" became widely popular, according to Hebdige, because they freed design from the paternalism of Old World formalism. Decades later these same formal European designs resurface as a distinctive style that provide a symbolic weight, credibility, and authenticity to goods. They are appreciated by the culturati, for they offer distinction from the "common" pleasures of surface styling.

The industrialization of the domestic sphere, noted by Zukin (1982/1989), appears in our sample of advertisements. Goods with industrial capacities are promoted to the everyday user. Again, the watch category proves interesting in this regard. The promotion of watches for men highlights their great craftsmanship and technical excellence, not their fashion. Advertisers endlessly emphasize the amount of water pressure the watches could withstand, even though few such timepieces would likely endure more water pressure that the sweat produced in a corporate board meeting. Watches are associated with the extreme work environments of the pilot or astronaut. Home entertainment systems have "concert hall quality" and barbeque grills are strong enough to roast an entire pig on. The detailing of the good's functionality is lovingly listed, supporting connoisseurship. These "industrial strength" objects are above the common cycles of mass produced goods—they have a professional status. There is seriousness about these objects. They are not trivial goods of leisure, but important goods of function and work, worn and used by deep thinking people.

Figure 15.13 Advertisers refer to the "classics" to disassociate goods from commodity cycles.

The Valuing of the Cultural Industries

Advertisers shifted away from associating goods with the power of the economic realm, re-linking them instead to the ascendant media and cultural sphere. This was achieved in three different ways: goods appeared in front of the camera; they were associated with media representations; and most profoundly, goods were linked to those who worked behind the cameras and design boards—cultural intermediaries.

In the past Hollywood filmmakers had taken great pains to hide their filmmaking apparatus—the camera, microphone—so as not to disturb their audience's suspension of disbelief. Yet for the culturati the "behind the scene" world is as interesting, if not more so, than what is in front of the camera. In the mediated world esteem is bestowed on those able to draw the attention of the camera and microphone—able to make a cultural "buzz." The media world confers as much, if not greater, value to this quality as to exotic landscapes, high art, diamonds, pearls, and bowls of caviar. The camera and the microphone are exposed to build esteem for the commodity. A jewelry ad depicts a woman being driven in a car and shielding herself from the paparazzi; on her wrist is the commodity captured in the flash. The goods are given value not because they are rare or special, but because those who are photographed wear them.

In another campaign for Boss Man fashion, the models are depicted behind microphones in a simulated press conference; the microphone signifies status. A liquor advertisement shows a woman in the frame of a 35mm camera. She warns her male companion: "Hush, Vincenzo. Remember there is much your wife and I could discuss over biscotti and a glass of Frangelico. (Addenda: Although he apologized profusely, Sophia and Vincenzo's wife still had lunch together)." The commodity is situated in the celebrity gossip stream of great cultural interest in the mediated market place. "Candid shots" are rare in these ads, as the vast majority of individuals "pose" for the camera. The models offer themselves knowingly to the camera as emblems of beauty and objects through which cultural capital is acquired and associated.

Advertisers have long associated goods with art and celebrities (Twitchel 1997; Berger 1995), but in our *Vanity Fair* sample, writers, filmmakers, architects, photographers, and designers were pressed into promotional service. A DKNY ad shows its model walking through a movie set; Guess Jeans models prop themselves up beside an old movie camera, as does a Virginia Slim cigarette model; shoes are placed on top of film reels. Commodity makers aligned themselves with artists to create esteem. IBM tells the story of Gavin, who "just finished his epic poem the iceberg, the walrus, and the fisherman's elbow. It took nineteen years to complete; his publisher said, you are brilliant. You are profound, but you've got to get faster on the keyboard." IBM insinuates that it

Figure 15.14 Advertisers shifted away from associating goods with the power of the economic realm, re-linking them instead to the ascendant media and cultural sphere.

is more supportive of creative work than publishers are, asserting that "you'd rather be a poet than a typist" and claiming to provide the technological tools necessary for the poet to be both.

Advertisers wove past and present media references into their work. Louis Vuitton's campaign depicts women walking down the street with their reflections posted on billboards above them. These images suggest the complex cycling of media promotion, the blurring of the real and the represented world. Another ad uses film and photographic footage from the past to stir media nostalgia and tap into audience media meanings to secure esteem for the brand. Tiffany's employs images of Audrey Hepburn to promote its jewelry, referencing the famous film, *Breakfast at Tiffany's*, to capture the aura of the silver screen and tout its most famous product placements. Tommy Hilfiger includes clips of Marilyn Monroe and Peter Fonda, icons of Hollywood cinema that powerfully speak a sense of American identity. These romantically charged individuals—Monroe dies, drowning in her own celebrity sorrow; Fonda's rebellious and free character in *Easy Rider* is killed by the massifying middle class—celebrate distinction. These ads are intertexutal, popular cultural montages put in the service in promotional montage.

We have seen the attention drawn to the cultural intermediary's lifestyle in contemporary culture. Yet what cycles in these ads is not simply the taste but the cultural intermediaries themselves, who became promotional subjects. Unlike celebrities who are known because they appear in front of the camera, those who appear behind must be labeled. Unknown characters are labeled with cultural industry occupations. For example, one ad showed three people labeled "designer, architect, demolition expert." There is a shoe ad with all the occupations of the people listed below, and in another a picture of a model who is labeled a "stylist." Advertisers display the tools of the cultural industries to signify the cultural intermediary: They are shown at their work. For example, an alcohol ad and a television ad depict almost an identical motif of a man working on a metal sculpture: "Inspiration doesn't keep office hours" (Johnnie Walker Black Label). The reader is told in a Hanes panty hose advertisement that the woman on top of the TV is the creator of a successful television program.

Speaking to a cultured consumer, advertisers made frequent reference to the world of the intellect, using literary references including quotations from literary figures and philosophers such as Plato and Nietzsche. The promotional copy articulates argumentative reasoning or social scientific hypothesis. Models are shown reading books, or engaged in thinking sports such as chess. Literary and artistic heroes and their family members are used to promote products, sometimes without reference to their works. One brand uses the name of Earnest Hemingway to sell its chairs. The Moroccan novelist

Figure 15.15 These ads are intertextual, popular cultural montages put in the service of product promotion.

Bernadette Trinidad is depicted in front of a dining room table and the copy reads: "In her writings as well as her life, she defines romance as imagination. And nothing sparks the imagination quite like the sinuous lines and elegant extravagance of the Bellasera dining room" (Thomasville). Susan Sontag and Salman Rushdie pose for Absolute Vodka. Coach models its bags with reference to literary greats of the past, Ralph Waldo Emerson. Tiffany's employs Paloma Picasso as one of its designers to add cultural cachet to its jewelry.

The designer plays a key role in the promotion of goods. The technique of using an individual to promote a product line is a very old and initially helped to humanize the commodity and the abstract corporation (Marchand 1986). Designers offer something more than personalization, for they signify a "creator," removing the good from mass production cycles and invoking the idea that the object has sprung from a fertile mind, skilled hands, and a creative impulse, not a tawdry grab for profit. Fashion designers have a long history as promotional subjects. Coco Chanel and Christian Dior were legends in the *Vanity Fair* of the 1920s, not simply the current publication. The media gossiped in the 1960s about Roy Halston's party exploits with artists and musicians; this designer's name, and others, were recycled in the 1990s as part of an intensified concentration on the exploits of designers old and new.

The blur between artist and designer, which had begun in the 1920s, was also largely complete by this time. The media promoted Calvin Klein the man as heavily as his underwear. Stories of his party exploits, his affairs, and his addictions circulated through celebrity gossip circuits. Advertisers used images of the new designer Tommy Hilfinger to launch the brand in the early 1980s, helping the audiences to believe that the clothing was produced by a creative force. As the brand grew popular images of the designer disappeared.

The cult of the designer spread beyond clothing, as automobile manufacturers highlighted design to distance their cars from those that were mass produce. For example, a car manufacturer updated its brand with a six-page spread showing various cultural intermediaries (actors, composers, designers) beyond the scenes at their work. The truck is presented as a fellow performer in this exciting world of creativity. Another manufacturer showcased designers who imparted their creative wisdom to readers: "I like to take a classic and recreate it. The classics give me my foundation." "Everybody has the potential to be successful, you just have to believe that you can be." "It's so much harder to do something really simple than to do something very complicated. The ultimate in creativity is simplicity." "The secret to our success is a strong belief in ourselves and our product." "We strive for a balance of a clean and functional collection with no unnecessary details." "A sense of longevity and endurance is important to me. If people are wearing my watches 20 years from now without looking dated, I've been successful" (TAG Heuer). In these ads

Figure 15.16 Speaking to a cultured consumer, advertisers made frequent reference to the world of the intellect, using literary references including quotations from literary figures and philosophers. Models are shown reading books or engaged in thinking sports such as chess.

the creative genius displaces the scientist and therapist as the most important source of wisdom for how to live life and achieve self-actualization. The mobilization of cultural intermediaries as celebrities by advertisers taps into the lives of that segment of the middle class which hungers for the lifestyles of artists (Campbell 1989, Zukin 1982/1989).

Cultural Capital and Romanticism

In our sample advertisements made more appeals to cultural as opposed to economic capital. The unique object eclipsed the "rare" object, as attention was placed on what was socially, not materially, distinctive. We find an aestheticization of everyday life, as commodities are no longer placed beside art, for they had became art, and designer brands stand in for the signature of the artist.

We might understand the motifs designed for the culturati as largely a collective reference to the Romantic period in modern history. The Romantic movements of the nineteenth century rejected rationality and prized emotion over reason, the senses over the intellect. Romanticism deeply values the individual, feeling that subjective truths are more pertinent to guiding one's life course than scientific truths. The exotic, the remote, and the mysterious were prized. Romantic movements cherished the artist and the creator. We saw how many advertisements used the cultural intermediary to instill goods with value. Romantic movements sought to create a space beyond the trials of industrial society, and in their "landscapes of escape" advertisers gave readers images of a fantasy world stripped of urban references.

"Showing in" is itself a romantic gesture, revealing oneself to the other through aesthetic display. Folk culture, primitivism, national and ethnic origins, and medieval culture fascinated those in romantic movements, who nostalgically searched for lost objects of history. The sample displayed romantic longings for the farm, craft labor, and handwriting. Due to its focus on subjective states, romanticism offers advertisers a way of removing goods from economic cycles and blatant status appeals. But the advertisers' version of romanticism was insubstantial. The most profound tenet of romanticism was the embrace of nature, but advertisers showed little reverence to nature in their designs. They also steered clear of the more difficult aspects of romanticism, particularly the valuing of rebellion, the demonic, the monstrous, and the diseased. The ads also reflect anti-romantic styles as well, including classicism (against which the romantic movements arose), modernism, and functionalism.

Perhaps most powerfully, the ads were "anti-mass" and "anti-fashion" (particularly those directed to males). Contemporary romantic movements, particularly the counter-culture movements of the 1960s, saw mass society and mass

Figure 15.17 Designers offer something more than personalization, for they signify a "creator," removing the good from mass production cycles and invoking the idea that the object has sprung from a fertile mind, skilled hands, and a creative impulse, not a tawdry grab for profit.

produced goods as deadening the spirit of the individual. Advertisers worked hard to cleanse their messages of references to mass production by associating goods with craft production, functionalism, and communicating an anti-fashion position—intriguing, given that *Vanity Fair* is largely a fashion magazine. To fight against the rapid cycling of fashion, objects were made symbolically "weighty"—images of chunky jewelry, heavy glass bowls, and similar objects reappeared throughout the sample.

The designer brand infiltrated itself neatly into the consciousness of audiences fearful of mass culture, linking the good to a "craftsperson" or an "artist," symbolically rendering the product unique, new, one of a kind. The "creator" was held in higher esteem than the movie star—who perhaps too easily inspired thoughts of tawdry, massified, conformist tastes. Advertisers obviously believed their audiences were more interested in those behind the camera than in front of it. The culturati secure their place of privilege in the cultural field by their ability to recite, and have an opinion on, not only the design, but the makers name and style. The advertisements support the idea of demassification in that one of the central themes was distinction or distinctiveness. Fables of austerity replaced fables of abundance as the advertisements presented single goods for careful reflective study.

In the ads we found also a privileging of national stereotypes and ethnic origins over universalizing principles. Advertising provides opportunities to escape into exotic landscapes and replay the traditional fashion circuit, referencing Paris, London, New York, and Milan. It is indeed a most profound irony that the sentiments of anti-mass consumption were used to sell mass-produced goods: Demassification has not shown itself as a force in opposition to the continued intensification of commodity-based satisfaction of needs. Instead, it was seamlessly incorporated into the further promotion of goods.

Conclusion

In a recent study of 3,000 late 1990s television ads, Goldman, Papson, and Kersey try to show that commercials are not simply rhetorical appeals but contribute to a pervasive, coherent, hegemonic vision of the future. They found that advertisers promote the dominant values of modernity and science and noted how this ideology was "cleansed of the ravages of Capital—the shantytowns and barrios, unemployment lines, soup kitchens, polluted air and water.... What remains is less a contested terrain than a reflection of the wonderment brought on by Capital." Corporate ads leave out the social costs and political-economic contradictions of capital and "in the imaginary landscapes of Capital that are assembled in advertising the transformative force of Capital appears always to enable and never to disrupt." Although this narrative of capital is false, it possesses a mythic coherence and pervasiveness which alternative discourses of history lack. The clusters of signifiers in advertising do not invite our "ability to conceptualize and discriminate" (Goldman, Papson, and Kersey 1998–2003). Mueller argued in a similar vein that advertising makes us more accepting of our position by "immunizing" us from "perceived alternatives" (cited in Cross 1996, 6).

Advertising is a myth machine that produces a "simplified, abstracted, decontextualized, and exclusionary" discourse, to use Goldman and Papson's words. But we would raise one corrective to build upon their study: Advertising produces multiple myths. It is clear from Goldman and Papson's results that even in this postmodern time goods continue to be promoted with reference to the wonders of modernity, science, and technology. But our own study, detailed above, reveals the power of an anti-modern myth which values romanticism, authenticity and naturalness. This myth too flowed through the discourses through and about goods during the 1990s. As Wernick (1992) points out, advertisers draw upon a variety of symbols to "discharge" their one overriding concern, which is to sell commodities by animating the world of goods.

The nature of the specific product sector appears to have a considerable impact on the values used by advertisers. Looking mainly at technology, financial services, and automobiles, Goldman and Papson found appeals to modernity to be dominant. On the other hand, we found that cosmetic, fashion and apparel advertisements struggled to disassociate products from scientific ways of knowing and progress by linking them to nostalgia, purity, and naturalness. The discourse of the "natural," as Judith Williams showed long ago, is as much a myth as modernity is, but it is a different myth. In a world of skin cancer scares, mad cow disease, and genetic engineering of minds and bodies, skepticism toward appeals to the wonders of science, technology and progress have taken root.

Because advertising flashes around us constantly, its contradictory ideological themes are not always readily apparent. Part of what fuels these differing myths is the marketers' knowledge that consumers can hold contradictory values. While we might like our computers to be "high tech," but we also demand that the commodities we put on or in our bodies be "pure" and "natural." And, as this study has shown, perhaps no other consumer group holds a more contradictory relationship to goods than does the culturati.

CHAPTER 16

The Fifth Frame

The Promotional Context

During the last twenty years a new cultural frame has been deposited atop the sedimentary layers of its predecessors. In this period the commercial media expanded and consolidated, new media technologies (Internet, wireless) emerged, and more global media links were secured. High costs for television network space, lower audience sizes, advertising clutter, competition from cable, satellite and new personal television devices, promotionally jaded viewers, and questions about advertising effectiveness, all caused the leading role of the thirty-second broadcast TV ad—although still important—to be challenged, supplemented, or replaced by other media.

The early 1990s' recession increased advertisers' interest in exploring new promotional techniques. Advertisers competed to sponsor sports stars, wrote promotional press releases for newspapers, staged branded music concerts, and updated their in-store promotions. Among other things, here were great hopes that branded entertainment events and promotional mementos (hats, T-shirts, key chains) would find their way into the lifestyle narratives of individuals. Against this backdrop of great commercial media experimentation, advertising was entering a period of mixed-media campaigns, as messages were coordinated across media and promotional platforms. Although products continued to be showcased, efforts were focused increasingly on the building, maintenance, and extension of brands. Lury (2004), who calls brands the "logos of the global economy," has recently argued that brands have become the key medium of exchange between companies and consumers and a primary force of globalization. As the processes of globalization were refined, niche communication businesses emerged, and the power of media planners and brand managers rose as the sun set on the full service agency model.

Advertisers believed consumer lifestyles were becoming more idiosyncratic, and devised means for addressing a demassifying culture. The distinctiveness of early sub-cultural groupings gave way to hybrid or indeed promiscuous taste cultures, where consumers grazed across music genres and fashion statements, or move in and out of them, to forge a sense of distinctive identity. Totems became transitory, group formations more fluid. A new anthropological perspective came to the fore in the research departments that had previously been preoccupied with the psychology of consumer behavior or segmenting markets via psychographics. Listening to consumers in qualitative interviews, marketers began to appreciate that their target audiences were much more diverse than they had realized, and were situated in far more complex networks of social meanings and relationships than they had thought. Goods and brand meanings were informed by individual histories, used to map social worlds, and woven intricately into lifestyles.

Advertisers came to appreciate lifecycles as much as lifestyles, attending to temporality and the fluid stages of concern and desires consumers moved through from childhood to old age. Yet, despite advertisers' wishes, consumers refused to adhere to clear-cut developmental stages. Teens hated to be targeted as teens, for they believed themselves to be young adults, while baby boomers recoiled at being labeled middle-aged or even adult. Thus advertisers learned to target their audiences more subtly by referring to concrete experiences, nostalgic motifs, and retro imagery, or unique aesthetic appeals, instead of by age profile. They found there were some shared cohort events that could provide a common ground. These generational passion points were replayed until they became so iconic that they were subjected to parody in order to keep them interesting.

Researchers became forward-thinking, seeking to forecast and preempt trends, styles, and changes in values. The traditional concern for maintaining a coherent set of brand values was augmented by a new interest in keeping a brand "fresh" and culturally relevant. Campaigns were precisely timed, new symbols were released more strategically, and emergent cultural happenings were carefully tracked and recycled. New scanner technology made possible the continuous recording of actual buying decisions, enabling the construction of consumer-specific profiles for marketing strategies. The drive to marry this information with media data and to use new technology to transmit personalized messages was no longer just a dance of sugar-plum fairies in advertisers' heads, but rather a plausible reality—albeit one marred by serious privacy issues.

The traditional status goods of the rich were popularized, to be sure, but explosive growth in global communications and travel threatened to transform the exoticism of the foreign into the universal bland consistency represented by the franchised outlets now found on every boulevard, high street, and strip mall. A more complex game of status competition came to prevail, played not simply on the field of economic standing, but in social and cultural fields where winning demands fame or the exercise of cultural knowledge: It is not the goods one possesses that count, but rather the enactment of consumption sensibility or taste as carried out through them. In this period of demassification social uniqueness and distinction were the new gold standards, and creativity the currency of choice. Innovations of cool were as likely to be found at the end of the block as across the globe, in the domain of the poor as much

Table 16.1 Evolution of Cultural Frames for Goods in Relation to the Development of Media, Marketing, and Advertising.

Media for Advertising	Newspapers/ Magazines	Radio	Television	Television	Television	Media Mix
Marketing Strategy	Rational	Non-rational	Behaviorist	Segmentation		Anthropological
Advertising Strategy	Utility[a]	Product Symbols[b]	Personification[c]	Lifestyle[d]		Demassifying[e]
Period	1890 1910	1920 1940	1950 1960	1970 1980		1990 2000
Elements in Ads	Product qualities/ price/use	Product qualities	Product	Product		Brand image
		Symbolic attributes	Person prototype	Activity: person-setting		Media world niches
Metaphoric-Emotive Themes in Ads	Quality, useful, descriptive	Status, family, health; white magic; social authority	Glamor, romance; sensuality; black magic, self-transformation	Leisure, health; groups, friendship		Authenticity; spotlighting; reflexivity; diversity; transformation of objects
Cultural Frames for Goods	Idolatry: Products are abstracted from process of production, presented as pure use-values	Iconology: Products are embodiments of attributes, configured in social judgment	Narcissism: Products are personalized and satisfaction is judged in interpersonal terms	Totemism: Products are emblems of group-related consumption practices		Mise-en-Scène: Products are props for the self-construction of changing scenes and life-scripts

* Pre-1890: Posters and billboards.

[a] See Figure 1.2. [b] See Figure 1.3. [c] See Figure 1.4. [d] See Figure 1.5. [e] See Figure 1.6.

as those of the rich. The opening of new status domains expanded competition and envy. But the cultural field demanded that one keep one's social aspirations carefully hidden. To appear earnestly engaged in social competition—to be a victim of social influence, persuasion, or fashion—is the kiss of social death. To play the game it is necessary to appear all-knowing about the practices of promotion, to seem to be disinterested in goods and impervious to social rivalry—in short, to be cool.

The media is one of the few areas where this new definition of social success could be reflected, and despite monopoly control and heavy gatekeeping, the media—unlike many other social institutions—was able to project the sense of meritocracy so valued by popular culture. The media became the reception area where the popular dream of "making it," based upon innate guile, talents, looks, or ability to capture the popular imagination, was projected. *Pop Idol*, talk shows, and reality television celebrated the triumph of meritocracy, where everyday reluctant heroes were lifted out of the crowd and the shadows of obscurity into the bright light of fame. Andy Warhol's apocryphal 1968 statement—"In the future everyone will be famous for fifteen minutes"—took on a profound resonance thirty years later. The American Dream had been fully absorbed by the Hollywood Fantasy.

The Fifth Phase of Advertising: Mise-en-Scène

The French phrase *mise-en-scène* (literally, "to put into the scene") originated in the nineteenth century to describe what happens on the stage and is now often applied to film composition. The tenth edition of *Merriam Webster's Collegiate Dictionary* defines mise-en-scène as "the arrangement of actors and scenery on a stage for a theatrical production; stage setting; the physical setting of an action," and suggests the words "context" and "milieu" as synonyms. We can also think of mise-en-scène as an arrangement of elements in a setting in order to achieve a unique style, or as setting the stage for action.

As discussed earlier, the idea of "cultural frames for goods" is our most general analytical construct in this book. In a nutshell, a cultural frame is the representation of the relation between persons, products, and images of well-being that is most characteristic of a specific epoch in marketing and advertising history. The first, called "idolatry" (1890–1920), emphasizes above all the useful characteristics of the goods themselves; when images of persons appear, they are usually highly stylized drawings. In the second cultural frame, "iconology" (1920–1950), products and persons appear together in settings that are heavily determined by symbolic attributes, such as status and social authority. In the third, "narcissism" (1950–1970), persons come to the fore in ads: products are personalized in terms of feelings such as romance, sensuality, and self-transformation. In the fourth, "totemism" (1970–1990), the social grouping is the core representation, and products form the emblems of various group consumption practices.

Each of the successive cultural frames for goods forms an expanding platform on which later ones are erected. The thematic elements in earlier frames do not disappear; rather, they are incorporated into a gradually more complex ensemble of strategies. In the section that follows we concentrate on the most recent of these transitions.

Transition from Totemism (Fourth Cultural Frame) to Mise-en-Scène (Fifth Frame)

As we have shown earlier, in the totemistic phase images of social groupings predominate. These images were carefully structured by ad designers, who were offering to consumers what they hoped would be seen as an authoritative and persuasive reading of interpersonal relationships, at different levels of material success, as those relationships were mediated through the possession of goods. Above all, these images served as concrete representations of certain abstractions, namely, defining social norms (gender relations, limited ethnic mixing, socio-economic class distinctions, and a hierarchy of cultural activities). We can use another French term, namely, *tableau* (plural *tableaux*), defined in *Webster's* tenth edition as "a graphic description or representation; a striking or artistic grouping," to characterize this style. A variant is the phrase *tableau vivant*, or "living picture," referring to "a depiction of a scene, usually presented on a stage by silent and motionless costumed participants." The persons represented in marketing tableaux are the passive carriers of those abstractions we listed just above.

Totemism is a fixed representation of "approved" social distinctions; the purpose of these representations is to reaffirm and reinforce specific, enduring forms of social differentiation. An ordering of "higher" and "lower" is also one of the essential features of totemism: In what we call primitive societies, this ordering signifies a hoped-for stability over time; as used within the inherently fluid nature of marketplace relations, however, it forms a guide to ceaseless aspirations, and to the ever-changing material markers of relative success, for individuals. It marks out the pathways that define the meaning of "moving up" in the social world.

The fifth cultural frame for goods, mise-en-scène, contrasts sharply with its predecessor, the totemistic tableau vivant, in every essential detail. Where the earlier one appears stilted and passive, the contemporary frame is fluid and relentlessly active, and the sense of rigidity is replaced by one of limitless possibilities for fast-paced rearrangements of the setting. Most importantly, the mise-en-scène style promises, to every individual who is willing to take the plunge, full participation in the successive "definitions of the situation" that supposedly form the basis of social life.

In the fifth cultural frame goods or commodities are the stage-props for the scenes and settings. The "directors" for the scenes are not the marketers or their brands, however, but the consumers themselves, who can use these props in the service of a virtually unlimited set of creations and re-creations of value and shared meanings. This is why we can call it a demassifying process: Although the props are themselves mass-produced commodities, and thus bear all the signs of goods fashioned with the labor and material resources of a vast industrial empire, their significance is transformed by their emplacement in this new cultural frame, which encourages individuals to regard themselves as the true artisans of meaning-creation.

The individual as director is encouraged to believe that she or he can begin with a blank slate, an empty stage of life, on which can then be arrayed—and continuously reshuffled—the elements of personality, freely assembled from the person's inner psyche; the desired type of social grouping and role-playing; the subtle signals of group identity emanating from an idiosyncratic blend of goods and their many characteristics; a natural or built environment, possibly exotic; and a set of actions, made possible by the fast-paced video formats transmitted by television or the Internet. New technologies are essential for the success of this phase: animation, graphical design software, digitized and edited images, higher-resolution imagery, composite (collage) scene construction, rapid-fire editing for scene transitions, easy access to musical accompaniment, and a re-mastering of the earlier heritage of cultural property for an infinite supply of "retro" designs, an entire electronic universe riding on ever-faster processors and video cards and huge hard-drive storage capacities.

In the fifth phase life presents itself to the individual as a script-writing exercise. But seen from the vantage-point of reflection and analysis, the observation immediately arises that there are tens of millions, and potentially billions, of scripted lives. The act of scripting does not and cannot make the surrounding density of the human world disappear. Thus, inevitably, one of the strongest urges is to find a way to "stand out from the crowd," to have one's self-created uniqueness recognized and celebrated, in an environment where everyone else, or at least many others, has the same agenda (see Figure 16.1, Alfred Dunhill Fragrance). In such an environment, originality, uniqueness, and "notice" are fleeting phenomena. This is why Andy Warhol's famous remark about fame, made many decades ago, is such a prescient anticipation of the mise-en-scène cultural frame. Alas, however, there are far too many competitors to assign each a full fifteen minutes of fame—the allotment is more likely to be about fifteen milliseconds.

Thus most of the life-scripts will never rise above the level of local significance. But, so what? Whatever its inherent limitations may be, the *mise-en-scène* frame offers a highly distinctive form of sensibility within the endless permutations of the high-intensity marketplace, one that holds the potential

Figure 16.1 Alfred Dunhill Fragrance.

for rich forms of personal satisfaction for many individuals, different in kind from its four predecessors.

The totemic phase retained a devotion and earnest willingness to adhere to a group badge. In the fifth phase group devotion is more tentative, while maintaining identity and individuality in relation to the group is more highly valued. Goods are part of the mise-en-scène of ever-transformed lifestyle plays. Advertisers here recognize the consumers' interests in directing and orchestrating their own commodity displays, in the advancement of their promotional selves and thus focus on putting commodities "in the scene." There is also an increased "knowingness" about commodity exchange and the constructed nature of mise-en-scène relations. The intense materialism of this period is driven less by a worship of goods than by a willingness to continually let go of existing goods and embrace the new. While some items are cherished, many become disposable props. The emphasis is above all upon recombining commodities to expand experience and express distinctive consumption sensibility (see Figure 16.2.)

In this phase the relationship between people and things becomes increasingly animated by media references. Advertising reflects the media cultural dynamic by "spotlighting," a cultural frame in which individuals or commodities are highlighted, conferring prestige, honor, and value because the warm glow of the camera shines upon them, however briefly. Designers draw from the palettes of color offered by film and popular music. Digital technology, improvements in sound, and airbrushing link goods to fantastical myths and make possible visual acrobatics; everyday settings are supplemented by "hyper-real" environments. Advertisers used the media networks to create promotional "buzz" and global brand recognition. They expose the metacodes of their practice to prove to cynical audiences they are not giving them a "sales job." The backstage of the cultural intermediary is promotionally rendered as front, and the act of deconstructing promotional realism brings pleasure to viewers who delight in seeing advertising emperors wearing no clothes. At the same time these motifs feed the deep romantic interest in the work and lifestyles of creative people.

Ever mindful of the savviness of consumers, advertisers avoid directly dictating to them; instead using their promotional formats more to offer resources, ideas, or moments of pleasure. Faced with audiences that were increasingly withdrawing their interpretive labor, advertisers shifted their focus toward getting consumers' attention and testing more complex formats with which to engage them. Because they prove most useful in this regard, reflexive messages that use irony, puns, humor, and entertainment increased. Sales messages were subtler, cinema and television advertisements became bolder, and branded entertainment expanded. Phillips and McQuarrie (2002) found that the rhetorical structures of advertising changed significantly during this moment. While

Figure 16.2 "Fight Sameness," NextMonet.

in the 1950s and 1960s U.S. advertisers offered simple and singular metaphorical devises and made efforts to explain their tropes to audiences, in the 1980s and 1990s "advertisers increased their usage of the most demanding kind of figure, placed further demands on consumers by adding tropes to the body copy, and hiked these demands still further by offering fewer literal explanations of these figures." (McQuarrie, 2002) These authors found a great increase in "destabilizing tropes" such as puns, irony, and metaphors that deconstruct commonplace sensibilities. In both of our own case studies presented earlier, we found advertisers employing reflexivity in their messages, acknowledging the capabilities of a visually literate audience fully aware of the symbolics on offer, and keenly interested in deconstructing them.

While bringing a constant parade of new objects onto the stage of one's life can be a radical and thrilling experience, it also causes a fear of missing out, on not discovering something new, developing further, achieving more. The construction and regular maintenance of lifestyles calls for steeling oneself against long-term attachments, a letting go, and an openness to fluidity and constant change. While brands profited from the willingness of consumers to animate their lifestyles through an ever-changing set of commodities, they also paid a price for this service. Evidence suggests that particularly the new generation of consumers had become less brand loyal, more fickle, and more willing to dip in and out of brand experiences unburdened by personal commitment.

Promotional Folklore

It is useful to recall that these new advertising formats occurred while the traditional regulatory, conceptual, and practical fences—erected to separate popular culture from advertising, art from commercial speech, culture from economy, above from below the line—lost many of their gates. A more intensive communication system permeated culture; advertising gave way to promotional communication, and to this extent, the former died. But as Celia Lury (2002, 232) points out, speaking in relation to the work of British artist Damien Hirst, these changes do not necessarily mean a complete or inevitable collapse of categories: "Rather it suggests that the interdependence of the categories may be made visible and productive for a particular position for the author." Bringing traditional categories into question has proven to be highly productive; advertisers embraced this constructive area, playing with the distinction between commodity persuasion and "authentic" messaging, celebrating noncommercial values within their commercials.

Within a culture where the advertiser's role had been so heavily privileged, it is hardly surprising that a popular folklore about advertising would emerge. Just as advertisers depend upon their conceptions of consumers to engage in dialogues with audiences, so did consumers build template of marketers and advertisers, through which they filtered their own interpretations of market-ing strategies. Consumer templates designed by marketers and advertisers (for example, that of the yuppie and Generation X) became a part of public dis-course used to map and criticize cultural values and exclusion. The belief that lifestyles should be unfettered contributed to greater skepticism toward media and marketing institutions at the same moment that those institutions became more intimately interwoven into people's life-ways, ensuring cultural contra-diction, paradox, and irony.

Advertising addresses the central anxiety of how to maintain individual-ity under the pressures of the massifying forces of the market and the media, while at the same time contributing to that very anxiety. We use the term "folk-lore" to acknowledge that the shifting templates advertisers and consumers have constructed of one another were often fantastically mythic; but like all great mythic creations they also resonate with kernels of acute insight. As the work of advertising historians remind us, advertising folklore is very old, but what we take as distinctive is how advertisers became more attentive to con-sumers' judgments, how institutionalizing practices became more sensitive to the diversity of audience taste, perception, and resistance.

These meta-exchanges between producers and consumers are neither fully rational nor transparent, but rather subject to a great deal of misunderstand-ing. Despite the interpretive strengths of consumers and the obvious efforts made by marketers to please audiences, advertisers retain a final control over the images represented. While the rhetoric of diversity and sensitivity blazed through the industry, fuelled by the processes of globalization, we find evi-dence that advertisers concentrated most upon mobilizing and addressing consumer categories they believed would yield the greatest market benefit; hence the concentrated efforts to target the yuppie, the child, the youth mar-ket, and the urban cultural elite (which included advertisers and other cul-tural intermediaries). Advertisers paid top dollar for these audiences, seeing them (although sometimes wrongly) as the most valuable consumers in the marketplace. Media environments were shaped in the interest of these groups. And while there is no doubt that advertisers made many concessions to audi-ence tastes, we also found instances of blatant disregard for newly-emerging values. The representations of women, for example, often remain tethered to highly traditional motifs despite evidence that they caused offense to female (and increasingly male) consumers: In our sophisticated age one can still see, for example, a TV ad for a new type of floor-mop which so enthralls a house-wife that she waltzes into her neighbor's home and begins madly cleaning it. Advertisers have also shied away from fully empowering minority characters, leaving them safety tethered to traditional stereotypes and assigning them the role of adding color to the group, instead of furnishing them with individual identities. It must be said that a great many advertisements remain insulting to the audiences' intelligence, insensitive to their tastes, poorly made, and boring: Thus it is unsurprising that they are quickly zapped.

A Matter of Satisfaction

Recently Nobel prize-winning economists, Western governments, nongovernmental organizations, and the United Nations have shown increased interest in the dynamics of satisfaction and contentment. The work of Frey and Stutzer (2001), which explored the relationship between economics and happiness, has been highly acclaimed. Their study was undertaken in Switzerland, a mature marketplace with a world-respected system of public provisioning. The researchers were able to isolate key variables, as they took sound measurements of both expanding financial wealth and political empowerment. The research confirmed pervious studies showing that rising levels of income and material prosperity have a fleeting and minimal impact on personal happiness. The authors stressed that their study clearly challenges the economic orthodoxy that continues to see the expansion of corporate value as making the greatest contribution to social welfare. The more dramatic finding was the influence authentically democratic institutions and local autonomy had on happiness: A sense of political empowerment contributes to higher levels of reported satisfaction and sustained contentment than material wealth. Well-being substantially rises when individuals feel personally involved in politics, believe they exercise some control over their lives, and when changes occur in relationship to their input. Where these sources of satisfaction are absent or inadequate, does advertising serve to fill the gap?

Our relationship to advertising remains profoundly ambivalent. In their long-term study Calfee et al. (1994) found that the U.S. public's attitude toward advertising has remained surprisingly consistent over time. The majority of the public consistently reported that they found aspects of advertising informative and helpful and felt that the benefits of advertising outweigh its deficits. Yet, across a multitude of studies 70 percent of the public also consistently reported that they thought advertising was often untruthful and that advertisers generally sought to "persuade people to buy things they do not want." Very similar findings were revealed in a recent British study (*Marketing Week*, 8 July 2004).

The public and governments have shown great concern about the role advertising plays in encouraging unhealthy lifestyles. Advertising has been implicated in encouraging the public to smoke, binge-drink, and dull their pain with extraordinarily expensive pharmaceutical drugs; in preying upon the ill, taking advantage of children's vulnerabilities, and alienating children from their parents; in promoting unhealthy eating habits and encouraging individuals to take on high levels of personal debt. Advertisers of risk products have been threatened with bans and regulation to encourage them to be good corporate citizens. Indeed, the folklore of advertising encompassed a rising belief that, far from contributing to well-being, advertisers are also contributing to its destruction (see Cronin 2004).

The advertising controversies of this period (tobacco, fast food and obesity, prescription drug issues) have been interwoven with rising anxieties about health (expansion of fitness industry, organics, alternative health, and vitamins) and extended expectations toward well-being. Conceptions of well-being have been inflated to encompass body, mind, emotion, and sprit, as the mantra of quality of life that began to be chanted in the 1960s expanded steadily. As much as money, people want time and serenity; space to roam and be to alone; information to aid their well-being and self development—all of which is in short supply in urban centers. Yet, great confusion remains about how exactly to achieve this well-being, and there is profound confusion toward the nostrums that experts and advertising offers—not only because we are skeptical, but because the advice given is contradictory and subject to continual change and revision. This contested terrain will continue to plague promotional practices well into the twenty-first century.

Still, throughout the history of their profession, advertisers have displayed great flexibility to both stir and sooth social and cultural anxieties. Roland Marchand calls the world of advertising a "therapeutic practice," wherein anxieties and problems created by rapid social change are diagnosed and treated with "talk therapy." In his study of 1920s and 1930s American advertising messages, Marchand found in the fantastical scripts astute representations of social malaise. He agrees that the casts of characters offered in advertisements are clearly distorted representations of social circumstances, and that the specific prescriptions and advice offered by advertisers that promise "equality and autonomy through acts of consumption" should quite rightly be seen as manipulative and fanciful. However, concentrating on the "perceptions of social and cultural dilemmas" revealed in advertising, Marchand found there acute insights into the broad underlying dynamics of early twentieth-century society. Marchand's research revealed that early-twentieth-century advertisers detected discontent toward the massive scale, abstractness, and impersonal relations of modernity.

In those more recent advertisements of the fifth phase that we analyzed earlier, advertisers appear to have diagnosed a desire on the part of consumers—young consumers especially—to disentangle themselves from intensive promotion and commodity circulation. Consider the address to youth and the culturati we explored: Advertisers have been turning themselves inside out to acknowledge their young audiences' interests in promotional honesty, consumer autonomy, and soft sales ambience. In the formats designed specifically

They don't know me.

I get these catalogues for kids clothes and I don't have kids.

I get discounts for car repair, I take the subway.

I get offers for aluminum siding . . .

I live in an apartment.

Hey, you behind the glass. You're the one with the computers and data bases. You don't know me. You don't know them.

Figure 16.3   IBM "Getting to Know You" campaign,

You ought to know what we are.

(Song: Getting to know you . . .
Getting to know all about you . . .)

Hey, I think they've got sandwiches
in there . . .

Figure 16.3 Continued.

for the culturati, promotional efforts concentrated on presenting objects as untainted by the processes of commodification.

Marchand argued that, working through a process of trial and error, advertisers have come to continually diagnose and respond to social and cultural dilemmas and thus can be understood to have adopted a therapeutic role (1986, 360): "No longer patent medicine 'hawkers,' advertising men had now become broader social therapists who offered, within the advertising tableaux themselves, balms for the discontents of modernity." Yet, as the IBM ad (Figure 16.3) demonstrates, despite advertisers' sophisticated research apparatus, cracks remain in the diagnosis of our needs.

Policy

CHAPTER **17**

Issues in Social Policy

Through our cultural-historical analysis, we have drawn attention to how the emergence of advertising forms within mediated communication radically changed the cultural discourse of modern industrial societies, and how these forms assumed a privileged place in that discourse. As such advertising impinges directly upon some very sensitive and important areas of life, and forces policy makers to think very carefully about its proper place within a democratic society. The uniqueness of advertising agencies, and the regulatory issues confronting them, is that they have emerged as the point of mediation between the industrial, cultural, and communications sectors of society. Accordingly, advertising has encountered three different sets of social policy considerations—those connected with business, the media, and social relations.

In North America and Europe throughout the 1960s and 1970s several regulatory initiatives were legislated and enacted to limit and or control advertising. However, during the 1980s we witnessed a reversal of this trend, bringing a broad drift toward the "business perspective," especially in the United States and the UK, including the deregulation of advertising and media industries and increasing commercialization of broadcasting systems in other Western countries such as France. To advance the global marketplace and to facilitate new technology, industry officials argued that the consumer was best suited to shape and monitor the marketplace. Consumers (including children) were recognized as being intelligent enough to select their own pleasures and to use their critical capacities to protect themselves against being manipulated. The active consumer view also came from academics in the arts, humanities, and social sciences who felt critics exaggerated the role of advertising and who were overly scornful toward the popular pleasures afforded by it (Nava and Nava 1992; Featherstone 1991; Twitchell 1997; Cronin 2004). Advertisers, these commentators believed, had reached an institutional maturity—and so too have audiences.

Yet advertising remains a point of friction among a number of controversial issues and social policy debates (Singer 1986). In the twenty-first century Western liberal democracies continue to grapple with these changes. For example, as the power and prevalence of advertising grew, many nations called for increased regulation to mitigate the potentially adverse effects of high-risk products on consumers, particularly on vulnerable constituencies such as the elderly (Nikoltchev, Prosser, and Scheuer 2000). In fact the regulatory system is in a state of constant revision. In this chapter we explore some of the changes and recurring themes of the post-1970s regulatory environment. We explore the implications of our rethinking of advertising's role for the broader questions of social policy that arise in market societies, and we consider how regulatory systems are responding to the intensive processes of globalization, new technology, and increased emphasis on cross media and integrated campaigns of the last twenty years.

A Narrow and Wide View of Regulation

The policy debates about advertising have evolved historically, both as the broader climate of opinion changed and in response to particular changes in the advertising industry. For example, advertising representations continue to agitate feminists and civil rights activists, parents, university students and the not for profit sector. Debate continued over advertising to children and the promotion of tobacco and alcohol, even as new concerns were raised about the promotion of pharmaceutical drugs, fast food, and financial services. There have been regular calls for advertising to take responsibility for some of its perceived social and cultural impacts. According to Anne Cronin (2004), advertising has become a lightening rod for our discontents about negative consumption habits. And yet, after more than a century of modern advertising the uncertainties about its social role and mandate continue, and we still have little understanding of how, within a free and democratic society, we may define reasonable limits to marketing's social communication. One way to analyze the varied advertising regulation debates is to consider the assumptions made about the role of advertising.

The history of regulation has been heavily shaped by assumptions about its role in the marketplace. Advertising, from this perspective, is seen as a means of distributing product information that supports consumer choice. So important is this contribution considered that many nation states protect the rights of commercial speech in the same manner as they do the speech rights of citizens and the press. This narrow role of advertising and the corresponding regulatory stance was recently reaffirmed by a current member of the U.S. Federal Trade Commission (FTC), Mary L. Azcuenaga (1997):

> Some might say that the very idea of regulation of advertising is incompatible with the concept of a free market. In fact, I believe, the opposite is true. One of the fundamentals of a market economy is the free flow of information about goods and services offered for sale. The underlying theory is that the more fully consumers are informed, the better equipped they will be to make purchase decisions appropriate to their own needs. The phrase "appropriate to their own needs" expresses an important point. The appropriateness of a purchasing choice in a free-market economy depends on consumer preference, not governmental fiat. It is the exercise of informed choice by consumers that

ensures that unwanted goods and services eventually will disappear from the market, and that prices that are too high to induce purchase ultimately will be lowered as selling firms seek to attract buyers.

The central argument of this book, on the other hand, is that advertising extends well beyond an economic function, for contemporary advertising provides much more than product information and utilitarian features. Studies confirm that consumers do not look to advertising solely in order to evaluate the performance, durability, and effectiveness of products. The narrow view also fails to appreciate the structural relationship between advertisers and the media, upon which democracy and culture has become overwritten, as well as the complex relationship between advertising and over consumption, cultural values, socialization, identity formation, environmental degradation, erosion of the public sphere, and distortion of social communication. The policy arena has had difficulty in addressing these problem issues.

Advertising is more than a mechanism for communicating product information to individuals: It is in truth an entire cultural system, a social discourse whose unifying theme is the meaning of consumption. The primary field of the content of modern advertising is contemporary culture itself, and advertising represents a contested discourse precisely for this reason. This we see as the "broad perspective" of advertising as a form of social communication. We argue that the institutionalization of advertising and its vast role in modern life requires our conception of advertising to accommodate the unintended social consequences of marketing communication, as well as the broader cultural effects of our particular market communication system, which narrower regulatory approaches will continually fail to approach.

Regulatory Systems

Most Western countries have developed formalized sets of regulatory activities, beyond legislation and the law courts, to supervise the advertising and media industries. The United States, the United Kingdom, Canada, Australia, and New Zealand, for example, all have established legislation applicable to advertising, as well as self-regulatory bodies through which industry attempts to encourage members to adhere to particular codes of conduct. Some of the regulatory activities include guidelines established by the industry associations; pre-clearing and review panels (especially for food and drugs); watchdog groups (Media Watch); standards councils; complaints procedures; codes of ethics; and formal regulatory agencies such as the Canadian Radio-television and Telecommunications Commission (CRTC). National regulatory systems are informed by specific historical, social, cultural, and political economic characteristics of a given nation, and thus specific approaches differ, of course.

The United States, where almost half of all global advertising originates, has one of the least restrictive advertising regulatory frameworks of all liberal democracies, perhaps stemming from a deeply rooted distrust toward government intervention, and a widely-held belief that the positive contribution advertising makes to the economy should not be censored. The United States also has strong constitutional protection of free speech, which advertisers call upon regularly to protect or defend their commercial expressions. Self-regulatory models have been seen as a means of circumventing the constitutional challenges that might accompany government-legislated advertising regulation. Ironically, however, self-regulatory models, which require that affiliations to be made between advertisers and their industry associations, have been challenged by anti-trust laws that limit the rights of corporations to form alliances (derived from an interest in preventing monopolies).

Canada and Britain appear to have a higher tolerance toward government initiatives than does the United States and both these countries have sought to balance private and public interests in the sphere of advertising oversight. Canada, for example, has demonstrated concern about government control over broadcasting and advertising in mandating its key regulatory body, the CRTC, to operate at arm's-length from the government. The CRTC has nevertheless been endowed with considerable power to speak for the public interest should it choose to do so.

In the UK the rights of commercial speech is also acknowledged, but at the same time a history of collectivist rights supports restrictions of that speech. The Office of Communication (Ofcom) is responsible for regulating the communications industries, including television, radio, telecommunication, and wireless communication. While Ofcom has considerable power over communication providers that power is not unlimited. The UK government recently reaffirmed its right to ban advertising by sector and overrule the decisions of official regulatory bodies, on the grounds that only democratically elected authorities should be the final arbitrators in decisions about public goods (*Campaign*, July 23, 2004).

The situations in non-Western countries differ widely. For example, during the years of the Cultural Revolution 1966–1976, China banned advertising in an effort to achieve the Chinese revolutionary radicals' socialist goal of ridding the country of capitalist evil. It was believed that "advertising is a necessary evil for the capitalist countries caused by overproduction and under-consumption" (Chu 1982, 40). By 1979, however, China had begun easing restrictions on advertising and foreign-company businesses; shortly thereafter, Coca-Cola, Rado, Seiko, Kodak, Gillette, Phillips, and other firms established their brands in the country. The economic reforms of 1992 endorsed the construction of "a socialist market economy with Chinese characteristics," opening China to much more foreign advertising. The number of foreign advertising agencies climbed from 98 in 1992 to 280 in 1993 (Chadwick 1997).

Still the government controls over half of all the promotional information, vets all advertising, and censors what it finds inappropriate. While the central concern of Chinese regulation, similar to the West, has been truth and comparative claims, some ads have been censored for seemingly unique reasons. For example, during the 1990s Budweiser beer entered the Chinese market with the slogan "the king of beers." This was changed to "America's favorite" because the word "king" was thought to propagandize in favor of an aristocratic world-view (Chadwick 1997).

The evolution of advertising in non-Western countries is an important and expanding area of advertising study in the globalization mediated marketplace. A useful overview of aspects of global, and especially Asian, advertising regulation can be found in Frith (1996, 2003). To harmonize with the scope of our study, however, here we confine our exploration primarily to regulatory development in North America and Western Europe.

Policy History: The Business of Honesty

Contemporary regulation carries the legacy of past concerns. Industry self-regulation emerged quite early in the twentieth century, when the extravagant claims in patent-medicine ads threatened to arouse a backlash against all advertising. "Truth in advertising" was one of the first professional rallying cries to help advertisers organize their initial programs for self-regulation. Although the principles of *caveat emptor* ("buyer beware") and freedom of commercial speech have been articulated throughout the history of business, the ravages of unrestrained industrialism in the late nineteenth century created a climate of opinion, at the beginning of the twentieth century, in which restrictions on advertising appeared necessary to ensure the maintenance of fair business practices. Indeed, concerns about honest business communication date back to the medieval period, when merchants and shopkeepers were threatened with the rack for shortening the standard measure of bread or diluting beer, on the grounds that consumers deserved some assurance about the measure they were buying. With the advent of industrial production and the resulting proliferation of new products in the marketplace, the relationship between the claims of producers and the actual quality, price, and quantity of goods became a matter of ongoing interest for both consumers and competitors.

Advertisers and the neophyte agencies reasoned that the deceptions of a few (particularly the extravagant claims in patent-medicine ads) were detrimental to the credibility and legitimacy of the rest. Thus they began to develop codes of ethics, promoting them as vehicles for self-regulation, and urged governments

to legislate in those areas where the worst infractions were occurring. In 1924, in Wembley, England, the Associated Advertising Clubs of the World adopted the "Wembley Code of Ethics," which reads in part as follows:
We pledge ourselves:

1. To dedicate our efforts to the cause of better business and social service;
2. To seek the truth and to live it;
3. To tell the Advertising story simply and without exaggeration and to avoid even a tendency to mislead;
4. To refrain from unfair competitive criticism;
5. To promote a better international understanding based upon a recognition of our mutual responsibility and our interdependence;
6. To conserve for ourselves and for posterity ideals of conduct and standards of Advertising practice born of the belief that truthful advertising builds both character and good business. (Turner 1952, 184)

For all their overblown rhetoric, advertisers and agencies shared consumers' concerns with the matters of truthful product claims, unfair or deceptive business practices, competitive advertising, and false pricing, and they saw distinct benefits for themselves in the enactment of legal sanctions against gross abuses of rogue marketers or fringe sectors of the economy. Ad agencies have accepted the longstanding business concerns about fair and competitive practices that became entrenched in both legislated and industry generated guidelines and procedures (Greyser 1972).

"Fairness" in advertising became part of American industrial law as early as 1914, as a component of the codification of competitive business practice, with the formation of the Federal Trade Commission (FTC). The notions of unfair and deceptive advertising were further articulated in the Wheeler-Lea amendment (1938) to the FTC Act. In Canada, shortly thereafter, the Combines and Monopolies Act was extended to include advertising; and the Department of Consumer and Corporate Affairs was later given jurisdiction over complaints about misleading and deceptive advertisements.

In the United States, the relationship between these trade restrictions and the First Amendment were contested in the courts over a number of years, leading to the landmark *Virginia v. Citizens Consumer Council Inc.* decision, which appears to have entrenched the constitutional rights of commercial speech. As Ashman et al. (1979, 23) noted: "On May 24,1976, the Supreme Court of the United States handed down what well may be the most important document in the recent history of advertising in this country. . . . While still subject to regulation on a variety of grounds under administrative law, advertising that tells what is available and at what price is also in the public interest for a variety of reasons, including the fact that it is indispensable to the operation of a free enterprise marketplace."

Part of the professionalization of advertising brought it under the constraints our society imposes on all economic activities, the aegis of "fair business practice." Like any other business sector, advertisers had to learn to align their interests to respond to the perceived need to make the marketplace function efficiently and fairly. Advertising has generally been accorded a place of honor among economic activities, because most people believe that it aids consumer choice and generally supports competitiveness in the marketplace. For this reason it has been indirectly subsidized through the tax system, an obvious acknowledgment of advertising's legitimate place in the industrial firmament: a fully tax-deductible expense of doing business.

In 1976 Canada's notorious Bill C-58 denied this tax benefit to Canadian advertisers who placed advertising in "foreign" magazines distributed in Canada; it took an occasion such as this, when tax law was used to make cultural policy, to bring the issue of advertising's key role in the sphere of cultural production to public attention. This measure, designed to bolster Canada's national culture, was rescinded in 1999 by Bill C-55, which acknowledged the expansion of foreign-owned media ownership and permitted Canadian advertisers half the tax exemption for placing ads in publications that did not meet the 80 percent Canadian content rule. A press release from the 1999 Department of Foreign Affairs and International Trade outlined the change:

> Tax deductibility is currently only available for ads placed in periodicals with a minimum of 75% Canadian ownership and that contain at least 80% original content. This will now be changed to provide full deductibility, regardless of the nationality of ownership, in any periodical that contains at least 80% original or Canadian content. Canadian advertisers will receive half the deduction for ads placed in foreign magazines under the *de minimis* exemption, as well as for ads placed in magazines created by foreign investors that include less than 80% original or Canadian content.

The legitimacy and survival of advertising may well have rested on the advertising industry's acceptance of some limitations on commercial speech. Restrictions against falsifying a product, or misleading the consumer about its characteristics and price, have, in fact, not proven onerous to the industry. As Brian Philcox (1989), president of the Association of Canadian Advertisers, acknowledged in his public defense of the newly won constitutional protection for commercial free speech in Canada, "Commercial free speech simply means the right to inform the consumer of what's for sale. It is also the right of the consumer to be informed. At no time does an advertiser have license to misinform. Let's not forget that advertising, along with all the other facets of marketing communication, is a deeply rooted part of our cultural heritage." Accepting these limitations was thought to make good business sense, because advertisers also believe that consumers base decisions about products on rational performance criteria. Philcox went on to suggest that "advertising must be the most vulnerable business activity in existence. If the product doesn't live up to the copywriter's promise, then the consumer will trash it. That product will die, and deservedly so."

As Alan Rae of the Canadian Advertising Foundation (CAF) has stated, all policy for advertising (both regulation and self-regulation) is presented "as ways of attaining one or two common goals-to protect the consumer and ethical business against false, misleading or even unfair advertising" (*Marketing* 1986). The acceptance of honest advertising and its interpretation as the absence of deception or false beliefs brought about a significant reduction in truly misleading advertisements; those that do occur are adequately reported and dealt with by the available complaints mechanisms. Most potential offenders are eliminated by the various official and unofficial pre-release review processes. Correction of offending ads that slip through the net is usually swift. Rae concluded, "The fact that in recent years complaints received by CAF deal more with social issues, indicates that the battle against deceptive advertising is increasingly successful."

But the definitions of deception and unfairness in advertising turn out to have been more controversial than was imagined when advertising was more textual than visual. The nature of "dishonesty" had to be worked out in the changing context of social communication, as performance and pricing claims for products became infrequent. The broader, still contentious issues concerning what is implied by modern advertising imagery form the basis for many of the recent critiques of advertising practices. For example, it has been repeatedly suggested that alcohol advertising encourage young people to take up these habits, because the advertising designs are "youth oriented" in their choice of models, stylistic devices, and references to the symbols of youth subcultures.

Attempts to operationalize honesty, in the context of modern visual media, imply an interpretive response on the part of the recipient of the message, as well as something about the intention of the advertising designer. The advertisers have been adamant in arguing that any attempts to regulate communication formats would be a violation of their freedom of speech. During the 1970s, the FTC attempted to expand the purview of the honest advertising edict by opening up the matter of substantiation of product claims, and by attempting to develop trade regulation rules concerning disclosure of information and inferred claims in advertisements. But as influential advertising creator Tony Schwartz (1974) pointed out, advertisers can only run afoul of regulatory agencies or industry codes if they make overt claims about their products that cannot be substantiated; an ad that does not involve a claim cannot be false or deceptive in this sense. Thus Schwartz advised advertisers to make no claims at all about the product, but rather to use imagery and symbols to create a message that resonated with "social truths" for the target audience. Our own historical analysis of advertising messages shows that the language of implication and creative allusion supplanted product claims as the standard practice in advertising. The decline in "hard" information and the concomitant rise of imagery and lifestyle advertising as a mode of communication has likewise promoted more ambiguity in advertising and made most guidelines for deceptive and misleading advertising of little consequence to advertising practitioners.

U.S. regulatory models subsume many of the actual claims made within the content of advertisements under the heading of "puffery," defined as those exaggerated points made by advertisers that are considered so routine and obvious that consumers are well aware of them and view them critically. According to FTC commissioner Mary L. Azcuenaga (1997), the Commission does not focus on advertising's "softer," subjective claims:

> Although, in principle, the FTC may challenge any deceptive advertising claim, it is the Commission's long established practice not to challenge claims that are purely subjective (e.g., "best," "brightest," "great taste," "feels and looks great"). This type of claim generally is considered "puffery." Instead, the FTC concentrates on challenging false or misleading claims about objective facts (e.g., "fat-free," "proven effective by scientific tests").

In his well-researched and well-argued 1996 book, *The Great American Blowup: Puffery In Advertising and Selling*, Ivan Preston makes a convincing argument against the blanket immunity provided to advertisers by the concept of puffery, calling for the inclusion of much of what passes for puffery under the ban on deceptive advertising. Advertising would be highly restricted indeed were it to be mandated to discuss only scientifically proven selling points for products. And yet, clearly there are cases in which doubts exist about the capacity of the receivers of information to understand and evaluate all types of advertising messages. But advertisers themselves admit to no charge of dishonesty, arguing that deception lies in the eye of the beholder; the consumer is assumed to be a person fully capable of rational evaluation of messages. The advertising industry itself has, for the most part, accepted the criteria of fairness and honesty when they are narrowly defined, but resisted broader interpretations of these principles for fear that they may become entrenched in regulatory processes. By and large, the industry has been successful, such that regulation of advertising has to date remained narrowly based on the issue of false or misleading communication.

High-Risk Products

Deceptive advertising has proven to be a particular concern in relation to products considered to pose health risks or those commodities that require special knowledge to understand their impact, such as pharmaceuticals. The history of control over these substances has illustrated that when advertising bans are threatened or put into place, advertisers are quick to protest the innocence of their craft in creating or stimulating demand. One professional told the CRTC that most of the research studies he had seen did not show a link between advertising spending and increased consumption. For example, beer advertising was designed for brand switching: "Marketers can only promote a brand that fulfills a consumer demand in a manner that is superior to the competition. . . . The sole objective of advertising is to gain brand share at the expense of the competition" (*Marketing* 1987). This issue lies at the center of disputes concerning products whose consequences are or can be harmful to health and socially costly (for example, tobacco, alcohol, or drugs). In this section we explore the special regulation of high-risk products.

Alcohol

The case of advertising for alcoholic products has been one of the longest-running battlegrounds of advertising regulation. In the wake of Prohibition, the Canadian government restricted all advertising for alcoholic beverages. During the Second World War (after December 1942), however, the spirit beverage producers were allowed, like many other advertisers, to engage in corporate and public service advertisements under the War Time Alcoholic Beverage Order. This order was rescinded in 1947, and thereafter broadcast ads for beer and wine were permitted provided that they were acceptable to the provincial governments. Under pressure from manufacturers and broadcasters, in November 1963 the Canadian government issued "General Guidelines" for the advertising of beer and wine, which, among other things, stated that the ads could not present drinking as a necessary part of social activity or as a status symbol. They also could not show their product, except incidentally during the manufacturing process, and could include no family scenes, minors, glasses, bottles, or people engaged in consumption of alcohol. A pouring sound could not be used as a sound effect.

These guidelines were adjusted slightly over the next two decades to allow the showing of bottles and "pouring" sound effects. Moreover, in 1972, following the U.S. broadcasting ban on spirit alcohol advertising, advertisers in Canada reached a voluntary agreement with broadcasters to restrict the advertisement of distilled spirit products to print media (mainly magazines). A preliminary evaluation of the results of the guidelines on distilled spirit advertising revealed that advertisers, however constrained they felt, committed few infractions; the study also indicated that the range of social imagery, social relations, settings, and values in such advertising was narrower than it was for other product categories. Some years ago brewers tried to counter bad publicity by launching a public education campaign which highlighted moderation in drinking (see Figure 17.1). Thereafter the Canadian Association of Broadcasters, fully aware of the income broadcasters receive from beer advertising, undertook the production of television public-service ads that focus on drinking and driving.

Arguments about the implications of advertising design are much more difficult to resolve. The fact is that advertisers count on viewers' abilities to construct, from the symbolic clues they provide in the ad, an interpretation of the promise of their products. Generally speaking, advertisers would like to imply that such interpretations are subjective, that is, the responsibility of the viewer alone. Ashman et al. (1979) remarked, with regard to the issue of the limits of communication formats in advertising, that "there is a difference between false advertising and the advertising which maybe considered as misleading upon the application of value judgments." Most of modern advertising communication falls into this latter category, making few falsifiable claims but invoking many value judgments. The problem of modern advertising policy is that the ground upon which the issue of dishonesty first rested has shifted, from the matter of overt verbalized deceptions (the advertiser lying about the qualities, price, or effectiveness of the product) to the implied claims or the potential inferences and interpretations that a viewer or reader is led to make, as a result of the complex language and imagery used in advertisements. Does an ad that alludes, in overblown and poetic language, to sensuous or sexual attributes imply that erotic gratification is a consequence of that product's use? Does an image that shows a "housewife" using a product imply that working women do not? Does a picture that shows a partially dressed woman struggling to be free of a man in a car imply rape or sexual domination?

Legal to Sell: Legal to Advertise

Over the twentieth century as a whole regulation of tobacco advertising, for example, was less restrictive than that of alcohol advertising, perhaps because the idea of responsible smoking is less convincing than is moderate drinking. When consumed in moderation, and often with a meal, alcohol is considered a normal part of life in many cultures. In Italy and France wine is a central every day life, just as a pint in the pub is a ritual in Britain. Doctors even advocate wine, in moderate amounts, as a healthy elixir for the heart. Alcohol producers in the United States have thus questioned why they have been restricted from advertising their perfectly legal product to adults (Starek 1997c). Still, alcohol producers have shown a willingness to self-regulate, to undertake campaigns

Taking the message to the people.

request: "Please Drink Responsibly." They will be seen along streets in communities across the country.

Please drink responsibly.

The Brewers of Canada

The television campaign has reached Canadians, literally from coast to coast, and has done an effective job of changing people's attitudes. However, to ensure that the Responsible Use message reaches people when and where it's most crucial, the Brewers have extended the campaign to include outdoor boards and posters. The outdoor boards feature scenes from the TV commercials, and the simple

In addition, posters with the same message can be seen in distribution outlets for alcoholic beverages everywhere. Together with the TV campaign, these public service messages are reaching Canadians wherever they go.

Figure 17.1 In response to criticism of their industry's advertising, brewers promote a different perspective on drinking from their branded campaigns. *Source:* Courtesy of the Brewers Association of Canada.

of "responsible drinking" messages, and—in the case of spirit alcohol—agreed for a period of time to a ban on broadcast advertising. It seems that spirit producers traditionally had more difficulty making the case for moderate drinking, due to the alcoholic strength of their product, and after World War II they volunteered to accept tighter advertising restrictions than were imposed on beer and wine producers. Yet in the 1990s the special bans on sprit alcohol advertising were drawn into question in both North America and Europe.

Part of the reasons for this stems from the unfortunate irony that advertising bans have encouraged producers to be more creative in other areas of their marketing. For example, many of the increasingly prevalent below the line techniques that now appear to be new (sponsorship, product placement, viral marketing) were pioneered by tobacco manufacturers, who were searching for ways to market their products without broadcast media advertising. Such was also the case with spirit producers.

In the 1990s, finding their fortunes dwindling, spirit producers sought an alternative to advertising, by developing a line of products known as "alcopops" (fruit or sparkling flavored beverages spiked with spirits), packaged like bottled beer and containing a similar alcohol content. Uniquely packaged and sweet-tasting, alcopops proved attractive to young drinkers. Alcopops quickly became controversial, since they blurred the line between alcoholic and non-alcoholic beverages, yet from a regulatory perspective alcopops presented a challenge by eroding the traditional distinctions between spirits, beer, and wine. In the mid-1990s, amidst a regulatory environment where singling out of one product for special treatment was considered a negative intervention in marketplace dynamics, spirit alcohol producers had a very strong case for breaking their forty-year-old advertising ban agreement. Spirit alcohol now appears in various media in several European counties and North America.

Yet it is well known that alcohol consumption is an important risk factor in motor vehicles accidents, crime, suicide, domestic violence, and a variety of serious illnesses (sclerosis of the liver, alcohol poisoning, heart disease, and high blood pressure). According to Rice (1995), in 1995 in the United States $22.5 billion was spent on health care directly related to alcohol consumption. Factoring both health and social costs, the bill for alcohol consumption rises to an estimated $175.9 billion per year, higher than the costs of other drug problems ($114.2 billion) and smoking ($114.2). In 1997 the World Health Organization (WHO) called for a coordinated effort to address the health and social problems associated with alcohol:

> Current responses are piecemeal and inadequate, and have done little to control the marketing of alcohol products. Evidence suggests that self-regulation by the alcohol, advertising and media industries is ineffective. Media literacy, training young people to de-code and resist marketing messages, by

> itself is insufficient to address the emotional and non-logical appeal of the marketing. New responses are required. The global nature of the marketing demands a response at international, national and local levels. (Institute of Alcohol Studies, 2004)

Stemming from this recommendation, the European Union has sought to harmonize alcohol advertising regulation across its member nations such that "no one within the European television market shall promote alcohol to minors, link alcohol consumption to driving or create impression alcohol enhances physical performance or contributes to social or sexual success." (Institute of Alcohol Studies 2005). On the basis of the WHO's estimate that alcohol producers spend three times more on sponsorship, product tie-ins, contests and special promotions than they do on advertising, the new regulation also limits promotional activity (Jernigan and O'Hara 2004).

In the UK the Portman Group has enacted an industry self-regulatory code since 1996, and the Independent Television Producers have their own code. Each code clearly restricts the types of alcohol ads that can be produced. These codes appear quite severe in principle: alcohol cannot be associated with toughness or bravado, with sexual attractiveness, with a desire to overcome loneliness, quick drinking, driving, or drinking at work; ads cannot associate alcohol with a celebrity likely to be respected by those under eighteen. And yet these principles are commonly stretched or breached in practice.

A 2003 advertisement for Bacardi Rum offers an example: Advertisers used Vinnie Jones, ex-footballer, film actor in their advertisements. The spot featured Jones (tough, macho, respected by those under eighteen), and a beautiful young woman (sexual attractiveness) competing against one another (peer pressure) to see who could make the fastest rum drink (why make drinks so quickly unless they will be drunk quickly?), while a crowd of young and hip party goers undulate stimulation) around them (social status), drenched by the backsplash of the drinks-making contest.

This advertisement was pulled from the air, not because it was considered to violate regulatory codes, but because Bacardi got nervous about the reputation of their product spokesperson after Jones was charged in an air rage incident in which he "attacked a fellow passenger and informed the crew he could have them 'murdered for £3,000'" (*Brand Republic*, December 16, 2003).

Since 2000 mounting media coverage in Britain of the "lad and laddett" cultures of binge drinking, and the antics of drunken football hooligans running amok during tournaments on the Continent, along with concern about the link between alcopops and youth drinking, increasingly called the self-regulatory measures into question, and encouraged the government in mid-2004 to test the waters of opinion for a motion to strengthen UK alcohol advertising. EU officials applauded this initiative, seeing the UK as a key nation in the success of their regulatory harmonization plans. Yet those within the advertising industry voiced what is now a well-rehearsed refrain: The legal director for The Institute of Practitioners in Advertising, Marina Palomba, stated, "What we see in the proposals to change the codes are assumptions without evidence. This goes against what the government has said on this subject, which is that any steps to restrict freedom of commercial expression and the right to advertise legal products has to be evidence-based" (in Lepper 2004, 15). The Advertising Association (2000), an umbrella organization of UK advertising agencies, continued to hold the position that alcohol advertising does not contribute to consumption, but simply to brand maintenance and switching:

> In general, companies advertise their own brands in order to increase the overall market share of their brands alone and to protect that market share against brand switching by consumers. Brand advertising, of the type seen in the alcoholic drinks market sector, is a tool of competition between brands, not a means to ensure overall increases in total consumption of a product type.

Despite this, new creative restrictions were instated in 2005.

Tobacco Product Marketing

Until recently in North America, restrictions on the content and placement of tobacco advertising—for example, its exclusion from radio and television—were the result of voluntary agreements between governments and the industry. However, in the United States the more recent trend, stemming largely from the terms of the settlements of the massive lawsuits settled between the industry and state and federal governments, has been a move toward limiting tobacco advertising, especially advertising directed at young persons.

In 1988 Canada took the unprecedented step of completely banning advertising for a product which was legal to sell. The Tobacco Products Control Act (TPCA), "an act to prohibit the advertising and promotion and respecting the labeling and monitoring of tobacco products," became law on June 28, 1988 (Health Canada Online 2005). The act focused on protecting Canadians' health from the consequences of tobacco use, by seeking to protect young persons from becoming dependent on tobacco and by raising public awareness of the hazards of tobacco use. Tobacco advertising was banned from magazines, newspapers, broadcasts, outdoor ads, retail signs, as well as sponsorship and promotional initiatives, including the use of tobacco brand names on merchandise. Section 9(3) of the Act stated, "This section does not affect any obligation of a distributor, at common law or under any Act of Parliament or of a provincial legislature, to warn purchasers of tobacco products of the health effects of those products." Thus, the Act attempts to prevent tobacco firms

Figure 17.2 Bacardi "Latin Quarter" campaign.

Figure 17.2 Continued.

from using the hazard-warning requirement as a defense against civil liability claims. Finally, the Tobacco Products Control Act contains elaborate stipulations on reporting by manufacturers to the Minister of National Health and Welfare on such matters as sales, product constituents (including prescriptions on testing methods), and controlled expenditures (e.g., for sponsorships).

Almost immediately upon passage of the Act, Canada's tobacco manufacturers—Rothmans, Benson & Hedges, RJR-Macdonald, and Imperial Tobacco—filed lawsuits against the federal government, claiming among other things that the prohibition on advertising and promotion in the Act was a violation of the Charter of Rights and Freedoms in the Canadian constitution, which contains protections for freedom of speech and expression similar to those guaranteed in the First Amendment to the U.S. Constitution. Advertising is sometimes called "commercial free speech," in order to distinguish it from "political speech," which encompasses all comments on social and political issues made by individuals and organizations. Thus the two main issues to be decided by the courts were: (1) whether commercial speech is entitled to exactly the same kind of protection, as a fundamental freedom, as is political speech; and (2) if not, what restrictions on commercial speech are "reasonable" in a "free and democratic society."

The federal government's legislation was based on its understanding of the very serious health risks incurred by users of tobacco products. The government's position could be summarized as follows: Even though the effects of advertising and other promotional activities cannot be identified with precision, because human behavior is complex, and there are so many influences (such as peer approval) on a person's attitudes and behavior, advertising must be presumed to have some persuasive effect on consumers. These presumed effects are: helping to encourage persons to begin using tobacco products; encouraging them to continue doing so, even when tobacco users become aware of the associated health risks; and, finally, promoting the erroneous belief that switching to brands that are lower in tar and nicotine content will significantly reduce those health risks. Due to such effects, consumption of tobacco products and the consequent health risks are higher than they would be if people were not exposed to promotional activities (including advertising) on behalf of tobacco products.

In responding to the government's position, the tobacco industry made three basic points. First, selling tobacco products remains a legal activity, and it is therefore unfair and unwarranted to ban outright promotional activities on their behalf. Second, there are many other products, such as alcoholic beverages and motor vehicles (especially off-road vehicles and motorcycles), whose use and misuse give rise to serious health risks, and yet the government has not imposed a total advertising and promotion ban on these product groups.

Third, it is not the intention of tobacco-product marketing to attempt to persuade non-users to begin using their products; rather, tobacco-product advertising is aimed at encouraging existing smokers to switch brands, either among competing manufacturers or among product lines by the same manufacturer. From this perspective, the government's prohibition will not, therefore, have the desired effect in lowering health risks. However, during the long time in which the TPCA was before the courts, the government had enforced it ban on tobacco advertising.

The TPCA was ruled unconstitutional by the Quebec Superior court in 1991, a decision overturned in the Quebec Court of Appeal. In 1995 the ruling of the Appeal court had made its way to the Supreme Court of Canada, where in a narrow 5–4 decision, the court struck down key sections of the Act, once again allowing tobacco advertising to appear in Canada. Immediately Health Canada drafted new legislation to ban tobacco advertising and promotion, particularly anything that was targeted at minors, once again, and in fact the government prohibition still stayed in effect. This new legislation was introduced in 1996 as Bill C-71, the Tobacco Act, which was given Royal Assent in 1997. The current legislation introduced, for the first time, tighter restrictions on the *content* of tobacco ads: First, "no person shall promote a tobacco product by means of an advertisement that depicts, in whole or in part, a tobacco product, its package or a brand element of one or that evokes a tobacco product or a brand element." Second, "lifestyle advertising" was prohibited; the Act defines it as "advertising that associates a product with, or evokes a positive or negative emotion about or image of, a way of life such as one that includes glamour, recreation, excitement, vitality, risk or daring." (Government of Canada Tobacco Act 2005) Furthermore, all advertising is to be carefully targeted to adults; mailed promotional material must not be directed to young people, nor may events marketing expose young people to signs that promote tobacco.

The United States was one of the first nations to impose restrictions on cigarette advertising. Concerns about the health risk of tobacco began to surface in the 1960s, and one of the first regulatory responses was to utilize the so-called "Fairness Doctrine," which required anti-smoking messages to be given equal weight in broadcast media. This arrangement ended in 1971, when cigarette advertisers—unwilling to face the prospect of seeing effective anti-smoking ads running on television—voluntarily removed all tobacco advertising from the broadcast media. Advertisers continued to get their messages televised through promotion in sports stadiums and cultural events. Despite its pioneering regulation, however, tobacco proved difficult to regulate because tobacco corporations have a considerable stake in the economy and are protected under constitutional doctrines of rights and freedoms. As Hugh Bayley, Member of the Select Committee, British MP and Minister of State for Health pointed out, "If cigarettes were introduced today, their production and sale would probably be banned." (House of Commons Hansard January 27, 1993) Yet one of the strongest arguments tobacco manufacturers have had around the world against those that attempt to restrict their marketing practices is that they are selling a legal product.

In 1996 President Clinton charged the Food and Drug Administration with control over a comprehensive program that sought to restrict the distribution of tobacco products and their advertising to children and adolescents. Part of the program required tobacco companies to educate young people about the hazards of their products. The tobacco industries brought a lawsuit against the FDA on the following grounds: (1) the FDA does not have authority over tobacco products, (2) tobacco products are not drugs, (3) FDA marketing restrictions violate First Amendment rights. Four years later the plan was struck down by the Supreme Court in a 5–4 ruling which stated that that FDA lacked legal authority over tobacco and its marketing. The ruling stated both that the Congress had "clearly precluded the FDA from asserting jurisdiction to regulate tobacco products," but the decision also noted this was so despite the fact "tobacco use, particularly among children and adolescents, poses perhaps the single most significant threat to public health in the United States" (*Food and Drug Administration et al. v Brown & Williamson Tobacco Corp. et al.* 2000).

In the summer of 2004 the U.S. Senate voted 78 to 15 in favor of a new bill to empower the FDA to regulate advertising. The bill, which also provided funds to tobacco producers to change the crops they grow, was celebrated by public interest groups, but yet again condemned by marketing industry organizations as a "content-based censorship of advertising" that violated the First Amendment (Teinowitz 2004). Until new legislation is written it appears the ping-pong game between the government and tobacco companies will continue, and until then the government will have to negotiate advertising restrictions with the tobacco companies.

The regulation of tobacco advertising in the United States has important implications for other countries throughout the globe, due to the dominance of U.S. programming in the global marketplace. In 1991 the European Commission proposed a ban to end all tobacco advertising and promotion. While most member countries supported the ban, Germany, The Netherlands, Denmark, and the UK initially opposed it, primarily on constitutional grounds. But by the turn of the twentieth century most European countries had agreed to the ban, including Denmark, The Netherlands, and the UK.

Direct-to-Consumer Drug Advertising

As the sun was setting on the Marlboro Man and Joe Camel, a new regulatory debate emerged about the marketing of prescription drugs direct to consumers. Advertising of pharmaceutical products had been confined to specialty publications directed to doctors. Promoting pharmaceuticals to the public was banned throughout the twentieth century in most Western countries. In 1997 the US Food and Drug Administration began to ease these restrictions, allowing direct to consumer drug advertisements to appear. Pharmaceuticals are a very big business spending $21.5 billion in 2002 on promotion and advertising directed to consumers and professionals. (Branch Jr. 2003) The change in the regulation saw a rapid rise in advertising investment. At TBWA World Health Europe, the chairman, Nick Baum, noted, "In the US, DTC (direct-to-consumer) has gone from $670 million in 1996 to $2.5 billion in 2002 to become the fastest growing sector of the ad market. It's the fastest-growing sector of the ad industry" (in Considine 2004). The communication conglomerates formed over the last twenty years have assumed a major stake in health care promotions and advertising. WPP has formalized its Health at JWT brand, which works from within the main agency. Euro RSCG Life has been formalized by Havas, Omnicom formed DDB Health, and Publicis Groupe has reorganized its health concerns under an umbrella firm dubbed Publicis Healthcare Group. While industry and advertisers celebrate the new initiatives, generally arguing it allows consumers to take control of information about their health, health activists have expressed many concerns; studies reveal that consumers are likely to act upon advertising information and that the number of direct requests for prescription drugs is on the rise. In a recent study by the Kaiser Family Foundation, 30 percent of a representative sample of 1,872 reported asking about a drug they had seen advertised on TV or in the press; doctors were found to honor up to 80 percent of these requests.

Pharmaceutical advertising is prohibited in all European Union member states, although so-called "awareness ads," which promote drugs without mentioning the brand, are permitted. Pharmaceutical companies and some regulator argue that the ban of direct to consumer advertising is overly "nanny-ish," arguing that advertising is one of the best means to promote "self-health." They also note that the EU measures are ineffective in the Internet era where consumer have access to a wide variety of information about drugs. They also maintain that consumers are at greater risk, given the misinformation about drugs communicated through the Internet, since drug producers are barred from providing accurate information about their commodities to consumers (Pfanner 2004).

According to the managing director of DDB Health, Jonathan Hoare, "There's a sea change in the way the pharmaceutical business is conducted. In the past two-and-a-half years, there's been a real surge in globalization." Because patents run out in seven years, companies seek to sell their products to the widest number of consumers as possible. Jeff Daniels, who is responsible for European operations at Grey Healthcare Group, says,. "More and more look early on, even before a product is launched, at how they will keep the brand going" (in Considine 2004). Given that advertising is the primary means by which brands are kept going, and that a single creative account, such as the Sanofi-Synthelabo account won by Publicis, can be worth $235 million, this area of regulation will remain contentious.

Lifestyle Risks: Of Credit Cards and Hamburgers

The penetration of marketing and promotion into lifestyles during the last two decades also brought into question advertiser's responsibility not only for the more obvious risky commodities, such as alcohol and tobacco, but also for everyday commodities such as financial products and fast food, some of what are now considered to represent potential risks to the consumer's well being.

Britain has witnessed considerable debate about the regulation of these goods. The complex nature of many financial products makes this service sector particularly liable to a charge of deceptive advertising. Any misrepresentation in this sector carries the potential for having devastating impacts on consumers. Rising levels of personal debt, particularly amongst the young, and exposure of unfair marketing practices and pension scandals in the UK financial industry, have led to the development of special regulatory codes for the advertising of financial products, which state that financial service advertising must be clear and must not profit from people's inexperience. Financial service providers must make their calculated rates and projections clear, and arm the consumer with the knowledge that values on investments go up and down, and also that earnings in the past do not necessarily imply earnings in the future. Regulation to date has been narrowly defined around the concept of deception, avoiding more complex questions such as the relationship between advertising and rising personal debt levels.

In the opening years of the twenty-first century a great deal of attention became focused on the promotion of food. Advocacy groups called for increased regulation of sugary, salty, and fatty foods because of their implication in childhood obesity (Sustain, 2002). These debates have played out dramatically in Britain. The recent release of a World Health Organization report, which spelled out in hard numbers the rising obesity rates, and which encouraged nation states to reduce the amount of sugar in people's diets, led to the charge that junk food manufacturers had stolen the crown of peddlers of bad health once held by the tobacco companies. In 2002 £500 million was spent on food advertising, £178 million of that on sweets and snacks (Lee, 2004). Concern coalesced around the marketing of junk food to children, and in November 2004 Labour MP Debra Shiply rallied one hundred backbenchers around a private member's bill to ban junk food and drink to those under five years of age. During the hearings of a select committee of Parliament on obesity that same month, Cilla Snowball, managing director of Abbott Media Vickers DDBO, caused a bit of panic when she noted that some campaigns targeted kids based upon "pester power," despite the existing restriction that "advertisers must not directly advise or ask children (defined as those under fifteen) to ask their parents or others to enquiries or purchases" (Independent Television Commission 2003). By December Culture Minister Tess Jowel had instructed Ofcom, the new regulatory body in Britain which oversees broadcasting, to explore "strengthening the existing code on advertising food to children" (Department of Culture, Media and Sport 2003). Current regulation restricts advertising that contravenes the public promotion of a varied and balanced diet or the inculcation of bad dietary habits, or that promotes excessive consumption. The government debated the idea of banning fast food advertising to children.

In September 2003 the Hastings Report, a comprehensive study of the research literature undertaken to explore the influence of food promotion on children's diets, was published. The authors presented evidence to the effect that food advertising influenced children's nutritional knowledge and shaped their food preferences and purchase behavior; the study found a clear link between television viewing, diet, obesity, and cholesterol levels. The authors stressed the point that the studies upon which they drew their conclusions had used sound methodological procedures which assured confidence in the data produced. Although they noted that it was is impossible to attain incontrovertible proof of the link between advertising and childhood obesity, due to the number of complex variables involved, the authors nevertheless felt confident concluding that "food promotion is influencing children's diets in a number of ways" (Hastings et al. 2003, 3; see also Livingstone 2004, and Livingstone and Helsper 2004). They went on to argue that the influences was likely to be even stronger than suggested in the literature, because the studies reviewed did not account for the influence of food promotion on the purchase behavior of parents, and because most studies focused primarily on television advertising, and therefore the impact of food advertising in other media and through promotion was not factored into the measure.

Throughout 2004 the issue was covered intensely by the British media (see Kline 2004), and the advertising industry eventually entered the debate, downplaying the role of advertising in child obesity and arguing that sedentary lifestyles stemming from the government's decision to eliminate physical fitness from the school curriculum was more to blame. By the summer of 2004 the government had stepped back from its threat to ban food advertising. Based upon this and other research findings, the Food Standards Association (FSA) in July 2004 agreed to take action which concentrated on concentrated providing more information about healthy diets through schools, media, and governmental initiatives. (Food Standards Association July 6, 2004). Advertising in relation to potential lifestyle risks has come under increasing scrutiny.

Persuasive Discontents

Concern with unfair business practices also gave rise to a debate about persuasive techniques that appear to violate the assumption of rational communication. The impetus for this issue was the identification of formats or techniques of communication that gave advertising an unfair advantage as a means of persuasive communication. In the 1950s, as advertisers changed their formats with the advent of TV, there was a growing sense that advertising agencies possessed increasing power and influence over the consumer. Since then, agencies have competed in the marketplace based on their special abilities to break through clutter and utilize effective powers of persuasion—that is, on their ability to psychologically "grab" the audience. In this context critics perceived the need for higher ethical standards for communication practice that could define restraints on the use of new media formats. Probably the greatest impetus for the suggestion of limitations on advertising's range of communication practices was the emerging belief that advertising provided excessive advantages to the corporate sphere.

Vance Packard's famous attack on the depth-psychology techniques being adapted to marketing strategy, *The Hidden Persuaders* (1957), created a widespread desire to define the boundaries of honest persuasion, and hence the limits on the formats that advertisers should be permitted to use. So, for example, although it has never been shown conclusively that subliminal messages (assuming their use in real campaigns) inserted in ads can affect product choices, fears about the subversion of personal autonomy resulted in quick government action; there are laws against using subliminal advertising in a number of jurisdictions, and, although the industry, in the words of one of our interviewees, regards the issue as the "UFO of business," this particular limitation on expression gained widespread industry support.

By the 1980s attention had shifted from subliminal messages to the invasion of advertising forms within editorial and programming content. Deregulation, the desire to reach resistant audiences, and the opportunities afforded by new technology, an empowered media planner, and public relations sector fuelled cross-promotion, viral marketing campaigns, and advertorials (advertising editorials); shopping channels and interactive advertising; and a renewal of old promotional approaches, specifically product placement and sponsorship—all of which challenged the mid-twentieth century agreements to cordon off advertising practices within regulatory constraints. Concerns about the audiences' ability to distinguish latent corporate persuasion communicated through new advertising techniques grew: How could audiences make rational choices if the information was camouflaged as popular culture content, for example?

The issue was debated widely in 2002 when, fearing a backlash, media providers (including CNN and ABC) went public with the story of celebrity drug plugs. Sarah Cohn, a CNN spokeswoman, noted in a press release that several celebrities who discussed illnesses and the specific medication they used while being interviewed on news programs had been paid by pharmaceutical companies: "In light of recent attention involving paid celebrity endorsements, CNN became aware that some celebrities were interviewed about their health problems might be paid. We decided it was important for our viewers to be aware of that as part of any future interviews or features about a celebrity" (in Petersen 2002). The news channels promised to better screen celebrities to ascertain whether they would make an impromptu promotion, and to educate hosts to respond on air with a balanced statement such as "this is only one of many potential drugs available to treat this illness." This example demonstrates that a narrow definition of promotion, focusing on "fair business practices," remains a primary motivation of marketing regulation into the twenty-first century.

Indeed there is nothing under current U.S. regulations to prevent the practice. The line between media interview and advertisement has been blurred from some time: A media interview can technically be a spot for a full range of commodity promotion, from drugs to diapers to soup. Celebrities have long used their privileged media access to promote movies, music, pet causes and themselves. The difference is the types of commodities that are now being promoted, and the financial exchanges made in their wake. There is good reason to believe that the twenty-first century will mark a new era of fusion between promotional and popular cultural content that we have not begun to imagine. In the age of media mix and the merger of above and below the line practices, an estimated 170,000 well-paid, well-trained public relations specialists, along with scores of advertisers and media planners, are working to erase the traditional divide between editorial and advertising content, as 40,000 tired and overworked journalists punch the clock.

Not all countries however, believe the fairness doctrine is adequate to protect citizens from twenty-first century promotional techniques. In 1989 the European Commission created Television without Frontiers (TVWF) to "ensure the free movement of broadcasting services within the internal market and at the same time to preserve certain public interest objectives, such as cultural diversity, the right of reply, consumer protection and the protection of minors" (EEC 1989). Along with a mandate to facilitate a European television market, TVWF sought to harmonize audiovisual regulation across member states. Limits were placed on the duration of advertising: Advertising could not exceed 15 percent of daily transmission time or 20 percent of hourly amount (approx twelve minutes), and the number of interruptions to programming was also fixed (approximately forty-five minutes of programming prior to an ad break). Advertising was to be fair, honest, and respectful of the vulnerabilities of children. Tobacco and medical product advertising was banned and alcohol advertising, while permitted, was subject to regulations, specifically to protect minors.

But what was most interesting, and would turn out to be most controversial about the TVWF initiatives, was its attempts through the 1990s to address some of the changes taking place in the media environment. The directive establishing TVWF required advertisers to clearly distinguish their messages from programming content through visual or auditory means recognizable to audiences. In other words, audiences had to understand exactly when they were being "pitched to." TVWF banned what it called "surreptitious" advertising, defined as "the representation in words or pictures of goods, services, the name, the trade mark or the activities of the producer of goods or a provider of services in programs when such representation is intended by the broadcaster to serve as advertising and might mislead the public as to its nature," and stated that this is not permitted particularly "if it is done in return for payment or for similar consideration" (European Union, Audio Visual Policy). TVWF also has sought to regulate new advertising techniques, including interactive, split-screen and virtual advertising, despite the minimal use of these techniques (an estimated 96–99 percent of advertising revenue is still spent on traditional media advertising). Soon thereafter comments began to be heard from advertisers and EU research firms, noting that in the interest of the advancement of new technologies, and because of the complications in separating content and advertising within some of the new techniques (as well as the threat of legal challenge), TVWF should consider bringing to bear what the industry likes to call a "light touch" to regulation (Kelloggs Report). In short, this area remains highly contentious and unresolved.

Children

The long-standing rationale for regulating children's advertising is based on the principle that children, due to their immaturity, are incapable of identifying advertising as commercial persuasion, and moreover do not have the experiential and conceptual abilities to evaluate advertisements and evaluate commercial messages rationally (Roberts, 1983). This argument has been at the heart of repeated attempts to restrict or ban advertising to children. This principle was confirmed as providing reasonable grounds for limiting broadcast advertising for children in Quebec, where a ban on advertising directed at children under age thirteen has been in place since 1976. The ban was upheld in a Canadian Supreme Court (1989) ruling as a reasonable limitation on commercial speech, because it accords with consumer protection legislation that strives to "protect a group that is most vulnerable to commercial manipulation." The court went on to state that "in sum, the evidence sustains the reasonableness of the legislature's conclusion that a ban on commercial advertising directed to children was the minimal impairment of free expression consistent with the pressing and substantial goal of protecting children against manipulation through such advertising."

The debates about protecting children have also focused upon restricting the amount of children's advertising. In the United States in 1974, the FCC limited Saturday morning network television to nine-and-one-half minutes of advertising per broadcast hour. This was rescinded in 1980, when the FCC reasoned in its suspension of the guidelines that market forces and industry self-regulation would prevent the "overcommercialization" of media, believing there would be limited demand for children's advertising and that self-regulatory codes established for children's broadcasting would suffice to restrain children's advertisers. Contrary to this expectation, children became a key market for advertisers and expenditure on U.S. children's advertising increased dramatically between 1982 and 1987, particularly among toy advertisers, who became the leading children's advertisers and also used the de facto deregulation to launch product-based animated programs, dubbed the "30-minute commercial."

The deregulating commercial time in conjunction with the general industry deregulation taking place in the 1980s, resulted in the production of new opportunities for children's merchandising, which decreased the role of network broadcasters in children's advertising while increasing the intensity of marketing communication initiatives. The result was network revenue losses from children's programming. Explaining his own network's threats to withdraw from children's network production because they could not compete, NBC executive Brandon Tartikoff explained in 1988, "For the last three years we have not made the kinds of profits that we did five or six years ago.... The shrinking profits are due to the boom in recent years of children's shows sold in syndication to independent TV stations" (in Boyer 1988). By using syndications of television stations in impromptu networks, toy marketing consortia were able to both compete with network children's programming and to short-circuit the broadcaster-based guidelines for the self-regulation of children's advertising that had been developed independently of the FCC. For example, the broadcast industry codes restricted the use of children's TV heroes in the advertisement and required that children's advertisements not take advantage of children's inability to distinguish fantasy and reality, or programming from advertising. Many of the advertisements for character toys, however, use scenes from the animated TV series interspersed with images of children playing with their character toys; in one ad, for example, a young boy is shrunk, climbs into a toy plane, and flies off into a GI Joe program (Kline 1988). By reorganizing the economic basis of communications, toy marketers have been able to circumvent the system of self-regulation set up by network broadcasters.

The regulation of children's advertising and programming has remained a contested sphere since the 1980s. In August 1996, responding to concerns that children's programming in the United States had become an advertorial ghetto, the FCC introduced new rules to encourage more educational and informational programs for children. The new initiatives sought to achieve the following:

- Adopt several public information initiatives designed to give parents greater information about the core educational programs being aired by TV stations.
- Set forth a clear definition of what type of programs qualify as core programs: they generally must have serving the educational and informational needs of children as a significant purpose; be aired between the hours of 7 a.m. and 10 p.m.; be a regularly scheduled weekly program; and be at least 30 minutes in length.
- Establish a guideline that calls for every TV station to air at least three hours per week of core educational programming. (Federal Communications Commision 2005)

Still, the array of marketing communication options available in commercialized media renders policies or regulatory programs that operate with a narrow understanding of the synergistic mediated marketplace futile. Cross-promotions, for example in thirty-minute cartoons in which the toy is the star, remain on the air.

In recent years social critics have moved beyond a focus on television advertising to examine the much broader issues involved in marketing goods to children, beginning with Stephen Kline's 1993 book, *Out of the Garden: Toys, TV, and Children's Culture in the Age of Marketing,* and continuing to the present, with the appearance in Fall 2004 of Juliet Schor's *Born to Buy: The Commercialized Child and the New Consumer Culture.*

Advocacy Advertising as Commercial Speech

In this book we have focused on the development of product advertising and its changing dynamics within the broader system of mediated communication. This by no means implies that the practices of governmental advertising, corporate public relations, social marketing, and political campaigning are incidental to the advertising system. As we have noted in chapter 8, around the world policy makers have noted that paid advertising is not merely the exclusive domain of merchandisers competing in the market to sell their brands, but now is the broader privileged modality of social communication generally, adapted by governments to solve social problems and to promote their programs, by political parties to win votes, and by interest groups and social advocates to articulate their concerns and to critique aspects of the global market culture. Advocacy campaigns in the commercial media have increasingly become an important means of influencing social discussion for corporate, government, and public-interest groups alike.

We have also noted that some of the consequences of these broader applications of the marketing communication model have been part of the evolving role of advertising more generally, leading to a blurring of lines between commercial, social, and political speech specifically. For this reason we suggested that the role of advertising must be conceived of generally as a modality of social communication generally, as a form of persuasive discourse which can be distinguished less by its content, form, or purpose than by the fact that it involves the transmission of a message through paid access to the audience of various media. Advertising has a dual life, therefore: as a commodity on the market and as a forum of cultural expression.

This blending of commercial and political speech has engendered some of the most difficult regulatory issues facing market democracies today. The problem is that once unfettered from the narrow confines of marketing's four Ps (person, place, product, price), advertising's social influence has been extended to embrace broader social issues, controversial lifestyles, and the political crises confronting the modern world. Nonprofit societies and interest groups use advertising to communicate their messages to the public, including environmental organizations such as Greenpeace and the World Wildlife Fund, children's charities such as Banados in Britain and the Save the Children Foundation in North America, animal rights organizations such as the Society for the Prevention of Cruelty to Animals, and anti-smoking and drug coalitions (see Figure 17.3). Yet through the resources available to them to buy time and space in media, large corporations appear to have considerable potential to constrain or skew public debate (Bellant 1988).

Although such advocacy advertising—the selling of ideas, ideological viewpoints, or corporate images—has been around for a long time (Marchand 1987), modern states became worried in the 1950s that there might be a need to regulate it. If companies simply talked about the benefits of their products in a competitive business sense, the principles of fair business practices would suffice. But when hi-tech companies advocate social revolution, or clothing manufactures condone anarchy and rebellion to appear "cool" in the minds of their young target consumers, or oil companies position themselves as green advocates and banks identify human rights with ethical banking, is regulation necessary with respect to the ideological content of advertising speech acts? In other words, advertising's growing diffusion as a form of both commercial and

WILL TOBACCO INDUSTRY DECEPTION OUTMUSCLE PARLIAMENT?

DEAR MEMBERS OF PARLIAMENT:

What may be the most expensive and deceptive lobbying campaign in Canadian history is underway to block perhaps the most important health bill ever tabled in Parliament. And while it is going on, our Members of Parliament, remain almost silent about the offensiveness of this campaign.

The foreign-controlled tobacco industry is threatening the autonomy of Parliament with an unprecedented multi-million dollar phoney letter campaign. And while the industry's deceptive letters and lobbying behind the scenes muscles many MPs off their commitment to the health of young Canadians, you, Canada's leaders, have not informed the public about the industry's tactics.

IT'S TIME TO SPEAK OUT

After a major struggle, the Tobacco Products Control Act has just received Second Reading in Parliament. But many Canadians are unaware that Bill C-51 is still in trouble. The Government's promise to Canadian youth to stop the industry's deceptive marketing practices faces a monumental uphill struggle.

Bill C-51 would ban tobacco advertising and promotion, a measure strongly recommended by the Canadian Cancer Society, Canadian Medical Association and by virtually every other major medical body.

To be candid, the industry's deceptive campaign has shaken the resolve of some MPs. Parliament knows that tobacco products are both addictive and lethal and that virtually all of the industry's new customers come from the child and adolescent market. In the name of decency, we are asking you not to let the industry's phoney letters destroy the chance for thousands of youngsters to make it through adolescence without being hooked by this industry's wares.

MUSCLING PARLIAMENT

Tell Canadians what is going on. A foreign-controlled industry is using an estimated $4 to 6 million to run an unprecedented campaign to defeat a proposed bill of the Government of Canada.

To put this in perspective, the cigarette manufacturers are spending more money to defeat Bill C-51 than the Progressive Conservative Party national office spent on advertising in the last election.

Brazenly, industry spokesmen denied their involvement in the letter campaign and misled the press with respect to the amount of funding for the lobby to defeat Bill C-51.

Such a massive attempt to subvert the will of Parliament has enormous implications. If the cigarette manufacturers are successful with this deceptive campaign (see boxed

The Fake Spontaneous Letter Campaign

Many Canadians would like to know how MPs feel about an industry campaign that tries to fake spontaneous letters against Bill C-51. Here's how the industry operates. Using huge phone and mail crews, the manufacturers target hundreds of thousands of Canadians. Using massive purchased lists, a postal gram is sent to each target informing the recipient that the industry will soon be in contact.

An expensive misinformation package is then delivered to the potential sympathizer. It includes a pre-typed letter ready for the target's signature and a pre-stamped envelope both addressed to the local MP. All the target has to do is sign and mail what is really a form letter in disguise. In order to increase the chance of a return, the industry phones once, twice, three times, even if across

text), think of the potential distortions to the democratic process which may take place. The precedent will be an open invitation for all industries wishing to avoid regulation to use muscle in this manner.

How can charitable agencies combat this massive disinformation? You, our MPs, know how to counter unfounded attacks when you want to. Millions of dollars have been spent to defend other legislation. How much will you spend to prevent 35,000 deaths every year?

ATTEMPTS TO GUT BILL C-51

A few MPs are seeking amendments which could destroy this legislation.

1 In 1972, the industry agreed to a voluntary code of self-regulation in order to evade the ban on advertising recommended by an all-party

Canada. Given the industry's low success rate in obtaining signatures, we estimate that each letter which reaches an MP is costing the industry $50 or more.

Each letter is made to look different. Form, text, colour of paper, are all varied by using automated equipment. Why? To deceive the local MP, of course. To give the impression of a spontaneous, grass-roots rebellion to the bill.

The real message here for MPs is not the letters from the industry's enormous campaign. The real message for MPs is being sent by the hundreds of thousands of thoughtful Canadians who refuse to sign. They refuse to sign despite letters being placed under their noses, despite coercing phone calls, and despite the absence of balanced information. Over 80 percent of those contacted will not sign.

committee of Parliament. After 15 years of increasing medical evidence and years of flagrant violation of its own code by the industry, some MPs are seeking to resurrect this voluntary process.

2 Some MPs have a fall-back position. They agree to ban tobacco advertising but they want to protect arts and sports sponsorship. This would provide the industry with the perfect escape route. The money which now goes to advertising would simply shift to sponsorship effectively gutting the legislation.

Canadian health organizations are saying "No compromises!" Each trade-off could ultimately condemn tens of thousands of youngsters to an early death at the hands of tobacco industry products.

TACTICS TO BLOCK BILL C-51

Tactic No. 1. Equate illegitimate industry claims of a right to promote a lethal drug with emotion-laden concepts like "freedom of choice" and "censorship." Don't mention that a product which is as addictive as heroin regains freedom of choice. There is no "censorship" involved in Bill C-51. The law recognizes differences between the right of citizens to express themselves and the right of a corporation to advertise what it pleases to whom it pleases.

Tactic No. 2. Divert attention. As long as the debate focuses on arts and sports sponsorship, the public will not be talking about 35,000 tobacco-caused deaths a year.

Tactic No. 3. Publicize discredited research and industry-funded scientists. Claim that it has not been "proven," that tobacco products cause lung cancer or other deadly diseases.

Tactic No. 4. Claim that "tobacco ad bans have not worked in other countries." Confuse the public by misrepresenting data and withholding key information. Fail to explain why, if ad bans don't work, the industry is spending millions to defeat Bill C-51.

From the industry's fishy studies to its offensive references to civil liberties issues, the industry campaign is a monstrous piece of misinformation. Is it too much to ask that you, our MPs, fight for the kids in the face of tobacco industry intimidation?

"We are extremely pleased that you plan to expose the tobacco industry's phoney letter campaign. If the industry is successful in blocking Bills C-51 and C-204, tens of thousands of deaths may be the ultimate cost."

Canadian Medical Association

A FEW OF THE ORGANIZATIONS WHICH SUPPORT BILLS C-51 AND C-204*
Canadian Medical Association • Canadian Cancer Society • Canadian Public Health Association
National Action Committee on the Status of Women • Canadian Nurses Association • Canadian Teachers Federation
* This ad was funded in part by the Community Health Department of the Montreal General Hospital

HOW TO HELP

1 Write your Member of Parliament. Ask your MP to support Bill C-51 and Bill C-204. MP Lynn McDonald's private member's bill which has received 2nd Reading in the House of Commons. Both bills would bring an end to tobacco advertising and promotion. For the name of your MP, call the toll free number for Elections Canada, at 1-800-267-4480. Write your

TO THE NSRA — "LET'S GIVE KIDS A CHANCE"

[ ] Here's my membership cheque for $40 payable to the NSRA
[ ] And/or $ _____ in support of the national campaign to pass Bill C-51
[ ] Enclosed is $8 for "Give Kids a Chance" your $8 page letter to MPs on Bill C-51 and tobacco industry deception

Name _____ Age _____
Address _____
City _____ Postal Code _____
Mail to: NON-SMOKERS' RIGHTS ASSOCIATION
Suite 408, 344 Bloor Street West, Toronto, Ontario M5S 1W9

MP, House of Commons, Ottawa K1A 0A6 – no postage is required.

2 Join and/or support the Non-Smokers' Rights Association. The NSRA is much more than a clean air rights group. The NSRA is a hard-hitting national, non-profit organization pressing for preventive medical approaches to the entire tobacco issue.

NON-SMOKERS' RIGHTS ASSOCIATION
Suite 408, 344 Bloor Street West, Toronto, Ontario M5S 1W9

Figure 17.3
Source: Courtesy of Non-Smokers' Rights Association.

political expression in a democratic society has gotten people worried about the communicative power and privilege enjoyed by those organizations that have the money to use advertising as a forum for political expression .

To date, only those organizations with a considerable funding base are able to get access to the media. And it is this potential connection between money and social communication that makes advertising markets a problem for the assumptions about "free speech" and a "level playing field" in markets. In order for there to be fairness in the treatment of subjects of political importance in our media, there should be no bias in the access to the expression of ideas. Since restricting the content of political speech is constitutionally proscribed, the U.S. Federal Communications Commission first attempted to deal with the growth of social marketing and advocacy advertising by applying its "Fairness Doctrine," which in effect justified broadcasters in restricting advocacy advertising or, granted to opponents a "right of response" to them. But during the 1980s the fairness criterion was dropped under the general Reagan-inspired deregulation ethos, making the exercise of advocacy a matter of broadcaster (and advertiser) self-restraint. It was up to the broadcaster's discretion to determine whether ads were too controversial or not.

There have also been instances in which broadcasters have refused to sell media space to ads organizations. ABC and Fox also do not accept what they deem to be "advocacy ads." An advertisement produced by the left-leaning Move-On.org was denied access to 2004 Super Bowl audiences on CBS for its thirty-second spot called "Child's Pay," which presented an ad critical of the rising federal budget deficit under the Bush administration and the legacy it would have for the nation's children. CNN, which agreed to show the ad, garnered huge publicity merely by broadcasting it during the controversy over CBS's refusal to do so, showing that broadcasters have great power over what is deemed by some to be controversial. CBS defended its position by noting its policy on such ads had been in place since the early 1970s and had been used to screen out hundreds of ads by anti-abortionists, free-trade campaigners, and pro-gun lobbyists. The station was also criticized for airing a message by an anti-drug organization during the Super Bowl; however, CBS claimed that there was a clear public interest in preventing drug use, and thus the ad was not considered by the network to fall under the controversial heading.

In Canada, Adbusters, an anti-commercialization organization, was denied access to several media channels despite having pre-cleared its ads with regulators. Like Move-On.org, Adbusters was informed that their messages, which addressed over-consumption and media addiction, were considered controversial. The case was taken to court in 2004 to test both the controversy restrictions imposed by the broadcasters and denial of oppositional political speech opportunities in a society in which media have usurped the town hall and street as the key streams of message exchange (Friesen 2004).

The questions of how to distinguish controversial issues within advertisements, or more generally how to differentiate corporate advocacy from political information, is further complicated within a commercial media system in which sweater producers like Benneton, and shoemakers like Kenneth Cole, sell their goods with reference to controversial issues such as the death penalty, AIDS, and racism, but where social advocates cannot do the same. The guarantees of commercial free speech imply that those organizations with substantial financial backing can use public airwaves to influence the public discussion of social issues. And so anarchy and rebellion can be celebrated by corporations, while special interest groups are dismissed as unacceptable advocates or as too controversial by broadcasters. Given that media are considered vital to democratic discourse, the undue influence of public debate by corporate and social interests within commercial media systems remains an unresolved issue. Likewise, corporate advocacy forces public interest group to enter the debate about social policy and social behavior through the gateway of advertising. And this confusion of political and commercial speech rights all come to a head in the debates about advertising's role in elections and referenda.

Political Advertising

Indeed nothing speaks more powerfully of the ascendance of the promotional system or the blurring of lines between consumers and citizens within market society, than advertising's role within contemporary democratic politics, particularly in the USA (McGovern 1997). With the advent of mass television audiences in the 1950s, advertising personnel began to play an ever more strategic role in orchestrating the Eisenhower presidential campaign—leading to the quip that American's were now being sold their leaders like a bar of soap (Thorson et al. 1991). A prescient thought, however, as it seems fair to say that the television spot has replaced the soapbox and the rear platform of the train in political life. Small children are now not just kissed from the back of the campaign train but rather in slow-motion splendor during highly stylized presidential "image campaigns" or depicted picking daisies—to the soundtrack of an ominous nuclear countdown in a notorious as in ad directed against Barry Goldwater during the 1964 presidential election campaign—in hard hitting attack spots (Diamond and Bates 1992, Jamieson 2000).

The bars of soap quip barely captures the profound impact that advertising has on contemporary elections, where increasing amounts of party funds are directed at three strategic uses of political advertising for electioneering: acclaiming (branding) the candidates and their policies (61 percent), attacking the opposition and its policies (38 percent), and defending the candidates and their policies against the attacks of opponents (1 percent). By the time of the 1996 presidential campaign, over $200 million was spent on election advertising and by 2000 over one million political spots were aired on television alone in the election year. Although negative campaigning is as old as democracy, vicious attack spots designed not simply to discredit but to demoralize political opposition, or to call into question the integrity of the opposition, are growing more common in each election (Benoit et al. 2003). Studies of presidential campaigns in the United States indicate that image-related claims and attacks (related to personality, leadership potential, and character) aired on television outweigh policy related messages by 3 to 2 (Kaid and Johnstone 2000). The Bush–Kerry confrontation led each campaign to spend upwards of US$60 million each on pre-election campaigning even before the "race" even began. It has been estimated that total political advertising expenditures for the election year of 2004 would climb to $2.68 billion (PQ Media Report, August 2004). With national politics now played out through a marketing system, the now-familiar questions of promotional "image politics" (Diamond and Bates 1992; Jamieson 2000; Wernick 1991), negative advertising (Kline 1997), and the cynicism of voters (Ansolabehere and Iyengar 1995) are all discussed critically within the academic literatures as presenting problems for democratic nations. Yet the content and style of campaign advertising—and the relationship between media and politics—is largely beyond the reach of regulation because it is regarded as "political speech" and thus entitled to virtually unlimited constitutional protection. It is worth remembering, too, that political ads are not subject to the "substantiation" requirements of truth, any more than candidates can be held to the promises they make when seeking election. Caveat emptor, rather than truth in advertising, is a principle that applies to political marketing as well as consumer sales.

This does not mean that political advertising is completely unregulated, however, for there remains a long-held democratic principle that fears the link between money and social influence. In the interests of insuring a "level playing field" for electoral campaigning, most democratic governments have therefore imposed limits on the amounts of money that can be raised and spent on political advertising during an election. Although the definition of an election period and the specific limitations vary, most democracies impose caps on advertising expenditures and have created organizations for ensuring that corporations or parties cannot unduly influence votes by dominating the air-waves. Canada's Elections Act, for example, places ceilings on expenditures and monitors each party's advertising spends (donations to parties receive tax credits) in the period before the election (thirty-three days), as well as allocating each party a right of access to "unpaid" party political time within the media according to a very complex formula, which ascribes a weight to each official party and candidate based on previous votes cast and seats held in Parliament. Similar policies limiting advertising spends are found in most democratic nations, with a $75 million cap placed on the hard money advertising spends in the United States, which comes into effect after a party has officially chosen its candidate—but all spending prior to that time is exempt.

What has become truly controversial about the rise of political marketing however is the potential for "third-party" groups—whether industry, advocacy, or interest groups—to use so-called "soft money" funds to influence public debate during an election. The concerns grew in the wake of Richard Nixon's 1974 Federal Election Campaign Act, which rendered ineffective restrictions on contribution limits and disclosure requirements. It had become common practice to organize campaign activities under the auspices of Political Action Groups (PACs) which functioned at arm's-length from the official party, thus escaping the "hard money" spending limits and accounting imposed in the period before an election. Thereafter political parties began to develop new ways of fundraising to support advertising campaigns which could both be more negative and more focused on particular controversial issues that the party did not wish to address in their own advertising or campaigning. This method was sanctified by a Supreme Court ruling after the 1996 presidential campaign which distinguished between "express advocacy" and "issue advocacy" advertising. Express advocacy required an explicit "vote for" or "party specific recommendation," whereas ads that left out these magic words were considered to be issue advocacy and remained beyond public scrutiny or control as acts of free political speech. In 2000 it is estimated that over $250 million of soft advertising was spent on the Gore–Bush campaign.

Although there has been a protracted debate about third party campaigning in the USA for thirty years, little seems to have changed in the practices of third-party political marketing, in spite of a U.S Supreme Court Case, *McConnell v. Federal Election Commission*, challenging the constitutionality of the Bipartisan Campaign Reform Act, which had reaffirmed Congressional authority to regulate campaign funding. The main issues heard by the Court were whether the limits imposed on party finances and independent advertising campaigns by parties and interest groups were permissible restrictions on the rights of free speech and association guaranteed by the First Amendment. The Court held that the constitutional interest served by campaign finance laws is "to prevent corruption or the appearance of corruption—understood as any exchange of cash for votes, including the undue influence over the electorate." The courts therefore approved broader standards for defining types of campaign activity such as political advertising, and expanded the reach of the law to encompass the federal election related activities of local party committees and political groups (Corrado and Mann 2004, 26; Elections Canada 2004). Although laws in the United States and elsewhere have confirmed that spending restraints on advertising during elections are a valid way of ensuring fairness in democracy, they can be of little consequence, as the case of the

"Swift Boat Veterans" and MoveOn.org demonstrated during the 2004 presidential race.

A recent supreme court decision in Canada handed down a similar judgment on the ambiguous role of third party advertising as a form of political influence open to citizens and corporations, in upholding the constitutionality of the sections of the *Canada Elections Act* limiting third party election advertising expenses to $3,000 in a given electoral district and $150,000 nationally, and requiring a third party to identify itself in all of its election advertising, to appoint financial agents and auditors, and to register with the chief electoral officer (Third Party Election Advertising Parliament of Canada 2005). In making this finding in 2004 in *Harper v. Canada*, the court noted that there are two ways for the government to ensure freedom of expression in advertising so that there is proper political discourse: The government can take steps to provide a voice to those who might otherwise not be heard; or it can take steps to restrict the voices which dominate the political discourse so that others may be heard as well.

The court concluded that the provisions of the *Canada Elections Act* that restricted voices that could otherwise dominate the discourse should be upheld as constitutional. In rendering its decision, the court made the following observations in acknowledging the legitimate place of advertising in political discourse: (a) the right of citizens to act in a meaningful way includes the right to act in an informed manner; (b) that, when there is an unequal dissemination of views, the ability of citizens to become informed is undermined; (c) that advertising enhances political discourse; (d) that the greater the number of voices that are heard, the more citizens are empowered to act meaningfully; (e) that advertising influences citizens; (f) that, if one side of a debate is able to dominate another, this is to the detriment not only of other speakers but also of the listeners. In the words of Chief Justice Beverly McLachlin:

> The ability to engage in effective speech in the public square means nothing if it does not include the ability to attempt to persuade one's fellow citizens through debate and discussion. This is the kernel from which reasoned political discourse emerges. Freedom of expression must allow a citizen to give voice to her vision for her community and nation, to advocate change through the art of persuasion in the hope of improving her life and indeed the larger social, political and economic landscape. (2004, A12)

The classic example of how important third-party advertising has become was evidenced clearly in the United States during the 2004 presidential campaign when the "Swift Boat Veterans for Truth" launched its $7 million attack on John Kerry's Vietnam War record. "Texans for Truth" responded with a similarly loaded counter-blast against Bush's stint in the National Guard, adding to the alleged $60 million dollars spent by anti-Bush campaigners—all soft money. Although court cases were launched against the Federal Electoral Commission by both Republicans and Democrats protesting soft money spending, the damage was already done. In this sense caps on party political advertising expenditures during elections do not ensure a level playing field when advocacy groups and corporate interests are free to use public airwaves to lobby on behalf of political parties.

However, it is not just concerns about third-party advertising potentially influencing an election that have become the subject of public debate. Although advertising (information campaigns) became an accepted tool of state power early in the twentieth century, governmental advertising budgets have risen significantly recently, making the modern state itself into a leading advertiser. In Canada during the 1970s, when Pierre Trudeau allocated $370 million to fight a national unity battle against Quebec separatism, the state became the country's leading single advertiser (Rose and Rutherford 2000). Currently the War on Drugs, anti-tobacco campaigns, and military recruiting all have billion-dollar budgets in U.S. markets. The magnitude of these communication budgets clearly presents a temptation to governments in power to use advertising less to inform citizens about programs than to win support or legitimate policies—or as part of a system of political patronage of the advertising sectors. Researchers have noticed that government spending on advertising tends to increase significantly just before an election.

This issue erupted into public controversy in Australia when, during the run-up to the 1995 election in New South Wales, four government campaigns were aired discussing issues from clean water and energy health to forestry policies and safety at train stations. The Australian Broadcasting Authority (ABA) was asked by the leader of the opposition in that state to determine whether these ads should be permitted in the period prior to the election, because, he charged, they were in fact "political matter," regulated under the Broadcasting Services Act of 1992. In reviewing the case, the ABA agreed that ad messages which are informational may also be political because they pertain to matters of public importance, and that campaigns conducted by governments in the normal course of their duties are not exempted from this provision in the act. The determination of what constitutes political matter therefore resulted from the consideration of the ads' proximity to an election, and also the "contextual background" of whether the subject is a prominent political issue at the time of broadcast. Using this contextual definition, the ABA panel ruled that none of the four governmental campaigns were "political matter" that would be covered under the act's provisions, because there was insufficient evidence of substantial debate about the issues at the time of their broadcast or because they did not make reference to governmental actions.

Mediated Practices

Because advertising emerged at a time of great uncertainty about the cultural role of the media, special concerns about community standards and values have been raised and acknowledged by advertisers. As Canadian Advertising Foundation Chairman Frank Philcox has stated, "Commercial free speech does not come without constraints. . . . Corporations must operate within the ethical standards of honesty and good taste our society demands [of public communications]." Thus, like all public expressions of opinion, advertising is also subject to legislated limits to public discourse, including sedition, libel, slander, and copyright restrictions (varying by country), and to other laws and regulatory frameworks that govern the media in general. There are very few instances worldwide in which advertisements have violated these general principles. In this context the controversy over advertising's communicative practices has centered around the industry's special obligations to respect community standards and values. In many cases, broadcasters use community standards to reject controversial advocacy advertising. It is not in any broadcaster's interest to deeply offend community standards or public taste, and most advertisers respect such provisions as ultimately working in their own interest—although they are sometimes chastened for adopting such a mainstream and bland view of life.

A closer review of social policy disputes reveals, however, that the social concerns expressed by the critics of advertising have gone well beyond the narrow issues of honesty and good taste that are readily acknowledged by industry spokespersons. For example, the industry has been accused of being insensitive to how its images degrade or objectify women or diminish particular racial and ethnic groups with unrealistic and limited images of their social life. Feminist accusations have been the most vociferous. As we saw in chapter 12, commentators have launched many criticisms against the representations of women and racial groups in advertising. Although these criticisms have been voiced since the 1970s, on the whole advertising has not changed a great deal in the intervening period. Advertising as a whole continues to be accused of reinforcing a biased and predominantly male view of life and male fantasies in its representation of women, and more generally of giving priority to white, middle-class community standards. The dynamics of "addressing the market" also underscore the disputes of ethnic and racial stereotypes reviewed in chapter 12. Advertisers' limited attempts to address blacks and Hispanics in the United States, along with the industry's disinterest in supporting minority media, remain contentious issues. Despite the serious consideration given to this issue, new guidelines and self-regulation appear to have failed to change advertising practices; public policy seems to be at a loss as to how to deal with problems like gender imagery beyond monitoring and chastening advertisers (CRTC 1992).

Identifying stereotypical misrepresentation in advertisements is relatively easy to do, but attempting to remedy the situation is harder than would appear at first glance. Perhaps one could require matching representations to social statistics. Would advertisers be allocated proportional characterizations—say, one child-minding ethnic father, three yuppie lawyers, and two working businesswomen? Such a directive would not really solve the problems of stereotypical misrepresentation because, of course, it would only perpetuate whatever inequities still exist in society. The problem lies not so much in the relationship that advertising content bears to reality, as in the reasons that advertising uses condensed codes of characterization and in the strategies for targeting particular audiences. In other words, stereotyping in advertising cannot be solved by treating it as a matter of inaccurate representation. Advertising personnel are no more sexist or racist than people in other areas; their overriding concern is with forms of communication that will sell products. Operating in a cluttered environment with severe time restrictions and targeting to segmented audiences, advertisers draw upon generalized representations of social groupings to enhance communication. As Erving Goffman (1979, 84) has said of advertisers, "their hype is hyper-ritualization." However, ads are not only about selling, for they operate in a social context and have social effects. Thus, we must try to sift out the aspects of advertising practice that have potentially negative social effects and seek to address them as precisely as possible.

The questions of greatest societal import that advertising raises are best summed up in disputes about the industry's role in the socialization of children. The issues—which emerge in clear relief because this particular audience is still in a process of formation and occupies an uncertain position in the population of consumers—touch on all of the three domains to which we have called attention in this chapter. First, the stereotyped and unrealistic representations common in children's advertising can become templates that shape children's social attitudes and development, particularly in the way they interact with their peers and parents. Second, the commercialization of programming has profoundly influenced the quality and emphasis of children's television. Third, the industrial sectors (toys, snacks, and cereal manufacturers) with interests in children's marketing are very limited. In short, the fundamental issue at stake is the flow of culture to children.

To date, we have dealt with this issue in only a piecemeal way. For example, we fully recognize that television is the dominant children's medium of communication, largely because American snack, soft-drink, cereal, and toy manufacturers are willing to spend approximately one billion dollars annually in the United States to support children's advertising and marketing promotions through television. We have no estimates of how much the advertising subsidy contributes to the channeling of children's cultural production effort into television alone, or how successful similarly low-cost books, movies, or radio programs would be in the children's market. Certainly, the evidence suggests that limits on commercial time or attempts to ban advertising in particular time slots (especially Saturday mornings) are likely to fail in the current broadcasting environment. Besides, this approach does not recognize that children watch adult programming and advertising at least as much as they watch children's programming. As a TV station owner bragged in an interview, "I have the largest share of the children's audience because I never run children's programs." Likewise, it would be easy to open up new children's "ghettos" (such as weekday mornings), provided the advertising revenue was there. Indeed, syndication and licensing arrangements are making the network broadcast self-regulation increasingly inconsequential to children's marketing. Similarly, attempts to restrict particular types of testimonials for products by the characters in children's programs have been undermined by a new marketing strategy in which the program is itself the advertisement (for example, the "Gem" or "Transformers"). Even attempts to ban advertising to children altogether, as in Quebec, have been undermined by the transmission, by cable, of uncensored foreign broadcasting into the regulated environment. The real problem is that the child's socialization is formulated within a wide cultural kaleidoscope, and in order to be effective our policy formulations must address the entire realm of commercially mediated culture, not just the part of it represented by advertisements.

Advertising as an enormously versatile and attractive genre of social communication, and with its overall relation to culture and society raises difficult policy questions. How does advertising itself affect the development of personal identity and the social aspects of consumption? We have traced the historical process in which the meaning of goods and the nature of the satisfactions to be derived through them have been systematically reformulated by economic institutions. These transformations were, in part, responses to changes in social composition such as the blurring of class distinctions, but more directly they were an internal response by the advertising industry to the problem of selling goods in the environment of mediated communication. Both factors gave rise to a great increase in the number of portrayals of human relationships in advertisements. The systematic emphases and obsessions in these portrayals show clearly that advertising is less at ease with depicting some types of human relationships or consumption patterns than others.

No matter what gave rise to the bias, however, there are calls to supplement current restrictions on misleading advertising content and inference (implied claims) with restrictions on "irrational" advertising, lifestyle advertising (for beer and cigarettes especially), and stereotyping; matters of advertising's "rhetorical forms" and appeal approaches may, as a result, become part of a regulatory policy agenda.

The case of stereotypic representation of people in advertising is especially instructive. We usually understand discrimination in this respect as involving the under representation of a particular category of people or groups—for example, not enough working women or blacks in middle-class occupations. Two factors are responsible for the attention given to advertising stereotypes: (1) advertising is so visible that people have come to regard criticism of it as an effective way to address the broader social problem of inequality; and (2) advertising is such a compressed form of communication that its dramas, characterizations, and role structures are both clearer and more "typical" than what is shown during programming time.

An Unfair Burden of Blame?

Advertisers maintain that many of the ads criticized by activists and watchdog groups do not, in fact, violate community standards but only the personal, somewhat prudish, and highly politicized taste of the critics. Advertisers also claim that the admittedly erotic or ambiguous images of women used in many campaigns are similar to arts and fashion photography and do not violate community standards. They claim that, according to their own research findings, many women like and respond positively to the images in these advertisements. Truly offensive ads, they contend, would receive complaints and be quickly withdrawn.

Advertisers also wonder why, among so many communication practices that treat life similarly, their industry is singled out. Advertising professionals often react to suggestions of a connection between "larger" social issue and their own creative activities on behalf of their clients with a mixture of contempt, wariness, and surprise. As one of our interviewees said, "I think advertising can play a role in helping to integrate people, though not a very substantial role. But I don't think advertising should be saddled with the various social problems." And yet the number of people complaining to regulators about UK advertising, for example, is rising; in 2003 "the ITC received a record number of complaints about ads—nearly 10,000 compared with 8300 in 2002." (Independent Television Commission 2002) These changes might reflect new procedures that made it easier for people to lodge a complaint. In the UK, unlike the United States, regulatory bodies are required to undertake community outreach and promotion to inform the public their rights to complain and the procedures for doing so.

Some in the advertising industry do feel unfairly singled out and ask why advertisers are expected to be such good citizens when other cultural programmers behave badly. Raoul Pinnell, vice president of global brand and communications at Shell, was so incensed by what he took to be the unjust differences between television programming and advertising regulation that he commissioned an independent research firm to undertake research. A panel watched and coded ninety hours of television for "instances of mismatches in behavior under the categories of smoking, drinking, drugs, driving, language, sex and nudity, and violence and crime, using twenty-one levels of offence ranging from "harmless" to "disgusting." The assertion that programming was more offensive than advertising on the first examination of the data was confirmed. However, when analyzed per hour of instances, the differences narrowed, and in a given hour of advertising programming audiences were found to be more likely to encounter nudity and sexuality, or violence and crime, than an hour of television programming. However, the intensity of offense material was greater within programming, particularly aggressive violence and crime. In sum, advertising potentially offends more often, programming offends more powerfully. While the forces that motivate public complaints about advertisements are difficult to untangle, it is clear that people are more likely to complain about advertisements. Broadcast regulators received less than half the complaints about their programming than advertisers, despite more explicit programming content.

We also know that complaints tend to cluster around a small number of ads, and the number of flashpoint ads remains constant over time. This suggests that the vast majority of advertising does not motivate people to complain to regulators, that there is a considerable overlap in what people find offensive, that a core cluster of individuals with common values complain. It might also indicate that the regulatory system in the UK is healthy, that most UK advertisers abide by the rules, perhaps out of fear of more harsh censorship, and that flashpoint ads stem from a small number of creatives who seek controversy as a strategy for obtaining notoriety among their peers, attention among their jaded audiences, free media exposure for their clients, or a combination of these potential benefits.

As we saw in chapter 12, when advertisers find themselves in the heat of controversy, few claim that they purposely court controversy. The Wrigley's "Xcite" advertisement (Figure 17.4), in which a young man vomits up a live dog, produced by Abbott Mead Vickers BBDO, is an example of a flashpoint ad, producing 863 complaints, largely from animal lovers and mothers with young children.

It became the most notorious advertisement in the history of British television. Mead Vickers BBDO and Leagas Delaney, the agency that produced the ad, has long marketed itself as an "ethical" agency, refusing to accept tobacco accounts because, according to AMV's Cilla Snowball, "We believe tobacco advertising encourages smoking." Agency founder David Abbot has publicly

Figure 17.4 Wrigley's Xcite, UK ad, 2003.

Figure 17.4 Continued.

voiced his disdain toward TBWA/London's work for French Connection, particularly its FCUK campaign (Palmer, 2001). Thus, when the dog breath ad broke as a news story, the agency quickly pulled the advertisement and made public statements denying that they had set out deliberately to offend the public, arguing that the problem stemmed from poor targeting of the message to its intended youth audience. Peter Knowland, new business and client service director at AMV, said, "We could have been cleverer in reaching our audience in a more targeted way. Though our specific target audience was youth, we trespassed unintentionally into the mainstream, which is what caused so much offence. We are now much more conscious of media-placement issues and work hard at ensuring that, despite greater fragmentation among agencies, that message doesn't get lost" (in Simms 2004).

Clearly, however, not everyone at major agencies holds the same attitude toward the question of good corporate citizenship. Leagas Delaney chairman Bruce Hains, speaking in his capacity as President of the Institution of Advertising Practitioners, stressed that agencies must put business concerns before complex social issues. He noted, "Advertising agencies and the people who run them are not social workers. We are there to work with clients for the best possible outcome for their brands" (in Palmer 2001). Hamish Pringle, director-general of the IPA and a member of the Advertising Association taskforce on self-regulation, agreed. He too feels there is an unfair regulatory double standard between advertising and programming. He argues that we delude ourselves in believing that cultural producers are more altruistic and less commercial than advertisers: Those who make television programming and newspapers are in business, he notes, and use salacious material to keep their industries afloat. Thus, he wonders, "Why is a glimpse of a nipple in a Neutrogena shower gel ad any more "commercial" than a naked page-three girl in *The Sun* [newspaper]?" Pringle believes that the media should be subject to the same codes of conduct as advertisers are. Raoul Pinnell of Shell takes the debate a step further: "There is a danger that we have created a regulated adland that pays for the promotion of a wide range of behavior in programs, for which advertising gets the blame."

There is a familiar ring to the industry arguments against regulation. Hains clearly articulates the long-held industry argument that advertisers are simply "in business" and advocates that rights to commercial speak should override public offense—a position which nicely ignores advertising's broader cultural role. Pringle also upholds the economic doctrine of fairness, equating cultural producers and advertisers, which leads him to conclude that lack of regulations on programming content represents an unfair competitive advantage. Statements such as these illustrate the point that advertisers no longer see other brands, but also the entire media system, as their competitive environment. Pinnell also subscribes to a narrow economic definition of advertising, focusing on its role as a media subsidy: because advertisers pick up the tab, they deserve to have their say, unencumbered by legal controls.

There are many limitations to these arguments. First, as our systemic analysis of the promotional system makes clear, it is wholly incorrect to assert that advertising pays for the media. Consumers pay for the media through the promotional costs that make up the price of goods. Agencies redirect or bridge this money to the media. Because consumers pay for advertising, their interests should be acknowledged. Even if we look at advertising from a strictly marketing position, many of the assertions above do not hold. One of the principles of the market is that consumer choice is paramount for market efficiency and individual satisfaction. Yet audience ad choice is limited, particularly in broadcasting media and public spaces. Studies have consistently shown that audiences find radio, television, and billboard advertising to be the most intrusive of all media (Cronin and Menelly 1992; Elliott and Speck 1999; Sepeck and Elliott 1997). Programming guides are provided for the television schedule, and audiences have the power to select what they want. But audiences have little ability to select advertising, particularly on broadcasting and public space advertising; their only good option is to avoid it, which they have done in increasing numbers with their zappers.

We have stated our reasons for concluding that the economic view is too narrow a framework to support useful debates about the role of advertising. The economic perspective fails to recognize that advertising is an accomplished and versatile form of social communication. Commercial messages have permeated the entire fabric of life during the course of the twentieth century, subtly blending their materials and techniques with those of the consumer culture as a whole, until they became virtually identical with it. As a result, the meaning and impact of advertisements considered in isolation is difficult to pin down. The significance of advertising is not confined to specific ads, to particular product categories or brands, or even to specific effects on a single medium. Advertising should be viewed as part of the institutionalization of marketing communication in our society, for its implications extend to the whole realm of mediated communication and popular culture. Whatever limitations we impose on marketing communication must, likewise, be grounded in a recognition of advertising as a robust form of social communication.

Because they are governed by the marketing concept, most advertisers claim that, at worst, they are reflecting partial images of reality. Advertising may not accurately depict society as a whole, but neither is it a total distortion, for its reflected images represent fragments of the population, market clusters, or lifestyle images that exist among significant components of the market. Advertisers often claim they are simply responding to consumer demand in their advertising. It is for this reason that Michael Ray (1982, 482) believes that effective targeting can eliminate most of advertising's offenses:

> [The] underlying mission that is central to the questions of society and the future...is to produce communication campaigns in marketing that get to the right people with the right message at the right time....If this kind of communication was accomplished, advertising could be one of the most pleasurable, effective, and moral forms of communication....If such efficient communication is achieved, most of the problems of advertising and marketing communication and society disappear.

Attempts by the advertising industry to address a specific market segment do not, of course, excuse it from the consequences of doing so through public media. In a perfect world, all advertisements would be directed only toward willing targets, but the growth of "zapping," and numerous complaints about junk-mail advertising and automated telephone sales—the most targeted forms of advertising—remind us that advertising remains a deeply intrusive act. Consumers are not always given the opportunity to seek out or choose the advertising information they want. By virtue of their power of dispersal throughout media, advertisers avoid this most important condition of being in the marketplace: namely, that audiences would choose them in preference to other cultural activities. Although advertisers hate to be "saddled with the problems of society," their selective and limited depiction of social groups and ideologies continues to draw criticism. Advertising is chastened for reinforcing racial, ethnic, and sexual stereotypes; for disrupting the normal socialization process; for perpetuating environmentally inappropriate behavior; and generally for promoting goals, values, and imagery that oppress, objectify, or dehumanize people.

Our own research has confirmed that advertising is a form of communication that adopts a very limited perspective on our society and the way people aspire, act, and interact in it. In reflecting an image of life governed by merchandising objectives, advertising has inherited all our cultural uncertainties about the consequences of consumerism, about cultural diversity, and about the role that social inequality plays in modern life. Although they are under no legal obligation to provide a view of life that authentically reflects the situations and conditions in society, advertisers should not be surprised by the number of people who find fault with a public discourse of social life solely determined by marketing criteria.

The above debates about representation serve to provide a clearer sense of both the unresolved issues in our system of advertising communication and our general discomfort with censorship when it borders on matters of depicting social life. Our society seems unable to attack the issue of social representation directly, precisely because it is both a highly controversial and deeply rooted social problem. Conceiving of communication as a marketplace, we are content to let consumers' preferences be the best judge of cultural preference. So why are the same criteria not extended to advertising representation?

This question reminds us that it is not simply the representation of a group in the advertisements, but the relationship of advertising to the media system as a whole that is truly at stake when a group is excluded from marketing's view. And this, perhaps, explains why advertising fails to provide any sense of social diversity and change. In the current commercial arrangements for media, targeted programming formats and alternative images survive only when that audience is of interest to a sufficient group of advertisers.

Because advertising is the economic fulcrum of the commercial media system, its influence on media markets has also been a matter of public policy debate. To the degree that commercialized media adopt a biased view in their productions, marketing dynamics appear to be one of the causes of this bias. A clear example of this systemically biased relationship occurred in 1999, when the FCC expressed concern over research that indicated advertisers spent less on minority media (Ofori 1996). The FCC reminded everyone that all audiences are created equal before the eyes of the law, and that the First Amendment supports diversity of speech. Wally Snyder, president and CEO of the American Advertising Federation, took a stand, arguing to his members, "It is time to acknowledge the problem" (American Advertising Association 1999).

But this situation is very difficult to address, for it is a structural in nature. Media in the United States operate as a marketplace in which audiences are bought and sold. Market principles are based on choice and price differentials. Through their purchases consumers support commodities that match their interests and needs and drive out those that do not. Despite their rhetoric advertisers certainly do not see all audiences as equal; whether this is a function of monopoly control, racism, stereotyping, or sound market data, pressures to turn profits for shareholders, scrutiny of promotional budgets, and target marketing force media buyers to be selective and strategic in their purchases. Thus, while it is unpalatable to face the biases of the marketplace, audiences are commodities, advertisers are shoppers, and the Hispanic audience commodity, at least as of 1999, was not considered to be as valuable as other audiences were. To force advertisers to pay the same price for all audiences would be to suppress the highly cherished market element in media.

Advertising throws back at us deep and unresolved tensions about the representation of social life in media. Attacking advertising for its biased view, and for its undoubted contribution to perpetuating regressive social practices, is one thing; but actually seeking to modify or eliminate practices enshrined in public attitudes, behavior, and institutional structures by reforming advertising representation alone is another. Actions directed at correcting social problems, in domains where advertising is only a bit player in a much more grand drama, will inevitably prove frustrating and inept. It seems far simpler for critics to focus on the representations of contested social relations as they appear in advertising than to confront the deeply rooted afflictions in our society that lie at their source. Advertising is particularly vulnerable as a system of social imagery because it is so prominent and intrusive, and because its condensed format implies greater simplification and typification in its representations, which leaves advertisers open to accusations of distorting real social conditions and denying the authentic experiences of ordinary people.

There may be good reasons for limiting certain sorts of persuasive techniques, for controlling stereotyped representations, or for regulating economic demand, but these are policy matters that cannot be addressed solely by controlling advertisements. Where social policy demands it, advertising policy should be seen rather as an integral part of more general economic, communications, and social initiatives. Questions about the economic function of advertising are not easily resolved, but one thing is clear: We cannot criticize advertising independently of the social context in which it performs. The focus should be, not on advertising practices, but on the specific set of institutional relationships through which advertising is tied to the social issues that concern us most.

Watching the Watchers

Advertisers, media, and ad agencies have struggled hard to define and articulate what their larger social role might be. Recent, highly publicized public tragedies have revealed that advertisers do think reflexively about the cultural impact of their messages. In Britain in 1997, after the death of Princess Diana, several advertisers chose not to run particular ads. Upon finding out that the Princess was killed in a Mercedes-Benz by a driver under the influence of alcohol, the Mercedes automobile company, along with several alcohol producers, pulled or changed their scheduled messages: "Mercedes-Benz people in England are quite shocked and just want to show a sign of respect," said Birgit Zaiser, a press officer at Mercedes headquarters in Stuttgart. At the same time, the UK television networks stated that they would refrain from showing ads depicting speeding cars or screeching tires and requested alcohol advertisements be moved in the schedule so that they did not appear next to direct news coverage of the death. Other major companies which altered their advertising in light of the event included Volkswagen, Allied Dunbar (which had a "grim reaper" ad), and Renault Clio (an advertisement featuring couples taking trips to France). The London–Paris rail line, Eurostar, pulled its radio advertisements and Cadbury delayed the display of its candy tag line, "The nation's favorite," because it has been used to refer to the princess (Bidlake and Pollack 1997). After the September 11, 20001 tragedy, advertisers in the United States were mindful of how their messages might be reinterpreted in light of the event. O. Burtch Drake, president and CEO of the American Association of Advertising Agencies stated, "Advertising can and will play a crucial role moving the country forward as we continue our recover." But he also counseled his members "to exercise sensitivity" as they carried on their business (Bogle 2001).

Examples such as these illustrate not only that advertisers feel that they need to be sensitive to the cultural mood in light of tragic events, but that they feel that their messages do have the potential to cause broad unease. But when threatened with sanctions advertisers tend to change their tone, minimizing the impact of their craft and narrowing the definition of their service. As the Libertad campaign declares, this means locating the arguments about advertising in debates on freedom of commercial speech (see Figure 17.5). But it is also the case that the advertising sector has sought to do so through codes of conduct they consider appropriate to their business.

The formulation of self-regulation codes helped advertisers to articulate the industry's perspective on advertising's role, and also helped to legitimize advertising by promoting a sense of professionalism among the majority of practitioners. Indeed, their own stand against extravagant claims, unfair competition, and misleading communication became absorbed into advertisers' working practice. Among the arguments about commercial free speech, one never hears an ad executive claim that misrepresentation is an inherent part of the freedom of commercial speech. Advertisers were not averse to government attempts to establish monitoring and regulatory structures that receive complaints about "unfair and deceptive" advertisements, because they quickly recognized that such mechanisms work in the interests of the industry as a whole by exposing the few "bad apples" before they taint the whole barrel. The profusion of regulatory agencies led one of our Canadian industry sources to comment, "We are the most regulated business in the world. The lawyers check every word that goes out of here. Health Canada has an enormous staff checking what we write. The Canadian Broadcasting Corporation has a whole department of taste." To advertisers, who feel that their trade is just a business like any other in the marketplace, the elaborate systems of guidelines and regulations appear cumbersome and restraining. Yet the irony of all this regulation is that the advertising business is very little influenced by regulations. As another of our interviewees stated, "I've never been very affected by regulations. We're self-policing."

The advertising industry has always responded emphatically, and often deftly, to issues of special concern that threaten its autonomy, by urging self-regulatory mechanisms as the best means of controlling the potential for abuses. But the industry's attempts at self-regulation, beyond the rather simple issues of "truth in advertising" and "fair business practice," have not always been effective or long-lasting. In the 1980s the FCC and FTC in the United States, after many years of lobbying and submissions by the advertising industry, began the process of deregulating commercial television and advertising

Figure 17.5 To forestall regulation, advertisers have narrowed the discussion of advertising to issues linked to freedom of expression.
Source: Libertad, Inc. All rights reserved.

in the hope that market forces and industry self-regulation would eliminate the need for regulation, particularly in the controversial area of children's advertising. They did so without much appreciation of how the industry would react, and in the face of some clear warnings that self-regulation was not likely to be successful. Yet the deregulation did not bring about a reduction in the intensity of debates about advertising. As Armstrong and Brucks (1988, 111) noted in their review of children's advertising policy:

> Self-regulation alone cannot deal effectively with the complex problems of children's advertising....Neither government regulation, consumer education for children and parents, advertiser and media efforts, nor self-regulation can work alone. But if all of the parties could work together—under a delicate blend of checks, balances and compromise—then these issues may finally be resolved.

Such cooperation rarely occurs. More often bitter critics, who accuse advertising of all manner of evil, are ranged against self-appointed advertising spokespersons set to defend unwaveringly their right to regulate themselves. In this context, one should keep in mind Kottman's (1964, 153) view proposed long ago, but still followed today, that "competitive selling is a kind of game played in the marketplace. Though there is a need for rules, there is also a need for sportsmanship and social responsibility within the context of the present culture, which is far from perfect and has created advertising as we know it."

In her exhaustive review of the effectiveness of several self-regulatory measures in the U.S., Campbell (1999) found some instances of success as well as evidence of a failure of self-regulation to live up to its promises. For example, this approach was promoted as a means to achieve quicker protective measures, and Campbell found that the video games industry did indeed rapidly regulate itself out of concern that governments would impose controls on them. In the case of protecting children's privacy on the Internet, however, industry response has lagged. In the United States self-regulation is promoted as a means to address issues that government could not deal with without infringing upon constitutional protections of freedom of expression; however, Campbell found "limited support for the claim." Moreover, many self-regulation initiatives turned out to be hindered by lack of resources, expertise, and enforcement of sanctions necessary to ensure widespread compliance.

Campbell's study discerned some key factors related to self-regulatory compliance. First, she notes that industry needs to be strongly motivated: The threat of legal sanctions has proved to be the most useful form of discipline. Economics is also a motivator. For example, while U.S. broadcasters were not happy to see the loss of advertising revenue from tobacco advertisers in 1989, since they made up roughly 10 percent of the total advertising revenue, they willingly upheld (at least until recently) limits on the number of non-programming minutes per hour because it allowed media space prices to be raised. Second, self-regulation also worked best when practices were subject to audit and accountability, and involved a limited number of industry participants. This did not mean that the overall size of the industry was an issue, but rather that good structural links between the participants were essential to success.

Finally, compliance with self-regulation was best achieved when codes were "relatively narrow and susceptible to output-based standards." While industry was able to comply with advertising time limits during children's programming and bans on particular products, they were much less successful in adjudicating "more subjective obligation to provide a variety of education and cultural programming" or regulating against violence and offensive material. In short, the broader social and cultural issues involved in advertising do not appear to be dealt with adequately by self-regulation (Campbell 1999).

Campbell's recommendations, derived from her careful survey of the literature, suggest the need for a broad-scale approach to regulation, one that combines self-regulation and government approaches. Yet it appears from the following comment, made in 1997 by a commissioner at the FTC, Roscoe B. Starek III, that self-regulation remains the preferred regulatory option in the United States:

> Self-regulation and consumer education can go a long way toward accomplishing this goal [protecting children], and I can predict that the Commission will continue to encourage private efforts to empower parents and protect children. We cannot and should not dictate the form of self-regulation, however, or attempt to regulate by threat of Commission action in areas where we lack authority. To do so needlessly risks stifling the burgeoning innovative efforts of the private sector. (Starek 1997)

While critics are quick to point the figure at the failures of self-regulatory measures, there are also instances where governments have failed to live up the sprit of their own advertising codes. The regulation of pharmaceutical advertising in the United States offers an example. Although direct to consumer advertising was permitted to appear in 1997, this type of advertising remained quite heavily regulated. After George W. Bush was sworn in as president in early 2001, concerns began to be raised about the level of enforcement of these regulations, since the number of false or misleading advertising cases was dropping: "In total, the number of enforcement actions initiated by FDA in 2003 was 75% lower than the average number initiated during the last years of the Clinton Administration" (Waxman 2004). The FDA was found to be taking an undue length of time to warn advertisers of their violations, and a warning letter was the only type of deterrent used, even though the FDA has the power to bring court action and fine drug producers (Dembner 2002).

Few Clear Answers

The fact that advertising does not fit within neat policy categories helps to explain why there is so little consensus on how to regulate it. Because it stands at the intersection of industry and culture, advertising can (and has) come under attack from diverse perspectives. At the same time, and perhaps as a result, comparatively little critical attention has been paid to the cultural and institutional nexus within which advertising works. It is easier, of course, simply to lay blame for everything that is going wrong with our market-driven society at the feet of advertising. But the result is a chaotic litany of unrelated complaints that fails to provide a framework in which to set policy.

The absence of guidelines has made it difficult for both supporters and opponents of advertising interests. Because so many different social issues are bound up with advertising one way or another, the rights or restrictions applicable in some cases do not appear to be relevant in others. This was evident when Canada's then Department of National Health and Welfare banned tobacco advertising from all media in 1989. In presenting its reasons for going to court over the legislated ban, Bob Foss of the Association of Canadian Advertisers (ACA) asked, "What will be next? We know there are many places people would like to see [an ad ban]. Numerous products have been targets, like tobacco and children's toys and alcoholic beverages....We're afraid it could come about if a precedent is set." The clear implication behind Foss's question is that there is a unitary principle for advertising's role and impacts that extends to all forms of advertising, in all media, and for all purposes. But should advertisements for hazardous products like cigarettes not be regulated differently from those for milk? Should television not be more restrictive in the way it advertises beer than it does cookies? Are not children less able than adults to understand the purposes and messages of advertising? To suggest that the protective mantle of free speech covers all cases equally is to overlook the very significant practical differences between the social issues involved in each of them.

Such differences arise precisely because, as we emphasized in earlier chapters, advertising is not just about the goods it displays; it also communicates much about the meaning and desirability of those particular goods, the social context in which consumption takes place, and the use and purposes of products and their production. In short, advertising orients people to goods, provides images of users, and conveys a mood, tempo, and stylistic that can be associated with various consumption patterns and images of well-being. The policy debates about advertising should now assimilate this understanding and recognize that the increasing sophistication of marketing communication demands a new way of thinking about the consequences of the unique combination of economic and cultural forces at work in our society.

Advertising is the apex of a cultural subsystem, a distinctive pattern of social communication that continues to alter our society in a number of important ways: It has transformed the institutional framework for market society, enhancing the power of large-scale corporate entities who undertake strategic marketing communications; it has created a highly concentrated and increasingly narrowly owned group of agencies that are experts in the new practices and forms of persuasive communications and the audience research upon which they are based; it has radically reordered the economics and audience bases of communications media; and it has changed many of the forms and practices of socialization in our society generally, including the television commercial itself, programming formats such as the rock video or children's television, as well as the entire spectrum of social, governmental, and political marketing. If we are to assess the controversies surrounding advertising, we can do so only by understanding the full scale and cultural significance of all this communications activity.

We have seen some efforts in this review of regulatory measures that have sought to address the new regulatory challenges posed by the mediated marketplace specifically globalization, new technologies, and promotional and cross marketing techniques that erode the line between commercial messages and media and cultural content. Recognizing the global spread of media, there have been efforts to extend regulatory measures across national boarders. Efforts have also been made to try to understand and regulate emergent forms of advertising channeled through new media technologies such as interactive advertising and mobile phone marketing. Cognizant of the erosion of the line between above the line advertising techniques and below the line promotion techniques many regulators today are aware that banning and regulating advertising alone is not effective unless promotional efforts (sponsorship, product placement, public relations) are also taken into account.

We can imagine a discourse about satisfaction and the meaning of products that is under the direct influence of the corporate sphere to a lesser degree a more democratically determined discourse in which commercial interests have a reduced but still prominent role. The logic of this argument could lead to tighter limitations on the amount of advertising, or even to its outright banning. We need to achieve a fuller range of influences in the discussion and evaluation of goods and their role in our lives. Just as we do not believe that the party in power should control the political dialogue in a democratic society, we do not believe that any single institution should control the public discourse about goods. We have sought to safeguard democracy through such means as the autonomy of the press, but we have not sufficiently secured the workings of democracy in the marketplace.

The rise of mediated communication and its close affiliation with advertising has meant that for some time now the most visible public discourse on consumption has been orchestrated through the media. (Interpersonal influence and individual evaluation are still important aspects of consumer behavior; however, they tend to be confined to private actions.) Possibly, then, it is to the media that we must turn to open other avenues to expand this discourse. Alternative channels could, if expanded, provide both a noncommercial voice for the discussion of goods and an opportunity for manufacturers of new products to present their goods to the public (consumer magazines, programs, associations). Support and amplification of the outlook represented by the consumer movement in the discourse on products is one way of counteracting the distortion that now leaves that discourse largely under the sway of commercial interests.

Media Controls

As we have seen, the media work within broad parameters established primarily to serve the needs of advertisers who wish to create and gain access to particular kinds of audiences. Has the commercialization of the media optimized the quality and potential uses of these media themselves? There is no doubt that advertising influences the performance of media, not only in the exercise of direct control over content, but also in the avoidance of controversial subjects, banal program formats, stereotyping of audience segments, and ownership concentration in media industries—broader issues that should draw more attention.

The question of how well the media function under largely commercialized conditions is related to a number of our most cherished beliefs about democracy. With media output controlled by the audience logic of advertising, there is no real marketplace for ideas—that is, no public forum where widely different types of social actors can buy and sell information, opinion, and images that express their interests. One serious consequence flowing from advertising's predominance in the media marketplace is that the combination of economic and audience logistics has led to a high degree of concentrated ownership and control in the media industries, prompting many commentators to ask whether diversity of views, quality of programming, and attention to minority interests or special audience needs have been sacrificed in the mad scramble for large or "upscale" audiences (Curran 1977; Murdock 1982; Campaign 1979; Urry and Lash 1994; Turow 1997). Certainly, the transition from small and politically committed audiences for newspapers to massive general-interest ones was a byproduct of commercialization. The light entertainment bias and other programming rigidities are all based on the competition for audiences within and among media; this affects public broadcasters, as well, because they must compete for audiences in order to justify receiving government funds.

Conclusion

Advertising professionals, throughout their history and into the twenty-first century, continue to react to suggestions of a connection between this type of "larger" social issue and their own creative activities on behalf of their clients with a mixture of contempt, wariness, and surprise. As one of our interviewees said, "I think advertising can play a role in helping to integrate people, though not a very substantial role. But I don't think advertising should be saddled with the various social problems." And yet, we cannot continue to talk about advertising as if it were still nothing but "salesmanship in print," or as a form of persuasive communication that is exclusively concerned with merchandising concerns, for it now impinges upon many dimensions of politics, education, and society. To talk about advertising demands that we deal with a wide array of promotional communication activities that have been mobilized, by those who have access to the mass media, to extend various channels of influence over social life.

References

Aaker, D. A., and Myers, J. G. 1975. *Advertising management.* Englewood Cliffs, NJ: Prentice-Hall.

Abercombie, N. 1994. Authority and consumer society. In *The authority of the consumer,* eds. R. Keat, N. Whiteley, and N. Abercrombie, 43–57. London: Routledge.

*Abernethy, A., and Franke, G. 1996. "The information content of advertising: A meta-analysis." *Journal of Advertising,* vol. 25, no. 2:1–16.

*Abernethy, A., and Wicks, J. L. 2001. "Self-regulation and television advertising: A replication and extension." *Journal of Advertising Research,* vol. 41, no. 3: 31–37.

˙Adamson, A. 2001. "Mapping a route for uncertain times." *Advertising Age,* vol. 72, no. 39: 36.

Aden, M. 1981. *Thirty seconds. New York, Penguin.*

Admap. 2003c."Best practice—how to get attention." December.

Adorno, T. W., and Adorno, G. 1955. *Benjamin's schriften. Amsterdam, Suhrkamp.*

Advertising Age. 1992."U.S. Advertising volume." Vol. 63, no. 18: 51.

Advertising Age. 2000a. "Clutter talk." Vol.71, no.11: 42.

Advertising Age. 2000b."Just put on a good show." Vol.71, no. 36: 18.

Advertising Age. 2001. "New style agency hiring." Vol.72, no. 4: 22.

Advertising Age. 2003. "Agency family trees: The 2003 guide to the top six advertising organizations." http://www.adage.com.

Advertising Age. 2003."10 top purchaser influencers." *Advertising Age,* vol. 74, no. 51: 27.

Advertising Association. 2000. *Executive briefs: Alcohol advertising. December 2000. London: Advetising Association.*

Advertising Standards Association. 2000. Annual report. London: Advertising Standards Association.

Advertising Standards Association. 2001a. *Annual report—40 years of effective self regulation.* London: Advertising Standards Association.

Advertising Standards Association. 2001b. *Annual report—a year in review. London: Advertising Standards Association.*

*Agency Magazine. 2001. "Guerrilla marketing grows up." Spring. London.

Ainslie, P. 1989. *The new TV viewer. In How Americans watch TV? A nation of grazers,* ed. R. Gilbert. New York: C. C. Publishing.

Akert, R. M. 2001. "Interview with Nina Disesa.".*Advertising & Society Review,* vol. 2, no. 4.

*Al-Deen, H. N. 1991. "Literacy and information content of magazine advertising: USA versus Saudi Arabia." *International Journal of Advertising,* vol. 10, no. 3: 251–258.

Albion, M., and Ferris, P. 1981. *The advertising controversy.* Boston: Auburn House.

*Alden, D., Hoyer, W., and Lee, C. 1993. "Identifying global and culture-specific dimensions of humor in advertising: A multinational analysis."*Journal of Marketing,* vol. 57, no. 2: 64–76.

Aldridge, S. 2004. *Prime minister's strategy unit life changes & social mobility: An overview of the evidence.* London: The Cabinet Office, UK.

Allen, F. L. 1931. *Only yesterday,* New York: Harper & Brothers.

*Allen, P. 2000. "Establishing successful customer relationships amid all the volume.".*The Advertiser.*

*Allison, A. 2001. "Interview with Douglas Porter." *Advertising & Society Review,* vol. 2, no. 2.

*American Demographics. 1985. "The big chill (revisited) or whatever happened to the baby boom?" American Demographics, vol. 7, no. 9: 23.

Anderson, M. 1984. *Madison avenue in Asia: Politics and transnational advertising.* Cranbury, NJ: Associated University Presses.

Andren, G., Ericsson, L., Ohlsson, R., and Tannsjo, T. 1978. *Rhetoric and ideology in advertising.* Stockholm: AB Grafiska.

Ang, I. 1991. *Desperately seeking the audience.* London: Routledge.

---

*Obtained from one of the following databases: World Advertising Research Centre (WARC); American Business Index (ABI); Brandrepublic, UK; Guardian On-line. Business Source Primer Publications.

Ansolabehere, S., and Iyengar, S. 1995. *Going negative: How attack ads shrink and polarize the electorate.* New York, Free Press.

Appadurai, A. 1988. *The social life of things: Commodities in cultural perspective.* Cambridge: Cambridge University Press.

*Appelbaum, U., and Halliburton, C. 1993. "How to develop international advertising campaigns that work: The example of the European food and beverage sector." *International Journal of Advertising,* vol. 12, no. 3: 223–244.

*Appiah, O. 2001a. "Black, white, hispanic, and Asian American adolescents' responses to culturally embedded ads." *Howard Journal of Communications,* vol. 12, no. 1: 29–48.

*Appiah, O. 2001b. "Ethnic identification on adolescents' evaluations of advertisements." *Journal of Advertising Research,* vol. 41, no. 5: 7–23.

Applegate, E. 1998. *Personalities and products: A historical perspective on advertising in America.* Westport, CT: Greenwood Press.

Arvidsson, A. 2003. *Marketing modernity: Italian advertising from fascism to postmodernity,* New York: Routledge.

*Assael, H. and Poltrack, D. 1991. "Using single source data to select TV programs based on purchasing behavior." *Journal of Advertising Research,* vol. 31, no. 4: 9–17.

Atwan, R., Mcquade, D., and Wright, J. W. 1979. *Edsels, Luckies and Frigidaires: Advertising the American way.* New York: Dell Publishing Company.

Australian Government Attorney-General's Department. 1992. Commonwealth of Australia law: Broadcasting services act. Australian Broadcasting Authority.

Azcuenaga, M. 1992. Whether FTC regulation of advertising claims concerning health, nutrition, and the environment? Speech by Federal Trade Commissioner Mary l. Azcuenaga, before the grocery manufacturers of America. Washington, DC.

Azcuenaga, M. 1994. Advertising: Interpretation and enforcement policy: Remarks by Federal Trade Commissioner Mary l. Azcuenaga before the American Advertising Federation 1994 national government affairs conference. Washington DC.

Azcuenaga, M. 1997. The role of advertising and advertising regulation in the free market: Speech by Federal Trade Commissioner Mary l. Azcuenaga before the Turkish Association of Advertising Agencies. Conference on Advertising for Economy and Democracy. Istanbul, Turkey.

*Backhaus, K., Muhlfeld, K., and Vandoorn, J. 2001. "Consumer perspectives on standardization in international advertising: A student sample." *Journal of Advertising Research,* vol. 41, no. 5: 53–61.

*Banerjee, S., Gulas, C., and Iyer, E. 1995) "Shades of green: A multidimensional analysis of environmental advertising." *Journal of Advertising,* vol. 24, no. 2: 21–32.

Barbour 1982. *Those amazing people! The story of the Canadian magazine industry, 1778–1967.* Toronto: Crucible.

Barnouw, E. 1978. *The sponsor: Notes on a modern potentate.* New York: Oxford University Press.

*Barry, D. E., Paterson, R. L., and Todd, W. B. 1987. "The role of account planning in the future of advertising agency research." *Journal of Advertising Research,* vol. 27, no.1: 15–21.

Barthes, R. 1973/1993. *Mythologies.* London: Vintage.

*Bartos, R. 1995. "How to advertise to women." *Admap* September. NTC Publication Ltd.

*Batty, D. 2004. "Call for EU-wide junk food ban." *Guardian,* May 27.

Baudrillard, J. 1970/1998. *The consumer society: Myths and structures.* London: Sage.

Baudrillard, J. 1981. *For a critique of the political economy of the sign.* St. Louis MO: Telos.

Baudrillard, J. 1983. *Simulations.* New York: Semiotext(e).

Baudrillard, J. 1988. *Ecstacy of communication.* Paris: Semiotext(e)/Pluto.

Bauman, Z. 1998. *Globalization: The human consequences.* New York: Columbia University Press.

BBC News (December 15 2003) 'Bacardi pulls Vinnie Jones TV ads. BBC News World Edition. http://news.bbc.co.uk

Beasley, R., and Danesi, M. 2002. *Persuasive signs: The semiotics of advertising (approaches to applied semiotics, 4).* Berlin: Walter de Gruyter Inc.

Beck, U. 1992. *Risk society: Towards a new modernity.* London: Sage.

Belch, G. F., and Belch, M. A. 1998. *Advertising and promotion: An integrated marketing communications perspective.* New York: Irwin McGraw-Hill.

*Belk, R. 1986. Yuppies as arbiters of the emerging consumption style. In *Advances in consumer research,* ed. L. Lutz, S14–S19. Provo, UT: Association for Consumer Research.

Bell, D. 1976/1979. *The coming of post-industrial society: A venture in social forecasting.* New York: Basic Books.

Bell, D. 1976/1996. *The cultural contradictions of capitalism*. New York: HarperCollins Publishers.

Bell, D. 1980. *Sociological journeys: Essays 1960–1980*. London: Heinemann.

Bell, M. 1966. *Marketing: Concepts and strategy*. New York: Houghton Mifflin.

Bellah, R. N., Madsen, R., Sullivan, W., Weidler, A. and Tipton, S. 1985. *Habits of the heart: Individualism and commitment in American life*. Berkeley: University of California Press.

Bellant, R. 1988. *The Coors connection: How Coors family philanthropy undermines democratic pluralism*. Cambridge, MA: South End Press.

Beltrame, J. 1996. *New regulation on tobacco advertising and sales*. Washington, DC: CanWest News.

*Benezra, K. (1995) Don't mislabel gen x. *Brandweek*.

Bennett, S. and Rademacher, E. 1997. The 'age of indifference' revisited: Patterns of political interest, media exposure, and knowledge among generation x. In *After the boom: The politics of generation x*, eds. S. Craig and S. Bennett. Lanham, MD: Rowman & Littlefield.

*Benoit, W. L., Hansen, G. J., and Verser, R. M. 2003. "A meta-analysis of the effects of viewing U.S. Presidential debates." *Communication Monographs*, vol. 70: 335–350.

Berelson, P., and Mcphee, M. 1954. *Voting: A study of opinion formation in a presidential campaign*, Chicago: University of Chicago Press.

Berger, A. 2003/2004. *Ads, fads and consumer culture: Advertising's impact on American character and society*. New York: Rowman & Littlefield.

Berger, J. 1972. *Ways of seeing*. London: Penguin.

Bergreen, L. 1978. *Look now, pay later*. New York: Russell Sage Foundation.

*Bidlake, S., and Pollack, J. 1997. "Marketers rethink ads in wake of Diana tragedy." *Advertising Age*, vol. 68, no. 36: 8.

Bird, B. 2002. *Evolution of new advertising techniques: Germany*. Brussells, Belgium: Bird and Bird.

*Biu Tse, A. C., and Lee, R. P. W. 2001. "Zapping behavior during commercial breaks." *Journal of Advertising Research*, vol. 41, no. 3: 25–30.

Blackley, N., and Capel, J. 1989. *The global advertising marketplace*, 2nd ed.

*Block, V. 2003. "Jingle biz rocked by licensed pop in ads." *Advertising Age*, vol. 74, no. 5: 6.

*Boddewyn, J. J. 1982. "Advertising regulation in the 1980s: The underlying global forces." *Journal of Marketing*, vol. 46: 27–35.

*Boddewyn, J. J. 1991. "Controlling sex and decency in advertising around the world." *Journal of Advertising*, vol. 20, no. 4: 25–36.

Boddewyn, J. J., Soehl, R., and Picard, J. 1986. "Standardization in international marketing: Is ted levitt in fact right?" *Business Horizons*, vol. 29, no. 6: 69–75.

*Boedecker, K., Morgan, F., and Wright, L. B. 1995. "The evolution of first amendment protection for commercial speech." *Journal of Marketing*, vol. 59, Issue 1: 38–48.

*Bogle, N. 2001. The day the advertising had to change. *The Independent*. September 29.

Bohannan, P. 1963. *Social anthropology*. New York: Holt, Rinehart and Winston.

Boorstin, D. 1962. *The image*. New York: Atheneum.

Boorstin, D. 1973. *The Americans: The democratic experience*. New York: Random House.

Borden, N. 1945/1947. *Advertising in our economy*: Chicago IL: Ayer Co.

Botterill, J. 2001. *Money goes to market: The marketing and promotion of British joint stock banks, 1950–2000*. London: University of East London.

Bourdieu, P. 1979/1987. *A social critique of the judgment of taste*. Boston: Harvard University Press.

Bourdieu, P. 1993. *Editor's introduction: Pierre Bourdieu on art, literature and culture. The field of cultural production*. New York: Columbia University Press.

Bradburn, N. 1969. *The structure of psychological well-being*. Chicago: Aldine Press.

Bradburn, N., and Caplovitz, D. 1965. *Reports on happiness*. Chicago: Aldine Press.

*Brady, J. 2000. "Brady's bunch." *Advertising Age*, vol. 71, no. 39: 68.

*Branch, A. 2003. "Media spend trends." *Pharmaceutical Executive*, vol. 23, no. 9: 142.

Bridge, G., and Watson, S. 2002. *A companion to the city*. London: Blackwell Publishers.

Briggs, A. 1961. *The birth of broadcasting*. London: Oxford University Press.

Bristor, J., Lee, R., and Hunt, M. 1995. "Race and ideology: African-American images in television advertising." *Journal of Public Policy & Marketing*, vol. 14, no. 1: 48–60.

Broadcasters' Audience Research Board (January 2002) Viewing summary, network viewing share (%). http://www.barb.co.uk

Brown, L. 1972. *The business behind the box*. New York: Harcourt Brace Jovanovich.

*Bruce, D. 1987. *Marketing*, December 14.

Buchan, J. 1997. *Frozen desire: The meaning of money*. New York: Farrar Straus & Giroux.

Buckingham, D. 1997. *Teaching popular culture: Beyond radical pedagogy.* London: Routledge.

Buckingham, D., Davies, H., Jones, K., and Kelley, P. 1999. *Children's television in Britain: History, discourse and policy.* London: British Film Institute.

Buckingham, D., and Sefton-Green, J. 1994. *Cultural studies goes to school: Reading and teaching popular media.* Bristol, PA: Taylor & Francis.

Bunyan, J. 2003. *The pilgrim's progress.* Oxford: Oxford University Press.

*Burke, M. C., and Edell, J. A. 1989. "The impact of feelings on ad-based affect and cognition." *Journal of Marketing Research,* vol. 26, February: 69–83.

Burke, P. 1978. *Popular culture in early modern Europe.* London: Temple Smith.

*Burnett, M. S. and Lunsford, D. A.(1994. "Conceptualizing guilt in the consumer decision-making process." *Journal of Consumer Marketing,* vol. 11, no. 3: 33–43.

Butler, J. 1989. *Gender trouble: Feminism and the subversion of identity.* London: Routledge.

*Byles, D. 1992. "Effectiveness and evolution." *Admap.* May, NTC Publictions Ltd.

*Caillat, Z., and Mueller, B. 1996. "The influence of culture on American and British advertising: An exploratory comparison of beer advertising." *Journal of Advertising Research,* vol. 36, no. 3: 79–89.

*Calfee, J. E., and Ringold, D. J. 1994. "The 70% majority: Enduring consumer beliefs about advertising." *Journal of Public Policy & Marketing,* vol. 13, no. 2: 228–239.

Callon, M. 1998. *The laws of the markets.* London: Blackwell Publishers.

Marchand, R. 1985/1986. *Advertising the American dream: Making way for modernity, 1920–1940.* Berkeley: University of California Press.

*Campaign. 2004. Government reserves power to ban categories of ads. *May, 16.*

Campbell, A., Gurin, G., and Miller, W. 1954. *The voter decides.* Chicago: Row, Peterson.

Campbell, A. J. 1999. "Self-regulation and the media." *Federal Communications Law Journal,* vol. 51, no. 3: 711–773.

Campbell, C. 1987/1989. *The romantic ethic and the spirit of modern consumerism.* Oxford: Basil Blackwell.

Canadian Radio-Television and Telecoommunications Commision 1978. *Proposed CRTC procedures and practices relating to broadcasting matters.* Public Notice. Ottawa, Canadian Radio-Television and Telecoommunications Commision.

Canadian Radio-Television and Telecoommunications Commision 1992. *Public notice 1992-58 1992 policy on gender portrayal.* Ottawa, Canadian Radio-Television and Telecoommunications Commision.

Cantrol, H. 1965. *The pattern of human concerns.* New Brunswick, NJ: Rutgers University Press.

*Cardona, M. M., Chura, H., Fine, J., Friedman, W., Halliday, J., and Thomaselli, R. 2002. "2002: Lookout." *Advertising Age,* vol. 73, no. 1: 1–2.

*Carlson, L., Grove, S., and Kangun, N. 1993. "A content analysis of environmental advertising claims: A matrix method approach." *Journal of Advertising,* vol. 22, no. 3: 27–40.

*Carpini, M. D. and Sigelman, L. 1986. "Do yuppies matter: Competing explanations of their political distinctiveness." *Public Opinion Quarterly,* vol. 50, no. 4: 502–518.

Castagnoli, N. 1992. "Speaking out: Let's consider self-regulation of rx advertising." *Medical Marketing and Media,* vol. 27, no. 8: 6–9.

Castells, M. 1996. *The rise of the network society: Vol. 1.* London: Blackwell Publications.

Castells, M. 1997. *The power of identity: Information age economy, society and culture: Vol. 2.* London: Blackwell Publishers.

Cateora, P. R. and Graham, J. L. 1999. *International marketing.* Boston: Irwin McGraw-Hill.

*Chadwick, J. 1997. "Navigating through china's new advertising law: The role of market research." *International Journal of Advertising,* vol.16, no. 4: 284–294.

*Chan, K. 1999. Cultural values in Hong Kong's print advertising, 1946–96." *International Journal of Advertising,* vol. 18, no. 4: 537–555.

*Cheng, H. 1994. "Reflections of cultural values: A content analysis of Chinese magazine advertisements from 1982–1992." *International Journal of Advertising,* vol. 13, no. 2: 167–184.

*Cheng, H. and Schweitzer, J. C. 1996. "Cultural values reflected in Chinese and US television commercials." *Journal of Advertising Research,* vol. 36, no. 3: 27–46.

*Chiarelli, N. 2003. "Has the global consumer changed?" *Admap,* no. 439.

Chief, C. B. 2003. Big tobacco pulls cigarette ads from mags. Hartford, UK: *New Britain Herald.*

Childs, N. 2003. "Gender in food advertising to children: Boys eat first." *British Food Journal,* vol. 105, no. 7: 408–419.

*Chu, J. 1982. "Advertising in china: Its policy, practice and evolution." *Journalism Quarterly*, vol. 59: 40–45

*Circus, P. 1989. "Alcohol advertising—the rules." *International Journal of Advertising*, vol. 8: 159-165.

*Cobb-Walgren, C. J. 1991. "The changing commercial climate." *Journal of Current Issues and Research in Advertising*, vol. 13, no. 102: 343–368.

Coen, R. 2003. *Insider's report: On advertising expenditure*. New York: Universal McCann.

Coleman, R. and Rainwater, L. 1978. Social standing in America. New York: Basic Books.

Commons, H. O. 1993. Hansard debates for 27 January 27, 1993. House of Commons.

*Confer, M. and Mcclathery, D. 1991. "The research study: The advertising impact of magazines in conjunction with television." *Journal of Advertising Research*, vol. 31, no. 1: RC2-RC6.

*Considine, P. 2004. World: Analysis—consumer demand for drugs fuels healthcare sector's rise. *Campaign*. March 26, 13: 20.

Control, C. C. F. T. 1997. Canadian law and tobacco: Government of Canada tobacco act. Ottawa. ON.

Converse, J. M. 1987. Survey research in the United States: Roots and emergence, 1890–1960. Berkeley: University of California Press.

Cook, G. 1992. *The discourse of advertising (interface)*. London: Routledge.

Corrado, A. and Mann, T. 2004. "Mcconnell v. Fec: A new world of campaign finance in the United States?" *Electoral Insight*, April: 26–31.

Coupland, D. 1991. *Generation x: Tales for an accelerated culture*. New York: St. Martin's Griffen.

*Craig, R. S. 1992. "The effect of television daytime programs on gender portrayals in television commercials: A content analysis." *Sex Roles*, vol. 26, no. 5-6: 197–211.

*Crain, R. 2001. "Philips, lexus choices highlight the diminished role of agencies." *Advertising Age*, vol. 72, no. 29: 18.

*Hatfield, Stefano 2002. "London's new gold rush." *Creativity Magazine*, May.

Cronin, A. 2004. *Advertising myths: The strange half-lives of images and commodities*. London: Routledge.

*Cronin, J. J. and Menelly, N. E. 1992. "Discrimination vs. Avoidance: 'zipping' of television commercials." *Journal of Advertising*, vol. 21, no. 2: 1–7.

Cross, G. 2002/2003. *An all consumer century*. New York: Columbia University Press.

Cross, M. 1996. *Advertising and culture: Theoretical perspectives*. Westport, CT: Praeger Publishers.

Croteau, D. and Hoynes, W. 2001. *The business of media: Corporate media and the public interest*. Thousand Oaks, CA: Pine Forge Press.

Csikszentmihalyi, M. and Rochberg-Halton, E. 1981. *The meaning of things*. Cambridge: Cambridge University Press.

Curran, J. 1977. Capitalism and the control of the press, 1800–1975. In *Mass communication and society*. eds. J. Curran, M., Gurevitch,.& J. Woollacott. London: Arnold.

Curti, M. 1967. "The changing concept of human nature in the literature of American advertising." *Business History Review*, vol. 41.

*Danaher, P. J. 1995. "What happens to television ratings during commercial breaks?" *Journal of Advertising Research*, vol. 35, no.1: 37–48.

Danesi, M. and Perron, P. 1999. *Analyzing cultures: An introduction and handbook.*, Indianapolis: Indiana University Press.

Danziger, S. and Gottschalk, P. 1997) *America unequal*. Boston: Harvard University Press.

Davidson, M. 1992. *The consumerist manifesto: Advertising in postmodern times*. London: Routledge.

De Certeau, M. 2002. *The practice of everyday life*. Berkeley: University of California Press.

De Mooij, M.1994. *Advertising worldwide: Concepts, theories, and practice of international, multinational, and global advertising*. Oxford: Philip Allan

*De Mooij, M. 1997. "Mapping cultural values for global marketing and advertising." Amsterdam, NL: ESOMAR Marketing Research.

De Mooij, M. 1998. *Global marketing and advertising: Understanding cultural paradoxes*. Thousand Oaks, CA: Sage Publications.

*De Mooij, M. 2003. "Convergence and divergence in consumer behavior." *International Journal of Advertising*, vol. 22, no. 2: 183 202.

Debord, G. 1970. *Society of the spectacle*. Detroit. MI: Black and Red.

*Decock, B. and De Pelsmacker, P. 2000. *Emotions matter*. Amsterdam, NL: ESOMAR.

Dee, J. 2002. "The myth of '18-34.'" *New York Times*. October 13: 58-61

*Deeken, A. 2003. "Magazine monitor.",*Mediaweek*, vol. 13, no. 9: 46.

Defleur, M. 1970. Mass communication and social change. In *Media sociology*, ed. J.Tunstall. London: Constable.

Defleur, M. and Ball-Rokeach, S. 1989. *Theories of mass communication*, New York: Longman.

*Deighton, J., Romer, D., and Mcqueen, J. 1989. "Using drama to persuade." *Journal of Consumer Research*, vol. 16, no. 3: 335–344.

Delany, P. 1994. *Representing the postmodern city*. Vancouver: Arsenal Pulp Press.

Dembner, A. 2002. "Going backwards: Bush's FDA action on drugs ads declining." October 19, *Boston Globe.*, 4.

US Department of Advertising 2004. *Texasadvertising: Current issues*. Austin TX: University of Texas at Austin.

UK Department of Culture Media and Sport. 2003. Press notice: Secretary of State requests strengthening existing code on advertising food to children. London: Department of Culture, Media and Sport.

Canadian Department of Foreign Affairs and International Trade. 1999a. "Ottawa and Washington agree on access to the Canadian advertising services market." Ottawa, ON: Department of Foreign Affairs and International Trade.

Canadian Department of Foreign Affairs and International Trade. 1999b. "Ottawa and Washington agree on access to the Canadian advertising services market." Ottawa, ON.

*Deyoung, S. and Crane, F. G. 1992. "Females' attitudes toward the portrayal of women in advertising: A Canadian study." *International Journal of Advertising*, vol. 11, no. 3: 249–256.

Diamond, E. and Bates, S. 1992. *The spot — the rise of political advertising on television*. Cambridge, MA: MIT Press.

Dickason, R. 2000. *British television advertising: Cultural identity and communication*, Luton: University of Luton Press.

Dickens, C. (1844/2002) *A Christmas carol*. Mineola NY: Dover Publications Inc.

Diener, E. (1984) "Subjective well being." *Psychological Bulletin*, vol. 95.

*Donaton, S. 2000a. "Media experts strut their stuff but creativity rules the roost." *Advertising Age*, vol. 71, no. 25: 36.

*Donaton, S. 2000b. "Pull the plug on upfront market or drop media-neutral pretense." *Advertising Age*, vol. 71, no. 21: 50.

*Donaton, S. 2001. "The presence of a sure thing." *Advertising Age*, vol. 72, no. 11: 4

*Donaton, S. and Levin, G. 1993. "The media wakes up to generation x." *Advertising Age*, vol. 64, no. 5: 16–17.

Douglas, M. and Isherwood, B. 1978/1981. *The world of goods*. London: Routledge.

Douglas, S. P. and Wind, Y. 1987. "The myth of globalization." *Columbia Journal of World Business*, vol. 22, Winter: 19–29.

*Drexler, M. D. 2002. "Unraveling the media myth." *Advertising Age*, vol. 73, no. 45: 22.

Driver, J. C. and Foxall, G. R. 1984. *Advertising policy and practice*. London: Holt, Rinehart and Winston.

*Dube, L., Chattopadhyay, A., and Letarte, A. 1996. "Should advertising appeals match the basis of consumers' attitudes?" *Journal of Advertising Research*, vol. November/December: 82–89.

Dugay, P. (Ed.) 2002. *Cultural economy: Cultural analysis and commercial life* Thousand Oaks CA: Sage Publications.

*Eagle, B. and Ambler, T. 2002. "The influence of advertising on the demand for chocolate confectionery." *International Journal of Advertising*, vol. 21, no. 4: 455–481.

Easterlin, R. 1974. Does economic growth improve the human lot? Some empirical evidence. In *Nations and households in economic growth*, eds. P. David and N. Reder. New York: Academic Press.

Eco, U. 1981. *The role of the reader: Explorations in the semiotics of texts*. London: Hutchinson.

*Edell, J. A., and Burke, M. C. 1987. "The power of feelings in understanding advertising effects." *Journal of Consumer Research*, vol. 14, December: 421–433.

*Elkin, T. 2001a. "AOL opens its tool box." *Advertising Age*, vol. 72, no. 51: 8.

*Elkin, T. 2001b. "Upgrade for RCA TV brand." *Advertising Age*, vol. 72, no. 42: 4–5.

*Elkin, T. 2002. "Getting viewers to opt in, not tune out." *Advertising Age*, vol. 44, no. 10: 10–11.

*Elkin, T. and Linnett, R. 2001. "Media moves up." *Advertising Age*, vol. 72, no. 28: 3–4.

*Elkin, T., Cuneo, A., Linnett, R., and Thomaselli, R. 2002. "Hewlett Packard consolidated its global media buys in 2002." *Advertising Age*, vol. 73, no. 23: 1–2.

*Eller, S. 1999 "Media outlook — outdoor." *The Advertiser* . February.

Elliot, B. 1962. *A history of English advertising*. London: Batsford.

*Elliott, M. T. and Speck, P. S. 1998. "Consumer perceptions of advertising clutter and its impact across various media." *Journal of Advertising Research*, vol. 38, no. 1: 29–42.

Ellis, B. E. 2000. *American psycho*. New York: Vintage Books.

*Ellis, J. 1999. "Web TV, cable reassemble content, ads with client base." *Advertising Age*, vol. 70, no. 16: S12–S13.

*Ellsworth, S. 2001. "Interview with Amil Gargano." *Advertising & Society Review*, vol. 2, no. 4.

Engle, J. F., Blackwell, R. D., and Miniard, P. W. 1993. *Consumer behaviour*. Fort Worth, TX: The Dryden Press.

*Englis, B. G. and Solomon, M. R. 1995, "To be and not to be? Lifestyle imagery, reference groups, and the clustering of America." *Journal of Advertising*, vol. 24, no. 1: 13–26.

*Ephron, E. 2002a. "Media shaker." *Advertising Age*, vol. 73, no. 6: 18.

*Ephron, E. 2002b. "Planning's next step." *Advertising Age*, vol. 73, no.19: 36.

*Erdogan, B. Z. and Baker, M. J. 2000. "Towards a practitioner-based model of selecting celebrity endorsers." *International Journal of Advertising*, vol. 19, no. 1: 25–44.

*Erdogan, B. Z., Baker, M. J., and Tagg, S. 2001. "Selecting celebrity endorsers: The practitioner's perspective." *Journal of Advertising Research*, vol. 41, no. 3: 39–49.

Ester, P. and Vinken, H. 1993. "Yuppies in cross-national perspective: Is there evidence for a yuppie value syndrome?" *Political Psychology*, vol. 14, no. 4: 667–696.

Europa: The European Commission. 2005. Audiovisual policy. The European Commission.

European Commission. 2004. *Audio visual policy*. The European Commission, Brussels.

Ewen, S. 1976. *Captains of consciousness*. New York: McGraw-Hill.

Ewen, S. 1988/1990. *Consuming images: The politics of style in contemporary culture*. New York: Basic Books.

*Ewing, M. T., Duplessis, E., and Foster, C. 2001. "Cinema advertising re-considered." *Journal of Advertising Research*, vol. 41, no. 1: 78–86.

Faircloth, A. 1998. "Meanwhile, in France." *Fortune*, vol. 137, no. 8: 40–41.

Faludi, S. 1992. *Backlash: The undeclared war against American women*. New York: Anchor.

Farganis, J. 1993. *Readings in social theory: The classic tradition to post-modernism*. New York: McGraw Hill.

Featherstone, M. 1991. *Consumer culture and postmodernism*. Thousand Oaks CA: Sage Publications.

Federal Communications Commission. 2005. http://www.fcc.gov/. Washington, DC.

Federal Election Commission. 2002 Bipartisan campaign reform act of 2002, public law no. 107-155. Washington DC, Federal Election Commission of the United States of America. http://www.fec.gov/pages/bcra/bcra_update.shtml.

Federal Trade Commission Bureau of Consumer Protection (2000). *Advertising and marketing on the internet: Rules of the road*. FTC: Washington, DC.

*Fine, J. 2000. "Cross-media catches fire." *Advertising Age*, vol. 71, no. 44: S2–S3.

*Fine, J. 2001. "Teen title angst." *Advertising Age*, vol. 72, no. 11: 3–4.

*Firat, A. F. and Venkatesh, A. 1995. "Liberatory postmodernism and the reenchantment of consumption." *Journal of Consumer Research*, vol. 22, no. 3: 239–268.

Firth, R. 1959. *Economics of the New Zealand maori*. Wellington, NZ: Government Printer.

Fish, S. E. 1980. *Is there a text in this class? The authority of interpretive communities*. Boston: Harvard University Press.

Fiske, J. 1987. *Television culture: Popular pleasures and politics*. London: Methuen.

Fiske, J. 1989. *Understanding popular culture*. London: Routledge.

Fitzgerald, K. 2000. "Dot-coms: The critical upfront unknown." *Advertising Age*, vol. 71, no. 21: S60.

*Fitzgerald, N. 1998. "The general's $1 billion gamble." *Adweek*, vol. 39, no. 23: 24–31.

*Fletcher, D. 2002/2003. "Reaching the ethnic consumer." *Admap*, vol. March, no. 437.

Food Marketing Institute 1999. *Trends in supermarket retailing*. Washington, DC: Food Marketing Institute.

Food Standards Association. 2004. Press release: Food promotion action plan agreed. London: Food Standards Association.

*Forbes, T. 1999. "Diagnosing the networks: Media pros say the prognosis is clear — they're multiplying." *Agency Magazine*. Winter.

*Ford, G. and Calfee, J. 1986. "Recent developments in FTC policy on deception." *Journal of Marketing*, vol. 50: 82–103.

*Ford, J. B. and Latour, M. S. 1993. "Differing reactions to female role portrayals in advertising." *Journal of Advertising Research*, vol. 33, no. 5: 43–53.

Ford-Hutchinson, S. and Rothwell, A. 2002. *The public's perception of advertising in today's society*. London: Advertising Standards Authority.

Forgas, J. 1981. *Social cognition: Perspectives on everyday understanding*. New York: Academic Press.

Forty, A. 1986. *Objects of desire: Design and society from Wedgewood to IBM*. New York: Pantheon.

*Foster, R. 2002. "Interview with Myra Stark." *Advertising & Society Review*, vol. 2, no. 2.

Foucault, M. 1980. *Power/knowledge: Selected interviews and other writings, 1972–1977*. New York: Pantheon Books.

Foucault, M. 1982. The subject of the power. In *Beyond structuralism and hermeneutics*, eds. H Dryfus and P. Rabinow. Brighton: Harvester.

Foucault, M. 1999. *Religion and culture*. New York: Routledge.

Fowles, J. 1996. *Advertising and popular culture*. Thousand Oaks, CA: Sage Publications.

Fox, R. and Lears, J. 1983. *The culture of consumption*. New York, Pantheon.

Fox, S. 1980/1997. *Mirror makers: A history of American advertising and its creators*. Chicago: University of Illinois Press.

Fox, S. 1984. *The mirror makers*. New York: William Morrow.

Frank, T. 1997. *The conquest of cool: Business culture, counterculture, and the rise of hip consumerism*. Chicago: University Press.

Cairncross-Gow, G. 2003. Secrets and spies, *Guardian*. May 15.

*Freeman, L.(1995). "No tricking the media savvy." *Advertising Age*, vol. 66, no. 6.

*Freeman, L. 1997. "Added theories drive need for client solutions." *Advertising Age*, vol. 68, no. 31: S18.

*Freeman, L. 2001. "Taking media apart." *Agency Magazine* . Winter.

*Freeman, L., Diaz, A.-C., Beardi, C., and Webster, N. C. 2000. "Decade in review." *Advertising Age*, vol. 71, no. 11: S14.

Frey, B. and Stutzer, A. 2001a. *Happiness and economics: How the economy and institutions affect human well-being*. Princeton, NJ: Princeton University Press.

Frey, B. S. and Stutzer, A. 2001b. *Happiness and economics: How the economy and institutions affect human well-being*. Princeton, NJ: Princeton University Press.

*Friedman, W. 2002. "Economy improves, but health of TV ads uncertain." *Advertising Age*, vol. 73, no. 19: 75

*Friedman, W. and Goetzl, D. 2001. "Billion-dollar bust: Upfront sale freefall." *Advertising Age*, vol. 72, no. 26: 1–2.

*Friedman, W., Halliday, J., and Neff, J. 2001. "TV networks hit hard by soft ad buys." *Advertising Age*, vol. 72, no. 6: 1–2.

Friesen, J. 2004. Adbusters suing networks for not airing its TV spots. Toronto: *Globe and Mail*.

*Friestad, M. and Wright, P. 1994. "The persuasion knowledge model: How people cope with persuasion attempts." *Journal of Consumer Research*, vol. 21, no. 1: 1–31.

Frith, K. 1996. *Advertising in Asia: Communication, culture and consumption*. New York: P. Lang.

Frith, K. and Sengupta, S. 1991. "Individualism and advertising: A cross cultural analysis from three countries." *Media Asia*, vol. 18, no. 4: 191–197.

Frith, K. T. and Mueller, B. 2003. *Advertising and societies: Global issues*. New York: P. Lang.

Galbraith, J. K. 1958. *The affluent society*. Boston: Houghton Mifflin.

Galbraith, J. K. 1967. *The new industrial state*. Boston: Houghton Mifflin.

Gay, P. D. and Pryke, M. (Eds.). 2002. *Cultural economy: Cultural analysis and commercial life*. Thousand Oaks, CA: Sage Publications.

Georges, C. 1993. "The boring twenties: Grow up crybabies, you're America's luckiest generation," *Washington Post* Sept 12, C1.

Giddens, A. 1991. *Modernity and self-identity: Self and society in the late modern age*. Stanford, CA: Stanford University Press.

Giddens, A. 1995. Living in a post-traditional society. In *Reflexive modernization: Politics, tradition and aesthetics in the modern social order,* eds. U. Beck, A. Giddens, and S. Lash, S. Stanford, CA" Stanford University Press.

Giddens, A. 2003. *The runaway world: How globalization is reshaping our lives*. London: Routledge.

*Gilbert, J. 2000. "Adforce sees future in mainstream media." *Advertising Age*, vol. 71, no. 34: 18–19.

*Giles, J. and Miller, S. 1994. "Generalizations x." *Newsweek* June 6: 62–72.

*Gilly, M. 1988. "Sex roles in advertising: A comparison of television advertisements in Australia, Mexico, and the United States." *Journal of Marketing*, vol. 52, no. 2: 75–86.

Gimein, M. 2002. Program-free commercials. *Fortune—European Edition*, April 1.

Gitlin, T. 1980. *The whole world is watching*. Berkeley: University of California Press.

Gitlin, T. 1983. *Inside prime-time*. New York: Pantheon.

Gladwell, M. 1997. The coolhunt. March 17. http://www.gladwell.com.

*Gleason, K. 2002. "Outdoor comes of age." *The Advertiser* April.

*Godin, S. 1997. "Permission key to successful marketing." *Advertising Age*, vol. 68, no. 45: S31.

*Goetzl, D. 2002. "Novartis unites at mindshare." *Advertising Age*, vol. 73, no. 2: 1–2.

*Goetzl, D., and Linnett, R. 2001). "Pfizer is right RX for carat." *Advertising Age*, vol. 72, no. 8: 10.

Goffman, E. 1979. *Gender advertisements*. New York: Harper and Row.

Goldberg, M., Fishbein, M., and Middlestadt, S. 1997. *Social marketing: Theoretical and practical perspectives*. Cambridge, MA: Lea.

Goldman, R. and Papson, S. 1994, *Advertising in the age of hypersignification. Theory, culture & society*. London: Sage Publications.

Goldman, R. and Papson, S. 1996. *The sign wars: Cluttered landscape of advertising*.New York: Guilford Press.

Goldman, R., Papson, S., and Kersey, N. 1998–2003a. *Landscapes of capital: Representing time, space, & globalization in corporate advertising http://it.stlawu.edu/~global/*.

Googins, B. 1991. *Work/family conflict: Private lives public responses*. New York: Auburn House.

Gossage, H. L. 1967. The gilded bough: Magic and advertising. In *The human dialogue*, eds. F. Matson and A. Montague. New York: Free Press.

Gottschalk, P. and Danziger, S. 1997. Family income mobility—how much is there and has it changed? Boston College Working Papers in Economics.

Government of Canada. 1997. "Canadian parliament tobacco act, bill c-71." Vol. Royal Assent: April 25, 1997.

Government of Canada. 2001. Parliament of Canada bill c-2: Canada elections act: Part 16, election advertising, third party advertising. Ottawa, ON.

Government of Canada. 2005. Part 17 third party election advertising: Parliament of Canada. Ottawa, ON. http://laws.justice.gc.ca/en/E-2.01/15202.html

*Graham, D. E. 1999. "1999 media outlook: Newspapers." *The Advertiser*. February.

*Green, A. 1992. "Death of the full-service agency?" *Admap*.

Greenberg, B. S. and Heeter, C.(1987. "VCRs and young people." *American Behavioral Scientist*, vol. 30, no. 5: 509.

Gross, D. M. and Scott, S. 1990. "Proceeding with caution." *Time*.

*Gruner, J. H. 1998. "Media outlook: Magazines." *The Advertiser*. March .

*Guccione, B., Jr. 1995. "Topspin." *Spin*, April: 24.

Haak, C. 1996. "German broadcast advertising law: Overview of the statutory regulations governing broadcast advertising." *Recht*, http://www.ojr.de/, vol. 36.

*Hackley, C. 2003. "How divergent beliefs cause account team conflict." *International Journal of Advertising*, vol. 22, no. 3: 313–332.

Haineault, D.-L., and Roy, J.-Y. 1993. *Unconscious for sale: Advertising, psychoanalysis, and public life*. Minneapolis: University of Minnesota Press.

Hakuhodo Institute of Life and Living. 1982. *Hitonami: Keeping up with the satos*. Kyoto PHP Research Institute.

Hales, P. B. 2004. *Documents of an ideal American suburb*. Chicago, Art History Department, University of Illinois at Chicago.

Hall, S. 1973/1980. *Encoding/decoding. Centre for contemporary cultural studies*. London: Hutchinson.

Hall, S.1988. *The hard road to renewal*. New York: Verso.

Hall, S. 1997. *Representation: Cultural representations and signifying practices*. London: Sage Publications.

*Halliday, J. 2000. "Bcom3 staffs up dedicated gm planning unit." *Advertising Age*, vol. 71, no. 42: 3.

*Halliday, J. 2003. "Study claims TV advertising doesn't work on car buyers." *Advertising Age*, vol. 74, no. 41: 8.

Harper, M., Harper, P., and Young, J. 1963. *The advertising agency. Printer's ink advertising: Today/yesterday/tomorrow*. New York: McGraw-Hill.

Harris, N. 1981. The drama of consumer desire. In *Yankee enterprise*, eds. O.Mayr and R. C. Post. Washington, DC: Smithsonian Institution Press.

Harrison, L., and Godfrey, C. 1989. "Alcohol advertising controls in the 1990s." *International Journal of Advertising*, vol. 8: 167.

Harron, M. 2000. "Die yuppie scum!" *Filmmaker: Independent Film*. Winter.

Harvey, D. 1989. *The condition of postmodernity: An enquiry into the origins of cultural change*. Oxford: Blackwell Publishers.

Hasting, G., Stead, M., Mcdermott, L., Forsyth, A., Mackintosh, A. M., Rayner, M., Godfrey, C., Caraher, M. and Angus, K. 2003. *Review of research on the effects of food promotion to children, prepared for the food standards agency*. Glasgow, Scotland: University of Strathclyde.

*Hatfield, S. 2002. "Creative departments need to regain stature, confidence." *Advertising Age*, vol. 73, no. 47: 20.

Health Canada. 2005. http://www.hc-sc.gc.ca/english/. Ottawa, ON: Health Canada.

*Heath, R. P. 1996."The frontiers of psychographics." *American Demographics*.

*Heaven, R. 1999. "Post-global advertising: The archetypal approach." *Admap*, .May.

Hebdige, D. 1981. *Subculture: The meaning of style*. London: Routeledge.

Hebdige, D. 1988. *Hiding in the light: On images and things*. Oxford: Routledge.

Heighton, E., and Cunningham, D. 1976. *Advertising in the broadcast media*. Belmont, CA: Wadsworth.

Henley Centre 2004. "The debt industry goes global." *The Henley Centre Newsletter*.

Herman, E. and Mcchesney, R. 1997/1998. *The global media: The new missionaries of corporate capitalism*. London: Cassell Academic.

Hernandez, D. G. 1995. "Restructions on cigarette advertising." *Editor & Publisher*, vol. 128, no. 33; 12–14.

Hettinger, H. 1933. *A decade of radio advertising*. Chicago: University of Chicago Press.

Hillier, B. 1983. *The style of the century: 1900–1980*. New York: E.P. Dutton.

Hindley, D. and Hindley, G. 1972. *Advertising in Victorian England*. London:,Wayland.

Hirsch, F. 1976. *Social limits to growth*. Cambridge: Harvard University Press.

Hirschberg, L. 1983. "When you absolutely, positively want the best." *Esquire*.

Hirschman, A. 1982. *Shifting involvements*. Princeton, NJ: Princeton University Press.

*Hite, R. E. and Fraser, C. 1988. "International advertising strategies of multinational corporations." *Journal of Advertising*, August/September: 9–17.

Hoffman, K. 1980. *A history of vanity fair: A modernist journal in America*. Toronto, University of Toronto.

Hofstede, G. 1984. *Culture's consequences: International differences in work related values*. Thousand Oaks CA: Sage.

*Holbrook, M. B. and Batra, R. 1987. "Assessing the role of emotions as mediators of consumer responses to advertising." *Journal of Consumer Research*, vol.1 4: 404–420.

*Holbrook, M. B. and Hirschman, E. C. 1982. "The experiential aspects of consumption: Consumer fantasies, feelings, and fun." *Journal of Consumer Research*, vol. 9, September: 132–140.

Hollander, S. C. and Germain, R. 1992. *Was there a Pepsi generation before Pepsi discovered it? Youth-based segmentation in marketing*. Chicago: American Marketing Association.

Holt, D. 2003. "How to build an iconic brand." *Market Leader*, .Summer, no. 21.

*Holt, D. B. 1998. "Does cultural capital structure American consumption?" *Journal of Consumer Research*, vol. 25.

*Holt, D. B. 2002. "Why do brands cause trouble? A dialectical theory of consumer culture and branding." *Journal of Consumer Research*, vol. 29: 70-90.

Holtz, G. 1995. *Welcome to the jungle: The why behind generation x*. New York: St. Martin's Griffin.

Hornblower, M. 1997. "Great xpectations." *Time*, vol. 129, no. 23: 58.

Horowitz, D. 1980. "Consumption and its discontents." *Journal of American History*, vol. 67.

Hotchkiss, G. B. 1950. *An outline of advertising*. New York: Macmillan.

*Howard, D. and Barry, T. 1988. "The prevalence of question use in print advertising: Headline strategies." *Journal of Advertising Research*, vol. 28, no. 4: 20–28.

*Howard-Spink, J. 2002. "Using archetypes to build stronger brands." *Admap* .October.

*Huang, M.-H. 1998. "Exploring a new typology of advertising appeals: Basic versus social emotional advertising in a global setting." *International Journal of Advertising*, vol. 17, no. 2: 145–169.

*Hughes, L. Q. 2001. "Buyers demand more data." *Advertising Age*, vol. 72, no. 25: T2-T3.

Hurvitz, D. 1984a. "Broadcast ratings: The missing dimension." *Critical Studies in Mass Communication*, vol. 1.

Hurvitz, D. 1984b. U.S. Market research and the study of radio in the 1930's. Meeting of the International Association of Mass Communication Research. Prague.

Hurvitz, D. 1985. The culture of business and the business of culture: Social research, scientific management and the collection of media-audience data. Second Workshop on Historical Research in Marketing. East Lansing, Michigan, Michigan State University, Department of Marketing and Transportation.

*Hutt, P. B. 1993. "FDA regulation of product claims in food labeling." *Journal of Public Policy & Marketing,* vol. 12, no. 1: 132–134.

Independent Television Commission. 2002. Annual report and accounts for 2002, London.

Independent Television Commission. 2003. ITC code rule 7.2.2. London, Independent Television Commission.

Inglehart, R. 1977. *The silent revolution: Changing values and political styles among western publics.* Princeton, NJ: Princeton University Press.

Inglehart, R. 1997. Modernization and postmodernization. Princeton, NJ: Princeton University Press.

Inglis, F. 1972. *The imagery of power: A critique of advertising.* London: Heinemann.

*Ingram, C. 1998. "Media specialist merit their seat at advertising's top table." Campaign, no. 38: 30.

Innis, H. 1951. *The bias of communication.* Toronto: University of Toronto Press.

Institute of Alcohol Studies. 2004. Fact sheet: Advertising and alcohol. London.

Institute of Alcohol Studies. 2005. Instittute of alcohol studies 'fact sheet'. London, Institute of Alcohol Studies. http://www.ias.org.uk

Institute of International Studies. 2002. *A dissenting voice — Christopher Hitchens interview: Conversations with history.* Berkeley: University of California.

*International Journal of Advertising. 1999. "Regional advertising expenditure & media share." Vol. 18, no. 2: 269.

International Labour Office. 2004. Market trends and globalization's impact on them. Geneva: Bureau for Workers' Activities.

Ippolito, P. and Mathios, A. 1990. "The regulation of science-based claims in advertising." *Journal of Consumer Policy,* vol. 13, no. 4: 413–445.

Jackson, J. 2001. Their man in Washington: Big media have an ally in new FCC chair Michael Powell. *Extra!.* September/October.

*Jacobs, B. 1995. "Advertising agencies and the management of media." *Admap.*April.

*Jaffe, A. 1990."Show and sell." *Channels.*

*Jaffe, L. and Berger, P. D. 1988. "Impact on purchase intent of sex-role identity and product positioning." *Psychology & Marketing,* vol. 5, no. 3: 259–271.

*Jaffe, L. J. 1991. "Impact of positioning and sex-role identity of women's responses to advertising." *Journal of Advertising Research,* vol. 31, June/July: 57–64.

*Jaffe, L. J. and Berger, P. D. 1994. "The effect of modern female sex role portrayals on advertising effectiveness." *Journal of Advertising Research,* vol. 34, July/August: 32–42.

Jameson, F. 1991. *Postmodernism, or, the cultural logic of late capitalism.* New York: Verso.

Jamieson, K. H. 1984. *Packaging the presidency.* Oxford: Oxford University Press.

Jamieson, K. H. 2000. *Everything you think you know about politics—and why you're wrong.* New York: Basic Books.

Janowitz, M. .1978. *The last half-century.* Chicago: University of Chicago Press.

Jansson, A. 2001. *Image culture: Media, consumption & everyday life in reflexive modernity.* Goteborgs: Universitet Acta Univ.

Janus, N. 1980. *The making of the global consumer: Transnational advertising and the mass media in Latin America.* Stanford, CA: Stanford University Press.

Jernigan, D. and O'Hara, J. 2004. Reducing underage drinking: A collective responsibility. In *Alcohol advertising and promotion,* eds. R. J. Bonnie and M. E. O'connell. Washington, DC: Institute of Medicine.

Jhally, S. 1987. *The code of advertising.* New York: St. Martin's Press.

Jhally, S. 1995. *Desire, sex and power in music video. Dreamworlds 2.* Northhampton, MA: Media Education Foundation.

Jhally, S. 1997. *Advertising & the end of the world.* Northhampton, MA: Media Education Foundation.

Jhally, S., Kline, S., and Leiss, W. 1985. "Magic in the marketplace." *Canadian Journal of Political and Social Theory,* vol. 9, no. 3.

Jhally, S. and Lewis, J. 1992. Enlightened racism: The Cosby show, audiences, and the myth of the American dream. Boulder, CO: Westview Press.

Joyce, W.(1963. *The role of mass media today. Printer's ink advertising: Today/yesterday/tomorrow.* New York: McGraw-Hill.

Kaid, L. L. and Johnston, A. 2000. *Videostyle in presidential campaigns: Style and content of televised political advertising.* Westport, CT: Praeger.

*Kaikati, J. 1987. "Celebrity advertising: A review and synthesis." *International Journal of Advertising,* vol. 6, no. 2.93–106.

*Kanso, A. and Nelson, R. A. 2002. "Advertising localization overshadows standardization." *Journal of Advertising Research,* vol. 42, no. 1: 79–89.

*Kanter, D. L. 1988. "Cynical marketers at work." *Journal of Advertising Research,* vol. 28, no. 6: 28–34.

*Kaplan, B. 1985. "Zapping: The real issue is communication." *Journal of Advertising Research,* vol. 25: 9–12.

*Karrh, J. 2001. "Audience attitudes towards brand (product) placement: Singapore and the United States." *International Journal of Advertising,* vol. 20, no. 1: 3–25.

*Kassan, M. 1998. "Let's all hail the new star of ad world." *Advertising Age,* vol. 69, no. 39: 38

Kasser, T. 2003. *The high price of materialism.* Cambridge, MA: MIT Press.

*Katz, H. and Lee, W.-N. (1992. "Oceans apart: An initial exploration of social communication differences in the US and UK prime-time television advertising." *International Journal of Advertising,* vol. 11, no. 1, 69–83.

Kellner, D. 1995. *Media culture.* London: Routledge.

Kellog, S. 2003. Response to the dg eac consultation on the review of the television without frontiers (twf) directive. http://www.europa.eu.int/comm/avpolicy/ regul/review-twf2003/wc_kellogg.pdf

Kemper, S. 2001. *Sri Lankan advertising and consumers in a transnational world.* Chicago: University of Chicago Press.

*Keown, C. F., Jacobs, L. W., Schmidt, R. W., and Ghymn, K.-I. 1992. "Information content of advertising in the United States, Japan, South Korea, and the People's Republic of China." *International Journal of Advertising,* vol. 11, no. 3: 257–268.

Kermode, M. 2004. Pop goes the movie. *The Observer,* March 21.

Kern-Foxworth, M. 1994. *Aunt Jemima, Uncle Ben, and Rastus.* New York: Praeger.

*Kerwin, A. M. 1998a. "Celebrity touch golden for fashion-oriented title." *Advertising Age,* vol. 69, no. 8: S14.

*Kerwin, A. M. 1998b. "Publishers cautiously optimistic about '98." *Advertising Age,* vol. 69, no. 8: 3–4.

*Kerwin, A. M. 1998c. "Revamp of magazine research eyed." *Advertising Age,* vol. 69, no. 27: 3.

*Kerwin, A. M. 1998d. "Teen version of 'people' to face powerful rivals." *Advertising Age,* vol. 69, no. 1: 4.

*Kerwin, A. M. 1999. "'in style' plots growth via web, spinoff titles." *Advertising Age,* vol. 70, no. 29: 6.

Key, W. B. 1972. *Subliminal seduction.* New York: Signet.

Key, W. B. 1976. *Media sexploitation,* New York: Signet.

Key, W. B. 1989. *The age of manipulation: The con in confidence, the sin in sincere.* New York: H. Holt.

Kilbourne, J. 2000a. *Advertising's image of women. Killing us softly 3.* Northampton MA: Media Education Foundation.

Kilbourne, J. 2000b. *Killing us softly 3: Advertising's image of women.* Northampton MA: Media Education Foundation.

*Klassen, M., Wauer, S., and Cassel, S. 1990/1991. "Increases in health and weight loss claims in food advertising in the eighties." *Journal of Advertising Research,* 32–37.

*Klassen, M. L., Jasper, C., and Schwartz, A. 1993. "Men and women: Images of their relationships in magazine advertisements." *Journal of Advertising Research,* vol. 33, no. 2: 30–40.

Klein, N. 2001/2002. *No logo: Taking aim at the brand bullies.* Toronto: A. A. Knopf Canada.

Kline, S. 1977. *The characteristics and structure of television news broadcasting: Their effects upon opinion change.* London: London School of Economics.

Kline, S. 1983. Images of well-being in Canadian magazine advertising. Meeting of the Canadian Communication Association. Vancouver, BC.

Kline, S. 1993/1995. *Out of the garden: Toys, TV and children's culture in the age of marketing.* New York: Verso.

Kline, S. 1995. "The play of the market: On the internationalization of children's culture." *Theory, Culture, and Society,* vol. 12, no. 2: 103–30.

Kline, S. 1996. Image politics: Negative advertising strategies and the election audience. In *Buy this book: Studies in advertising and consumption*, eds. M. Nava, A. Blak, I. Macrury, and B. Richards Oxford: Routledge.

Kline, S. 2004. Fast food, sluggish kids: Moral panics and risky lifestyles. Working paper, cultures of consumption. Cultures of Consumption Working Paper Series. London. http://www.consume.bbk.ac.uk/

Kline, S. and Leiss, W. 1978. "Advertising, needs and commodity fetishism." *Canadian Journal of Political and Social Theory*, vol. 2, no. 1.

Kotler, P. and Turner, R. E. 1981. *Marketing management*. Scarborough, On.: Prentice-Hall Canada.

*Kover, A. J., James, W. L., and Sonner, B. S. 1997. "To whom do advertising creatives write? An inferential answer." *Journal of Advertising Research*, vol. 37, no. 1: 41–54.

*Kramer, L. 1998, "McD's, Disney: Year-old pact is a happy deal." *Advertising Age*, vol. 69, no. 19: 24.

Kratzer, L. and Hodgins, S. 1997. "Adult outcomes of child conduct problems: A cohort study." *Journal of Abnormal Child Psychology*, vol. 25, no. 1: 65–81.

Kristeva, J. 1984. *Revolution in the poetic*. New York: Columbia University.

*Lahey, A., Careless, J., Caffyn, E., and Hodgins, B. 1997. Report on youth marketing. *Marketing Magazine*.

Laing J.(2001). *Saskatoon Star Phoenix Group Inc. v. Noton*. S.J. No. 275. Saskatchewan Court of Queen's Bench. Saskatoon, Canada: Judicial Centre of Saskatoon. March 28.

Lane, R. E. 1978. "Markets and the satisfaction of human wants." *Journal of Economic Issues*, vol. 12.

*Lannon, J.and Quelch, J. 2003. "When east meets west." *Market Leader*, vol. 20.

Lasch, C. 1979. *The culture of narcissism*. New York: Warner Books.

Lash, S. 2002. *Critique of information*. London: Sage Publications.

Lash, S. and Urry, J. 1987. *The end of organized capitalism*. Cambridge, MA: Polity Press.

Lash, S. and Urry, J. 1993/1994. *Economies of signs and space*. Thousand Oaks, CA: Sage.

*Laskey, H., Fox, R. and Crask, M. 1995. "The relationship between advertising message strategy and television commercial effectiveness." *Journal of Advertising Research*, vol. 35: 31–39.

Leadbeater, C. 1999. *Living on thin air: The new economy*. London: Penguin.

Lears, J. 1994/1995. *Fables of abundance: A cultural history of advertising in America*. New York: Basic Books.

*Leather, P., Mckechnie, S., and Amirkhanian, M. 1994. "The importance of likeability as a measure of television advertising effectiveness." *International Journal of Advertising*, vol. 13, no. 3: 265–280.

Leavis, F. R. and Thompson, D. 1933/1977. Culture and environment: The training of critical awareness. Westport, CT: Greenwood Press.

Lee, J. 2004. Food advertisers unite to avert ban. *Campaign*, June 4, Issue 23: 1.

Lee, M. 1993. *Consumer culture reborn: The cultural politics of consumption*. New York: Routledge.

*Leigh, T. W., Rethans, A. J., and Whitney, T. R. 1987. "Role portrayals of women in advertising: Cognitive responses and advertising effectiveness." *Journal of Advertising Research*, Oct./Nov.: 54–63.

Leiss, W. 1976/1988. *Limits to satisfaction: An essay on the problem of needs and commodities*. McGill Queens Press.

*Lepper, J. 2004. "Ipa slams ofcom's alcohol advertising clampdown plans." *Brand Republic*, September 24, 2004.

Levitt, T. 1970. "The morality of advertising." *Harvard Business Review*, vol. 48.

Levitt, T. 1983. *The globalization of markets. The marketing imagination*. New York: Macmillan.

Levitt, T. 1993. "The globalization of markets." *Harvard Business Review*, vol. 70, no. 3: 92–102.

Levy, S. J. 1969. Symbols by which we buy. In *Advancing marketing efficiency*, ed. L. H. Stockman. Chicago: American Marketing Association.

Levy, S. J. 1981. "Interpreting consumer mythology: A structural approach to consumer behavior." *Journal of Marketing*, vol. 45.

Levy, S. J. and Zaltman, G. 1975. *Marketing, society, and conflict*, Englewood Cliffs, NJ: Prentice-Hall.

Lewis, G. H. 1977. "Taste cultures and culture classes in mass society: Shifting patterns in American popular music." *International Review of the Aesthetic and Sociology of Music*, vol. 8.

Leymore, V. 1975. *Hidden myth: Structure and symbolism in advertising*. London: Heinemann.

Lin, C. A. 1993) "Cultural differences in message strategies: A comparison between American and Japanese TV commercials." *Journal of Advertising Research*, vol. 33, no. 4: 40–49.

Lindblom, C. 1977. *Politics and markets: The world's political-economic systems*. New York: Basic Books.

*Linnett, R. 2000a. "Generation media a hit." *Advertising Age*, vol. 71, no. 32: S2–S3.

*Linnett, R. 2000b. "Media planning strives for right fit." *Advertising Age*, vol. 71, no. 32: S4.

*Linnett, R. 2001a. "Media shop gets diversity unit." *Advertising Age*, vol. 72, no. 19: 8.

*Linnett, R. 2001b. "Starcom's new light." *Advertising Age*, vol. 72, no. 42: 4.

*Linnett, R., Friedman, W., and Halliday, J. 2001. "No gain." *Advertising Age*, vol. 72, no. 3: 1–3.

*Linnett, R. and Halliday, J. 2002. "Birth of a media-buying behemoth." *Advertising Age*, vol. 73, no. 10: 43.

*Linnett, R. and Thompson, S. 1999. "Kraft sizes up $800 mil media move." *Advertising Age*, vol. 71, no. 26: 1–2.

Lipset, S. and Rokkan, S. 1967. *Party systems and voter alignments*. New York: Free Press.

Lipsky, D. and Abrams, A. 1994. "The packaging (and re-packaging) of a generation." *Harper's Magazine*.

Livingstone, S.(1990. *Making sense of television*. London: Pergamon.

Livingstone, S. 2004. A commentary on the research evidence regarding the effects of food promotion on children—report prepared for ofcom. London: London School of Economics.

Livingstone, S. and Helsper, E. 2004. Advertising hfss foods to children: Understanding promotion in the context of children's daily lives—report prepared for ofcom. London: London School of Economics.

Lloyd, C. 1997/1998/1999. Advertising media: A changing marketplace. In *The advertising business: Operations, creativity, media planning, integrated communications*, ed. J. P. Jones. London: Sage Publications.

*Locks, I. 2002. "Why the big increase in magazines' market share?" *WARC*, no. 426.

Lodziak, C. 2002. *The myth of consumerism*. London: Pluto Press.

Loeb, L. A. 1994. *Consuming angels: Advertising and Victorian women*. New York: Oxford University Press.

Loewy, R. 2002. *Never leave well enough alone*. Baltimore, MD: Johns Hopkins University Press.

Longman, P. 1985. "The downwardly mobile baby boomers." *Wall Street Journal*. Eastern edition. New York.

*Lord, R. 2004. "Asian markets learn to accept different faces in advertising." Campaign. 1/30/2004 Issue 5: 16–18

*Love, T. 2002. "In times of challenge, creativity to the rescue." *Advertising Age*, vol. 73, no. 18: 30.

Lundberg, C. 1995. "Regulation of lawyer advertising." Bench & Bar of Minnesota.

Lunt, P. and Livingstone, S. 1992. *Mass consumption and personal identity: Every day economic experience*. Maidenhead, UK: Open University Press.

Lury, C. 1996. *Consumer culture*. Cambridge: Polity Press.

Lury, C. 2002. Portrait of the artist as a brand. In *Dear images: Art, copyright and culture*, eds. D. Mcclean and K. Schubert. London: Institute of Contemporary Arts.

Lury, C. 2004) *Brands: The logos of the global economy*. London: Routlege.

Lynd, H. and Lynd, R. 1929. *Middletown*. New York, Macmillan.

Lysonski, S. and Pollay, R. W. 1990. "Advertising sexism is forgiven, but not forgotten: Historical, cross-cultural and individual differences in criticism and purchase boycott intentions." *International Journal of Advertising*, vol. 9, no. 4: 317

*Macarthur, K. 2004. "Coke commits $400m to fix it." *Advertising Age*, vol. 75, no. 46.

*Mackenzie, S. B., Lutz, R., and Belch, G. 1986."The role of attitude toward the ad as a meadiator of advertising effectiveness: A test of competing explanations." *Journal of Marketing Research*, vol. 23: 130–143.

*Maclachlan, J. and Logan, M. 1993. "Camera shot length in TV commercials and their memorability and persuasiveness." *Journal of Advertising Research*, vol. 33, no. 2: 57–62.

Macmanus, S. A. and Turner, P. A. 1995. *Young v. Old: Generational combat in the 21st century (transforming American politics)*. Boulder, CO: Westview Press.

*Magiera, M. and Wells, M. 1993. "The coke saga: The rise and fall of peter sealy." *Advertising Age*, vol. 64, no. 42: 22–23.

Mandel, E. 1976. *Late capitalism*. London: NLB.

*Mandese, J. 1995) "In new growth phase, cable feeding on itself." *Advertising Age*, vol. 66, no. 13: S1–S3.

*Mandese, J. 1998. "Marketers want to justify plan strategy." *Advertising Age*, vol. 69, no. 31: S2–S3.

*Mandese, J. 2002. "Media ink consolidation or consolation? Madison avenue's big get bigger", *Admap*, July, Issue 430.

Marchand, R. 1986. *Advertising and the American dream: Making way for mondernity, 1920-1940.* Berkeley, University of California Press.

Marchand, R. 1998. Customer research as public relations: General motors in the 1930s. In *Getting and spending: American and European consumer society in the twentieth century,* eds. S. Strasser, C. Mcgovern, M. Judt, D. S. Mattern, C. Mauch, and D. Lazar. Cambridge, MA: Cambridge University Press.

Marchand, R. 2000. *Creating the corporate soul.* Berkeley: University of California Press.

*Marchetti, M. 1995. "Talkin' 'bout my generation." *Sales and Marketing Management,* vol. 147, no. 12: 64–67.

Marcuse, H. 1964. *One-dimensional man.* Boston: Beacon Press.

Marketing News. 1989. "Time-Warner deal could create media hypermarket for advertisers."

*Marketing Week 2004. "Factfile: Is advertising proving irresistible?" February 2: 34

*MarketFacts. (1997. "Generation x: Who are they?" LIMRA's MarketFacts, vol. 16, no. 4: 4.

*Marney, J. 1988. *Marketing.* March 28.

Marshall, J. and Werndly, A. 1997/2002. *The language of television (intertext).* London: Routledge.

Martenson, R. 1987. "Advertising strategies and information content in American and Swedish advertising: A comparative content analysis in cross-cultural copy research." *International Journal of Advertising,* vol. 6, no. 2: 133–144.

Marx, K. 1867/1976. *Capital.* Harmondsworth, Middlesex: Penguin.

Maslow, A. 1987. *Motivation and personality,* (3rd ed.). New York: Harper and Row.

May, T. 2001) *Social research: Issues, methods and process.* Maidenhead, UK : Open University Press.

Mcallister, M. 1995/1996/1997). *The commericalization of American culture: New advertising control and democracy.* Thousand Oaks, CA: Sage Publications.

Mcallister, M. P. and Mazzarella, S. R. 2000. "Special issue: Advertising and consumer culture." *Mass Communication & Society,* vol. 3, no. 4.

Mcchesney, R. 1997. "The global media giants: The nine firms that dominate the world." *Extra!* November/December.

Mccracken, G. 1990/1991. *Culture and consumption: New approaches to the symbolic character of consumer goods and activities.* Bloomington: Indiana University Press.

Mccullough, L. S. 1993. "Leisure themes in international advertising: A content analysis." *Journal of Leisure Research,* vol. 25, no. 4: 380–387.

*Mcdaniel, C., Jr. 1982 *Marketing,* (2nd ed.). New York: Harper and Row.

*Mcevoy, D. 2001. "Outdoor advertising effectiveness." *Admap,* vol. 423.

Mcfall, L. 2004. *Advertising: A cultural economy.* Thousand Oaks, CA: Sage.

Mcguire, W. J. 1968. Personality and attitude change: An information processing theory. In *Psychological foundations of attitudes,* eds. A. G. Greenwald, T. Brock, and T. M. Ostrom. San Diego, CA, Academic Press.

Mcluhan, M. 1951/2002. *The mechanical bride: Folklore of industrial man.* Corte Medera, CA, Ginko Press.

Mcluhan, M. 1962. *The Gutenberg galaxy.* London: Routledge and Kegan Paul.

Mcluhan, M. 1964. *Understanding media: The extensions of man.* London: Routledge and Kegan Paul.

*Mcquarrie, E. F. and Mick, D. G. 1992. "On resonance: A critical pluralistic inquiry into advertising rhetoric." *Journal of Consumer Research,* vol. 19, no. 2: 180–197.

Mcrobbie, A. 2002. From holloway to hollywood: Happiness at work in the new cultural economies. In *Cultural economy: Cultural analysis and commercial life,* ed. P. D. Gay, 97–114. Thousand Oaks, CA: Sage Publications.

Media, P. 2004. *Political media buying 2004: Analysis of spending on political advertising and marketing communication.* Stamford, CT: PQ Media.

*Meech, P. 1999. "Regional advertising expenditure and media share." *International Journal of Advertising,* vol. 18, no. 2: 269–272.

Mica, N. 1992. *Changing culture,* London: Sage Publications.

*Michell, P. and Haug, S. 1990. "Why advertisers change their agencies", *Admap.*

Miller, D. 1987. *Material culture and mass consumption (social archaeology).* Oxford: Blackwell Publishers.

Miller, D. 1998. *A theory of shopping.* Ithaca, NY: Cornell University Press.

Miller, D. 2002. The unintended political economy. In *Cultural economy: Cultural analysis and commercial life,* ed. P. D. Gay. Thousand Oaks, CA: Sage Publications.

Miller, P. and Rose, N. 1994. "Mobilizing the consumer, assembling the object of consumption." *Theory, Culture and Society,* vol. 14, no. 1: 1–36.

Miller, W. and Levitin, T. 1976a. *Leadership and change.* Cambridge. MA: Winthrop.

Miller, W. E. and Levitin, T. E. 1976b. *Leadership and change: The new politics and the American electorate.* University Press of America.

Mitchell, A. A. 1983. *The nine American lifestyles.* New York: Macmillan.

Mitchell, A. A. 1986. Theoretical and methodological issues in developing and individual level model of advertising effects. In *Advertising and consumer psychology,* eds. J. C. Olson and K. Sentis. New York: Praeger Publishing Co.

Miyagi, M. and Tanaka, F. 1999. "Peripheral communication: Description of how young Japanese view TV commercials and the media." European Society of Opinion and Marketing Research.

Moeran, B. 1996. *A Japanese advertising agency: An anthropology of media and markets.* Honolulu: University of Hawai'i Press.

*Moore, D. J. and Harris, W. D. 1996. "Affect intensity and the consumer response to high impact emotional advertising appeals." *Journal of Advertising,* vol. 25, no. 1: 37–50.

*Morgan, A. I. 1984/1985. "Point of view: Who's killing the great advertising campaigns of America?" *Journal of Advertising Research,* vol. 24, no. 6: 33–35.

Morgenson, G. 1991. "The trend is not their friend." *Forbes,* vol. 16, September: 118.

Morley, D. 1993. "Active audience theory: Pendulums and pitfalls." *Journal of Communication,* vol. 43, no. 4: 13–19.

Morris, J. and Pai, F.-W. 1997. "Where east meets west. A design for measuring and interpreting emotional response to standardized advertisement across cultures." Amsterdam: ESOMAR Marketing Research.

*Morrison, D. A. 1994. "More than new label, gen x need research." *Advertising Age,* vol. 65, no. 45: 27.

*Morrison, D. A. 1997. "Beyond the gen x label." *Brandweek,* vol. 38, no. 11: 23–25.

Mort, F. 1996. *Cultures of consumption: Masculinities and social space in late twentieth-century Britain (comedia).* Oxford: Routledge.

*Morton, L. P. 2003. "Targeting generation x." *Public Relations Quarterly,* vol. 48, no. 4: 43–45.

Moscovici, S. 1981. On social representations. In *Social cognition: Perspectives on everyday understanding,* ed. J. Forgas. New York: Academic Press.

Moskin, J. 1973. *The case for advertising.* New York: American Association of Advertising Agencies.

Muir, H. 2004. "Advertisement denounced as racist." *The Guardian.* May 19.

*Muncy, J. 1991. "The journal of advertising: A twenty-year appraisal." *Journal of Advertising,* vol. 20, no. 4: 1–11.

Murdock, G. 1982. Large corporations and the control of the communications industries. In *Culture, society and the media,* eds. M. Gurevitch, T., Bennett, J., Curran, and J. Woollacott. London, Methuen.

Nadin, M. and Zakia, R. D. 1994. *Creating effective advertising: Using semiotics.* New York: Consultant Press Ltd.

*Nancarrow, C., Nancarrow, P., and Page, J. 2002) "An analysis of the concept of cool and its marketing implications." *Journal of Consumer Behaviour,* vol. 1, no. 4: 311 –323.

Nava, M. 1997. Framing advertising: Cultural analysis and the incrimination of visual texts. In *Buy this book: Studies in advertising and consumption,,* eds. M. Nava, A. Blake, I., Macrury, and B. Richards. London: Routledge.

Nava, M. and Nava, O. 1992. Discriminating or duped? Young people as consumers of advertising and art. In *Changing cultures: Feminism, youth and consumerism,* ed. M Nava. London, Sage.

*Neff, J. 2000. "Ad giants tweak media mix." *Advertising Age,* vol. 71, no. 42: S2–S3.

Negrine, R. 1988. *Satellite broadcasting: The politics and implications of the new media.* London: Routledge.

Nelson, J. and Young, D. 2003. Meta-analysis of alcohol advertising bans. Working Paper. Montana State University.

Nelson, P. 1974. The economic value of advertising. In *Advertising and society,* ed. Y. Brozen. New York: New York University Press.

*Neuborne, E., Browder, S., and Anderson, S. 1998. "Welcome to yuppie hardware; restoration's formula draws upscale buyers in droves." *Business Week.*

*Nevett, T. 1992. "Differences between American and British television advertising: Explanations and implications." *Journal of Advertising,* vol. 21, no. 4: 61–72.

Nevitte, N. 1996. *The decline of deference: Canadian value change in cross national perspective*. Peterborough, ON: Broadview.

Nikoltchev, S., Prosser, T., and Scheuer, A. 2000. *Regulation on advertising aimed at children in EU-member states and some neighbouring states: The legal framework.* : Strasbourg: European Audio Visual Observatory.

Nixon, S. 1996. Hard looks: Masculinities, spectatorship and contemporary consumption. New York: St. Martin's Press.

Nixon, S. 2003. Advertising cultures: Gender, commerce, creativity. Thousand Oaks CA: Sage Publications.

Nielsen Media Research 1999. Media release: Number of internet users and shoppers surges in United States and Canada Nielsen Media Research.

Nussenbaum, E. 2004. Products slide into more TV shows, with help from new middlemen. *New York Times*, September 6: C1.

O'barr, W. M. 1994. *Culture and the ad: Exploring otherness in the world of advertising (institutional structures of feeling)*. New York: Westview Press.

O'barr, W. M. 2001. "Interview with Paul Cappelli." *Advertising & Society Review, vol. 2, no. 4.*

*Observer. 2003b. "All the spin doctors' news that's fit to leak." November 9.

O'donohoe, S. 1996. "Collusion or collision? The advertising practitioner-consumer relationship." *Irish Marketing Review*, vol. 9: 17–27.

O'donohoe, S. 1997. "Raiding the postmodern pantry: Advertising and the young adult audience." *European Journal of Marketing*, vol. 31, no. 3-4: 234–254.

Ofori, K. A.(1996. When being no. 1 is not enough: The impact of advertising practices on minority-owned and minority-formatted broadcast stations. Tides Center Civil Rights Forum on Communications Policy. Washington D.C., Office of Communications Business Opportunities, Federal Trade Commission.

Oliver, R. 1981. Advertising and society.In *Advertising in Canada: Its theory and practice*, eds. P. Zarry and R. Wilson. Toronto: McGraw-Hill Ryerson.

Orwell, G. 1936/1969. *Keep the aspidistra flying*. Harvest Book.

Owen, R. 1997. *Gen x TV: The Brady Bunch to Melrose Place*. Syracuse, NY: Syracuse University Press.

Packard, V. 1957. *The hidden persuaders*. New York: D. McKay.

Packard, V. 1959. *The status seekers: An exploration of class behavior in America and the hidden barriers that affect you, your community, your future*. New York: David McKay Co.

*Palmer, C. 2001. Does advertising have a conscience? *Campaign* September 21, 38: 22.

Palmer, W. 2004. The eighties club: The politics of popular culture of the 1980's. http://www.eighties-club.tripod.com/.

Palmer, W. J. 1993. *The films of the eighties: A social history*. Carbondale, IL: SIU Press.

*Parker, C. W. and Young, S. M. 1986. "Consumer response to television commercials: The impact of involvement and background music on brand attitude formation." *Journal of Marketing Research*, vol. 23: 11–24.

Patten, S. 1907/1969. *The new basis of civilization*. Boston, MA: Harvard University Press.

Paulin, G. and Riordin, B. 1998. "Making it on their own: The baby-boom meets generation x." *Monthly Labor Review*, vol. 121, no. 2: 10–21.

*Pechmann, C. 1996. "Do consumers overgeneralize one-sided comparative price claims, and are more stringent regulations needed?" *Journal of Marketing Research*, vol. 33, no. 2: 150–163.

Petersen, M. 2002. CNN to reveal when guests promote drugs for companies. *New York Times* August 21: 1.

Peterson, E. 1963) *The magazine. Printer's ink advertising: Today/yesterday/tomorrow*. New York, McGraw-Hill.

Peterson, R. A. and Dimaggio, P. 1975. "From region to class: The changing locus of country music." *Social Forces*, vol. 53.

Petty, R. 1997. "Advertising law in the United States and European Union." *Journal of Public Policy & Marketing*, vol. 16, Spring: 2–13.

Petty, R. E. and Cacioppo, J. T. 1986. "The elaboration likelihood model of persuasion." *Advances in Experimental Social Psychology*, vol. 19: 123–205.

Pfanner, E. 2004. On advertising: Strategies vary for pill-pushers. *International Herald Tribune*, February 2.

*Phillips, B. J. and Mcquarrie, E. F. 2002. "The development, change, and transformation of rhetorical style in magazine advertisements 1954–1999." *Journal of Advertising*, vol. 31, no. 4: 1–13.

Piesman, M. and Hartley, M. 1984. *The yuppie handbook: The state-of-the-art manual for young urban professionals*. New York: Pocket Books.

Pinkus, K. 1995. *Bodily regimes: Italian advertising under fascism*. Minnesota: University of Minnesota Press.

Pitofsky, R. 1996. "Advertising regulation's 'state of the union.'" *Editor & Publisher*, vol. 129, no. 14: 56.

Policies, I. C. F. A. 2001. "Self-regulation of beverage alcohol advertising." *ICAP Reports 9*.

Politics4us.Org. 2004. http://www.Move-on.org/.

Pollay, R. 1979a. Information sources in advertising history. Westport, CT: Greenwood Press.

Pollay, R. 1983. The identification and distribution of values manifest in print advertising, 1900–1980. Working papers and research reprints, History of Advertising Archives. Vancouver, University of British Columbia.

Pollay, R. n.d. The the editors for the buy-ology urge! American magazine, advertising and the consumer culture, working paper 831. University of British Columbia.

*Pollay, R. and Gallagher, K. 1990. "Advertising and cultural values: Reflections in the distorted mirror." *International Journal of Advertising*, vol. 9, no. 4: 359–372.

Pollay, R. and Mainprize, S. 1984. Headlining of visuals in print advertising. In *Proceedings of the American Academy of Advertising*, ed. J. Glover. Denver, American Academy of Advertising.

Pollay, R. W. 1979b. *Information sources in advertising history*. Westport, CT: Greenwood Press.

Polonsky, M. J., Bailey, J., Baker, H., and Basche, C. 1998. "Communicating environmental information: Are marketing claims on packaging misleading?" *Journal of Business Ethics*, vol. 17, no. 3: 281–294.

Polonsky, M. J. and Waller, D. S. 1995. "Does winning advertising awards pay? The australian experience." *Journal of Advertising Research*, vol. 35, no. 1: 25–36.

Pope, D. 1983. *The making of modern advertising*. New York: Basic Books.

Prensky, D. and Wright-Isak, C. 1997. Advertising, values, and the consumption community. In *ChiagourisValues, lifestles, and psychographics*, eds. L. R. Kahle and L. Chiagounis. Mahwah, NJ: Lawrence Erlbaum Associates.

Presbrey, F. 1968. *The history of development of advertising*. New York: Greenwood Press.

Preston, I. L. 1996. *The great American blowup: Puffery in advertising and selling*. Madison: University of Wisconsin Press.

Pulos, A. 1986. *American design aesthetic: A history of industrial design to 1940*. Cambridge, MA: MIT Press.

Querles, R., Jeffres, L., and Schnuerer, A. 1980. Advertising and the management of demand: A cross-national test of the Galbraithian argument. International Communication Association Conference. Acapulco.

*Quinlan, M.-L. 2000. "Are you talking to me?" *The Advertiser*, March.

Radway, J. 1988."Reception study: Ethnography and the problem of dispersed and nomadic subjects." *Cultural Studies*, vol. 2, no. 4: 359–376.

Ratan, S. 1993. "Generational tension in the office: Why busters hate boomers." *Fortune*.

Real, M. 1971. *Mass-mediated culture*. Englewood Cliffs, NJ: Prentice-Hall.

*Redhead, D. 1997. "Generation next." Marketing, Jan 16: 25–26.

*Reinhard, K. 2001. "Mr. Reinhard is chairman, omnicom group's ddb worldwide, New York." *Advertising Age*, vol. 72, no. 37: 26.

*Rhea, M. J. 1995. "Advertising infrastructure in Romania." *Journal of European Marketing*, vol. 5, no. 4: 37–57.

*Rhea, M. J. 1996. "The emergence of an advertising industry in Romania." *Journal of European Marketing*, vol. 5, no. 2: 53–77.

Rice, D. P. 1995. "Economic costs of substance abuse." *Proceedings of the Association of American Physicians*, vol. 111, no. 2: 119–125.

Richards, B., Macrury, I., and Botterill, J. 2000. The dynamics of advertising. New York: Harwood Academic Press.

Ricoeur, P. 1977. *The rule of metaphor*. Toronto: University of Toronto Press.

Riesman, D. 1950. *The lonely crowd*. New Haven, CT: Yale University Press.

Ritchie, K. 1995. *Marketing to generation x*. New York: Lexington Books.

Ritzer, G. 1993. *The McDonaldization of society*. London: Pine Forge Press.

Robertson, R. 1992. *Globalization: Social theory and global culture*. London, Sage Publications.

Rose, J. and Rutherford, P. 2000. "Making pictures in our head: Government advertising in Canada." *Canadian Journal of Communication*, vol. 26, no. 1: 176–178.

Rosenthal, M. B., Berndt, E. R., Donohue, J. M., Epstein, A. M., and Frank, R. G. 2003. Demand effects on recent changes in prescription drug promotion. Kaiser Family Foundation.

Roslow, P. and Nicholls, J. A. F. 1996. "Targeting the Hispanic market: Comparative persuasion of TV commercials in Spanish and English." *Journal of Advertising Research*, vol. 36, no. 3: 67–78.

*Ross, C. 1997. "Media buying & planning." *Advertising Age*, vol. 68, no. 31: S1–S2.

*Ross, C. 1998. "E-study: Commercials battle all-time-high TV clutter." *Advertising Age*, vol. 69, no. 50: 4.

*Ross, C. 1999a) "Nielsen defends research showing drop in key demo." *Advertising Age*, vol. 70, no. 3: 3–4.

*Ross, C. 1999b. "R&g shifts $142 mil in media buys." *Advertising Age*, vol. 70, no. 51: 1–2.

*Ross, C. 1999c. "TV commercial clutter has ad buyers worried." *Advertising Age*, vol. 70, no. 50: 77.

*Ross, C. 2000a. "Data crowns ABC clutter king." *Advertising Age*, vol. 71, no. 10: 68.

*Ross, C. 2000b. "NBC blasts beyond the 15-minute barrier." *Advertising Age*, vol. 71, no. 33: 3–4.

*Ross, C. and Friedman, W. 1999. "Big advertisers, shops bristle at net TV ad clutter." *Advertising Age*, vol. 70, no. 38: 2.

Rothenberg, R. 1991. "Critics seek FTC. Action on products as move stars." *New York Times*.

Rothenberg, R. (1994). *Where the suckers moon*. New York: Knopf.

*Rothenberg, R. 2001. "To survive, ad agencies must join accountability revolution." *Advertising Age*, vol. 72, no. 45: 12.

*Rothenberg, R. 2002. "Marty Cooke finds a calling; it's bigger than advertising." *Advertising Age*, vol. 73, no. 45: 20.

*Rothenberg, R. (2002) Before it goes 'Hollywood,' some cautions for Mad Ave, Advertising Age. March 4. Vol. 73 Issue 9: 32.

Rotzoll, K., Haefner, J., and Sandage, C. 1976. *Advertising and society: Perspectives towards understanding*. Columbus, OH: Copywright Grid.

*Rugman, A. 2003, "The myth of globalization." *Market Leader*, vol. 20.

Rushkoff, D. 1994. *The gen x reader*. New York: Ballantine.

Sahlins, M. 1972. *Stone age economics*. Chicago: Aldine Press.

Sahlins, M. 1976. *Culture and practical reason*. Chicago: University of Chicago Press.

Said, E. W. 1979. *Orientalism*. New York: Vintage Books.

Said, E. W. 2000. *Out of place: A memoir*. New York: Vintage Books.

Salisbury, R. 1962. *From stone to steel*. London: Cambridge University Press.

Salmon, J. 2000. "Stamp out unintelligible ads." *Admap*.

Sampson, H. 1974. *A history of advertising from the earliest times*. London: Chatto and Windus.

Sanders, L. 2004. "NY city council to audit federal biz." *Advertising Age*, vol. 75, no. 15: 3–4.

Sandler, D. M. and Secunda, E. 1993. "Point of view: Blurred boundaries - where does editorial end and advertising begin?" *Journal of Advertising Research*, vol. 33, no. 3: 73–81.

Savva, S. 2002. "News and notes." *Addiction*, vol. 97, no. 9: 1232–1236.

Scammon, D. and Mayer, R. 1995. "Agency review of environmental marketing claims: Case-by-case decomposition of the issues." *Journal of Advertising*, vol. 2 4, no. 2: 33–44.

Scandiffio, M. 1999. "Selling the government's message now priority for cabinet: Public works minister wants communcations to have a higher profile in government planning." *Hill Times* (Public Works & Government Services Canada), vol. 94.

Schoemer, K. 1995. "Talking 'bout our generation." *Newsweek*.

Schor, J. 1998/2000. *The overspent American: Upsacaling, downshifting and the new consumer*. New York: Basic Books.

Schor, J. 1999. *The overspent American: Why we want what we don't need*. New York: Perennial.

Schor, J. 2004. *Born to buy: The commercialized child and the new consumer culture*. New York: Scribner.

Schudson, M. 1984. *Advertising the uneasy persuasion: Its dubious impact on American society*. New York: Basic Books.

Schuessler, K. F. and Fisher, G. A. 1985. "Quality of life research and sociology." *Annual Review of Sociology*, vol.1 1: 129–149.

Schwartz, T. 1974. *The responsive chord*. New York: Anchor.

Scitovsky, T. 1976. *The joyless economy*. New York: Oxford University Press.

Seager, A. 2004. "Be happy, says Dr. Doom." *Guardian*, May 8.

Segall, S. 1971. *Imagery: Current cognitive approaches*. New York: Academic Press.

Seldin, S. 1963. *The golden fleece: Selling the good life to Americans*. New York: Macmillan.

Sennett, R. 1978. *The fall of public man — on the social psychology of capitalism.* New York: Vintage Books/Randon House.

*Serafin, R. and Hume, S. 1992. "Chrysler may switch off prime time ads." *Advertising Age*, vol. 63, no. 12: 1–2.

Shapiro, B. P. 1981. Marketing for nonprofit organizations. In *The marketing of library and information services*, ed. B. Cronin. London: Aslib.

Shapiro, W. 1991. "The birth and - maybe - death of yuppiedom." *Time*, vol.137, no.14.

Sheehan, P. 1972. *The function and nature of imagery.* New York: Academic Press.

Shenk, J. W. 1997. "The new anti-ad." *U.S. News & World Report.*

Shepard, T. M. 1942. "What the war theme is doing to advertising readership." *Advertising & Selling.*

Shergill, S. 1988. Supermarket UPC scanners and TV people meters: A study of the impact of electronic technologies on consumer research, media planning and retail shelf space management. Syracuse, NY, Syracuse University.

Shergill, S. 1989. "Will the basis of television media planning change from demographics to product usage data?" *Journal of Midwest Marketing*, vol. Fall.

Shergill, S. 1990. Uses of single source data in advertising and marketing research. *Social Science Perspectives Journal: Proceedings of the National Social Science Association Conference.*

*Shergill, S. 1993. "The changing us media and marketing environment: Implications for media advertising expenditures in the 1990s." *International Journal of Advertising*, vol.12, no. 2: 95–116.

Shimp, T. 2000. *Advertising, promotion: Supplemental aspects of integrated marketing communications.* Fort Worth, TX: The Dryden Press.

Simmel, G. 1905/2002. The metropolis and mental life. In *The Blackwell city reader—2002*, eds. G. Bridge and S. Watson. Glencoe, IL: Free Press.

Simmel, G. 1971. The metropolis and mental life. In *On individuality and social forms*, eds. D. N. Levine and Georg Simmel. Chicago: University of Chicago Press.

Simmel, G. 1971/1990. *The philosophy of money.* London: Routledge.

*Simms, J. 2004. "Shock advertising: Double standards." *Marketing*, March 18.

Skornia, H. 1965. *Television and society.* New York: McGraw-Hill.

Slater, D. 1997. *Consumer culture and modernity.* London: Polity.

Smart, B. 2003. *Resisting McDonaldization.* Thousand Oaks, CA: Sage Publications.

Smith, A. 1979. *The newspaper: An international history.* London: Thames and Hudson.

Smith, J., Clurman, A., and Yankelovichandpartners. 1997. *Rocking the ages: The Yankelovich report of generational marketing.* New York: Harperbusiness.

Solomon, M. and Englis, B. 1997. Breaking out of the box: Is lifestyle a construct or a construction? In *Consumer research: Postcards from the edge*, eds. S. Brown and D. Turley. London, Routledge.

Sommers, M. 1983. The evolution of marketing thought and its implications for the study of advertising. Meeting of the Canadian Communication Association. Vancouver, BC.

*Sommerville, A. and Fuller, K. 2002. "Trouble in paradise: Getting to grips with the gender game." *Admap*, January.

*Speck, P. S. and Elliott, M. T. 1997. "Predictors of advertising avoidance in print and broadcast media." *Journal of Advertising*, vol. 26, no. 3: 61–76.

*Staff and agencies 2002. "Consumer debt reaches record levels." *Guardian* December 13.

Starek, R. 1997a. The ABSCs at the FTC: Marketing and advertising to children: Summary of prepared remarks of commissioner Roscoe B. Starek III, Federal Trade Commission, to the Minnesota Institute of Legal Education.

Starek, R. 1997b. Unfairness, internet advertising, and innovative remedies: Prepared remarks of Commissioner Roscoe B. Starek III. Presented before the American Advertising Federation Government Affairs Conference. Washington, DC.

Starek, R. B. 1997c. Advertising alcohol and the first amendment. Prepared remarks of Roscoe B. Starek III, Commissioner Federal Trade Commission. Presented before the American Bar Association Section of Administrative Law and Regulatory Practice Committee on Beverage Alcohol Practice. San Francisco, CA.

Starek, R. B. 1997d. Advertising alcohol and the first amendment: Prepared remarks of Roscoe B. Starek III, Commissioner Federal Trade Commission. Presented before the American Bar Association Section of Administrative Law and Regulatory Practice Committee on Beverage Alcohol Practice. San Francisco, CA.

States, S. C. O. T. U. 2000. *Food and drug administration et al. v. Brown & Williamson tobacco corp. et al.* Certiorari to the United States Court of Appeals for the Fourth Circuit, vol. No. 98-1152, no. Argued December 1, 1999; Decided March 21, 2000.

*Stern, B. 1993. "Feminist literary criticism and the deconstruction of ads: A postmodern view of advertising and consumer responses." *Journal of Consumer Research*, vol. 19, March: 556–566.

*Stern, B. 1999a. "Gender and multicultural issues in advertising: Stages on the research highway." *Journal of Advertising*, vol. 28, no. 1: 1–9.

*Stern, B. and Resnik, A. 1991. "Information content in television advertising: A replication and extension." *Journal of Advertising Research*: 36–46.

*Stern, B. B. 1999b. "Gender and multicultural issues in advertising: Stages on the research highway." *Journal of Advertising*, vol. 28, no. 1: 1–9.

Stewart, D. W. and D.H., F. 1986. *Effective television advertising: A study of 1000 commercials.* Lexington, MA: Lexington Books.

Stewart, M. 1993. "The effect on tobacco consumption of advertising bans in oecd countries." *International Journal of Advertising*, vol. 12: 155–180.

Stigler, G. 1961. "The economics of information." *Journal of Political Economy*, vol. 69: 213–225.

Stole, I. L. 2001. "The 'salesmanship of sacrifice': The advertising industry's use of public relations during the second world war." *Advertising and Society*, vol. 2, no. 2.

Stone, O. 1987. *Wall street.* (Twentieth Century Fox).

Strasser, S. 1995. *The making of the American mass market.* Washington, DC: Smithsonian Books.

Strasser, S. 2004. *Satisfaction guaranteed: The making of the American mass market.* Washington, DC: Smithsonian Institution Press.

Strasser, S., Mcgovern, C., and Judt, M. 1997/1998. *Getting and spending: American and European consumption in the twentieth century.* Cambridge, MA: Cambridge University Press.

Strauss, W. and Howe, N. 1991. *Generations.* New York: William Morrow Publisher.

Strauss, W. and Howe, N. 1997. *The fourth turning.* New York: Broadway Books Publisher.

*Strazewski, L. 1984. "Well-to-do market keeps shifting." *Advertising Age.*

Stuart, E. 1988. *All-consuming images: The politics of style in contemporary culture.* New York: Basic Books.

Stuart, E. 2001. *Captains of consciousness.* New York: Harper-Collins.

*Sumner, D. E. 2001. "Who pays for magazines? Advertisers or consumers?" *Journal of Advertising Research*, vol. 41, no. 6.

Sutherland, M. 1993. *Advertising and the mind of the consumer.* Sydney: Allen & Unwin.

Sylvester, A. K. 1990. "Controlling remote." *Marketing and Media Decisions*, vol. 25, no. 2: 54.

*Tauber, E. 1985. "Editorial: Zapping." *Journal of Advertising Research*, vol. 25, no. 2: 5.

Taussig, M. 1980/1981. *The devil and commodity fetishism in South America.* Chapel Hill: University of North Carolina Press.

*Taylor, C. and Lee, J. Y. 1994. "Not in vogue: Portrayals of Asian Americans in magazine advertising." *Journal of Public Policy & Marketing*, vol. 13, no. 2: 239–246.

*Taylor, C. and Taylor, J. 1994. "Regulatory issues in outdoor advertising: A content analysis of billboards." *Journal of Public Policy & Marketing*, vol. 13, Spring: 97–107.

*Teinowitz, I. 2002. "Fda reviews policies on ad regulation." *Advertising Age*, vol. 73, no. 20: 1–2.

Teinowitz, I. 2004. Senate passes bill curbing tobacco: Measure would empower FDA to regulate advertising. http://www.AdAge.com.

Thackeray, W. M. 1848/2003. *Vanity fair.* New York: Penguin.

Thompson, J. Walter Advertising Agency 2003. *Advertising effectiveness.* Promotional video. London

*Thompson, S. 2002. "Lifesavers effort gets personality." *Advertising Age*, vol. 73, no. 3: 42.

Thorson, E., Christ, W. G., and Caywood, C. 1991. "Effects of issue and image strategies, attack and support appeals, music, and visual content in political commercials." *Journal of Broadcasting & Electronic Media*, vol. 35; 465–486.

*Tiegel, E. 2000. "Loosening the grasp of 30-second spots." *Advertising Age*, vol. 71, no. 32: S6.

Time. 1997. "Defining gen x."

Tjernlund, A. and Wiles, C. R. 1991. "A comparison of role portrayal of men and women in magazine advertising in the USA and Sweden." *International Journal of Advertising*, vol. 10, no. 3: 259–268.

Tobacco Manufacturer's Association. 2003. Advertising and sponsorship regulation. Tobacco Manufacturer's Association.

Toffler, A. 1980. *Future shock: The third wave.* New York: William Morrow.

Tomlinson, A. (Ed.) 1990. *Consumption, identity and style: Marketing, meanings, and the packaging of pleasure.* London: Routledge.

Toncar, M. 2001. "The use of humour in television advertising: Revisiting the US-UK comparison." *International Journal of Advertising*, vol. 20, no. 4.

Torres, I. and Gelb, B. 2002. "Hispanic-targeted advertising: More sales?" *Journal of Advertising Research*, vol. 42, no. 6: 69–76.

Tse, D., Belk, R., and Zhou, N. 1989. "Becoming a consumer society: A longitudinal and cross-cultural content analysis of print ads from Hong Kong, the People's Republic of China, and Taiwan." *Journal of Consumer Research*, vol. 15, March: 457–472.

Tsui, B. 2000. "Yoga magazine gets boost from spirituality surge." *Advertising Age*, vol. 71, no. 37: 20

Tunstall, J. and Machin, D. 1999. *The Anglo-American media connection*. Oxford: Oxford University Press.

*Turnbull, Mike 1997. "Future of the ad agency: Full service—and a little bit more." *Admap* January. NTC Publications Ltd.

Turner, E. 1952. *The shocking history of advertising*. London: Michael Joseph.

Turner, R. 1976.,"The real self: From institution to impulse." *American Journal of Sociology*, vol. 81: 989–1016.

Turow, J. 1997/1998. *The breaking up of America: Advertisers and the new media world*. Chicago: University of Chicago Press.

Twitchell, J. 1995/1996/1997. *Adcult USA: The triumph of advertising in American culture*. New York: Columbia University Press.

Twitchell, J. 2000. Two cheers for materialism. In *The consumer society reader*, ed. J. S. A. D. B. Holt. New York: New Press.

*Tylee, J. 1998. "Public turns against swearing in ads." *Campaign*, .July 31: 4.

*Tylee, J. 1999. "Govt to target smokers rather than the tobacco companies." *Campaign*, 12.

U.S. Bureau of the Census. 1999. *Current population reports, nos. 311, 917, 1095. P-25*. Washington, DC, U.S. Bureau of the Census.

*Unwin, S. 1982. "The style is the ad." *International Journal of Advertising*, vol. 1, no. 2: 157–168.

Vagnoni, A. 2002. "We have seen advertising's future—but do we like it?" *Print*, vol. 55, no. 6: 41–43.

Valin, M. 1999. American advertising federation responds to FCC study into advertising and minority media buying practices. Press release. Washington, DC: American Advertising Federation.

Vanmeurs, L. 1998. "Zap! A study on switching behavior during commercial breaks." *Journal of Advertising Research*, vol. 38, no. 1: 43–53.

Varcoe, J. B. 1981. The advertising agency. In *Advertising in Canada: Its theory and practice*, eds. P. Zarry and R. Wilson. Toronto: McGraw-Hill Ryerson.

*Vaughn, R. L. 1982. "Point of view: Creatives versus researchers: Must they be adversaries?" *Journal of Advertising Research*, vol. 22, no. 6: 45–48.

Veblen, T. 1899/1902/1994/2000. *The theory of the leisure class: An economic study of institutions*. New York: Macmillan.

Veroff, J., Douvan, E., and Kulka, R. 1981 *The inner American: A self-portrait from 1957–1976*. New York: Basic Books.

Walker, J. 1983. *Art in the age of mass media*. London: Pluto Press.

Walker, M. 2002. "Humiliation sells." *New York Times*, September 22: 9–1,12.

Walsh, C. 2004. Things go bitter with coke: Conan Walsh. *The Observer Business*. April 18.

*Wang, J. 1997., "From four hundred million to more than one billion consumers: A brief history of the foreign advertising industry in China." *International Journal of Advertising*, vol.16, no. 4: 241–261.

Warde, A. 2002. Production, consumption and 'cultural economy.' *Cultural economy: Cultural analysis and commercial life*, ed. P. D. Gay. Thousand Oaks CA: Sage Publications.

Warlaumont, H. 2000. *Advertising in the 60s: Turncoats, traditionalists, and waste makers in America's turbulent decade*. New York: Praeger Publishers.

Wasko, J. 2001. *Understanding Disney: The manufacture of fantasy*. Cambridge: Polity.

Waters, J. and Ellis, G. 1996. The selling of gender identity. In *Advertising and culture*, ed. R. Cross. Westport, CT: Praeger Publishers.

Waxman, H. 2004. FDA enforcement actions against false and misleading prescription drugs declined in 2003. Washington, D.C., United States House of Representatives Committee on Government Reform (Minority staff).

*Webster, R. 2000. "Case study shows it's time to take action and cut clutter." *The Advertiser*, May.

*Weinberger, M. and Spotts, H. 1989. "A situational view of information content in TV advertising in the US and UK." *Journal of Marketing*, vol. 53, January: 89–93.

*Wells, W. D. 1983. "Point of view: How to end the never ending." *Journal of Advertising Research*, vol. 23, no. 2: 67–68.

Wells, W. D. 1988. Lectures and dramas. In Cognitive and affective responses to advertising, eds. P. Cafferata, and A Tybout. Lexington, MA: DC Heath.

*Wentz, L. 1985. "Time's yup for Europeans." *Advertising Age*.

Wernick, A. 1990/1991/1992. *Promotional culture: Advertising, ideology and symbolic expression.* Thousand Oaks, CA: Sage.

*West, C. 1994. "The 80s." *Newsweek*, vol. 123, no. 1.

West, C. 2000. *The Cornel West reader.* New York: Cornel West Publisher, Basic Civitas Books.

*Wheeler, B. 2000. "High price of support for refugee campaign." *Marketing Week*, vol. 23, no. 27: 21.

*White, R. 2002. "Advertising to women." *WARC Quick Briefs*, .November.

*White, R. 2003. "Using humour in advertising." *WARC Quick Briefs*, February.

*Whitelock, J. and Chung, D. 1989. "Cross-cultural advertising: An empirical study." *International Journal of Advertising*, vol. 8, no. 3: 291.

*Wiles, C., Wiles, J., and Tjernlund, A. 1996. "The ideology of advertising: The Uunited States and Sweden." *Journal of Advertising Research*, vol. 36, no. 3: 57–66.

*Wilkes, R. E. and Valencia, H. 1989. "Hispanics and blacks in television commercials." *Journal of Advertising*, vol. 18, no. 1: 19–25.

Williams, R. 1961. *The long revolution.* London: Penguin.

Williams, R. 1962/1980. *Advertising: The magic system. Problems of materialism and culture.* London: New Left Books.

Williams, R. 1982. *Dream worlds.* Berkeley: University of California Press.

Williamson, J. 1978. *Decoding advertisement: Ideology and meaning in advertising.* London: Marion Boyars Publisher Ltd.

Winship, J. 2000. "Women outdoors: Advertising, controversy and disputing feminism." *Journal of International Cultural Studies*, vol. 3, no. 1: 27–55.

*Witkowski, T. and Kellner, J. 1998. "Convergent, contrasting, and country-specific attitudes towards television advertising in germany and the united states." *Journal of Business Research*, vol. 42, no. 2: 167–174.

Wolf, M. 2003. *The entertainment economy.* New York: Three Rivers Press.

Wolfe, E. N. 2000. *Recent trends in wealth ownership, 1983-1998.* New York: New York University Press.

Wolfe, T. 1990a. *Bonfire of the vanities.* Toronto: HarperCollins Canada.

Wolfe, T. 1990b. "Late boomers." *American Spectator*, vol. 23, Nov.

*Wolin, L. D. 2003. "Gender issues in advertising—an oversight synthesis of research: 1970-2002." *Journal of Advertising Research*, vol. 43, no. 1, 111–130.

Wynne, D. 1998. *Leisure, lifestyle and the new middle class: A case study.* Oxford: Routledge.

Yankelovich, D. 1981. *New rules: Searching for self-fulfillment in a world turned upside down.* New York: Random House.

*Yankelovich, D. 1982. "New rules: Some implications for advertising: A luncheon address given at the 28th Annual ARF Conference." *Journal of Advertising Research*, vol. 22, no. 5: 9–14.

*Yorke, D. A. and Kitchen, P. J. 1985. "Channel flickers and video speeders." *Journal of Advertising Research*, vol. 25, no. 2: 21–25.

Zajoc, R. B. 1980. "Feeling and thinking: Preferences need no inferences." *American Psychology*, vol. 35: 151–175.

Zandpour, F., Campos, V., Catalano, J., Chang, C., Cho, Y. D., Hoobyar, R., Jiang, S.-F., Lin, M.-C., Madrid, S., Scheideler, H., and Osborn, S. 1994. "Global reach and local touch: Achieving cultural fitness in TV advertising." *Journal of Advertising Research*, vol. 5: 35–63.

*Zeltner, H. 1984. "Media buying calls for tight controls." *Advertising Age*, vol. 55, no. 65: 3–5.

*Zinkhan, G. M. and Carlson, L. 1995. "Green advertising and the reluctant consumer." *Journal of Advertising*, vol. 24, no. 2: 1–6.

*Zinn, L. and Power, C. 1992. "Move over, boomers." *Business Week*.

Zukin, S. 1982/1989. *Loft living: Culture and capital in urban change.* Piscataway, NJ: Rutgers University Press.

Zukin, S. 2004. *Point of purchase: How shopping changed American culture.* Oxford: Routledge.

Zyman, S. and Brott, A. 2002. *The end of advertising as we know it.* New York: Wiley Publishers.

Index

Page numbers in italics refer to Figures or Tables.